Opel Kadett
Service and Repair Manual

Matthew Minter and Mark Coombs

Models covered
Opel Kadett Hatchback Saloon and Estate, with petrol engines,
including special/limited editions

1196 cc, 1297 cc, 1389c cc, 1598 cc, 1796 cc & 1998 cc (inc 16-valve)

Covers most features of Convertible and Vans (including 1992 Convertible)

Does not cover Diesel engine

(3196/1136-288-5AC10)

ABCDE
FGHIJ
KLM

Printed in the USA

© Haynes Publishing 1999

A book in the **Haynes Service and Repair Manual Series**

ISBN 1 85960 246 0

British Library Cataloguing in Publication Data
A catalogue record for this book is available from the British Library.

Haynes Publishing
Sparkford, Nr Yeovil, Somerset BA22 7JJ, England

Haynes North America, Inc
861 Lawrence Drive, Newbury Park, California 91320, USA

Editions Haynes S.A.
Tour Aurore - La Défense 2, 18 Place des Reflets,
92975 PARIS LA DEFENSE Cedex, France

Haynes Publishing Nordiska AB
Box 1504, 751 45 UPPSALA, Sweden

Contents

LIVING WITH YOUR VAUXHALL ASTRA

Roadside Repairs

MAINTENANCE

Weekly checks

Routine Maintenance and Servicing

Contents

REPAIRS & OVERHAUL

Engine and Associated Systems

Transmission

Brakes and Suspension

Body Equipment

Wiring Diagrams

REFERENCE

Index

Introduction to the Vauxhall Astra and Belmont

The second generation Vauxhall Astra/Belmont is available with four petrol engines: 1.2 litre OHV and 1.3, 1.6 and 1.8 litre OHC. The 1.8 litre versions are fitted with fuel injection. A 1.6 diesel engine is also available, but is not dealt with in this manual. Both OHV and OHC engines are well proven designs and, provided regular maintenance is carried out, are unlikely to give trouble.

The Estate is only fitted with the 1.3 or 1.6 engine. A Van is available, and with the exception of the version which has leaf spring rear suspension, closely resembles the passenger car range.

Transmission and running gear follow established Opel front-wheel-drive practice. Manual transmission is either four or five-speed; automatic transmission is available on most models.

These are attractive, comfortable, well-equipped vehicles, requiring minimal maintenance, with most service and repair tasks being straightforward.

References to the 'left' or 'right' are in the sense of a person in the driver's seat, facing forward.

Astra GTE

Acknowledgements

Thanks are due to Champion Spark Plug, who supplied the illustrations showing spark plug conditions. Thanks are also due to Draper Tools Limited, who provided some of the workshop tools, and to all those people at Sparkford who helped in the production of this manual.

We take great pride in the accuracy of information given in this manual, but vehicle manufacturers make alterations and design changes during the production run of a particular vehicle of which they do not inform us. No liability can be accepted by the authors or publishers for loss, damage or injury caused by errors in, or omissions from, the information given.

Working on your car can be dangerous. This page shows just some of the potential risks and hazards, with the aim of creating a safety-conscious attitude.

General hazards

Scalding

• Don't remove the radiator or expansion tank cap while the engine is hot.
• Engine oil, automatic transmission fluid or power steering fluid may also be dangerously hot if the engine has recently been running.

Burning

• Beware of burns from the exhaust system and from any part of the engine. Brake discs and drums can also be extremely hot immediately after use.

Crushing

• When working under or near a raised vehicle, always supplement the jack with axle stands, or use drive-on ramps. *Never venture under a car which is only supported by a jack.*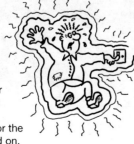
• Take care if loosening or tightening high-torque nuts when the vehicle is on stands. Initial loosening and final tightening should be done with the wheels on the ground.

Fire

• Fuel is highly flammable; fuel vapour is explosive.
• Don't let fuel spill onto a hot engine.
• Do not smoke or allow naked lights (including pilot lights) anywhere near a vehicle being worked on. Also beware of creating sparks (electrically or by use of tools).
• Fuel vapour is heavier than air, so don't work on the fuel system with the vehicle over an inspection pit.
• Another cause of fire is an electrical overload or short-circuit. Take care when repairing or modifying the vehicle wiring.
• Keep a fire extinguisher handy, of a type suitable for use on fuel and electrical fires.

Electric shock

• Ignition HT voltage can be dangerous, especially to people with heart problems or a pacemaker. Don't work on or near the ignition system with the engine running or the ignition switched on.

• Mains voltage is also dangerous. Make sure that any mains-operated equipment is correctly earthed. Mains power points should be protected by a residual current device (RCD) circuit breaker.

Fume or gas intoxication

• Exhaust fumes are poisonous; they often contain carbon monoxide, which is rapidly fatal if inhaled. Never run the engine in a confined space such as a garage with the doors shut.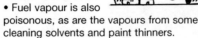
• Fuel vapour is also poisonous, as are the vapours from some cleaning solvents and paint thinners.

Poisonous or irritant substances

• Avoid skin contact with battery acid and with any fuel, fluid or lubricant, especially antifreeze, brake hydraulic fluid and Diesel fuel. Don't syphon them by mouth. If such a substance is swallowed or gets into the eyes, seek medical advice.
• Prolonged contact with used engine oil can cause skin cancer. Wear gloves or use a barrier cream if necessary. Change out of oil-soaked clothes and do not keep oily rags in your pocket.
• Air conditioning refrigerant forms a poisonous gas if exposed to a naked flame (including a cigarette). It can also cause skin burns on contact.

Asbestos

• Asbestos dust can cause cancer if inhaled or swallowed. Asbestos may be found in gaskets and in brake and clutch linings. When dealing with such components it is safest to assume that they contain asbestos.

Special hazards

Hydrofluoric acid

• This extremely corrosive acid is formed when certain types of synthetic rubber, found in some O-rings, oil seals, fuel hoses etc, are exposed to temperatures above 400°C. The rubber changes into a charred or sticky substance containing the acid. *Once formed, the acid remains dangerous for years. If it gets onto the skin, it may be necessary to amputate the limb concerned.*
• When dealing with a vehicle which has suffered a fire, or with components salvaged from such a vehicle, wear protective gloves and discard them after use.

The battery

• Batteries contain sulphuric acid, which attacks clothing, eyes and skin. Take care when topping-up or carrying the battery.
• The hydrogen gas given off by the battery is highly explosive. Never cause a spark or allow a naked light nearby. Be careful when connecting and disconnecting battery chargers or jump leads.

Air bags

• Air bags can cause injury if they go off accidentally. Take care when removing the steering wheel and/or facia. Special storage instructions may apply.

Diesel injection equipment

• Diesel injection pumps supply fuel at very high pressure. Take care when working on the fuel injectors and fuel pipes.

⚠ *Warning: Never expose the hands, face or any other part of the body to injector spray; the fuel can penetrate the skin with potentially fatal results.*

Remember...

DO

• Do use eye protection when using power tools, and when working under the vehicle.

• Do wear gloves or use barrier cream to protect your hands when necessary.

• Do get someone to check periodically that all is well when working alone on the vehicle.

• Do keep loose clothing and long hair well out of the way of moving mechanical parts.

• Do remove rings, wristwatch etc, before working on the vehicle – especially the electrical system.

• Do ensure that any lifting or jacking equipment has a safe working load rating adequate for the job.

DON'T

• Don't attempt to lift a heavy component which may be beyond your capability – get assistance.

• Don't rush to finish a job, or take unverified short cuts.

• Don't use ill-fitting tools which may slip and cause injury.

• Don't leave tools or parts lying around where someone can trip over them. Mop up oil and fuel spills at once.

• Don't allow children or pets to play in or near a vehicle being worked on.

Jacking and vehicle support

The jack supplied with the vehicle tool kit should only be used for changing the roadwheels - see "Wheel changing" later in this Section. When carrying out any other kind of work, raise the vehicle using a hydraulic jack, and always supplement the jack with axle stands positioned under the vehicle jacking points **(see illustrations)**.

When using a hydraulic jack or axle stands, always position the jack head or axle stand head under one of the relevant jacking points.

To raise the front of the vehicle, position the jack with an interposed block of wood underneath the front section of the sill. **Do not** jack the vehicle under the sump or any of the steering or suspension components. To raise the rear of the vehicle, position the jack head underneath the rear section of the sill. **Do not** attempt to raise the vehicle with the jack positioned under the suspension components.

The jack supplied with the vehicle, locates in the jacking points in the ridge on the underside of the sill. Ensure that the jack head is correctly engaged before attempting to raise the vehicle **(see illustration)**.

Never *work under, around, or near a raised vehicle, unless it is adequately supported in at least two places.*

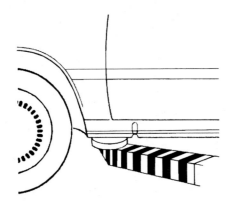

Workshop jack front location point

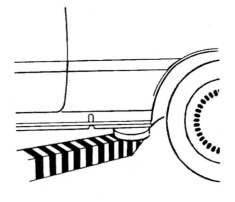

Workshop jack rear location point

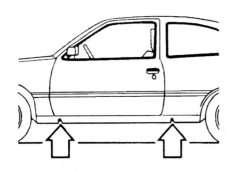

Sill jacking points for use with vehicle jack - arrowed

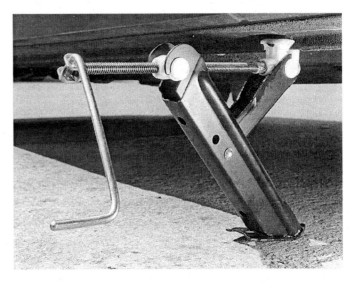

Vehicle jack in use

Towing

Towing eyes are fitted to the front and rear of the vehicle for attachment of a tow rope. The front towing eye is accessed through a slot in the bumper and the rear towing eye is located underneath the body. On models with a front spoiler, the towing point is situated behind an access cover in the spoiler and a shackle and pin are provided **(see illustrations)**. Always turn the ignition key to position I when the vehicle is being towed, so that the steering lock is released, and that the direction indicator and brake lights will work.

Before being towed, release the handbrake and select neutral on the transmission. Note that greater-than-usual pedal pressure will be required to operate the brakes, since the vacuum servo unit is only operational with the engine running. Similarly, on models with power steering, greater-than-usual steering effort will be required.

On models with an automatic transmission to prevent the transmission being damaged, the vehicle should be towed with its front wheels off the ground. If the vehicle is being towed with its front wheels on the ground the car must not be towed for more than 60 miles (100 km) and should never be towed at speeds in excess of 50 mph (80 kmh).

Rear towing eye

On models with a front spoiler, unclip the access cover . . .

. . . then fit the shackle and secure it in position with the retaining pin

Wheel changing

The spare wheel, jack and wheel brace are located in the luggage compartment.

To change a wheel, remove the spare wheel, jack and wheel brace and proceed as follows.

Apply the handbrake, and place chocks at the front and rear of the wheel diagonally opposite the one to be changed. Select first or reverse gear and make sure that the vehicle is located on firm, level ground. Prise off, and remove, the wheel trim (if applicable). Slightly loosen the wheel bolts with the brace provided. Locate the jack head in the jacking point nearest to the wheel to be changed, and raise the jack by turning the handle **(see illustrations)**. On certain models, it may be necessary to unclip access covers to reveal the jacking points. When the wheel is clear of the ground, remove the bolts and lift off the wheel. Fit the spare wheel and moderately tighten the bolts. Lower the vehicle, and then tighten the bolts fully in a diagonal sequence. Refit the wheel trim, where applicable. If possible, check the tyre pressure on the spare wheel. Remove the chocks and stow the jack, tools and the damaged wheel in the luggage compartment. Have the damaged tyre or wheel repaired, or renew it, as soon as possible.

2.8 Unclipping the wheel trim

2.9 Slackening a wheel bolt

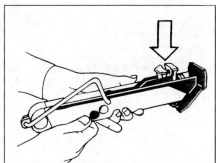

2.10 Ensure the groove in the jack head (arrowed) is engaged with the seam on the sill

Identifying leaks

Puddles on the garage floor or drive, or obvious wetness under the bonnet or underneath the car, suggest a leak that needs investigating. It can sometimes be difficult to decide where the leak is coming from, especially if the engine bay is very dirty already. Leaking oil or fluid can also be blown rearwards by the passage of air under the car, giving a false impression of where the problem lies.

 Warning: Most automotive oils and fluids are poisonous. Wash them off skin, and change out of contaminated clothing, without delay.

 HAYNES HiNT *The smell of a fluid leaking from the car may provide a clue to what's leaking. Some fluids are distictively coloured. It may help to clean the car carefully and to park it over some clean paper overnight as an aid to locating the source of the leak.*
Remember that some leaks may only occur while the engine is running.

Sump oil

Engine oil may leak from the drain plug...

Oil from filter

...or from the base of the oil filter.

Gearbox oil

Gearbox oil can leak from the seals at the inboard ends of the driveshafts.

Antifreeze

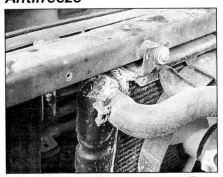

Leaking antifreeze often leaves a crystalline deposit like this.

Brake fluid

A leak occurring at a wheel is almost certainly brake fluid.

Power steering fluid

Power steering fluid may leak from the pipe connectors on the steering rack.

Jump starting

HAYNES HiNT

Jump starting will get you out of trouble, but you must correct whatever made the battery go flat in the first place. There are three possibilities:

1 *The battery has been drained by repeated attempts to start, or by leaving the lights on.*

2 *The charging system is not working properly (alternator drivebelt slack or broken, alternator wiring fault or alternator itself faulty).*

3 *The battery itself is at fault (electrolyte low, or battery worn out).*

When jump-starting a car using a booster battery, observe the following precautions:

✔ Before connecting the booster battery, make sure that the ignition is switched off.

✔ Ensure that all electrical equipment (lights, heater, wipers, etc) is switched off.

✔ Take note of any special precautions printed on the battery case.

✔ Make sure that the booster battery is the same voltage as the discharged one in the vehicle.

✔ If the battery is being jump-started from the battery in another vehicle, the two vehicles MUST NOT TOUCH each other.

✔ Make sure that the transmission is in neutral (or PARK, in the case of automatic transmission).

1 Connect one end of the red jump lead to the positive (+) terminal of the flat battery

2 Connect the other end of the red lead to the positive (+) terminal of the booster battery.

3 Connect one end of the black jump lead to the negative (-) terminal of the booster battery

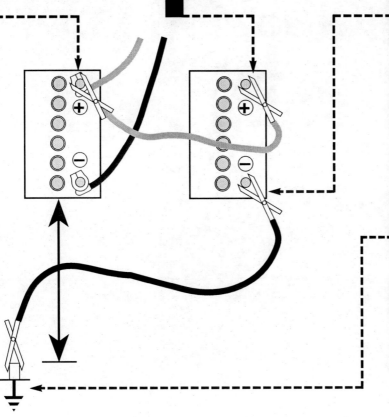

4 Connect the other end of the black jump lead to a bolt or bracket on the engine block, well away from the battery, on the vehicle to be started.

5 Make sure that the jump leads will not come into contact with the fan, drive-belts or other moving parts of the engine.

6 Start the engine using the booster battery and run it at idle speed. Switch on the lights, rear window demister and heater blower motor, then disconnect the jump leads in the reverse order of connection. Turn off the lights etc.

Introduction

There are some very simple checks which need only take a few minutes to carry out, but which could save you a lot of inconvenience and expense.

These "Weekly checks" require no great skill or special tools, and the small amount of time they take to perform could prove to be very well spent, for example;

☐ Keeping an eye on tyre condition and pressures, will not only help to stop them wearing out prematurely, but could also save your life.

☐ Many breakdowns are caused by electrical problems. Battery-related faults are particularly common, and a quick check on a regular basis will often prevent the majority of these.

☐ If your car develops a brake fluid leak, the first time you might know about it is when your brakes don't work properly. Checking the level regularly will give advance warning of this kind of problem.

☐ If the oil or coolant levels run low, the cost of repairing any engine damage will be far greater than fixing the leak, for example.

Underbonnet check points

◀ 1.6 litre

A *Engine oil level dipstick*

B *Engine oil filler cap*

C *Coolant expansion tank*

D *Brake fluid reservoir*

E *Screen washer fluid reservoir*

F *Battery*

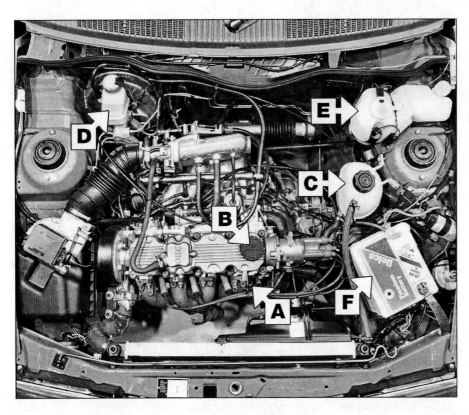

◀ 1.8 litre

A *Engine oil level dipstick*

B *Engine oil filler cap*

C *Coolant expansion tank*

D *Brake fluid reservoir*

E *Screen washer fluid reservoir*

F *Battery*

◀ 2.0 litre (16-valve)

A *Engine oil level dipstick*

B *Engine oil filler cap*

C *Coolant expansion tank*

D *Brake fluid reservoir*

E *Screen washer fluid reservoir*

F *Battery*

Engine oil level

Before you start

✔ Make sure that your car is on level ground.
✔ Check the oil level before the car is driven, or at least 5 minutes after the engine has been switched off.

 HAYNES HiNT *If the oil is checked immediately after driving the vehicle, some of the oil will remain in the upper engine components, resulting in an inaccurate reading on the dipstick!*

The correct oil

Modern engines place great demands on their oil. It is very important that the correct oil for your car is used (See "Lubricants and Fluids").

Car Care

● If you have to add oil frequently, you should check whether you have any oil leaks. Place some clean paper under the car overnight, and check for stains in the morning. If there are no leaks, the engine may be burning oil (see "Fault Finding").

● Always maintain the level between the upper and lower dipstick marks (see photo 3). If the level is too low severe engine damage may occur. Oil seal failure may result if the engine is overfilled by adding too much oil.

1 The dipstick top is often brightly coloured for easy identification (see "Underbonnet check points" on page 0•10 for the exact location). Withdraw the dipstick.

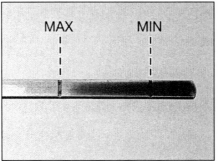

3 Note the oil level on the end of the dipstick, which should be between the upper ("MAX") mark and lower ("MIN") mark. Approximately 1.0 litre of oil will raise the level from the lower mark to the upper mark.

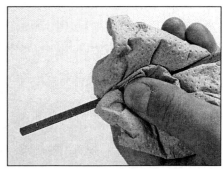

2 Using a clean rag or paper towel remove all oil from the dipstick. Insert the clean dipstick into the tube as far as it will go, then withdraw it again.

4 Oil is added through the filler cap. Unscrew the cap and top-up the level; a funnel may help to reduce spillage . Add the oil slowly, checking the level on the dipstick frequently. Avoid overfilling (see "Car Care").

Coolant level

 Warning: DO NOT attempt to remove the expansion tank pressure cap when the engine is hot, as there is a very great risk of scalding. Do not leave open containers of coolant about, as it is poisonous.

Car Care

● With a sealed-type cooling system, adding coolant should not be necessary on a regular basis. If frequent topping-up is required, it is likely there is a leak. Check the radiator, all hoses and joint faces for signs of staining or wetness, and rectify as necessary.

● It is important that antifreeze is used in the cooling system all year round, not just during the winter months. Don't top-up with water alone, as the antifreeze will become too diluted.

1 The coolant level varies with the temperature of the engine. When the engine is cold, the coolant level should be as shown. When the engine is hot, the level may rise slightly above the "COLD" mark.

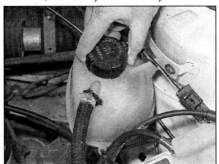

2 If topping-up is necessary, **wait until the engine is cold**. Slowly turn the expansion tank cap anti-clockwise to relieve the system pressure. Once any pressure is released, turn the cap anti-clockwise unti it can be lifted off.

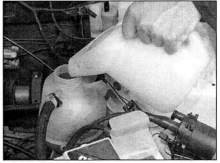

3 Add a mixture of water and antifreeze through the expansion tank filler neck until the coolant reaches the "COLD" level mark. Refit the cap, turning it clockwise as far as it will go until it is secure.

Screen washer fluid level

Screenwash additives not only keep the winscreen clean during foul weather, they also prevent the washer system freezing in cold weather - which is when you are likely to need it most. Don't top up using plain water as the screenwash will become too diluted, and will freeze during cold weather. On no account use engine antifreeze in the washer system - this could discolour or damage paintwork.

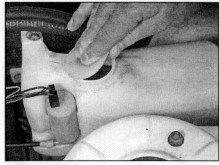

1 The windscreen/tailgate washer fluid reservoir is located at the rear left-hand corner of the engine compartment. An additional reservoir is fitted for those models having a headlamp washer system.

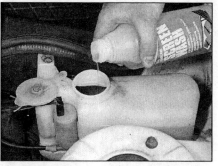

2 When topping-up the reservoir(s), a screenwash additive should be added in the quantities recommended on the bottle.

Brake fluid level

Warning:Brake hydraulic fluid can harm your eyes and damage painted surfaces, so use extreme caution when handling and pouring it.

● *Do not use fluid that has been standing open for some time, as it absorbs moisture from the air which can cause a dangerous loss of braking effectiveness.*

 HAYNES HiNT

● *Make sure that your car is on level ground.*
● *The fluid level in the master cylinder reservoir will drop slightly as the brake pads wear down, but the fluid level must never be allowed to drop below the 'MIN' mark.*

Safety first

● If the reservoir requires repeated topping-up this is an indication of a fluid leak somewhere in the system, which should be investigated immediately.

● If a leak is suspected, the car should not be driven until the braking system has been checked. Never take any risks where brakes are concerned.

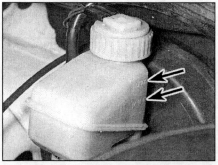

1 The "MAX" and "MIN" marks are indicated on the side of the reservoir. The fluid level must be kept between the marks.

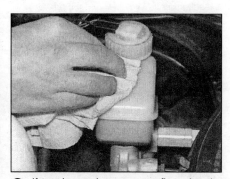

2 If topping-up is necessary, first wipe the area around the filler cap with a clean rag before removing the cap.

3 When adding fluid, it's a good idea to inspect the reservoir. The system should be drained and refilled if dirt is seen in the fluid (see Chapter 9 for details).

4 Carefully add fluid avoiding spilling it on surrounding paintwork. Use only the specified hydraulic fluid; mixing different types of fluid can cause damage to the system. After filling to the correct level, refit the cap securely, to prevent leaks and the entry of foreign matter. Wipe off any spilt fluid.

Power steering fluid level

Before you start:
✔ Park the vehicle on level ground.
✔ Set the steering wheel pointing straight-ahead.
✔ The engine should be turned off.

 For the check to be accurate the steering must not be turned once the engine has been stopped.

Safety First:
● The need for frequent topping-up indicates a leak, which should be investigated immediately.

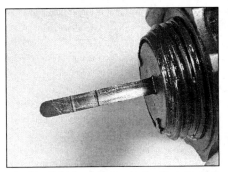

1 The fluid level is checked with a dipstick attached to the reservoir filler cap. The reservoir is located in the front left-hand corner of the engine compartment behind the headlight unit.

2 Clean the area around the reservoir. Remove the cap and wipe the dipstick with a clean rag. When the engine is cold, the fluid should come up to the lower ADD mark; when hot, it should come up to the FULL mark.

3 When topping-up, use the specified type of fluid. and do not overfill the reservoir. When the level is correct, refit the cap.

Electrical system

✔ Check all external lights and the horn. Refer to the appropriate Sections of Chapter 12 for details if any of the circuits are found to be inoperative.

✔ Visually check all wiring connectors, harnesses and retaining clips for security, and for signs of chafing or damage.

 If you need to check your brake lights and indicators unaided, back up to a wall or garage door and operate the lights. The reflected light should show if they are working properly.

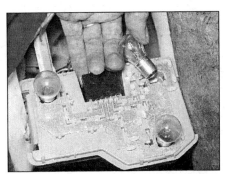

1 If a single indicator light, brake light or headlight has failed it is likely that a bulb has blown and will need to be replaced. Refer to Chapter 12 for details.
If both brake lights have failed, it is possible that the brake light switch above the brake pedal needs adjusting. This simple operation is described in Chapter 9.

2 If more than one indicator light or headlight has failed it is likely that either a fuse has blown or that there is a fault in the circuit (refer to "Electrical fault-finding" in Chapter 12).
The fuses are mounted in a panel located at the lower right-hand corner of the facia under a removable cover.

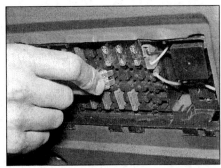

3 To replace a blown fuse, simply pull it out. Fit a new fuse of the same rating, available from car accessory shops.
It is important that you find the reason that the fuse blew - a checking procedure is given in Chapter 12.

Battery

Caution: Before carrying out any work on the vehicle battery, read the precautions given in "Safety first" at the start of this manual.

✔ Make sure that the battery tray is in good condition, and that the clamp is tight. Corrosion on the tray, retaining clamp and the battery itself can be removed with a solution of water and baking soda. Thoroughly rinse all cleaned areas with water. Any metal parts damaged by corrosion should be covered with a zinc-based primer, then painted.

✔ Periodically (approximately every three months), check the charge condition of the battery as described in Chapter 5A.

✔ If the battery is flat, and you need to jump start your vehicle, see *"Roadside Repairs"*.

1 The battery is located on the left-hand side of the engine compartment. The exterior of the battery should be inspected periodically for damage such as a cracked case or cover.

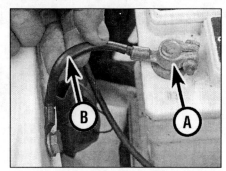

2 Check the tightness of battery clamps (A) to ensure good electrical connections. You should not be able to move them. Also check each cable (B) for cracks and frayed conductors.

Battery corrosion can be kept to a minimum by applying a layer of petroleum jelly to the clamps and terminals after they are reconnected.

3 If corrosion (white, fluffy deposits) is evident, remove the cables from the battery terminals, clean them with a small wire brush, then refit them. Accessory stores sell a useful tool for cleaning the battery post ...

4 ... as well as the battery cable clamps

Wiper blades

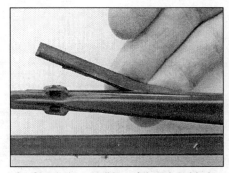

1 Check the condition of the wiper blades; if they are cracked or show any signs of deterioration, or if the glass swept area is smeared, renew them. For maximum clarity of vision, wiper blades should be renewed annually, as a matter of course.

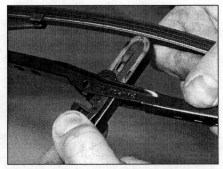

2 To remove a wiper blade, pull the arm fully away from the glass until it locks. Swivel the blade through 90°, press the locking tab(s) with your fingers, and slide the blade out of the arm's hooked end. On refitting, ensure that the blade locks securely into the arm.

Tyre condition and pressure

It is very important that tyres are in good condition, and at the correct pressure - having a tyre failure at any speed is highly dangerous. Tyre wear is influenced by driving style - harsh braking and acceleration, or fast cornering, will all produce more rapid tyre wear. As a general rule, the front tyres wear out faster than the rears. Interchanging the tyres from front to rear ("rotating" the tyres) may result in more even wear. However, if this is completely effective, you may have the expense of replacing all four tyres at once!

Remove any nails or stones embedded in the tread before they penetrate the tyre to cause deflation. If removal of a nail does reveal that the tyre has been punctured, refit the nail so that its point of penetration is marked. Then immediately change the wheel, and have the tyre repaired by a tyre dealer.

Regularly check the tyres for damage in the form of cuts or bulges, especially in the sidewalls. Periodically remove the wheels, and clean any dirt or mud from the inside and outside surfaces. Examine the wheel rims for signs of rusting, corrosion or other damage. Light alloy wheels are easily damaged by "kerbing" whilst parking; steel wheels may also become dented or buckled. A new wheel is very often the only way to overcome severe damage.

New tyres should be balanced when they are fitted, but it may become necessary to re-balance them as they wear, or if the balance weights fitted to the wheel rim should fall off. Unbalanced tyres will wear more quickly, as will the steering and suspension components. Wheel imbalance is normally signified by vibration, particularly at a certain speed (typically around 50 mph). If this vibration is felt only through the steering, then it is likely that just the front wheels need balancing. If, however, the vibration is felt through the whole car, the rear wheels could be out of balance. Wheel balancing should be carried out by a tyre dealer or garage.

Tread Depth - visual check

1 The original tyres have tread wear safety bands which will appear when the tread depth reaches approximately 1.6 mm. The band positions are indicated by a triangular mark on the tyre sidewall.

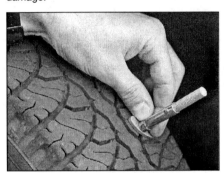

Tread Depth - manual check

2 Alternatively tread wear can be monitored with a simple, inexpensive device known as a tread depth indicator gauge.

Tyre Pressure Check

3 Check the tyre pressures regularly with the tyres cold. Do not adjust the tyre pressures immediately after the vehicle has been used, or an inaccurate setting will result. Tyre pressures are shown on the next two pages.

4 ***Tyre tread wear patterns***

Shoulder Wear

Underinflation (wear on both sides)
Under-inflation will cause overheating of the tyre, because the tyre will flex too much, and the tread will not sit correctly on the road surface. This will cause a loss of grip and excessive wear, not to mention the danger of sudden tyre failure due to heat build-up.
Check and adjust pressures
Incorrect wheel camber (wear on one side)
Repair or renew suspension parts
Hard cornering
Reduce speed!

Centre Wear

Overinflation
Over-inflation will cause rapid wear of the centre part of the tyre tread, coupled with reduced grip, harsher ride, and the danger of shock damage occurring in the tyre casing.
Check and adjust pressures

If you sometimes have to inflate your car's tyres to the higher pressures specified for maximum load or sustained high speed, don't forget to reduce the pressures to normal afterwards.

Uneven Wear

Front tyres may wear unevenly as a result of wheel misalignment. Most tyre dealers and garages can check and adjust the wheel alignment (or "tracking") for a modest charge.
Incorrect camber or castor
Repair or renew suspension parts
Malfunctioning suspension
Repair or renew suspension parts
Unbalanced wheel
Balance tyres
Incorrect toe setting
Adjust front wheel alignment
Note: *The feathered edge of the tread which typifies toe wear is best checked by feel.*

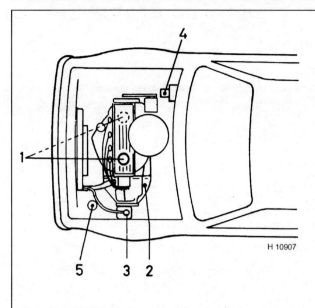

H 10907

Lubricants and fluids

Component or system	Lubricant type/specification
1 Engine	Multigrade engine oil, viscosity range SAE 10W/40 to 20W/50, to API SF/CC, SF/CD, SG/CC or SG/CD
2 Manual transmission	SAE 80EP gear oil or GM gear oil 90 188 629
2 Automatic transmission	Dexron II type automatic transmission fluid
3 Cooling system	Ethylene glycol-based antifreeze
4 Braking system	Hydraulic fluid to DOT 4 or SAE J1703
5 Power steering fluid	Dexron II type automatic transmission fluid

Capacities

Engine oil

Capacity (all engines - oil change, including filter):
1.3 and 1.4 litre engines . . . . .3.0 litres
1.6 litre engine . . . . .3.5 litres
1.8 and 2.0 litre (8-valve) engines . . . . .4.0 litres
2.0 litre (16-valve) . . . . .4.5 litres
Difference between "MAX" and "MIN" dipstick marks . . . . . . .1.0 litre

Cooling system

Capacity (approximate)
1.3 and 1.4 litre engines . . . . .6.7 litres
1.6, 1.8 and 2.0 litre engines . . . . .7.0 litres

Manual gearbox

Capacity (approximate) . . . . .2.1 litres

Automatic transmission

Capacity (approximate):
From dry . . . . .9.0 litres
Drain and refill . . . . .7.0 litres

Fuel tank

Capacity models . . . . .50 litres

Tyre pressures

Hatchback models

Pressures (tyres cold):	Front	Rear
1.2, 1.3 and 1.4 litre carburettor models:		
Up to 3 passengers:		
145 R 13 tyres	1.9 bars (28 psi)	1.7 bars (25 psi)
155 R 13 tyres	1.8 bars (26 psi)	1.6 bars (23 psi)
165 R 13 tyres	1.7 bars (25 psi)	1.7 bars (25 psi)
175/70 R 13 tyres	1.8 bars (26 psi)	1.6 bars (23 psi)
Full load:		
145 R 13 tyres	2.0 bars (29 psi)	2.3 bars (33 psi)
155 R 13 tyres	1.9 bars (28 psi)	2.1 bars (31 psi)
165 R 13 tyres	1.8 bars (26 psi)	2.0 bars (29 psi)
175/70 R 13 tyres	1.9 bars (28 psi)	2.1 bars (31 psi)
1.4 litre and 1.6 litre fuel injection models:		
Up to 3 passengers:		
155 R 13, 165 R 13 or 175/70 R 13 tyres	1.8 bars (26 psi)	1.6 bars (23 psi)
175/65 R 14 tyres	2.1 bars (30 psi)	1.9 bars (28 psi)
185/60 R 14 tyres	1.7 bars (24 psi)	1.7 bars (24 psi)
Full load:		
155 R 13	1.9 bars (28 psi)	2.2 bars (32 psi)
165 R 13 or 175/70 R 13 tyres	1.9 bars (28 psi)	2.1 bars (30 psi)
175/65 R 14 tyres	2.2 bars (32 psi)	2.4 bars (35 psi)
185/60 R 14 tyres	1.8 bars (26 psi)	2.0 bars (29 psi)
1.6 litre carburettor models:		
Up to 3 passengers	2.0 bars (29 psi)	1.8 bars (26 psi)
Full load	2.1 bars (31 psi)	2.3 bars (33 psi)

Hatchback models (continued)

   1.8 litre models:
      Up to 3 passengers . . . .   2.1 bars (31 psi)   1.9 bars (28 psi)
      Full load . . . .   2.2 bars (32 psi)   2.4 bars (35 psi)
   2.0 litre models:
     16-valve models:
      Up to 3 passengers . . . .   2.3 bars (33 psi)   2.1 bars (30 psi)
      Full load . . . .   2.4 bars (35 psi)   2.6 bars (38 psi)
     8-valve models:
      Up to 3 passengers . . . .   2.1 bars (30 psi)   1.9 bars (28 psi)
      Full load . . . .   2.2 bars (32 psi)   2.4 bars (35 psi)

Saloon models

Pressures (tyres cold):   **Front**   **Rear**
   1.3 and 1.4 litre carburettor models:
      Up to 3 passengers . . . .   1.8 bars (26 psi)   1.6 bars (23 psi)
      Full load:
        155 R 13 tyres . . . .   1.9 bars (28 psi)   2.4 bars (35 psi)
        175/70 R 13 tyres . . . .   1.9 bars (28 psi)   2.1 bars (30 psi)
   1.6 litre carburettor models:
      Up to 3 passengers . . . .   2.0 bars (29 psi)   1.8 bars (26 psi)
      Full load:
        155 R 13 tyres . . . .   2.1 bars (30 psi)   2.5 bars (36 psi)
        175/70 R 13 tyres . . . .   2.1 bars (30 psi)   2.3 bars (33 psi)
   1.4 and 1.6 litre fuel-injected models . . . .   See Hatchback information
   1.8 litre models:
      Up to 3 passengers . . . .   2.1 bars (30 psi)   1.9 bars (28 psi)
      Full load . . . .   2.2 bars (32 psi)   2.4 bars (35 psi)
   2.0 litre models . . . .   See Hatchback information

Estate and Van models

Pressures (tyres cold):   **Front**   **Rear**
   1.3 and 1.4 litre models:
      Up to 3 passengers . . . .   1.8 bars (26 psi)   1.8 bars (26 psi)
      Up to 4 passengers and 60 Kg load . . . .   1.9 bars (28 psi)   2.3 bars (33 psi)
      Full load . . . .   2.0 bars (29 psi)   2.8 bars (41 psi)
   1.6 litre models:
      Up to 3 passengers . . . .   1.8 bars (26 psi)   1.8 bars (26 psi)
      Up to 4 passengers and 60 Kg load . . . .   1.9 bars (28 psi)   2.3 bars (33 psi)
      Full load . . . .   2.0 bars (29 psi)   2.8 bars (41 psi)
   1.8 litre models:
      Up to 3 passengers . . . .   2.1 bars (30 psi)   2.3 bars (33 psi)
      Up to 4 passengers and 60 Kg load . . . .   2.2 bars (32 psi)   2.6 bars (38 psi)
      Full load . . . .   2.2 bars (32 psi)   3.2 bars (46 psi)

Astramax models

Pressures (tyres cold):   **Front**   **Rear**
   Up to 2 passengers and 100 kg load:
      155 R 13 tyres . . . .   2.0 bars (29 psi)   2.2 bars (32 psi)
      165 R13 and 165 R 14 tyres . . . .   1.8 bars (26 psi)   2.2 bars (32 psi)
   Full load:
      155 R 13 tyres . . . .   2.2 bars (32 psi)   3.0 bars (44 psi)
      165 R13 and 165 R 14 tyres . . . .   1.8 bars (26 psi)   3.0 bars (44 psi)

Convertible models

Pressures (tyres cold):   **Front**   **Rear**
   1.6 litre models:
     Up to 3 passengers:
        175/70 R 13 tyres . . . .   1.8 bars (26 psi)   1.6 bars (23 psi)
        175/65 R 14 tyres . . . .   2.1 bars (30 psi)   1.9 bars (28 psi)
        185/60 R 14 tyres . . . .   1.7 bars (24 psi)   1.7 bars (24 psi)
     Full load:
        175/70 R 13 tyres . . . .   1.9 bars (28 psi)   2.1 bars (30 psi)
        175/65 R 14 tyres . . . .   2.2 bars (32 psi)   2.4 bars (35 psi)
        185/60 R 14 tyres . . . .   1.8 bars (26 psi)   2.0 bars (29 psi)
   2.0 litre models:
     Up to 3 passengers:
        185/60 R 14 tyres . . . .   2.1 bars (30 psi)   1.9 bars (28 psi)
        185/55 R 15 tyres . . . .   2.5 bars (36 psi)   2.3 bars (33 psi)
     Full load:
        185/60 R 14 tyres . . . .   2.2 bars (32 psi)   2.4 bars (35 psi)
        185/55 R 15 tyres . . . .   2.7 bars (39 psi)   2.9 bars (42 psi)

Note: *Pressures apply only to original-equipment tyres, and may vary if any other make of tyre is fitted; check with the tyre manufacturer or supplier for correct pressures if necessary*

Chapter 1
Routine maintenance and servicing

Contents

Degrees of difficulty

Easy, suitable for novice with little experience	Fairly easy, suitable for beginner with some experience	Fairly difficult, suitable for competent DIY mechanic	Difficult, suitable for experienced DIY mechanic	Very difficult, suitable for expert DIY or professional

1 Vauxhall Astra/Belmont maintenance schedule

The maintenance intervals in this manual are provided with the assumption that you, not the dealer, will be carrying out the work. These are the minimum maintenance intervals recommended by the manufacturer for vehicles driven daily. If you wish to keep your vehicle in peak condition at all times, you may wish to perform some of these procedures more often. We encourage frequent maintenance, because it enhances the efficiency, performance and resale value of your vehicle. If the vehicle is driven in dusty areas, used to tow a trailer, or driven frequently at slow speeds (idling in traffic) or on short journeys, more frequent maintenance intervals are recommended.

When the vehicle is new, it should be serviced by a factory-authorised dealer service department, in order to preserve the factory warranty.

Every 250 miles (400 km) or weekly

☐ See Weekly checks

Every 9000 miles (15 000 km) or 6 months, whichever comes first

☐ Renew the engine oil and filter - early (pre-1987) models (Section 6)

Every 9000 miles (15 000 km) or 12 months, whichever comes first

☐ Renew the engine oil and filter - later (1987-on) models (Section 6)
☐ Renew the spark plugs (Section 7)
☐ Check and adjust the valve clearances - 1.2 litre models (Chapter 2A)
☐ Check all underbonnet and underbody components, pipes and hoses for leaks (Section 8)
☐ Check the condition of the auxiliary drivebelt, and renew if necessary (Section 9)
☐ Check the ignition system components and renew the contact breaker points (Section 10)
☐ Check idle speed and mixture adjustments (Section 11)
☐ Clean the fuel pump filter (carburettor models) (Section 12)
☐ Check the throttle cable adjustment (Chapter 4A or 4B)
☐ Check the automatic transmission fluid level (Section 13)
☐ Check the operation of the horn, all lights, and the wipers and washers (Section 14)
☐ Check the condition of the wiper blades (Section 15)
☐ Check the tightness of the roadwheel bolts (Section 16)
☐ Check the condition of the front, and rear (where fitted) brake pads (renew if necessary), and the calipers and discs (Section 17)
☐ Check the rear wheel bearings adjustment (Section 18)
☐ Check the handbrake adjustment (Section 19)
☐ Check the driveshaft CV joints and gaiters for condition (Section 20)
☐ Lubricate locks and hinges (Section 21)
☐ Check the exhaust system for condition and security (Section 22)
☐ Road test the vehicle (Section 23)

Every 18 000 miles (30 000 km) or 12 months, whichever comes first

In addition to all the items listed previously, carry out the following:

☐ Renew the air cleaner filter element (Section 24)
☐ Renew the fuel filter (fuel injection models) (Section 25)
☐ Clean the carburettor fuel inlet filter (Section 26)
☐ Check the manual transmission oil level (Section 27)
☐ Check the clutch adjustment (Section 28)
☐ Check the condition of the rear brake shoes (renew if necessary), wheel cylinders and drums (Section 29)
☐ Renew the brake fluid (Section 30)
☐ Check the headlamp alignment (Section 31)

Every 2 years (regardless of mileage)

In addition to all the relevant items listed previously, carry out the following:

☐ Renew the coolant (Section 32)

Every 36 000 miles (60 000 km) or 4 years, whichever comes first

In addition to all the relevant items listed previously, carry out the following:

☐ Renew the automatic transmission fluid (Section 33)
☐ Renew the camshaft toothed belt -
   1.3, 1.4, 1.6, 1.8 and 2.0 litre 8-valve engines (Chapter 2B),
   2.0 litre 16-valve engines (Chapter 2C)

Every 54 000 miles (90 000 km) or 3 years, whichever comes first

In addition to all the relevant items listed previously, carry out the following:

☐ Renew the braking system seals and hose (Chapter 9)

Underbonnet view of an early 1.6 litre model (air cleaner removed for clarity)

1 Wiper motor
2 Heater blower motor
3 Heater blower motor resistor
4 Windscreen washer tube
5 Screen washer reservoir
6 Suspension turrets
7 Coolant expansion tank
8 Ignition coil
9 Battery
10 Coolant hose

11 Radiator cooling fan
12 Distributor cover
13 Engine oil filler
14 Bonnet catch
15 Radiator
16 VIN plate
17 Engine breather
18 Air cleaner hot air pick-up
19 Thermostat housing
20 Fuel hoses

21 Fuel pump
22 Alternator
23 Accelerator cable
24 Carburettor
25 Choke cable
26 Servo non-return valve
27 Steering rack bellows
28 Air cleaner breather hose
29 Brake fluid reservoir
30 Brake servo

Underbonnet view of an early 1.8 litre model

1 Screen washer reservoir
2 Headlamp washer filler cap
3 Headlamp washer relay and fuse
4 Suspension turrets
5 Coolant expansion tank filler
6 Control relay (fuel injection system)
7 Ignition coil
8 Horn
9 Battery
10 Coolant hose

11 Radiator fan
12 Distributor
13 Engine oil filler
14 Bonnet catch
15 Radiator
16 VIN plate
17 Engine breather
18 Thermostat housing
19 Air cleaner
20 Airflow meter

21 Breather hose
22 Throttle valve housing
23 Fuel rail
24 Fuel pressure regulator
25 Servo non return valve
26 Steering rack bellows
27 Accelerator cable
28 Brake fluid reservoir
29 Brake servo

Underbonnet view of a 2.0 litre 16-valve model

1 Radiator top hose
2 Air cleaner
3 Suspension turrets
4 Coolant filler cap
5 Brake fluid reservoir
6 Air mass meter
7 Fuel pressure regulator
8 Breather hoses
9 Throttle cable

10 Engine oil filler cap
11 Pre-volume chamber
12 Brake servo non-return valve
13 Power steering hoses
14 Windscreen washer reservoir
15 Headlamp washer relay
16 ABS hydraulic unit
17 ABS surge arrester relay

18 Fuel injection control relay
19 Ignition coil
20 Battery
21 Power steering fluid reservoir
22 Distributor
23 Radiator
24 Vehicle identification plate
25 Horn

Front underbody view of a 1.8 litre model - other models similar

1 Control arm rear bush
2 Control arm
3 Anti-roll bar link
4 Driveshaft damper weight
5 Engine oil filter
6 Oil cooler hose
7 Air induction trunking

8 Radiator
9 Exhaust downpipes
10 Sump drain plug
11 Radiator fan
12 Gearbox sump
13 Driveshaft bellows
14 Brake hose

15 Steering balljoint attachment
16 Engine/transmission rear mounting
17 Gearchange tube
18 Exhaust pipe
19 Brake pipe
20 Brake and fuel pipes

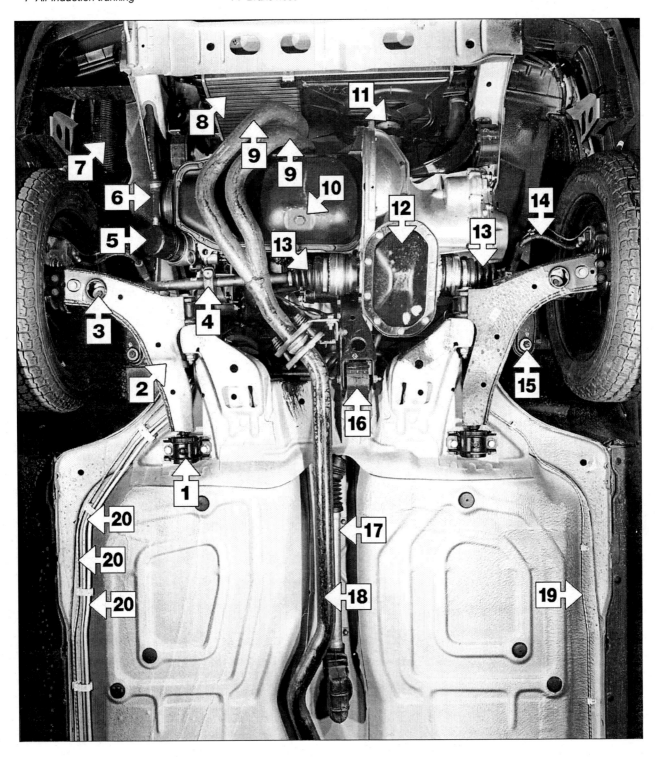

Rear underbody view of a 1.8 litre model - other models similar

1 Centre silencer
2 Handbrake adjuster
3 Handbrake cables
4 Fuel tank
5 Brake pipe
6 Brake and fuel pipes
7 Brake hoses
8 Axle beam
9 Axle mountings
10 Spring
11 Shock absorber mounting
12 Fuel filler pipe
13 Fuel gauge sender/fuel tank outlet
14 Fuel tank breather
15 Fuel filter*
16 Fuel pressure regulator*
17 Fuel pump*
18 Towing eye
19 Rear silencer
20 Rear brake pipes
*Fuel injection models only

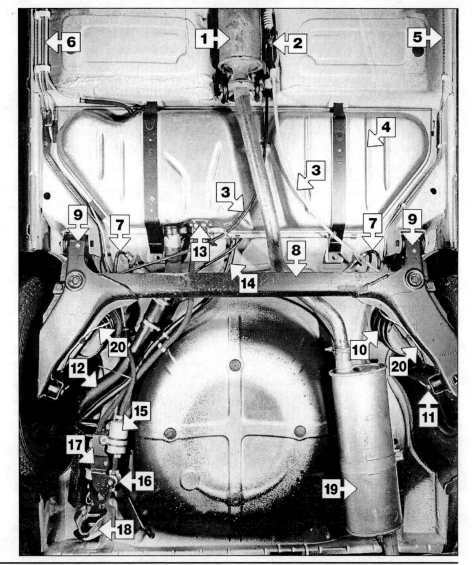

2 Introduction

General information

This Chapter is designed to help the home mechanic maintain his/her vehicle for safety, economy, long life and peak performance.

The Chapter contains a master maintenance schedule, followed by sections dealing specifically with each task on the schedule. Visual checks, adjustments, component renewal and other helpful items are included. Refer to the accompanying illustrations of the engine compartment and the underside of the vehicle for the locations of the various components.

Servicing of your vehicle in accordance with the mileage/time maintenance schedule and the following sections will provide a planned maintenance programme, which should result in a long and reliable service life. This is a comprehensive plan, so maintaining some

items but not others at the specified service intervals, will not produce the same results.

As you service your vehicle, you will discover that many of the procedures can - and should - be grouped together, because of the particular procedure being performed, or because of the close proximity of two otherwise-unrelated components to one another. For example, if the vehicle is raised for any reason, the exhaust can be inspected at the same time as the suspension and steering components.

The first step in this maintenance programme is to prepare yourself before the actual work begins. Read through all the sections relevant to the work to be carried out, then make a list and gather together all the parts and tools required. If a problem is encountered, seek advice from a parts specialist, or a dealer service department.

Intensive maintenance

If, from the time the vehicle is new, the routine maintenance schedule is followed closely, and frequent checks are made of fluid

levels and high-wear items, as suggested throughout this manual, the engine will be kept in relatively good running condition, and the need for additional work will be minimised.

It is possible that there will be times when the engine is running poorly due to the lack of regular maintenance. This is even more likely if a used vehicle, which has not received regular and frequent maintenance checks, is purchased. In such cases, additional work may need to be carried out, outside of the regular maintenance intervals.

If engine wear is suspected, a compression test (Chapter 2) will provide valuable information regarding the overall performance of the main internal components. Such a test can be used as a basis to decide on the extent of the work to be carried out. If for example a compression test indicates serious internal engine wear, conventional maintenance as described in this Chapter will not greatly improve the performance of the engine, and may prove a waste of time and money, unless extensive overhaul work (Chapter 2) is carried out first.

The following series of operations are those most often required to improve the performance of a generally poor-running engine:

Primary operations

a) Clean, inspect and test the battery (Section 4).
b) Check all the engine-related fluids (Section 3).
c) Check the condition and tension of the auxiliary drivebelt (Section 9).

d) Renew the spark plugs (Section 7).
e) Inspect the ignition system components (Section 10).
f)l Inspect the ignition HT leads (Section 10).
g) Check the condition of the air filter, and renew if necessary (Section 24).
h) Check the condition of all hoses, and check for fluid leaks (Section 8).

If the above operations do not prove fully effective, carry out the following secondary operations:

Secondary operations

All items listed under "Primary operations", plus the following:

a) Check the charging system (Chapter 5A).
b) Check the fuel system (Chapter 4A or 4B).
c) Renew the air filter (Section 24).
d) Renew the distributor cap and rotor arm (Section 10).
e) Renew the ignition HT leads (Section 10).

Every 250 miles or weekly

3 Fluid level checks

See "Weekly checks"

4 Battery check

See "Weekly checks"

5 Tyre checks

See "Weekly checks"

Every 9000 miles

6 Engine oil and filter renewal

1 Frequent oil and filter changes are the most important preventative maintenance procedures which can be undertaken by the DIY owner. As engine oil ages, it becomes diluted and contaminated, which leads to premature engine wear.
2 Before starting this procedure, gather together all the necessary tools and materials. Also make sure that you have plenty of clean rags and newspapers handy, to mop up any spills. Ideally, the engine oil should be warm, as it will drain more easily, and more built-up sludge will be removed with it. Take care not to touch the exhaust or any other hot parts of the engine when working under the vehicle. To avoid any possibility of scalding, and to protect yourself from possible skin irritants and other harmful contaminants in used engine oils, it is advisable to wear gloves when carrying out this work. Access to the underside of the vehicle will be greatly improved if it can be raised on a lift, driven

onto ramps, or jacked up and supported on axle stands (see "Jacking and Vehicle Support"). Whichever method is chosen, make sure that the vehicle remains level, or if it is at an angle, that the drain plug is at the lowest point. The drain plug is located at the rear of the sump.
3 Remove the oil filler cap from the camshaft cover (twist it through a quarter-turn anticlockwise and withdraw it).
4 Using a spanner, or preferably a socket and bar, slacken the drain plug about half a turn **(see illustration)**. Position the draining container under the drain plug, then remove the plug completely. If possible, try to keep the plug pressed into the sump while unscrewing it by hand the last couple of turns. As the plug releases from the threads, move it away sharply, so that the stream of oil from the sump runs into the container, not up your sleeve!
5 Allow some time for the oil to drain, noting that it may be necessary to reposition the container as the oil flow slows to a trickle.
6 After all the oil has drained, wipe the drain plug and the sealing washer with a clean rag. Examine the condition of the sealing washer,

and renew it if it shows signs of scoring or other damage which may prevent an oil-tight seal. Clean the area around the drain plug opening, and refit the plug complete with the washer. Tighten the plug securely, preferably to the specified torque, using a torque wrench.
7 The oil filter is located at the right-hand end of the engine.
8 Move the container into position under the oil filter.
9 Use an oil filter removal tool to slacken the filter initially, then unscrew it by hand the rest of the way **(see illustration)**. Empty the oil from the old filter into the container.
10 Use a clean rag to remove all oil, dirt and sludge from the filter sealing area on the engine. Check the old filter to make sure that the rubber sealing ring has not stuck to the engine. If it has, carefully remove it.
11 Apply a light coating of clean engine oil to the sealing ring on the new filter, then screw the filter into position on the engine. Tighten the filter firmly by hand only - **do not** use any tools.
12 Remove the old oil and all tools from under the vehicle then, if applicable, lower the vehicle to the ground.
13 Fill the engine through the filler hole in the camshaft cover, using the correct grade and type of oil (refer to Section 3 for details of topping-up). Pour in half the specified quantity of oil first, then wait a few minutes for the oil to drain into the sump. Continue to add oil, a small quantity at a time, until the level is up to the lower mark on the dipstick. Adding a further 1.0 litre (approx.) will bring the level up to the upper mark on the dipstick.
14 Start the engine and run it for a few minutes, while checking for leaks around the oil filter seal and the sump drain plug. Note that there may be a delay of a few seconds before the low oil pressure warning light goes out when

6.4 Removing the sump drain plug

6.9 Using an oil filter removal tool to unscrew the oil filter

the engine is first started, as the oil circulates through the new oil filter and the engine oil galleries before the pressure builds up.

15 Stop the engine, and wait a few minutes for the oil to settle in the sump once more. With the new oil circulated and the filter now completely full, recheck the level on the dipstick, and add more oil as necessary.

16 Dispose of the used engine oil safely, with reference to "General repair procedures".

Note: It is antisocial and illegal to dump oil down the drain. To find the location of your local oil recycling bank, call this number free.

7 Spark plug renewal

1 The correct functioning of the spark plugs is vital for the correct running and efficiency of the engine. It is essential that the plugs fitted are appropriate for the engine, the suitable type being specified at the end of this Chapter. If the correct type of plug is used and the engine is in good condition, the spark plugs should not need attention between scheduled renewal intervals, except for adjustment of their gaps. Spark plug cleaning is rarely necessary, and should not be attempted unless specialised equipment is available, as damage can easily be caused to the firing ends.

2 To remove the plugs, first open the bonnet. On 1.2 litre models remove the air cleaner as described in Chapter 4A. On 2.0 litre 16-valve engines undo the retaining screws and remove the spark plug lead cover from the engine.

3 Mark the HT leads 1 to 4, to correspond to the cylinder the lead serves (No 1 cylinder is nearest the timing belt end of the engine). Pull the HT leads from the plugs by gripping the end connectors, not the leads, otherwise the lead connections may be fractured.

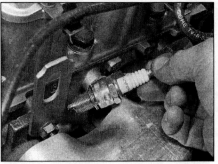

7.5 Removing a spark plug - 1.6 litre engine shown

4 It is advisable to remove any dirt from the spark plug recesses using a clean brush, vacuum cleaner or compressed air, before removing the plugs, to prevent the dirt dropping into the cylinders.

5 Unscrew the plugs using a spark plug spanner, a suitable box spanner, or a deep socket and extension bar **(see illustration)**. Keep the socket in alignment with the spark plugs, otherwise if it is forcibly moved to either side, the porcelain top of the spark plug may be broken off. As each plug is removed, examine it as follows.

6 Examination of the spark plugs will give a good indication of the condition of the engine. If the insulator nose of the spark plug is clean and white, with no deposits, this is indicative of a weak mixture or too hot a plug (a hot plug transfers heat away from the electrode slowly, while a cold plug transfers heat away quickly).

7 If the tip and insulator nose are covered with hard black-looking deposits, then this is indicative that the idle mixture is too rich. Should the plug be black and oily, then it is likely that the engine is fairly worn, as well as the mixture being too rich.

8 If the insulator nose is covered with light-tan to greyish-brown deposits, then the mixture is correct and it is likely that the engine is in good condition.

9 The spark plug gap is of considerable importance as, if it is too large or too small, the size of the spark and its efficiency will be seriously impaired. For the best results, the spark plug gap should be set in accordance with the Specifications at the end of this Chapter.

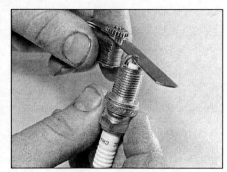

7.10a Measuring a spark plug electrode gap using a feeler blade

10 To set the spark plug gap, measure the gap between the electrodes with a feeler blade, and then bend open, or close, the outer plug electrode until the correct gap is achieved **(see illustrations)**. The centre electrode should never be bent, as this may crack the insulation and cause plug failure, if nothing worse.

11 Special spark plug electrode gap adjusting tools are available from most motor accessory shops **(see illustration)**.

12 Before fitting the new spark plugs, check that the threaded connector sleeves on the top of the plug are tight, and that the plug exterior surfaces and threads are clean.

13 Screw in the spark plugs by hand where possible, then tighten them to the specified torque. Take extra care to enter the plug threads correctly, as the cylinder head is of light alloy construction.

TOOL TiP

It is very often difficult to insert spark plugs into their holes without cross-threading them. To avoid this, fit a short length of 5/16-inch internal diameter hose over the end of the spark plug. The flexible hose acts as a universal joint to help align the plug with the plug hole. Should the plug begin to cross-thread, the hose will slip on the spark plug, preventing thread damage to the aluminium cylinder head.

14 Reconnect the HT leads in their correct order. On 1.2 litre models refit the air cleaner (Chapter 4A) and on 2.0 litre 16-valve models, refit the spark plug lead cover.

7.10b Measuring a spark plug electrode gap using a wire gauge

7.11 Adjusting a spark plug electrode gap using a special tool

8 Hose and fluid leak check

1 Visually inspect the engine joint faces, gaskets and seals for any signs of water or oil leaks. Pay particular attention to the areas around the camshaft cover, cylinder head, oil filter and sump joint faces. Bear in mind that, over a period of time, some very slight seepage from these areas is to be expected; what you are really looking for is any indication of a serious leak. Should a leak be found, renew the offending gasket or oil seal by referring to the appropriate Chapters in this manual.

2 Also check the security and condition of all the engine-related pipes and hoses. Ensure that all cable-ties or securing clips are in place, and in good condition. Clips which are broken or missing can lead to chafing of the hoses pipes or wiring, which could cause more serious problems in the future.

3 Carefully check the radiator hoses and heater hoses along their entire length. Renew any hose which is cracked, swollen or deteriorated. Cracks will show up better if the hose is squeezed. Pay close attention to the hose clips that secure the hoses to the cooling system components. Hose clips can pinch and puncture hoses, resulting in cooling system leaks. If wire-type hose clips are used, it may be a good idea to replace them with screw-type clips.

4 Inspect all the cooling system components (hoses, joint faces etc.) for leaks. Where any problems of this nature are found on system components, renew the component or gasket with reference to Chapter 3.

A leak in the cooling system will usually show up as white- or rust-coloured deposits on the area adjoining the leak.

5 Where applicable, inspect the automatic transmission fluid cooler hoses for leaks or deterioration.

6 With the vehicle raised, inspect the petrol tank and filler neck for punctures, cracks and other damage. The connection between the filler neck and tank is especially critical. Sometimes, a rubber filler neck or connecting hose will leak due to loose retaining clamps or deteriorated rubber.

7 Carefully check all rubber hoses and metal fuel lines leading away from the petrol tank. Check for loose connections, deteriorated hoses, crimped lines and other damage. Pay particular attention to the vent pipes and hoses, which often loop up around the filler neck and can become blocked or crimped. Follow the lines to the front of the vehicle, carefully inspecting them all the way. Renew damaged sections as necessary.

8 From within the engine compartment, check the security of all fuel hose attachments and pipe unions, and inspect the fuel hoses and vacuum hoses for kinks, chafing and deterioration.

9 Where applicable, check the condition of the power steering fluid hoses and pipes.

9 Auxiliary drivebelt check and renewal

Alternator drivebelt

Checking and adjustment

1 Correct tensioning of the auxiliary drivebelt will ensure that it has a long life. Beware, however, of overtightening, as this can cause excessive wear in the alternator.

2 The belt should be inspected along its entire length, and if it is found to be worn, frayed or cracked, it should be renewed as a precaution against breakage in service. It is advisable to carry a spare drivebelt of the correct type in the vehicle at all times.

3 Although special tools are available for measuring the belt tension, a good approximation can be achieved if the belt is tensioned so that there is approximately 13 mm of free movement under firm thumb pressure at the mid-point of the longest run between pulleys. If in doubt, err on the slack side, as an excessively-tight belt may cause damage to the alternator or other components.

4 If adjustment is required, loosen the alternator upper mounting nut and bolt - use two spanners, one to counterhold the bolt. Lever the alternator away from the engine using a wooden lever at the mounting bracket until the correct tension is achieved, then tighten the bolt securing the adjuster bracket, and the alternator mounting nuts and bolts. On no account lever at the free end of the alternator, as serious internal damage could be caused to the alternator.

Removal, renewal and refitting

5 To remove the belt, simply loosen the mounting nuts and bolts, and the bolt securing the adjuster bracket, as described previously, and slacken the belt sufficiently to slip it from the pulleys. On models with power steering it will first be necessary to remove the power steering pump drivebelt as described below.

6 Refit the belt, and tension it as described previously. Note that when a new belt has been fitted it will probably stretch slightly to

start with and the tension should be rechecked, and if necessary adjusted, after about 5 minutes running.

Power steering pump drivebelt

Checking and adjustment

7 Refer to the information given in paragraphs 1 to 3, noting that there should be approximately 8 mm of free movement in the belt.

8 If adjustment is required, slacken the adjuster bolt locknut (situated on the base of the pump) and rotate the adjuster nut as necessary to tension the belt. Once the belt tension is correct, securely tighten the locknut.

Removal, renewal and refitting

9 To remove the belt, simply loosen the locknut and fully slacken the adjuster nut sufficiently to slip the drivebelt from the pulleys.

10 Refit the belt, and tension it as described previously. Note that when a new belt has been fitted it will probably stretch slightly to start with and the tension should be rechecked, and if necessary adjusted, after about 5 minutes running.

Alternator/power steering pump drivebelt - later 1.6 litre models

Checking and adjustment

11 From March 1987 onwards, a single drivebelt is used for the alternator and power steering pump on 1.6 litre engines. The drivebelt is of the ribbed type and runs at a higher tension than the previous (V) belt.

12 To set the tension accurately, make up or obtain an adapter as shown **(see illustration)**.

13 Slacken the alternator pivot and adjusting strap bolts and fit the adapter. Using a torque wrench apply a load of 55 Nm (40 lbf ft) for a new belt, or 50 Nm (37 lbf ft) for an old belt. Keep the tension applied and securely tighten the alternator bolts.

Removal, renewal and refitting

14 To remove the belt, simply loosen the alternator pivot and strap bolts and slip the drivebelt from the pulleys.

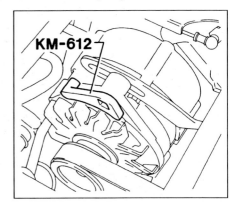

9.12 Adapter KM-612 used for setting drivebelt tension on later 1.6 litre models

15 Refit the belt, and tension it as described previously. Note that when a new belt has been fitted it will probably stretch slightly to start with and the tension should be rechecked, and if necessary adjusted, after about 5 minutes running.

10 Ignition system check

Models with contact breaker ignition system

1 Renew the contact breaker points and adjust the gap and dwell angle as described in Chapter 5B. After adjustment put one or two drops of engine oil into the centre of the cam recess where appropriate and smear the surfaces of the cam itself with petroleum jelly. Do not over-lubricate as any excess could get onto the contact point surfaces and cause ignition difficulties.

2 The spark plug (HT) leads should also be checked.

3 Ensure that the leads are numbered before removing them, if not make identification marks to avoid confusion when refitting. Pull the leads from the plugs by gripping the end fitting, not the lead, otherwise the lead connection may be fractured.

4 Check inside the end fitting for signs of corrosion, which will look like a white crusty powder. Push the end fitting back onto the spark plug ensuring that it is a tight fit on the plug. If not, remove the lead again and use pliers to carefully crimp the metal connector inside the end fitting until it fits securely on the end of the spark plug.

5 Using a clean rag, wipe the entire length of the lead to remove any built-up dirt and grease. Once the lead is clean, check for burns, cracks and other damage. Do not bend the lead excessively or pull the lead lengthwise - the conductor inside might break.

6 Disconnect the other end of the lead from the distributor cap. Again, pull only on the end fitting. Check for corrosion and a tight fit in the same manner as the spark plug end. If an ohmmeter is available, check the resistance of the lead by connecting the meter between the spark plug end of the lead and the segment inside the distributor cap. Refit the lead securely on completion.

7 Check the remaining leads one at a time, in the same way.

8 If new spark plug (HT) leads are required, purchase a set for your specific car and engine.

9 Remove the distributor cap, wipe it clean and carefully inspect it inside and out for signs of cracks, carbon tracks (tracking) and worn, burned or loose contacts; check that the cap's carbon brush is unworn, free to move against spring pressure and making good contact with the rotor arm. Also inspect the cap seal for signs of wear or damage and

10.9a Remove the distributor cap . . .

renew if necessary. Remove and inspect the rotor arm **(see illustrations)**. It is common practice to renew the cap and rotor arm whenever new spark plug (HT) leads are fitted. When fitting a new cap, remove the leads from the old cap one at a time and fit them to the new cap in the exact same location - do not simultaneously remove all the leads from the old cap or firing order confusion may occur. On refitting ensure that the arm is securely pressed onto the shaft and the cap is securely fitted.

10 Even with the ignition system in first class condition, some engines may still occasionally experience poor starting attributable to damp ignition components. To disperse moisture a moister dispersant aerosol can be very effective.

Models with an electronic ignition system

> ⚠ **Warning: Voltages produced by an electronic ignition system are considerably higher than those produced by conventional ignition systems. Extreme care must be taken when working on the system with the ignition switched on. Persons with surgically-implanted cardiac pacemaker devices should keep well clear of the ignition circuits, components and test equipment.**

11 Check the condition of the HT leads and distributor components as described above in paragraphs 3 to 10.

12 Check the ignition timing (Chapter 5C).

11 Idle speed and mixture adjustments

1 Before checking the idle speed and mixture setting, always check first the following.
 a) *Check that the ignition timing is accurate (Chapter 5B or 5C).*
 b) *Check that the spark plugs are in good condition and correctly gapped (Section 25).*
 c) *Check that the accelerator cable and, on carburettor models, the choke cable*

10.9b . . . and pull off the rotor arm from the distributor shaft (1.6 litre model shown)

 (where fitted) is correctly adjusted (see relevant Part of Chapter 4).
 d) *Check that the crankcase breather hoses are secure with no leaks or kinks (Chapter 2).*
 e) *Check that the air cleaner filter element is clean (Section 31).*
 f) *Check that the exhaust system is in good condition (see relevant Part of Chapter 4).*
 g) *If the engine is running very roughly, check the compression pressures as described in Chapter 2.*

2 Take the car on a journey of sufficient length to warm it up to normal operating temperature. Proceed as described under the relevant sub-heading.

Note: *Adjustment should be completed within two minutes of return, without stopping the engine. If this cannot be achieved, or if the radiator electric cooling fan operates, wait for the cooling fan to stop and clear any excess fuel from the inlet manifold by racing the engine two or three times to between 2000 and 3000 rpm, then allow it to idle again.*

Carburettor models

3 Connect a tachometer in accordance with the manufacturer's instructions.

4 If the idle speed is outside the specified tolerance (see Specifications), turn the adjustment screw as necessary **(see illustrations)**. This will not alter the CO content of the exhaust gas to any extent.

5 If an exhaust gas analyser is available, check the exhaust gas CO content as follows.

11.4a Idle speed adjustment screw (arrowed) - 32TL carburettor

11.4b Idle speed adjustment screw (arrowed) - 2E3 carburettor

11.4c Adjusting the idle speed - Varajet carburettor

11.4d Idle speed adjusting screw (A) - 1B1 carburettor

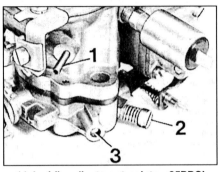

11.4e Idle adjustment points - 35PDSI carburettor

6 Remove the tamperproof cap (where fitted) from the mixture adjustment screw. Satisfy yourself that you are not breaking any local or national laws by so doing.

7 With the engine at normal operating temperature, check the CO content of the exhaust gas. If it is outside the permitted tolerance, turn the mixture adjusting screw as necessary to correct it **(see illustrations)**.

8 When the adjustments are correct, fit a new tamperproof cap to the screw and disconnect the tachometer. **Note:** On 32TL and Varajet II carburettors, if it proves difficult to adjust the idle speed and/or mixture setting then it is likely that the base idle speed is incorrect. Setting of this requires the use of an accurate vacuum gauge and should therefore be entrusted to a Vauxhall/Opel dealer.

Fuel-injected models

1.8 litre models

9 With the engine at normal operating temperature, connect a tachometer in accordance with its manufacturer's instructions.

10 Allow the engine to idle, and compare the idle speed with that given in the Specifications. If adjustment is necessary, slacken the locknut and turn the idle speed adjusting screw until the specified speed is obtained. The adjusting screw is situated on the throttle valve housing. Tighten the locknut on completion.

11 If an exhaust gas analyser is available, check the mixture (CO level) as follows.

12 With the engine idling at the specified speed, read the CO level and compare it with that specified.

13 If adjustment is necessary, remove the tamperproof cap from the mixture adjusting screw on the airflow sensor **(see illustration)**. Turn the screw clockwise to enrich the mixture, and anti-clockwise to weaken it.

14 On completion, re-adjust the idle speed if necessary. Note that failure to bring the CO level within the specified range indicates a fault in the injection system, or a worn engine.

2.0 litre models

15 On all models the idle speed is automatically controlled by the electronic control unit and is not adjustable. If it is found to be incorrect then a fault is present in the fuel injection/ignition system (Chapter 4B).

16 On models without a catalytic converter, the mixture (CO level) can be adjusted as described above in paragraphs 9 and 11 to 14. On 16-valve models the adjusting screw is on the air mass meter **(see illustration)**.

1 Distributor vacuum take-off
2 Idle speed adjustment screw
3 Mixture (CO level) adjustment screw

11.7a Mixture (CO) adjustment screw - 32TL carburettor

11.7b Mixture (CO) adjustment screw cap (arrowed) 2E3 carburettor

11.7c Adjusting the mixture (CO) setting - Varajet carburettor

11.7d Mixture (CO) adjustment screw (B) - 1B1 carburettor

11.13 On 1.8 litre fuel-injected models the mixture adjustment screw is located under the cap on the airflow sensor

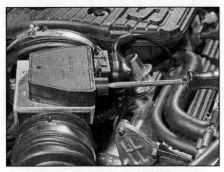

11.16 Adjusting the mixture (CO) setting - 2.0 litre 16-valve models

17 On models fitted with a catalytic converter, the mixture (CO level) is also automatically controlled by the electronic control unit and is not adjustable. If it is found to be incorrect then a fault is present in the fuel injection/ignition system (Chapter 4B).

1.4 and 1.6 litre models

18 On 1.4 and 1.6 litre models both the idle speed and mixture CO content are automatically controlled by the control unit and cannot be manually adjusted (See Chapter 4B). If necessary, they can be checked by if they are found to be incorrect then a fault is present in the fuel injection/ignition system.

12 Fuel pump filter cleaning - carburettor models

 Warning: Before carrying out the following operation refer to the precautions given in Safety first! and follow them implicitly. Petrol is a highly dangerous and volatile liquid and the precautions necessary when handling it cannot be overstressed

Note: *On some models the fuel pump may be a sealed unit, in which case this procedure is not necessary.*

1 Place a wad of rag underneath the fuel pump to catch the fuel which will be spilt during the following operation.
2 Undo the retaining screw and remove the end cover from the fuel pump. Recover the rubber seal **(see illustration)**.

12.2 Removing the fuel pump cover, filter and rubber seal - carburettor models

3 Remove the filter from the cover and wash it fresh fuel to remove any debris from it. Inspect the filter for signs of clogging or splitting and renew it if necessary.
4 Locate the filter in the cover and fit the rubber seal.
5 Refit the cover to the pump and securely tighten its retaining screw.
6 Start the engine and check for signs of fuel leakage.

13 Automatic transmission fluid level check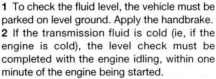

1 To check the fluid level, the vehicle must be parked on level ground. Apply the handbrake.
2 If the transmission fluid is cold (ie, if the engine is cold), the level check must be completed with the engine idling, within one minute of the engine being started.
3 With the engine idling, fully depress the brake pedal, and move the gear selector lever smoothly through all positions, finishing in position "P".
4 With the engine still idling, withdraw the transmission fluid level dipstick (located at the left-hand side of the engine compartment, next to the engine oil level dipstick). Pull up the lever on the top of the dipstick to release it from the tube. Wipe the dipstick clean with a lint-free rag, re-insert it and withdraw it again.
5 If the transmission fluid was cold at the beginning of the procedure, the fluid level should be on the "MAX" mark on the side of the dipstick marked "+20°C". Note that 0.4 litres of fluid is required to raise the level from the "MIN" to the "MAX" mark.
6 If the transmission fluid was at operating temperature at the beginning of the procedure (ie, if the vehicle had been driven for at least 12 miles/20 km), the fluid level should be between the "MIN" and "MAX" marks on the side of the dipstick marked "+94°C". Note that 0.2 litres of fluid is required to raise the level from the "MIN" to the "MAX" mark.
7 If topping-up is necessary, stop the engine, and top-up with the specified type of fluid through the transmission dipstick tube.
8 Re-check the level, and refit the dipstick on completion.

14 Electrical system check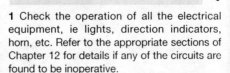

1 Check the operation of all the electrical equipment, ie lights, direction indicators, horn, etc. Refer to the appropriate sections of Chapter 12 for details if any of the circuits are found to be inoperative.
2 Note that stop-light switch adjustment is described in Chapter 9.
3 Check all accessible wiring connectors, harnesses and retaining clips for security, and for signs of chafing or damage. Rectify any faults found.

15 Wiper blade check

Check the condition of the wiper blades. If they are cracked, or show any signs of deterioration, or if they fail to clean the glass effectively, renew the blades. Ideally, the wiper blades should be renewed annually as a matter of course.

To remove a wiper blade, pull the arm away from the glass until it locks. Swivel the blade through 90°, then squeeze the locking clip, and detach the blade from the arm. When fitting the new blade, make sure that the blade locks securely into the arm, and that the blade is orientated correctly.

16 Roadwheel bolt tightness check

Using a torque wrench on each wheel bolt in turn, ensure that the bolts are tightened to the specified torque.

17 Brake pad, caliper and disc check

Front brakes

1 Apply the handbrake, then jack up the front of the vehicle and support securely on axle stands; remove the roadwheels (see "Jacking and Vehicle Support ").
2 For a quick check, the thickness of friction material remaining on each pad can be measured through the slot in the front of the caliper body **(see illustration)**. If any pad is worn to the minimum thickness or less, all four pads must be renewed (see Chapter 9).
3 For a complete check, the brake pads should be removed and cleaned. This will allow the operation of the caliper to be checked, and the condition of the brake disc itself to be fully examined on both sides (see Chapter 9).

Rear brakes

4 Chock the front wheels, then jack up the rear of the vehicle and support securely on axle stands; remove the roadwheels (see "Jacking and Vehicle Support "). Inspect the pads as described in paragraphs 2 and 3.

17.2 The thickness of the brake pads are visible through the caliper aperture

18 Rear wheel bearing adjustment

Refer to Chapter 10, Section 9.

19 Handbrake adjustment

Rear drum brake models

1 Normal adjustment of the handbrake takes place automatically due to the self-adjusting mechanism of the rear brakes. To compensate for cable stretch, or after a new cable has been fitted or the adjustment has otherwise been disturbed, proceed as follows.
2 Chock the front wheels, release the handbrake and raise and support the rear of the vehicle so that the rear wheels are clear of the ground.
3 Tighten the nut on the handbrake cable yoke until the rear wheels start to become stiff to turn, then back it off until they are free again **(see illustration)**.
4 Check that the handbrake starts to take effect at the second notch of lever movement, and is fully applied by the fourth or fifth notch.
5 A further check may be made by removing the plug in the brake backplate **(see illustration)**. When adjustment is correct, the pin on the handbrake operating lever is clear

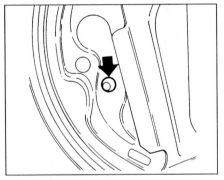

19.5 Check the handbrake lever pin (arrowed) is correctly positioned as described in text

19.11a On models with rear disc brakes the handbrake shoe adjuster wheel is accessible through the hole in the disc . . .

19.3 Handbrake cable adjusting nut (arrowed) on yoke - rear drum brake models

of the shoe web by approximately 3 mm with the handbrake released.
6 When adjustment is correct, apply a smear of grease to the threads of the cable end fitting to prevent corrosion. Lower the vehicle, apply the handbrake and remove the wheel chocks.

Rear disc brake models

7 Before checking handbrake adjustment, drive for approximately 300 metres at low speed with the handbrake lightly applied. This will clean off any rust or glaze from the drums and shoes.
8 Chock the front wheels and engage a gear. Slacken the rear wheel bolts. Raise and support the rear of the vehicle and remove the rear wheels.
9 Release the handbrake, then reapply it by two notches.
10 Slacken off the adjuster nut on the handbrake cable yoke (located to the left of the silencer) until it is at the end of its travel. If a silencer heat shield is fitted, access will be improved by removing it.
11 Turn a brake disc to bring the adjuster hole (the large unthreaded hole) into line with the adjuster at the bottom of the brake shoes. Using a screwdriver through the hole, turn the adjuster wheel until the shoes are against the disc, then back it off again until the disc is just free to turn without the shoes dragging **(see illustrations)**.

19.11b . . . and can be adjusted using a suitable screwdriver

12 Repeat the operation on the other brake.
13 Tighten the cable adjuster nut until the shoes start to drag again. This should happen on both sides.
14 Release and fully reapply the handbrake a couple of times. Check that the discs turn freely when the control is fully released, and that the brake is fully applied at the sixth notch.
15 Refit the exhaust heat shield if it was removed. Refit the wheels, lower the vehicle and tighten the wheel bolts.

20 Driveshaft CV joint and gaiter check

Refer to Chapter 8, Section 5.

21 Hinge and lock lubrication

Lubricate the hinges of the bonnet, doors and tailgate with a light general-purpose oil. Similarly, lubricate all latches, locks and lock strikers. At the same time, check the security and operation of all the locks, adjusting them if necessary (see Chapter 11).

Lightly lubricate the bonnet release mechanism and cable with a suitable grease.

22 Exhaust system check

1 With the engine cold (at least an hour after the vehicle has been driven), check the complete exhaust system from the engine to the end of the tailpipe. The exhaust system is most easily checked with the vehicle raised on a hoist, or suitably supported on axle stands (see "*Jacking and Vehicle Support*"). so that the exhaust components are readily visible and accessible.
2 Check the exhaust pipes and connections for evidence of leaks, severe corrosion and damage. Make sure that all brackets and mountings are in good condition, and that all relevant nuts and bolts are tight. Leakage at any of the joints or in other parts of the system will usually show up as a black sooty stain in the vicinity of the leak. Reputable exhaust repair systems can be used for effective repairs to exhaust pipes and silencer boxes, including ends and bends. Check for an MOT-approved permanent exhaust repair.
3 Rattles and other noises can often be traced to the exhaust system, especially the brackets and mountings. Try to move the pipes and silencers. If the components are able to come into contact with the body or suspension parts, secure the system with new mountings. Otherwise separate the joints (if possible) and twist the pipes as necessary to provide additional clearance.

23 Road test

Instruments and electrical equipment

1 Check the operation of all instruments and electrical equipment.
2 Make sure that all instruments read correctly, and switch on all electrical equipment in turn, to check that it functions properly.

Steering and suspension

3 Check for any abnormalities in the steering, suspension, handling or road "feel".
4 Drive the vehicle, and check that there are no unusual vibrations or noises.
5 Check that the steering feels positive, with no excessive "sloppiness", or roughness, and check for any suspension noises when cornering and driving over bumps.

Drivetrain

6 Check the performance of the engine, clutch (where applicable), gearbox/ transmission and driveshafts.

7 Listen for any unusual noises from the engine, clutch and gearbox/transmission.
8 Make sure that the engine runs smoothly when idling, and that there is no hesitation when accelerating.
9 Check that, where applicable, the clutch action is smooth and progressive, that the drive is taken up smoothly, and that the pedal travel is not excessive. Also listen for any noises when the clutch pedal is depressed.
10 On manual gearbox models, check that all gears can be engaged smoothly without noise, and that the gear lever action is not abnormally vague or "notchy".
11 On automatic transmission models, make sure that all gearchanges occur smoothly, without snatching, and without an increase in engine speed between changes. Check that all the gear positions can be selected with the vehicle at rest. If any problems are found, they should be referred to a Vauxhall/Opel dealer.
12 Listen for a metallic clicking sound from the front of the vehicle, as the vehicle is driven slowly in a circle with the steering on full-lock. Carry out this check in both directions. If a clicking noise is heard, this indicates wear in a driveshaft joint, in which case renew the joint if necessary.

Check the operation and performance of the braking system

13 Make sure that the vehicle does not pull to one side when braking, and that the wheels do not lock prematurely when braking hard.
14 Check that there is no vibration through the steering when braking.
15 Check that the handbrake operates correctly without excessive movement of the lever, and that it holds the vehicle stationary on a slope.
16 Test the operation of the brake servo unit as follows. With the engine off, depress the footbrake four or five times to exhaust the vacuum. Hold the brake pedal depressed, then start the engine. As the engine starts, there should be a noticeable "give" in the brake pedal as vacuum builds up. Allow the engine to run for at least two minutes, and then switch it off. If the brake pedal is depressed now, it should be possible to detect a hiss from the servo as the pedal is depressed. After about four or five applications, no further hissing should be heard, and the pedal should feel considerably harder.

Every 18 000 miles

24 Air cleaner filter element renewal

Carburettor models

1 To remove the air cleaner element, remove the air cleaner cover. This is secured by a centre nut or bolt, or by three screws. Additionally, release the spring clips around the edge of the cover or, if spring clips are not fitted, carefully prise around the lower edge of the cover with your fingers to release the retaining lugs **(see illustrations)**.
2 With the cover removed, lift out the element **(see illustrations)**.
3 Wipe inside the air cleaner, being careful not to introduce dirt into the carburettor throat. It is preferable to remove the air cleaner completely. Remember to clean the inside of the air cleaner cover.
4 Fit the new element, then refit and secure the cover. Observe any cover-to-body alignment lugs or slots.

Fuel injection models

1.4 and 1.6 litre models

5 Refer to paragraphs 1 to 4.

1.8 and 2.0 litre 8-valve models

6 The air cleaner on these models is contained within the airflow sensor housing.

24.1a On carburettor models, undo the retaining nut (on some models the lid will be retained by screws) . . .

24.1b . . . and release the retaining clips . . .

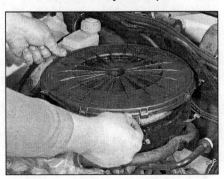
24.2a . . . then lift off the air cleaner lid . . .

24.2b . . . and withdraw the filter element

24.7 On 1.8 and 2.0 litre 8-valve models, disconnect the airflow sensor wiring connector . . .

24.8a . . . then release the retaining clips . . .

24.8b . . . and remove the air cleaner housing cover, complete with the filter element

24.9 On fitting, ensure the element is correctly seated in the cover groove

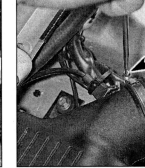
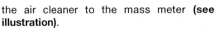

24.10 Disconnecting the trunking from the air cleaner - 2.0 litre 16-valve models

24.13 Fitting a new air cleaner element - 2.0 litre 16-valve models

7 Release the locking clip, and disconnect the plug from the airflow sensor **(see illustration)**. Disconnect the air trunking.

8 Release the spring clips, and lift off the air cleaner cover with airflow sensor attached. The element will probably come away with the cover **(see illustrations)**. Do not drop or jar the airflow sensor.

9 Wipe clean the inside of the air cleaner an fit a new element to the cover, engaging the element seal in the cover recess **(see illustration)**. Refit and secure the cover, then reconnect the airflow sensor plug. Refit the air trunking.

2.0 litre 16-valve models

10 Disconnect the trunking which connects

25.3 Fuel filter showing mounting and hose connections

the air cleaner to the mass meter **(see illustration)**.

11 Release the four spring clips which secure the air cleaner lid. Remove the lid.

12 Remove the element and wipe clean the inside of the filter housing and lid.

13 Fit a new element, sealing lip uppermost **(see illustration)**. Refit and secure the lid and trunking.

25 Fuel filter renewal - fuel injection models

⚠️ **Warning: Before carrying out the following operation refer to the precautions given in Safety first! and follow them implicitly. Petrol is a highly dangerous and volatile liquid and the precautions necessary when handling it cannot be overstressed.**

1 The fuel filter is located under the rear of the vehicle. Chock the front wheels, jack up the rear of the vehicle, and support securely on axle stands (see *"Jacking and Vehicle Support"*).

2 Disconnect the battery negative lead and position a suitable container below the fuel filter, to catch spilt fuel.

3 Slacken the retaining clips and, bearing in mind the information given in Chapter 4B on depressurising the fuel system, disconnect both hoses. To minimise fuel loss clamp the hoses either side of the filter or be prepared to

plug the hose ends as they are disconnected **(see illustration)**.

4 Loosen the clamp bolt, and withdraw the filter from its clamp. Note the orientation of the fuel flow direction indicator on the filter. This will be in the form of an arrow which points in the direction of the fuel flow, or the filter will have AUS (out) stamped on its outlet side **(see illustration)**.

5 Recover the mounting rubber from the old filter, and transfer it to the new filter.

6 Fit the new filter making sure its fuel flow direction indicator is facing the right way.

7 Reconnect the hose and securely tighten their retaining clips.

8 Start the engine and check the disturbed hose connections for signs of leakage.

25.4 Fuel filter directional marking

26 Carburettor fuel inlet filter cleaning

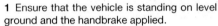

⚠️ **Warning: Before carrying out the following operation refer to the precautions given in Safety first! and follow them implicitly. Petrol is a highly dangerous and volatile liquid and the precautions necessary when handling it cannot be overstressed.**

Referring to the relevant Section of Chapter 4A, remove the filter, wash it fresh fuel to remove any debris from it. Inspect the filter for signs of clogging or splitting and renew it if necessary. Refit the filter and reconnect the fuel hose.

27 Manual transmission oil level check

1 Ensure that the vehicle is standing on level ground and the handbrake applied.
2 Working underneath the vehicle, unscrew the transmission oil level plug **(see illustration)**. The level plug is located beside the driveshaft inner CV joint; on 1.2, 1.3, 1.4 and later 1.6 litre models the plug is on the left-hand side of the transmission, and on all other models it is on the right-hand side.
3 The oil level should be up to the lower edge of the level plug hole.
4 If necessary, top-up with oil through the breather/filler orifice in the gear selector cover. Unscrew the breather/filler plug, and top-up with the specified grade of oil, until oil just begins to run from the level plug hole. A funnel may be helpful, to avoid spillage **(see illustrations)**. Do not overfill - if too much oil is added, wait until the excess has run out of the level plug hole. Refit the level plug and the breather/filler plug on completion.

28 Clutch adjustment check

Refer to Chapter 6

29 Rear brake shoe, wheel cylinder and drum check

1 Chock the front wheels, then jack up the rear of the vehicle and support it on axle stands (see 'Jacking and vehicle support').
2 The thickness of friction material remaining on one of the brake shoes can be observed through the hole in the brake backplate that is exposed by prising out the sealing grommet **(see illustration)**. A torch or inspection light will probably be required to help observation. When viewing through the inspection holes, the rivet heads cannot easily be seen. In this case, if there is less than approximately 2 mm

27.2 Removing the manual transmission level plug - early 1.6 litre model shown

thickness of friction material visible, remove the drums and inspect the shoes. If any of the shoes is excessively worn, all four shoes must be renewed as a set.
3 For a comprehensive check, the brake drum should be removed and cleaned. This will allow the wheel cylinders to be checked, and the condition of the brake drum itself to be fully examined (see Chapter 9).

30 Brake fluid renewal

⚠️ **Warning: Brake hydraulic fluid can harm your eyes and damage painted surfaces, so use extreme caution when handling and pouring it. Do not use fluid that has been standing open for some time as it absorbs moisture from the air. Excess moisture can cause a dangerous loss of braking effectiveness.**

1 The procedure is similar to that for the bleeding of the hydraulic system as described in Chapter 9, except that the brake fluid reservoir should be emptied by siphoning, using a clean poultry baster or similar before starting, and allowance should be made for the old fluid to be expelled when bleeding a section of the circuit.
2 Working as described in Chapter 9, open the first bleed screw in the sequence and pump the brake pedal gently until nearly all the old fluid has been emptied from the master cylinder reservoir. Top-up to the `MAX'

29.2 Removing the sealing grommet from the inspection hole in the rear brake backplate

27.4a To top up, unscrew the breather/filler plug from the top of the transmission . . .

27.4b . . . then top up via the breather/filler plug orifice

level with new fluid and continue pumping until only the new fluid remains in the reservoir and new fluid can be seen emerging from the bleed screw. Tighten the screw and top the reservoir level up to the `MAX' level line.

> **HAYNES HiNT**
> *Old hydraulic fluid is invariably much darker in colour than the new, making it easy to distinguish the two.*

3 Work through all the remaining bleed screws in sequence until new fluid can be seen at all of them. Be careful to keep the master cylinder reservoir topped up to above the `MIN' level at all times or air may enter the system and greatly increase the length of the task.
4 When the operation is complete, check that all bleed screws are securely tightened and that their dust caps are refitted. Wash off all traces of spilt fluid and recheck the master cylinder reservoir fluid level.
5 Check the operation of the brakes before taking the car on the road.

31 Headlamp aim check

Accurate adjustment of the headlight beam is only possible using optical beam-setting equipment, and this work should therefore be carried out by a Vauxhall/Opel dealer or service station with the necessary facilities.

Basic adjustments can be carried out in an emergency, and further details are given in Chapter 12.

Every 2 Years

32 Coolant renewal

Cooling system draining

⚠️ **Warning: Wait until the engine is cold before starting this procedure. Do not allow antifreeze to come in contact with your skin or painted surfaces of the vehicle. Rinse off spills immediately with plenty of water. Never leave antifreeze lying around in an open container or in a puddle in the driveway or on the garage floor. Children and pets are attracted by its sweet smell. Antifreeze is fatal if ingested.**

1 To drain the cooling system, remove the expansion tank filler cap. Turn the cap anti-clockwise until it reaches the first stop. Wait until any pressure remaining in the system is released then push the cap down, turn it anti-clockwise to the second stop and lift off.
2 Position a suitable container beneath the radiator bottom hose union.
3 Slacken the hose clip and ease the hose from the radiator stub. If the hose joint has not been disturbed for some time, it will be necessary to gently manipulate the hose to break the joint. Do not use excessive force, or the radiator stub could be damaged. Allow the coolant to drain into the container.
4 As no cylinder block drain plug is fitted and the radiator bottom hose union may be situated halfway up the radiator, this may not fully drain the cooling system.
5 If the coolant has been drained for a reason other than renewal, then provided it is clean and less than two years old, it can be re-used.
6 Reconnect the hose and securely tighten its retaining clip on completion of draining.

Cooling system flushing

7 If coolant renewal has been neglected, or if the antifreeze mixture has become diluted, then in time, the cooling system may gradually lose efficiency, as the coolant passages become restricted due to rust, scale deposits, and other sediment.
8 The cooling system efficiency can be restored by flushing the system clean.
9 The radiator should be flushed independently of the engine to avoid unnecessary contamination.

Radiator flushing

10 To flush the radiator, drain the cooling system then proceed as follows.
11 Slacken the retaining clips and disconnect the top and bottom hoses from the radiator.
12 Insert a garden hose into the radiator top inlet. Direct a flow of clean water through the radiator, and continue flushing until clean water emerges from the radiator bottom outlet.
13 If after a reasonable period, the water still does not run clear, the radiator can be flushed

32.19a On 1.2 litre models, bleed the cooling system through the cylinder head heater hose outlet

with a good proprietary cleaning agent. It is important that the manufacturers instructions are followed carefully. If the contamination is particularly bad, insert the hose in the radiator bottom outlet, and flush the radiator in reverse.

Engine flushing

14 To flush the engine, remove the thermostat as described in Chapter 3, then temporarily refit the thermostat cover.
15 With the top and bottom hoses disconnected from the radiator, insert a garden hose into the radiator top hose. Direct a clean flow of water through the engine, and continue flushing until clean water emerges from the radiator bottom hose.
16 On completion of flushing, refit the thermostat and reconnect the hoses with reference to Chapter 3.

Cooling system filling

17 Before attempting to fill the cooling system, make sure that all hoses and clips are in good condition, and that the clips are tight. Note that an antifreeze mixture must be used all year round, to prevent corrosion of the engine components (see following sub-Section). Also check that the radiator and cylinder block drain plugs are in place and tight.
18 Remove the expansion tank filler cap.
19 On 1.2 litre models, disconnect the heater hose from the cylinder head, on 1.3, 1.4 and later 1.6 litre engines models, disconnect the wire and unscrew the coolant temperature sender from the inlet manifold. On early 1.6, and all 1.8 and 2.0 litre models, unscrew the bleed screw which is situated in the thermostat housing cover (where no bleed screw is fitted, unscrew the temperature sender unit) **(see illustrations)**.
20 Fill the system by slowly pouring the coolant into the expansion tank to prevent airlocks from forming.
21 If the coolant is being renewed, begin by pouring in a couple of litres of water, followed by the correct quantity of antifreeze, then top-up with more water.
22 When coolant free of air bubbles emerges from the orifice, reconnect the heater hose (1.2 litre models) or refit the coolant temperature

32.19b On 1.3 litre models, unscrew temperature gauge sender unit from the manifold to bleed the cooling system

sender/bleed screw (as applicable) and tighten it securely (all other models).
23 Top-up the coolant level to the "KALT" (or "COLD") mark on the expansion tank, then refit the expansion tank cap.
24 Start the engine and run it until it reaches normal operating temperature, then stop the engine and allow it to cool.
25 Check for leaks, particularly around disturbed components. Check the coolant level in the expansion tank, and top-up if necessary. Note that the system must be cold before an accurate level is indicated in the expansion tank. If the expansion tank cap is removed while the engine is still warm, cover the cap with a thick cloth, and unscrew the cap slowly to gradually relieve the system pressure (a hissing sound will normally be heard). Wait until any pressure remaining in the system is released, then continue to turn the cap until it can be removed.

Antifreeze mixture

26 The antifreeze should always be renewed at the specified intervals. This is necessary not only to maintain the antifreeze properties, but also to prevent corrosion which would otherwise occur as the corrosion inhibitors become progressively less effective.
27 Always use an ethylene-glycol based antifreeze which is suitable for use in mixed metal cooling systems. The quantity of antifreeze and levels of protection are indicated in the Specifications.
28 Before adding antifreeze the cooling system should be completely drained, preferably flushed, and all hoses checked for condition and security.
29 After filling with antifreeze, a label should be attached to the expansion tank stating the type and concentration of antifreeze used and the date installed. Any subsequent topping up should be made with the same type and concentration of antifreeze.
30 Do not use engine antifreeze in the screen washer system, as it will cause damage to the vehicle paintwork. A proprietry screen should be added to the washer system in the recommended quantities.

Every 36 000 miles

33 Automatic transmission fluid renewal

1 Allow the transmission to cool down before draining, as the fluid: can be very hot indeed.
2 Remove all the fluid pan screws except one which should be unscrewed through several turns.
3 Release the fluid pan from its gasket and as the end of the pan tilts downwards, catch the fluid in a suitable container.
4 Remove the remaining screw and the pan. Peel off the gasket (where fitted) or remove all traces of sealant (as applicable).
5 Pull the filter mesh from its securing clips and recover its sealing ring. Clean the filter in a high flash-point solvent and allow it to dry. If the filter is clogged or split it must be renewed.
6 Fit a new O-ring and refit the filter securely.
7 Ensure that the fluid pan and transmission mating surfaces are clean and dry and bolt on the fluid pan using a new gasket. Where no gasket is fitted, apply a bead of sealant about 5.0 mm thick to clean surfaces. The fluid pan which is fitted with a gasket can be identified by the strengthening ribs on the pan flanges. The pan for use with silicone sealant has plain flanges.
8 Fill the transmission with the specified quantity of fluid and then check the level as described in Section 13.

Specifications

Cooling system

Antifreeze mixtures:
Protection down to -15ºC	28% antifreeze
Protection down to -30ºC	50% antifreeze

Note: *Refer to antifreeze manufacturer for latest recommendation*

Fuel system

Idle speed:
Carburettor models:	
Manual transmission	900 to 950 rpm
Automatic transmission	800 to 850 rpm
Fuel-injected models:	
1.4 litre models	830 to 990 rpm*
1.6 litre models	720 to 880 rpm*
1.8 litre models:	
Early (pre 1987) models:	
Manual transmission	900 to 950 rpm
Automatic transmission	800 to 850 rpm
Later (1987 onwards) models	800 to 900 rpm
2.0 litre models	720 to 780 rpm*

Idle mixture CO content:
Carburettor models	1.0 to 1.5%
Fuel-injected models	Less than 1.0%**

*Not adjustable - controlled by ECU
**On all 1.4 and 1.6 litre fuel injection models, and 2.0 litre models with a catalytic converter the exhaust gas CO content is regulated by the control unit and is not adjustable

Ignition system

Spark plugs:
Type:	
1.2 litre models	Champion RL82YCC or RL82YC
1.3, 1.4, 1.6 and 1.8 litre models	Champion RN9YCC or RN9YC
2.0 litre models:	
8-valve models	Champion RN9YCC or RN9YC
16-valve models	Champion RC9MCC
Electrode gap:	
RL82YCC, RN9YCC and RC9MCC plugs	0.8 mm
RL82YC and RN9YC plugs	0.7 mm

*The spark plug gap quoted is that recommended by Champion for their specified plugs listed above. If spark plugs of any other type are to be fitted, refer to their manufacturer's spark plug gap recommendations.

Braking system

Brake pad minimum thickness (including backing plate)	7.0 mm
Rear brake shoe minimum friction material-to-rivet head depth	0.5 mm

Torque wrench settings

	Nm	lbf ft
Sump drain plug	45	33
Spark plugs	20	15
Roadwheel bolts	90	66

Notes

Chapter 2 Part A:
OHV engine

Contents

Degrees of difficulty

Easy, suitable for novice with little experience	Fairly easy, suitable for beginner with some experience	Fairly difficult, suitable for competent DIY mechanic 	Difficult, suitable for experienced DIY mechanic	Very difficult, suitable for expert DIY or professional

Specifications

General
Maker's designation	12 SC
Bore x stroke	79.0 x 61.0 mm
Cubic capacity	1196 cc
Compression ratio	9.0: 1

Valve clearances (warm)
Inlet	0.15 mm
Exhaust	0.25 mm

Cylinder head
Identification mark	E
Valve seat width:	
Inlet	1.25 to 1.50 mm
Exhaust	1.60 to 1.85 mm
Overall height	81 ± 0.25 mm

Valves and guides

	Inlet	Exhaust
Overall length	99.3 mm	101.1 mm
Head diameter	32 mm	29 mm
Stem diameter (nominal, ± 0.005 mm):		
Standard	7.005 mm	6.995 mm
Oversize 1	7.080 mm	7.060 mm
Oversize 2	7.155 mm	7.1 35 mm
Oversize A	7.255 mm	7.235 mm
Valve guide bore (± 0.01 mm):		
Standard	7.035 mm	
Oversize 1	7.110 mm	
Oversize 2	7.185 mm	
Oversize A	7.285 mm	
Valve clearance in guide:		
Inlet	0.01 5 to 0.045 mm	
Exhaust	0.035 to 0.065 mm	
Sealing face angle	44°	

Camshaft

Radial run-out	0.03 mm max
Endfloat	0.17 to 0.43 mm
Cam lift	6.45 mm

Pistons and bores

	Diameters	Marking
Production size 1	78.95 mm	5
	78.96 mm	6
	78.97 mm	7
	78.98 mm	8
Production size 2	78.99 mm	99
	79.00 mm	00
	79.01 mm	01
	79.02 mm	02
Production size 3	79.03 mm	03
	79.04 mm	04
	79.05 mm	05
	79.06 mm	06
Production size 4	79.07 mm	07
	79.08 mm	08
	79.09 mm	09
	79.10 mm	1
Oversize (+0.5 mm nominal)	79.47 mm	79.47/7 +0.5
	79.48 mm	79.48/8 +0.5
	79.49 mm	79.49/9 +0.5
	79.50 mm	79.50/0 + 0.5
Pistons clearance in bore	0.1 to 0.3 mm estimated	
Bore out-of-round and taper	0.013 mm max	

Piston rings

Quantity (per piston)	2 compression, 1 oil control (scraper)
Thickness:	
Compression	2.0 mm
Oil control	5.0 mm
End gap:	
Compression	0.30 to 0.45 mm
Oil control	0.40 to 1.40 mm
Ring gap offset	180° (see text)
Ring vertical clearance in groove	Not specified - typically 0.06 mm

Gudgeon pins

Length	65 mm
Diameter	20 mm
Clearance in piston	0.0015 to 0.0195 mm
Clearance in connecting rod	None (interference fit)

Crankshaft and bearings

	Colour code	Embossed code
Number of main bearings	3	
Main bearing journal diameters - standard:		
Front	53.997 to 54.010 mm	
Centre and rear	54.007 to 54.020 mm	
Centre journal width - standard	29.000 to 29.052 mm	
Main bearing shell identification - standard:		
Front, top	Brown	1 ON or 701-N
Front, bottom	Brown	1 UN or 702-N
Centre, top	Brown	20+UN or 705-N
Centre, bottom	Green	20+UN or 725-N
Rear, top	Green	631-N
Rear, bottom	Green	635-N
Main bearing shell identification - standard journal, oversize housing:		
Front, top	U1 -OB	
Front, bottom	U1-U	
Centre, top and bottom	U	
Rear, top	U3-OB	
Rear, bottom	U3-U	
Big-end bearing journal diameter - standard	4.971 to 44.987 mm	
Big-end bearing shell identification - standard	None	
Main and big-end bearing undersizes	0.25 mm production and service; 0.50 mm service only	

Main bearing shell identification - 0.25 undersize:	Colour code	Embossed code
Front, top	Brown-blue	1 OA or 006-A
Front, bottom	Brown-blue	1 UA or 008-A
Centre, top	Brown-blue	20+UA or 014-A
Centre, bottom	Brown	20+UA or 034-A
Rear, top	Green-blue	632-A
Rear, bottom	Green-blue	636-A
Main bearing shell identification - 0.50 undersize:		
Front, top	Brown-black	1 OB or 027 B
Front, bottom	Brown-black	1 U or 029 B
Centre, top	Brown-black	2 OB 0.35 B
Centre, bottom	Green-black	2 UB 035 B
Rear, top	None	3 OB 0,50
Rear, bottom	None	3 U 0,50
Big-end bearing shell identification:		
0.25 undersize	A	
0.50 undersize	B	
Main and big-end bearing journal out-of-round	0.006 mm max	
Main and big-end bearing journal taper	0.01 mm max	
Crankshaft endfloat	0.09 to 0.20 mm	
Connecting rod endfloat	0.02 to 0.06 mm	
Main bearing running clearance:		
Front	0.020 to 0.046 mm	
Centre	0.010 to 0.036 mm	
Rear	0.01 0 to 0.032 mm estimated	
Big-end bearing running clearance	0.11 to 0.24 mm	
Crankshaft radial run-out (at centre journal, shaft in block)	0.03 mm max	

Flywheel

Ring gear run-out	0.5 mm max	
Refinishing limit - depth of material which may be removed from		
clutch friction surface	0.3 mm max	

Lubrication system

Oil pump tolerances:		
Teeth backlash	0.1 to 0.2 mm	
Teeth projection	0.04 to 0.10 mm	
Oil pressure at idle (engine warm)	1.5 bar	

Torque wrench settings

	Nm	lbf ft
Flywheel bolts (Use new bolts every time):		
Stage 1	35	26
Stage 2	Angle-tighten a further 50° to 90°	
Main bearing caps	62	46
Big-end bearing caps	27	20
Sump bolts (with locking compound)	5	4
Cylinder head bolts (use new bolts every time):		
Stage 1	25	18
Stage 2	Angle-tighten a further 60°	
Stage 3	Angle-tighten a further 60°	
Stage 4	Angle-tighten a further 60°	
Camshaft sprocket	40	30
Crankshaft pulley	40	30
Engine mounting bracket, RH:		
To block (use sealant on lower bolt)	20	15
To damping pad	40	30
Engine mountings to body:		
LH rear	65	48
RH rear	40	30
Sump drain plug	45	33
Oil pump mounting bolts	20	15

1 General description

The engine is of four-cylinder. in-line overhead valve type, mounted transversely at the front of the car.

The crankshaft is supported in three shell type main bearings. Thrustwashers are incorporated in the centre main bearing to control crankshaft endfloat.

The connecting rods are attached to the crankshaft by horizontally split shell type big-end bearings. and to the pistons by gudgeon pins which are an interference fit in the connecting rod small-end bore. The aluminium alloy pistons are of the slipper type and are fitted with three piston rings: two compression rings and an oil control ring.

The camshaft is chain driven from the crankshaft and operates the rocker arms via tappets and short pushrods. The inlet and exhaust valves are each closed by a single valve spring and operates in guides, integral with the cylinder head. The valves are actuated directly by the rocker arms.

Engine lubrication is by a gear type oil pump. The pump is mounted beneath the crankcase and is driven by a camshaft, as are the distributor and fuel pump.

Many of the engine component retaining bolts are of the socket-headed type and require the use of Torx type multi-tooth keys or socket bits for removal. These are readily available from retail outlets and should be obtained if major dismantling or repair work is to be carried out on the engine.

2 Compression test - description and interpretation

1 When engine performance is down, or if misfiring occurs which cannot be attributed to the ignition or fuel systems, a compression test can provide diagnostic clues as to the engine's condition. If the test is performed regularly, it can give warning of trouble before any other symptoms become apparent.
2 The engine must be fully warmed-up to normal operating temperature, the battery must be fully charged, and all the spark plugs must be removed (Chapter 1). The aid of an assistant will also be required.
3 Disable the ignition system by disconnecting the ignition HT coil lead from the distributor cap and earthing it on the cylinder block. Use a jumper lead or similar wire to make a good connection.
4 Fit a compression tester to the No 1 cylinder spark plug hole - the type of tester which screws into the plug thread is best.
5 Have the assistant hold the throttle wide open, and crank the engine on the starter motor; after one or two revolutions, the compression pressure should build up to a maximum figure, and then stabilise. Record the highest reading obtained.
6 Repeat the test on the remaining cylinders, recording the pressure in each.
7 All cylinders should produce very similar pressures; a difference of more than 2 bars between any two cylinders indicates a fault. Note that the compression should build up quickly in a healthy engine; low compression on the first stroke, followed by gradually-increasing pressure on successive strokes, indicates worn piston rings. A low compression reading on the first stroke, which does not build up during successive strokes, indicates leaking valves or a blown head gasket (a cracked head could also be the cause). Deposits on the undersides of the valve heads can also cause low compression.
8 Although Vauxhall do not specify exact compression pressures, as a guide, any cylinder pressure of below 10 bars can be considered as less than healthy. Refer to a Vauxhall dealer or other specialist if in doubt

as to whether a particular pressure reading is acceptable.
9 If the pressure in any cylinder is low, carry out the following test to isolate the cause. Put a teaspoonfull of clean oil into that cylinder through its spark plug hole, and repeat the test.
10 If the addition of oil temporarily improves the compression pressure, this indicates that bore or piston wear is responsible for the pressure loss. No improvement suggests that leaking or burnt valves, or a blown head gasket, may be to blame.
11 A low reading from two adjacent cylinders is almost certainly due to the head gasket having blown between them; the presence of coolant in the engine oil will confirm this.
12 If one cylinder is about 20 percent lower than the others and the engine has a slightly rough idle, a worn camshaft lobe could be the cause.
13 If the compression reading is unusually high, the combustion chambers are probably coated with carbon deposits. If this is the case, the cylinder head should be removed and decarbonised.
14 On completion of the test, refit the spark plugs and reconnect the ignition system.

3 Operations possible with the engine in the car

The following operations may be carried out without having to remove the engine:
a) Adjustment of the valve clearances.
b) Removal and refitting of cylinder head.
c) Removal and refitting of sump.
d) Removal and refitting of oil pump.
e) Removal and refitting of the timing gear components.
f) Removal and refitting of pistons and connecting rods.
g) Removal and refitting of the flywheel.
h) Removal and refitting of the engine/transmission mountings.

4 Operations requiring engine removal

The following operations can only be carried out after removal of the engine:
a) Removal and refitting of the camshaft and tappets.
b) Removal and refitting of the crankshaft and main bearings.
c) Removal and refitting of the crankshaft rear oil seal.

5 Engine dismantling and reassembly - general information

1 If the engine has been removed from the car for major overhaul, or if individual components have been removed for repair or renewal, observe the following general hints on dismantling and reassembly.

2 Drain the oil into a suitable container and then thoroughly clean the exterior of the engine using a degreasing solvent or paraffin. Clean away as much of the external dirt and grease as possible before dismantling.
3 As parts are removed, clean them in a paraffin bath. However, do not immerse parts with internal oilways in paraffin as it is difficult to remove, usually requiring a high pressure hose. Clean oilways with nylon pipe cleaners.
4 Avoid working with the engine or any of the components directly on a concrete floor, as grit presents a real source of trouble.
5 Wherever possible, work should be carried out with the engine or individual components on a strong bench. If the work must be done on the floor, cover it with a board or sheets of newspaper.
6 Have plenty of clean, lint-free rags available and also some containers or trays to hold small items. This will help during reassembly and also prevent possible losses.
7 Always obtain a complete set of gaskets if the engine is being completely dismantled, or all those necessary for the individual component or assembly being worked on. Keep the old gaskets with a view to using them as a pattern to make a replacement if a new one is not available.
8 If possible refit nuts, bolts and washers in their locations after removal; this helps to protect the threads and avoids confusion or loss.
9 During reassembly thoroughly lubricate all the components, where this is applicable, with engine oil, but avoid contaminating the gaskets and joint mating faces.
10 Where applicable, the following Sections describe the removal, refitting and adjustment of components with the engine in the car. If the engine has been removed from the car, the procedures described are the same except for the disconnection of hoses, cables and linkages, and the removal of components necessary for access, which will already have been done.

6 Ancillary components - removal and refitting

If the engine has been removed from the car for complete dismantling, the following externally mounted ancillary components should be removed. When the engine has been reassembled these components can be refitted before the engine is installed in the car, as setting up and adjustment is often easier with the engine removed. The removal and refitting sequence need not necessarily follow the order given:
a) Alternator (Chapter 5A).
b) Distributor and spark plugs (Chapters 1 and 5).
c) Inlet and exhaust manifolds and carburettor (Chapter 4A).
d) Fuel pump (Chapter 4A).
e) Water pump and thermostat (Chapter 3).
f) Clutch assembly (Chapter 6).

7 Valve clearances - adjustment

1 This adjustment should be carried out with the engine at its normal operating temperature. If it is being done after overhaul when the engine is cold, repeat the adjustment after the car has been driven a few kilometres when the engine will then be hot.

2 Begin by removing the air cleaner, as described in Chapter 4A.

3 Mark the spark plug leads to ensure correct refitting and then pull them off the spark plugs.

4 Disconnect the engine breather hoses at the rocker cover **(see illustration)**.

5 Undo the four bolts securing the rocker cover to the cylinder head and lift off the shaped spreader washers.

6 Withdraw the rocker cover from the cylinder head. If it is stuck give it a tap with the palm of your hand to free it.

7 Turn the engine by means of the crankshaft pulley bolt, or by engaging top gear and pulling the car forward, until No 1 piston is approaching TDC on the firing stroke. This can be checked by removing No 1 spark plug and feeling for compression with your fingers as the engine is turned, or by removing the distributor cap and checking the position of the rotor arm which should be pointing to the No 1 spark plug lead segment in the cap. The ignition timing marks on the pulley and timing cover must be aligned **(see illustration)**.

8 With the engine in this position the following valves can be adjusted - counting from the timing cover end of the engine.

1 exhaust
2 inlet
3 inlet
5 exhaust

9 Now turn the engine crankshaft through one complete revolution and adjust the following remaining valves:

4 exhaust
6 inlet
7 inlet
8 exhaust

10 As each clearance is being checked, slide a feeler blade of the appropriate size, as given in the Specifications, between the end of the

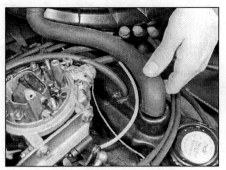

7.4 Removing the breather hose from the rocker cover

valve stem and the rocker arm **(see illustration)**. Adjust the clearance by turning the rocker arm retaining nut using a socket or ring spanner until the blade is a stiff sliding fit.

11 It is also possible to check and adjust the clearances with the engine running. This is done in the same way, but each valve is checked in turn. It will of course be necessary to refit the plug leads and No 1 spark plug if this method is adopted. To reduce oil splash place a piece of cardboard, suitably cut to shape, between the pushrod side of the rocker arms and the edge of the cylinder head.

12 After adjustment remove all traces of old gasket from the cylinder head mating face and renew the rocker cover gasket if it is cracked or perished.

13 Refit the rocker cover and secure with the retaining bolts and shaped spreader washers.

14 Refit the spark plug and plug leads, reconnect the engine breather hoses and refit the air cleaner, as described in Chapters 1 and 4.

8 Cylinder head - removal and refitting

Removal

1 Make sure that the engine is cold before commencing operations to avoid any chance of the head distorting.

2 Disconnect the battery negative terminal

3 Drain the cooling system, as described in Chapter 1, and remove the air cleaner, as described in Chapter 4A.

4 From behind the engine, undo the two bolts securing the exhaust front pipe to the manifold. Remove the bolts and tension springs; then separate the pipe joint from the manifold.

5 Slacken the retaining clip and disconnect the radiator top hose from the thermostat housing in the water pump.

6 Slacken the alternator mounting and adjustment arm bolts, move the alternator towards the engine and slip the drivebelt off the pulleys.

7 Slacken the retaining clips and disconnect the heater hose and radiator bottom hose from the water pump.

7.7 Ignition timing marks (arrowed) in alignment

8 Disconnect the other heater hose at the cylinder head outlet after slackening the retaining clip.

9 Undo the union nut and disconnect the brake servo vacuum hose from the inlet manifold.

10 Note the location of the plug leads to aid refitting and pull them off the spark plugs. Disconnect the HT lead at the coil, undo the distributor cap retaining screws and remove the cap and leads.

11 Refer to Chapter 4A and disconnect the choke and accelerator cables from the carburettor. Detach the distributor vacuum advance pipe.

12 Disconnect the fuel hose from the carburettor and plug its end after removal.

13 Disconnect the engine breather hoses from the rocker cover.

14 Undo the three socket-headed screws securing the inlet manifold to the cylinder head. Note the spark plug lead support brackets fitted to the two end retaining bolts.

15 Lift the inlet manifold complete with carburettor from the cylinder head and recover the gasket.

16 Undo the four bolts and shaped spreader washers and lift off the rocker cover.

17 Slacken the rocker arm retaining nuts, move the rocker arms to one side and lift out the pushrods **(see illustration)**. Keep the pushrods in order after removal.

18 Undo the cylinder head retaining bolts, half a turn at a time in the reverse sequence to that shown in **illustration 8.26**. Unscrew the bolts fully and remove them. Obtain new bolts for use when refitting.

7.10 Checking a valve clearance

8.17 Removing the pushrods

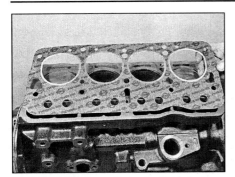

8.24 Fitting a cylinder head gasket

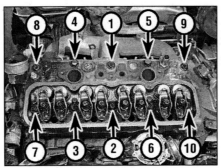

8.26 Cylinder head bolt tightening sequence

8.29 Inlet manifold gasket in position

19 Lift the cylinder head from the block. If it is stuck, tap it free with a soft-faced mallet. Do not insert a lever into the gasket joint - you may damage the mating surfaces.

20 With the cylinder head removed, recover the gasket.

21 If the cylinder head has been removed for decarbonising or for attention to the valves or springs, reference should be made to Sections 9 and 10.

Refitting

22 Before refitting the cylinder head, ensure that the cylinder block and head mating faces are spotlessly clean and dry with all traces of old gasket removed. Use a scraper and wire brush to do this, but take care to cover the water passages and other openings with masking tape or rag to prevent dirt and carbon falling in. Remove all traces of oil and water from the bolt holes, otherwise hydraulic pressure created by the bolts being screwed in could crack the block or give inaccurate torque settings. Ensure that the bolt threads are clean and dry.

23 When all is clean, screw two guide studs into the cylinder block. These can be made from the two old cylinder head bolts by cutting off their heads and sawing a screwdriver slot in their ends.

24 Locate a new gasket in position on the block as shown **(see illustration)**. Do not use any jointing compound on the gasket

25 Lower the cylinder head carefully into position. Screw in new bolts finger tight, remove the guide pins and screw in the two remaining bolts.

26 Tighten the cylinder head bolts in the order shown **(see illustration)** to the first stage specified torque. Now tighten the bolts through three further stages as given in the Specifications. No further retightening will be required.

27 Refit the pushrods, making quite sure that each one is located in its tappet.

28 Reposition the rocker arms over the ends of the pushrods and then adjust the valve clearances, as described in Section 7.

29 Place a new gasket in position and refit the inlet manifold and carburettor **(see illustration)**.

30 Refit the rocker cover, using a new gasket, and secure with the four bolts and spreader washers.

31 Refit the heater hoses and radiator hoses to the outlets on the water pump and cylinder head.

32 Refit the fuel hose to the carburettor, the vacuum advance pipe to the distributor and the breather hoses to the rocker cover.

33 Refit and adjust the accelerator and choke cables, as described in Chapter 4A.

34 Refit the brake servo vacuum hose to the inlet manifold.

35 Refit the distributor cap and reconnect the plug leads and coil lead.

36 Slip the drivebelt over the pulleys and adjust its tension, as described in Chapter 1.

37 Reconnect the exhaust front pipe to the manifold and tighten the bolts to compress the tension springs.

38 Refill the cooling system as described in Chapter 1, refit the air cleaner as described in Chapter 4A and connect the battery negative terminal.

9 Cylinder head - overhaul

1 Unscrew the rocker arm retaining /adjustment nuts and withdraw the rocker arms from the studs. Keep them in order as they are removed.

2 To remove the valves, the springs will have to be compressed to allow the split collets to be released from the groove in the upper section of the valve stems. A valve spring compressor will therefore be necessary.

3 Locate the compressor to enable the forked end of the arm to be positioned over the valve spring collar whilst the screw part of the clamp is situated squarely on the face of the valve.

4 Screw up the clamp to compress the spring and release the pressure of the collar acting on the collets. If the collar sticks, support the head and clamp frame and give the end of the clamp a light tap with a hammer to help release it.

5 Extract the two collets and then release the tension of the clamp. Remove the clamp, withdraw the collar and spring and extract the valve. Remove the valve stem seals and the exhaust valve rotators.

6 As they are released and removed, keep the valves in order so that if they are to be refitted they will be replaced in their original positions in the cylinder head. A piece of stiff card with eight holes punched in it is a sure method of keeping the valves in order.

7 Examine the head of the valves for pitting and burning, especially the heads of the exhaust valves. The valve seating should be examined at the same time. If the pitting on valve and seat is very slight, the marks can be removed by grinding the seats and valves together with coarse, and then fine, valve grinding paste.

8 Where bad pitting has occurred to the valve seats it will be necessary to recut them and fit new valves. The latter job should be entrusted to the local agent or engineering works. In practice it is very seldom that the seats are so badly worn. Normally it is the valve that is too badly worn for refitting, and the owner can easily purchase a new set of valves and match them to the seats by valve grinding.

9 Valve grinding is carried out as follows. Smear a trace of coarse carborundum paste on the seat face and apply a suction grinder tool to the valve head. With a semi-rotary motion, grind the valve head to its seat, lifting the valve occasionally to redistribute the grinding paste. When a dull matt even surface is produced on both the valve seat and the valve, wipe off the paste and repeat the process with fine carborundum paste, lifting and turning the valve to redistribute the paste as before. A light spring placed under the valve head will greatly ease this operation. When a smooth unbroken ring of light grey matt finish is produced, on both valve and valve seat faces, the grinding operation is complete.

10 Scrape away all carbon from the valve head and the valve stem. Carefully clean away every trace of grinding compound; take great care to leave none in the ports or in the valve guides. Clean the valves and valve seats with a paraffin-soaked rag, then with a clean rag and finally, if an air line is available, blow the valves, valve guides and valve ports clean.

11 Check that all valve springs are intact. If any one is broken, all should be renewed. Check the free height of the springs against new ones. If some springs are not within

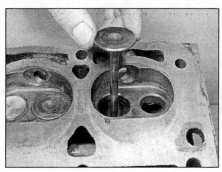

9.15 Fitting a valve to its guide

9.17 Fitting an exhaust valve rotator

9.18a Fit the valve spring . . .

specification, replace them all. Springs suffer from fatigue and it is a good idea to renew them even if they look serviceable.

12 Check that the oil supply holes in the rocker arm studs are clear.

13 The cylinder head can be checked for warping either by placing it on a piece of plate glass or using a straight-edge and feeler blades. Slight distortion may be corrected by having the head machined to remove metal from the mating face.

14 Valve guide renewal is necessary if the valve stem clearance in the guide exceeds that specified. Renewal, or reaming to accept oversize valves, should be left to a GM dealer.

15 Commence reassembly by lubricating a valve stem and inserting it into its guide **(see illustration)**.

16 Fit the valve stem oil seal, using the protective sleeve supplied with the new seals over the valve stem to avoid damage.

9.20 Compress the spring and fit the collets

Lubricate the sleeve and push on the seal, ring downwards. Recover the sleeve.

17 On exhaust valves, fit the valve rotator **(see illustration)**.

18 Fit the valve spring and collar, with the recessed part of the collar inside the spring **(see illustrations)**.

19 Place the end of the spring compressor over the collar and valve stem and, with the screw head of the compressor over the valve head, screw up the clamp until the spring is compressed past the groove in the valve stem. Then put a little grease round the groove.

20 Place the two halves of the split collar (collets) into the groove with the narrow ends pointing towards the spring **(see illustration)**. The grease will hold them in the groove.

21 Release the clamp slowly and carefully, making sure that the collets are not dislodged from the groove. When the clamp is fully released the top edges of the collets should be in line with each other. Give the top of each spring a smart tap with a soft-faced mallet when assembly is complete to ensure that the collets are properly settled.

22 Repeat the above procedure for the other 7 valves.

23 The rocker gear can be refitted with the head either on or off the engine. The only part of the procedure to watch is that the rocker nuts must not be screwed down too far or it will not be possible to refit the pushrods.

24 Next put the rocker arm over the stud followed by the pivot ball **(see illustrations)**. Make sure that the spring fits snugly round the rocker arm centre section and that the two

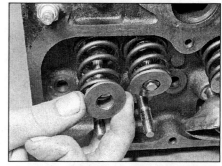

9.18b . . . followed by the spring collar

bearing surfaces of the interior of the arm and the ball face, are clean and lubricated with engine oil.

25 Oil the stud thread and fit the nut with the self-locking collar uppermost **(see illustration)**. Screw it down until the locking collar is on the stud.

10 Cylinder head and pistons - decarbonising

1 This can be carried out with the engine either in or out of the car. With the cylinder head removed, carefully use a wire brush and blunt scraper to clean all traces of carbon deposits from the combustion spaces and the ports. The valve head stems and valve guides should also be freed from any carbon deposits. Wash the combustion spaces and ports down with petrol and scrape the cylinder head surface free of any foreign

9.24a Fitting a rocker arm . . .

9.24b . . . and its pivot ball

9.25 Fit the nut with the self-locking collar uppermost

11.7 Insert the cork strips in the main bearing cap grooves

11.9 Refitting the sump

12.2a Undo the two socket-headed bolts (arrowed) . . .

matter with the side of a steel rule or a similar article.

2 If the engine is installed in the car, clean the pistons and the top of the cylinder bores. If the pistons are still in the block, then it is essential that great care is taken to ensure that no carbon gets into the cylinder bores as this could scratch the cylinder walls or cause damage to the piston and rings. To ensure this does not happen, first turn the crankshaft so that two of the pistons are at the top of their bores. Stuff rag into the other two bores or seal them off with paper and masking tape. The waterways should also be covered with small pieces of masking tape to prevent particles of carbon entering the cooling system and damaging the water pump.

3 Press a little grease into the gap between the cylinder walls and the two pistons which are to be worked on. With a blunt scraper carefully scrape away the carbon from the piston crown, taking great care not to scratch the aluminium. Also scrape away the carbon from the surrounding lip of the cylinder wall. When all carbon has been removed, scrape away the grease which will now be contaminated with carbon particles, taking care not to press any into the bores. To assist prevention of carbon build-up the piston crown can be polished with a metal polish. Remove the rags or masking tape from the other two cylinders and turn the crankshaft so that the two pistons which were at the bottom are now at the top. Place rag or masking tape in the cylinders which have been decarbonised and proceed as just described. Decarbonising is now complete.

11 Sump - removal and refitting

Removal

1 Jack up the front of the car and securely support it on axle stands (see "*Jacking and Vehicle Support*").

2 Drain the engine oil into a suitable container (Section 2) and refit the plug after draining.

3 Undo the bolts securing the flywheel cover plate and side support braces and remove the cover.

4 Undo the retaining bolts and lift away the sump. It will probably be necessary to tap the sump from side to side with a hide or plastic mallet to release the joint face.

Refitting

5 Thoroughly clean the sump in paraffin or a suitable solvent and remove all traces of external dirt and internal sludge. Scrape away all traces of old gasket from the sump and crankcase faces and ensure that they are clean and dry. Also clean the bearing cap grooves.

6 Apply a thick bead of jointing compound to the crankcase flange and at the joints of the front and rear main bearing caps

7 Position the cork side gaskets on the crankcase flanges and then insert the cork and sealing strips to the main bearing cap grooves (**see illustration**)

8 Apply a further bead of jointing compound to the gasket faces and to the gasket joints at the bearing caps.

9 Refit the sump (**see illustration**) and secure it in place with the retaining bolts which should be progressively tightened in a diagonal sequence.

10 Refit the flywheel cover plate, lower the car and fill the engine with oil as described in Chapter 1.

12 Oil pump - removal and refitting

Removal

1 Remove the sump. as described in Section 11.

2 Undo the two socket-headed bolts and withdraw the pump from the crankcase (**see illustrations**).

Refitting

3 Refitting the pump is the reverse sequence to removal, but engage the pump shaft in the distributor driveshaft slot, and tighten the retaining bolts to the specified torque.

13 Oil pump - overhaul

1 Remove the oil pump, as described in Section 12.

2 Undo the two pump cover bolts and lift off the cover and oil pick-up tube. Remove the cover gasket.

3 Take out the driving gear and driven gear (**see illustrations**).

12.2b . . . and remove the oil pump

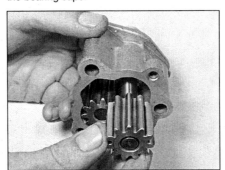

13.3a Removing the oil pump driving gear . . .

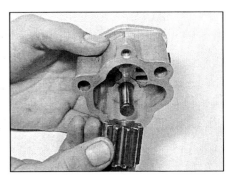

13.3b . . . and the driven gear

13.4 Oil pump and pressure relief valve components

13.8 Check the pump gear teeth backlash

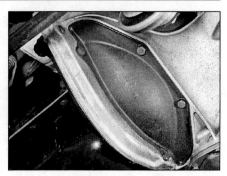

14.2 Clutch access plate

4 Undo the large nut on the side of the housing and remove the sealing washer and oil pressure relief spring and ball valve **(see illustration)**.

5 Clean all the parts in paraffin and dry with a lint-free cloth.

6 Inspect the pump gears, housing, cover and relief valve ball for scoring, scuff marks or other signs of wear and renew the pump if these signs are evident.

7 If the pump condition is satisfactory, check the pump clearances as follows.

8 Using a feeler blade, check the backlash between the gear teeth. Place a straight-edge across the top edge of the gears and check their projection. If any of the clearances exceeds the tolerances given in the Specifications, renew the pump **(see illustration)**.

9 If the clearances are satisfactory, refit the

relief valve assembly and assemble the pump gears. Fill the pump with oil and refit the cover using a new gasket. Tighten the cover securing bolts and refit the pump.

14 Timing gear components - removal and refitting

Removal

1 For greater access remove the front right-hand wheel trim and slacken the wheel bolts. Jack up the front of the car, support it securely on axle stands (see "*Jacking and Vehicle Support*") and remove the roadwheel.

2 Undo the four retaining bolts and remove the clutch access plate at the base of the bellhousing **(see illustration)**.

3 Slacken the alternator mounting and adjustment arm bolts, move the alternators

towards the engine and slip the drivebelt off the pulleys.

4 Lock the flywheel by wedging a screwdriver between the ring gear teeth and the side of the bellhousing.

5 Using a socket or spanner undo the crankshaft pulley retaining bolt and withdraw the pulley.

6 Undo the bolts securing the timing cover to the front of the engine and lift off the cover.

7 Withdraw the oil slinger from the crankshaft, noting which way round it is fitted **(see illustration)**.

8 Temporarily refit the pulley and turn the crankshaft until the crankshaft sprocket keyway is uppermost and the timing marks on the two sprockets are in alignment **(see illustration)**. Remove the pulley.

9 Undo the two retaining bolts and remove the timing chain tensioner. One of two types of tensioner may be fitted: simple spring-operated, or oil pressure assisted. With the oil pressure assisted type, restrain the thrust pad to prevent premature ejection of the tensioner components **(see illustration)**.

10 Undo the camshaft sprocket retaining bolt and remove the bolt and washer **(see illustration)**. Place a screwdriver through one of the sprocket holes and in contact with the camshaft retaining plate behind the sprocket to stop it turning as the bolt is undone.

11 Withdraw the camshaft sprocket and crankshaft sprocket from their respective locations, using a screwdriver as a lever if necessary, then remove the sprockets complete with chain **(see illustration)**.

12 Thoroughly clean all the components in

14.7 Crankshaft oil slinger

14.8 Crankshaft sprocket keyway (A) and sprocket timing marks (B)

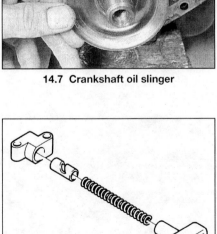

14.9 Timing chain tensioner - oil pressure assisted type

14.10 Camshaft sprocket retaining bolt and washer

14.11 Removing the sprockets and timing chain

14.13 Using a drift to remove the timing cover oil seal

14.14a Fit the new seal to the holder

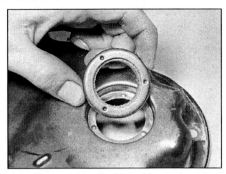

14.14b . . . and refit the holder and seal to the timing cover

paraffin and dry them with a lint-free cloth. Remove all traces of old gasket from the faces of the timing cover and engine.

Refitting

13 To renew the oil seal in the timing cover, place the cover outer face downwards over two blocks of wood and drive out the old seal and holder using a hammer and drift **(see illustration)**.

14 Place the new seal (which must have been soaked in engine oil for 24 hours) in the holder and then tap the holder into the cover using a block of wood **(see illustrations)**. The seal holder must be fitted flush with the outer edge of the timing cover.

15 Commence reassembly by engaging the chain around the crankshaft sprocket.

16 Engage the camshaft sprocket within the loop of the chain so that it can be fitted to the

camshaft and will have its timing mark in alignment with the one on the crankshaft sprocket. Adjust the camshaft sprocket as necessary within the chain loop to achieve this.

17 Fit the sprocket to the camshaft, screw in the bolt and washer and tighten the bolt while holding the sprocket with a screwdriver, as was done during removal.

18 Refit the timing chain tensioner. With the oil pressure assisted type, compress the thrust pad by hand, secure the tensioner and release the thrust pad.

19 To refit the spring-operated chain tensioner, place the tensioner in position and fit the lower retaining bolt finger tight. Move the spring blade away from the tensioner body with a screwdriver, pivot the tensioner into position and fit the upper retaining bolt, then release the springs and tighten both bolts **(see illustrations)**.

20 Position the oil slinger over the crankshaft and place a new gasket on the front of the engine **(see illustration)**. Apply jointing compound to both sides of the gasket.

21 Refit the cover and the retaining bolts, but only screw the bolts in two or three turns **(see illustration)**. Position the crankshaft pulley on the crankshaft to centralise the cover and then tighten the bolts progressively in a diagonal sequence.

22 Refit the pulley retaining bolt and tighten to the specified torque.

23 Refit the drivebelt and adjust its tension, as described in Chapter 1.

24 Refit the roadwheel and lower the car to the ground. Tighten the wheel bolts.

15 Pistons and connecting rods
- removal and refitting

Removal

1 Remove the cylinder head, the sump and the oil pump, as described in earlier Sections.

2 The connecting rod big-end caps and rods may not be marked numerically for location when new and therefore they must be inspected for identification marks before dismantling. If no marks are evident, punch, scribe or file identification marks on the caps and rods starting with No 1 at the timing cover end. Mark them all on the same side to avoid confusion during reassembly. If they have already been marked then this will not, of course, be necessary.

3 Undo and remove the big-end cap retaining bolts and keep them in order for correct refitting.

4 Detach the big-end bearing caps. If stuck, lightly tap them free using a soft-faced mallet.

5 To remove the bearing shells for inspection and/or renewal, press the bearing end opposite the groove in both connecting rod and bearing cap and the shells will slide out. Again keep the shells in order of removal.

6 The piston rod assemblies are removed through the top of each cylinder bore, being pushed upwards from underneath using a wooden hammer handle which is pushed against the connecting rod. Rotate the crankshaft accordingly to gain suitable access to each rod assembly. Note that, if there is a pronounced wear ridge at the top of the

14.19a Fit the tensioner lower bolt . . .

14.19b . . . then push back the spring, pivot the tensioner and fit the upper bolt

14.20 Fitting a new timing cover gasket

14.21 Refitting the timing cover

15.11 Offering the piston to the bore

15.12 Piston ring compressor fitted

cylinder bore, there is a risk of piston ring damage unless the ridge is first removed using a ridge reaming tool, or scraper.

7 The pistons should not be separated from their connecting rods unless they or the gudgeon pins are to be renewed. The gudgeon pin is a press fit and special tools are required for removing and installation. This task should therefore be entrusted to your local agent or automotive machine shop.

8 If for any reason the pistons are separated from their rods, mark them numerically on the same side as the rod markings to ensure correct refitting.

Refitting

9 If new pistons or piston rings are being fitted to the old bores, it is essential to roughen the cylinder bore walls slightly with medium grit emery cloth to allow the rings to bed in. Do this with a circular up-and-down action to produce a criss-cross pattern on the cylinder bore walls. Make sure that the bearing journal on the crankshaft is protected with masking tape during this operation. Thoroughly clean the bores with a paraffin-soaked rag and dry with a lint-free cloth Remove the tape from the crankshaft journals and clean them also.

10 Commence reassembly by lubricating the cylinder bores and crankshaft journals.

11 Space the piston rings around the pistons so that their end gaps are 180° apart. In the case of the oil scraper ring, offset the gaps in the upper and lower rails by 25 to 50 mm to right and left of the end gap of the central section. Offer a piston/connecting rod

assembly to its bore, making sure that it is the right way round **(see illustration)**.

12 Oil the piston and rings, then fit a piston ring compressor to the piston and tighten it to compress the rings **(see illustration)**.

13 Gently tap the piston through the ring compressor and into its bore using the hammer handle. Guide the connecting rod near to its crankshaft journal and then fit the bearing shell upper half.

14 Ease the connecting rod onto the journal, fit the lower shell to the cap and fit the cap to the rod **(see illustration)**. Refit and tighten the retaining bolts to the specified torque **(see illustration)**.

15 Repeat the sequence described for the remaining three piston/ connecting rods.

16 Refit the cylinder head, oil pump and sump, as described in earlier Sections.

16 Flywheel - removal and refitting

Removal

1 Remove the clutch assembly and the release bearing, as described in Chapter 6.

2 Undo the three bolts and remove the release bearing guide tube.

3 Mark the position of the flywheel in relation to the crankshaft mounting flange or pulley.

4 Wedge a screwdriver between the ring gear teeth and transmission casing and then undo the socket-headed retaining bolts using a multi-tooth key or socket bit **(see illustration)**. Remove the bolts and withdraw the flywheel.

Refitting

5 Refitting is the reverse sequence to removal. Tighten the flywheel retaining bolts to the specified torque.

17 Engine/transmission mountings - removal and refitting

Removal

1 The engine/transmission assembly is supported in a triangular arrangement of three mountings: one on the right-hand side supporting the engine, one on the left-hand side supporting the transmission and a third centrally sited mount supporting the complete assembly at the rear.

2 To remove either of the front mountings position a jack under the engine or transmission adjacent to the mounting and just take the weight of the engine or transmission.

3 Undo the bolts securing the support bracket to the engine or gearbox and the bolts securing the mounting to the bodyframe. Lift off the bracket and remove the relevant mounting.

4 To remove the rear mounting jack up the front of the car and support it on axle stands (see "Jacking and Vehicle Support").

5 Support the engine/transmission assembly under the differential cover plate using a jack and interposed block of wood.

6 Undo the two bolts securing the mounting to the underbody and the through-bolt and nut securing the mounting to the support bracket. Slide the mounting rearwards out of the bracket and remove it from under the car.

Refitting

7 In all cases refitting is the reverse sequence to removal, but tighten the retaining bolts to the specified torque. Where thread locking compound was evident on the old bolts, clean out the bolt holes using a tap (or an old bolt with a slot cut in its threads); clean the bolt threads and apply thread locking compound.

8 If there is an arrow stamped on the rear mounting, it should point to the front when the mounting is fitted.

15.14a Fitting a big-end bearing cap

15.14b Tightening a big-end bearing cap bolt

16.4 Flywheel retaining bolts are socket-headed

18.4a Camshaft retaining plate bolts (arrowed)

18.4b Removing the engine front plate

18.5 Removing the camshaft

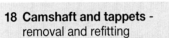

18 Camshaft and tappets - removal and refitting

Removal

1 Remove the engine from the car, as described in Section 23, and then remove the sump and timing gear components, as described in earlier Sections.

2 If the cylinder head is still in place, slacken the rocker arm nuts, move the rocker arms to one side and lift out the pushrods, keeping them in order.

3 Invert the engine or, if the cylinder head is still in place, lay the engine on its side.

4 Undo the two bolts securing the camshaft retaining plate in position and lift off the plate **(see illustrations)**. The engine front plate should also be removed as all the bolts securing it in place have now been undone.

5 Carefully withdraw the camshaft from the cylinder block, taking care not to scratch the bearing journals with the sharp edges of the cam lobes **(see illustration)**.

6 From within the crankcase withdraw each tappet from its bore and keep them in order for refitting **(see illustration)**.

Refitting

7 Scrape away all traces of old gasket from the engine front plate and cylinder block. Make sure that both mating faces are clean and dry.

8 Lubricate the tappet bores in the crankcase and insert each tappet into its respective bore.

9 Lubricate the camshaft bearing journals and carefully insert the camshaft.

10 Place a new gasket in position and then locate the front plate, patterned side outward, over the gasket **(see illustration)**. Temporarily refit two or three of the timing cover bolts to act as alignment guides, but only tighten them finger tight.

11 Now position the camshaft retaining plate with its forks located into the groove in the boss on the end of the camshaft. Note that the fork section faces upwards. Secure the retaining plate with the two bolts.

12 Check that the camshaft is free to turn.

13 Refit the timing gear components and the sump, as described in earlier Sections. If the cylinder head is in place, refit the pushrods and adjust the valve clearances.

14 Refit the engine to the car.

19 Crankshaft rear oil seal - removal and refitting

Removal

1 Remove the engine from the car, as described in Section 23, and then remove the sump and flywheel, as described in earlier Sections.

2 Slacken the rear main bearing cap bolts slightly and withdraw the oil seal from its location.

Refitting

3 Lubricate the lips of a new oil seal and carefully ease it over the crankshaft boss and

into position. Make sure that the seal is fully entered into its location so that its outer face is flush with the edge of the bearing cap and cylinder block.

4 Apply jointing compound to the contact edges of the main bearing cap and then tighten the retaining bolts to the specified torque.

5 Refit the sump and flywheel, as described earlier, and then refit the engine to the car, as described in Section 23.

20 Crankshaft and main bearings - removal and refitting

Removal

1 With the engine removed from the car, as described in Section 23, and all the components removed from it, as described in earlier Sections, the crankshaft can be removed as follows.

2 Invert the engine. The three main bearing caps are all different so note their locations.

3 Undo the retaining bolts and remove the bearing caps.

4 Lift out the crankshaft and remove the rear oil seal from the crankshaft boss.

5 Remove the main bearing shells from the crankcase and bearing caps and identify them for location.

Refitting

6 Commence reassembly as follows.

7 Ensure that the crankcase and crankshaft are thoroughly clean and that all oilways are clear. If possible blow the drillings out with compressed air, and then inject clean engine oil through them to ensure that they are clear.

8 Avoid using old bearing shells; wipe the shell seats in the crankcase clean and then fit the upper halves of the main bearing shells into their seats.

9 Note that there is a tab on the back of each bearing which engages with a groove in the shell seating (in both crankcase and bearing cap) **(see illustration)**.

10 Wipe away all traces of protective grease on the new shells.

11 The central bearing shell also takes up the crankshaft endfloat. Note that the half-shells fitted to the cylinder block all have oil duct

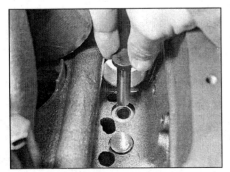

18.6 Removing a tappet

18.10 Fitting a new front plate gasket

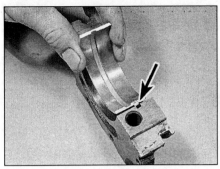

20.9 Bearing shell tab engages with groove (arrowed)

20.12 Lubricate the bearing shells

20.13 Fitting the crankshaft

20.14 Fitting the centre main bearing cap

holes, while only the centre main bearing cap half-shells has an oil duct hole.

12 When the shells are fully located in the crankcase and bearing caps, lubricate them with clean engine oil (see illustration).

13 Carefully install the crankshaft into position in the crankcase (see illustration).

14 Lubricate the crankshaft main bearing journals and then refit the centre main bearing cap (see illustration). Tighten the retaining bolts to the specified torque wrench setting.

15 Locate the new oil seal onto the rear end of the crankshaft, and apply jointing compound to the block mating flange. Also fill the grooves on both sides of the rear main bearing cap with sealant (see illustrations).

16 Fit the rear main bearing cap and tighten the retaining bolts to the specified torque (see illustration).

17 Fit the front main bearing cap, but before fitting the retaining bolts smear them with jointing compound and then tighten to the specified torque wrench setting. Check that the bearing cap is exactly flush with the end face of the crankcase as it is tightened.

18 Now rotate the crankshaft and check that it turns freely, and shows no signs of binding or tight spots. Check that the crankshaft endfloat is within the limits specified using a feeler blade as shown (see illustration). No provision is made for adjusting crankshaft endfloat; if it is outside the specified limits, the most likely reasons are wear or incorrect regrinding (assuming that the correct shells have been fitted).

21 Engine components -
examination and renovation

Crankshaft

1 Examine the crankpin and main journal surfaces for signs of scoring or scratches, and check the ovality and taper of the crankpins and main journals. If the bearing surface dimensions do not fall within the tolerance ranges given in the Specifications at the beginning of this Chapter, the crankpins and/or main journals will have to be reground.

2 Big-end and crankpin wear is accompanied by distinct metallic knocking, particularly noticed when the engine is pulling from low revs, and some loss of oil pressure.

3 Main bearing and main journal wear is accompanied by severe engine vibration rumble - getting progressively worse as engine revs increase - and again by loss of oil pressure.

4 If the crankshaft requires regrinding take it to an engine reconditioning specialist, who will machine it for you and supply the correct undersize bearing shells.

5 On some engines, the crankshaft journal diameters are machined undersize in production to allow for greater manufacturing tolerances.

Big-end and main bearing shells

6 Inspect the big-end and main bearing shells for signs of general wear, scoring, pitting and scratches. The bearings should be matt grey in colour. With lead-indium bearings, should a trace of copper colour be noticed, the bearings are badly worn as the lead bearing material has worn away to expose the indium underlay. Renew the bearings if they are in this condition or if there are any signs of scoring or pitting.

20.15a Crankshaft rear oil seal

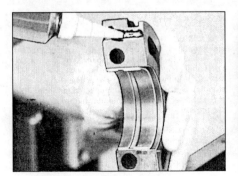

20.15b Fill the rear main bearing cap grooves with sealant

20.16 Fitting the rear main bearing cap

20.18 Checking the crankshaft endfloat

You are strongly advised to renew the bearings - regardless of their condition - at time of major overhaul. Refitting used bearings is a false economy.

7 The undersizes available are designed to correspond with crankshaft regrind sizes. The bearings are in fact, slightly more than the stated undersize as running clearances have been allowed for during their manufacture.

Cylinder bores

8 The cylinder bores must be examined for taper, ovality, scoring and scratches. Start by carefully examining the top of the cylinder bores. If they are at all worn a very slight ridge will be found on the thrust side. This marks the top of the piston travel. The owner will have a good indication of the bore wear prior to dismantling the engine, or removing the cylinder head. Excessive oil consumption accompanied by blue smoke from the exhaust can be caused by worn cylinder bores and piston rings.

9 Measure the bore diameter across the block and just below any ridge. This can be done with an internal micrometer or a dial gauge. Compare this with the diameter of the bottom of the bore, which is not subject to wear. If no measuring instruments are available, use a piston from which the rings have been removed and measure the gap between it and the cylinder wall with a feeler blade.

10 Refer to the Specifications. If the cylinder wear exceeds the permitted tolerances then the cylinders will need reboring.

11 If the cylinders have already been bored out to their maximum it may be possible to have liners fitted. This situation will not often be encountered.

Connecting rods

12 Examine the mating faces of the big-end caps to see if they have ever been filed in a mistaken attempt to take up wear. If so, the offending rods must be renewed.

13 Check the alignment of the rods visually, and if all is not well, take the rods to your local agent for checking on a special jig.

Pistons and piston rings

14 If the pistons and/or rings are to be re-used, remove the rings from the pistons. Three strips of tin or 0.38 mm feeler blades should be prepared and the top ring then sprung open just sufficiently to allow them to be slipped behind the ring. The ring can then be slid off the piston upwards without scoring or scratching the piston lands.

15 Repeat the process for the second and third rings.

16 Mark the rings or keep them in order so they may be refitted in their original locations.

17 Inspect the pistons to ensure that they are suitable for re-use. Check for cracks, damage to the piston ring grooves and lands, and scores or signs of picking-up the piston walls.

18 Clean the ring grooves using a piece of old piston ring ground to a suitable width and scrape the deposits out of the grooves, taking care not to remove any metal or score the piston lands. Protect your fingers - piston rings are sharp.

19 Check the rings in their respective bores. Press the ring down to the unworn lower section of the bore (use a piston to do this, and keep the ring square in the bore). Measure the ring end gap and check that it is within the tolerance allowed (see Specifications). Also check the ring's side clearance in its groove. If these measurements exceed the specified tolerances the rings will have to be renewed, and if the ring grooves in the pistons are worn new pistons may be needed.

20 Proprietary piston rings are available which are reputed to reduce oil consumption due to bore wear without the expense of a rebore. Depending on the degree of wear, the improvement produced by fitting such rings may be short-lived.

21 If new rings (or pistons and rings) are to be fitted to an existing bore the top ring must be stepped to clear the wear ridge at the top of the bore, or the bore must be de-ridged.

22 Check the clearance and end gap of any new rings, as described in paragraph 19. If a ring is slightly tight in its groove it may be rubbed down using an oilstone or a sheet of carborundum paper laid on a sheet of glass. If the end gap is inadequate the ring can be carefully ground until the specified clearance is achieved.

23 If new pistons are to be installed they will be selected from the grades available (see Specifications), after measuring the bores as described in paragraph 9. Normally the appropriate oversize pistons are supplied by the repairer when the block is rebored.

24 Removing and refitting pistons on the connecting rod is a job for your dealer or specialist repairer. Press equipment and a means of accurately heating the connecting rod will be required for removal and insertion of the gudgeon pin.

Camshaft and bearings

25 With the camshaft removed, examine the bearings for signs of obvious wear and pitting. If there are signs, then the three bearings will need renewal. This is not a common requirement and to have to do so is indicative of severe engine neglect at some time. As special tools are necessary to do this work properly, it is recommended that it is done by your dealer. Check that the bearings are located properly so that the oilways from the bearing housings are not obstructed.

26 The camshaft itself should show no marks on either the bearing journals or the profiles. If it does, it should be renewed.

27 Examine the skew gear for signs of wear or damage. If this is badly worn it will mean renewing the camshaft.

28 The thrust plate (which also acts as the locating plate) should not be ridged or worn in any way. If it is, renew it.

Timing chain sprockets and tensioner

29 Examine the teeth of both sprockets for wear. Each tooth is the shape of an inverted V and if the driving (or driven) side is concave in shape, the tooth is worn and the sprocket should be renewed. The chain should also be renewed if the sprocket teeth are worn. It is sensible practice to renew the chain anyway.

30 Inspect the chain tensioner, which is automatic in operation. The most important item to check is the shoe which wears against the chain. If it is obviously worn, scratched or damaged in any way, then it must be renewed. Check the spring for signs of wear and renew the unit if generally worn or defective, or when a new chain is being fitted.

Valve rocker arms, pushrods and tappets

31 Each rocker arm has three wearing surfaces, namely the pushrod recess, the valve stem contact, and the centre pivot recess. If any of these surfaces appear severely grooved or worn the arm should be renewed. If only the valve stem contact area is worn it is possible to clean it up with a fine file.

32 If the rocker ball is pitted, or has flats in it, this should also be renewed.

33 The nut on the rocker stud is a self-locking type. If it has been removed or adjusted many times, the self-locking ring may have become ineffective and the nut may be slack enough to turn involuntarily and alter the tappet clearance.

34 The rocker studs should be examined to ensure that the threads are undamaged and that the oil delivery hole in the side of the stud at the base of the thread is clear. Place a straight-edge along the top of all the studs to ensure that none is standing higher than the rest. If any are, it means that they have pulled out of the head some distance. They should be removed and replaced with an oversize stud. As this involves reaming out the stud hole to an exact size to provide an interference fit for the replacement stud, you should seek professional advice and assistance to ensure that the new oversize stud is securely fitted at the correct angle.

35 Any pushrods which are bent should be renewed. On no account attempt to straighten them. They are easily checked by rolling over a perfectly flat surface such as a sheet of glass.

36 Examine the bearing surfaces of the tappets which lie on the camshaft. Any indentation in these surfaces or any cracks indicate serious wear and the tappets should be renewed. Thoroughly clean them out, removing all traces of sludge. It is most unlikely that the sides of the tappets will prove worn but, if they are a very loose fit in their bores and can readily be rocked, they should be exchanged for new ones. It is very unusual to find any wear in the tappets, and any wear present is likely to occur at very high mileages, or in cases or neglect. If the tappets are worn, examine the camshaft carefully as well!.

Flywheel

37 If the teeth on the flywheel starter ring are badly worn, or if some are missing, then it will be necessary to remove the ring and fit a new one.

38 Either split the ring with a cold chisel after making a cut with a hacksaw blade between two teeth, or use a soft-headed hammer (not steel) to knock the ring off, striking it evenly and alternately at equally spaced points. Take great care not to damage the flywheel during this process, and protect your eyes from flying fragments.

39 Clean and polish with emery cloth four evenly spaced areas on the outside face of the new starter ring.

40 Heat the ring evenly with a flame until the polished portions turn dark blue. Alternatively heat the ring in a bath of oil to a temperature of 200°C. (If a naked flame is used take adequate fire precautions.) Hold the ring at this temperature for five minutes and then quickly fit it to the flywheel, so the chamfered portion of the teeth faces the gearbox side of the flywheel. Wipe all oil off the ring before fitting it.

41 The ring should be tapped gently down onto its register and left to cool naturally when the contraction of the metal on cooling will ensure that it is a secure and permanent fit. Great care must be taken not to overheat the ring, indicated by it turning light metallic blue. If this happens the temper of the ring will be lost.

42 If the driven plate contact surface of the flywheel is scored or on close inspection shows evidence of small hair cracks, caused by overheating, it may be possible to have the flywheel surface ground provided the overall thickness of the flywheel is not reduced too much. Consult a specialist engine repairer and if it is not possible, renew the flywheel complete.

43 If the needle bearing in the centre of the crankshaft flange is worn, fill it with grease and tap in a close-fitting rod. Hydraulic pressure will remove it. Tap the new bearing into position and apply a little grease.

22 Engine lubrication system - general description

The engine lubrication system is quite conventional. A gear type oil pump draws oil up from the sump, via the suction pipe and strainer, and pumps the oil under pressure in the cartridge oil filter. From the oil filter the oil flows into galleries drilled in the engine block to feed the main bearings on the crankshaft and the moving components of the cylinder head. Oil is bled from the main bearing journals in the crankshaft to supply the big-end bearings.

Therefore, the bearings which receive pressure lubrication are the main crankshaft bearings, the big-end bearings, the camshaft bearings, and the rocker arms.

The remaining moving parts receive oil by splash or drip feed and these include the timing chain and associated items, the distributor and fuel pump drive, the tappets, the valve stems and to a certain extent the pistons.

The lubrication system incorporates two safeguards. The first is a pressure operated ball valve situated in the gallery between the oil and oil filter. This is in effect a filter bypass valve and allows oil to pass directly into the engine block gallery, downstream of the filter, when the filter is clogged up and resists the flow of oil.

The second system is an oil pressure relief valve, located in the oil pump casing, which controls the oil pressure to the specified maximum.

23 Engine - removal and refitting

Removal

1 The makers recommend that the engine be removed from above, leaving the gearbox in the vehicle.

2 Disconnect the battery positive and negative terminals. Remove the bonnet (Chapter 11).

3 Remove the air cleaner (Chapter 4A).

4 Drain the cooling system (Chapter 1). Disconnect the coolant hoses from the water pump, thermostat housing and cylinder head. not forgetting the heater hoses.

5 Disconnect and plug the fuel pump feed hose, and (when fitted) the fuel return hose. Be prepared for fuel spillage.

6 Disconnect the throttle and choke cables from the carburettor (Chapter 4A).

7 Disconnect the brake servo vacuum hose, either from the servo or from the manifold. Secure the hose so that it will not be damaged.

8 Release the electrical connectors for the oil pressure switch and the coil LT terminals. Unplug the coil-to-distributor HT lead at the distributor cap.

9 Disconnect the engine wiring harness multi-plug, pressing its locking device to release it.

10 Withdraw the clutch input shaft (see Chapter 6).

11 Unbolt the exhaust downpipe from the manifold.

12 Remove the three flywheel cover plate bolts, which are accessible from below.

13 Secure the lifting tackle to the engine and take its weight.

14 Support the gearbox with a jack or blocks, then remove the right-hand mounting completely.

15 Remove the remaining engine-to-clutch housing bolts.

16 Make sure that no attachments have been overlooked, then carefully draw the engine away from the clutch housing and lift it out.

Refitting

17 Refit in the reverse order to removal, referring to the appropriate Chapters for guidance if necessary. If the clutch has been disturbed, make sure that the driven plate is centralised (Chapter 6), otherwise it will not be possible to refit the clutch input shaft.

18 Refer to Section 24 before starting the engine.

24 Engine - initial start-up after overhaul

1 Make sure the battery is fully charged and that all lubricants, coolant and fuel are replenished.

2 If the fuel system has been dismantled it will require several revolutions of the engine on the starter motor to pump the petrol up to the carburettor.

3 As soon as the engine fires and runs, keep it going at a fast tickover only (no faster) and bring it up to the normal working temperature.

4 As the engine warms up there will be odd smells and some smoke from parts getting hot and burning off oil deposits. The signs to look for are leaks of water or oil which will be obvious if serious. Check also the exhaust pipe and manifold connections, as these do not always 'find' their exact gastight position until the warmth and vibration have acted on them, and it is almost certain that they will need tightening further. This should be done, of course, with the engine stopped.

5 When normal running temperature has been reached adjust the engine idling speed, as described in Chapter 1, and check the valve clearances, as described in Section 7 of this Chapter.

6 Stop the engine and wait a few minutes to see if any lubricant or coolant is dripping out when the engine is stationary.

7 Road test the car to check that the timing is correct and that the engine is giving the necessary smoothness and power. Do not race the engine - if new bearings and/or pistons have been fitted it should be treated as a new engine and run in at a reduced speed for the first 500 miles (800 km).

8 If many new internal components have been fitted, it will be beneficial to change the engine oil and oil filter after the first 1000 miles (1600 km).

Notes

Chapter 2 Part B:
OHC engines

Contents

Degrees of difficulty

Easy, suitable for novice with little experience	Fairly easy, suitable for beginner with some experience	Fairly difficult, suitable for competent DIY mechanic	Difficult, suitable for experienced DIY mechanic	Very difficult, suitable for expert DIY or professional

Specifications

General

Type	Four-cylinder, in-line, water-cooled, single overhead camshaft, transversely mounted

Engine codes:
1.3 litre models	13N, 13NB or 13 S
1.4 litre models	14NV or C14NZ
1.6 litre models	16SH, 16SV or C16NZ
1.8 litre models	18E or 18SE
2.0 litre models	20NE, 20SEH, 20SER or C20NE

Note: *The engine code forms the first digits of the engine number*

Bore x Stroke:
1.3 litre models	75.0 x 73.4 mm
1.4 litre models	77.6 x 73.4 mm
1.6 litre models:	
16SH engine	80.0 x 79.5 mm
16SV and C16NZ engine	79.0 x 81.6 mm
1.8 litre models	84.8 x 79.5 mm
2.0 litre models	86.0 x 86.0 mm

Capacity:
1.3 litre models	1297 cc
1.4 litre models	1389 cc
1.6 litre models	1598 cc
1.8 litre models	1796 cc
2.0 litre models	1998 cc

Firing order	1-3-4-2 (No.1 cylinder at timing belt end)
Crankshaft rotation	Clockwise

Compression ratio:
13N and 13NB engines	8.2 : 1
13S, 16SH, 20NE and C20NE engines	9.2 : 1
14NV or C14NZ	9.4 : 1
18E engine	9.5: 1
16SV, C16NZ, 18SE, 20SEH and 20SER engines	10.0 : 1

Camshaft toothed belt tension (using gauge KM-510-A):	**1.3 and 1.4 litre**	**1.6, 1.8 and 2.0 litre**
New belt, cold	6.0	3.0
New belt, warm	8.0	8.0
Used belt, cold	5.0	3.0
Used belt, warm	7.5	8.0

Cylinder head

Material	Light alloy
Maximum permissible distortion of sealing face	0.025 mm
Overall height of cylinder head	95.75 to 96.25 mm

Valve seat width:
Inlet:
All 1.3, 1.4, 1.6 litre and 18E engines	1.3 to 1.4 mm
18SE and all 2.0 litre engines	1.0 to 1.5 mm

Exhaust:
All 1.3, 1.4, 1.6 litre and 18E engines	1.7 to 1.8 mm
18SE and all 2.0 litre engines	1.7 to 2.2 mm

Valves and guides

Valve clearance	Automatic by hydraulic valve lifters (cam followers)

Valve length:
1.3 litre engine	105.3 mm
1.4 litre engine	105.0 mm

1.6 litre engines:
16SH engine	106.5 mm
16SV and C16NZ engines	101.5 mm

1.8 litre engines:
18E engine	106.5 mm
18SE engine	104.2 mm
2.0 litre engines	104.2 mm

Valve stem-to-guide clearance:

	Inlet	Exhaust
1.3 and 1.4 litre engines	0.020 to 0.050 mm	0.040 to 0.070 mm

1.6 litre engine:
	Inlet	Exhaust
16SH and 16SV engines	0.015 to 0.042 mm	0.030 to 0.060 mm
C16NZ engine	0.020 to 0.050 mm	0.020 to 0.050 mm

1.8 litre engine:
	Inlet	Exhaust
18E engine	0.015 to 0.042 mm	0.030 to 0.060 mm
18SE engine	0.018 to 0.052 mm	0.040 to 0.070 mm
2.0 litre engine	0.018 to 0.052 mm	0.040 to 0.070 mm

Valve guide installed height:
1.3 and 1.4 litre engines	80.85 to 81.25 mm
All 1.6 litre and 18E engines	80.95 to 81.85 mm
18SE and all 2.0 litre engines	83.50 to 83.80 mm

Valve stem diameter:

	Inlet	Exhaust
1.3 litre engine	7.000 to 7.010 mm	6.980 to 6.990 mm
1.4 litre engine	6.998 to 7.012 mm	6.978 to 6.992 mm

1.6 litre engine:
	Inlet	Exhaust
16SH and 16SV engines	7.795 to 7.970 mm	7.957 to 7.970 mm
C16NZ engine	6.998 to 7.012 mm	6.978 to 6.992 mm

1.8 litre engine:
	Inlet	Exhaust
18E engine	7.795 to 7.970 mm	7.957 to 7.970 mm
18SE engine	6.998 to 7.012 mm	6.978 to 6.992 mm
2.0 litre engine	6.998 to 7.012 mm	6.978 to 6.992 mm

Oversizes	0.075, 0.150, 0.250 mm

Valve guide bore diameter:
1.3 and 1.4 litre engines	7.030 to 7.050 mm
1.6, 1.8 and 2.0 litre engines	8.000 to 8.017 mm

Camshaft

Radial run-out	0.03 mm max
Endfloat	0.09 to 0.21 mm

Camshaft journal diameters:
1.3, 1.4 and 1.6 (C16NZ) litre engines:
No 1	39.435 to 39.450 mm
No 2	39.685 to 39.700 mm
No 3	39.935 to 39.950 mm
No 4	40.125 to 40.200 mm
No 5	40.435 to 40.450 mm

1.6 litre (16SH and 16SV), 1.8 and 2.0 litre engines:
No 1	42.455 to 42.470 mm
No 2	42.705 to 42.720 mm
No 3	42.955 to 42.970 mm
No 4	43.205 to 43.220 mm
No 5	43.455 to 43.470 mm

Camshaft bearing (direct in housing) diameters:
  1.3, 1.4 and 1.6 (C16NZ) litre engines:
    No 1 . . . .   39.500 to 39.525 mm
    No 2 . . . .   39.750 to 39.775 mm
    No 3 . . . .   40.000 to 40.025 mm
    No 4 . . . .   40.250 to 40.275 mm
    No 5 . . . .   40.550 to 40.525 mm
  1.6 litre (16SH and 16SV), 1.8 and 2.0 litre engines:
    No 1 . . . .   42.500 to 42.525 mm
    No 2 . . . .   42.750 to 42.775 mm
    No 3 . . . .   43.000 to 43.025 mm
    No 4 . . . .   43.250 to 43.275 mm
    No 5 . . . .   43.500 to 43.525 mm

Piston rings

Number of piston rings . . . .   2 compression, 1 oil control
Ring end gap:
  Compression . . . .   0.3 to 0.5 mm
  Oil control (rail) . . . .   0.40 to 1.40 mm
Ring gap offset (to gap of adjacent ring) . . . .   180°

Gudgeon pins

Length:
  1.3 and 1.4 litre engines . . . .   65 mm
  1.6, 1.8 and 2.0 litre engines . . . .   70 mm
Diameter:
  1.3 and 1.4 litre engines . . . .   20 mm
  1.6, 1.8 and 2.0 litre engines . . . .   23 mm
Clearance in piston:
  1.3 and 1.4 litre engines . . . .   0.007 to 0.010 mm
  1.6, 1.8 and 2.0 litre engines . . . .   0.011 to 0.014 mm
Clearance in connecting rod . . . .   None (interference fit)

Crankshaft and bearings

Number of main bearings   5
Main bearing journal diameter:
  1.3, 1.4, and 1.6 (16SV and C16NZ) litre engines . . . .   54.972 to 54.985 mm
  1.6 (16SH), 1.8 and 2.0 litre engines . . . .   57.982 to 57.995 mm
Crankpin diameter:
  1.3, 1.4, and 1.6 (16SV and C16NZ) litre engines . . . .   42.971 to 42.987 mm
  1.6 (16SH), 1.8 and 2.0 litre engines . . . .   48.971 to 48.987 mm
Undersizes . . . .   0.25 and 0.50 mm
Crankshaft endfloat:
  1.3, 1.4, and 1.6 (16SV and C16NZ) litre engines . . . .   0.1 to 2.0 mm
  1.6 (16SH), 1.8 and 2.0 litre engines . . . .   0.07 to 0.3 mm
Main bearing running clearance:
  1.3, 1.4, and 1.6 (16SV and C16NZ) litre engines . . . .   0.025 to 0.05 mm
  1.6 (16SH), 1.8 and 2.0 litre engines . . . .   0.015 to 0.04 mm
Big-end running clearance:
  1.3, 1.4, and 1.6 (16SV and C16NZ) litre engines . . . .   0.019 to 0.071 mm
  1.6 (16SH) and 1.8 litre engines . . . .   0.019 to 0.063 mm
  2.0 litre engine . . . .   0.006 to 0.031 mm
Big-end side-play:
  1.3, 1.4, and 1.6 (16SV and C16NZ) litre engines . . . .   0.11 to 0.24 mm
  1.6 (16SH), 1.8 and 2.0 litre engines . . . .   0.07 to 0.24 mm
Bearing shell identification:
  Top shells:
    Main bearings, standard . . . .   Brown
    Main bearings, 0.25 mm undersize . . . .   Brown/blue
    Main bearings, 0.5 mm undersize . . . .   Brown/white
    Big-end bearings, standard . . . .   None
    Big-end bearings, 0.25 mm undersize . . . .   Blue
    Big-end bearings, 0.5 mm undersize . . . .   White
  Bottom shells:
    Main bearings, standard . . . .   Green
    Main bearings, 0.25 mm undersize . . . .   Green/blue
    Main bearings, 0.5 mm undersize . . . .   Green/white
    Big-end bearings, standard . . . .   None
    Big-end bearings, 0.25 mm undersize . . . .   Blue
    Big-end bearings, 0.5 mm undersize . . . .   White
Main and big-end bearing journal out-of-round . . . .   0.04 mm max
Crankshaft radial run-out (at centre journal, shaft in block) . . . .   0.03 mm max

Flywheel

Refinishing limit - depth of material which may be removed from
clutch friction surface .... 0.3 mm max

Lubrication system

Oil pump tolerances:
  Teeth backlash .... 0.1 to 0.2 mm
  Gear-to-housing clearance (endfloat):
    1.3, 1.4 and 1.6 (16SV and C16NZ) litre engines .... 0.08 to 0.15 mm
    1.6 (16SH), 1.8 and 2.0 litre engines .... 0.03 to 0.10 mm
Oil pressure at idle (engine warm) .... 1.5 bar

Torque wrench settings

	Nm	lbf ft
Flywheel to crankshaft:		
1.3 litre engine	60	44
1.4 and 1.6 (16SV and C16NZ) litre engines:		
Stage 1	35	26
Stage 2	Angle tighten a further 30 to 45°	
1.6 (16SH), 1.8 (18E) engines:		
Stage 1	50	37
Stage 2	Angle tighten a further 25 to 35°	
1.8 (18SE) and 2.0 litre engines:		
Stage 1	65	48
Stage 2	Angle tighten a further 30 to 45°	
Driveplate to crankshaft	60	44
Main bearing cap bolts:		
1.3 litre engine:		
Bolts Part No. 11 082 602*	65	48
Bolts Part No. 90 215 694:		
Stage 1	50	37
Stage 2	Angle tighten a further 45 to 60°	
1.6 (16SH) and 1.8 (18E) litre engine:		
Bolts Part No. 90 215 047*	65	48
Bolts Part No. 90 234 048:		
Stage 1	50	37
Stage 2	Angle tighten a further 45 to 60°	
1.4 and 1.6 (16SV and C16NZ) litre engines:		
Stage 1	50	37
Stage 2	Angle tighten a further 45 to 60°	
1.8 (18SE) and 2.0 litre engines:		
Stage 1	50	37
Stage 2	Angle tighten a further 40 to 50°	
*Use these bolts only if the angle-tightening bolts are not available		
Oil pump relief valve cap	30	22
Oil pressure switch	30	22
Oil pump bolts	6	4
Oil drain plug	45	33
Sump pan bolts	5	4
Big-end cap bolts:		
1.3, 1.4 and 1.6 (16SV and C16NZ) litre engines		
Bolts with 15 mm thread length	28	21
Bolts with 40 mm thread length:		
Stage 1	25	18
Stage 2	Angle tighten a further 30°	
1.6 (16SH) and 1.8 (18E) engines	45	33
1.8 (18SE) and 2.0 litre engines:		
Stage 1	35	26
Stage 2	Angle tighten a further 45°	
Cylinder head bolts:		
1.3, 1.4 litre and 1.6 (16SV and C16NZ) litre engines:		
Stage 1	25	18
Stage 2	Angle tighten a further 60°	
Stage 3	Angle tighten a further 60°	
Stage 4	Angle tighten a further 30°	
Warm the engine up to normal operating temperature then	Angle tighten a further 30°	
1.6 (16SH), 1.8 and 2.0 litre engines:		
Stage 1	25	18
Stage 2	Turn bolt through 60°	
Stage 3	Turn bolt through 60°	
Stage 4	Turn bolt through 60°	
Warm the engine up to normal operating temperature then	Angle tighten a further 30°	

Torque wrench settings (continued)

	Nm	lbf ft
Camshaft sprocket bolt	45	33
Crankshaft pulley bolt:		
1.3, 1.4 and 1.6 (16SV and C16NZ) litre engine:		
Bolt with 23 mm thread length	55	41
Bolt with 30 mm thread length:		
Stage 1	55	41
Stage 2	Angle tighten a further 45 to 60°	
1.6, 1.8 and 2.0 litre engine	20	15
Crankshaft sprocket bolt - 1.6 (16SH), 1.8 and 2.0 litre engines:		
Stage 1	130	96
Stage 2	Angle tighten a further 40 to 50°	
Starter motor bolts:		
1.3 litre engine	25	18
1.6, 1.8 and 2.0 litre engines	45	33
Engine mounting bracket to crankcase	50	37
Engine mounting bracket to transmission	30	22
Engine mountings to bodyframe	40	30
Alternator bracket to block	40	30
Fuel pump to camshaft housing	18	13

Note: *All bolts which are angle tightened must be renewed whenever they are disturbed*

1 General description

The engine is of four-cylinder, in-line overhead camshaft type, mounted transversely at the front of the car.

The crankcase is supported in five shell type main bearings. Thrustwashers are incorporated in the centre main bearing to control crankshaft endfloat.

The connecting rods are attached to the crankshaft by horizontally split shell type main bearings, and to the pistons by gudgeon pins which are an interference fit in the connecting rod small-end bore. The aluminium alloy pistons are fitted with three piston rings: two compression rings and an oil control ring.

The camshaft is driven by a toothed rubber belt from the crankshaft and operates the valves via rocker arms. The rocker arms are supported at their pivot end by hydraulic self-adjusting valve lifters (ball studs) which automatically take up any clearance between the camshaft, rocker arm and valve stems. The inlet and exhaust valves are each closed by a single spring and operate in guides pressed into the cylinder head.

Engine lubrication is by a gear type pump located in a housing attached to the front of the cylinder block. The oil pump is driven by the crankshaft, while the fuel pump (on carburettor models) and the distributor are driven by the camshaft.

2 Compression test - description and interpretation

Refer Chapter 2A, Section 2.

3 Operations requiring engine removal

The design of the engine is such that great accessibility is afforded and it is only necessary to remove the engine for attention to the crankshaft and main bearings. It is possible to renew the crankshaft rear oil seal with the engine in the car, but this entails the use of the manufacturer's special tools and it is quite a difficult operation due to lack of working clearance. For this reason this operation is described with the engine removed.

4 Engine dismantling and reassembly - general information

Refer to Chapter 2A, Section 5.

5 Ancillary components - removal and refitting

Refer to Chapter 2A, Section 6. For fuel injection models, refer to the appropriate Sections of Chapter 4B.

6 Oil pressure regulator valve - removal and refitting

Removal

1 From just to the rear of the crankshaft pulley, unscrew the pressure regulator valve and extract the spring and plunger.
2 Renew the spring if it is distorted or weak (compare it with a new one if possible).
3 If the plunger is scored, renew it.

Refitting

4 Clean out the plunger hole and reassemble using a new plug sealing washer.

7 Camshaft toothed belt - removal, refitting and adjustment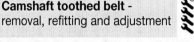

Note: *The following procedure will necessitate re-positioning of the water pump which, in turn, is likely to cause leakage from around the sealing flange. Minor leakage can normally be rectified by using a proprietry radiator sealing product in the cooling system, although it is preferable to remove the water pump completely and fit a new sealing ring (for further information see Chapter 3).*

Removal

1 Undo the belt cover retaining bolts (early models) or release the retaining clips (later models) and remove the cover.
2 Turn the crankshaft until No 1 piston is at its firing point, indicated (on models up to June 1990) by the notch on the crankshaft pulley being in line with the oil pump housing pointer, and/or by the camshaft sprocket mark being in line with the camshaft housing rib **(see illustrations)**.
3 Slacken the alternator mounting and adjustment bolts, move the alternator towards the engine and remove its drivebelt. Where

7.2a Crankshaft pulley notch and oil pump pointer in alignment (arrowed)

7.2b Camshaft sprocket mark and housing rib (both arrowed) should be aligned

7.4 Jamming the flywheel ring gear

7.8 Slackening a water pump bolt

7.9 Swivelling the water pump using a spanner on the flats

necessary, unscrew the union nuts and disconnect the oil cooler pipes from the filter housing to improve access to the crankshaft pulley.

4 On 1.3, 1.4 and 1.6 (16SV and C16NZ) litre engines, release the crankshaft pulley central bolt without disturbing the set position of the crankshaft. To prevent the crankshaft turning it may be sufficient to engage a gear (manual gearbox only) and apply the handbrake; a better way is to remove the flywheel bottom cover plate and jam the flywheel ring gear with a large screwdriver or a tyre lever **(see illustration)**. Remove the bolt and the pulley.

5 On 1.6 (16SH), 1.8 and 2.0 litre engines, remove the four Allen screws which secure the pulley to the sprocket. Remove the pulley.

6 On all models, drain the cooling system as described in Chapter 1.

7 On later (June 1990 onwards) 1.4 litre and 1.6 (16SV and C16NZ) litre engines which are fitted with a spring-loaded automatic tensioner, lock the tensioner in its slackest position. To do this move the tensioner indicator arm clockwise until the holes in the baseplate and arm align and lock the tensioner in position with a suitable rod **(see illustration 7.15)**.

8 On all models, slacken the three bolts which secure the water pump. The bolts are accessible through holes in the belt backplate **(see illustration)**.

9 Swivel the pump to release the tension on the toothed belt. There are flats behind the pump sprocket for this purpose **(see illustration)**. Note the belt's running direction if it is to be used again, then slip it off the sprockets. At this point, also note the statement at the beginning of this Section.

10 A new belt, or one which is to be re-used, must not be kinked or be contaminated with oil, grease etc

Refitting

Later (June 1990 onwards) 1.4 litre and 1.6 (16SV and C16NZ) litre engines

11 Fit the new belt without disturbing the set position of the crankshaft and camshaft sprockets. Apply some tension by moving the water pump and check that the timing marks are correctly aligned **(see illustration)**.

12 Refit the crankshaft pulley bolt and withdraw the locking rod from the spring-loaded automatic tensioner.

13 Rotate the water pump and set the belt tension so that the automatic tensioner indicator arm and backplate holes are aligned (the tensioner arm will have moved fully

clockwise). Tighten the water pump bolts securely.

14 Rotate the crankshaft smoothly through two complete turns clockwise until the timing marks are realigned **(see illustration 7.11)**.

15 Slacken the water pump bolts and rotate the pump anti-clockwise slightly until the automatic tensioner arm is positioned in the centre of backplate notch **(see illustration)**. When the tensioner is correctly positioned, tighten the water pump bolts to the specified torque setting.

16 Rotate the crankshaft through two more complete turns clockwise (so that the timing marks are aligned again) and check that the tensioner arm and backplate notch are still correctly aligned. If not, repeat the operation in paragraph 15.

17 Once the tensioner position is correct, remove the crankshaft pulley bolt.

18 Refit all disturbed components by reversing the removal sequence. Adjust the auxiliary drivebelt and refill the cooling system as described in Chapter 1.

All other models

19 Fit the new belt without disturbing the set position of the crankshaft and camshaft sprockets. Apply some tension by moving the water pump.

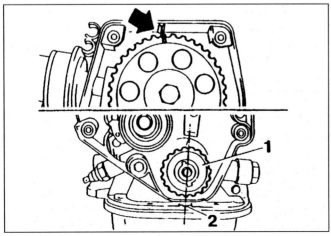

7.11 On 1.4 and 1.6 (16SV and C16NZ) litre engines, align the camshaft sprocket mark with the backplate rib and the notch or dot on the crankshaft sprocket (1) is aligned with the backplate/oil pump housing groove (2)

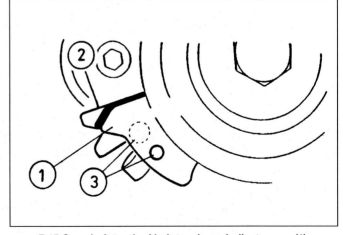

7.15 Camshaft toothed belt tensioner indicator arm (1), baseplate (2) and locking holes (3) - later 1.4 litre and 1.6 (16SV and C16NZ) litre engines

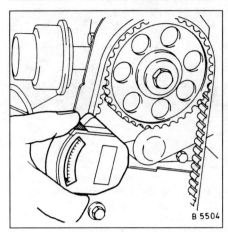

7.21 Checking the camshaft toothed belt tension with gauge KM-510-A

20 Refit the crankshaft pulley and check that the pulley and camshaft sprocket marks are still correctly aligned (paragraph 2). If not, release the belt tension and align the sprockets correctly. Tighten the crankshaft pulley bolt to the specified torque, using locking compound on the bolt threads.

21 To adjust the tension of the belt, ideally the tension gauge specified by the makers (KM-51 0-A) should be used (**see illustration**). If this is available, proceed as follows.

22 Turn the crankshaft through at least half a turn in the normal direction of rotation. Set the tension gauge, apply it to the 'slack' side of the belt (above the alternator) and release it. Read the gauge and compare the figure with that given in the Specifications.

23 If adjustment is necessary, move the water pump to increase or decrease belt tension, rotate the crankshaft through one full turn and take another gauge reading. Repeat as necessary until the desired tension is achieved.

24 In the absence of the belt tension gauge, an approximation to the correct tension can be judged by twisting the belt in the middle of its 'slack' side (between water pump and camshaft sprocket). It should just be possible to twist the belt through 90º (a quarter turn) by hand (**see illustration**), A belt which is too tight will normally be heard to hum or honk when running,

8.19 Removing a rocker arm

7.24 Checking the belt tension by twisting it between the water pump and camshaft sprockets

25 When adjustment is correct, tighten the water pump bolts to the specified torque. Refit and secure the belt cover.

26 Refit and tension the alternator drivebelt and refill the cooling system, both as described in Chapter 1. Refit the flywheel bottom cover if it was removed.

8 Cylinder head - removal and refitting

Removal

Note: *The procedure given here is for carburettor models. The procedure for fuel injection models is similar; refer to Chapter 4B for details of fuel injection component removal and wiring disconnection.*

1 The cylinder head may only be removed when the engine is cold, otherwise there is a risk of distortion.

2 Disconnect the battery earth lead.

3 Remove the air cleaner, (Chapter 4).

4 Drain the cooling system, (Chapter 1).

5 Disconnect the radiator and heater hoses from the cylinder head and inlet manifold.

6 Disconnect and plug the fuel lines and unbolt the fuel pump. Also disconnect the fuel return line from the T-piece or carburettor. Be prepared for fuel spillage.

7 Unbolt and remove the camshaft cover, noting the location of the clips which secure the HT leads and fuel lines. Also disconnect the breather hose (when fitted). Recover the gasket.

8 Disconnect the control cables and electrical cables (as applicable) from the carburettor, referring to Chapter 4A if necessary.

9 Release the coolant pipe bracket at the inlet manifold.

10 Disconnect the brake servo vacuum hose from the inlet manifold.

11 Slacken the alternator pivot bolt, remove the adjusting strap bolt at the engine end and remove the alternator drivebelt.

12 Align the timing marks, slacken the camshaft toothed belt and remove it from the camshaft sprocket, as described in Section 7. Unless it is wished to remove the belt entirely, there is no need to remove the crankshaft pulley.

13 Disconnect the HT leads, identifying them if necessary. Remove the distributor cap and the distributor itself, (Chapter 5).

14 Disconnect the temperature gauge wire from the sender on the thermostat housing or inlet manifold.

15 Unbolt the exhaust downpipe(s) from the exhaust manifold.

16 Following the reverse sequence to that shown in **illustration 8.26a**, slacken each cylinder head bolt by a quarter turn. Following the same order, slacken each bolt by a half turn, then remove them completely. The bolts should by discarded, and new ones used for refitting.

17 Lift off the camshaft housing and camshaft, disconnecting any breather hoses which are connected to the housing.

18 Lift off the cylinder head using the manifolds as handles if it is stuck. Do not prise between the head and block or damage may result.

19 Remove the rocker arms and thrust pads from the cylinder head. Withdraw the hydraulic valve lifters and immerse them in a container of clean engine oil to avoid any possibility of them draining. Keep all components in their original order if they are to be refitted (**see illustration**).

20 If the cylinder head has been removed for decarbonising or for attention to the valves, hydraulic valve lifters and springs, reference should be made to Sections 10 and 11.

Refitting

21 Before refitting the cylinder head, ensure that the block and head mating faces are spotlessly clean and dry with all traces of old gasket removed. Use a scraper to do this, but take care to cover the water passages and other openings with masking tape or rag to prevent dirt and carbon falling in. Remove all traces of oil and water from the bolt holes otherwise hydraulic pressure created by the bolts being screwed in could crack the block or give inaccurate torque settings. Ensure that the bolt threads are clean and dry.

22 When all is clean locate a new gasket on the block so that the worn OBEN or TOP can be read from above (**see illustration**). Do not use any jointing compound on the gasket.

23 Refit the hydraulic valve lifters, thrust pads and rocker arms to the cylinder head in

8.22 Head gasket must be fitted with the word OBEN (or TOP) uppermost

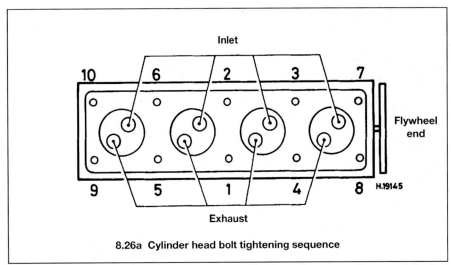

Inlet

10 6 2 3 7

Flywheel end

9 5 1 4 8

H.19145

Exhaust

8.26a Cylinder head bolt tightening sequence

8.26b Using a marked card to measure angular rotation when tightening cylinder head bolts

their original positions. If new hydraulic valve lifters are being used, or if they were dismantled for cleaning, immerse each one in a container of clean engine oil and compress it (by hand) several times to charge it.
24 Locate the cylinder head on the block so that the positioning dowels engage in their holes.
25 Apply a uniform bead of jointing compound to the mating face of the cylinder head and lower the camshaft housing into place. Position the sprocket with the timing marks aligned.
26 Fit the new cylinder head bolts and tighten them in the order shown, in the stages given in the Specifications. The required angular measurement can be marked on a card and then placed over the bolt as a guide to the movement of the bolt (see illustrations).
27 Refit the distributor, as described in Chapter 5.
28 Refit and secure the exhaust downpipe(s). Apply a little anti-seize compound to the bolts.
29 Refit the camshaft cover, using a new gasket. Tighten the bolts in diagonal sequence, remembering to fit the HT lead and fuel line brackets (see illustrations).
30 Reconnect the HT leads and refit the distributor cap.
31 Refit the fuel pump, using new gaskets on

each side of the spacer. Reconnect the fuel supply and return lines.
32 Refit and tension the camshaft toothed belt, as described in Section 7, then refit the belt cover.
33 Refit and tension the alternator drivebelt, as described in Chapter 1.
34 Refit the coolant hoses and refill the cooling system, as described in Chapter 1. Secure the coolant pipe bracket to the inlet manifold.
35 Reconnect the throttle and choke cables to the carburettor, as described in Chapter 4A. On models with automatic choke, reconnect the electrical lead to the choke.
36 Refit the brake servo vacuum hose, the temperature gauge wire and the crankcase breather hose(s).
37 Check that nothing has been overlooked, then refit the air cleaner.
38 Reconnect the battery and start the engine. There may be considerable valve gear noise until the hydraulic tappets pressurise with oil.
39 Run the engine until it reaches normal operating temperature, then check the ignition timing, as described in Chapter 5.
40 Switch off the engine, immediately remove the air cleaner and tighten the cylinder head bolts through the final specified angle, following the outward spiral pattern previously used. No further tightening is necessary.

9 Camshaft - removal and refitting

Removal

1 The camshaft can only be removed without disturbing the housing if special tool 603 850, or equivalent, is available to depress the cam followers whilst the camshaft is withdrawn.
2 Assuming that the special tool is not available, the camshaft housing must be removed. Since the cylinder head bolts will be removed, it would certainly be good practice to fit a new cylinder head gasket; however, if the cooling system is drained and the housing is removed gently, there is a good chance that the head gasket seal will not be broken. It is the reader's choice whether to undertake the extra work of renewing the head gasket as a precaution, or to risk the vexation of finding that the old gasket has 'blown' after reassembly.
3 With the camshaft housing removed, as described in Section 8, clamp the cylinder head with four head bolts and some spacers if the head is not to be disturbed (see illustration).
4 Undo the camshaft sprocket bolt, using an open-ended spanner on the flats of the camshaft to stop the shaft turning. Remove the bolt, washer and sprocket.
5 At the other end of the housing, remove the two Allen screws which secure the thrust

8.29a Fitting a new camshaft cover gasket

8.29b HT lead bracket is secured by one of the camshaft cover bolts

9.3 Cylinder head bolt, with washers and nuts for spacers, used to clamp head

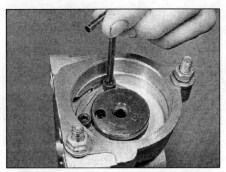

9.5a Removing the Allen screws which secure the camshaft thrust plate

9.5b Removing the camshaft thrust plate

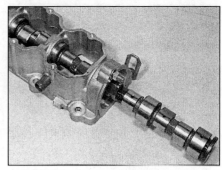

9.6 Removing the camshaft from the housing

plate. Push the camshaft rearwards and extract the plate **(see illustrations)**.

6 Carefully withdraw the camshaft from the distributor end of the housing. Be careful not to damage the bearing surfaces in the housing **(see illustration)**.

7 Where necessary, undo the bolts which secure the belt cover backplate and remove the plate **(see illustration)**.

Refitting

8 Prise out the oil seal with a screwdriver. Drive in a new seal until it is flush with the housing, using a piece of wood or a suitably sized socket **(see illustrations)**.

9 Liberally lubricate the camshaft bearings and the oil seal lip. (If special lubricant has been supplied with a new camshaft, use it; otherwise use clean engine oil, perhaps with a molybdenum disulphide additive.) Carefully insert the camshaft.

10 Refit the thrust plate and tighten its screws. Check the camshaft endfloat using a feeler blade **(see illustration)**. If the endfloat exceeds that specified, renew the thrust plate.

11 Refit the belt backplate (where necessary).

12 Refit the camshaft sprocket, engaging the peg on the shaft with the hole in the sprocket. Tighten the sprocket bolt to the specified torque, holding the camshaft as before **(see illustrations)**.

13 Refit the camshaft housing, (Section 8).

14 If a new camshaft has been fitted, it is most important to observe the following running-in schedule (unless otherwise specified by the manufacturer) immediately after start-up:

One minute at 2000 rpm
One minute at 1500 rpm
One minute at 3000 rpm
One minute at 2000 rpm

15 Change the engine oil (but not the filter, unless due in any case) approximately 1000 km after fitting a new camshaft.

10 Cylinder head - overhaul

1 With the cylinder head removed, clean away external dirt.

2 Remove the valves, springs and associated components, as described in Section 9 of Chapter 2A. Note that both inlet and exhaust valve springs have seats, but they are different **(see illustration)**.

3 Inspect the valves, valve seats, guides and springs, also as described in Section 9, Chapter 2A. Regrind or renew as necessary.

4 Check the head sealing surface for warping by placing in on a piece of plate glass, or using a straight-edge and feeler blades. Slight

9.7 Camshaft belt cover backplate (1.3 litre engine shown)

9.8a Prising out the camshaft housing oil seal

9.8b Fitting a new camshaft housing oil seal

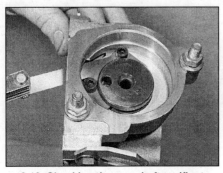

9.10 Checking the camshaft endfloat

9.12a Fitting the camshaft sprocket. Peg locating hole is arrowed

9.12b Tightening the camshaft sprocket bolt

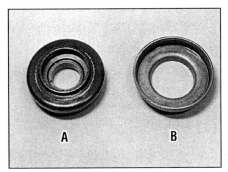

10.2 Exhaust valve spring rotator seat (A) and inlet valve spring seat (B)

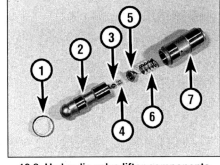

10.6 Hydraulic valve lifter components

1 Collar
2 Plunger
3 Ball
4 Small spring
5 Plunger cap
6 Large spring
7 Cylinder

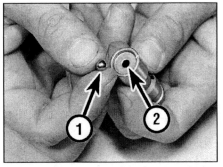

10.12 Locate the ball (1) on its seat (2) in the base of the plunger

distortion, or corrosion, may be corrected by machining. Seek expert advice if this is necessary: the removal of too much metal will render the head useless.

5 Check the valve lifter bores in the cylinder head for wear which, if evident, will mean renewal of the cylinder head. Also check the valve lifter oil supply holes in the cylinder head for any sign of contamination.

6 On engines which have covered a high mileage, or for which the service history (particularly oil changes) is suspect, it is possible for the valve lifters to suffer internal contamination, which in extreme cases may result in increased engine top-end noise and wear. To minimise the possibility of problems occurring later in the life of the engine, it is advisable to dismantle and clean the hydraulic valve lifters as follows whenever the cylinder head is overhauled. Note that no spare parts are available for the valve lifters, and if any of

the components are unserviceable, the complete assembly must be renewed **(see illustration)**.

7 Carefully pull the collar from the top of the valve lifter cylinder. It should be possible to remove the collar by hand-if a tool is used, take care not to distort the collar.

8 Withdraw the plunger from the cylinder, and recover the string.

9 Using a small screwdriver, carefully prise the cap from the base of the plunger. Recover the spring and ball from under the cap, taking care not to lose them as the cap is removed.

10 Carefully clean all the components using paraffin or a suitable solvent, paying particular attention to the machined surfaces of the cylinder (internal surfaces), and piston

(external surfaces). Thoroughly dry all the components using a lint-free cloth. Carefully examine the springs for damage or distortion- the complete valve lifter must be renewed if the springs are not in perfect condition.

11 Lubricate the components sparingly with clean engine oil of the correct grade, then reassemble as follows.

12 Invert the plunger, and locate the ball on its seat in the base of the plunger **(see illustration)**.

13 Locate the smaller spring on its seat in the plunger cap, then carefully refit the cap and spring, ensuring that the spring locates on the ball. Carefully press around the flange of the cap, using a small screwdriver if necessary, until the flange is securely located in the groove in the base of the plunger **(see illustrations)**.

14 Locate the larger spring over the plunger cap, ensuring that the spring is correctly seated, and slide the plunger and spring assembly into the cylinder **(see illustrations)**.

15 Slide the collar over the top of the plunger, and carefully compress the plunger by hand, until the collar can be pushed down to engage securely with the groove in the cylinder **(see illustration)**.

16 On some engines an oil pressure regulating valve in the head stabilises the oil pressure applied to the valve lifters **(see illustration)**. To renew the valve, access is gained via the circular plug covering the end of the valve. The old valve must be crushed and its remains extracted, and a thread (M10) cut in the valve seat to allow removal using a suitable bolt. A new valve and plug can then

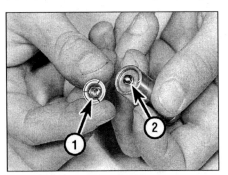

10.13a Spring (1) located in plunger cap, and ball (2) located on seat in plunger

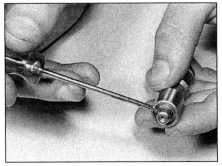

10.13b Locate the cap flange in the plunger groove

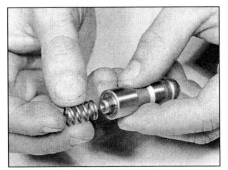

10.14a Locate the spring over the plunger cap . . .

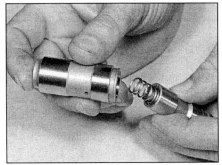

10.14b . . . then slide the plunger and spring assembly into the cylinder

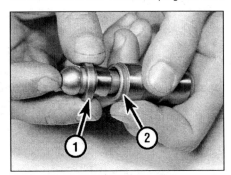

10.15 Slide the collar (1) over the top of the plunger and engage with the groove (2)

10.16 Cylinder head oil pressure regulating valve (arrowed)

12.6 Oil pick-up support bracket

12.7a Removing the oil baffle plate. This model has two cork gaskets . . .

be driven into position. Care must be taken to keep foreign matter and swarf out of the oilways; it is probably best to have the valve renewed by a GM dealer if necessary.

17 Refit the valves, springs etc, as described in Section 9 of Chapter 2A. Remember to fit new valve stem seals.

18 On 1.6 (16SH), 1.8 and 2.0 litre engines, take the opportunity to renew the thermostat housing sealing ring whilst the head is removed.

11 Cylinder head and pistons - decarbonising

Refer to Chapter 2A, Section 10; bearing in mind also that the head is of light alloy construction and is easily damaged.

12 Sump - removal and refitting

Removal

1 Jack up the front of the car and support it on axle stands (see "*Jacking and Vehicle Support*").

2 Drain the engine oil into a suitable container and refit the plug after draining.

3 Unbolt the exhaust downpipe(s) from the exhaust manifold.

4 Undo the bolts securing the flywheel cover plate to the transmission bellhousing and remove the plate.

5 Undo the retaining bolts and lift away the sump. It will probably be necessary to tap the

sump from side to side with a hide or plastic mallet to release the joint face.

6 On later models, where necessary, unbolt the oil pick-up pipe support bracket (see illustration). If the engine is in the car, it will be easier to remove the baffle plate if the oil pick-up pipe is removed completely.

7 Remove the baffle plate and recover the gasket(s). On some models a double-sided rubber gasket is used; on other models there are two cork gaskets (see illustrations).

Refitting

8 On later models, where the baffle plate has been removed, ensure that the surfaces are clean and dry and refit the plate using new gasket(s) (as applicable). Refit the oil pick-up pipe bracket and securely tighten its retaining bolts.

9 On all models, thoroughly clean the sump in paraffin or a suitable solvent and remove all traces of external dirt and internal sludge. Scrape away the remains of the old gasket from the sump and crankcase faces and ensure that they are clean and dry.

10 Apply jointing compound to the oil pump housing joint, the crankcase mating face and the rear main bearing cap joint, then place a new gasket in position.

11 Apply jointing compound to the sump face and retaining bolt threads, place the sump in position and refit the bolts. Progressively tighten the bolts in a diagonal sequence.

12 Refit the exhaust downpipe(s) and flywheel cover plate, lower the car to the ground and fill the engine with oil.

13 Oil pump - removal and refitting

Removal

1 Remove the camshaft toothed belt and the sump, as described in earlier Sections of this Chapter.

2 Slacken and remove the crankshaft sprocket centre bolt (if not already done - see Section 7, paragraph 4) and remove the sprocket and spacers, noting their correct fitted locations. Extract the Woodruff key (where fitted) (see illustrations).

3 Undo the retaining bolts and remove the toothed belt cover backplate. On later models, in order to remove the backplate it will first be necessary to remove the remaining camshaft toothed belt sprockets to allow this.

4 Undo the two bolts securing the oil pick-up pipe to the oil pump housing and the bolt securing the support bracket to the centre main bearing cap (see illustration). Remove the pick-up pipe. On models with an oil cooler, slacken the union nuts and disconnect the pipes from the oil pump housing.

5 Undo the retaining bolts and withdraw the oil pump housing from the front of the engine.

Refitting

6 Refitting is the reverse of removal, noting the following points.

a) Ensure that the pump housing mating faces are clean and place a new gasket which is smeared with jointing compound on both sides in position.

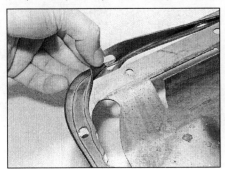

12.7b . . . while this one has one double-sided rubber gasket

13.2a Removing the crankshaft sprocket

13.2b Woodruff key (arrowed) in crankshaft nose

13.4 Oil pick-up pipe retaining bolts (arrowed)

13.6 Tape the crankshaft nose

14.1 Using an impact screwdriver to undo the oil pump rear cover screws

b) *Steps must be taken to protect the seal lips from damage or turning back on the shoulder at the front end of the crankshaft. To do this, grease the seal lips and then bind tape around the crankshaft to form a gentle taper* (see illustration).

c) *Refit the sump and camshaft toothed belt and sprockets as described in earlier Sections of this Chapter.*

14 Oil pump - overhaul

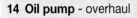

1 With the oil pump removed from the vehicle, withdraw the rear cover. The cross-head fixing screws are very tight and an impact driver will be required to remove them (see illustration).

2 Check the backlash between the inner and outer gear teeth (see illustration).

3 Check the endfloat between the gear outer faces and the housing (see illustration).

4 If any of the clearances are outside the specified tolerance, renew the components as necessary. Note that the outer gear face is marked for position (see illustration).

5 The pressure regulator valve can be unscrewed from the oil pump housing and the components cleaned and examined (see illustration).

6 Always renew the oil seal; a socket is useful to remove and install it (see illustration).

15 Pistons and connecting rods - removal and refitting

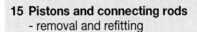

Proceed as described in Chapter 2A, noting also that the piston crowns are not marked to show their direction of fitting, but the underside of the piston is (see illustration).

16 Flywheel - removal and refitting

Refer to Chapter 2A, noting that the flywheel securing bolts are hexagon-headed. On 1.6 (16SV and C16NZ), 1.8 (18SE) and all 2.0 litre engines note that it will be necessary to remove the transmission or engine in order to remove the flywheel. On all engines, on refitting, use thread locking compound on the flywheel bolts and tighten them to the specified torque.

17 Crankshaft front oil seal - removal and refitting

Removal

1 Remove the camshaft toothed belt, as

14.2 Checking oil pump gear teeth backlash

14.3 Checking oil pump gear endfloat

14.4 Gear outer face identification mark (arrowed)

14.5 Oil pressure regulator valve components

14.6 Fitting a new front oil seal

15.1 Large land (arrowed) faces the flywheel end of the engine

described in Section 7. On 1.6 (16SH), 1.8 and 2.0 litre models, note that it will also be necessary to undo the crankshaft sprocket centre bolt (see Section 7, paragraph 4) and remove the sprocket and spacers, noting their correct fitted locations.

2 On later models, remove the remaining camshaft toothed belt sprockets then undo the retaining bolts and remove the toothed belt cover backplate.

3 Remove the crankshaft sprocket, using two screwdrivers to lever it off if it is tight. Remove the Woodruff key.

4 Punch or drill a small hole in the metal face of the oil seal, screw in a self-tapping screw and use this to lever out the seal. Several attempts may be necessary. Be careful not to damage the sealing face of the crankshaft.

Refitting

5 Apply PVC tape to the step on the crankshaft nose to protect the seal lip as it is fitted.

6 Lubricate the lip of the seal and, using a suitable tube, tap the seal into its location. Remove the masking tape.

7 Refit the toothed belt cover backplate, sprockets and belt as described in the earlier Sections of this Chapter.

18 Engine/transmission mountings - removal and refitting

Refer to Chapter 2A, Section 17.

19 Crankshaft rear oil seal - removal and refitting

Remove the engine from the car, as described in Section 23 and renew the oil seal. as described in Chapter 2A, Section 19.

20 Crankshaft and main bearings - removal and refitting

Removal

1 With the engine removed from the car, as described in Section 23, and all the

20.3 Identification number on No 3 main bearing cap

components removed from it, as described in earlier Sections, the crankshaft can be removed as follows.

2 Invert the engine so that it is standing on the top surface of the cylinder block.

3 The main bearing caps are numbered 1 to 4 from the toothed belt end of the engine. The rear cap is not marked. To ensure that the caps are fitted the correct way round, note that the numbers are read from the water pump side when the crankcase is inverted (see illustration).

4 Unscrew and remove the main bearing cap bolts and tap off the caps. If the bearing shells are to be used again, keep them with their respective caps. The original shells are colour-coded and if used again must be returned to their original locations.

5 Note that the centre bearing shell incorporates thrust flanges to control crankshaft endfloat.

6 Lift the crankshaft from the crankcase. Extract the upper half shells and again identify their position in the crankcase if they are to be used again.

7 The rubber plug location adjacent to the bellhousing flange on the crankcase covers the aperture for installation of a TDC sensor. This sensor when connected to a suitable monitoring unit, indicates TDC from the position of the contact pins set in the crankshaft counterbalance weight (see illustration).

Refitting

8 Ensure that the crankcase and crankshaft are thoroughly clean and that all oilways are

20.7 TDC sensor contact pins (arrowed) in crankshaft web

clear. If possible blow the drillings out with compressed air, and then inject clean engine oil through them to ensure that they are clear.

9 Wipe the shell seats in the crankcase and bearing caps clean and then fit the upper halves of the main bearing shells into their seats.

10 Note that there is a tag on the back of each bearing which engages with a groove in the shell seating in both crankcase and bearing cap (see illustration).

11 Wipe away all traces of protective grease on the new shells.

12 The central bearing shell also takes up the crankshaft endfloat (see illustration). Note that the half shells fitted to the cylinder block all have oil duct holes, while only the centre main bearing cap half shell has an oil duct hole.

13 When the shells are fully located in the crankcase and bearing caps, lubricate them with clean engine oil.

14 Fill the lips of a new crankshaft oil seal with grease and fit it to the end of the crankshaft (see illustration).

15 Carefully install the crankshaft into position in the crankcase (see illustration).

16 Lubricate the crankshaft main bearing journals and then refit the centre and intermediate main bearing caps. Tighten the retaining bolts to the specified torque wrench setting (see illustrations).

17 Coat the inner surfaces of the rear main bearing cap with sealant to GM spec 15 04 200/8 983 368. (This sealant is available in 200 ml tubes from GM parts departments.) Fill the side grooves of the bearing cap with RTV

20.10 Main bearing shell correctly fitted, with tag and groove (arrowed) engaged

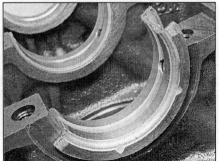
20.12 Centre main bearing shell, showing thrust flanges

20.14 Crankshaft rear oil seal

20.15 Fitting the crankshaft

20.16a Fitting a main bearing cap

20.16b Tightening a main bearing cap bolt

20.17 Inject jointing compound into the cap side grooves

20.19 Checking crankshaft endfloat

jointing compound. After fitting the bearing cap and tightening its securing bolts, inject further RTV jointing compound into the side grooves until it is certain that they are full (see illustration).

18 Fit the front main bearing cap, but before fitting the retaining bolts, smear them with jointing compound, and then tighten to the specified torque wrench setting. Check that the bearing cap is exactly flush with the end face of the crankcase as it is tightened.

19 Now rotate the crankshaft and check that it turns freely, and shows no signs of binding or tight spots. Check that the crankshaft endfloat is within the limits specified, using a dial gauge or with feeler blades inserted between the flange of the centre bearing shell and the machined surface of the crankshaft (see illustration). Before measuring, make sure that the crankshaft has been forced fully towards one end of the crankcase to give the widest gap at the measuring location. Incorrect endfloat will most likely be due to wear or to incorrect regrinding (assuming that the correct shells have been fitted).

21 Engine components -
examination and renovation

1 Refer to Chapter 2A Section 21, noting the following additional information

Camshaft

2 With the camshaft removed, examine the bearings for signs of obvious wear and pitting. If evident, a new camshaft housing will

probably be required.

3 The camshaft itself should show no marks or scoring on the journal or cam lobe surfaces. If evident, renew the camshaft. When renewing a camshaft, it should be noted that, in some instances, a camshaft with undersize bearing journals and appropriately-machined carrier journals may have been fitted by the manufacturer. Where applicable, such camshafts are colour-coded violet for identification, and this should be checked to ensure that the correct replacement is obtained.

4 The retaining plate should appear unworn and without grooves. In any event, check the camshaft endfloat and fit a new plate where necessary.

5 The housing front oil seal should always be renewed at major overhaul.

Camshaft toothed belt

6 Closely inspect the belt for cracking, fraying or tooth deformation. Where evident, renew the belt.

7 If the belt has been in use for 30 000 miles or more, it is recommended that it is renewed even if it appears in good condition.

8 Whenever the original belt is to be removed, but is going to be used again, always note its running direction before removing it. It is even worthwhile marking the tooth engagement points on each sprocket. As the belt will have worn in a set position, refitting it in exactly the same way will prevent any increase in noise which might otherwise occur when the engine is running.

Valve lifters, rockers and thrust pads

9 Any signs of wear in a hydraulic lifter can only be rectified by renewal, the unit cannot be dismantled.

10 Inspect the rockers and thrust pads for wear or grooving. Again, renew if evident.

Piston/bore grade marks

11 The number or code denoting the piston and bore grade (see Specifications) will be found on the sump sealing surface of the smaller engines, and near the engine number on the larger engines.

22 Engine lubrication and crankcase ventilation systems -
general description

1 Oil pressure for all moving components is provided by a gear type oil pump which is driven from the front end of the crankshaft. The crankshaft has flats for this purpose.

2 The pump draws oil from the sump through a pick-up pipe and strainer and pumps it through the oil filter and oil galleries to the engine friction surfaces.

3 A pressure regulator valve is screwed into the body of the oil pump. A relief valve, located in the oil filter mounting base, opens should the filter block due to clogging caused by neglected servicing. An oil pressure switch is screwed into the pump casing.

4 The cylinder bores are lubricated by oil splash from the sump.

5 The hydraulic valve lifters are pressurised with oil to maintain optimum valve clearance at all times.

6 The crankcase ventilation system is designed to draw oil fumes and blow-by gas (combustion gas which has passed the piston rings) from the crankcase into the air cleaner, whence they are drawn into the engine and burnt during the normal combustion cycle.

7 On larger engines, one of the crankcase ventilation hoses is attached to the camshaft cover. Inside the cover is a filter which should be cleaned in paraffin periodically (see illustrations).

8 On smaller engines, the ventilation system incorporates an oil separator bolted to the

22.7a Crankcase ventilation hose attached to camshaft cover (1.8 litre engine shown)

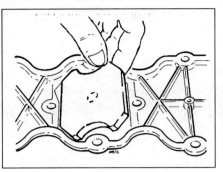

22.7b Camshaft housing filter

22.8 Crankcase ventilation system oil separator - 1.3 litre engine

block. Although it is not a specified maintenance task, the separator can be removed for cleaning (see illustration).

9 On all engines, the breather hoses should be cleaned out periodically and renewed if necessary. Investigate the cause of any build-up of white sludge - sometimes this indicates a cooling system fault or a blown head gasket, although it may simply mean that the engine is not reaching operating temperature (eg short runs in winter).

10 The lubrication system of some larger engines incorporates an oil cooler. Oil leaves and returns via an adapter mounted between the oil filter and its housing (see illustrations). The adapter contains a thermostatic valve which prevents the oil from circulating in the cooling circuit until it has warmed up. The oil cooler itself is mounted in front of the radiator.

11 The oil cooler pipes and hoses should be inspected regularly for signs of deterioration or leakage. The oil cooler fins will benefit from an occasional cleaning with solvent, followed if possible by blowing through the fins with compressed air.

12 At time of engine overhaul, consideration should be given to renewing the oil cooler, especially if major mechanical failure has occurred. If the old cooler is to be re-used it should be flushed with several changes of clean oil in an attempt to remove metal particles and other contaminants.

13 Access to the oil cooler is gained by removing the radiator (Chapter 3) or the front trim panel (Chapter 11).

22.10a Oil cooler adapter (arrowed) above oil filter

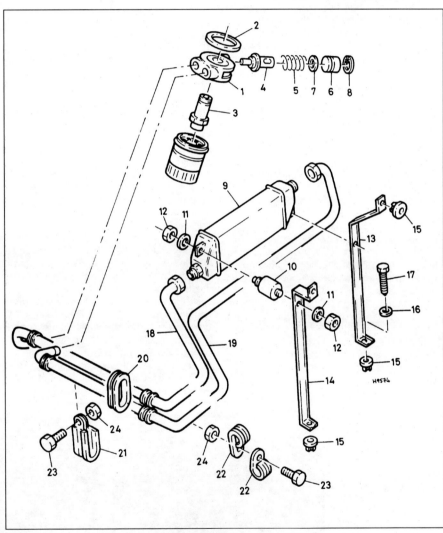

22.10b Oil cooler and associated components

1 Adapter	9 Oil cooler	17 Screw
2 Sealing ring	10 Mounting rubber	18 Flow pipe
3 Hollow screw	11 Washer	19 Return pipe
4 Thermostatic valve	12 Nut	20 Grommet
5 Spring	13 Bracket	21 Clamp
6 Plug	14 Bracket	22 Clamps
7 Seal	15 Nuts	23 Screws
8 Circlip	16 Washer	24 Nuts

23 Engine - removal and refitting

Removal

1 The OHC engines may be removed either with or without the manual gearbox. To remove the engine alone, proceed as described in Chapter 2A, Section 23, making allowances for differences in the attachment of components such as the carburettor or fuel injection items.

2 Removal of the engine and automatic transmission together may be possible, but it is not recommended because of the weight and unwieldiness of the combined units.

3 To remove the engine and manual gearbox together, first disconnect both battery terminals. Remove the bonnet (Chapter 11).

4 Remove the air cleaner, as described in Chapter 4.

5 Drain the cooling system as described in Chapter 1. Disconnect all coolant hoses from the engine, not forgetting the heater hoses and (if fitted) the inlet manifold/carburettor heating hoses.

6 Disconnect the throttle cable and (if fitted) the choke cable, as described in Chapter 4.

7 Disconnect the brake servo vacuum hose. Either remove the hose completely, or secure it so that it will not be damaged.

8 Disconnect and plug the fuel feed and return lines. Be prepared for some fuel spillage.

9 Disconnect the engine wiring harness plug. On models so equipped, disconnect the dipstick sensor wiring also (see illustrations).

10 Disconnect the HT lead, LT leads and multi-plug from the ignition coil and module.

11 Disconnect the gearchange remote control rod at the pinch-bolt.

12 Disconnect the speedometer cable at the gearbox end.

13 Disconnect the clutch cable, as described in Chapter 6.

23.9a Engine wiring harness plug

23.9b Dipstick sensor plug

14 Slacken the front wheel bolts, raise and securely support the front of the car and remove the front wheels.

15 Unbolt and remove the exhaust downpipe(s). Also disconnect the earth strap from the gearbox.

16 Where applicable, disconnect the oil cooler hoses from the oil filter housing. Be prepared for some oil spillage and plug the hoses.

17 Separate the control arm balljoints from the steering knuckles. See Chapter 10 for details.

18 Separate the driveshafts from the final drive housing, as described in Chapter 8. Be prepared for some oil spillage; plug the driveshaft holes and tie the shafts up out of the way.

19 Attach the lifting tackle to the engine and gearbox and take the weight of the assembly.

20 Unbolt the engine/transmission mountings from the body members (see illustrations).

21 Carefully lower the assembly through the engine bay to the ground. Depending on the type and reach of the vehicle lifting gear, it may be necessary to lift the vehicle off the engine to enable it to be withdrawn.

22 To separate the engine and gearbox, support the latter and unbolt the starter motor and flywheel bottom cover. Remove the

remaining engine-to-bellhousing bolts and carefully withdraw the gearbox from the engine. Do not allow the weight of the gearbox to hang on the clutch input shaft.

Refitting

23 When refitting, tighten the engine/transmission mounting bolts finger tight at first, then to the specified torque, in the following order:

a) RH front mounting.
b) LH front mounting.
c) Rear mounting.

24 The remainder of the refitting process follows the reverse order to removal. Refer to the appropriate Chapters for guidance if necessary. Remember to replenish the gearbox oil after refitting.

24 Engine - initial start-up after overhaul

Refer to Chapter 2A, Section 24. There is no need to adjust the valve clearances, but remember to tighten the head bolts (Section 8) if the head has been disturbed. Expect some initial noise from the hydraulic valve lifters, until they are properly pressurised with oil.

23.20a Engine/transmission left-hand mounting

23.20b Engine/transmission right-hand mounting

Chapter 2 Part C:
DOHC (16-valve) engine

Contents

Degrees of difficulty

Easy, suitable for novice with little experience	Fairly easy, suitable for beginner with some experience	Fairly difficult, suitable for competent DIY mechanic	Difficult, suitable for experienced DIY mechanic	Very difficult, suitable for expert DIY or professional

Specifications

General

Type	Four-cylinder, in-line, water-cooled, double overhead camshaft, transversely mounted
Engine code*	20XE, C20XE* or 20XEJ
Bore	86.0 mm
Stroke	86.0 mm
Capacity	1998 cc
Firing order	1-3-4-2 (No 1 cylinder at crankshaft pulley end)
Direction of crankshaft rotation	Clockwise
Compression ratio	10.5: 1

Note: *The engine code forms the first digits of the engine number*

Cylinder block

	Diameter	Marking
Cylinder bore diameter:		
Standard size 1	85.98 mm	8
	85.99 mm	99
	86.00 mm	00
	86.01 mm	01
Standard size 2	86.02 mm	02
Oversize (0.5 mm)	86.47 mm	7 + 0.5
	86.48 mm	8 + 0.5
	86.49 mm	9 + 0.5
	86.50 mm	0 + 0.5
Maximum cylinder bore ovality	0.013 mm	
Maximum cylinder bore taper	0.013 mm	

Crankshaft

Number of main bearings	5
Main bearing journal diameter	57.982 to 57.995 mm
Crankpin diameter	48.971 to 48.987 mm
Undersizes	0.25 and 0.50 mm
Crankshaft endfloat	0.07 to 0.3 mm
Main bearing running clearance	0.015 to 0.04 mm
Big-end running clearance	0.019 to 0.063 mm
Big-end side-play	0.07 to 0.24 mm

Bearing shell identification:

Top shells:

Main bearings, standard	Brown
Main bearings, 0.25 mm undersize	Brown/blue
Main bearings, 0.5 mm undersize	Brown/white
Big-end bearings, standard	None
Big-end bearings, 0.25 mm undersize	Blue
Big-end bearings, 0.5 mm undersize	White

Bottom shells:

Main bearings, standard	Green
Main bearings, 0.25 mm undersize	Green/blue
Main bearings, 0.5 mm undersize	Green/white
Big-end bearings, standard	None
Big-end bearings, 0.25 mm undersize	Blue
Big-end bearings, 0.5 mm undersize	White
Main and big-end bearing journal out-of-round	0.04 mm max
Crankshaft radial run-out (at centre journal, shaft in block)	0.03 mm max

Pistons and piston rings

Piston diameter	0.03 mm less than bore diameter
Piston-to-bore clearance	0.02 to 0.04 mm

Gudgeon pins

Length	61.5 mm
Diameter	21 mm
Clearance in piston	0.003 to 0.010 mm
Clearance in connecting rod	0.015 to 0.030 mm

Cylinder head

Minimum acceptable height after machining	135.63 mm
Maximum acceptable gasket face distortion	0.025 mm
Camshaft bearing bore diameter	28.000 to 28.021 mm

Valve seat width:

Inlet	1.0 to 1.4 mm
Exhaust	1.4 to 1.8 mm

Camshafts

Drive	Toothed belt

Number of bearings:

Inlet	5
Exhaust	6
Bearing journal diameter	27.939 to 27.960 mm
Bearing journal running clearance	0.061 mm
Camshaft endfloat	0.04 to 0.144 mm
Cam lift	9.5 mm

Valves

Operation	Bucket tappet incorporating hydraulic adjuster
Seat angle	44° 40'

Length:

Production	105 mm
Service	104.6 mm

Head diameter:

Inlet	33 mm
Exhaust	29 mm

Stem diameter (standard):

Inlet	6.955 to 6.970 mm
Exhaust	6.945 to 6.960 mm
Stem diameter (oversize)	0.075 and 0.150 mm

Stem-to-guide clearance:

Inlet	0.045 mm
Exhaust	0.055 mm
Valve clearance	Automatic adjustment by hydraulic adjusters

Valves (continued)

Valve guide internal diameter:
Standard .... 7.000 to 7.015 mm
Oversizes .... 0.075 and 0.150 mm
Valve guide installed height .... 10.70 to 11.00 mm

Torque wrench settings

	Nm	lbf ft
Starter motor-to-block bolts	45	33
Starter motor bracket-to-block bolts	25	18
Manifold nuts	20	15
Alternator mounting-to-block bolts	40	30
Steering pump mounting-to-block bolts	40	30
Crankshaft pulley-to-sprocket screws with splined heads	20	15
Crankshaft sprocket central bolt (greased threads):		
Stage 1	250	184
Stage 2	Angle-tighten a further 40 to 50°	
Main bearing caps:		
Stage 1	50	37
Stage 2	Angle-tighten a further 40° to 50°	
Big-end bearing caps:		
Stage 1	35	26
Stage 2	Angle-tighten a further 45° to 60°	
Engine mountings (use thread-locking compound)	75	55
Camshaft bearing caps:		
M8 nuts	20	15
M6 nuts	10	7
Oil drain plug	45	33
Oil pump housing-to-block bolts	6	4
Sump bolts (use thread-locking compound)	15	11
Flywheel bolts (use thread-locking compound):		
Stage 1	65	48
Stage 2	Angle-tighten a further 30° to 45°	
Water pump-to-block bolts	25	
Camshaft sprocket bolts:		
Stage 1	50	37
Stage 2	Angle-tighten a further 40° to 50°	
Camshaft drivebelt tensioner and idler rollers-to-block bolts:		
Stage 1	25	
Stage 2	Angle-tighten a further 45° to 60°	
Camshaft cover screws	8	6
Cylinder head bolts:		
Stage 1	25	18
Stage 2	Angle-tighten a further 65°	
Stage 3	Angle-tighten a further 65°	
Stage 4	Angle-tighten a further 65°	
Warm the engine up to normal operating temperature then	Angle tighten a further 30° to 45°	

Note: All bolts which are angle tightened must be renewed whenever they are disturbed

1 General description

The 2.0 litre 16-valve engine differs from the other 2 litre engines fitted to the range in the areas of the cylinder head, camshaft drive and associated components. The block, crankshaft and pistons are essentially unchanged, except for the use of fully floating gudgeon pins secured by circlips.

The cylinder head carries two camshafts, both driven by the same toothed belt. The front camshaft operates the exhaust valves, the rear camshaft the inlet valves. The cam lobes bear directly onto bucket tappets which incorporate hydraulic adjuster mechanisms. The front camshaft also drives the distributor.

There are four valves per cylinder, two inlet and two exhaust. The exhaust valves are sodium-filled; at operating temperature the sodium melts and improves the conduction of heat away from the valve head. The combustion chambers are of pent roof pattern, with the spark plugs centrally placed between the valve rows.

The camshaft toothed belt also drives the water pump, as in the other engines, but a separate roller is used to adjust belt tension. An idler roller is used to complete the belt run.

The engine is pleasing in appearance and obviously well-engineered. Extensive use has been made of aluminium castings, not only for components such as the sump and camshaft toothed belt cover but even for the flywheel cover and spark plug lead cover.

2 Compression test - description and interpretation

Refer Chapter 2A, Section 2.

3 Operations requiring engine removal

The design of the engine is such that great accessibility is afforded and it is only necessary to remove the engine for attention to the crankshaft and main bearings.

4 Engine dismantling and reassembly - general

Refer to Chapter 2A, Section 5.

5 Ancillary components - removal and refitting

Refer to Chapter 2A, Section 6. For information on the fuel injection components, refer to the appropriate Sections of Chapter 4B.

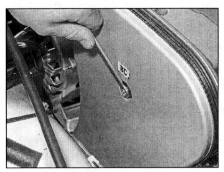

7.6a Removing a belt cover bolt . . .

7.6b . . . and the rubber bush

7.6c The belt cover seal

6 Oil pressure regulating valve - removal and refitting

Refer to Chapter 2B, Section 6.

7 Camshaft toothed belt - removal and refitting

Note: *The camshaft toothed belt must be renewed every time it is removed, even if it is apparently in good condition.*

Removal

1 Raise and support the front of the vehicle (see "*Jacking and Vehicle Support*"). Remove the engine undertray and the wheel arch splash shields as a unit.
2 Disconnect the battery negative lead.
3 Unclip the throttle cable from the air cleaner-to-air mass meter trunking. Slacken the clips and remove the trunking.
4 Remove the air cleaner as described in Chapter 4B.
5 Remove the steering pump drivebelt (when applicable) and the alternator drivebelt.
6 Remove the three bolts and rubber bushes which secure the camshaft toothed belt cover. Remove the cover and its seal **(see illustrations)**.
7 Working through the wheel arch, slacken the six screws with splined heads which secure the crankshaft pulley to the sprocket. For better access, unbolt the oil cooler hose clip from the inner wing.
8 Turn the crankshaft until the timing mark on the pulley is in line with the pointer and the timing marks on the camshaft sprockets are in line with the notches on the backplate **(see illustrations)**. (To turn the crankshaft by means of the central bolt, a Torx socket, size E20, will be needed. If this is not available, engage 4th or 5th gear and turn the crankshaft by turning a front wheel. It is easier to do this smoothly if the spark plugs are removed).
9 Remove the six screws with splined heads and lift off the crankshaft pulley. The screw holes are offset so it will only fit one way.
10 Slacken the camshaft belt tensioner screw using a 6 mm Allen key **(see illustration)**. Move the tensioner to slacken the belt and slip the belt off the sprockets and rollers.
11 Do not turn the crankshaft or camshafts while the belt is removed, or piston/valve contact may occur.

Refitting

12 Commence refitting by checking that the pulley and sprocket timing marks are still correctly aligned. Temporarily refit the pulley and secure it with two screws to do this. When satisfied, remove the pulley.
13 Fit the new belt over the sprockets and rollers, being careful not to kink it. Observe any arrows or other indication of running direction.
14 Refit the crankshaft pulley. Secure it with the six screws with splined heads, tightened to the specified torque **(see illustration)**.
15 The belt tension must now be set. The makers specify the use of a special tool (KM-666); if this is available, proceed as follows **(see illustration)**.
16 Fit the special tool to the tensioner. Make sure the tensioner is free to move.
17 Make a mark on the exhaust camshaft sprocket, seven teeth anti-clockwise from the timing mark. Turn the crankshaft clockwise

7.8a Pulley notch and pointer must be aligned . . .

7.8b . . . and sprocket marks align with backplate notches (arrowed)

7.10 Slackening the camshaft belt tensioner screw

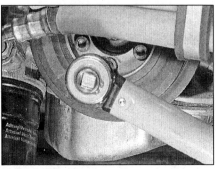

7.14 Tightening one of the crankshaft pulley screws

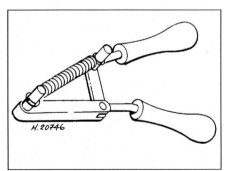

7.15 Special tool KM-666 for tensioning the camshaft toothed belt

7.18 Checking the belt tension using a spring balance and ruler

until the new mark is aligned with the notch on the belt backplate. In this position tighten the tensioner screw to the specified torque, then remove the special tool.

18 If the special tool is not available, belt tension must be set by hand. Move the tensioner using a square drive in the hole provided, nip up the screw and check the tension. As a guide, tension is correct when the belt cannot quite be twisted through 90° by hand in the middle of the run between the exhaust camshaft sprocket and the idler roller. If a spring balance is available, correct tension is indicated when in the same place the belt is deflected 10 mm by a load of 9 kg **(see illustration)**. When tension is correct, tighten the tensioner screw to the specified torque.

19 It must be emphasised that the method of setting belt tension without the special tool is given as a guide only. The consequences of a belt slipping or breaking in service could be

10.3a Removing a camshaft sprocket bolt and washer

10.3b Removing a camshaft sprocket

serious. The only way to be certain that tension is correct is to use the maker's tool, or to have a Vauxhall garage carry out the work.

20 Whichever tensioning method was used, now turn the crankshaft through two full turns clockwise and check that the pulley and sprocket timing marks come back into correct alignment. If they do not, remove the belt and start again.

21 The remainder of refitting is the reverse of the removal procedure.

8 Camshaft toothed belt tensioner and idler rollers - removal and refitting

Removal

1 Remove the toothed belt as described in Section 7.

2 Remove the Allen screw which secures the belt tensioner. Lift off the tensioner and its mounting plate and recover the spacer sleeve.

3 Similarly unbolt and remove the idler roller and recover its sleeve.

4 Renew the rollers if they show roughness when spun, or if they have been noisy in operation.

Refitting

5 Refitting is the reverse of the removal procedure, noting the following points:
a) *Make sure the spacer sleeves are the right way round. The smaller diameter of the tensioner sleeve goes towards the block. The smaller diameter of the idler sleeve goes away from the block.*
b) *Tighten the screws to the specified torque.*
c) *Fit a new camshaft toothed belt.*

9 Camshaft sprocket oil seals - renewal

1 Remove the camshaft toothed belt as described in Section 7.

2 Remove the camshaft cover and the camshaft sprockets, as described in paragraphs 1 to 4 of Section 10.

3 Punch or drill a small hole in the face of one of the oil seals. Screw in a self-tapping screw

9.4a Fitting a new camshaft oil seal

9.4b Seating a camshaft oil seal

and use this to lever the seal out. Clean the seal seat.

4 Grease the lips of a new seal and fit it, lips inwards. Seat the seal by tapping it home using a mallet and a large socket or a piece of tube **(see illustrations)**.

5 Repeat the operations on the other oil seal.

6 The remainder of refitting is the reverse of the removal procedure. Fit a new camshaft toothed belt as described in Section 7.

10 Camshafts - removal and refitting

Removal

1 Remove the camshaft toothed belt as described in Section 7.

2 Remove the spark plug cover, which is retained by two Allen screws. Disconnect the breather hoses from the camshaft cover, remove the 20 Allen screws and the camshaft cover itself.

3 Hold a camshaft using an open-ended spanner on the flats provided towards the sprocket end. Without allowing the camshaft to move (risk of piston-to-valve contact) slacken the sprocket bolt. Remove the bolt, washer and sprocket **(see illustrations)**.

4 Repeat the operation on the other camshaft. Although both sprockets appear to be identical, it is good practice not to get them mixed up. The exhaust sprocket on the engine shown here is marked 'L'; the inlet sprocket is unmarked **(see illustration)**.

5 Remove the distributor (Chapter 5C).

10.4 Exhaust camshaft sprocket is marked 'L'

10.6 Matching numbers on bearing cap and cylinder head

10.7 Distributor housing bearing cap has two extra nuts

10.11 Fitting a camshaft bearing cap

6 Check that the camshaft bearing caps carry identification numbers, and note which way round they are fitted. The inlet camshaft caps are numbered 1 to 5, the exhaust camshaft caps 6 to 10. Corresponding numbers are cast in the cylinder head (see illustration).

7 Progressively slacken the bearing cap nuts, half a turn at a time until the valve spring pressure has been released. Do not overlook the two extra nuts on the cap which forms part of the distributor housing (see illustration). Remove the nuts and washers and lift off the caps. Be careful that a camshaft does not spring up suddenly when removing the caps.

8 Remove the camshafts with their oil seals. Be careful when handling them, as the edges of the lobes are sharp. Remove the oil seals.

Refitting

9 Commence refitting by generously oiling the camshaft bearing surfaces and lobes. If fitting new camshafts, apply the special assembly lubricant provided.

10 Apply sealant to the mating faces of the bearing caps which house the oil seals (Nos 1 and 6) and to the one which houses the distributor drive (No 11).

11 Place the camshafts in position with the sprocket locating pins uppermost. Fit the bearing caps, in their correct positions and the right way round, and the nuts and washers (see illustration).

12 Tighten the bearing cap nuts half a turn at a time in progressive sequence so the camshafts are pulled down evenly. Finally tighten them to the specified torque (see illustration).

13 Fit new oil seals as described in Section 9.

14 Refit the sprockets to their respective camshafts. Fit the sprocket bolts and tighten them to the specified torque, holding the camshafts with a spanner on the flats to prevent rotation (see illustration).

15 Using a strap wrench on the sprocket or a spanner on the sprocket bolt, carefully move each camshaft a little way to verify that it is free to turn. If the cylinder head is installed on the engine, be careful that piston-to-valve contact does not occur. If a camshaft will not turn, it may be that the bearing caps have been fitted the wrong way round.

16 Refit the distributor and the camshaft cover.

10.12 Tightening a camshaft bearing cap nut

17 Fit a new camshaft toothed belt as described in Section 7.

18 If new camshafts have been fitted, it is suggested that the running-in schedule specified in Chapter 2B, Section 9, paragraph 14, be observed.

11 Cylinder head - removal and refitting

Note: The procedure described here is the removal of the cylinder head leaving the inlet manifold and fuel injection equipment in place. If preferred, the manifold can be removed with the head after making the appropriate disconnections.

Removal

1 Remove the camshaft toothed belt as described in Section 7.

11.7 Disconnecting the small breather hoses from the camshaft cover

10.14 Tightening a camshaft sprocket bolt

2 Disconnect the multi-plug from the air mass meter. Undo the four or five Allen screws, release the idle speed adjuster hose and remove the volume chamber and air mass meter together.

3 Drain the cooling system by disconnecting the radiator bottom hose (see Chapter 1).

4 Disconnect the accelerator cable.

5 Remove the nine nuts which secure the inlet manifold. They have deformed threads so they are stiff. A socket with a universal joint or 'wobble drive' will be needed to reach some of the nuts.

6 Cut the cable-tie which secures the injector wiring harness to the cylinder head.

7 Disconnect the two small breather hoses from the camshaft cover (see illustration).

8 Unbolt the support bracket from the base of the inlet manifold (see illustration). Slide the manifold off the cylinder head studs. Be careful not to strain the fuel hoses or the wiring.

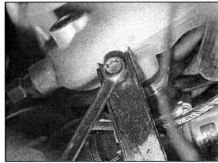

11.8 Unbolting the inlet manifold support bracket (seen from below)

11.11 Disconnecting the heater hose from the cylinder head

11.15 Disconnecting the large breather hose

11.16 Removing a camshaft cover screw

9 Remove the exhaust manifold (Chapter 4B).
10 Remove the radiator top hose.
11 Disconnect the heater hose from below the distributor **(see illustration)**.
12 Remove the spark plug lead cover secured by two Allen screws. Disconnect the HT leads from the plugs and move them aside.
13 Remove the distributor (Chapter 5C).
14 Remove the thermostat housing (Chapter 3).
15 Disconnect the large breather hose from the camshaft cover **(see illustration)**. Unbolt the hose bracket from the cylinder head.
16 Remove the 20 Allen screws which secure the camshaft cover **(see illustration)**. Remove the cover.
17 Remove the camshaft sprockets (Section 10).
18 Remove the two Torx screws which

secure the top of the belt backplate to the cylinder head. Also remove the rubber bush and unscrew the belt cover mounting stud **(see illustrations)**.
19 Using a size E12 Torx socket, slacken the cylinder head bolts a quarter-turn each in the sequence shown. In the same sequence slacken the bolts a further half-turn, then undo them completely and remove them **(see illustrations)**. Recover the washers. New bolts must be used when refitting.
20 Lift off the cylinder head, pulling the inlet manifold back towards the bulkhead slightly if necessary **(see illustration)**. Be careful not to bend the belt backplate. Put the head down on two blocks of wood so that it does not rest on the protruding valves.
21 Recover the gasket from the cylinder block and clean the mating surface, being

careful not to get any debris into the cylinder bores. Cover the open bores, or stuff oily rags into them, to protect them if the head is going to be off for more than a few hours.

Refitting

22 Commence refitting by placing a new head gasket onto the block, making sure that it fits over the locating dowels and that it is the right way up **(see illustration)**. It is marked 'OBEN/TOP'.
23 Lower the head onto the block and fit it onto the dowels. Fit the washers to the new bolts, fit the bolts and tighten them finger tight.
24 Following the sequence shown, tighten the bolts through the first four stages given in the Specifications **(see illustrations)**.

11.18a Remove the rubber bush . . .

11.18b . . . and the belt cover mounting stud

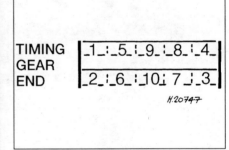

11.19a Cylinder head bolt slackening sequence

11.19b Removing a cylinder head bolt and washer

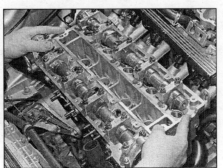

11.20 Lifting off the cylinder head

11.22 New head gasket in position

TIMING
GEAR
END

10 6 2 3 7

9 5 1 4 8

H.20748

11.24a Cylinder head bolt tightening sequence

11.24b Angle tightening a cylinder head bolt

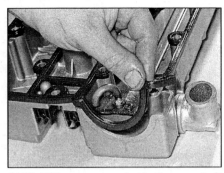

11.25 Fitting a new gasket to the camshaft cover

25 The remainder of refitting is a reversal of the removal procedure, noting the following points:

a) *Use new gaskets on the thermostat housing, the manifolds and the camshaft cover* **(see illustration).**

b) *Use a new camshaft toothed belt and tension it as described in Section 7.*

c) *Tighten all fastenings to the specified torque.*

d) *Run the engine until the cooling fan cuts in. If the hydraulic tappets have been disturbed, they may be noisy for a few minutes until they settle down. Switch the engine off, remove the camshaft cover again and tighten the cylinder head bolts through the final specified stage.*

12 Cylinder head - overhaul

1 Remove the manifold gaskets
2 Remove the camshafts, slackening the bearing cap nuts progressively until the valve spring pressure is released.
3 Remove the spark plugs.

4 Using a sucker or a magnet, remove the hydraulic tappet buckets from their bores **(see illustration).** If they are to be re-used, keep them in order so that they can be refitted to their original locations. To stop the oil draining out of them, store them in a bath of clean engine oil with the oil ring lowermost.
5 Prepare a box with 16 compartments to receive the valve components. Using a valve spring compressor and a piece of tube with two slots cut in it, compress a valve spring **(see illustration).** Extract the collets from the top of the valve stem using a pencil magnet or a magnetic screwdriver.
6 Carefully release the compressor and remove the valve, the spring upper seat and the spring. Pull off the valve stem oil seal with longnosed pliers and recover the valve spring seat. Place all the components in the appropriate compartment in the box **(see illustrations).**

12.4 Removing a tappet. Note the oil ring (arrowed)

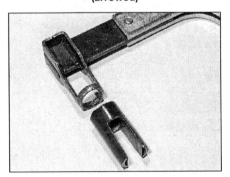

12.5 Detail of valve spring compressor head and tube

12.6a Remove the valve . . .

12.6b . . . the spring upper seat . . .

12.6c . . . the valve spring . . .

12.6d . . . the valve stem oil seal (arrowed) . . .

12.6e . . . and the valve spring seat

12.12a Fit a valve stem oil seal into a socket or tube . . .

12.12b . . . and press it home

12.13 Fitting a valve collet

7 Repeat the operations on the other 15 valves.

8 Clean the combustion chambers and the gasket mating faces with a wooden or plastic scraper. Finish up with a rag or toothbrush and a solvent such as a proprietary carburettor cleaner.

9 Inspect the valves, springs and seats as described in Chapter 2A, Section 9, paragraphs 7 to 11. Note however that the exhaust valves on these engines are filled with sodium to improve heat transfer. Sodium is a highly reactive metal which will ignite or explode spontaneously on contact with air or water. Valves containing sodium must not be disposed of in ordinary scrap.

10 Check the head gasket mating face for distortion using a straightedge and feeler blades. Check crosswise, lengthwise and diagonally. Warp limits are given in the Specifications.

11 Inspect the camshafts and their bearing surfaces and caps as described in Section 24.

12 Commence reassembly by fitting a valve spring seat to its location. Fit a new valve stem oil seal to the top of the valve guide, using a deep socket or a piece of tube **(see illustrations)**.

13 Oil the valve stem and insert the valve into its guide, passing it gently through the stem oil seal to avoid damage. Fit the valve spring and upper seat. Compress the spring and fit the collets using a magnetic screwdriver this is a fiddly business. A dab of grease on each collet will keep them in position on the valve stem **(see illustration)**.

14 Carefully release the valve spring

compressor. Apply a solid tube or piece of wood (eg a hammer handle) to the top of the valve and tap smartly with a hammer to settle the components.

15 Repeat the operations on the other valves.

16 Refit the tappets, with the oil ring lowermost, oiling them generously **(see illustrations)**. If new camshafts are to be fitted, apply some of the assembly lubricant supplied with new camshafts to the top surfaces of the tappets.

17 Fit the camshafts and their oil seals as described in Section 10.

18 The distributor and spark plugs may be refitted now, or if preferred left until after the head has been refitted.

13 Sump and oil baffle plate - removal and refitting

Removal

1 Raise and support the front of the vehicle (see *"Jacking and Vehicle Support"*). Disconnect the battery earth (negative) lead.

2 Drain the engine oil.

3 Remove the exhaust manifold (Chapter 4).

4 Disconnect the multi-plug from the engine oil level sensor.

5 Remove the flywheel cover plate.

6 Remove the sump retaining bolts. Remove the sump, tapping it with a hide or plastic mallet if necessary to break the joint.

7 Remove the oil pick-up pipe and its bracket, followed by the baffle plate.

8 Remove the old gaskets and clean the mating surfaces.

Refitting

9 Commence refitting by applying sealant to the oil pump housing joint and the rear main bearing cap joint.

10 Apply sealant to a new gasket and fit the gasket to the block. Make sure that the locating dowels are in position.

11 Fit the baffle plate to the block. Refit the oil pick-up pipe and bracket, using a new O-ring between the pipe and the pump and applying sealant to the bolt threads.

12 Fit another new gasket, this time without sealant, between the baffle plate and the sump. Fit the sump, apply sealant to the bolt threads and insert and tighten the bolts.

13 The remainder of refitting is the reverse of the removal procedure. Remember to refit and tighten the drain plug and to refill the engine with oil on completion.

14 Oil pump - removal and refitting

Removal

1 Remove the camshaft toothed belt as described in Section 7.

2 Disconnect the oil cooler lines from the filter housing and move them aside. Be prepared for oil spillage.

3 Remove the camshaft cover and both camshaft sprockets (see Section 10).

4 Remove the belt tensioner and idler rollers.

5 Remove the crankshaft sprocket central bolt, using an E20 Torx socket. The bolt is very tight prevent the crankshaft turning by engaging a gear, chocking the wheels and applying the handbrake, or remove the flywheel cover plate and have an assistant jam the ring gear teeth.

6 Remove the crankshaft sprocket, using a puller if necessary. Note how the tang on the sprocket engages with the keyway in the crankshaft. Recover the spacer from behind the sprocket. Remove the timing belt backplate.

7 Remove the sump, oil pick-up pipe and baffle plate as described in Section 13.

8 Unbolt the oil pump from the block and remove it. Clean the pump and block mating faces.

12.16a Oiling a tappet . . .

12.16b . . . and fitting it to its bore

Refitting

9 Commence refitting by smearing a new gasket with grease and placing it on the pump. Grease the lips of the oil seal and refit the pump, being careful not to damage the oil seal as it passes over the crankshaft.

10 Insert the pump securing bolts. Position the bottom of the pump flush with the sump mating face of the block and tighten the bolts to the specified torque.

11 Thinly coat the outer face of the spacer with sealant to GM spec 15 04 200/8 983 368 (see Chapter 2B, Section 20, paragraph 17). Push the spacer onto the crankshaft.

12 The remainder of refitting is the reverse of the removal procedure. Remember to fit a new camshaft toothed belt.

15 Oil pump - overhaul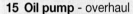

Refer to Chapter 2B, Section 14.

16 Oil cooler thermostatic valve - removal and refitting

Removal

1 The thermostatic valve is mounted in the oil cooler adapter, just above the oil filter.

2 Place a drain tray under the filter housing. Remove the circlip from the end of the valve **(see illustration)**.

3 Recover the plug, spring and thermostatic element. There will be some oil spillage.

4 Clean and examine the components: renew any which are obviously worn or damaged.

Refitting

5 Refitting is the reverse of the removal procedure. Check the engine oil level and top-up if necessary.

17 Crankshaft front oil seal - renewal

1 Remove the crankshaft sprocket as described in the procedure for oil pump removal. There is no need to remove the camshaft sprockets or belt backplate. Recover the spacer from behind the sprocket.

2 Drill or punch a small hole in the face of the oil seal. Screw in a self tapping screw and use this to lever out the seal. Clean the seal seat.

3 Grease the lips of a new oil seal. Fit the seal, lips inwards, and seat it using a piece of tube, some washers and the crankshaft sprocket bolt.

4 Thinly coat the outer face of the spacer with sealant to GM spec 15 04 200/8 983 368 (see Chapter 2B, Section 20, paragraph 17). Push the spacer onto the crankshaft.

5 The remainder of refitting is the reverse of the removal procedure. Remember to fit a new camshaft toothed belt.

16.2 Circlip securing oil cooler thermostatic valve

18 Pistons and connecting rods - removal and refitting

Refer to Chapter 2A, Section 15, but note that the pistons and rods may be separated if wished, as described in Section 19.

19 Pistons and connecting rods - dismantling and reassembly

1 With the pistons and connecting rods removed they may be separated if necessary as follows.

2 Note the relative orientation of rod and piston. When fitted, the arrow on the piston crown points to the camshaft sprocket end of the engine, and the bosses on the connecting rod face towards the flywheel.

3 Remove one of the circlips which secure the gudgeon pin. Push the gudgeon pin out of the piston and connecting rod using a wooden or brass rod. No great force should be necessary.

4 When refitting, fit the connecting rod into the piston and make sure they are the right way round. Oil the gudgeon pin and push it home, then secure it with the circlip.

20 Flywheel - removal and refitting

Removal

1 Remove the clutch assembly as described in Chapter 6.

2 Mark the position of the flywheel relative to the crankshaft. Jam the ring gear teeth and slacken the flywheel retaining bolts (see Chapter 2A, Section 16).

3 Remove the bolts and lift off the flywheel. Do not drop it, it is heavy. Obtain new bolts for reassembly.

Refitting

4 Refitting is the reverse of the removal procedure. Tighten the bolts to the specified torque.

21 Crankshaft rear oil seal - renewal

Remove the flywheel as described in Section 20.

Renew the oil seal as described in Chapter 2A, Section 19.

22 Engine/transmission mountings - removal and refitting

Refer to Chapter 2A, Section 17.

23 Crankshaft and main bearings - removal and refitting

Refer to Chapter 2B, Section 20.

24 Engine components - examination and renovation

1 The cylinder head and oil pump have been considered earlier in this Chapter. For other components refer to Chapter 2A, Section 21, and note the following additional information.

Camshafts

2 With the camshafts removed, examine the bearing surfaces and lobes for wear, pitting and scuffing. Measure the bearing journals with a micrometer. Dimensions are given in the Specifications.

3 Wear or damage to a camshaft means that it must be renewed. If there is corresponding wear in the bearing seats and caps, a complete new cylinder head will be required. The bearing caps are line bored in position on the head and cannot be renewed separately.

4 With the camshafts fitted to the head, check their endfloat using a dial gauge or feeler blades. Endfloat outside the limits specified means that the camshaft(s) and/or cylinder head must be renewed.

Camshaft toothed belt

5 As mentioned earlier, the belt must be renewed every time that it is removed, even if it appears to be in good condition.

Piston/bore grade marks

6 The number or code denoting the piston and bore grade (see Specifications) is stamped on the block near the engine number.

25 Engine - removal and refitting

Removal

1 The engine is removed with the transmission by lowering the two out of the engine bay. They can then be separated on the bench.

2 Disconnect both leads from the battery.
3 Depressurise the fuel system (Chapter 4B).
4 Remove the bonnet.
5 Remove the air cleaner (Chapter 4B).
6 Disconnect the idle adjuster hose from the pre-volume chamber. Remove the screws from the pre-volume chamber, disconnect the multi-plug from the air mass meter and remove the pre-volume chamber and air mass meter together.
7 Drain the cooling system (Chapter 1).
8 Disconnect all coolant and heater hoses from the engine.
9 Disconnect the brake servo vacuum hose at the servo.
10 Disconnect the accelerator cable.
11 Disconnect the fuel supply and return pipes from the fuel injector rail. Be prepared for fuel spillage. Release the pipes from any clips or ties and move them out of the way.
12 Remove the exhaust manifold securing nuts and heat shield.
13 Disconnect the engine wiring harness multi-plug next to the expansion tank.
14 Disconnect the multi-plugs from the fuel injectors and the throttle valve switch. Also unbolt the earth straps from the fuel rail.
15 Disconnect the HT distributor-to-ignition coil lead and the LT multi-plug from the distributor.
16 Disconnect the wiring harness multi-plug at the left-hand suspension turret.
17 In the area of the right-hand suspension turret, disconnect the multi-plugs for the inductive pulse sensor and (if applicable) the vent valve and the oxygen sensor.
18 Disconnect the wiring from the two temperature sensors on the thermostat housing.
19 On the rear of the engine disconnect the multi-plugs from the knock sensor, the idle speed adjuster and the oil temperature switch.
20 Disconnect the oil level sensor and the reversing light switch.

21 Unbolt the earth strap from the transmission.
22 Disconnect the speedometer cable, or disconnect the speedometer sender multi-plug, as applicable **(see illustration)**.
23 Engage second gear, then disconnect the gearchange remote control by undoing the pinch-bolt.
24 Disconnect the clutch cable.
25 Slacken the front wheel bolts, raise and securely support the front of the car and remove the front wheels (see *"Jacking and Vehicle Support"*).
26 On models with power steering, remove the pump drivebelt. Unbolt the pump and move it aside without disconnecting its hoses. Support it so that the hoses are not strained.
27 Disconnect the oil cooler lines from the filter housing. Be prepared for oil spillage.
28 Remove the exhaust manifold (Chapter 4B).
29 Separate the control arm balljoints from the steering knuckles (see Chapter 10).
30 Separate the driveshafts from the final drive housing (see Chapter 8). Be prepared for oil spillage. Plug the holes and tie the driveshafts up out of the way.
31 Attach the lifting tackle to the engine/transmission and take the weight. Check that no cables, hoses etc are still attached or are otherwise in the way.
32 Unbolt the engine/transmission mountings in the following order:
  a) LH front.
  b) Rear.
  c) RH front.
33 Carefully lower the assembly through the engine bay to the ground. If necessary lift the vehicle off the engine to enable it to be withdrawn.

Refitting

34 When refitting, apply thread-locking compound to the engine/ transmission mounting bolts. Tighten them finger tight at

25.22 Speedometer sender (used with digital instrument panel)

first, then to the specified torque in the following order:
  a) LH front.
  b) RH front.
  c) Rear
35 The remainder of refitting is the reverse of the removal procedure.

26 Engine - initial start-up after overhaul

1 Refer to Chapter 1, Section 24, but disregard the instructions to check the idle speed and valve clearances.
2 If new camshafts have been fitted, it is suggested that the running-in schedule specified in Chapter 2B, Section 9, paragraph 14, be observed.
3 Run the engine until the cooling fan cuts in. If the hydraulic tappets have been disturbed, they may be noisy for a few minutes until they settle down.
4 Switch the engine off, remove the camshaft cover and tighten the cylinder head bolts through the final specified stage.

Notes

Notes

Chapter 3
Cooling, heating and ventilation systems

Contents

Degrees of difficulty

Easy, suitable for novice with little experience	Fairly easy, suitable for beginner with some experience	Fairly difficult, suitable for competent DIY mechanic	Difficult, suitable for experienced DIY mechanic	Very difficult, suitable for expert DIY or professional

Specifications

Thermostat
Opening temperature:
    1.3 litre models . . . . 91°C
    All other models . . . . 92°C
Fully open temperature:
    1.3 litre models . . . . 103°C
    All other models . . . . 107°C

Expansion tank cap
Opening pressure . . . . 1.20 to 1.35 bar

Fan thermoswitch
Switches on at:
    Early models . . . . 97°C
    Later models . . . . 100°C
Switches off at . . . . 93°C

Torque wrench settings

	Nm	lbf ft
Coolant pump bolts:		
1.2, 1.3 and 1.4 litre models	8	6
1.6, 1.8 and 2.0 litre models	25	18
Thermostat housing bolts:		
1.3 and 1.4 litre models	10	7
1.6, 1.8 and 2.0 litre models	15	11
Temperature sender in manifold	10	7
Temperature sender in thermostat housing	8	6

1 General information and precautions

General information

The cooling system is of pressurised type, comprising of a pump driven by the timing belt, an aluminium crossflow radiator, electric cooling fan, and a thermostat. The system functions as follows. Cold coolant from the radiator passes through the hose to the coolant pump where it is pumped around the cylinder block and head passages. After cooling the cylinder bores, combustion surfaces and valve seats, the coolant reaches the underside of the thermostat, which is initially closed. The coolant passes through the heater and is returned via the cylinder block to the coolant pump.

When the engine is cold the coolant circulates only through the cylinder block, cylinder head, expansion tank and heater. When the coolant reaches a predetermined temperature, the thermostat opens and the coolant passes through to the radiator. As the coolant circulates through the radiator it is cooled by the inrush of air when the car is in forward motion. Airflow is supplemented by the action of the electric cooling fan when necessary. Upon reaching the radiator, the coolant is now cooled and the cycle is repeated.

The electric cooling fan mounted on the rear of the radiator is controlled by a thermostatic switch. At a predetermined coolant temperature the switch actuates the fan.

Precautions

Warning: Do not attempt to remove the expansion tank filler cap or disturb any part of the cooling system while the engine is hot, as there is a high risk of scalding. If the expansion tank filler cap must be removed before the engine and radiator have fully cooled (even though this is not recommended) the pressure in the cooling system must first be relieved. Cover the cap with a thick layer of cloth, to avoid scalding, and slowly unscrew the filler cap until a hissing sound can be heard. When the hissing has stopped, indicating that the pressure has reduced, slowly unscrew the filler cap until it can be removed; if more hissing sounds are heard, wait until they have stopped before unscrewing the cap completely. At all times keep well away from the filler cap opening.

Warning: If the engine is hot, the electric cooling fan may start rotating even if the engine is not running, so be careful to keep hands, hair and loose clothing well clear when working in the engine compartment.

Warning: Do not allow antifreeze to come into contact with skin or painted surfaces of the vehicle. Rinse off spills immediately with plenty of water. Never leave antifreeze lying around in an open container or in a puddle in the driveway or on the garage floor. Children and pets are attracted by its sweet smell. Antifreeze can be fatal if ingested.

2 Cooling system hoses - disconnection and renewal

Note: *Refer to the warnings given in Section 1 of this Chapter before proceeding.*

1 If the checks described in Chapter 1 reveal a faulty hose, it must be renewed as follows.
2 First drain the cooling system (see Chapter 1). If the coolant is not due for renewal, it may be re-used if it is collected in a clean container.
3 To disconnect a hose, use a screwdriver to slacken the clips, then move them along the hose, clear of the relevant inlet/outlet union. Carefully work the hose free. While the hoses can be removed with relative ease when new, or when hot, **do not** attempt to disconnect any part of the system while it is still hot.
4 Note that the radiator inlet and outlet unions are fragile; do not use excessive force when attempting to remove the hoses. If a hose proves to be difficult to remove, try to release it by rotating the hose ends before attempting to free it. If all else fails, cut the hose with a sharp knife, then slit it so that it can be peeled off in two pieces. Although this may prove expensive if the hose is otherwise undamaged, it is preferable to buying a new radiator.
5 When fitting a hose, first slide the clips onto the hose, then work the hose into position. If clamp type clips were originally fitted, it is a good idea to replace them with screw type clips when refitting the hose. If the hose is stiff, use a little soapy water as a lubricant, or soften the hose by soaking it in hot water.
6 Work the hose into position, checking that it is correctly routed, then slide each clip along the hose until it passes over the flared end of the relevant inlet/outlet union, before tightening the clips securely.
7 Refill the cooling system with reference to Chapter 1.
8 Check thoroughly for leaks as soon as possible after disturbing any part of the cooling system.

3 Radiator - removal, inspection and refitting

Removal

Note: *The radiator can be removed with the cooling fan still attached, but due to the limited space available care must be taken to*
avoid damaging the radiator If preferred, the cooling fan may be removed first, as described in Section 6, to provide greater access.

 If leakage is the reason for wanting to remove the radiator, bear in mind that minor leaks can be often be cured using a propriety radiator sealant, with the radiator in situ.

1 Drain the cooling system, (Chapter 1), and disconnect the battery earth terminal.
2 Slacken the retaining clips and detach the radiator top and bottom hoses and also the smaller diameter expansion tank vent hose.
3 Disconnect the two electrical leads at the thermal switch on the side of the radiator.
4 If the cooling fan is still in position, disconnect the electrical leads at the multi-plug adjacent to the fan motor. Release the cable clips securing the wiring harness to the fan cowl bracket and move the harness to one side.
5 On automatic transmission models equipped with a fluid cooler, disconnect and plug the cooler lines at the radiator side tank. Be prepared for fluid spillage, and take care not to allow dirt to enter the cooler lines.
6 Remove the radiator mounting bolts (one on each side at the top). Carefully lift out the radiator, with fan and shroud if not previously removed.

Inspection

7 With the radiator assembly removed it is easier to examine for leaks which will show up as corroded stains. Permanent repairs with this type of radiator are not possible due to the light alloy and plastic composition. A proprietary sealant compound may be tried, but it is better to renew a defective assembly.
8 Clean out the inside of the radiator by flushing (Chapter 1), and also clean the matrix, removing all the dead flies and bugs which reduce the radiator's efficiency. Take this opportunity to inspect the hoses and clips, making sure that all are fit for further use.

Refitting

9 Refitting the radiator is the reverse of the removal procedure. Check that the rubber mountings are in good condition and ensure that the bottom location pegs fit correctly on installation. On completion, refill the cooling system and, on automatic transmission models, check the transmission fluid level and top-up if necessary. See Chapter 1 for details.

4 Thermostat - removal, testing and refitting

Removal

1 Drain the cooling system, saving the coolant if it is fit for re-use (see Chapter 1). Disconnect the battery earth lead and proceed as described under the relevant sub-heading.

4.3a Remove the thermostat retaining snap-ring . . .

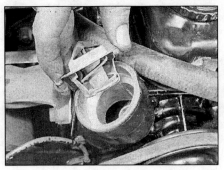

4.3b . . . and withdraw the thermostat - 1.2 litre model

4.6 Removing the thermostat housing . . .

1.2 litre models

2 Disconnect the radiator top hose from the outlet connection at the top of the water pump. This exposes the thermostat and it will be seen that it is retained by a snap-ring.

3 Prise the snap-ring free using a suitable screwdriver blade and then remove the thermostat from the pump outlet (see illustrations).

1.3 and 1.4 litre models

4 Remove the camshaft toothed belt cover, which is secured by five screws.

5 Slacken the clip and detach the radiator top hose from the thermostat housing.

6 Remove the two bolts and detach the thermostat housing (see illustration). On later models the thermostat housing may not be accessible until the camshaft toothed belt back plate has been removed, if necessary remove the plate as described in Chapter 2.

7 Remove the thermostat from its recess, noting how the projections on the thermostat fit in cut-outs in the recess (see illustration).

1.6, 1.8 and 2.0 litre models

8 Slacken the clip and detach the radiator top hose from the thermostat housing (see illustration).

9 Unbolt and remove the thermostat cover and extract the thermostat (see illustrations). On 2.0 litre 16-valve models the thermostat is a bayonet fitting in the housing; release it by depressing it and turning with a pair of pointed-nose pliers.

Testing

10 A rough test of the thermostat may be made by suspending it with a piece of string in a container full of water. Heat the water to bring it to the boil - the thermostat must open by the time the water boils. If not, renew it.

11 If a thermometer is available, the precise opening temperature of the thermostat may be determined, and compared with the figures given in the Specifications. The opening temperature is also marked on the thermostat (see illustration).

12 A thermostat which fails to close as the water cools must also be renewed.

Refitting

1.2 litre models

13 Refitting the thermostat is the reverse sequence to removal, but use a new rubber seal and install the thermostat with the arrow on the web pointing upwards. Refill the cooling system, as described in Chapter 1.

All other models

14 Refit in the reverse order to removal; use a new rubber seal on the thermostat (see illustration). Refill the cooling system, as described in Chapter 1.

4.7 . . . and withdraw the thermostat from its recess - 1.3 litre model

4.8 Slackening the hose clip at the thermostat housing (1.6 litre model shown)

4.9a Removing the thermostat cover . . .

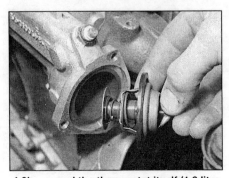

4.9b . . . and the thermostat itself (1.6 litre model shown)

4.11 Testing the thermostat

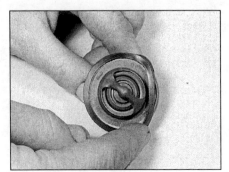

4.14 Fitting a new seal to the thermostat

5.4 Removing the water pump - 1.2 litre model

5 Water pump - removal and refitting

Removal

1 Drain the cooling system as described in Chapter 1 then disconnect the battery earth lead. Proceed as described under the relevant sub-heading.

1.2 litre models

2 Remove the auxiliary drivebelt, as described in Chapter 1.
3 Slacken the hose clips and disconnect the three hoses from the pump
4 Remove the six retaining bolts and carefully pull the pump off the head (see illustration). Recover the gasket.
5 If a new pump is being fitted, unbolt and transfer the pump pulley. Transfer the thermostat also, or fit a new one if the old one has seen much service.
6 Before refitting the water pump clean away all traces of old gasket from the pump and cylinder head mating faces.
7 Apply a little grease to a new gasket and place it in position on the pump. Refit the pump and secure the unit with the six bolts tightened progressively to the specified torque.
8 Refit the three hoses and tighten the clips securely. Refit the drivebelt and adjust the tension, as described in Chapter 1. Finally, refill the cooling system, as described in Chapter 1, and reconnect the battery.

1.3, 1.4, 1.6, 1.8 and 2.0 litre 8-valve models

9 Remove the camshaft toothed belt and the toothed belt backplate as described in Chapter 2 Part B.
10 Remove the three securing bolts and withdraw the water pump (see illustration). Note that it may be necessary to remove the alternator completely (see Chapter 5A) to provide enough room to remove the pump from the engine bay.

2.0 litre 16-valve models

11 Working as described in Chapter 2 Part C, removing the following components.
a) Camshaft toothed belt.

5.10 Removing the water pump - 1.8 litre model shown

b) Camshaft cover.
c) Camshaft sprockets.
d) Toothed belt tensioner and idler rollers.
e) Crankshaft sprocket.
f) Toothed belt backplate.
12 Remove the three bolts which secure the water pump to the block. Remove the pump and clean the recess in the block.

Refitting

1.2 litre models

13 If a new pump is being fitted, unbolt and transfer the pump pulley. Transfer the thermostat also, or fit a new one if the old one has seen much service.
14 Before refitting the water pump clean away all traces of old gasket from the pump and cylinder head mating faces.
15 Apply a little grease to a new gasket and place it in position on the pump. Refit the pump and secure the unit with the six bolts tightened progressively to the specified torque.
16 Refit the three hoses and tighten the clips securely. On completion, refit the drivebelt and refill the cooling system (Chapter 1).

1.3, 1.4, 1.6, 1.8 and 2.0 litre 8-valve models

17 Refitting is the reverse of removal, noting the following points.
a) Fit a new sealing ring to the pump (see illustration).
b) Ensure that the pump and its recess are clean and dry and coat the sealing ring and cylinder block mating surface with silicone grease or petroleum jelly. This will prevent contact corrosion between the pump and the block, and make things easier if the pump has to be moved for adjustment of the camshaft toothed belt.
c) Fit the camshaft toothed belt and tension it as described in Chapter 2 Part B and tighten the pump bolts to the specified torque.
d) On completion refill the cooling system and adjust the alternator drivebelt as described in Chapter 1.

2.0 litre 16-valve models

18 Refitting is the reverse of removal using a new sealing ring. Tighten the pump mounting bolts to the specified torque then refit all

disturbed components as described in Chapter 2 Part C. On completion refill the system as described in Chapter 1.

6 Radiator electric cooling fan - testing, removal and refitting

Testing

1 The cooling fan is supplied with current via the ignition switch, relay and a fuse (see Chapter 12). The circuit is completed by the cooling fan thermostatic switch, which is mounted in the side of the radiator.
2 If a fan does not appear to work, run the engine until normal operating temperature is reached, then allow it to idle. If the fan does not cut in within a few minutes, switch off the ignition and disconnect the wiring plug from the cooling fan switch. Bridge the two contacts in the wiring plug using a length of spare wire, and switch on the ignition. If the fan now operates, the switch is probably faulty and should be renewed.
3 If the fan still fails to operate, check that full battery voltage is available at the feed wire to the switch; if not, then there is a fault in the feed wire (possibly due to a fault in the fan motor, or a blown fuse). If there is no problem with the feed, check that there is continuity between the switch earth terminal and a good earth point on the body; if not, then the earth connection is faulty and must be re-made.
4 If the switch and the wiring are in good condition, the fault must lie in the motor itself. The motor can be checked by disconnecting the motor wiring connector and connecting a 12 volt supply directly to the motor terminals. If the motor is faulty, it must be renewed, as no spares are available.

Removal

5 Disconnect the battery negative terminal.
6 Disconnect the fan motor electrical leads at the multi-plug adjacent to the motor. Release the wiring harness cable-ties at the fan cowl bracket and move the harness to one side.
7 Undo and remove the two small bolts securing the fan cowl to the top of the radiator. Lift the fan and cowl assembly upwards to release the lower mounting lugs and remove the unit from the car.

5.17 Fitting a new sealing ring to the pump

8 To separate the fan motor from the cowl unscrew the three nuts. The fan blades may be withdrawn from the motor spindle after removal of the retaining clip.
9 Further dismantling of the assembly depends on the extent of the problem. If the motor is defective it would be better to have it overhauled by a specialist, as spare parts may be difficult to obtain. The alternative is to renew the motor which may prove cheaper and quicker in the long run.

Refitting

10 Reassembly, if the unit was dismantled, and refitting to the car are the reverse of the dismantling and removal sequences. On completion run the engine up to normal operating temperature and check the fan for correct functioning.

7 Cooling system electrical switches - testing, removal and refitting

Electric cooling fan thermostatic switch

Testing

1 Testing of the switch is described in Section 6, as part of the fan test procedure.

Removal

2 The switch is located in the side of the radiator (see illustration). The coolant should be cold before removing the switch.
3 Disconnect the battery negative lead. If necessary, firmly apply the handbrake then jack up the front of the vehicle and support it on axle stands (see "Jacking and Vehicle Support"). Access to the switch can then be gained from underneath the vehicle.
4 Either drain the cooling system to below the level of the switch (as described in Chapter 1), or have ready a suitable plug which can be used to plug the switch aperture in the radiator whilst the switch is removed. If a plug is used, take great care not to damage the radiator, and do not use anything which will allow foreign matter to enter the radiator.
5 Disconnect the wiring plug from the switch.
6 Carefully unscrew the switch from the radiator and recover the sealing ring/washer.

Refitting

7 Refitting is a reversal of removal using a new sealing ring/washer. Securely tighten the switch and top-up/refill the cooling system as described in Chapter 1.
8 On completion, start the engine and run it until it reaches normal operating temperature, then continue to run the engine and check that the cooling fan cuts in and functions correctly.

Coolant temperature gauge sender

Testing

9 The coolant temperature gauge, mounted in the instrument panel, is fed with a stabilised voltage supply from the instrument panel feed (via the ignition switch and a fuse), and its earth is controlled by the sender.
10 The sender is located in the cylinder head, behind the water pump on 1.2 litre engines, in the inlet manifold on 1.3 and 1.4 litre engines, and in the thermostat housing on 1.6, 1.8 and 2.0 litre engines (see illustration). The sender contains a thermistor, which consists of an electronic component whose electrical resistance decreases at a predetermined rate as its temperature rises. When the coolant is cold, the sender resistance is high, current flow through the gauge is reduced, and the gauge needle points towards the 'cold' end of the scale. If the sender is faulty, it must be renewed.
11 If the gauge develops a fault, first check the other instruments; if they do not work at all, check the instrument panel electrical feed. If the readings are erratic, there may be a fault in the voltage stabiliser, which will necessitate renewal of the stabiliser (see Chapter 12). If the fault lies in the temperature gauge alone, check it as follows.
12 If the gauge needle remains at the 'cold' end of the scale, disconnect the sender wire, and earth it to the cylinder head. If the needle then deflects when the ignition is switched on, the sender unit is proved faulty, and should be renewed. If the needle still does not move, remove the instrument panel (Chapter 12) and check the continuity of the wiring between the sender unit and the gauge, and the feed to the gauge unit. If continuity is shown, and the fault still exists, then the gauge is faulty, and the gauge unit should be renewed.

13 If the gauge needle remains at the 'hot' end of the scale, disconnect the sender wire. If the needle then returns to the 'cold' end of the scale when the ignition is switched on, the sender unit is proved faulty and should be renewed. If the needle still does not move, check the remainder of the circuit as described previously.

Removal

14 Either partially drain the cooling system to just below the level of the sender (Chapter 1), or have ready a suitable plug which can be used to plug the sender aperture whilst it is removed. If a plug is used, take great care not to damage the sender unit threads, and do not use anything which will allow foreign matter to enter the cooling system.
15 Disconnect the battery negative lead.
16 Disconnect the wiring from the sender, then unscrew the unit from its location.

Refitting

17 Ensure that the sender threads are clean and apply a smear of suitable sealant to them.
18 Refit the sender, tightening it securely, and reconnect the wiring.
19 Top-up the cooling system as described in "Weekly checks"
20 On completion, start the engine and check the operation of the temperature gauge. Also check for coolant leaks.

Fuel injection system coolant temperature sensor

21 Refer to Chapter 4.

8 Heater/ventilation system - general information

The heater operates by passing fresh air, drawn in from the area at the base of the windscreen, through a matrix which is heated by engine coolant.

Temperature regulation is achieved by mixing hot and cold air. Flap valves are used for this; other flap valves direct the air to the windscreen, floor or side outlets.

An electric fan is used to boost airflow through the heater when the normal ram airflow is insufficient, or in extreme climatic conditions.

Fresh air is available at the centre vents, regardless of the heater settings. Stale air is exhausted through grilles towards the rear of the vehicle.

9 Heater components - removal and refitting

Control panel

1 Remove the front half of the centre console, as described in Chapter 11.
2 Remove the radio (if fitted) and its surround, as described in Chapter 12. If a radio is not fitted, remove the blanking plate.

7.2 Cooling fan thermostatic switch screwed into side of radiator

7.10 Disconnecting the temperature gauge sender wire (1.8 litre model shown)

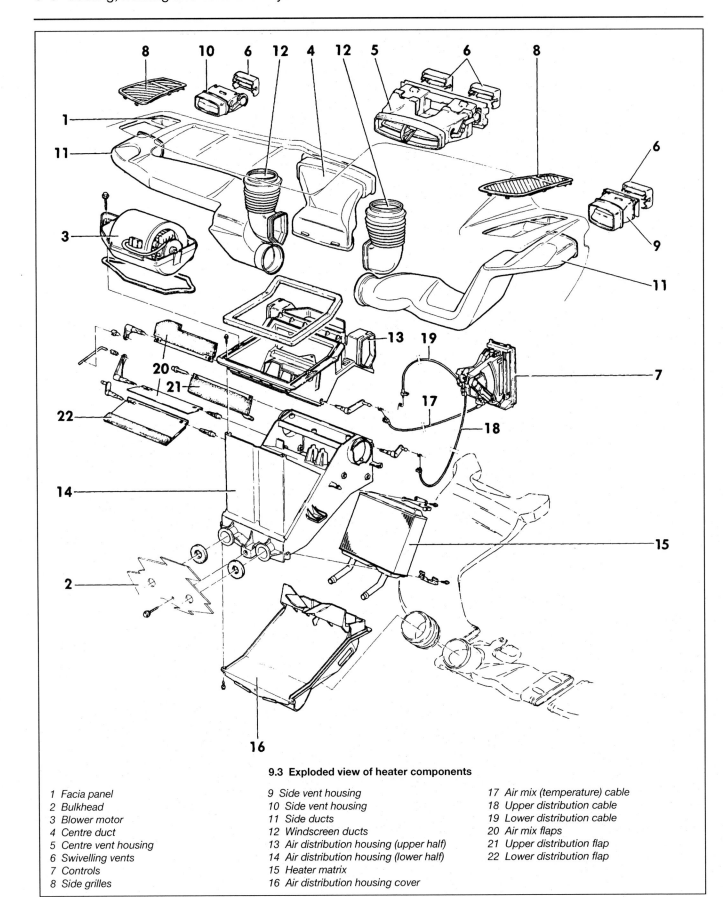

9.3 Exploded view of heater components

1 Facia panel	9 Side vent housing	17 Air mix (temperature) cable
2 Bulkhead	10 Side vent housing	18 Upper distribution cable
3 Blower motor	11 Side ducts	19 Lower distribution cable
4 Centre duct	12 Windscreen ducts	20 Air mix flaps
5 Centre vent housing	13 Air distribution housing (upper half)	21 Upper distribution flap
6 Swivelling vents	14 Air distribution housing (lower half)	22 Lower distribution flap
7 Controls	15 Heater matrix	
8 Side grilles	16 Air distribution housing cover	

9.4a Removing a screw from the top of the radio aperture

9.4b Heater control panel side screw

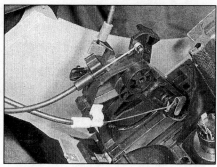

9.5 Removing the heater control panel

3 Detach the three control cables from the air distribution housing, noting their locations for refitting. Their sleeves are colour-coded as follows **(see illustration)**:

Brown - Foot level distribution
White - Hot/Cold air mix
Black - Screen level distribution

4 Remove the two screws from the top of the radio aperture and the two side screws, one on each side **(see illustrations)**.

5 Draw the control panel away **(see illustration)**. To remove it completely, disconnect the wires from the blower switch and (when fitted) the cigarette lighter.

6 Refit in the reverse order to removal. No adjustment of the cable is required: correct length is achieved by the precise location of the cable outer clamps.

Blower motor

7 Remove the wind deflector, (Chapter 11).

8 Remove the water deflector by freeing it from under the rubber seal and extracting its securing clip **(see illustrations)**. It may also be necessary to slacken or remove one of the wiper spindle nuts.

9 Disconnect the multi-plug, remove the two securing nuts and remove the motor **(see illustration)**.

10 If the housing halves are unclipped, the motor and ballast resistor can be removed by undoing the two screws at the resistor end **(see illustration)**. Spares for the meter are not available, but a competent auto-electrician may be able to repair certain types of fault.

11 Refit in the reverse order to removal.

Heater matrix

12 Remove the front half of the centre console, as described in Chapter 11.

13 Disconnect the control cables from the air distribution housing. Removal of the heater

control panel is recommended, as described earlier in this Section, to improve access.

14 Under the bonnet, clamp the coolant hoses at the heater matrix stubs (below the steering rack) and disconnect them. Be prepared for coolant spillage.

15 Remove the four screws which secure the air distribution housing cover **(see illustrations)**. The carpet will have to be turned back to get at the lower ones.

16 Disconnect the rear heating duct bellows, when fitted, and remove the air distributor housing cover.

17 Remove the three screws which secure the heater matrix **(see illustrations)**. The air mix flap will have to be moved in order to get at the top two screws. Remove the matrix brackets.

18 Withdraw the matrix into the car, keeping it as flat as possible to minimise coolant spillage.

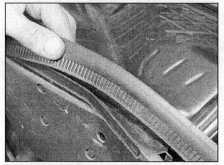

9.8a Lift the rubber seal to free the water

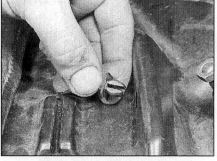

9.8b Water deflector clip

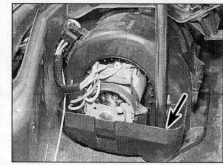

9.9 Removing a blower motor securing nut

9.10 Blower motor-to-housing screws (arrowed)

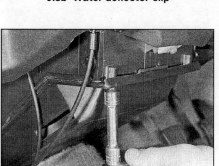

9.15a Removing an air distribution housing upper screw

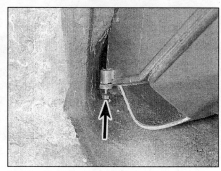

9.15b Air distribution housing lower screw (arrowed)

9.17a Removing the heater matrix lower screw

19 Refit in the reverse order to removal; top-up the cooling system on completion (*Weekly checks*).

Air distribution housing

20 Remove the blower motor and the heater matrix, as described earlier in this Section.
21 Remove the five nuts which secure the facia panel and the pedal bracket to the bulkhead.
22 Remove the steering column switch shrouds. On models with an adjustable column, also remove the adjuster knob and the column lower cover. Refer to Chapter 10 if necessary.

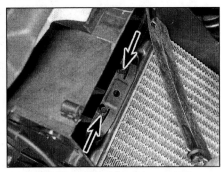

9.17b Heater matrix upper securing screws (arrowed)

23 Disconnect the hoses and ducts which connect the air distribution housing to the facia panel ducts.
24 Remove the two remaining screws, one at each end, which secure the facia panel. Pull the facia panel away on the passenger side and have an assistant withdraw the air distribution housing, also towards the passenger side.
25 Refit in the reverse order to removal. Use new self-locking nuts when securing the facia panel and pedal bracket to the bulkhead.
26 Top-up the cooling system on completion.

10 Vents and grilles - removal and refitting

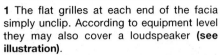

1 The flat grilles at each end of the facia simply unclip. According to equipment level they may also cover a loudspeaker (**see illustration**).
2 The swivelling vents can be unclipped after swivelling them downwards as far as possible. The side vent housings are secured by a single screw and clips (**see illustration**); the clips will probably be destroyed during removal.
3 The centre vent housing is secured by four screws, two above and two below (**see illustration**). The lower screws also secure the radio surround. This housing also carries the clock, when fitted, which must be disconnected when removing the housing.
4 The air extraction grilles on the outside of the vehicle can be carefully prised out of their locations with a wooden or plastic wedge, being careful not to damage the paintwork.
5 All these components can be refitted by simply clipping and/or screwing them back into position

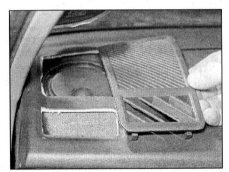

10.1 Removing an end grille and speaker

10.2 Removing a swivelling vent housing securing screw

10.3 Removing a centre vent housing screw

Chapter 4 Part A:
Fuel and exhaust systems - carburettor models

Contents

Degrees of difficulty

Easy, suitable for novice with little experience	Fairly easy, suitable for beginner with some experience	Fairly difficult, suitable for competent DIY mechanic	Difficult, suitable for experienced DIY mechanic	Very difficult, suitable for expert DIY or professional

Specifications

Fuel pump

Operation . . . . Mechanical from camshaft
Pressure . . . . 0.25 to 0.36 bar

Carburettor application

1.2 litre models . . . . 32 TL
1.3 litre models:
  13N engine . . . . 35 PDSI
  13SC engine 2E3
  13NB engine 1B1
1.4 litre models 2E3
1.6 litre models
  16SH engine . . . . Varajet II
  16SV engine 2E3

32TL Carburettor data - 12SC engine

Needle valve . . . . 1.75 mm
Venturi diameter . . . . 25 mm
Main jet 117
Mixture outlet . . . . 2.5 mm
Air correction jet 75
Mixture F96
Idle fuel jet 47
Idle air jet 90
Idle mixture jet 210
Auxiliary mixture fuel jet 35
Auxiliary mixture air jet 170
Auxiliary mixture jet 100
Full load enrichment jet 65
Partial load enrichment jet (idle) 40
Partial load enrichment jet (main) 40
Accelerator pump jet 45

32TL Carburettor data - 12SC engine (Continued)

Accelerator pump return jet	30
Accelerator pump delivery	6.5 to 9.5 cc per 10 strokes
Pull-down reduction jet	35
Pull-down adjustment (choke valve gap)	4.3 to 4.8 mm
Throttle valve gaps:	
Fast idle	0.6 to 0.7 mm
Mechanical pull-down	0.8 to 0.9 mm
Fast idle speed	3600 to 4000 rpm
Float level	23.5 to 24.0 mm
Vacuum at idle speed	1 to 20 mbar

35 PDSI Carburettor data - 13N engine

Needle valve	1.75 mm
Needle valve sealing ring	2.5 mm
Venturi diameter	26 mm
Mixture outlet	2.4 mm
Accelerator pump delivery:	
Manual gearbox	10 ± 1.0 cc per 1 0 strokes
Automatic transmission	7 ± 1.0 cc per 10 strokes
Accelerator pump arm	Throttle valve shaft
Main jet	X122.5
Air correction jet	80
Idle cut-off jet	50
Pump injector tube	50
Enrichment jet in float chamber:	
Manual gearbox	50
Automatic transmission	70
Enrichment jet in cover:	
Manual gearbox	100
Automatic transmission	80
Auxiliary fuel jet	35
Auxiliary mixture jet	5.0

2E3 Carburettor data - 13SC engine

	Primary	Secondary
Venturi diameter	20 mm	24 mm
Main jet	X97.5	X112.5
Air correction jet	80	100
Emulsion tube code number	88	60
Partial load enrichment orifice	0.5 mm	-
Pre-atomiser diameter	8 mm	7 mm
Mixture outlet orifice	2.5 mm	3.0 mm
Idle fuel jet	37.5	-
Idle air jet	130	-
Full load enrichment jet	-	85 to 105
Automatic choke adjustment data:		
Choke valve pull-down gap	2.1 to 2.5 mm	
Fast idle speed	2400 to 2800 rpm	
Throttle valve fast idle gap	1.1 to 1.2 mm	
Accelerator pump delivery:		
Manual transmission	10.3 to 12.7 cc per 10 strokes	
Automatic transmission	7.8 to 10.2 cc per 10 strokes	
Float level	29 to 30 mm	

1B1 Carburettor data - 13NB engine

Venturi	25 mm
Air correction jet/emulsion tube	57.5/18
Main jet	X112.5
Auxiliary jet	42.5/155
Idle jet	47.5/147.5
Part-load enrichment:	
In housing	100
In adapter	0.3
Float level (not adjustable)	28.5 ± 1 mm
Throttle valve gap:	
Manual	0.55 to 0.65 mm
Automatic	0.70 to 0.80 mm
Choke valve gap	3.1 to 3.5 mm
Accelerator pump delivery	4.5 to 7.5 ml per 10 strokes
Fast idle speed	3500 to 3900 rpm

2E3 Carburettor data - 14 NV engine

	Primary	Secondary
Venturi diameter	20 mm	24 mm
Main jet	X95	X110
Air correction jet	117.5	90
Emulsion tube	103	51
Part load enrichment	0.55 mm	-
Idle fuel jet	45	-
Idle air jet	130	-
Full load enrichment jet	-	57.5 to 77.5
Check valve gap (see text):		
Vacuum, small	1.7 to 2.1 mm	
Vacuum, large	2.5 to 2.9 mm	
Mechanical (full throttle)	1.5 to 3.5 mm	
Throttle valve gap	0.8 to 0.9 mm	
Accelerator pump delivery	10.5 to 13.5 ml per stroke	
Float level	29 ± 1 m	
Fast idle speed	2200 to 2600 rpm	

Varajet II Carburettor data - 16SH engine

Fast idle speed:	
Manual gearbox	2050 to 2150 rpm
Automatic transmission	2250 to 2350 rpm
Choke valve gaps (see text):	
A	2.8 to 3.4 mm
B	2.3 to 2.8 mm
C	9.5 to 10.5 mm
Automatic choke cover adjustment	1 mark towards L
Float level	4.5 to 6.5 mm
Idle jet	0.65 mm
Primary main jet	204
Primary main jet needle	151
Secondary main jet	3.20 mm
Secondary main jet needle	2.20 mm (marked G)
Float needle valve diameter	1.93 mm

2E3 Carburettor data - 16 SV engine

	Primary	Secondary
Venturi diameter	20 mm	24 mm
Main jet	X95	X105
Air correction jet	110	80
Emulsion tube	88	51
Idle fuel jet	42.5	-
Idle air jet	132.5	-
Full load enrichment jet	-	85 to 105
Choke valve gap (see text):	**Manual**	**Automatic**
Vacuum, small	1.3 to 1.7 mm	1.4 to 1.8 mm
Vacuum, large	1.9 to 2.3 mm	2.0 to 2.4 mm
Mechanical (full throttle)	1.5 to 3.5 mm	3.0 to 5.0 mm
Throttle valve gap	0.8 mm	
Accelerator pump delivery:		
Manual	10.5 to 13.5 ml per 10 strokes	
Automatic	7.5 to 10.5 ml per 10 strokes	
Fast idle speed:		
Manual	2000 to 2400 rpm	
Automatic	2500 to 2900 rpm	

Idle speed adjustment data

Idle speed:	
All models with manual gearbox	900 to 950 rpm
All models with automatic transmission	800 to 850 rpm (in P)
CO level at idle	1.0 to 1.5%

Recommended fuel grade

Minimum octane rating (see Section 2):	
1.2 litre models:	
Vehicles up to February 1985	98 RON leaded (4-star) or 95 RON unleaded (unleaded premium)**
Vehicles from February 1985 onwards	98 RON leaded (4-star) or 95 RON unleaded (unleaded premium)*
1.3 litre models:	
13N and 13NB engines	91 RON leaded (4-star) or 95 RON unleaded (unleaded premium)
13SC engine	98 RON leaded (4-star) or 95 RON unleaded (unleaded premium)*

Recommended fuel grade (Continued):

1.4 litre models	98 RON leaded (4-star) or 95 RON unleaded (unleaded premium)
1.6 litre models:	
16SH engines	98 RON leaded (4-star) or 95 RON unleaded (unleaded premium)*
16SV engines	98 RON leaded (4-star) or 95 RON unleaded (unleaded premium)***

*If the ignition timing is retarded by 3°, 95 RON unleaded (unleaded premium) petrol can be used (see Chapter 5 for details)
After 5 tankfuls of unleaded fuel, one tankful of leaded fuel **must be used
***If the octane rating plug is position correctly, 95 RON unleaded (unleaded premium) petrol can be used (see Section 2 for details)

Torque wrench settings

	Nm	lbf ft
Inlet manifold nuts or bolts:		
1.2 litre models	23	17
1.3 and 1.4 litre models	20	15
1.6 litre models	22	16
Carburettor securing nuts:		
1.2 litre models	18	13
1.3 and 1.4 litre models	20	15
1.6 litre models	15	11
Fuel pump to camshaft housing:		
1.3 and 1.4 litre models	20	15
1.6 litre models	15	11

1 General information

The fuel system consists of a fuel tank mounted under the rear of the car, a mechanical fuel pump and a carburettor. The fuel pump is operated by an eccentric on the camshaft and is mounted on the rear of the cylinder head. The air cleaner contains a disposable paper filter element and incorporates a flap valve air temperature control system which allows cold air from the outside of the car and warm air from the exhaust manifold to enter the air cleaner in the correct proportions.

The fuel pump lifts fuel from the fuel tank via a filter and supplies it to the carburettor. Excess fuel is returned from the anti-percolation chamber to the fuel tank.

 Warning: Many of the procedures in this Chapter require the removal of fuel lines and connections which may result in some fuel spillage.
Before carrying out any operation on the fuel system refer to the precautions given in Safety first! at the beginning of this Manual and follow them implicitly. Petrol is a highly dangerous and volatile liquid and the precautions necessary when handling it cannot be overstressed.

2 Unleaded petrol - general information and usage

Note: *The information given in this Chapter is correct at the time of writing and applies only to petrols currently available in the UK. If updated information is thought to be required check with a Vauxhall dealer. If travelling abroad consult one of the motoring organisations (or a similar authority) for advice on the petrols available and their suitability for your vehicle.*
1 The fuel recommended by Vauxhall is shown in the Specifications, followed by the equivalent petrol currently on sale in the UK.
2 RON and MON are different testing standards; RON stands for Research Octane Number (also written as RM), while MON stands for Motor Octane Number .
3 If it is wished to run the vehicle on 95 (RON) unleaded petrol the following operations **must** first be carried out; this is necessary to avoid detenation (knocking and pinking) which could lead to possible engine damage.

1.2 litre models

4 On 1.2 litre models produced prior to February 1985, unleaded fuel can be used in these models but note that to every five tankfuls of unleaded fuel used, one tankful of leaded fuel must also be used.
5 On later models, to allow the vehicle to run on 95 (RON) unleaded petrol, the ignition timing **must** be retarded by 3° (see Chapter 5 for details). Do not use 95 (RON) unleaded petrol if the ignition timing has not been retarded.

1.3 litre models

6 On models with 13N and 13NB engines, 95 (RON) unleaded fuel can be used without any modifications.
7 On models with a 13SC engine, to allow the vehicle to run on 95 (RON) unleaded petrol, the ignition timing **must** be retarded by 3° (see Chapter 5 for details). Do not use 95 (RON) unleaded petrol if the ignition timing has not been retarded.

1.4 litre models

8 All models can be run on 95 (RON) unleaded fuel can be used without modification.

1.6 litre models

9 On models with a 16SH engine, to allow the vehicle to run on 95 (RON) unleaded petrol, the ignition timing **must** be retarded by 3° (see Chapter 5 for details). Do not use 95 (RON) unleaded petrol if the ignition timing has not been retarded.
10 Later models with a 16SV engine have a fuel octane rating coding plug in the ignition system wiring harness **(see illustration)**. The plug which is located on the right-hand side of the engine compartment, is set during production to give optimum engine output and efficiency when run on 98 (RON) fuel. To run the vehicle on 95 (RON) unleaded fuel, make sure the plug is set to the "95" position (95 should be visible on the side of the plug). To reset the plug, release its locking clip then remove the plug and rotate it through half a turn (180°) before reconnecting it. **Note:** *If after making the adjustment, the octane rating of the fuel used is found to be so low that excessive knocking still occurs, seek the advice of your Vauxhall dealer.*

3 Air cleaner housing - removal and refitting

Removal

1 Remove the centre retaining nut or bolt or the three screws from the air cleaner cover.
2 Lift the air cleaner off the carburettor,

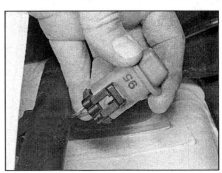
2.10 Octane plug in the "95" position - later 1.6 litre models

3.2a Hot air pick-up tube (arrowed) engages with air cleaner

3.2b Air cleaner vacuum hose connection

3.2c Air cleaner hose connection

disengaging the hot air pick-up from the manifold shroud (where necessary), together with the breather and vacuum hoses **(see illustrations)**.

Refitting

3 Refit by reversing the removal operations, making sure that the gasket or sealing ring is in place on the carburettor.

4 Air cleaner air temperature control system - general information

1.2 litre models

1 Inlet air pre-heating is controlled manually by a flap valve located in the side of air cleaner casing. The valve can be set in any one of three positions according to seasonal operating temperature as shown in the following table.

Summer position - above 10°C
Intermediate position - 10°C to -5°C
Winter position - below -5°C

2 In terms of fuel economy the engine will run most efficiently with the valve set in the summer position and least efficiently in the winter position. Providing the engine is running smoothly, and accelerates evenly, the summer position may be retained down to 0°C. If roughness or hesitation occurs, move the flap valve to the next position.
3 The three positions are shown on the air cleaner cover. In the winter position only hot air from the hot air box on the exhaust manifold enters the air cleaner. In the summer position only cold from the air cleaner inlet spout enters. In the intermediate position a blended supply from both sources enters the air cleaner.

1.3, 1.4 and 1.6 litre models

4 A thermostatically controlled air cleaner is used to regulate the temperature of the air entering the carburettor according to ambient temperatures and engine load. The air cleaner has two sources of supply, through the normal inlet spout (cold air) or from a hot air box mounted on the exhaust manifold (hot air).
5 The airflow through the air cleaner is controlled by a flap valve in the air cleaner spout, which covers or exposes the hot or

cold air ports according to temperature and manifold vacuum.
6 A vacuum motor operates the flap valve and holds it fully open when the temperature in the air cleaner is below a predetermined level. As the air inlet temperature rises the vacuum motor opens or closes the flap valve dependent entirely on manifold vacuum. Thus, during light or constant throttle applications, the flap valve will remain open, supplying the carburettor with hot air, and will close under heavy throttle application so that only cold air enters the carburettor.
7 As the temperature in the air cleaner rises further the vacuum motor closes the flap valve therefore allowing only cold air to enter the carburettor under all operating conditions.
8 The vacuum motor is operated by vacuum created in the inlet manifold and is controlled by a temperature sensing unit located inside the air cleaner.

5 Fuel pump - testing, removal and refitting

Note: *Refer to the warning note in Section 1 before proceeding.*

Testing

1 To test the fuel pump on the engine, disconnect the outlet pipe which leads to the carburettor, and hold a wad of rag over the pump outlet while an assistant spins the engine on the starter. *Keep the hands away from the electric cooling fan.* Regular spurts of fuel should be ejected as the engine turns.

5.4 Fuel inlet (A) and outlet (B) hose connections - typical

2 The pump can also be tested by removing it. With the pump outlet pipe disconnected but the inlet pipe still connected, hold a wad of rag by the outlet. Operate the pump lever by hand, moving it in and out; if the pump is in good condition the lever should move and return smoothly and a strong jet of fuel ejected.

Removal

3 Disconnect the battery earth lead.
4 Mark the pump inlet and outlet hoses, for identification purposes then slacken both retaining clips **(see illustration)**. Place wads of rag beneath the hose unions to catch any spilled fuel then disconnect both hoses from the pump and plug the hose ends to minimise fuel loss.
5 Remove the pump retaining nuts or bolts and washers and withdraw the pump from the engine. Recover the spacer and (where necessary) the gaskets on either side of it **(see illustration)**.

Refitting

6 Refitting is a reversal of removal, but use new flange joint gaskets (where necessary).

6 Fuel tank sender unit - removal and refitting

Note: *Refer to the warning note in Section 1 before proceeding.*

Removal

1 Proceed as described in Section 7, paragraphs 1 to 3.

5.5 Removing the fuel pump (1.3 litre engine shown)

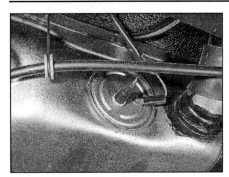

6.2 Fuel gauge sender unit (screw-fit sender unit)

6.3 Fuel gauge sender unit secured by bolts

7.11 Fuel tank filler pipe-to-neck junction

2 Disconnect the electrical leads from the sender unit **(see illustration)**.
3 To remove the sender unit, either engage a flat piece of steel as a lever between two of the raised tabs on the sender unit and turn it anti-clockwise to release it, or undo the retaining bolts (as applicable) **(see illustration)**.
4 Withdraw the sender unit carefully to avoid bending the float arm. Recover the sealing ring.

Refitting

5 Refit in the reverse order to removal, using a new sealing ring if necessary.

7 Fuel tank - removal and refitting

Note: *Refer to the warning note in Section 1 before proceeding.*

Removal

1 Disconnect the battery negative lead cap. Remove the fuel tank filler cap.
2 A drain plug is not provided and it will therefore be necessary to syphon or hand pump all the fuel from the tank before removal.
3 Having emptied the tank, jack up the rear of the car and support it on axle stands (see "*Jacking and Vehicle Support*").

Hatchback and Saloon models

4 Remove the exhaust system as described in Section 27.
5 Measure and record the length of exposed

thread protruding through the handbrake cable adjusting locknut at the compensating yoke on the rear axle.
6 Hold the cable with pliers or a spanner, unscrew the adjusting nut and remove the cable end from the yoke.
7 Remove the retainer and detach the cable from the connecting link located just to the rear of the handbrake lever rod.
8 Detach the cable from its retainers on the fuel tank and underbody and move it clear of the tank.
9 Disconnect the two electrical leads from the fuel gauge sender unit.
10 Remove the single bolt which secures the fuel filler pipe to the underbody.
11 Slacken the hose clips and disconnect the filler pipe from the tank neck **(see illustration)**. Unclip the vent hose.
12 Support the tank with a jack and suitable blocks of wood, or have an assistant hold it up, then undo the two retaining strap nuts **(see illustration)**.
13 Pivot the straps out of the way of the tank
14 Lower the tank slightly and, when sufficient clearance exists, disconnect the overflow and vent hoses from the top of the tank
15 Lower the tank fully and slide it out from under the car.
16 If the tank is contaminated with sediment or water, remove the sender unit and swill out the tank with clean fuel. If the tank is damaged, or leaks, it should be repaired by a competent specialist or renewed. **Do not** attempt to solder or weld a fuel tank yourself.

Estate and Van

17 The procedure is similar to that just described, but note the following points:
 a) *The fuel filler pipe must be unscrewed from the rear quarter panel* **(see illustration)**.
 b) *There is no need to disconnect the handbrake cable or to remove the exhaust system.*

Refitting

18 Refit in the reverse order to removal. Renew hoses, clips etc as necessary, and adjust the handbrake on completion, as described in Chapter 1.

8 Accelerator cable - removal, refitting and adjustment

Removal

1 Remove the air cleaner as described in Section 3.
2 Extract the spring clip (when fitted) and disconnect the cable ball end from the carburettor throttle lever **(see illustration)**.
3 Slide the cable outer bush out of the support bracket on the carburettor **(see illustration)**.
4 Inside the car, release the cable from the 'keyhole' fitting on the pedal by easing back the spring and prising the cable end out of the slot.
5 Release the grommet from the bulkhead and pull the cable into the engine compartment.

7.12 One of the fuel tank retaining strap nuts (arrowed)

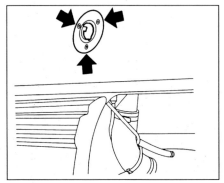

7.17 Fuel filler pipe retaining screws - Estate model

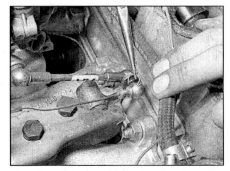

8.2 Accelerator cable ball and spring clip

8.3 Accelerator cable bracket and bush

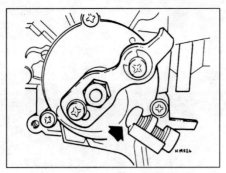

8.7 Accelerator cable adjustment to provide clearance at point arrowed

Refitting

6 Refit in the reverse order to removal.

Adjustment

7 Adjust the cable, by selecting the appropriate position of the spring clip behind the cable outer bush, to give a small amount of free play in the inner cable when the pedal is released. On 1.3 litre models with 13NB engine, make sure that with the choke control pushed fully home there is a small clearance between the fast idle adjuster screw and the choke cam plate **(see illustration)**.

9 Accelerator pedal - removal and refitting

Removal

1 If necessary, remove the under-dash trim on the driver's side to improve access.
2 Disconnect the accelerator cable from the pedal, as described in Section 8.
3 Prise the spring clip off the end of the accelerator pivot. Remove the pedal, recovering any spacers, washers, bushes etc, and unhooking the pedal return spring.

Refitting

4 Refit in the reverse order to removal. Adjust the accelerator cable if necessary on completion, as described in Section 8.

10 Choke cable - removal, refitting and adjustment

Removal

1 Disconnect the battery earth lead.
2 Tap out the small pin which secures the choke control knob to the cable end fitting. Unscrew and remove the knob.
3 Undo the retaining ring or nut which secures the choke control to the facia. Push the control into the facia and disconnect the warning light switch (when fitted).
4 Remove the air cleaner, as described in Section 3.
5 Disconnect the choke inner and outer cable from the carburettor **(see illustration)**. On some carburettors the inner cable is secured

by a grub screw which must be undone with an Allen key.
6 Release the bulkhead grommet and remove the cable.

Refitting

7 Refit in the reverse order to removal, adjusting the cable as follows.

Adjustment

8 Adjust the positions of the inner and outer cables at the carburettor so that, with the control knob pushed home, there is a small amount of slack in the inner cable. Secure the cable in position then operate the choke control knob and check that the choke linkage opens fully.

11 Carburettor - description

1 Several types and makes of carburettor are fitted to the vehicles covered by this manual. All are of the downdraught type.
2 The 32 TL carburettor fitted to the 1.2 engine is a fixed jet, single barrel instrument. The 35 PDSI and 1B1 fitted to low compression versions of the 1.3 engine are similar.
3 The 2E3 carburettor fitted to normal compression versions of the 1.3 engine is a fixed jet, twin barrel instrument. Opening of the throttle valves is sequential; the primary throttle valve is opened mechanically, but the secondary throttle valve is opened by vacuum developed in both venturis. Primary and secondary transition systems, and a part load

10.5 Choke cable inner clamp screw (arrowed)

enrichment valve, ensure efficient operation under all speed and load conditions.
4 The GM Varajet II carburettor fitted to 1.6 models is also a twin barrel type, but the main fuel jet is controlled by a tapered needle valve. The design is well proven and has been used on several earlier models.
5 All carburettors have a bypass system for providing idle mixture, and an accelerator pump for mixture enrichment when the throttle is opened rapidly.
6 When an automatic choke is fitted, the choke cover is heated electrically when the engine is running; as the cover warms up, the choke is released. On the 2E3 carburettor the choke cover is also heated by engine coolant. Both types of automatic choke need to be 'primed' by depressing and releasing the accelerator pedal before starting the engine from cold.

12 32 TL carburettor - adjustments

Note: *Under normal operating conditions only the carburettor idle adjustments described in Chapter 1 will need attention. Checking and adjustment of the following settings is not a routine operation and should only be necessary after carburettor overhaul or if the operation of the carburettor is suspect.*

Idle speed and mixture

1 Refer to Chapter 1.

Fast idle

2 This operation may be carried out with the carburettor installed or removed. If the carburettor is removed, rotate the choke linkage on the side of the carburettor until the linkage arm is against its stop and the choke valve is fully closed.
3 With the linkage held in this position a small drill bit, of diameter equal to the fast idle valve gap given in the Specifications, should just slide between the throttle valve and the carburettor barrel **(see illustration)**.
4 If adjustment is necessary slacken the locknut on the fast idle adjusting screw **(see illustration)** and turn the screw as necessary to achieve the specified setting. Tighten the locknut after adjustment.

12.3 Using a drill bit to check the fast idle gap

12.4 Fast idle adjusting screw (arrowed)

12.11a Using a drill bit to check the choke valve gap

12.11b Choke valve gap adjusting screw (arrowed)

5 If the carburettor is in the car, first allow the engine to reach normal operating temperature and then if necessary adjust the idle speed, as described in Chapter 1. Also make sure that, when the choke knob is pulled fully out, the linkage rotates to the fully closed position with the linkage arm against its stop. If necessary adjust the choke cable (Section 10).

6 Connect a tachometer to the engine in accordance with the manufacturer's instructions.

7 Start the engine and, with the choke knob pulled fully out, compare the engine speed with the fast idle speed setting given in the Specifications. If adjustment is necessary slacken the locknut and turn the fast idle adjusting screw to achieve the specified speed. Tighten the locknut after adjustment.

8 Switch off the engine and disconnect the tachometer.

Choke valve gap

9 Run the engine until normal operating temperature is reached and then switch off and remove the air cleaner.

10 Pull the choke knob fully out and check that the linkage rotates to the fully closed position with the linkage arm against its stop. If necessary adjust the choke cable (Section 10).

11 With the choke knob still pulled out, start the engine and check that a drill of diameter equal to the choke valve gap dimension will just slide between the valve and choke barrel. If necessary slacken the locknut and turn the adjusting screw above the vacuum unit until the correct gap is achieved **(see illustrations)**.

12 Switch off the engine, tighten the locknut and refit the air cleaner.

Accelerator pump delivery

13 With the carburettor installed, and the air cleaner removed, start the engine and allow it to idle for a few seconds, then switch it off.

14 Look down the carburettor barrel and open the throttle by hand. As the throttle is opened, a squirt of petrol should emerge from the accelerator pump jet. If no petrol is delivered, the pump is faulty or the jet is blocked.

15 The above check only serves to show whether or not the pump is working. For an accurate check, the carburettor must be removed.

16 With the carburettor assembled and the float chamber full of fuel, place the carburettor over a measuring cylinder. Take appropriate fire precautions.

17 Operate the throttle over its full stroke 10 times, taking about 3 seconds per stroke. Catch the fuel delivered by the pump in the measuring cylinder. The desired delivery is given in the Specifications. No adjustment is possible: cleaning or renewal of the pump components will be necessary if the delivery is incorrect.

13 35 PDSI carburettor - adjustments

Note: *Under normal operating conditions only the carburettor idle adjustments described in Chapter 1 will need attention. Checking and adjustment of the following settings is not a routine operation and should only be necessary after carburettor overhaul or if the operation of the carburettor is suspect.*

Idle speed and mixture

1 Refer to Chapter 1

Fast idle

2 The fast idle system comes into play when the choke control is operated. It is adjusted by a screw which acts on the throttle spindle lever **(see illustration)**.

3 Adjustment is correct when, with the choke control pushed in and the throttle released, the end of the screw is just in contact with the lever.

13.2 Fast idle adjustment screw (arrowed)

Accelerator pump delivery

4 The stroke of the accelerator pump can be adjusted by turning a nut on the end of the pump operating rod. The desired delivery is given in the Specifications.

5 Apart from the above points, the procedure is described in Section 12, paragraphs 13 to 17.

6 Check that the stream of fuel ejected from the accelerator pump delivery tube hits the throttle valve shaft. Adjust if necessary by careful bending of the delivery tube.

14 1B1 carburettor - adjustments

Note: *Under normal operating conditions only the carburettor idle adjustments described in Chapter 1 will need attention. Checking and adjustment of the following settings is not a routine operation and should only be necessary after carburettor overhaul or if the operation of the carburettor is suspect.*

Idle speed and mixture

1 Refer to Chapter 1.

Fast idle

2 Bring the engine to normal operating temperature and connect a tachometer (rev counter) to it. Stop the engine.

3 Pull the choke control fully out. Check that the choke lever on the carburettor is resting against its stop, and that the index notch on the cam plate is aligned with the mark on the adjuster screw **(see illustration)**. Slacken the

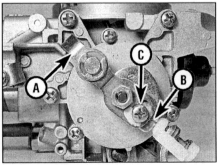

14.3 Fast idle adjustment

1 Lever against stop 3 Cam plate screw
2 Index notch

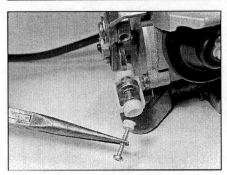

14.4 Removing the tamperproof cap from the fast idle adjustment screw

14.5 Notches on choke cover and carburettor housing (arrowed) aligned

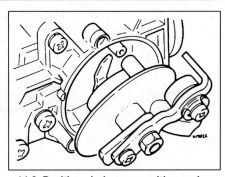

14.6 Position choke cover with opening lever to the left of drive lever

screw on the cam plate if necessary and correct the alignment, then retighten the screw.

4 Start the engine without touching the throttle. With the choke valve fully open, the fast idle speed should be as given in the Specifications. If adjustment is necessary, remove the tamperproof cap and turn the adjustment screw until the speed is correct **(see illustration)**.

Choke unit cover

5 The index notches on the cover and carburettor housing must align **(see illustration)**. Slacken the cover clamp screws if necessary to adjust, then retighten the screws.

6 If the choke cover is removed for any reason, ensure when refitting that the opening lever is positioned to the left of the drive lever **(see illustration)**.

14.8a Choke valve gap adjustment screw (arrowed)

14.8b Measuring the choke valve gap using a twist drill

Vacuum pull-down unit

7 If suspected of malfunction this unit can be checked using a hand vacuum pump and gauge. Disconnect the vacuum hose from the throttle body and connect the vacuum pump. Apply vacuum to the pull-down unit; if the vacuum drops, the unit is leaking and must be renewed.

Choke valve gap

8 Refer to Section 12, paragraphs 9 to 12 noting the adjustment and measurement points are shown here **(see illustrations)**. Lock the screw with paint on completion.

Throttle valve basic adjustment

9 This requires special measuring equipment and must be left to a Vauxhall dealer or a carburettor specialist.

Accelerator pump delivery

10 A rough check may be made without removing the carburettor as follows. Remove the air cleaner and run the engine for a few seconds, then switch it off. Look into the carburettor venturi and open the throttle fully by hand. As the throttle is opened, a clean double jet of fuel should be seen spraying from the delivery tube. If not, remove the carburettor and make further checks as follows.

11 Refer to Section 15, paragraphs 20 to 23 for the procedure noting that the adjustment point is as shown **(see illustration)**.

14.11 Accelerator pump adjustment point
Loosen clamp screw (under arrow) and rotate the cam plate

15 2E3 carburettor - adjustments

Note: *Under normal operating conditions only the carburettor idle adjustments described in Chapter 1 will need attention. Checking and adjustment of the following settings is not a routine operation and should only be necessary after carburettor overhaul or if the operation of the carburettor is suspect.*

Adjustments with carburettor fitted

Idle speed and mixture

1 Refer to Chapter 1.

Fast idle

2 The engine must be at operating temperature and the idle speed and mixture must be correctly adjusted. Remove the air cleaner to improve access.

3 Position the fast idle adjustment screw on the second highest step of the fast idle cam. Connect a tachometer to the engine. Make sure that the choke plate is fully open.

4 Start the engine without touching the throttle pedal and compare the engine speed with that given in Specifications. If adjustment is necessary, remove the tamperproof cap from the head of the fast idle screw by crushing it with pliers and adjust by means of the screw **(see illustration)**.

5 When adjustment is correct, stop the engine and disconnect the tachometer. Fit a new tamperproof cap where this is required by law.

15.4 Fast idle adjustment screw under tamperproof cap (arrowed)

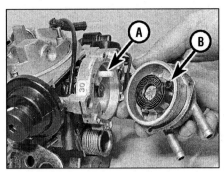

15.7 Choke drive lever (A) engages with loop (B)

Choke pull-down

Note: *This adjustment can also be done with the carburettor removed.*

6 Remove the air cleaner.

7 Remove the choke cover by removing the three screws and the securing ring. There is no need to disconnect the coolant hoses, just move the cover aside. Notice how the loop in the end of the bi-metallic spring engages in the choke drive lever **(see illustration)**.

8 Move the choke drive lever to close the choke valve completely. Position the fast idle screw on the highest step of the cam.

1.3 litre models

9 Apply vacuum to the choke pull-down unit (at the hose nearest the carburettor body) using a modified hand pump or by making a connection with a rubber hose or plastic tube between the choke vacuum unit of the carburettor and the inlet manifold of another vehicle (engine running). Apply light pressure to the choke drive lever in a clockwise direction (as if to close the choke valve) and check the choke valve gap by inserting a gauge rod or twist drill of the specified size. If adjustment is necessary, turn the adjusting screw on the side of the choke housing **(see illustrations)**.

1.4 and 1.6 litre models

10 Disconnect both vacuum hoses from the pull-down unit then, using a small screwdriver, press in the pull-down arm adjusting screw **(see illustration 15.9b)** until some resistance is felt. In this position the choke valve gap should correspond to the value given in the Specifications for the 'small' gap. Adjust if necessary by turning the screw on the pull-down unit.

15.12 Choke cover alignment marks (arrowed)

15.9a Checking the choke pull-down gap. Apply vacuum to hose arrowed

11 Press in the screw further until the arm moves to its stop. In this position the choke valve gap should correspond to the value specified for the 'large' gap. Adjust if necessary by turning the arm adjusting screw.

All models

12 Refit the choke cover, making sure that the spring loop engages in the choke drive lever. Align the notches in the choke cover and choke housing when tightening the screws **(see illustration)**.

Throttle damper adjustment - automatic transmission models

13 To adjust the damper, slacken the locknut and screw the damper in or out until there is a clearance of 0.05 mm between the end of the damper and the throttle lever. From this position, screw the damper towards the throttle lever by 2½ turns, then secure it with the locknut.

Adjustments with carburettor removed

Fast idle cam position

14 The choke pull-down adjustment previously described must be correct. If not already done, remove the choke cover.

15 Open the throttle, then close the choke valve by light finger pressure on the choke drive lever. Release the throttle.

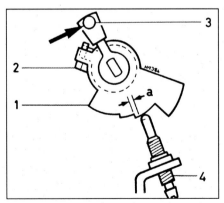

15.16 Fast idle cam adjustment

1 Fast idle cam	4 Fast idle
2 Adjustment lever	adjustment screw
3 Choke drive lever	a = 0.2 to 0.8 mm
(press in direction	(0.08 to 0.32 in)
arrowed)	

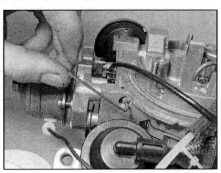

15.9b Choke pull-down adjusting screw

16 Check that the fast idle adjustment screw is resting on the second highest step of the fast idle cam, in the position shown **(see illustration)**. If not, first check that the choke return spring is correctly positioned. then adjust by bending the lever 2.

17 Refit and secure the choke cover, observing the alignment marks.

Throttle valve fast idle gap

18 Position the fast idle adjustment screw on the highest step of the fast idle cam.

19 Use a gauge rod or twist drill of the specified diameter to measure the opening of the primary throttle valve. Adjust if necessary at the fast idle adjustment screw. (This is a preliminary adjustment; final adjustment of the fast idle speed should take place with the engine running.)

Accelerator pump delivery

20 It will be necessary to feed the float chamber with fuel from a small reservoir during this test. Take all necessary fire precautions when dealing with fuel and fuel vapour.

21 Position the primary barrel over an accurate measuring glass. Fully open and close the throttle ten times, taking approximately one second for each opening and pausing for three seconds after each return stroke. Make sure that the fast idle cam is not restricting throttle travel at either end.

22 Measure the quantity of fuel delivered and compare it with the specified value.

23 If adjustment is necessary, release the clamp screw and turn the cam plate in the desired direction **(see illustration)**. Tighten the clamp screw and recheck the pump delivery.

15.23 Accelerator pump delivery adjustment: + to increase, - to decrease

16.4 Fast idle screw (arrowed) positioned on cam second highest step

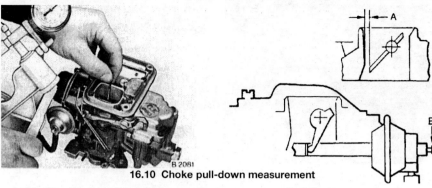

16.10 Choke pull-down measurement

A See Specifications (Choke valve gap A)
B Adjustment screw

16 Varajet II carburettor - adjustments

Note: *Under normal operating conditions only the carburettor idle adjustments described in Chapter 1 will need attention. Checking and adjustment of the following settings is not a routine operation and should only be necessary after carburettor overhaul or if the operation of the carburettor is suspect.*

Automatic choke carburettor

Idle speed and mixture

1 Refer to Chapter 1.

Fast idle speed

2 The engine must be at operating temperature and normal idle adjustments must be correct. The air cleaner must be removed and its vacuum hose plugged.
3 Connect a tachometer to the engine.
4 Slightly open the throttle valve plate so that the fast idle adjusting screw can be positioned on the second step of the cam (see illustration).
5 Start the engine without touching the accelerator. The engine speed should be as specified; if not, turn the fast idle adjusting screw as necessary.

Choke pull-down (gap A)

6 In order to be able to carry out this adjustment, a suitable vacuum pump must be available. It is possible to create sufficient vacuum using a modified hand pump or by making a connection with a rubber hose or plastic tube between the choke vacuum unit of the carburettor and the inlet manifold of another vehicle (engine running).
7 Remove the air cleaner.
8 Position the fast idle screw on the uppermost step of the cam. Check that the choke valve plate is fully closed. This may not be the case if the choke cover is still warm, in which case use a rubber band to close it.
9 Apply vacuum to the choke vacuum unit as described in paragraph 6.
10 Measure the gap A between the edge of the choke valve plate and the wall of the carburettor. Measure at the flatter side of the

valve plate. A twist drill or similar should be used as a gauge (see illustration). The gap should be as specified.
11 If necessary, turn the screw B to bring the gap to the specified clearance. If the gap was found to be too small, it will probably be necessary to bend the pullrod slightly to provide sufficient clearance for movement of the adjustment screw.
12 On completion of adjustment, lock the adjustment screw with a drop of suitable sealant.
13 Now check the play between the baffle flap lever and the pullrod with the vacuum source still connected so that the pullrod is in the fully extended position (see illustration). The clearance A must be as shown. Where necessary, bend the end of the pullrod to bring the clearance within tolerance.

Choke fast idle (gap B)

14 Close the choke valve with a rubber band.
15 Open the throttle and position the fast idle screw on the second highest step of the fast idle cam. Release the throttle and check that the screw stays on the step.
16 Open the choke valve slightly and release it in order to let it find its correct position. Check the choke valve gap B by the same method as when checking the pull-down gap.
17 If adjustment is necessary, remove the carburettor and take off the choke cover. Bend the rod which connects the fast idle cam to the choke valve lever until the gap is correct.

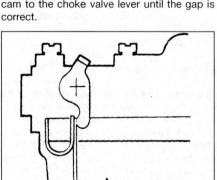

16.13 Baffle flap lever-to-pullrod clearance
A = 0.1 to 0.3 mm

18 If adjustment has been necessary, recheck the pull-down gap after refitting the carburettor.

Full throttle opening

19 Close the choke valve with a rubber band.
20 Open the throttle fully and hold it open while measuring the choke valve gap C.
21 If adjustment is necessary, carefully bend that part of the linkage shown (see illustration). Bend the tag to the right to increase the gap, to the left to decrease it.

Automatic choke cover

22 The pointer on the choke housing cover should be set against the mark given in the Specifications. If there is a tendency to stall or hesitate during warm-up, it is permissible to turn the cover through one or two divisions towards R (rich). The clamp ring screws must be slackened to do this.
23 If the ignition is switched on with the engine cold (approx 20°C), the choke valve should open fully in three to four minutes. If a longer time is required, check the choke valve for free movement; renew the choke cover if the valve is free.

Accelerator pump

24 With the engine at operating temperature and the accelerator released, no clearance should exist between the pump operating lever and the pump plunger.
25 Have an assistant depress the accelerator to its full extent and hold it there. Press the pump plunger with a screwdriver and check that it will move further downwards before resistance is encountered.

16.21 Full throttle opening adjustment - bend tang G to adjust choke gap

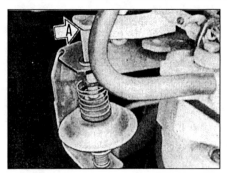

16.28 Carburettor throttle damper

A Damper pin   *B Locknut*

26 Bend the pump operating lever as necessary to achieve these conditions.
27 Check that when the pump plunger is depressed, a jet of fuel is delivered towards the inner venturi If not, dismantle the carburettor And clean or renew the pump components.

Throttle damper adjustment (automatic transmission only)

28 Automatic transmission models are equipped with a throttle linkage damper, the purpose of which is to stop the throttle snapping shut suddenly when the pedal is released **(see illustration)**.
29 Correct adjustment of the damper is carried out as follows. Release the damper locknut and unscrew the damper until the damper pin is only just touching the throttle lever. From this position, screw the damper back in between 3 and 4 complete turns, then secure with the locknut.

Part load regulator screw adjustment

30 Problems such as jerking or hesitation at light throttle openings, or excessive fuel consumption despite moderate driving habits, may be due to incorrect adjustment of the part load regulator screw.
31 It is emphasised that this adjustment should not be attempted until all other possible causes of the problems mentioned have been investigated.
32 Remove the carburettor from the vehicle.
33 Prise out the metal plug covering the part load regulator screw (adjacent to the fuel inlet union).
34 If stalling or hesitation is the reason for adjustment - ie the mixture is too weak - turn the screw one-quarter turn anti-clockwise.
35 If excessive fuel consumption is the problem ie the mixture is too rich turn the screw one-quarter turn clockwise.
36 Refit the carburettor and test drive the vehicle to see if any improvement has occurred. If necessary a further adjustment can be made, but **do not** deviate from the original setting by more than half a turn of the screw.
37 Fit a new metal plug on completion, where this is required by law.

Manual choke carburettor

Idle speed and mixture

38 Refer to Chapter 1.

Fast idle speed

39 The idle speed must be correct and the engine must be at operating temperature. Remove the air cleaner and plug its vacuum hose.
40 Pull out the choke until the mark on the fast idle cam is aligned with the tip of the fast idle adjustment screw **(see illustration)**. Hold the choke valve plate open with a rubber band.
41 Connect a tachometer to the engine.
42 Start the engine and check the fast idle speed against that given in the Specifications. If adjustment is necessary, turn the fast idle adjustment screw; the tamperproof cap over the screw head may be removed by crushing it with pliers.
43 Switch off the engine when adjustment is correct. Fit a new tamperproof cap where this is required by law.

Choke pull-down (gap A)

44 Remove the air cleaner.
45 Pull the choke control out fully. Apply vacuum to the choke vacuum unit, as described in paragraph 6. With the vacuum applied, measure gap A **(see illustration 16.11** and Specifications). Correction is by means of the adjusting screw on the vacuum unit.
46 Check the clearance between the baffle flap lever and the pullrod, as described in paragraph 13.

Other adjustments

47 Accelerator pump and part load regulator screw adjustments are as previously described for the automatic choke carburettor.

17 Idle cut-off solenoid - description and testing

1 Some of the carburettors described in this Chapter are fitted with an idle cut-off solenoid. This is an electrically-operated valve which interrupts the idle mixture circuit when the ignition is switched off, thus preventing the engine from running-on.
2 The idle cut-off solenoid is energised all the time that the ignition is switched on. A defective solenoid, or a break in its power supply, will cause the engine to stall or idle roughly, although it will run normally at speed.
3 If the operation of the solenoid is suspect, first check (using a 12 volt test lamp) that battery voltage is present at the solenoid terminal when the ignition is on.
4 With the solenoid unscrewed from the carburettor, connect the body of the solenoid to the negative terminal of a 12 volt battery. When the battery positive terminal is connected to the solenoid centre terminal,

16.40 Mark on the fast idle cam (arrowed) must be aligned with the tip of the screw

there should be an audible click and the needle at the tip of the solenoid should retract.
5 A defective idle cut-off solenoid must be renewed.

18 Carburettor - removal and refitting

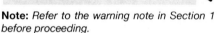

Note: *Refer to the warning note in Section 1 before proceeding.*

Removal

1 Disconnect the battery earth lead.
2 Remove the air cleaner, as described in Section 3.
3 Disconnect the choke cable (manual choke models) or the automatic choke electrical and/or coolant connections. Plug the coolant hoses to avoid spillage.
4 Disconnect the fuel supply hose from the carburettor or vapour separator. Be prepared for fuel spillage. On carburettors with a fuel return hose attached, disconnect that too. Plug the fuel hoses.
5 Disconnect the accelerator cable, as described in Section 8.
6 Disconnect the distributor vacuum hose.
7 Disconnect the idle cut-off solenoid wire (when fitted).
8 Disconnect any remaining hoses or wires, then remove the securing nuts and lift the carburettor off its studs. Recover the gasket.

Refitting

9 Refit in the reverse order to removal, noting the following.
a) Use a new gasket if the old one was damaged.
b) Adjust the accelerator cable and (when fitted) the choke cable, as described in Sections 8 and 10.
c) If coolant hoses were disturbed check the coolant level after running the engine and top-up if necessary.
d) Adjust the idle speed and mixture, as described in Chapter 1.

19.3 Removing the throttle return spring

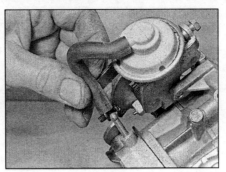

19.4 Disconnecting the vacuum hose

19.5a Four screws (arrowed) secure the carburettor cover to the float chamber housing

19.5b Separating the cover from the float chamber housing

19.6 Undo the screw (arrowed) to separate the throttle valve and float chamber housings

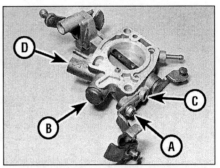

19.7 Throttle valve housing components support bracket screw (A), blanking plug (B), idle mixture screw (C) and idle speed screw (D)

19 32 TL carburettor - overhaul

Note: *In the rare event of a complete carburettor overhaul being necessary, it may prove more economical to renew the carburettor as a complete unit. Check the price and availability of a replacement carburettor and of its component parts before starting work; note that most sealing washers, screws and gaskets are available in kits, as are some of the major sub-assemblies. In most cases it will be sufficient to dismantle the carburettor and to clean the jets and passages.*

1 Remove the carburettor from the engine.
2 Clean the carburettor externally using a suitable cleaning solvent, or petrol in a well ventilated area. Wipe the carburettor dry with a lint-free cloth and prepare a clean uncluttered working area.
3 Disconnect the throttle return spring from the linkage and the support bracket on the side of the carburettor **(see illustration)**.
4 Disconnect the vacuum unit hose from the outlet on the throttle valve housing **(see illustration)**.
5 Undo the four retaining screws and separate the carburettor cover from the float chamber housing **(see illustrations)**.
6 At the base of the carburettor undo the single securing the throttle valve housing to the float chamber housing **(see illustration)**. Separate the two housings.
7 Undo the screw securing the choke cable support bracket to the throttle valve housing and lift off the bracket. Undo the blanking plug

and remove the seal ring from the housing **(see illustration)**.
8 As a guide to refitting, count and record the number of turns necessary to screw the auxiliary idle mixture screw and the basic idle mixture screw fully into the housing. Now remove the two screws.
9 Undo the four screws and remove the accelerator pump cover, diaphragm, and spring from the float chamber housing **(see illustration)**.
10 From the other side of the float chamber housing, undo the three screws and remove the enrichment valve cover, diaphragm and spring **(see illustration)**.
11 Carefully withdraw the fuel discharge nozzle from the housing **(see illustration)**.
12 Tap the float pivot pin out of the pivot

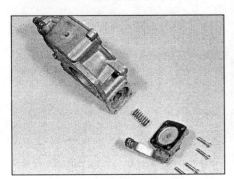

19.9 Accelerator pump components

19.10 Enrichment valve components

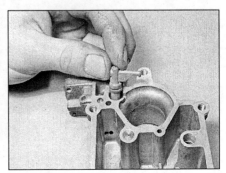

19.11 Removing the fuel discharge nozzle

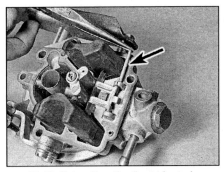

19.12 Extracting the float pivot pin

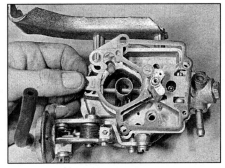

19.13 Lift off the gasket

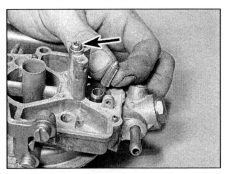

19.14 Removing the float needle valve. Main jet is arrowed

posts and withdraw the pin using long-nosed pliers **(see illustration)**.

13 Lift out the float and then remove the gasket from the carburettor top cover **(see illustration)**.

14 Lift out the float needle valve and then unscrew the main jet **(see illustration)**.

15 Unscrew all the jets and plugs from the carburettor cover, making a careful note of their locations **(see illustration)**. Remove the mixture tube from the air correction jet bore.

16 Withdraw the pre-atomiser from the top cover venturi **(see illustration)**.

17 Undo the retaining plug and withdraw the fuel filter adjacent to the inlet hose connection on the top cover.

18 If necessary the choke valve operating linkage and vacuum unit can be removed from the top cover. Undo the three retaining screws and the retaining clips for the operating cam

and choke valve rod. Remove the cam and spring, disengage the operating rod from the cam and choke valve lever and withdraw the assembly **(see illustration)**.

19 With the carburettor now dismantled, clean the components in petrol in a well ventilated area. Allow the parts to air dry.

20 Blow out all the jets and the passages in the housings using compressed air or a tyre foot pump. Never probe with wire.

21 Examine the choke and throttle valve spindles and linkages for wear or excessive side-play. If wear is apparent in these areas it is advisable to obtain an exchange carburettor.

22 Check the diaphragms and renew them if they are punctured or show signs of deterioration.

23. Examine the float for signs of deterioration and shake it, listening for fuel inside. If so renew it, as it is leaking and will give an incorrect float level height causing flooding.

24 Blow through the float needle valve assembly while holding the needle valve closed, then open. Renew the valve if faulty, or as a matter of course if high mileages have been covered.

25 Obtain the new parts as necessary and also a carburettor repair kit which will contain a complete set of gaskets, washers and seals.

26 Reassemble the carburettor using the reverse of the dismantling procedures, but carry out the settings and adjustments described in Section 12 as the work progresses.

27 Check the float level as shown after refitting the float **(see illustration)**. Bend the float arm if necessary to achieve the specified level.

28 After refitting the carburettor, carry out the basic idle adjustment then adjust the idle speed and mixture settings as described in Chapter 1.

20 35 PDSI carburettor - overhaul

Note: *In the rare event of a complete carburettor overhaul being necessary, it may prove more economical to renew the carburettor as a complete unit. Check the price and availability of a replacement carburettor and of its component parts before starting work; note that most sealing washers, screws and gaskets are available in kits, as are some of the major sub-assemblies.*

1 Major carburettor overhaul is not a routine operation and should only be carried out when components are obviously worn. Removing of the cover and mopping out the fuel and any sediment from the fuel bowl, and clearing the jets with compressed air is usually sufficient to keep a carburettor in good working order.

2 With the carburettor removed from the engine and cleaned externally, remove the clip which retains the fast idle rod to the lever on the choke valve plate spindle **(see illustration)**.

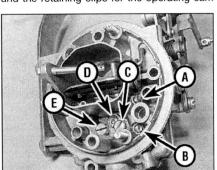

19.15 Plugs (A and B), idle jet (C), air correction jet (D) and auxiliary fuel/air jet (E) in carburettor cover

19.16 Removing the pre-atomiser

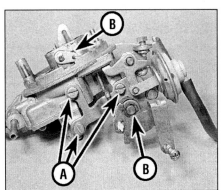

19.18 Choke linkage screws (A) and retaining clips (B)

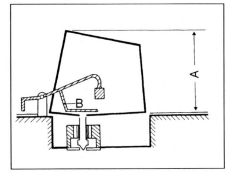

19.27 Float level measurement

A Measurement point
B Bend here to adjust

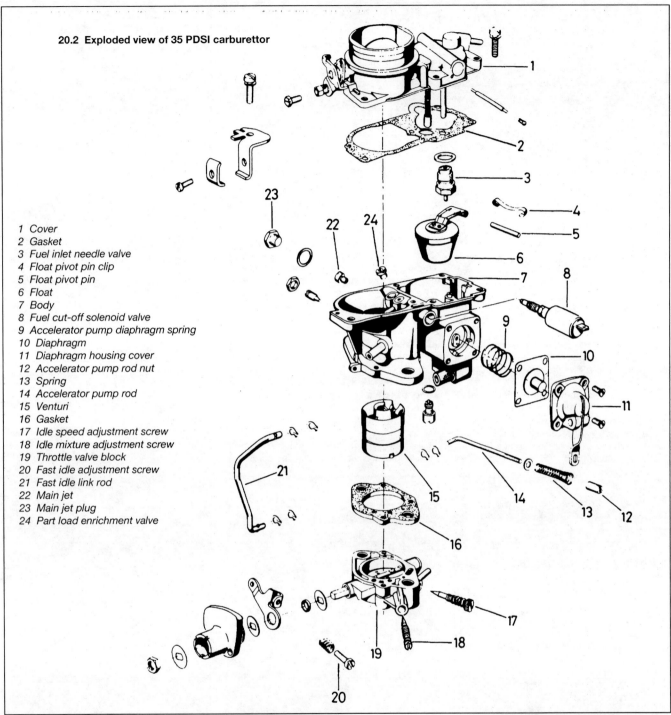

20.2 Exploded view of 35 PDSI carburettor

1 Cover
2 Gasket
3 Fuel inlet needle valve
4 Float pivot pin clip
5 Float pivot pin
6 Float
7 Body
8 Fuel cut-off solenoid valve
9 Accelerator pump diaphragm spring
10 Diaphragm
11 Diaphragm housing cover
12 Accelerator pump rod nut
13 Spring
14 Accelerator pump rod
15 Venturi
16 Gasket
17 Idle speed adjustment screw
18 Idle mixture adjustment screw
19 Throttle valve block
20 Fast idle adjustment screw
21 Fast idle link rod
22 Main jet
23 Main jet plug
24 Part load enrichment valve

3 Extract the six screws and remove the cover.
4 Use a socket wrench to unscrew the fuel inlet needle valve.
5 Extract the screw plug and withdraw the metering pin.
6 Extract the spring clip and withdraw the float from the carburettor bowl.
7 The part load enrichment valve is screwed into the base of the float bowl.
8 The main jet can be unscrewed if the plug in the float bowl is extracted and a screwdriver inserted through the hole.
9 The throttle valve housing is held to the main body of the carburettor by two securing screws. To remove the housing, first disconnect the accelerator pump link and then extract the screws.
10 The accelerator pump housing can be dismantled by extracting the four pump housing screws.
11 Clean all components and examine for wear or damage.
12 Blow through all jets and passages with air from a tyre pump; never probe them with wire in an attempt to clean them or their calibration will be ruined.
13 Renew all seals, gaskets, diaphragms etc; these will be available in the form of an overhaul kit.
14 No provision is made for float level adjustment, nor is any checking procedure or dimension specified.
15 Reassemble the carburettor in the reverse order to dismantling, observing the settings and adjustments described in Section 13.

21.3 Lifting off the carburettor top cover

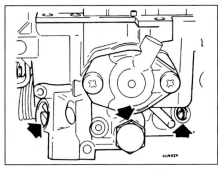

21.4 Adjustment screws and idle cut-off valve plug (arrowed)

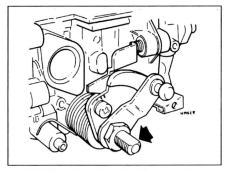

21.5 Throttle valve shaft lever and nut (arrowed)

21 1B1 carburettor - overhaul

Note: *In the rare event of a complete carburettor overhaul being necessary, it may prove more economical to renew the carburettor as a complete unit. Check the price and availability of a replacement carburettor and of its component parts before starting work; note that most sealing washers, screws and gaskets are available in kits, as are some of the major sub-assemblies. In most cases it will be sufficient to dismantle the carburettor and to clean the jets and passages.*

1 Remove the carburettor from the engine.
2 Detach the vacuum unit pull-down hose from the throttle body housing.
3 Remove the four retaining screws and separate the top cover from the carburettor body **(see illustration)**.

4 Remove the idle speed and mixture adjustment screws, and the idle cut-off valve or plug **(see illustration)**.
5 If necessary the throttle valve lever, cam plate and return spring can be removed after removal of the shaft nut **(see illustration)**. As they are removed, note their relative positions.
6 Remove the two retaining screws and lift off the part-load enrichment device cover, spring and diaphragm **(see illustration)**.
7 Remove the accelerator pump collar, piston and spring **(see illustrations)**.
8 Pull the accelerator pump delivery tube out of the carburettor body **(see illustration)**. Note the spring and ball.
9 Press out the float pin and remove the float and needle valve **(see illustrations)**.
10 Unscrew and remove the main jet **(see illustration)**.
11 Remove the choke thermal and vacuum units by undoing the three retaining screws.

21.6 Removing the part-load enrichment device

12 Unscrew and remove the idle fuel/air and auxiliary fuel/air jets from the carburettor body, taking note of the location of each **(see illustration)**.
13 Further dismantling is not recommended.

21.7a Removing the accelerator pump collar . . .

21.7b . . . the piston . . .

21.7c . . . and the spring

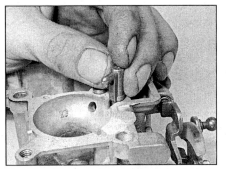

21.8 Removing the accelerator pump delivery tube

21.9a Removing the float . . .

21.9b . . . followed by the needle valve

Clean and inspect the various components as described in Section 19, paragraphs 19 to 25.
14 Reassembly is a reversal of the dismantling procedure. Note that float level is not adjustable on this carburettor.
15 After refitting, adjust the idle speed and mixture setting as described in Chapter 1 then carry out the other adjustments described in Section 14 of this Chapter.

22 2E3 carburettor - overhaul

Note: *Refer to the note at the beginning of Section 21.*
1 With the carburettor removed from the vehicle, drain the fuel from the float chamber and vapour separator. Clean the outside of the carburettor.
2 Remove the hoses and wires from the carburettor, making identifying marks or notes to avoid confusion on reassembly **(see illustrations)**.
3 Access to the jets and float chamber is obtained by removing the top half of the carburettor, which is secured by five screws. Blow through the jets and drillings with compressed air, or air from a foot pump - do not probe them with wire. If it is wished to remove the jets, unscrew them carefully with well-fitting tools.
4 Remove the fuel strainer from the inlet pipe by hooking it out with a small screwdriver, or by snaring it with a long thin screw. Renew the strainer **(see illustration)**.
5 Clean any foreign matter from the float chamber. Renew the inlet needle valve and

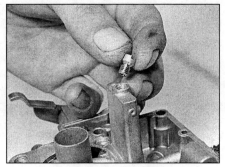
21.10 Removing the main jet

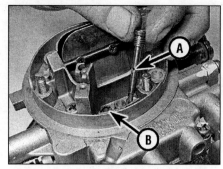
21.12 Idle (A) and auxiliary (B) fuel/air jets

seat if wear is evident, or if a high mileage has been covered. Renew the float if it is punctured or otherwise damaged.
6 No procedure has been specified for float level adjustment. Simply check that the inlet needle valve is closed completely before the float reaches the top of its stroke.
7 Renew the diaphragms in the part load enrichment valve and in the accelerator pump. If additional pump or valve parts are supplied in the overhaul kit, renew these parts also.
8 Further dismantling is not recommended. Pay particular attention to the throttle opening mechanism if it is decided to dismantle it: the interlocking arrangement is important.
9 Reassemble in the reverse order to dismantling. Use new gaskets and seals throughout; lubricate linkages with a smear of molybdenum based grease.
10 Before refitting the carburettor, carry out the checks and adjustments described in Section 15.

23 Varajet II carburettor - overhaul

Note: *Refer to the Note at the beginning of Section 21.*

Automatic choke type

1 It is rare for the carburettor to require complete dismantling; indeed, normally where this is required then it would probably be more economical to renew the complete unit.
2 It will usually be found that the first few operations described in the following paragraphs to remove the cover will be sufficient to enable cleaning of the jets and carburettor float chamber to be carried out.
3 With the carburettor removed and external dirt cleaned away, pull off the vacuum hose from the choke vacuum unit **(see illustration)**.
4 Extract the three screws from the automatic choke retaining ring and withdraw the assembly.

22.2a Top view of 2E3 carburettor

1 *Vapour separator*
2 *Choke cover*
3 *Choke pull-down unit*
4 *Fuel hose*
5 *Thermotime valve*
6 *Secondary throttle vacuum unit*

22.2b 2E3 carburettor - choke cover side view

22.2c Side view showing accelerator pump (1) and choke pull-down unit (2)

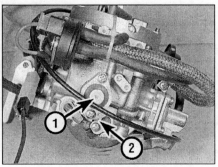
22.2d View showing part load enrichment valve (1) and accelerator pump cam (2)

22.4 Fuel inlet fuel strainer

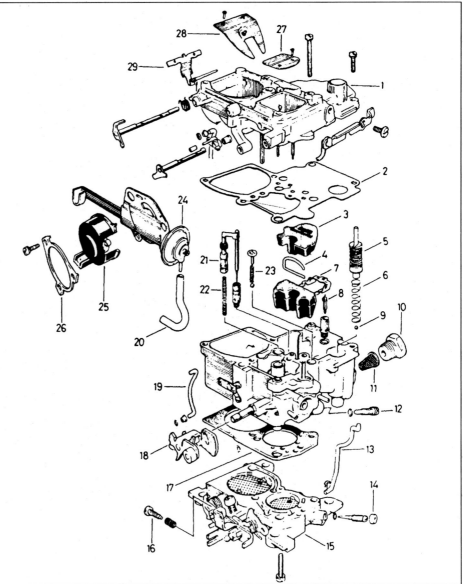

23.3 Exploded view of Varajet II carburettor

1 Cover
2 Gasket
3 Packing piece
4 Float pin
5 Accelerator pump piston
6 Spring
7 Float
8 Fuel inlet needle valve
9 Check ball (accelerator pump)
10 Fuel inlet union
11 Fuel filter
12 Idle speed adjustment screw
13 Link rod
14 Idle mixture adjustment screw
15 Throttle valve block
16 Fast idle screw and spring
17 Gasket
18 Fast idle cam
19 Fast idle link rod
20 Vacuum hose
21 Part load needle valve and piston
22 Spring
23 Suction valve and check ball
24 Choke vacuum unit
25 Choke housing cover
26 Cover retainer
27 Choke valve plate (primary barrel)
28 Baffle flap (secondary barrel)
29 Full load needle valve

5 Extract the split pin and disconnect the accelerator pump rod from the lever.
6 Unscrew the fuel inlet nozzle and extract the gauze filter from inside (see illustration).
7 Extract the retaining clip and disconnect the choke connecting rod from the cam.

8 Extract the three short and four long carburettor cover retaining screws (see illustration).
9 Remove the cover making sure that, as it is withdrawn, the gasket remains behind on the flange of the float chamber. Remember that

the accelerator pump plunger is under spring tension.
10 Remove the accelerator pump plunger and spring and carefully peel off the cover gasket. Remove the pump suction valve spring retainer (see illustration).

23.6 Fuel inlet union and gauze

23.8 Varajet II carburettor top cover

23.10 Accelerator pump plunger and spring

23.13 Float and needle valve

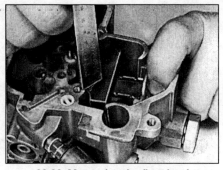

23.22 Measuring the float level

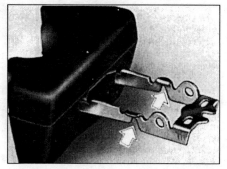

23.23 Float adjustment points (arrowed)

11 Pull or twist out the vacuum piston spring and needle of the carburettor first stage. Take care not to bend the retaining bracket or partial load needle.

12 If necessary, the partial load plunger may be withdrawn by gripping its rod with a pair of pliers.

13 Remove the packing piece, float and needle from the float chamber **(see illustration)**. Empty the fuel from the chamber.

14 Note their location and unscrew the jets.

15 Extract the four retaining screws and remove the throttle valve plate block.

16 Further dismantling is not recommended.

17 Clean all components and renew any that are worn or damaged. If the throttle valve plate spindle is worn then the complete throttle block must be renewed. Clean jets and passages with air pressure only; never probe with wire or their calibration will be ruined.

18 Obtain a repair kit which will contain all the necessary renewable items, including gaskets.

19 Reassembly is a reversal of dismantling, but observe the following points.

20 When assembling the accelerator pump, ensure that the check ball is correctly located.

21 Check that the needle valve spring is correctly located on the float arm bracket. There should be approximately 0.2 mm free play between the spring and the bracket. Correct if necessary by carefully bending one item or the other.

22 Refit the float, needle valve and pivot clips. Check the float level, with the gasket fitted, by applying moderate finger pressure to the float arms and pivot clip to close the needle valve **(see illustration)**. The top surface of the float should be the specified distance below the carburettor top flange.

23 Correct the float level if necessary by carefully bending the float arms at the points shown **(see illustration)**.

24 When installing the cover to the carburettor body, take care that the accelerator pump plunger does not become wedged.

25 Make sure that the breather screen is in position.

26 Check that the bi-metallic spring of the

automatic choke engages positively with the choke valve plate spindle arm.

27 Check the operation of the throttle valve plate lever. Remember that the secondary valve plate does not open until the primary valve plate has opened by two-thirds of its travel. The secondary throttle valve plate will not open until the choke valve plate is fully open after the engine has reached operating temperature.

28 Carry out those checks and adjustments in Section 15 which can be performed with the carburettor on the bench.

29 After refitting, set the idle speed and mixture, (Chapter 1), then carry out any adjustments outstanding from Section 15.

Manual choke type

30 The operations are very similar to those described in the preceding paragraphs, but the references to automatic choke components should be ignored.

24 Inlet manifold - removal and refitting

Removal

1.2 litre models

1 The manifold may be removed with or without the carburettor. In either case, refer to Section 18 and follow the steps preparing for carburettor removal.

2 Disconnect the brake servo vacuum hose.

3 Remove the three screws which secure the manifold to the cylinder head **(see illustration)**.

4 Remove the manifold and recover the gasket.

1.3, 1.4 and 1.6 litre models

5 Drain the cooling system, as described in Chapter 1.

6 Remove the alternator, as described in Chapter 5.

7 Release the coolant pipe from the inlet manifold and clutch housing.

8 On 1.3 models, disconnect the coolant temperature gauge lead.

9 Refer to Section 18 and either remove the carburettor, or follow the steps preparing for carburettor removal.

10 Disconnect the brake servo vacuum hose.

11 Remove the securing nuts and withdraw the manifold. Recover the gasket.

Refitting

12 Refit in the reverse order to removal, using a new gasket. Tighten the manifold nuts progressively to the specified torque. On 1.3, 1.4 and 1.6 litre models refill the cooling system and adjust the alternator drivebelt, as described in Chapter 1.

25 Exhaust manifold - removal and refitting

Removal

1.2 litre models

1 Raise and securely support the front of the car (see "*Jacking and Vehicle Support*").

2 From under the car, separate the manifold-to-downpipe joint by removing the two bolts and recovering the tension springs.

3 Remove the air cleaner, as described in Section 3.

4 Remove the six bolts which secure the exhaust manifold to the cylinder head. Remove the manifold and recover the gasket.

1.3, 1.4 and 1.6 litre models

5 Remove the air cleaner, as described in Section 3. Also remove the hot air shroud; noting how its sections fit over the manifold.

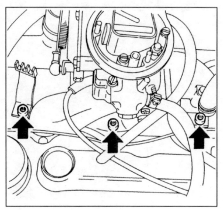

24.3 Three screws (arrowed) securing inlet manifold - 1.2 litre models

27.4a Exhaust system flexible joint

27.4b Exhaust system rubber mounting ring

27.5 Graphite sealing ring fitted at the flexible joint

6 Remove the securing nuts or bolts from the manifold-to-downpipe joint.

7 Remove the manifold securing nuts and withdraw the manifold from the studs. Recover the gaskets.

Refitting

1.2 litre models

8 Refit in the reverse order to removal, using a new gasket. Tighten the manifold securing bolts progressively, starting in the middle and working towards the ends, to avoid destructive stresses. Use a little anti-seize compound on the downpipe joint, and a new seal if necessary.

1.3, 1.4 and litre models

9 Refit in the reverse order to removal. Use a new gasket and tighten the nuts as described in paragraph 5. Also renew the gasket or seal at the downpipe joint.

26 Inlet manifold pre-heater (1.6 litre models with automatic transmission) - general information, removal and refitting

General information

1 An electric manifold pre-heater is fitted to some 1.6 litre models (fitted with a 16SH engine) with automatic transmission. If it malfunctions, warm-up time will be prolonged and cold driveability will suffer.

Removal

2 Disconnect the battery earth (negative) lead.

3 Disconnect the pre-heater wiring multi-plug.

4 Remove the screws which secure the pre-heater to the inlet manifold. Pull the pre-heater downwards and remove it.

Refitting

5 Refitting is the reverse of the removal procedure. Make sure that the pre-heater and manifold are clean, and use a new sealing ring.

27 Exhaust system - inspection, removal and refitting

Inspection

1 The exhaust system should be examined for leaks, damage and security at the intervals given in Routine Maintenance. To do this, apply the handbrake and allow the engine to idle. Lie down on each side of the car in turn, and check the full length of the exhaust system for leaks while an assistant temporarily places a wad of cloth over the end of the tailpipe. If a leak is evident repairs may be made using a proprietary exhaust repair kit. If the leak is excessive, or damage is evident, the relevant section should be renewed. Check the rubber mountings for condition and security and renew them if necessary.

Removal

2 To remove the exhaust system, jack up the front and/or rear of the car and support it securely on axle stands (see "*Jacking and Vehicle Support*"). Alternatively drive the front or rear wheels up on ramps or over a pit.

3 The system is made up of three or four sections. The front and rear sections can be removed independently, but to remove a middle section it will be necessary to remove an adjacent end section also. it is certainly easier to free stubborn joints with the complete system removed from the car.

4 To remove a front or rear section, remove the U-bolt clamps which hold the section together. Unhook the section from its rubber mounting rings, and for the front section unbolt the manifold or downpipe **(see illustrations)**. Free the joints and remove the section concerned. The application of penetrating oil will be of assistance in freeing seized joints. Heat from a blowlamp can also be helpful, but take great care to shield the fuel tank, fuel lines and other vulnerable or inflammable areas.

Refitting

5 Use a little exhaust jointing compound when assembling joints. Renew clamps, rubber rings, seals and gaskets as a matter of course unless they are in perfect condition **(see illustration)**.

6 When refitting the complete exhaust system, position it so that the mountings are evenly loaded before tightening the U-bolt clamps.

Chapter 4 Part B:
Fuel and exhaust systems - fuel-injected models

Contents

Degrees of difficulty

Easy, suitable for novice with little experience	Fairly easy, suitable for beginner with some experience	Fairly difficult, suitable for competent DIY mechanic 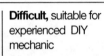	Difficult, suitable for experienced DIY mechanic	Very difficult, suitable for expert DIY or professional

Specifications

System type

1.4 and 1.6 litre models	Multec CFI (single-point injection)
1.8 litre models:	
Early (18E engine) models	Bosch LE Jetronic (multi-point injection)
Later (18SE engine) models	Bosch L3 Jetronic (multi-point injection)
2.0 litre models:	
8-valve models:	
Early (Pre 1990) models	Bosch Motronic ML4.1 (multi-point injection)
Later (1990 on) models	Bosch Motronic M1.5 (multi-point injection)
16-valve models	Bosch Motronic M2.5 (multi-point injection)

Fuel pump

Type	Electric
Pressure:	
1.4 and 1.6 litre models	1.0 bar
1.8 and 2.0 litre models	2.5 bar

Adjustment data

Idle speed:	
1.4 litre models	830 to 990 rpm
1.6 litre models	720 to 880 rpm
1.8 litre models:	
Early (pre 1990) models:	
Manual transmission	900 to 950 rpm
Automatic transmission	800 to 850 rpm
Later (1990 on) models	800 to 900 rpm
2.0 litre models	720 to 780 rpm (not adjustable - regulated by control unit)
Exhaust gas CO content (at idle)	Less than 1.0%*

On models equipped with a catalytic converter the exhaust gas CO content is regulated by the control unit and is not adjustable

Recommended fuel

Minimum octane rating:	
Models without a catalytic converter	98 RON leaded (4-star) or unleaded (Super unleaded)*
Models with a catalytic converter	95 RON unleaded (Unleaded premium) **only**

If the necessary precautions are taken, 95 RON unleaded (unleaded premium) petrol can be used (see Section 4 for details)

Torque wrench setting

	Nm	lbf ft
Multec CFI components:		
Throttle body/injector unit retaining nuts	22	16
Throttle body/injector housing upper section retaining screws	6	4
Inlet manifold	22	16
Throttle valve potentiometer screws	2	2
Injector valve bolt	3	2
Pressure regulator unit screws	3	2
Idle air control stepper motor retaining screws	3	2
Oxygen sensor unit	38	28
Inlet manifold nuts and bolts	22	16

1 General information and precautions

1 The fuel system consists of a fuel tank mounted under the rear of the car with an electric fuel pump immersed in it, a fuel filter, fuel feed and return lines. On 1.4 and 1.6 litre models, the pump supplies fuel to throttle body unit which incorporates the fuel injection valve and pressure regulator. On 1.8 and 2.0 litre models, the fuel pump supplies fuel to the fuel rail which acts as a reservoir for the four fuel injectors which inject fuel into the inlet tracts. On all models a fuel filter is incorporated in the feed line from the pump to the fuel rail to ensure the fuel supplied to the injectors is clean.
2 Refer to Section 5 for further information on the operation of the relevant fuel injection system.

Warning: Many of the procedures in this Chapter require the removal of fuel lines and connections which may result in some fuel spillage. Before carrying out any operation on the fuel system refer to the precautions given in Safety first! at the beginning of this Manual and follow them implicitly. Petrol is a highly dangerous and volatile liquid and the precautions necessary when handling it cannot be overstressed.

Note: *Residual pressure will remain in the fuel lines long after the vehicle was last used, when disconnecting any fuel line, depressurise the fuel system as described in Section 7.*

2 Air cleaner housing - removal and refitting

Removal

1.4 and 1.6 litre models

1 Refer to the information given for the carburettor models in Chapter 4A. For information on the air temperature control system refer to Chapter 4A, Section 4.

1.8 and 2.0 litre 8-valve models

2 Remove the air cleaner element as described in Chapter 1.
3 Disconnect the air intake tube then undo the retaining screws and remove the housing from the engine compartment.

2.0 litre 16-valve models

4 Remove the trunking which connects the air cleaner to the air mass meter.
5 Remove the three bolts which secure the air cleaner. Remove the air cleaner **(see illustrations)**.

Refitting

6 Refit by reversing the removal operations.

3 Accelerator cable - removal, refitting and adjustment

Refer to Chapter 4A, Section 9, substituting "throttle housing" in for all references to the "carburettor".

4 Unleaded petrol - general information and usage

Note: *The information given in this Chapter is correct at the time of writing and applies only to petrols currently available in the UK. If updated information is thought to be required check with a Vauxhall dealer. If travelling abroad consult one of the motoring organisations (or a similar authority) for advice on the petrols available and their suitability for your vehicle.*

1 The fuel recommended by Vauxhall is given in the Specifications Section of this Chapter, followed by the equivalent petrol currently on sale in the UK.
2 RON and MON are different testing standards; RON stands for Research Octane Number (also written as RM), while MON stands for Motor Octane Number. Fuel requirements are as follows.

1.4 and 1.6 litre models

3 All 1.4 and 1.6 litre fuel-injected models are fitted with catalytic converters and **must** therefore be run on 95 (RON) unleaded fuel only. Under no circumstances should leaded (UK "4-star") fuel be used as this will damage the catalytic converter.

1.8 litre models

4 All 1.8 litre models are designed to run on 98 (RON) octane leaded or unleaded petrol (see Specifications). If it is wished to run the vehicle on 95 (RON) unleaded petrol the following operations **must** first be carried out;

2.5a Two of the air cleaner securing bolts (arrowed) - 2.0 litre 16-valve

2.5b The third air cleaner bolt - 2.0 litre 16-valve

2.5c Removing the air cleaner - 2.0 litre 16-valve

this is necessary to avoid detenation (knocking and pinking) which could lead to possible engine damage

5 On early (18E engine) models, to allow the vehicle to run on 95 (RON) unleaded petrol, the ignition timing **must** be retarded by 3∞ (see Chapter 5 for details). **Do not** use 95 (RON) unleaded petrol if the ignition timing has not been retarded.

6 On later (18SE engine) models a fuel octane rating coding plug in the ignition system wiring harness **(see illustration)**. The plug which is located on the right-hand side of the engine compartment, is set during production to give optimum engine output and efficiency when run on 98 (RON) fuel. To run the vehicle on 95 (RON) unleaded fuel, the plug position can be reset to modify the timing characteristics of the ignition system. To reset the plug, release its locking clip then remove the plug and rotate it through half a turn (180°) before reconnecting it. **Note:** *If after making the adjustment, the octane rating of the fuel used is found to be so low that excessive knocking still occurs, seek the advice of your Vauxhall dealer.*

2.0 litre models

7 On all models with a catalytic converter, 95 (RON) unleaded fuel **must** be used. Under no circumstances should leaded (UK "4-star") fuel be used as this will damage the catalytic converter.

8 All models not equipped with a catalytic converter can be are designed to run on 98 (RON) octane leaded or unleaded petrol (see Specifications). If it is wished to run the vehicle on 95 (RON) unleaded petrol, the fuel octane rating plug must be set to the "95" position (see paragraph 6); this is necessary to avoid detenation (knocking and pinking) which could lead to possible engine damage

5 Fuel injection system - general information

1.4 and 1.6 litre models

1 The MULTEC Central Fuel injection (CFI) system is fitted to 1.4 litre (C14NZ) and 1.6 litre (C16NZ) engine models and provides a simple method of fuel metering whereby fuel is injected into the inlet manifold by a single solenoid operated fuel injector unit. The injector unit is located centrally in the top of the throttle valve housing and this is mounted on the top of the inlet manifold. The length of time for which the injector remains open determines the quantity of fuel reaching the cylinders for combustion. The electrical signals which determine the fuel injector opening duration are calculated by the Electronic Control Unit (ECU) from the information supplied by a network of sensors. The fuel pressure is regulated mechanically.

2 The signals fed to the ECU include inlet manifold vacuum from the Manifold Absolute Pressure (MAP) sensor; engine speed and

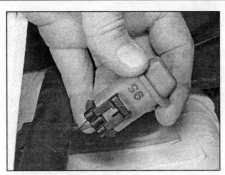

4.6 Octane rating plug in the "95" setting position

crankshaft position from the distributor; road speed from a sensor at the base of the speedometer cable; the position of the throttle valve plate from the throttle position sensor; engine coolant temperature; and the oxygen content in the exhaust gases via a sensor in the exhaust manifold. Battery voltage is also monitored by the ECU.

3 Using the information gathered from the various sensors, the ECU sends out signals to control the system actuators. The actuators include the fuel injector, the idle air control stepper motor, the fuel pump relay and the ignition control unit.

4 The ECU also has a diagnostic function which can be used in conjunction with special Vauxhall test equipment for fault diagnosis. With the exception of basic checks to ensure that all relevant wiring and hoses are in good condition and securely connected, fault diagnosis should be entrusted to a Vauxhall dealer.

5 The system incorporates a three-way catalytic converter to reduce exhaust gas pollutants, and a closed-loop fuel mixture control (by means of the exhaust gas oxygen sensor) is used. The mixture control remains in an open-loop mode (using pre-programmed values stored in the ECU memory) until the exhaust gas oxygen sensor reaches its normal operating temperature.

1.8 litre models

Early (18E engine) models

6 A Bosch LE Jetronic fuel injection system is fitted to all early 1.8 litre models fitted with the 18E engine.

7 By means of electronic control, the fuel injection system supplies the precise amount of fuel for optimum engine performance with minimum exhaust emission levels. This is achieved by continuously monitoring the engine using various sensors, whose data is input to an electronic control unit in the form of electrical signals. Based on this constantly-changing data, the control unit determines the fuel necessary to suit all engine speed and load conditions, which is then injected directly into the inlet manifold.

8 The main components of the system are:
  a) Control unit - the signals delivered by the various sensors are processed in the

control unit, and from these signals, the appropriate control impulses for the fuel injectors are generated Additional circuitry within the control unit operates an overrun fuel cut-off to reduce fuel consumption, and a cold start booster for cold starting fuel enrichment.
  b) Control relay - this comprises an electronic timing element and a switch relay, which cuts off the fuel supply immediately after the engine stops.
  c) Airflow sensor - the amount of air drawn in by the engine is measured by the airflow sensor to determine the engine load condition. This is achieved by using a flap valve attached to a spindle, which is free to pivot within the airflow sensor bore, and is deflected by the passage of intake air. Attached to the flap valve spindle is a potentiometer, which transforms the angular position of the flap valve into a voltage, which is then sent to the control unit. Airflow passing through the sensor is one of the main variables used by the control unit to determine the precise fuel requirement for the engine at any given time.
  d) Fuel injectors - each fuel injector consists of a solenoid-operated needle valve, which opens under commands from the control unit. Fuel from the fuel distribution pipe is then delivered through the injector nozzle into the inlet manifold. All four fuel injectors operate simultaneously; once for each turn of the crankshaft regardless of inlet valve position. Therefore, each injector will operate once with the inlet valve closed, and once with it open, for each cycle of the engine. The fuel injectors always open at the same time relative to crankshaft position, but the length of time in which they stay open, eg the injector duration, is governed by other variables, and is determined by the control unit. For a given volume of air passing through the airflow sensor, the control unit can enrich the air/fuel mixture ratio by increasing the injector duration, or weaken it by decreasing the duration.
  e) Fuel pump - the fuel pump is an electric self-priming roller cell unit, located at the rear of the car. Fuel from the tank is delivered by the pump, at a predetermined pressure, through the fuel filter to the fuel distribution pipe. From the fuel distribution pipe, the fuel is supplied to the four fuel injectors the excess being returned to the fuel tank via the fuel pressure regulator. A greater volume of fuel is circulated through the system than will be needed, even under the most extreme operating conditions, and this continual flow ensures that a low fuel temperature is maintained. This reduces the possibility of vapour lock, and ensures good hot starting characteristics.
  f) Fuel pressure regulator - the fuel pressure regulator Is fitted to the fuel distribution

pipe, and controls the operating pressure in the fuel system. The unit consists of a metal housing, divided into two chambers by a diaphragm. Fuel from the fuel distribution pipe fills one chamber of the regulator, whilst the other chamber contains a compression spring, and is subject to inlet manifold vacuum via a hose connected to the manifold, downstream of the throttle valve. A valve attached to the diaphragm opens a fuel return port in the fuel chamber of the regulator as the diaphragm deflects. When the fuel pressure in the regulator exceeds a certain value, the diaphragm is deflected, and fuel returns to the tank through the now open return port. This also occurs when the port is opened by the deflection of the diaphragm under the influence of manifold vacuum. Therefore, as manifold vacuum increases, the regulated fuel pressure is reduced in direct proportion.

g) *Throttle valve switch* - the throttle valve switch is attached to the throttle spindle on the throttle valve housing. As the throttle spindle turns in response to movement of the accelerator pedal, contacts within the switch are closed at the two extremes of shaft movement. One contact closes in the idle position, and one in the full-throttle position. These signals are then processed by the control unit to determine throttle valve position.

h) *Auxiliary air valve* - this device comprises a large-bore air channel, connected by hoses to the throttle housing and inlet manifold, and allowing intake air to bypass the throttle valve. In the centre of the air channel is a blocking plate attached to a bi-metal strip. When the engine is cold, the blocking plate is withdrawn from the air channel, allowing air to pass through the valve. As the engine warms up, a current is supplied to the valve, heating the bi-metal strip and causing the blocking plate to begin closing the air channel until, as engine temperature increases, the channel is closed completely. The additional air passing through the valve is measured by the airflow sensor, which compensates by increasing the injector duration to provide additional fuel. Therefore, the engine receives a greater air/fuel mixture during cold driveaway and warm-up conditions.

i) *Temperature sensors* - information on engine (coolant) temperature and intake air temperatures are measured by sensors, one located in the coolant jacket and the other in the intake air stream. The sensors consist of resistors whose resistance decreases as temperature increases. The change in electrical resistance of the sensors is measured by the control unit, and this information is used to modify injector duration accordingly.

Later (1987 onwards) 1.8 litre models

9 A Bosch L3 Jetronic fuel injection system is fitted to all later 1.8 litre models fitted with the 18SE engine.
10 The system is based on the LE system used previously, but it has a digital control system, rather than the analogue system used on the LE type. The L3 system control unit is housed within the engine compartment as part of the airflow sensor assembly, and the system wiring layout differs to suit.

2.0 litre models

11 The Motronic systems fitted to 2.0 litre models control the fuel injection and ignition systems as an integrated package. This has considerable advantages in terms of efficiency, performance and reduction of exhaust emissions.
12 Idle speed is regulated by the opening and closing of an electrically-operated valve which allows air to bypass the throttle butterfly. No manual adjustment is possible.
13 Ignition timing is advanced and retarded electronically in response to engine speed and load, engine temperature and inducted air temperature. Engine speed information comes from an inductive pulse sensor on the side of the cylinder block. The sensor is mounted close to the toothed lockwasher attached to the crankshaft No 1 counterweight. The passage of each lockwasher tooth produces an electrical pulse in the sensor. This signal is transmitted to the control unit.
14 The system fitted to 8-valve models before 1990 is known as Motronic ML4.1. The fuel injection side is very similar to the LE/L3 Jetronic systems fitted to 1.8 models. The control unit is located behind the trim panel in the driver's footwell.
15 1990 8-valve models are fitted with a system known as Motronic M1.5. The main difference is in the control unit, which triggers the injectors in pairs instead of all together as previously. There are also minor differences in the fixings of the fuel pressure regulator and the fuel injector rail. The fuel pump is now immersed in the tank instead of being fitted alongside.
16 The system fitted to 16-valve models is known as Motronic M2.5. The most significant difference from the other Motronic systems is in the way that intake air is measured. Where the other systems measure air volume by means of a flap, the M2.5 system measures air mass by its cooling effect on a hot wire. The M2.5 system also incorporates knock control, whereby detonation (pre-ignition or pinking) is sensed and causes the ignition timing to be retarded.
17 Injection on the M2.5 system is fully sequential. Each injector is individually controlled to deliver fuel at the optimum moment in the induction process. The ignition distributor carries a Hall Effect sensor which sends the control unit a cylinder recognition signal.
18 On all systems, the control unit incorporates self-testing and fault detection features. Fault codes are stored in the unit, but these are only accessible to Vauxhall

dealers or other specialists with the necessary test equipment.
19 If a fault is detected by the control unit, a 'limp home' program comes into operation by means of which an average value is substituted for the normal output of a defective or disconnected sensor. In this case the vehicle is still driveable, albeit with reduced performance and efficiency. A warning light on the instrument panel, carrying an outline of an engine and a lightning symbol, warns the driver that a fault has occurred.

6 Fuel system - depressurisation

Note: *Refer to the warning note in Section 1 before proceeding.*

⚠️ **Warning: The following procedure will merely relieve the pressure in the fuel system - remember that fuel will still be present in the system components and take precautions accordingly before disconnecting any of them.**

1 The fuel system referred to in this Section is defined as the tank-mounted fuel pump, the fuel filter, the fuel injectors, the fuel rail and the pressure regulator, and the metal pipes and flexible hoses of the fuel lines between these components. All these contain fuel which will be under pressure while the engine is running and/or while the ignition is switched on. The pressure will remain for some time after the ignition has been switched off and must be relieved before any of these components are disturbed for servicing work.
2 Disconnect the battery negative terminal.
3 Place a container beneath the relevant connection/union to be disconnected, and have a large rag ready to soak up any fuel not being caught by the container.
4 Slowly loosen the connection or union nut (as applicable) to avoid a sudden release of pressure and position the rag around the connection to catch any fuel spray which may be expelled. Once the pressure is released, disconnect the fuel line and insert plugs to minimise fuel loss and prevent the entry of dirt into the fuel system.

7 Fuel pump - removal and refitting

Note: *Refer to the warning note in Section 1 before proceeding.*

Removal

1.4, 1.6 and later (1990 on) 2.0 litre 8-valve models

1 The fuel pump is located inside the fuel tank. Before removing the pump, detach the battery earth lead.
2 Lift up the rear seat cushion and remove the access cover from the floor to reveal the pump.

7.6 Fuel pump, damper and filter assembly

3 Disconnect the electrical connectors from the pump.
4 Bearing in mind the information in Section 6, slacken the retaining clip and disconnect the fuel hose. Plug the hose end to minimise fuel loss.
5 Undo the retaining bolts and remove the pump assembly from the tank. Recover the rubber seal.

1.8 and 2.0 litre models (except later 1990 on 2.0 litre 8-valve models)

6 The fuel pump is located underneath the vehicle, just in front of the fuel tank (see illustration). Before removing the pump or associated components, detach the battery earth lead.
7 Clamp the fuel hoses on either side of the pump to prevent loss of fuel when they are disconnected. Self-locking grips are useful for this. Disconnect the hoses, bearing in mind the information given in Section 6.
8 Unscrew the pump mounting clamp bolts and withdraw the pump from its flexible insulator. Disconnect the electrical plug as the pump is withdrawn.
9 Alternatively, the pump can be removed complete with filter and damper diaphragm unit if the mounting strap nuts are unscrewed and the assembly removed from its flexible mountings.

Refitting

1.4, 1.6 and later (1990 on) 2.0 litre 8-valve models

10 Refitting is the reversal of removal using a new rubber seal. Prior to refitting make sure the pump filter is clean and undamaged. If necessary, unclip the filter and renew it.

1.8 and 2.0 litre models (except later 1990 on 2.0 litre 8-valve models)

11 Refitting is the reverse of removal, ensuring the hose clips are securely tightened. On completion, start the engine and check the hoses for signs of leakage.

8 Fuel gauge sender unit - removal and refitting

Refer to Chapter 4 Part A, Section 6.

9 Fuel tank - removal and refitting

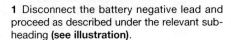

Refer to Chapter 4 Part A, Section 7.

10 Fuel injection system - testing and adjustment

Testing

1 If a fault appears in the fuel injection system first ensure that all the system wiring connectors are securely connected and free of corrosion. Then ensure that the fault is not due to poor maintenance; ie, check that the air cleaner filter element is clean, the spark plugs are in good condition and correctly gapped, the cylinder compression pressures are correct, the ignition timing is correct and the engine breather hoses are clear and undamaged, referring to Chapters 1, 2 and 5 for further information.
2 If these checks fail to reveal the cause of the problem the vehicle should be taken to a suitably equipped Vauxhall dealer for testing. Your dealer has access to special electronic diagnostic equipment which will locate the fault quickly and simply, alleviating the need to test all the system components individually (a time consuming operation that carries a high risk of damaging the control unit).

Adjustment

3 On 1.4 and 1.6 litre models, whilst experienced home mechanics with a considerable amount of skill and equipment (including a good-quality tachometer and a good-quality, carefully-calibrated exhaust gas analyser) may be able to check the exhaust CO level and the idle speed, if these are found to be in need of adjustment the car **must** be taken to a suitably-equipped Vauxhall dealer for testing. Neither the mixture (exhaust gas CO level) or idle speed are adjustable, and should either be incorrect then a fault must be present in the fuel injection system.
4 On 1.8 litre models, both the idle speed and idle mixture (exhaust gas CO level) are adjustable. Refer to Chapter 1 for information on the adjustment procedure.
5 On 2.0 litre models not equipped with a catalytic converter the idle mixture (exhaust gas CO level) can be adjusted as described in Chapter 1, however the idle speed is regulated by the control unit and is not adjustable. On models with a catalytic converter, both the idle speed and mixture (exhaust gas CO level) are regulated by the control unit (see paragraph 3). Should the idle speed/mixture (as applicable) be incorrect then a fault must be present in the fuel injection system.

11 Single-point fuel injection system components (1.4 and 1.6 litre models) - removal and refitting

1 Disconnect the battery negative lead and proceed as described under the relevant sub-heading (see illustration).

Throttle body/injector housing unit components

2 The following items can be removed from the throttle body/injector housing unit for inspection and where necessary, renewal. If the unit is in position in the car, first remove the air cleaner unit to allow suitable access to the appropriate component (see illustration).

Throttle valve potentiometer

3 Disconnect the wiring connector from the potentiometer, then undo the retaining screws and remove the potentiometer from the throttle housing (see illustrations).
4 Refitting is a reversal of the removal procedure. Ensure that the throttle valve is fully shut as the potentiometer is fitted into position and that the pick-up is properly seated on the throttle spindle. Tighten the retaining screws to the specified torque setting.
5 Reconnect the wiring plug and refit the air cleaner unit.

Injection valve

6 Disconnect the wiring plug. Undo the retaining screw then carefully lever the injection valve free using a suitable screwdriver. Remove the injection valve together with its holder (see illustrations).
7 Refit in the reverse order of removal. Always renew the seal rings and as the injection unit is pressed into position, ensure that the wiring connector is facing up (towards the retaining screw). If the retaining screw was fitted with a washer, discard the washer and apply a suitable locking compound to the screw threads before screwing it into position.

Throttle body upper injector housing

8 Detach the wiring connector, undo the retaining screws and lift the upper injector housing clear of the main body. Remove the seal.
9 Unscrew the union nuts and detach the fuel lines from the injector housing.
10 Refit in the reverse order of removal. Remove the seal located between the upper housing and the main body. Where the retaining screws were fitted with washers, discard the washers and coat the threads of the screws with a suitable locking compound. Tighten the retaining screws to the specified torque to secure the upper body to the main body.

Idle air stepper motor

11 Detach the wiring connector, undo the retaining screws and withdraw the idle air stepper motor unit from the injector unit housing (see illustrations).

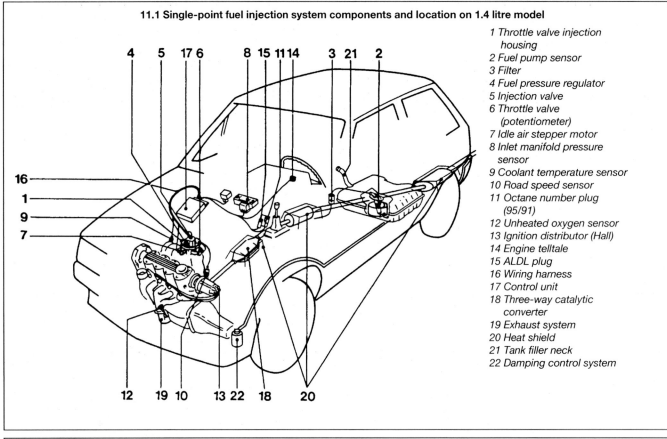

11.1 Single-point fuel injection system components and location on 1.4 litre model

1 Throttle valve injection housing
2 Fuel pump sensor
3 Filter
4 Fuel pressure regulator
5 Injection valve
6 Throttle valve (potentiometer)
7 Idle air stepper motor
8 Inlet manifold pressure sensor
9 Coolant temperature sensor
10 Road speed sensor
11 Octane number plug (95/91)
12 Unheated oxygen sensor
13 Ignition distributor (Hall)
14 Engine telltale
15 ALDL plug
16 Wiring harness
17 Control unit
18 Three-way catalytic converter
19 Exhaust system
20 Heat shield
21 Tank filler neck
22 Damping control system

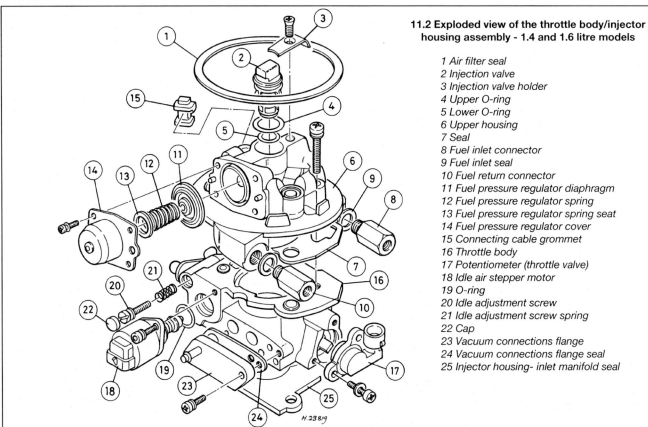

11.2 Exploded view of the throttle body/injector housing assembly - 1.4 and 1.6 litre models

1 Air filter seal
2 Injection valve
3 Injection valve holder
4 Upper O-ring
5 Lower O-ring
6 Upper housing
7 Seal
8 Fuel inlet connector
9 Fuel inlet seal
10 Fuel return connector
11 Fuel pressure regulator diaphragm
12 Fuel pressure regulator spring
13 Fuel pressure regulator spring seat
14 Fuel pressure regulator cover
15 Connecting cable grommet
16 Throttle body
17 Potentiometer (throttle valve)
18 Idle air stepper motor
19 O-ring
20 Idle adjustment screw
21 Idle adjustment screw spring
22 Cap
23 Vacuum connections flange
24 Vacuum connections flange seal
25 Injector housing- inlet manifold seal

H.238/9

11.3a Detach the wiring connector from the throttle valve potentiometer

11.3b Throttle valve potentiometer removal

11.6a Disconnect the wiring connector . . .

11.6b . . . undo the retaining screw . . .

11.6c . . . and remove the injector

11.11a Detach the wiring connector . . .

12 Refit in the reverse order of removal. To avoid damaging the injector housing as the motor unit is refitted, press the cone in against its stop and check that the top of the cone to the mating flange face is within 28 mm **(see illustration)**.

Throttle body/injector housing unit

13 Disconnect the wiring connectors from the throttle body/injector housing.

14 Disconnect the operating rod, then unscrew and remove the two retaining nuts from the studs and carefully lift the throttle body/injector housing from the inlet manifold. Remove the gasket and clean the mating surfaces.

15 Refit in the reverse order of removal, but be sure to fit a new gasket between the manifold and the throttle body/injector unit. Tighten the retaining nuts to the specified torque setting.

Pressure regulator

16 Prior to removal of the regulator unit, a new diaphragm must be obtained as this must be renewed whenever the cover is removed. Release the pressure in the fuel system as

described in Section 6.

17 Undo the four retaining screws and carefully withdraw the regulator unit cover, spring and diaphragm **(see illustrations)**.

18 Refit in the reverse order of removal.

11.11b . . . undo the retaining screws . . .

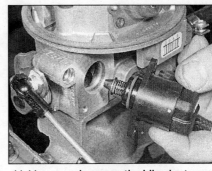

11.11c . . . and remove the idle air stepper motor

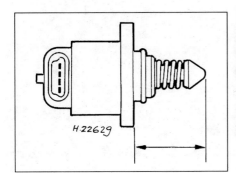

11.12 Idle air stepper motor cone tip-to-flange distance should be as specified

11.17a Undo the retaining screws . . .

11.17b . . . and remove the pressure regulator cover, spring and diaphragm

Ensure that the new diaphragm and its seatings are clean. Note that no adjustment to the regulator unit is necessary (or possible).

Inlet manifold pressure sensor

19 This unit is located on the engine side of the bulkhead. Disconnect the wiring connector and the vacuum hose, then detach and remove the unit from the bulkhead.

20 Refit in the reverse order of removal, ensuring that the vacuum hose and wiring plug are securely reconnected. Position the vacuum hose so that it progressively slopes down between the inlet manifold pressure sensor and the throttle housing.

Control unit

21 Detach and remove the trim panel from the right-hand footwell to gain access to the control unit.

22 Disconnect the wiring multi-plug connectors, undo the retaining screw then release and remove the control unit.

23 The control unit also contains a programmable memory (PROM) unit in which the engine/vehicle data and calibration are stored. If this unit is known to be faulty it can be removed from the control unit and renewed separately. If the control unit is at fault, the PROM unit should be removed from it, the control unit alone renewed and the original PROM unit fitted to the new control unit.

24 To separate the PROM from the control unit, detach and withdraw the cover from the end of the control unit, then press back the retaining clips, unplug and withdraw the PROM unit from the control unit. When removed, no attempt must be made to open and/or tamper with the PROM unit. Ensure that its plug contacts are clean and in good condition.

25 If renewing the control unit it is important that the part number/code sticker label is transferred to the new unit.

26 Refit in the reverse order of the removal procedure. On completion, switch on the ignition and check for satisfactory operation.

Coolant temperature sensor

27 Partially drain the cooling system to allow the temperature sensor to be removed without excessive coolant loss (Chapter 1).

28 Disconnect the multi-plug from the temperature sensor, then unscrew the sensor. Note the position of the sealing ring.

29 Refitting is a reversal of the removal procedure, using a new sealing ring and tightening the sensor securely.

Road speed sensor

30 Unclip the road speed sensor multi-plug, located near the base of the speedometer cable, and disconnect it. Unscrew and detach the speedometer cable from the sensor.

31 Unscrew the road speed sensor from its gearbox location and remove it.

32 Refitting is the reverse to removal.

12.4 Tightening a throttle valve switch screw

Oxygen sensor

33 Refer to Section 12, paragraphs 93 to 96.

12 Multi-point fuel injection system components (1.8 and 2.0 litre models) - removal and refitting

1 Disconnect the battery and proceed as described under the relevant sub-heading.

1.8 litre models

Throttle valve switch

2 Disconnect the wiring plug from the switch.
3 Remove the two mounting screws and pull the switch off the throttle valve spindle.
4 Refit in the reverse order to removal, adjusting the switch as follows. Release the switch mounting screws and rotate the switch in an anti-clockwise direction until resistance is felt. Tighten the screws **(see illustration)**. Have an assistant open the throttle valve slightly by depressing the accelerator pedal. A click should be heard from the switch as the throttle opens; another click should be heard when the pedal is released..

Fuel injectors

Early (pre 1990) models

5 Make sure that the engine is cool, and that all sources of external ignition (eg pilot lights) have been extinguished. Disconnect the battery earth lead.
6 Bearing in mind the information given in Section 6, release the hose clamps and

12.8 Undoing a fuel injector retaining bolt

12.6 Slackening a fuel rail hose clamp

withdraw the fuel rail from the injectors **(see illustration)**. Catch as much fuel as possible.

7 Disconnect the wiring plugs from the injectors.

8 Unscrew the retaining bolts (two per injector) and withdraw the injectors from their holders, being careful not to damage the needle valves **(see illustration)**.

9 Refit in the reverse order to removal; renew the injector sealing rings if their condition is at all doubtful.

Later (1990 on) models

10 Refer to paragraphs 5 to 9, noting that the fuel rail is retained by bolts and the injectors are secured to the fuel rail by clips.

Airflow meter

11 The airflow meter is located between the air cleaner and the throttle valve housing.
12 Disconnect the wiring harness plug from the airflow meter. Release the securing band and remove the rubber trunking **(see illustration)**.
13 Release the spring clips and remove the airflow meter with the upper part of the air cleaner housing.
14 Unbolt the airflow meter from the air cleaner housing **(see illustration)**.
15 Check the meter flap for free movement, without any jerkiness. If necessary, clean away any dirt in the area of the flap using a clean lint-free rag.
16 Refit in the reverse order to removal.

Control unit

Early (pre 1990) models

17 The control unit is located at the side of the front footwell, on the passenger side.

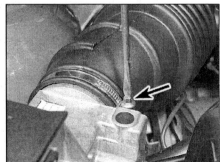

12.12 Disconnecting the airflow meter trunking

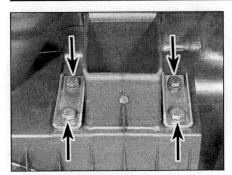

12.14 Airflow meter securing bolts (arrowed)

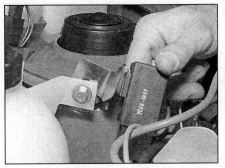

12.36a Removing the control relay and bracket

12.36b Unplugging the control relay

18 Remove the footwell trim panel.
19 Make sure that the ignition is switched off, then release the multi-plug spring clip and disconnect the multi-plug.
20 Remove the three securing screws and withdraw the control unit.
21 Refit in the reverse order to removal, but make sure that the ignition is switched off before reconnecting the multi-plug.

Later (1990 on) models
22 Remove the airflow meter as described earlier.
23 Remove the four screws which secure the cover to the top of the airflow meter (these may be hidden by blanking plugs). Remove the cover and insert, then the control unit.
24 Refitting is the reverse of removal.

Coolant temperature sensor

25 The coolant temperature sensor for the fuel injection system is located near the alternator. Because it is additional to the

temperature gauge sensor, it is known as temperature sensor II.
26 Partially drain the cooling system - about 3 litres should be sufficient.
27 Disconnect the electrical lead and unscrew the sensor.
28 Refit in the reverse order to removal. Use a little sealant on the sensor threads, and refill the cooling system on completion.

Auxiliary air valve

29 The auxiliary air valve is bolted to the side of the camshaft housing.
30 Disconnect the wiring plug from the valve.
31 Release the hose clips and disconnect the air hoses from the valve.
32 Unbolt and remove the valve.
33 The function of the valve may be checked by looking through the hose connecting stubs. A clear passage should exist between the stubs when the valve is cold. As the valve is heated (achieved by connecting its terminals to a 12 volt battery) the regulator disc should move round and block the hole.
34 Refit in the reverse order to removal, using new hose clips if necessary. An air leak on the intake side of the valve will raise the idle speed.

Control relay

35 The control relay is located on the front suspension strut turret. Unplugging the relay disables the fuel pump - this is necessary when performing a compression test.
36 Slacken the securing bolt, remove the relay and its bracket from the turret, and withdraw the relay from the plug **(see illustrations)**.

37 Refit in the reverse order to removal.

Fuel pressure regulator

38 The fuel pressure regulator is located between injectors 3 and 4 **(see illustration)**.
39 Disconnect the battery earth lead and take appropriate fire precautions.
40 Clamp the fuel hoses to minimise fuel loss, using self-locking grips with suitably protected jaws.
41 Disconnect the fuel and vacuum hoses form the pressure regulator and remove it. Be prepared for fuel spillage.
42 Refit in the reverse order to removal.

2.0 litre models

43 Refer to the information given earlier for the 1.8 litre models, information for additional components is as follows

Idle speed adjuster

44 Note the routing and positioning of the air hoses, then disconnect the multi-plug and the air hoses from the idle speed adjuster **(see illustrations)**. On the 16-valve engine the adjuster is located below the inlet manifold; access is not good but is easier from below.
45 Refitting is the reverse of the removal procedure.

Control unit

46 The control unit is located behind the side trim panel in the driver's footwell. To remove the trim panel, first remove the front two screws from the driver's 'kick plate' and peel back the door surround strip in the area next to the side trim panel **(see illustrations)**.

12.38 Fuel pressure regulator

12.44a Disconnect the idle speed adjuster multi-plug . . .

12.44b . . . and the air hoses (arrowed)

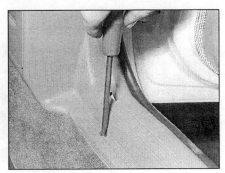

12.46a Remove the kick plate screws . . .

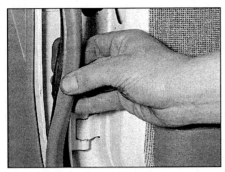

12.46b . . . and peel back the door surround strip

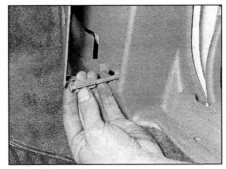

12.47 Prise out the clips to release the trim panel

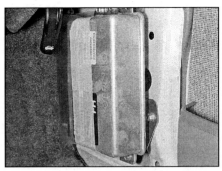

12.48 Motronic control unit location

47 Open the access panel in the side trim. Prise out the plastic retaining clips and withdraw the side trim panel **(see illustration)**.
48 Remove the retaining screws to release the control unit **(see illustration)**. Release the multi-plug catch and disconnect the multi-plug. Handle the control unit with care if it is to be re-used.
49 Refitting is the reverse of the removal procedure.

Inductive pulse sensor

50 Refer to Chapter 5.

Fuel injectors - Motronic ML4.1 and M1.5

51 Remove the idle speed adjuster.
52 Disconnect the wiring plugs from the fuel injectors.
53 Unbolt the fuel rail from the inlet manifold, bearing in mind the information in Section 6.
54 Remove the clips which secure the injectors to the fuel rail by prising them out.
55 Disconnect the brake servo hose from the throttle body housing.
56 Unbolt the fuel supply hose bracket.
57 Carefully lift the fuel rail away from the manifold and pull out the injectors.
58 Refitting is the reverse of the removal procedure. If the old injectors are being refitted, use new sealing rings.

Fuel injectors - Motronic M2.5

59 Remove the pre-volume chamber as described earlier.
60 Bearing in mind the information in Section 6, clean around the unions on the fuel rail, then disconnect the supply and return hoses from it **(see illustration)**. Be prepared for fuel spillage.
61 Disconnect the two crankcase ventilation hoses from the camshaft cover. To improve access, remove the larger of the two hoses completely.
62 Disconnect the vacuum hose from the fuel pressure regulator.

63 Disconnect the multi-plugs from the air mass meter and from the throttle valve switch.
64 Unbolt the throttle cable bracket and move it aside.
65 Remove the nuts securing the earth straps at each end of the fuel rail **(see illustration)**.
66 The injector multi-plugs must now be disconnected. Each plug is secured by a spring clip, which must be levered out with a small screwdriver or long-nosed pliers. With all the multi-plugs released, cut or undo cable ties as necessary and move the wiring rail forwards so that it rests on the camshaft cover **(see illustrations)**.
67 Remove the two bolts which secure the fuel rail to the inlet manifold.
68 Pull the rail and injectors away from the manifold.
69 Individual injectors may now be removed from the rail by removing their retaining clips and pulling them from the rail **(see illustrations)**.

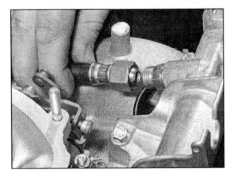

12.60 Disconnecting the fuel supply line from the fuel rail

12.65 One of the earth straps on the fuel rail

12.66a Removing the spring clip from an injector multi-plug

12.66b Lifting the wiring rail off the injectors

12.69a Remove the retaining clip

12.69b . . . and pull out the injector

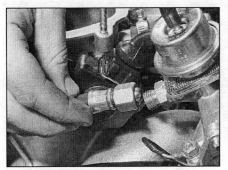

12.73 Disconnecting the fuel return line from the fuel pressure regulator

12.74 Disconnecting the vacuum hose

12.77 Removing a pre-volume chamber screw

70 Refitting is the reverse of the removal procedure. If the old injectors are being refitted, use new sealing rings.

Throttle valve potentiometer - Motronic M1.5

71 The throttle valve potentiometer is removed and refitted in the same way as the throttle valve switch (which it replaces) on earlier models. There is no need for adjustment.

Fuel pressure regulator - Motronic M1.5 and 2.5

72 On Motronic M2.5 systems, remove the pre-volume chamber.
73 Bearing in mind the information in Section 6, disconnect the fuel return union from the pressure regulator (see illustration). Be prepared for fuel spillage.
74 Disconnect the vacuum hose from the regulator (see illustration).

12.79 Idle speed adjuster hose attachment to pre-volume chamber

75 Remove the four Torx screws which secure the pressure regulator to the fuel rail. A small E6 Torx spanner will be needed for access to the screws. If this is not available the fuel rail will have to be removed so that the screws can be undone with a socket or (at a pinch) self-locking pliers. With the screws removed, the pressure regulator can be removed from the rail.
76 Refitting is the reverse the removal.

Pre-volume chamber - Motronic M2.5

77 Remove the four Allen screws which secure the pre-volume chamber to the throttle housing (see illustration). On some models there is a fifth screw to the left which must also be removed.
78 Release the hose clip which secures the air mass meter to the pre-volume chamber.
79 Lift the pre-volume chamber slightly and disconnect the idle speed adjuster hose from the left-hand end (see illustration). Remove the pre-volume chamber.
80 Refitting is the reverse of the removal procedure, but note that it is important that the ring which seals the throttle body to the pre-volume chamber is not displaced during fitting. Air leaks at this point will weaken the mixture and dirt may enter. Secure the ring to the chamber if necessary with a few dabs of sealant (see illustration).

Throttle valve switch - Motronic M 2.5

81 Remove the pre-volume chamber and the air mass meter.
82 Disconnect the multi-plug from the switch (see illustration). Remove the two screws and withdraw the switch.

83 Refitting is the reverse of the removal procedure. Adjust the switch before tightening the screws as described in paragraph 4 of this Section.

Air mass meter - Motronic M2.5

84 Disconnect the multi-plug from the air mass meter (see illustration).
85 Release the hose clips from each end of the meter and remove it. Do not drop it, it is fragile.
86 Refitting is the reverse of the removal procedure.

Coolant temperature sensor - Motronic M2.5

87 Partially drain the cooling system at the radiator bottom hose to bring the coolant level below the level of the thermostat housing.
88 Disconnect the multi-plug from the sensor on the thermostat housing. The Motronic sensor is the larger of the two the smaller one feeds the temperature gauge. Unscrew the sensor and remove it.
89 Refitting is the reverse of the removal procedure, noting the following points:
a) Use a new sealing ring on the sensor, and apply a little sealant to its threads.
b) Refill the cooling system as described in Chapter 1.

Knock sensor - Motronic M2.5

90 The knock sensor is on the rear of the cylinder block. Unless the inlet manifold has been removed, access is easiest from below.
91 Disconnect the multi-plug (coloured red or orange) from the knock sensor. Remove the securing screw and the sensor (see illustration).

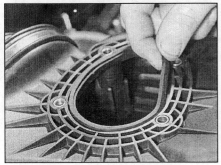

12.80 Pre-volume chamber sealing ring

12.82 Disconnecting the throttle valve switch multi-plug

12.84 Disconnecting the multi-plug from the air mass meter

12.91 Knock sensor multi-plug (arrowed) seen from below

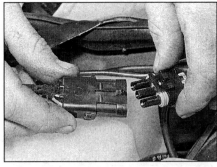

12.94 Disconnecting the oxygen sensor multi-plug

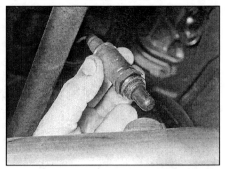

12.95 Removing the oxygen sensor

12.98a Canister clamp nut (arrowed)

12.98b Disconnecting a hose from the canister

12.100 Disconnecting the vent valve multi-plug

92 Refitting is the reverse of the removal procedure, but make sure that the sensor and its seat are perfectly clean and that the sensor is secured firmly. Failure to observe these points could lead to damage to the engine, because a poorly mounted sensor will not pick up knocking (pinking) and the appropriate ignition correction will not be applied.

Oxygen sensor - models with a catalytic converter

93 Bring the engine to operating temperature, then switch it off and disconnect the battery.
94 Disconnect the oxygen sensor multi-plug, which is located near the right-hand suspension turret **(see illustration)**. Free the wiring leading to the sensor.
95 Working under the vehicle, unscrew the sensor from the exhaust manifold **(see illustration)**.
96 Refitting is the reverse of the removal procedure. Note that the makers specify the use of a special anti-seize compound made of graphite and glass beads. New sensors are provided with their threads already coated with this compound. When refitting a used sensor, obtain some of the special compound from a Vauxhall dealer.

Carbon canister - 16-valve models with a catalytic converter

97 Raise the front of the vehicle and remove the left-hand roadwheel.
98 Slacken the canister clamp nut. Release the canister from the clamp, disconnect the

hoses from it and remove it **(see illustrations)**. Treat the canister with the same precautions as would apply to a fuel tank - it may be full of vapour.
99 Refitting is the reverse of the removal procedure.

Vent valve - 16-valve models with a catalytic converter

100 Disconnect the multi-plug and the hoses from the vent valve **(see illustration)**. Unbolt the valve bracket and remove the valve and bracket.
101 Refitting is the reverse of the removal procedure.

13 Inlet manifold - removal and refitting

Removal

1.4 and 1.6 litre models

1 Refer to the information given in Section 11, Chapter 4A, for information on the various electrical components which must be disconnected.

1.8 litre models

2 Disconnect the battery earth lead.
3 Disconnect the injection wiring harness plugs and earth connections as follows:
 a) Airflow meter plug.
 b) Coolant temperature sensor **(see illustration)**.
 c) Fuel injectors **(see illustration)**.
 d) Throttle valve switch **(see illustration)**.

 e) Auxiliary air valve **(see illustration)**.
 f) Cam cover earth tags.
4 Disconnect the distributor vacuum hose from the throttle valve housing **(see illustration)**.
5 Depressurise the cooling system by unscrewing the expansion tank cap, taking precautions against scalding if the system is hot. Disconnect and plug the coolant hoses from the throttle valve housing.
6 Disconnect the air inlet duct from the housing.
7 Disconnect the brake servo and crankcase ventilation hoses from the housing.
8 Disconnect and plug the fuel hoses from the fuel rail stubs. The hoses are different sizes and one of them carries a white band for identification. Be prepared for fuel spillage.
9 Disconnect the accelerator cable from the throttle levers. The cable inner is secured by a

13.3a Coolant temperature sensor plug (arrowed)

13.3b Disconnecting a fuel injector plug

13.3c Unplugging the throttle valve switch lead connector

13.3d Unplugging the auxiliary air valve

wire clip, and the outer is retained in its bracket by an E-clip **(see illustration)**.

10 Unscrew the nuts which secure the inlet manifold to the cylinder head. The lower nuts are different to reach: a small socket or ring spanner will be needed.

11 Lift away the manifold and recover the gasket **(see illustrations)**.

2.0 litre 8-valve models

12 Refer to the information given above in paragraphs 2 to 11, noting the hose connections shown **(see illustration)**.

2.0 litre 16-valve models

13 Disconnect the battery earth (negative) lead.

14 Drain the cooling system (see Chapter 1).

15 Remove the pre-volume chamber, the air mass meter and its trunking as described in Section 12.

16 Remove the alternator drivebelt and the

adjuster strap nut and bolt (see Chapter 1).

17 Disconnect the throttle cable from the throttle housing. Pull the cable out of the retainer and move it aside **(see illustration)**.

18 Remove the 9 nuts which secure the manifold to the cylinder head. These are all stiff and some are not easily accessible; a socket with a "wobble drive" or universal joint will be needed. Once the nuts are removed, slide the manifold back on its studs to improve access to the injector wiring rail.

19 Disconnect the two breather hoses from the camshaft cover.

20 Disconnect the injector wiring rail from the injectors as described earlier.

21 Release the earth straps from each end of the fuel rail.

22 If a vent valve is fitted, disconnect the multi-plug and the hose from it.

23 Disconnect the throttle position switch multi-plug.

24 Bearing in mind the information given in Section 6, disconnect the fuel supply and return unions from the fuel rail. Be prepared for fuel spillage.

25 Release the fuel supply hose bracket from the throttle housing.

26 Release the cable tie which secures the coolant hoses to the right-hand side of the manifold.

27 Disconnect the brake servo vacuum hose and the large coolant hose from the base of the manifold **(see illustrations)**.

28 Unhook the clutch cable from the bracket behind the manifold.

29 Disconnect the small coolant hose from the expansion tank.

30 Disconnect the air hose which connects the idle speed adjuster to the base of the manifold.

31 With the help of an assistant, lift the manifold to gain access to the idle speed

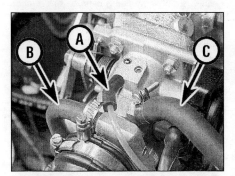

13.4 Distributor vacuum hose (A), coolant hose (B) and breather (C) on throttle housing

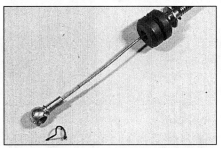

13.9 Accelerator cable at engine end

13.11a Removing the inlet manifold - 1.8 litre model

13.11b Inlet manifold showing injectors fuel rail and associated components

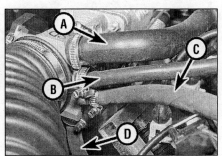

13.12 Throttle valve housing - ML4.1
A Hose from idle speed adjuster
B Crankcase ventilation hose
C Coolant hose
D Coolant hose

13.17 Pulling the throttle cable out of the retainer

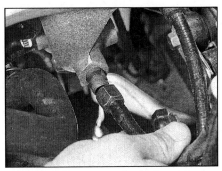

13.27a Disconnect the brake servo hose . . .

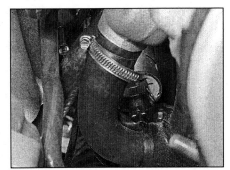

13.27b . . . and the large coolant hose

13.32 Removing the inlet manifold - 2. litre 16-valve model

adjuster and the knock sensor. Disconnect the multiplugs from these components and feed the wiring harness back through the manifold.

32 Remove the manifold complete with fuel rail and injectors **(see illustration)**. Recover the gasket.

Refitting

33 Refitting is the reverse of the removal procedure, noting the following points:

a) *Use a new manifold gasket* **(see illustration)**.

13.33 Fitting a new inlet manifold gasket

b) *Tighten the manifold nuts to the specified torque.*
c) *Refill and bleed the cooling system as described in Chapter 1.*

14 Exhaust manifold - removal and refitting

Removal

2.0 litre 16-valve models

1 Raise and securely support the front of the vehicle (see "*Jacking and Vehicle Support*").
2 Disconnect the battery earth (negative) lead.
3 Remove the manifold heat shield, which is secured by three bolts at the top and two of the manifold nuts at the bottom **(see illustration)**.
4 Remove the remaining 10 nuts which secure the manifold.
5 On models with an oxygen sensor, disconnect the sensor multiplug (near the right-hand suspension mounting) and free the wiring leading to the sensor.
5 Working under the vehicle, unbolt the manifold-to-exhaust system flexible joint and

support bracket **(see illustration)**.
6 Lift away the manifold and recover the gasket.

All other models

7 Refer to Chapter 4A. On models with an oxygen sensor, disconnect the sensor multi-plug and free the wiring to prevent it being strained whilst the manifold is removed.

Refitting

8 Refitting is the reverse of the removal procedure, using a new manifold gasket **(see illustration)**.

15 Exhaust system - inspection, removal and refitting

1 Refer to Chapter 4A. On models with an oxygen sensor, it will be necessary to disconnect the sensor multi-plug and free the wiring from its retaining clips before removal. On refitting ensure the sensor wiring is correctly routed and in no danger of contacting the exhaust system.

14.3 Removing an exhaust manifold heat shield bolt

14.5 Manifold-to-exhaust system joint and bracket

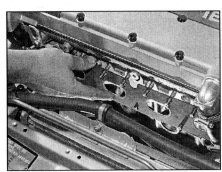

14.8 Fitting a new exhaust manifold gasket

Chapter 5 Part A:
Starting and charging systems

Contents

Degrees of difficulty

Easy, suitable for novice with little experience	Fairly easy, suitable for beginner with some experience	Fairly difficult, suitable for competent DIY mechanic 	Difficult, suitable for experienced DIY mechanic	Very difficult, suitable for expert DIY or professional

Specifications

System type . . . . 12V negative earth

Battery
Capacity . . . . 36 to 66 Ah (depending on model)
Charge condition:
  Poor . . . . 12.5 volts
  Normal . . . . 12.6 volts
  Good . . . . 12.7 volts

Alternator
Type . . . . Bosch or Delco
Output . . . . 45, 55 or 65A (depending on model)

Starter motor
Type . . . . Pre-engaged Bosch or Delco

Torque wrench settings	**Nm**	**lbf ft**
Alternator mounting bracket bolts*	40	30
Alternator pivot and adjustment bolts*	34	25
Starter motor mounting bolts*:		
1.3 litre models	25	18
1.6, 1.8 and 2.0 litre models	45	33

Torque wrench settings for the 1.2 litre models not available

1 General information and precautions

General information

The engine electrical system consists mainly of the charging and starting systems. Because of their engine-related functions, these components are covered separately from the body electrical devices such as the lights, instruments, etc (which are covered in Chapter 12). Refer to Part B or C for information on the ignition system.

The electrical system is of the 12-volt negative earth type.

The battery is of the low maintenance or "maintenance-free" (sealed for life) type and is charged by the alternator, which is belt-driven from the crankshaft pulley.

The starter motor is a pre-engaged type incorporating an integral solenoid. On starting, the solenoid moves the drive pinion into engagement with the flywheel ring gear before the starter motor is energised. Once the engine has started, a one-way clutch prevents the motor armature being driven by the engine until the pinion disengages from the flywheel.

Precautions

Further details of the various systems are given in the relevant Sections of this Chapter.

While some repair procedures are given, the usual course of action is to renew the component concerned. The owner whose interest extends beyond mere component renewal should obtain a copy of the *"Automobile Electrical & Electronic Systems Manual"*, available from the publishers of this manual.

It is necessary to take extra care when working on the electrical system to avoid damage to semi-conductor devices (diodes and transistors), and to avoid the risk of personal injury. In addition to the precautions given in the *"Safety first!"* section of this manual, observe the following when working on the system:

Always remove rings, watches, etc before working on the electrical system. Even with the battery disconnected, capacitive discharge could occur if a component's live terminal is earthed through a metal object. This could cause a shock or nasty burn.

Do not reverse the battery connections. Components such as the alternator, electronic control units, or any other components having semi-conductor circuitry could be irreparably damaged.

If the engine is being started using jump leads and a slave battery, connect the batteries *positive-to-positive* and *negative-to-negative* (see *"Booster battery (jump) starting"*). This also applies when connecting a battery charger.

Never disconnect the battery terminals, the alternator, any electrical wiring or any test instruments when the engine is running.

Do not allow the engine to turn the alternator when the alternator is disconnected.

Never "test" for alternator output by 'flashing' the output lead to earth.

Never use an ohmmeter of the type incorporating a hand-cranked generator for circuit or continuity testing.

Always ensure that the battery negative lead is disconnected when working on the electrical system.

Before using electric-arc welding equipment on the car, disconnect the battery, alternator and components such as the fuel injection/ignition electronic control unit to protect them from the risk of damage.

2 Electrical fault finding - general information

Refer to Chapter 12.

3 Battery - testing and charging

Standard and low maintenance battery - testing

1 If the vehicle covers a small annual mileage it is worthwhile checking the specific gravity of the electrolyte every three months to determine the state of charge of the battery. Use a hydrometer to make the check and compare the results with the following table. Note that the specific gravity readings assume an electrolyte temperature of 15°C (60°F); for every 10°C (48°F) below 15°C (60°F) subtract 0.007. For every 10°C (48°F) above 15°C (60°F) add 0.007.

Ambient temperature, 25°C (77°F)

	above	below
Fully-charged	1.21 to 1.23	1.27 to 1.29
70% charged	1.17 to 1.19	1.23 to 1.25
Fully-discharged	1.05 to 1.07	1.11 to 1.13

2 If the battery condition is suspect, first check the specific gravity of electrolyte in each cell. A variation of 0.040 or more between any cells indicates loss of electrolyte or deterioration of the internal plates.

3 If the specific gravity variation is 0.040 or more, the battery should be renewed. If the cell variation is satisfactory but the battery is discharged, it should be charged as described later in this Section.

Maintenance-free battery - testing

4 In cases where a "sealed for life" maintenance-free battery is fitted, topping-up and testing of the electrolyte in each cell is not possible. The condition of the battery can therefore only be tested using a battery condition indicator or a voltmeter.

5 A Delco type maintenance-free battery is fitted with a built-in charge condition indicator. The indicator is located in the top of the battery casing, and indicates the condition of the battery from its colour. If the indicator shows green, then the battery is in a good state of charge. If the indicator turns darker, eventually to black, then the battery requires charging, as described later in this Section. If the indicator shows clear/yellow, then the electrolyte level in the battery is too low to allow further use, and the battery should be renewed. **Do not** attempt to charge, load or jump start a battery when the indicator shows clear/yellow **(see illustration)**.

6 If testing the battery using a voltmeter, connect the voltmeter across the battery and compare the result with those given in the Specifications under "charge condition". The test is only accurate if the battery has not been subjected to any kind of charge for the previous six hours. If this is not the case, switch on the headlights for 30 seconds, then wait four to five minutes before testing the battery after switching off the headlights. All other electrical circuits must be switched off, so check that the doors and tailgate are fully shut when making the test.

7 If the voltage reading is less than 12.2 volts, then the battery is discharged, whilst a reading of 12.2 to 12.4 volts indicates a partially discharged condition.

8 If the battery is to be charged, remove it from the vehicle (Section 4) and charge it as described later in this Section.

Standard and low maintenance battery - charging

Note: *The following is intended as a guide only. Always refer to the manufacturer's recommendations (often printed on a label attached to the battery) before charging a battery.*

9 Charge the battery at a rate of 3.5 to 4 amps and continue to charge the battery at this rate until no further rise in specific gravity is noted over a four hour period.

10 Alternatively, a trickle charger charging at the rate of 1.5 amps can safely be used overnight.

11 Specially rapid 'boost' charges which are claimed to restore the power of the battery in 1 to 2 hours are not recommended, as they can cause serious damage to the battery plates through overheating.

12 While charging the battery, note that the temperature of the electrolyte should never exceed 37.8°C (100°F).

Maintenance-free battery - charging

Note: *The following is intended as a guide only. Always refer to the manufacturer's recommendations (often printed on a label attached to the battery) before charging a battery.*

13 This battery type takes considerably longer to fully recharge than the standard type, the time taken being dependent on the extent of discharge, but it can take anything up to three days.

14 A constant voltage type charger is required, to be set, when connected, to 13.9 to 14.9 volts with a charger current below 25 amps. Using this method, the battery should be usable within three hours, giving a voltage reading of 12.5 volts, but this is for a partially discharged battery and, as mentioned, full charging can take considerably longer.

15 If the battery is to be charged from a fully discharged state (condition reading less than 12.2 volts), have it recharged by your Vauxhall dealer or local automotive electrician, as the charge rate is higher and constant supervision during charging is necessary.

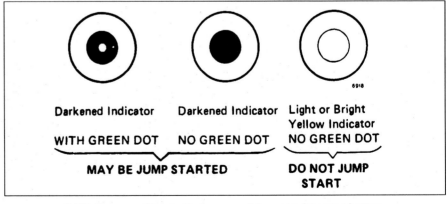

Darkened Indicator
WITH GREEN DOT

Darkened Indicator
NO GREEN DOT

MAY BE JUMP STARTED

Light or Bright Yellow Indicator
NO GREEN DOT

DO NOT JUMP START

3.5 Battery condition indicator on maintenance-free type battery

4 Battery - removal and refitting

Removal

1 The battery is located on the left-hand side of the engine bay.
2 Slacken the clamp nut and bolt on the negative (-) terminal clamp **(see illustration)**. Lift the clamp off the terminal post. If the clamp is stuck to the post, beware of using force to free it as the post may be broken. Warm water will usually do the trick.
3 Similarly disconnect the positive (+) terminal; this may be protected by a plastic cover.
4 Undo the clamp bolt at the base of the battery and lift out the battery. Be careful, it is heavy. Keep it upright and do not drop it.

Refitting

5 Refit in the reverse order to removal, connecting the earth (negative) lead last. Use a little proprietary anti-corrosion compound, or petroleum jelly, on the terminal posts. Do not overtighten the clamp bolt or the terminal clamps.

5 Charging system - testing

Note: *Refer to the warnings given in "Safety first!" and in Section 1 of this Chapter before starting work.*
1 If the ignition warning light fails to illuminate when the ignition is switched on, first check the alternator wiring connections for security. If satisfactory, check that the warning light bulb has not blown, and that the bulbholder is secure in its location in the instrument panel. If the light still fails to illuminate, check the continuity of the warning light feed wire from the alternator to the bulbholder. If all is satisfactory, the alternator is at fault and should be renewed or taken to an auto-electrician for testing and repair.
2 If the ignition warning light illuminates when the engine is running, stop the engine and check that the drivebelt is correctly tensioned (see Chapter 1) and that the alternator connections are secure. If all is so far satisfactory, have the alternator checked by an auto-electrician for testing and repair.
3 If the alternator output is suspect even though the warning light functions correctly, the regulated voltage may be checked as follows.
4 Connect a voltmeter across the battery terminals and start the engine.
5 Increase the engine speed until the voltmeter reading remains steady; the reading should be approximately 12 to 13 volts, and no more than 14 volts.
6 Switch on as many electrical accessories (eg, the headlights, heated rear window and heater blower) as possible, and check that the alternator maintains the regulated voltage at around 13 to 14 volts.

4.2 Disconnect the battery negative terminal first

7 If the regulated voltage is not as stated, the fault may be due to worn brushes, weak brush springs, a faulty voltage regulator, a faulty diode, a severed phase winding or worn or damaged slip rings. The alternator should be renewed or taken to an auto-electrician for testing and repair.

6 Alternator drivebelt - removal, refitting and tensioning

Refer to the procedure given for the auxiliary drivebelt(s) in Chapter 1.

7 Alternator - removal and refitting

Removal

1 Disconnect the battery earth (negative) lead.
2 Make a note of the electrical connections at the rear of the alternator, then disconnect the multi-plug, spade terminals or other connectors as appropriate.
3 Remove the alternator strap bolts, noting the short earth lead which links the alternator to the engine. Slacken the pivot bolt, swing the alternator towards the engine and remove the drivebelt.
4 Remove the pivot bolt and lift off the alternator. On one car examined, the pivot bolt had been inserted from the 'wrong' side so that it could not be withdrawn far enough to release the alternator: in this case it is necessary to unbolt the alternator mounting from the block.
5 Take care not to knock or drop the alternator.

Refitting

6 Refit in the reverse order to removal; tension the drivebelt as described in Chapter 1.

8 Alternator - testing and overhaul

If the alternator is thought to be suspect, it should be removed from the vehicle and taken to an auto-electrician for testing. Most auto-electricians will be able to supply and fit

brushes at a reasonable cost. However, check on the cost of repairs before proceeding as it may prove more economical to obtain a new or exchange alternator.

9 Starting system - testing

Note: *Refer to the precautions given in "Safety first!" and in Section 1 of this Chapter before starting work.*
1 If the starter motor fails to operate when the ignition key is turned to the appropriate position, the following possible causes may be to blame.
   a) *The battery is faulty.*
   b) *The electrical connections between the switch, solenoid, battery and starter motor are somewhere failing to pass the necessary current from the battery through the starter to earth.*
   c) *The solenoid is faulty.*
   d) *The starter motor is mechanically or electrically defective.*
2 To check the battery, switch on the headlights. If they dim after a few seconds, this indicates that the battery is discharged - recharge (see Section 3) or renew the battery. If the headlights glow brightly, operate the ignition switch and observe the lights. If they dim, then this indicates that current is reaching the starter motor, therefore the fault must lie in the starter motor. If the lights continue to glow brightly (and no clicking sound can be heard from the starter motor solenoid), this indicates that there is a fault in the circuit or solenoid - see following paragraphs. If the starter motor turns slowly when operated, but the battery is in good condition, then this indicates that either the starter motor is faulty, or there is considerable resistance somewhere in the circuit.
3 If a fault in the circuit is suspected, disconnect the battery leads (including the earth connection to the body), the starter/solenoid wiring and the engine/transmission earth strap. Thoroughly clean the connections, and reconnect the leads and wiring, then use a voltmeter or test lamp to check that full battery voltage is available at the battery positive lead connection to the solenoid, and that the earth is sound. Smear petroleum jelly around the battery terminals to prevent corrosion - corroded connections are amongst the most frequent causes of electrical system faults.
4 If the battery and all connections are in good condition, check the circuit by disconnecting the wire from the solenoid blade terminal. Connect a voltmeter or test lamp between the wire end and a good earth (such as the battery negative terminal), and check that the wire is live when the ignition switch is turned to the 'start' position. If it is, then the circuit is sound - if not the circuit wiring can be checked as described in Chapter 12.

5 The solenoid contacts can be checked by connecting a voltmeter or test lamp between the battery positive feed connection on the starter side of the solenoid, and earth. When the ignition switch is turned to the 'start' position, there should be a reading or lighted bulb, as applicable. If there is no reading or lighted bulb, the solenoid is faulty and should be renewed.

6 If the circuit and solenoid are proved sound, the fault must lie in the starter motor. In this event, it may be possible to have the starter motor overhauled by a specialist, but check on the cost of spares before proceeding, as it may prove more economical to obtain a new or exchange motor.

10 Starter motor - removal and refitting

Removal

1 Disconnect the battery earth lead.

1.2 litre models

2 Disconnect the battery positive leads; separate the starter motor lead from the other. Also disconnect the positive lead from the alternator.

3 Separate the gearshift linkage to improve access. Unbolt and remove the starter motor from above, disconnecting the solenoid command lead.

4 If a new starter motor is being fitted, transfer the electrical lead to it.

1.4, 1.6, 1.8 and 2.0 litre 8-valve models

5 Raise and support the front of the vehicle (see "*Jacking and Vehicle Support*").

6 Note the electrical connections to the starter solenoid, then disconnect them.

7 Unbolt the starter motor and remove it from below **(see illustration)**.

2.0 litre 16-valve models

8 Remove the starter motor-to-transmission bolts which are accessible from above.

9 Raise and support the front of the vehicle (see "*Jacking and Vehicle Support*"). Remove the inlet manifold bracing strap.

10 Disconnect the main feed and command leads from the starter motor.

11 Remove the remaining starter motor mounting bolts, not forgetting the bracket at the brushgear end of the motor. Remove the motor from below.

Refitting

12 Refitting is the reverse of the removal procedure.

11 Starter motor - testing and overhaul

If the starter motor is thought to be suspect, it should be removed from the vehicle and taken to an auto-electrician for testing. Most auto-electricians will be able to supply and fit brushes at a reasonable cost. However, check on the cost of repairs before proceeding as it may prove more economical to obtain a new or exchange motor.

12 Ignition switch - removal and refitting

Refer to Chapter 10.

13 Oil pressure warning light switch/gauge sender - removal and refitting

Removal

1 The switch/gauge sender is screwed into the cylinder block or oil filter carrier (depending on model).

2 Disconnect the battery negative lead and disconnect the wiring from the switch/sender **(see illustration)**.

3 Unscrew the switch/sender and recover the sealing washer. Be prepared for oil spillage, and if the switch is to be left removed from the engine for any length of time, plug the hole.

Refitting

4 Examine the sealing washer for signs of damage or deterioration and if necessary renew.

5 Refit the switch/sender, complete with washer, and tighten it securely. Reconnect the wiring.

6 Check and, if necessary, top-up the engine oil as described in Chapter 1.

14 Oil level sensor (16-valve models) - removal and refitting

Removal

1 Raise and support the front of the vehicle (see "*Jacking and Vehicle Support*").

2 Disconnect the battery earth (negative) lead.

3 Drain the engine oil, saving it if it is fit for re-use.

4 Follow the sensor wiring back to its connection with the main wiring harness and disconnect it. (Early type sensors have a wiring plug secured with two screws, which can be disconnected at the sensor.)

5 Remove the four screws which secure the sensor to the sump. Remove the sensor and recover the seal.

Refitting

6 Refitting is the reverse of the removal procedure. Use a new seal. Refill the engine with oil on completion.

10.7 Starter motor mounting bolts (arrowed) - engine removed for clarity

13.2 Oil pressure sender wires (arrowed)

Chapter 5 Part B:
Contact breaker ignition system

Contents

Degrees of difficulty

Easy, suitable for novice with little experience	Fairly easy, suitable for beginner with some experience	Fairly difficult, suitable for competent DIY mechanic 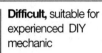	Difficult, suitable for experienced DIY mechanic	Very difficult, suitable for expert DIY or professional 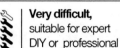

Specifications

General

Type	Distributor with mechanical contact breaker points
Firing order	1-3-4-2 (No 1 at crankshaft pulley end of engine)

Distributor

Rotational direction of rotor	Clockwise (viewed from cap)
Contact breaker points gap	0.4 mm
Dwell angle	47 to 53°
Timing*	10° BTDC (crankshaft pulley notch and timing cover rib in alignment)

Refer to text for information on usage of unleaded petrol

Ignition coil

Primary winding resistance (approximate)	1.2 to 1.6 ohm
Secondary winding resistance (approximate)	7k ohms

Torque wrench settings

	Nm	lbf ft
Spark plugs	40	30

1 General information

1 In order that the engine can run correctly it is necessary for an electrical spark to ignite the fuel/air mixture in the combustion chamber at exactly the right moment in relation to engine speed and load. The ignition system is based on feeding low tension voltage from the battery to the coil where it is converted to high tension voltage. The high tension voltage is powerful enough to jump the spark plug gap in the cylinders many times a second under high compression, providing that the system is in good condition and that all adjustments are correct.

2 The ignition system is divided into two circuits, low tension and high tension.

3 The low tension circuit (sometimes known as the primary) consists of the battery, lead to the ignition switch, lead from the ignition switch to the low tension or primary coil windings, and the lead from the low tension coil windings to the contact breaker points and condenser in the distributor.

4 The high tension circuit consists of the high tension or secondary coil winding, the heavy ignition lead from the centre of the coil to the centre of the distributor cap, the rotor arm, and the spark plug leads and spark plugs.

5 The system functions in the following manner. Low tension voltage is changed in the coil into high tension voltage by the opening and closing of the contact breaker points in the low tension circuit. High tension voltage is then fed via the carbon brush in the centre of the distributor cap to the rotor arm of the distributor cap, and each time it comes in line with one of the four metal segments in the cap, which are connected to the spark plug leads, the opening and closing of the contact breaker points causes the high tension voltage to build up, jump the gap from the rotor arm to the appropriate metal segment and so via the spark plug lead to the spark plug, where it finally jumps the spark plug gap before going to earth.

6 The ignition is advanced and retarded automatically, to ensure that the spark occurs at just the right instant for the particular load at the prevailing engine speed.

7 The ignition advance is controlled both mechanically and by a vacuum-operated system. The mechanical governor comprises two weights, which move out from the distributor shaft as the engine speed rises due to centrifugal force. As they move outwards they rotate the cam relative to the distributor shaft, and so advance the spark. The weights are held in position by two light springs and it is the tension of the springs which is largely responsible for correct spark advancement.

8 The vacuum control consists of a diaphragm, one side of which is connected via a small bore tube to the carburettor, and the other side to the contact breaker plate. Depression in the inlet manifold and carburettor, which varies with engine speed and throttle opening, causes the diaphragm to move, so moving the contact breaker plate, and advancing or retarding the spark.

9 A resistance wire in the low tension feed to the coil keeps the coil voltage down to 6V during normal running. This wire is bypassed when the starter motor is operating, to compensate for reduced battery voltage.

2 Ignition system - testing

1 By far the majority of breakdown and running troubles are caused by faults in the ignition system either in the low tension or high tension circuits.
2 There are two main symptoms indicating faults. Either the engine will not start or fire, or the engine is difficult to start and misfires. If it is a regular misfire, (ie the engine is running on only two or three cylinders), the fault is almost sure to be in the secondary or high tension circuit. If the misfiring is intermittent the fault could be in either the high or low tension circuits. If the car stops suddenly, or will not start at all, it is likely that the fault is in the low tension circuit. Loss of power and overheating, apart from faulty carburation settings, are normally due to faults in the distributor or to incorrect ignition timing.

Engine fails to start

3 If the engine fails to start and the car was running normally when it was last used, first check that there is fuel in the petrol tank. If the engine turns over normally on the starter motor and the battery is evidently well charged, then the fault may be in either the high or low tension circuits. First check the HT circuit.
4 One of the commonest reasons for bad starting is wet or damp spark plug leads and distributor. Remove the distributor cap. If condensation is visible internally dry the cap with a rag and also wipe over the leads. Refit the cap. If the engine fails to start due to either damp HT leads or distributor cap, a moisture dispersant can be very effective. To prevent the problem recurring, a proprietry damp start product can be used to provide a sealing coat, so excluding any further moisture from the ignition system. In extreme difficulty, a proprietry cold start product will help to start a car when only a very poor spark occurs.
5 If the engine still fails to start, check that voltage is reaching the plugs by disconnecting each plug lead in turn at the spark plug end, and holding the end of the cable with rubber or an insulated tool about 6 mm away from the cylinder block. Spin the engine on the starter motor. Note *Do not operate the starter system with the plug leads disconnected in any other way to that described, or damage to system components may result.*
6 Sparking between the end of the cable and the block should be fairly strong with a regular blue spark. If voltage is reaching the plugs, then remove them and clean and regap them. The engine should now start.
7 If there is no spark at the plug leads, take off the HT lead from the centre of the distributor cap and hold it to the block as before. Spin the engine on the starter once more. A rapid succession of blue sparks between the end of the lead and the block indicates that the coil is in order and that the

distributor cap is cracked, the rotor arm is faulty or the carbon brush in the top of the distributor cap is not making good contact with the spring on the rotor arm.
8 If there are no sparks from the end of the lead from the coil, check the connections at the coil end of the lead. If it is in order start checking the low tension circuit. Possibly, the points are in bad condition. Clean and reset them as described in this Chapter, Section 3.
9 Use a 12V voltmeter or a 12V bulb and two lengths of wire. With the ignition switched on and the points open, test between the low tension wire to the coil and earth. No reading indicates a break in the supply from the ignition switch. Check the connections at the switch to see if any are loose. Refit them and the engine should run. A reading shows a faulty coil or condenser, or broken lead between the coil and the distributor.
10 Take the condenser wire off the points assembly and with the points open test between the moving point and earth. If there is now a reading then the fault is in the condenser. Fit a new one and the fault is cleared.
11 With no reading from the moving point to earth, take a reading between earth and the distributor terminal of the coil A reading here shows a broken wire which will need to be replaced between the coil and the distributor. No reading confirms that the coil has failed and must be renewed, after which the engine will run once more. Remember to refit the condenser wire to the points assembly. For these tests it is sufficient to separate the points with a piece of dry paper while testing with the points open.

Engine misfires

12 If the engine misfires regularly, run it at a fast idling speed. Pull off each of the plug caps in turn and listen to the note of the engine. Hold the plug cap in a dry cloth or with a rubber glove as additional protection against a shock from the HT supply.
13 No difference in engine running will be noticed when the lead from the defective circuit is removed. Removing the lead from one of the good cylinders will accentuate the misfire.
14 Remove the plug lead from the plug which is not firing and hold it about 6 mm away from the block. Restart the engine. If the sparking is fairly strong and regular, the fault must lie in the spark plug.
15 The plug may be loose, the insulation may be cracked, or the points may have burnt away giving too wide a gap for the spark to jump. Worse still, one of the points may have broken off. Either renew the plug, or clean it, reset the gap, and then test it.
16 If there is no spark at the end of the plug lead, or if it is weak and intermittent, check the ignition lead from the distributor to the plug. If the insulation is cracked or perished, renew the lead. Check the connections at the distributor cap.

17 If there is still no spark, examine the distributor cap carefully for tracking. This can be recognised by a very thin black line running between two or more electrodes, or between an electrode and some other part of the distributor. These lines are paths which now conduct electricity across the cap thus letting it run to earth. The only answer is a new distributor cap.
18 Apart from the ignition timing being incorrect, other causes of misfiring have already been dealt with under the Selection dealing with the failure of the engine to start. To recap, these are that:
a) *The coil may be faulty giving an intermittent misfire.*
b) *There may be a damaged wire or loose connection in the low tension circuit.*
c) *The condenser may be faulty.*
d) *There may be a mechanical fault in the distributor (broken driving spindle or contact breaker spring).*
19 If the ignition timing is too far retarded, it should be noted that the engine will tend to overheat, and there will be a quite noticeable drop in power. If the engine is overheating and the power is down, and the ignition timing is correct, then the carburettor should be checked, as it is likely that this is where the fault lies.

3 Contact breaker points - gap and dwell angle adjustment

1 To adjust the contact breaker points so that the correct gap is obtained, first undo the two distributor cap retaining screws, lift off the cap and withdraw the rotor arm from the distributor shaft. At this stage it is a good idea to clean the inside and outside of the cap and inspect its condition. It is unlikely that the four segments inside the cap will be badly burned or corroded, but if they are the cap must be renewed. If only a small deposit is on the segments, it may be scraped away using a small screwdriver.
2 Push in the carbon brush located in the centre of the cap several times to ensure that it moves freely. The brush should protrude by at least 6 mm.
3 Gently prise the contact breaker points open to examine the condition of their faces. If they are rough, pitted or dirty it will be necessary to remove them to enable new points to be fitted.
4 Assuming that the points are in a satisfactory condition, or that they have been renewed, the gap between the two faces should be measured using feeler blades as follows.
5 Pull off the plug leads, after marking them to ensure correct refitment, and then remove the spark plugs.
6 With the transmission in gear and the handbrake released, slowly pull the car forward, while at the same time watching the distributor, until the heel of the contact

3.6 Checking the contact breaker points gap using a feeler blade

breaker arm is on the peak of one of the four cam lobes. A feeler blade equal to the contact breaker points gap, as given in the Specifications, should now just fit between the contact faces **(see illustration)**. Make sure that the feeler blade is clean - if the contact faces are contaminated with oil or grease, the LT current will be greatly reduced and malfunction will result.

7 If the gap varies from this amount, slacken the contact breaker plate retaining screw and move the breaker plate in or out to achieve the desired gap. The plate can be easily moved with a screwdriver inserted between the notch in the breaker plate and the two adjacent pips in the distributor baseplate.

8 When the gap is correct, tighten the retaining screw and then recheck the gap.

9 Refit the rotor arm, distributor cap, spark plugs and leads.

10 If a dwell meter is available, a far more accurate method of setting the contact breaker points gap is by measuring and setting the distributor dwell angle.

11 The dwell angle is the number of degrees of distributor cam rotation during which the contact breaker points are closed, ie the period from when the points close after being opened by one cam lobe until they are opened again by the next cam lobe. The advantages of setting the points by this method are that any wear of the distributor shaft or cam lobes is taken into account, and also the inaccuracies of using a feeler blade are eliminated. In general, a dwell meter should be used in accordance with the manufacturer's instructions. However, the use

of one type of meter is outlined as follows.

12 To set the dwell angle, remove the distributor cap and rotor arm and connect one lead of the dwell meter to the '+' terminal (15) on the coil and the other lead to the '-' terminal (1) on the coil.

13 Whilst an assistant turns on the ignition and operates the starter, observe the reading on the dwell meter scale. With the engine turning on the starter the reading should be as stated in the Specifications.

Note: *Fluctuation of the dwell meter needle indicates that the engine is not turning over fast enough to give a steady reading. If this is the case, remove the spark plugs and repeat the checks.*

14 If the dwell angle is too small, the contact breaker point gap is too wide, and if the dwell angle is excessive the gap is too small.

15 Adjust the contact breaker points gap, using the method described in paragraph 7, until the correct dwell angle is obtained.

16 When the dwell angle is satisfactory, disconnect the meter and refit the rotor arm, distributor cap and, if removed, the spark plugs and leads.

17 Check the ignition timing, as described in Section 8.

4 Contact breaker points - removal and refitting

1 When significant pitting or burning of the contact faces has occurred, the contact set should be renewed. It is not an expensive item and is worth renewing as a preventive measure at alternate service intervals, even if apparently still in good condition.

Removal

2 Undo the two distributor cap retaining screws, lift off the cap and withdraw the rotor arm from the distributor shaft **(see illustration)**.

3 Move the contact breaker arm spring blade away from the plastic insulator and slip the low tension and condenser lead terminals off the insulator **(see illustration)**.

4 Undo the retaining screw securing the contact breaker plate to the distributor baseplate and lift off the contact set **(see illustration)**.

Refitting

5 Locate the new contact set on the baseplate and refit the retaining screw.

6 Move the contact breaker spring blade away from the insulator, fit the low tension and condenser leads and allow the spring blade to slip back into place. Make sure that the leads and the blade locate squarely in the insulator.

7 Check and adjust the contact breaker points gap or dwell angle, as described in Section 3, then refit the rotor arm and distributor cap.

5 Condenser - testing, removal and refitting

Testing

1 The purpose of the condenser is to prevent excessive arcing of the contact breaker points, and to ensure that a rapid collapse of the magnetic field, created in the coil and necessary if a healthy spark is to be produced at the plugs, is allowed to occur.

2 The condenser is fitted in parallel with the contact breaker points. If it becomes faulty it will cause ignition failure, as the points will be prevented from cleanly interrupting the low tension circuit

3 If the engine becomes very difficult to start, or begins to miss after several miles of running, and the contact breaker points show signs of excessive burning, then the condition of the condenser must be suspect. A further test can be made by separating the points by hand, with the ignition switched on. If this is accomplished by an excessively strong flash, it indicates that the condenser has failed.

4 Without special test equipment, the only reliable way to diagnose condenser trouble is to renew the suspect unit and note if there is any improvement in performance. It is not an expensive component and it is worth considering periodic renewal on a preventive basis, to avoid the inconvenience entailed by failure in use.

Removal

5 To remove the condenser from its location in the distributor, undo the distributor cap retaining screws, lift off the cap and withdraw the rotor arm from the distributor shaft.

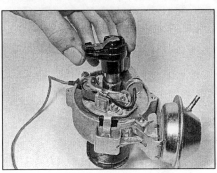

4.2 Removing the rotor arm

4.3 Slip the low tension and condenser leads out of the insulator

4.4 Undoing the points retaining screw

6.3 Ignition timing marks (arrowed) in alignment

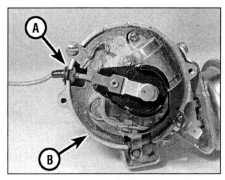

6.7 Distributor rotor position prior to refitting
A LT lead grommet   B No1 reference mark

6.8 Correct position of oil pump driveshaft prior to fitting distributor

6 Move the contact breaker arm spring blade away from the plastic insulator and withdraw the condenser lead.

7 Undo the screw securing the condenser to the distributor baseplate and lift the condenser off.

Refitting

8 Refitting is the reverse sequence to removal, but make sure that the condenser and low tension leads are securely located in the insulator behind the contact breaker arm spring blade.

6 Distributor - removal and refitting

Removal

1 Pull off the spark plug leads, after marking them to ensure correct refitment, and remove the spark plugs.

2 Undo the distributor cap retaining screws, lift off the cap and place it to one side.

3 With the transmission in gear and the handbrake released, pull the car forward until, with a finger over the plug hole, compression can be felt in No 1 cylinder (the cylinder nearest the crankshaft pulley). Continue moving the car forwards until the notch on the crankshaft pulley is in line with the raised mark on the timing cover (**see illustration**). The distributor rotor arm should now be pointing to the notch on the rim on the distributor body.

4 Disconnect the distributor low tension lead at the harness connector and detach the vacuum advance pipe from the distributor vacuum unit.

5 Undo the distributor clamp retaining bolt, lift off the clamp plate and withdraw the distributor from its location.

Refitting

6 Before refitting the distributor, check that the engine has not been inadvertently turned whilst the distributor was removed; if it has, return it to the original position, as described in paragraph 3.

7 As the distributor is refitted, the distributor shaft will rotate anti-clockwise slightly due to the meshing action of the skew gears on the distributor shaft and camshaft. To ensure that

the distributor shaft is in the correct position after fitting, ie with the rotor arm pointing towards the notch in the rim of the distributor body, set the shaft so that the rotor arm is pointing towards the low tension lead grommet in the side of the distributor body (**see illustration**), prior to fitting. As the skew gears mesh, the shaft will turn back to the correct position.

8 It is also necessary to position the oil pump driveshaft so that it engages with the slot in the distributor shaft as the distributor is inserted. The shaft should be positioned so that it is at approximately 90° to the crankshaft centreline (**see illustration**).

9 Make sure that the O-ring seal is in position at the base of the distributor and, with the shafts set as previously described, insert the distributor into its location. It may take two or three attempts to engage the oil pump driveshaft, and finish with the rotor arm pointing to the notch. If necessary move the distributor shaft very slightly one way or the other, until the correct position is achieved.

10 With the distributor in place, turn the distributor body clockwise a few degrees so that the contact breaker points are closed, and then slowly turn it anti-clockwise until they just open with the rotor arm once more pointing towards the notch in the distributor body rim. Hold the distributor in this position and refit the clamp plate and clamp bolt. Tighten the bolt securely.

11 Reconnect the low tension lead and the vacuum advance pipe. Refit the spark plugs, distributor cap and leads.

12 Refer to Section 8 and adjust the ignition timing.

7 Distributor - overhaul

1 Remove the distributor from the engine, as described in the previous Section, and then prepare a clean uncluttered working area.

2 Remove the rotor arm, ease the contact breaker arm spring blade away from the plastic insulator and slip the low tension and condenser leads off the insulator.

3 Withdraw the low tension lead grommet from the slot in the side of the distributor body (**see illustration**) and remove the lead.

4 Undo the retaining screw and lift off the contact set.

5 Undo the retaining screw and lift off the condenser (**see illustration**).

6 On the side of the distributor body, undo the two vacuum unit securing screws. Withdraw the vacuum unit and at the same time disengage the operating arm from the peg on the side of the baseplate (**see illustrations**).

7 Undo the two baseplate securing screws, noting the earth tag under one screw and the spade terminal under the other (**see illustration**). Withdraw the baseplate assembly from the distributor body.

8 This is the practical limit of dismantling of these distributors, as none of the components below the baseplate are renewable as separate items. If, however, it is necessary to remove the centrifugal advance springs and

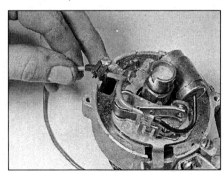

7.3 Removing the LT lead

7.5 Undoing the condenser retaining screw

7.6a Remove the vacuum unit retaining screws (arrowed) . . .

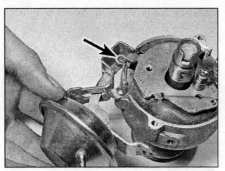

7.6b . . . and disengage the operating arm (arrowed) while withdrawing the unit

7.7 Undo the baseplate retaining screws (arrowed)

weights for cleaning or inspection, this can now be done. Mark each spring and its associated locating post with a dab of paint for identification and then carefully hook off the springs. Ensure that the springs and weights are refitted in the same positions otherwise the ignition advance characteristics of the engine will be altered. The weights can be withdrawn after extracting the small retaining clips **(see illustration)**.

9 With the distributor dismantled, clean the mechanical components in paraffin and dry with a lint-free cloth.

10 Check the condition of the contact breaker points, as described in Section 3. Check the distributor cap for corrosion of the segments and for signs of tracking, indicated by a thin black line between the segments. Make sure that the carbon brush in the centre of the cap moves freely and stands proud by at least 6 mm. Renew the cap if necessary.

11 If the metal portion of the rotor arm is badly burned or loose renew the arm. If slightly burnt, clean the arm with a fine file.

12 Check that the plates of the baseplate assembly move freely, but without excessive slackness. If defective the baseplate assembly must be renewed.

13 Suck on the end of the vacuum unit outlet and check that the operating arm moves in as the suction is applied. Release the suction and check that the arm returns to its original position. If this is not the case, renew the vacuum unit.

14 Inspect the distributor body and shaft assembly for excessive side movement of the shaft in its bushes. With the advance weights

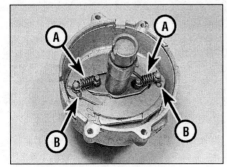

7.8 Centrifugal advance springs (A) and advance weight retaining clips (B)

and springs in position, hold the skew gear at the base of the shaft with one hand, and with the other hand turn the upper shaft clockwise as far as it will go and then release it. Check as this is done, that the advance weights move out and then return under the action of the springs. Finally check the drivegear for wear, chips or pitting of the teeth. It will be necessary to renew the complete distributor if the body, shafts, weights, springs or drivegear are worn or are in any way unsatisfactory.

15 Reassembly of the distributor is a direct reversal of the removal sequence, but apply a few drops of engine oil to the locating pivot posts of the advance weights and to the felt pad at the top of the distributor shaft. After reassembly adjust the contact breaker points, as described in Section 3, and then refit the distributor to the car, as described in Section 6.

8 Ignition timing - adjustment

Models using leaded (4-star) petrol

1 For prolonged engine life, efficient running performance and economy it is essential for the fuel/air mixture in the combustion chambers to be ignited by the spark plugs at precisely the right moment in relation to engine speed and load. For this to occur the ignition timing must be set accurately and should be checked at the intervals given in Chapter 1 or wherever the position of the distributor has been altered. To make an accurate check of the ignition timing it is necessary to use a stroboscopic timing light, whereby the timing is checked with the engine running at idling speed.

2 If the distributor has been removed, or if for any reason its position on the engine has been altered, obtain an initial setting to enable the engine to be run, as described in Section 6. Also make sure that the contact breaker points gap or dwell angle is correctly set, as described in Section 3.

3 To check the timing, first highlight the timing marks using white chalk or quick-drying paint. The marks are a notch on the crankshaft pulley and a raised mark on the timing cover **(see illustration 6.3)**. When they are aligned the engine is at the specified

number of degrees BTDC when the marks are aligned, not TDC.

4 Run the engine up to its normal operating temperature and then switch off.

5 Connect a timing light to the spark plug lead of No 1 cylinder, following the manufacturer's instructions.

6 With the engine idling, point the timing light at the timing marks. The marks will appear stationary, and if the timing is correct, they will be aligned.

7 If the marks are not aligned, slacken the distributor clamp bolts or retaining nuts and move the distributor body slowly in one direction or the other until the marks line up. Tighten the clamp bolt or retaining nuts and check that the setting has not altered.

8 Open the throttle slightly and note the movement of the timing marks. If the centrifugal advance in the distributor is working correctly the marks should appear to move away from each other as the engine speed increases. The same should happen if suction is applied to the vacuum advance pipe after disconnecting it from the carburettor, indicating that the distributor vacuum unit is satisfactory.

9 After checking the timing, switch off the engine and disconnect the timing light, if removed, refit the vacuum pipe to the carburettor.

Models using unleaded petrol

Early (pre February 1985) models

10 On models produced up to February 1985, no adjustment of the ignition timing is necessary if the vehicle is to be run on unleaded fuel (See Chapter 4A for fuel requirement).

Later (February 1985 on) models

11 All models produced after February 1985 are designed to run on unleaded, but the manufacturers state that the ignition should be retarded by 3°, to 7° BTDC.

12 The crankshaft pulley only has one timing mark (10° BTDC), so it will be necessary to make additional marks to accurately retard the ignition.

13 Turn the engine by means of the crankshaft pulley bolt, or by engaging top gear and pulling the car forward, until No 1 piston is at TDC on the firing stroke. This can be felt by removing No 1 spark plug and feeling for compression with your fingers as the engine is turned. The precise TDC point will have to be determined using a blunt probe (such as a knitting needle) inserted through No 1 spark plug hole.

14 Make a mark on the crankshaft pulley in alignment with the timing mark, or pointer, on the engine.

15 The original pulley mark indicates 10° BTDC, and the new mark TDC. Using these two markings, measure out a make a third mark on the pulley in the 7°BTDC position.

16 Using the new timing mark, adjust the ignition timing as described in paragraphs 4 to 7. If detonation occurs, it may be necessary to retard the ignition timing even further; some experimentation may be worthwhile to achieve satisfactory running.

9 Ignition HT coil - removal, testing and refitting

Removal

1 Disconnect the battery leads.
2 Disconnect the LT wiring connectors from the coil, noting there correct fitted positions.
3 Disconnect the HT lead from the coil.
4 Undo the retaining bolts and remove the coil from the car.

Testing

5 Testing of the coil consists of using a multimeter set to its resistance function, to check the primary (LT '+' to '-' terminals) and secondary (LT '+' to HT lead terminal) windings for continuity, bearing in mind that on the four output, static type HT coil there are two sets of each windings. Compare the results obtained to those given in the Specifications at the start of this Chapter. Note the resistance of the coil windings will vary slightly according to the coil temperature, the results in the Specifications are approximate values for when the coil is at 20°C.

6 Check that there is no continuity between the HT lead terminal and the coil body/mounting bracket.

7 If the coil is thought to be faulty, have your findings confirmed by a Vauxhall dealer before renewing the coil.

Refitting

8 Refitting is a reversal of the relevant removal procedure ensuring that the wiring connectors are correctly and securely reconnected.

Chapter 5 Part C:
Electronic (breakerless) ignition systems

Contents

Degrees of difficulty

Easy, suitable for novice with little experience	**Fairly easy,** suitable for beginner with some experience	**Fairly difficult,** suitable for competent DIY mechanic	**Difficult,** suitable for experienced DIY mechanic	**Very difficult,** suitable for expert DIY or professional

Specifications

General

Type	Breakerless electronic ignition system
System type:	
1.3 and 1.4 litre carburettor models	AC Delco system
1.4 and 1.6 litre fuel injection models	Multec MSTS-h Hall effect trigger, microprocessor controlled advance (integral with Multec CFi system)
1.6 litre carburettor models:	
16SH engine models	Hall effect trigger distributor
16SV engine models:	
Pre 1988 models	Inductive trigger, microprocessor controlled advance type MZV
1989 onwards models	Hall effect trigger, microprocessor controlled advance type E1 Plus (also known as EZ Plus)
1.8 litre models:	
18E engine models	Hall effect trigger distributor
18SE engine models	Inductive trigger, microprocessor controlled advance type E1 61 (formerly known as EZ 61)
2.0 litre models	Inductive trigger, microprocessor controlled advance (integral with Bosch Motronic system)
Firing order	1-3-4-2 (No 1 at timing belt end of engine)
Rotational direction of distributor rotor arm	Anti-clockwise (viewed from cap)

Ignition timing

At idle (with vacuum pipe disconnected - early models only):

1.4 litre models	5° BTDC
All other models	10° BTDC

Ignition coil

Primary winding resistance (approximate)	1.2 to 1.6 ohm
Secondary winding resistance (approximate)	7k ohms

Torque wrench settings

	Nm	lbf ft
Spark plugs	20	15

1 General information

1.3 and 1.4 litre carburettor models

On all 1.3 litre models a Delco breakerless electronic ignition system is used. The system comprises solely of the HT ignition coil and the distributor, the distributor being driven off the end of the camshaft.

The distributor contains an induction sensor (reluctor) mounted onto its shaft and an ignition module (pick-up) fixed to its body. The system operates as follows.

When the ignition is switched on but the engine is stationary the transistors in the module prevent current flowing through the ignition system primary (LT) circuit.

As the crankshaft rotates, the induction sensor moves through the magnetic field created by the module. When the teeth are in alignment with the module projections a small AC voltage is created. The module uses this voltage to switch the transistors in the unit and complete the ignition system primary (LT) circuit.

As the teeth move out of alignment with the module projections the AC voltage changes and the transistors are switched again to interrupt the primary (LT) circuit. This causes a high voltage to be induced in the coil secondary (HT) windings which then travels down the HT lead to the distributor and onto the relevant spark plug.

1.6 litre (16SH engine) models and 1.8 litre (18E engine) models

On these models a Bosch (Hall effect) ignition system is fitted. The system comprises of the HT ignition coil, the distributor and the ignition module.

The Hall effect system distributor incorporates a permanent magnet, a detector/amplifier, and four vanes. When a vane is masking the detector/amplifier no voltage is induced in the detector, and under these conditions the module passes current through the low tension windings of the coil.

Rotation of the distributor will uncover the detector and cause it to be influenced by the magnetic field of the permanent magnet. The Hall effect induces a small voltage in the detector plate which is then amplified and triggers the module to interrupt the low tension current in the coil.

The ignition module in the Hall effect system incorporates a circuit which switches off the low tension circuit if the time between consecutive signals exceeds 1.5 seconds. The coil and internal circuits are therefore protected if the ignition is left switched on inadvertently.

1.6 litre (16SV engine) models

Pre 1988 models

The MZV system is fitted to the 16SV engine in 1987 and 1988 model years. It is an electronic system in which the amount of ignition advance is controlled by a microprocessor which receives information on engine speed, temperature and load. A correction can also be applied for small changes in fuel octane rating by means of the octane rating coding plug. The initial ignition timing is still determined by distributor position. The distributor LT pulse generator is of the inductive sensor type.

A basic adjustment coding plug is provided for use when checking the initial ignition timing. When disconnected, this prevents the control unit from applying ignition advance.

1989 onwards models

The E1 Plus system (also known as EZ Plus) is a development of the MZV system. Externally the components are very similar, but the distributor LT pulses are now produced by a Hall Effect sensor instead of inductively. The microprocessor control unit incorporates a self-diagnosis facility for fault detection, but this is only accessible to Vauxhall dealers or other specialists with dedicated test equipment. The control unit also limits engine maximum speed by cutting off the LT pulses to the coil above 6000 rpm.

1.8 litre (18SE engine) models

The E1 61 system (also known as EZ 61) is fitted to all 1.8 litre engines from 1987 model year. Like the MZV and E1 Plus systems it uses a microprocessor control unit to calculate dynamic ignition advance. LT signals are derived from an inductive pulse sensor mounted on the front face of the cylinder block and a segmented disc attached to the crankshaft No 1 counterweight.

The distributor in this system serves only to distribute HT voltage to the correct cylinders. The distributor position is not adjustable and has no effect on ignition timing. The only alteration possible to the timing is by means of the octane rating coding plug.

1.4 and 1.6 litre fuel injection models

The MULTEC CFi engine management system is described in Chapter 4B. The system is regulated by an Electronic Control Unit (ECU) which is continuously supplied information from various engine, cooling system and fuel system sensors. The ECU is then able to make the necessary adjustments to the fuel and ignition systems in accordance with the continuously changing demands of the engine. The ECU also has a diagnostic function, which can be used in conjunction with special Vauxhall test equipment, for fault diagnosis in the ignition system.

With the exception of basic checks to ensure that all relevant wiring and connections are in good condition and securely connected, fault diagnosis should be entrusted to a Vauxhall dealer.

2.0 litre models

The Motronic systems are fully described in Chapter 4B. The ignition side is very similar to the E1 61 system described earlier. Again, no alteration to the timing is possible except via the octane rating plug.

The Motronic M2.5 system fitted to 16-valve models compensates for small changes in fuel octane rating automatically as part of the knock control function. The control unit contains two ignition timing 'maps', one for high octane fuel and one for lower octane. If the engine knocks frequently, the control unit switches to the low-octane map. A steady period free of knocking will cause a switch back to the high-octane map. On the C20XE engine the maps are for 91 and 95 octane fuel; on the others they are for 95 and 98 octane. 91 octane fuel must not be used in the engines which are not programmed for it.

2 Ignition system - testing

⚠ **Warning: Voltages produced by an electronic ignition system are considerably higher than those produced by conventional ignition systems. Extreme care must be taken when working on the system with the ignition switched on. Persons with surgically-implanted cardiac pacemaker devices should keep well clear of the ignition circuits, components and test equipment**

Carburettor models and 1.8 litre (18E engine) models

Note: *Refer to the warning given in Section 1 of Part A of this Chapter before starting work. Always switch off the ignition before disconnecting or connecting any component and when using a multi-meter to check resistances.*

General

1 The components of electronic ignition systems are normally very reliable; most faults are far more likely to be due to loose or dirty connections or to "tracking" of HT voltage due to dirt, dampness or damaged insulation than to the failure of any of the system's components. **Always** check all wiring thoroughly before condemning an electrical component and work methodically to eliminate all other possibilities before deciding that a particular component is faulty.

2 The old practice of checking for a spark by holding the live end of an HT lead a short distance away from the engine is not recommended; not only is there a high risk of a powerful electric shock, but the HT coil or amplifier unit will be damaged. Similarly, **never** try to "diagnose" misfires by pulling off one HT lead at a time.

Engine will not start

3 If the engine either will not turn over at all, or only turns very slowly, check the battery and starter motor. Connect a voltmeter across the battery terminals (meter positive probe to battery positive terminal), disconnect the ignition coil HT lead from the distributor cap and earth it, then note the voltage reading obtained while turning over the engine on the starter for (no more than) ten seconds. If the reading obtained is less than approximately 9.5 volts, first check the battery, starter motor and charging system as described in the relevant Sections of this Chapter.

4 If the engine turns over at normal speed but will not start, check the HT circuit by connecting a timing light (following the manufacturer's instructions) and turning the engine over on the starter motor; if the light flashes, voltage is reaching the spark plugs, so these should be checked first. If the light does not flash, check the HT leads themselves followed by the distributor cap, carbon brush and rotor arm using the information given in Chapter 1.

5 If there is a spark, check the fuel system for faults referring to the relevant part of Chapter 4 for further information.

6 If there is still no spark, check the voltage at the ignition HT coil "+" terminal; it should be the same as the battery voltage (ie, at least 11.7 volts). If the voltage at the coil is more than 1 volt less than that at the battery, check the feed back through the fusebox and ignition switch to the battery and its earth until the fault is found.

7 If the feed to the HT coil is sound, check the coil's primary and secondary winding

3.3 Crankshaft pulley timing notch (arrowed) aligned with pointer (1.3 litre model shown, others similar)

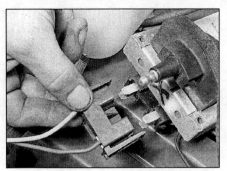

3.4 Disconnecting the distributor wiring connector at the ignition coil

3.5 Removing the distributor from the camshaft housing

resistance as described later in this Section; renew the coil if faulty, but be careful to check carefully the condition of the LT connections themselves before doing so, to ensure that the fault is not due to dirty or poorly-fastened connectors.

8 If the HT coil is in good condition, the fault is probably within the control unit or distributor assembly. Testing of these components should be entrusted to a Vauxhall dealer.

Engine misfires

9 An irregular misfire suggests either a loose connection or intermittent fault on the primary circuit, or an HT fault on the coil side of the rotor arm.

10 With the ignition switched off, check carefully through the system ensuring that all connections are clean and securely fastened. If the equipment is available, check the LT circuit as described above.

11 Check that the HT coil, the distributor cap and the HT leads are clean and dry. Check the leads themselves and the spark plugs (by substitution, if necessary), then check the distributor cap, carbon brush and rotor arm as described in Chapter 1.

12 Regular misfiring is almost certainly due to a fault in the distributor cap, HT leads or spark plugs. Use a timing light (paragraph 4 above) to check whether HT voltage is present at all leads.

13 If HT voltage is not present on any particular lead, the fault will be in that lead or

in the distributor cap. If HT is present on all leads, the fault will be in the spark plugs; check and renew them if there is any doubt about their condition.

14 If no HT is present, check the HT coil; its secondary windings may be breaking down under load.

1.8 litre (18SE engine) models and all 1.4, 1.6 and 2.0 litre fuel injection models

15 If a fault appears in the ignition system first ensure that the fault is not due to a poor electrical connection or poor maintenance; ie, check that the air cleaner filter element is clean, the spark plugs are in good condition and correctly gapped, that the engine breather hoses are clear and undamaged, referring to Chapter 1 for further information. Also check that the accelerator cable is correctly adjusted as described in the relevant part of Chapter 4. If the engine is running very roughly, check the compression pressures as described in Chapter 2.

16 If these checks fail to reveal the cause of the problem the vehicle should be taken to a suitably equipped Vauxhall dealer for testing using special diagnostic equipment. The tester will locate the fault quickly and simply alleviating the need to test all the system components individually which is a time consuming operation that carries a high risk of damaging the control unit.

17 The only ignition system checks which can be carried out by the home mechanic are

those described in Chapter 1, relating to the spark plugs, and the ignition coil test described in this Chapter. If necessary, the system wiring and wiring connectors can be checked as described in Chapter 12 ensuring that the control unit wiring connector(s) have first been disconnected.

3 Distributor - removal and refitting

Removal

1.3 and 1.4 litre carburettor models

1 Remove the spark plugs (Chapter 1).

2 Undo the distributor cap retaining screws, lift of the cap and place it to one side.

3 With the transmission in gear and the handbrake released, pull the car forwards, until, with a finger over the plug hole, compression can be felt in No 1 cylinder (the cylinder nearest the crankshaft pulley). Continue moving the car forwards until the notch on the crankshaft pulley is aligned with the timing pointer **(see illustration)**. (On automatic transmission models, turn the engine by means of a spanner on the crankshaft bolt.) If the distributor cap is temporarily placed in position, the distributor rotor should be pointing towards the No 1 spark plug lead segment in the cap.

4 Disconnect the distributor wiring connector at the ignition coil **(see illustration)**, and detach the vacuum advance pipe from the distributor vacuum unit.

5 Undo the distributor clamp retaining nut (or bolt), lift off the clamp plate, and withdraw the distributor from the camshaft housing **(see illustration)**.

1.6 litre carburettor models and 1.4, 1.6 and 1.8 litre (18E engine) fuel injection models

6 The procedure is similar to that just described in paragraphs 1 to 5, with the following differences.

 a) The wiring connector must be unplugged from the distributor, not from the coil **(see illustration)**.

 b) The distributor cap is secured by two spring clips, not by screws **(see illustration)**.

3.6a Unplugging the distributor LT connector (1.6 litre carburettor model shown)

3.6b Removing the distributor cap (1.6 litre carburettor model shown)

3.6c Removing the flash shield to expose the No 1 cylinder reference mark (arrowed) (1.6 litre carburettor model shown)

c) *There is a mark on the edge of the distributor body to indicate the rotor contact position for No 1 cylinder firing, but the rotor and flash shield must be removed to expose it* **(see illustration)**. *The rotor can then be refitted to confirm the alignment.*

d) *The distributor is secured by two nuts, not by a clamp plate. Where no mark is present make one with a scriber or dot of white paint* **(see illustration)**.

e) *The distributor drive is by means of an offset peg and hole, not by a slot and dogs* **(see illustration)**.

1.8 litre (18SE engine) models

7 Disconnect the battery leads.

8 Undo the retaining screws and remove the distributor cap from the distributor **(see illustration)**.

9 Extract the insulator. This is an interference

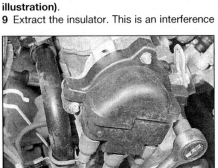

3.8 On 1.8 litre (18SE engine) models, undo the distributor cap retaining screws

3.10b . . . and remove the rotor

3.6d Removing the distributor upper securing nut (1.6 litre carburettor model shown)

fit in the housing, via an O-ring seal located in a groove on its outer edge, so ease it out of position taking great care not to damage the rotor arm **(see illustration)**.

10 Undo the two retaining screws and remove the rotor arm **(see illustrations)**.

11 If necessary, extract the rotor hub and carefully lever the oil seal out from the cylinder head **(see illustrations)**.

2.0 litre 8-valve models

12 Refer to paragraphs 7 to 11.

2.0 litre 16-valve models

13 Disconnect the battery earth (negative) lead.

14 Disconnect the Hall sensor multi-plug from the distributor **(see illustration)**.

15 Remove the spark plug lead cover and disconnect the leads from the plugs. Disconnect the HT distributor-to-coil lead

3.9 Extract the insulator

3.11a Extract the rotor hub . . .

3.6e Removing the distributor - note peg-and-hole drive (1.6 litre carburettor model shown)

from the coil or from the distributor cap.

16 Remove the two bolts which secure the distributor to the cylinder head **(see illustration)**.

17 Withdraw the distributor complete with cap and HT leads. Note how the offset peg on the distributor drive fits into the hole in the exhaust camshaft **(see illustration)**.

Refitting

1.3 and 1.4 litre carburettor models

18 Before refitting the distributor, check that the engine has not been inadvertently turned whilst the distributor was removed; if it has, return it to the original position as described in paragraph 3.

19 Position the distributor so that the rotor contact is in line with the arrow or notch in the distributor body. In this position, the offset lug on the distributor drive coupling will be in the

3.10a Undo the two Allen screws . . .

3.11b . . . and prise out the oil seal

3.14 On 2.0 litre 16-valve models, disconnect the Hall sensor wiring . . .

3.16 . . . then undo the retaining bolts . . .

3.17 . . . and remove the distributor

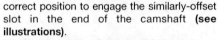

3.19a Distributor rotor contact, and arrow on distributor body (circled) in alignment . . .

3.19b . . . causing the drive coupling to be aligned like this . . .

3.19c . . . to engage the offset slot in the camshaft

correct position to engage the similarly-offset slot in the end of the camshaft (see illustrations).

20 Check that the O-ring seal is in place on the distributor body, then insert the distributor into its camshaft housing location. With the rotor contact and arrow on the distributor body still in line, refit and secure the distributor clamp.

21 Refit the distributor cap, spark plugs and leads, wiring plug and vacuum pipe.

22 Adjust the ignition timing (Section 5).

1.6 litre carburettor models and 1.4, 1.6 and 1.8 litre (18E engine) fuel injection models

23 Refer to paragraphs 18 to 22, bearing in mind the information given in paragraph 6.

1.8 litre (18SE engine) models

24 Lubricate the lips of the new seal and press the seal squarely into position in the

cylinder head, making sure its sealing lip is facing inwards. If necessary, tap the seal into position using a suitable tubular drift which bears only on its hard outer edge.

25 Carefully ease the rotor hub into position aligning its holes with the retaining bolt holes in the camshaft flange (see illustration).

26 Refit the rotor arm and securely tighten its retaining screws.

27 Fit a new O-ring to the groove in the insulator. Apply a smear of oil to aid installation and ease the insulator into position (see illustration).

28 Refit the distributor cap, making sure it is correctly located, and securely tighten its retaining screws.

2.0 litre 8-valve models

29 Refer to paragraphs 24 to 27.

2.0 litre 16-valve models

30 Refitting is the reverse of the removal

procedure. Renew the O-ring seal if necessary. The distributor can only be fitted in one position and its fixings are not slotted as it has no direct influence on the ignition timing.

4 Distributor - overhaul

1.3 and 1.4 litre carburettor models

1 Remove the distributor from the engine, as described in the previous Section.

2 Undo the two retaining screws and lift off the rotor (see illustration).

3 Disconnect the two electrical plugs, one at each end, from the ignition module (see illustration).

4 Undo the two module retaining screws (see illustration), and withdraw the unit from the distributor.

5 Undo the two vacuum unit retaining screws (see illustration), disengage the operating rod and remove the vacuum unit.

6 Due to its design and construction, this is the limit of dismantling possible on this distributor. It is possible to renew the rotor, vacuum unit, ignition module and distributor cap separately, but if inspection shows any of the components remaining on the distributor to be in need of attention, the complete distributor assembly must be renewed.

7 Check the distributor cap for corrosion of the segments, and for signs of tracking, indicated by a thin black line between the segments. Make sure that the carbon brush in

3.25 Align the camshaft and rotor hub bolt holes

3.27 Renewing the insulator sealing ring

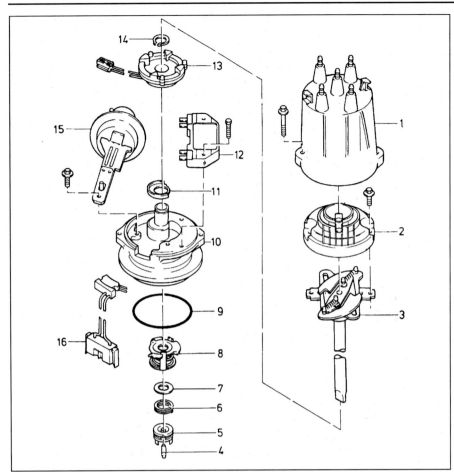

1 Distributor cap
2 Rotor
3 Shaft
4 Pin
5 Drive dog
6 Spring
7 Washer
8 Spring
9 O-ring
10 Body
11 Seal
12 Ignition module
13 Induction sensor
14 Circlip
15 Vacuum unit
16 Plug to coil

4.3 Disconnecting an electrical plug from the ignition module

the centre of the cap moves freely, and stands proud of its holder. Renew the cap if necessary.

8 If the metal portion of the rotor is badly burnt or loose, renew the rotor. If slightly burnt it may be cleaned with a fine file.

9 Suck on the end of the vacuum unit outlet, and check that the operating rod moves in as the suction is applied. Release the suction, and check that the rod returns to its original position. If this is not the case, renew the vacuum unit.

10 Inspect the distributor body and shaft assembly for excessive side movement of the shaft in its bushes. Check that the advance weights are free to move on their pivot posts,

and that they return under the action of the springs. Check the security of all the components on the distributor shaft, and finally check for wear of the lug on the drive coupling.

11 Reassembly of the distributor is the reverse sequence to dismantling, but apply a few drops of engine oil to the advance weight pivot posts before refitting the rotor. If a new ignition module is being fitted, the new module will be supplied with a small quantity of silicone grease. This should be applied between the module and its housing, to improve heat dissipation.

12 Refit the distributor as described in Section 3, after reassembly.

1.6 litre (16SH engine) and 1.8 litre (18E engine) models

13 Remove the distributor as described in Section 3.

14 Pull off the rotor arm, and unclip the flash shield **(see illustration)**.

15 Although the top bearing plate can be removed after undoing its retaining screws, this is of academic interest, since no spare parts are available, neither are there any items requiring adjustment.

16 The vacuum unit can be renewed separately if required. Remove it by undoing the two retaining screws and unhooking the operating arm from the baseplate **(see illustrations)**. Note that the screws are not of equal length; the longer screw also secures one of the distributor cap clips.

17 Test the vacuum unit, as described in paragraph 9.

18 Inspect the distributor cap and rotor, as described in paragraphs 7 and 8.

19 Reassemble the distributor in the reverse order to that followed when dismantling. Make sure that the vacuum unit operating arm is correctly engaged with the peg on the baseplate; several attempts may be needed to reconnect it.

20 Refit the distributor as described in Section 3, after reassembly.

4.4 Ignition module securing screws (arrowed)

4.5 Vacuum unit retaining screws (arrowed)

**4.14 Exploded view of the Bosch breakerless type distributor -
1.6 litre (16SH engine) and 1.8 litre (18E engine) models**

1 Vacuum unit
2 Body
3 Cap retaining clip
4 O-ring
5 Distributor cap
6 Rotor
7 Flash shield
8 Top bearing plate
9 Abutment ring

4.16a Removing a vacuum unit retaining screw

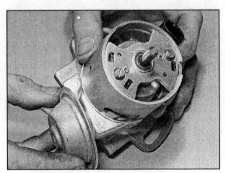

4.16b Removing the vacuum unit

1.6 (16SV engine) litre carburettor models and 1.4, 1.6 and 2.0 litre 16-valve fuel injection models

21 Overhaul of the distributor should be entrusted to a Vauxhall dealer.

1.8 litre (18SE engine) and 2.0 litre 8-valve models

22 Refer to Section 3.

5 Ignition timing - adjustment

⚠ *Warning: Voltages produced by an electronic ignition system are considerably higher than those produced by conventional ignition systems. Extreme care must be taken when working on the system with the ignition switched on. Persons with surgically-implanted cardiac pacemaker devices should keep well clear of the ignition circuits, components and test equipment*

1.3, 1.4 and 1.6 (16SH engine) litre carburettor models and 1.8 litre (18E engine) fuel injection models

Models using leaded (4-star) petrol

1 Static timing cannot be checked with the breakerless ignition system. However, if the

distributor is correctly refitted (Section 3), the timing should be accurate enough to start the engine and permit it to run.

2 Dynamic timing, using a stroboscopic timing light, is carried out as described in Part B, Section 8, paragraphs 10, 11 and 12. Note, however, that the distributor is secured by two nuts instead of a clamp bolt. Note also that on 1.4 litre models, there are two timing notches on the crankshaft pulley; the first represents 10ºBTDC and the second 5ºBTDC (see illustration).

3 Dwell angle checking and adjustment is not necessary with breakerless distributors.

Models using unleaded petrol

4 The engines used in Cavalier models are designed to run on high octane unleaded petrol.

5 On 1.3 litre (13N and 13NB engines) low compression engines, no modifications are required and the ignition timing remains unaltered. However, on all other models the manufacturers recommend that the ignition timing is adjusted in accordance with the following guidelines.

6 If detonation ("pinking" or "knock") occurs, the timing should be retarded by 3° (see Part B, Section 8). If detonation occurs, it may be necessary to retard the ignition timing even further; some experimentation may be worthwhile to achieve satisfactory running.

All other models

7 On these models the ignition timing can be checked using a stroboscopic light, but adjustment is not possible. If the ignition timing is incorrect, the car should be taken to a Vauxhall dealer for testing/adjustment (as applicable).

6 Ignition HT coil - removal, testing and refitting

Removal

1 Disconnect the battery leads.

2 Disconnect the LT wiring connectors from the coil, noting their correct fitted positions (see illustration).

3 Disconnect the HT lead from the coil. where

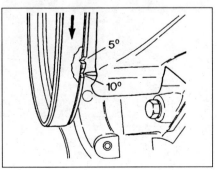

5.2 Crankshaft pulley timing marks - 1.4 litre carburettor models

6.2 Disconnecting a coil LT lead (1.8 litre model shown)

6.3 Ignition module wiring plug

6.4a Removing a coil securing bolt

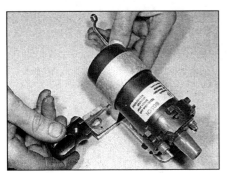

6.4b Undoing the coil clamp screw and nut

necessary, also disconnect the wiring connector from the ignition module (see illustration).

4 Undo the retaining bolts and remove the coil from the car. If necessary, undo the clamp screw and remove the coil from its mounting bracket (see illustrations).

Testing

5 Testing of the coil consists of using a multimeter set to its resistance function, to check the primary (LT '+' to '-' terminals) and secondary (LT '+' to HT lead terminal) windings for continuity, bearing in mind that on the four output, static type HT coil there are two sets of each windings. Compare the results obtained to those given in the

Specifications at the start of this Chapter. Note the resistance of the coil windings will vary slightly according to the coil temperature, the results in the Specifications are approximate values for when the coil is at 20ºC.

6 Check that there is no continuity between the HT lead terminal and the coil body/mounting bracket.

7 If the coil is thought to be faulty, have your findings confirmed by a Vauxhall dealer before renewing the coil.

Refitting

8 Refitting is a reversal of the relevant removal procedure ensuring that the wiring connectors are correctly and securely reconnected.

7 Ignition module (control unit) - removal and refitting

1.3 and 1.4 litre carburettor models

1 The ignition module is located in the distributor. See Section 4 for details.

1.6 (16SH engine) carburettor models and 1.8 litre (18E engine) fuel injection models

2 The ignition module is located on the coil mounting plate. To gain access, first remove

the coil, as described in Section 6.

3 With the coil removed from its bracket, the module can be unbolted from the mounting plate (see illustration).

4 If a new module is being fitted, it should be supplied with a small quantity of silicone grease, which must be applied to the mounting plate to improve heat dissipation (see illustration). Similar heat sink compounds can also be obtained from shops selling radio and electronic components.

5 Refit the ignition module in the reverse order to removal. Make sure that the locating pins engage with the holes in the mounting plate.

1.6 litre (16SV engine) carburettor models and 1.8 litre (18SE engine) fuel injection models

6 The ignition control unit is located in the engine compartment where it is mounted onto the suspension strut turret. To remove the unit, first disconnect the battery leads.

7 Release the spring retaining tangs and disconnect the wiring connector (see illustration).

8 Undo the retaining screws and remove the unit from its mounting bracket.

9 Refitting is the reverse of removal

1.4 and 1.6 fuel injection models and all 2.0 litre models

10 Refer to Chapter 4.

7.3 Unbolting the ignition module (1.8 litre model shown)

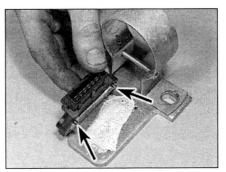

7.4 Ignition module and mounting plate - note locating pins (arrowed), and heat sink compound on baseplate (1.8 litre model)

7.7 Disconnecting the control unit wiring plug - later 1.8 litre model

Chapter 6
Clutch

Contents

Degrees of difficulty

Easy, suitable for novice with little experience	Fairly easy, suitable for beginner with some experience	Fairly difficult, suitable for competent DIY mechanic	Difficult, suitable for experienced DIY mechanic	Very difficult, suitable for expert DIY or professional

Specifications

Type . . . . Single dry plate with diaphragm spring. Cable actuation

Adjustment
Pedal stroke:
   Desired value . . . . 138 mm
   Permitted . . . . 129 to 145 mm

Torque wrench settings

	Nm	lbf ft
Clutch cover to transmission casing	7	5
Clutch pressure plate to flywheel	15	11
Release fork clamp bolt	35	26
Transmission end cover plug:		
4-speed	50	37
5-speed	30	22

1 General information

All models covered by this manual are fitted with a single plate diaphragm spring clutch which is enclosed in a pressed steel cover bolted to the flywheel. The gearbox input shaft projects through the clutch and is located at its forward end in a needle roller spigot bearing within the centre of the crankshaft.

The clutch driven plate is located between the flywheel and the clutch pressure plate and it can slide on splines on the gearbox input shaft. When the clutch is engaged, the diaphragm spring forces the pressure plate to grip the driven plate against the flywheel and drive is transmitted from the crankshaft, through the driven plate, to the gearbox input shaft. On disengaging the clutch the pressure plate is lifted to release the driven plate with the result that the drive to the gearbox is disconnected.

The clutch is operated by a foot pedal suspended under the facia and a cable connected to the clutch release lever mounted on the clutch bellhousing. Depressing the pedal causes the release lever to move the thrust bearing against the release fingers of the diaphragm spring in the pressure plate assembly. The spring is sandwiched between two rings which act as fulcrums. As the centre of the spring is moved in, the periphery moves out to lift the pressure plate and disengage the clutch. The reverse takes place when the pedal is released.

As wear takes place on the driven plate with usage, the foot pedal will rise progressively relative to its original position. Periodic adjustment is not required.

An unusual feature of the design of this particular clutch is that the driven plate, release bearing and seal can be renewed without having to remove either the engine or the transmission from the car.

2 Clutch - adjustment

1 Clutch adjustment is not a routine operation; it should only be necessary after the cable or pressure plate has been renewed. In use the clutch pedal will rise relative to the brake pedal as the clutch linings wear: this is normal and is not a reason for adjustment as long as the pedal stroke remains correct.
2 To perform the initial adjustment after component renewal, proceed as follows.
3 With the clutch pedal released, take a measurement from the outer edge of the steering wheel to the centre of the clutch pedal pad and record the dimension. Now take a second measurement with the clutch pedal fully depressed. These measurements can be taken using a suitable strip of wood or metal as the important figure is the difference between the two measurements, that is the

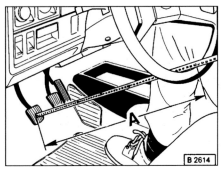

2.3a Clutch pedal released measurement (A)

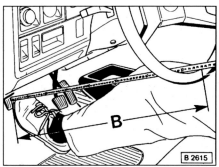

2.3b Clutch pedal depressed measurement (B)

Refitting

4 When refitting, coat the pedal shaft with a 'dry' lubricant (molybdenum disulphide paste, copper-based anti-seize compound, or equivalent).

5 Refit the pedal and spring and secure the shaft. Reconnect the clutch cable and check the adjustment, as described in the previous Section.

5 Clutch - removal, inspection and refitting

⚠️ *Warning: Dust created by clutch wear and deposited on the clutch components may contain asbestos which is a health hazard DO NOT blow it out with compressed air or inhale any of it. DO NOT use petrol or petroleum based solvents to clean off the dust. Brake system cleaner or methylated spirit should be used to flush the dust into a suitable receptacle. After the clutch components are wiped clean with rags, dispose of the contaminated rags and cleaner in a sealed, marked container.*

Removal

1 A good feature of these models is that of being able to renew the clutch pressure plate, the driven plate, the release bearing, the release pivot bushes and the clutch seal without having to remove either the engine or the transmission.

2 Although the maker's procedure requires the use of special tools, these are not essential and the work can be carried out using the tools normally available to the home mechanic.

3 Some of the operations are best carried out by working under the front of the vehicle, so apply the handbrake fully, jack up the front of the vehicle and support securely on axle stands (see "*Jacking and Vehicle Support*"). Bolt and remove the flywheel housing cover plate from the base of the clutch bellhousing.

4 On early models (up to approximately mid-1988), unscrew and remove the plug from the transmission casing end cover. On later models there is no plug in the end cover. On these models, unscrew the nut and disconnect the earth lead from the end cover. Position a suitable container beneath the end cover then undo the retaining bolts, noting each ones correct fitted location as it is removed, and remove the casing end cover and gasket from the transmission **(see illustrations)**.

5 Extract the circlip, now exposed, from the end of the input shaft using a pair of circlip pliers.

6 Underneath the circlip is a socket-headed (12-point) screw, which will require a 12-point splined key to extract it. Motor accessory tool shops usually stock this type of key. Remove the screw **(see illustrations)**.

---

movement (stroke) of the pedal itself **(see illustrations)**. This should be within the limits given in the Specifications. If adjustment is necessary, it is done at the release lever end.

4 To carry out the adjustment, first remove the spring clip from the threaded end of the cable at the release lever. Pull the end of the cable to gain some slack and turn the adjuster as necessary until the desired pedal stroke is obtained. Refit the spring clip when adjustment is correct **(see illustration)**.

5 Note that when correctly adjusted the clutch pedal will be slightly higher than the brake pedal and it is incorrect for the two pedals to be in alignment. Note also that there should be no play in the clutch pedal of these vehicles.

3 Clutch cable - removal and refitting

Removal

1 Before disturbing the clutch cable installation, take a measurement of the length of the threaded end of the cable protruding through the cable adjuster at the clutch release lever. This will enable an initial adjustment setting to be made when refitting the cable.

2 Remove the spring clip, slacken the cable adjuster and slip the cable out of the release lever slot. Move the cable assembly rearwards and withdraw it from the lug on the transmission casing.

2.4 Removing the spring clip from the clutch cable

---

3 Remove the cable from the support bracket behind the engine and, where applicable, release any clips or ties securing the engine wiring harness to the clutch cable.

4 If necessary to improve access, remove under-facia trim on the driver's side.

5 Unhook the return spring from the clutch pedal and disconnect the cable from the pedal lever **(see illustration)**.

6 The cable can now be withdrawn into the engine compartment by pulling it through the bulkhead.

Refitting

7 Refitting the clutch cable is the reverse sequence to removal. Position the cable adjuster initially so that the same amount of cable protrudes through the adjuster as noted during removal, then adjust the clutch, as described in Section 2.

4 Clutch pedal - removal and refitting

Removal

1 Disconnect the clutch cable from the release lever and from the pedal, as described in the previous Section.

2 Remove the wire locking clip from the pedal shaft retaining nut. Remove the nut and washers from the shaft.

3 Push the pedal shaft nut out of the pedal bush. Recover the return spring and remove the pedal.

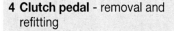

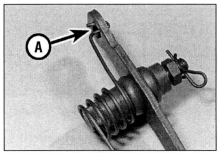

3.5 Clutch pedal components assembled as when in place on the vehicle. Clutch cable is retained by return spring (A) - shown with pedal removed for clarity

5.4a Threaded plug in transmission end cover (arrowed) (4-speed transmission)

5.4b Unscrewing threaded plug (4-speed transmission)

5.4c On later models, remove the transmission end cover to gain access to the input shaft end

7 The shaft can now be slid out of engagement with the splined hub of the clutch driven plate. To do this, the makers provide a special tool, but an effective substitute is to remove one of the four bolts which secure the

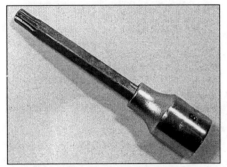

5.6a Splined key for removing 12-point socket-head screws

gearchange mechanism cover to the top of the transmission case. Using this bolt as a pattern, obtain one similar, but of at least 40 mm in length. Screw the bolt into the end of the input shaft and use the bolt to pull the shaft out of its stop. Refit the bolt to the cover on the transmission case. On some 5-speed transmissions, it is not unknown for the input shaft to be very tight, in which event it may prove difficult to withdraw it without using the special tool or a puller of some sort. In extreme cases a slide hammer will have to be attached to the end of the shaft to enable it to be withdrawn **(see illustrations)**.

8 Before the clutch can be removed the pressure plate must be compressed against the tension of the diaphragm spring, otherwise the clutch assembly will be too thick to pass through the space between the flywheel and the edge of the bellhousing when withdrawing it.

9 The vehicle makers can supply three special clamps (KM526) for this job, but substitutes can be made up from strips of 3 mm thick steel strip. The clamps should be U-shaped with a distance of approximately 15 mm between the inner faces of each side of the clamp **(see illustration)**.

10 Bevel the edges of the clamps to make it easier to fit them. Have an assistant depress the clutch pedal fully and then fit each clamp securely over the edge of the clutch cover/plate assembly engaging them in the apertures spaced around the rim of the clutch cover. Turn the crankshaft by means of the pulley bolt to bring each clip location into view.

11 Once the clips have been fitted, release the clutch pedal.

12 Progressively loosen and remove each of the six bolts which hold the clutch cover to the flywheel **(see illustration)**.

5.6b Removing the input shaft screw

5.7a Screwing bolt into input shaft

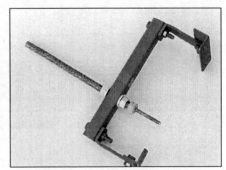

5.7b If the input shaft is tight, fabricate a tool similar to that shown . . .

5.7c . . . to disengage the shaft from the clutch

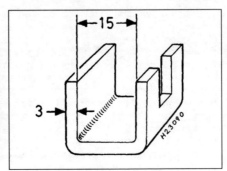

5.9 Clutch pressure plate retaining clamp dimensions - in mm

5.12 Unscrewing clutch cover bolts

13 Although positioning dowels are not used to locate the clutch cover to the flywheel, the coloured spot on the flywheel should be in alignment with the notch in the rim of the clutch cover.

14 Withdraw the clutch assembly downwards and out of the bellhousing. The pressure plate can be compressed in a vice in order to be able to remove the clips **(see illustration)**.

Inspection

15 In the normal course of events, clutch dismantling and reassembly involves simply fitting a new clutch pressure plate, driven plate and release bearing. Under no circumstances should the diaphragm spring clutch unit be dismantled. If a fault develops in the pressure plate assembly, a new or exchange replacement unit must be fitted.

16 Do not attempt to reline a driven plate yourself, it is just not worth it, but obtain a new component. The necessity for renewing the plate will be apparent if the lining material has worn down to the rivets or the linings are oil stained. If the latter, rectify the faulty engine or transmission oil seal which must be the cause. The driven plate may also have broken torsion springs or worn hub splines.

17 If a new clutch is being fitted, it is false economy not to renew the release bearing at the same time (see Section 6). This will preclude having to replace it at a later date.

18 Check the machined faces of the flywheel and the pressure plate. If either is badly grooved it should be machined until smooth, or replaced with a new item. If the pressure plate is cracked or split it must be renewed.

Refitting

19 Some clutch assemblies are supplied already compressed with the retaining clips fitted. If this is not the case, the pressure plate should be compressed evenly in a vice; using protectors to prevent damage to the machined face of the plate. Alternatively, use a heavy bolt and nut with two metal strips having a hole drilled in them to do the job. Fit the clips.

20 Apply a smear of molybdenum disulphide grease to the splines of the driven plate hub and then offer the plate to the flywheel so that the greater projecting side of it is away from the flywheel. Hold the plate against the flywheel while the clutch pressure plate assembly (compressed) is offered into position.

21 Push the input shaft through the hub of the driven plate and engage its end in the pilot bearing in the end of the crankshaft. Note that it is not permissible to use hammer blows to assist in refitting the input shaft.

22 If the input shaft cannot be pushed home by hand, steady pressure should be exerted by means of a screw or hydraulic device. The special tool KM-564, is produced expressly for the purpose, but it should be possible to press the shaft into position using the

5.14 Removing clutch with retaining clips fitted

improvised tool (or something similar) shown in **illustration 5.7c**. If the shaft is hammered home, transmission damage may result.

23 Bolt the clutch cover to the flywheel and tighten them to the specified torque.

24 Have your assistant depress the clutch pedal and then remove the temporary clips.

25 To the end of the input shaft, screw in the recessed screw and fit a new circlip.

26 On early models screw the plug into the transmission end cover, on four-speed transmissions apply a smear of sealant to the plug threads prior to installation. Tighten to the specified torque noting that the plug should not project more than 4.0 mm from the face of the end cover when correctly fitted.

27 On later models, ensure that the end cover and transmission mating surfaces are clean and dry and fit a new gasket. Refit the cover and screw in the retaining bolts, making sure each one is fitted in its original location. Tighten the bolts evenly and progressively to the specified torque setting then reconnect the earth strap and securely tighten its retaining nut.

28 Check the clutch adjustment (Section 2).

29 Fit the cover plate to the flywheel housing.

30 Lower the front of the vehicle to the ground and check the transmission oil level as described in Chapter 1.

6 Clutch release bearing, lever, bushes and seal - removal and refitting

Removal

1 Wear of the clutch release bearing is indicated by a squealing noise when the clutch pedal is depressed with the engine running.

2 To gain access to the release bearing it is necessary first to remove the clutch unit as described in Section 5.

3 After removing the clutch unit, undo the clamp bolt securing the release fork to the release lever pivot shaft. Disconnect the clutch cable from the release lever, see Section 3 for details if necessary, and then pull the release lever pivot shaft up and out of the housing and remove the release fork. Unscrew the three bolts securing the release

bearing guide to the transmission and remove the guide. Prise the old (input shaft) seal out of the release bearing guide location. If required, the bushes supporting the release lever pivot can be drifted out of the case using a suitable drift **(see illustrations)**.

Refitting

4 Refitting is the reverse of the removal procedure but the following points should be noted:

a) *After fitting a new input shaft seal to the release bearings guide fill the space between the lips of the seal with a good quality general purpose grease*

b) *When fitting the new O-ring seal to the casing at the release bearing guide location do not use any grease or oil as this seal should be fitted dry.*

c) *Lightly smear the release bearing guide surface, on which the bearing slides with molybdenum disulphide grease and tighten the bolts securely.*

d) *If being renewed, drift the new release lever bushes into their housings, ensure that their locating tongues are engaged in the slots in the case, and coat the inner surfaces of the bushes with molybdenum disulphide grease.*

e) *Fit the release bearing and the release fork together and tighten the release fork clamp bolt to the specified torque.*

f) *Refit the clutch as described in Section 5.*

g) *Check the adjustment as described in Section 2.*

6.3a Release lever shaft bushes

6.3b Clutch release bearing

Chapter 7 Part A:
Manual transmission

Contents

Degrees of difficulty

Easy, suitable for novice with little experience	Fairly easy, suitable for beginner with some experience	Fairly difficult, suitable for competent DIY mechanic	Difficult, suitable for experienced DIY mechanic	Very difficult, suitable for expert DIY or professional

Specifications

Type . . . . Four or five forward speeds (all with synchromesh) and reverse. Unit transversely mounted at front of car

Designation

1.2, 1.3 and 1.4 litre models	F10.4, F10.4W, F10.5 or F10.5W
1.6 litre models:	
Early models	F16.4W or F16.5W
Later models	F13.4, F13.5 or F13.5CR
1.8 litre models	F16.4W, F16.5W or F16.5C
2.0 litre models:	
8-valve models	F16.5W or F16.5C
16-valve models	F20.5CR

Note: *Four-speed transmissions have the suffix.4 and five-speed transmissions the suffix.5.*

Oil type/specification . . . . Gear oil, viscosity SAE 80EP, or GM gear oil 90 188 629

Oil capacity

F10.4 and F13.4	1.7 litres approx
F10.5, F13.5 and F20.5	1.8 litres approx
F16.4	2.0 litres approx
F16.5	2.1 litres approx

Torque wrench settings

	Nm	lbf ft
Differential cover plate bolts:		
4-speed transmission	30	22
5-speed transmission:		
Early (pre 1988) models	30	22
Later (1988 onwards) models	18	13
Transmission housing-to-engine bolts	75	55
Exhaust bracket to transmission casing	60	44
Mounting bracket bolts to transmission	30	22
Mounting bolts to bodyframe	40	29
Reverse lamp switch	20	15

1 General information

The transmission is contained in a cast-aluminium alloy casing bolted to the engine's left-hand end, and consists of the gearbox and final drive differential - often called a transaxle.

Drive is transmitted from the crankshaft via the clutch to the input shaft, which has a splined extension to accept the clutch friction plate, and rotates in sealed ball-bearings. From the input shaft, drive is transmitted to the output shaft, which rotates in a roller bearing at its right-hand end, and a sealed ball-bearing at its left-hand end. From the output shaft, the drive is transmitted to the differential crownwheel, which rotates with the differential case and planetary gears, thus driving the sun gears and driveshafts. The rotation of the planetary gears on their shaft allows the inner roadwheel to rotate at a slower speed than the outer roadwheel when the car is cornering.

The input and output shafts are arranged side by side, parallel to the crankshaft and driveshafts, so that their gear pinion teeth are in constant mesh. In the neutral position, the output shaft gear pinions rotate freely, so that drive cannot be transmitted to the crownwheel.

Gear selection is via a floor-mounted lever and selector rod mechanism. The selector rod causes the appropriate selector fork to move its respective synchro-sleeve along the shaft, to lock the gear pinion to the synchro-hub. Since the synchro-hubs are splined to the output shaft, this locks the pinion to the shaft, so that drive can be transmitted. To ensure that gear-changing can be made quickly and quietly, a synchro-mesh system is fitted to all forward gears, consisting of baulk rings and spring-loaded fingers, as well as the gear pinions and synchro-hubs. The synchro-mesh cones are formed on the mating faces of the baulk rings and gear pinions.

2 Transmission - draining and refilling

1 Since transmission oil draining and refilling is not specified by Vauxhall as a routine service operation, the transmission is regarded as a sealed unit and therefore has no drain plug. If, for any reason, it is wished to drain the oil, the differential cover plate must be removed as follows.
2 From underneath the vehicle, remove all traces of dirt from around the transmission differential cover plate.
3 Position a suitable container beneath the plate then slacken and remove the retaining bolts and allow the oil to drain into the container. Remove the cover plate and recover the gasket.
4 Once all the oil has drained, remove all traces of oil and dirt from the mating surfaces of the cover plate and transmission.

5 Fit a new gasket to the plate and refit the plate to the transmission. Tighten the plate retaining bolts evenly and progressively to the specified torque setting.
6 Fill the transmission with the specified type and quantity of oil via the breather/filler plug and check the oil level (see Chapter 1).

3 Gearchange lever - removal and refitting

Removal

1 Remove the centre console, when fitted, as described in Chapter 11. Put the gear lever in neutral.
2 Peel back the rubber boot from the base of the gear lever.
3 On 4-speed models, remove the circlip from the gear lever. Push the lever to the left and remove it.
4 On 5-speed models, it is probably best to remove the four screws which hold the gear lever housing to the floor, then remove the lever and housing complete. Check that spares are available before attempting to separate the housing components.

Refitting

5 Refit in the reverse order to removal, lubricating the contact surfaces with silicone grease.

4 Gearchange lever reverse blocker cable - removal and refitting

Removal

1 The reverse blocker mechanism prevents inadvertent selection of reverse gear. It is released by lifting the collar under the gear lever knob: this collar is connected to the top of a cable, the bottom end of which is attached to a finger or rod If the cable breaks it may be renewed as follows, but check first that spare parts are available.
2 Remove the gear lever, as described in Section 3. Pull the knob from the gear lever, first heating the knob in boiling water. Even after heating, it is likely that the knob will be

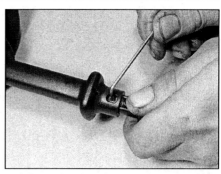

4.3 Removing a grub screw from the gear lever

destroyed during removal. Extract the spring from below the knob.
3 Remove the grub screw from the top of the gear lever. These may have a plain slotted head or a recessed hexagon head **(see illustration)**.
4 Drive out the roll pins which secure the plastic coupling and shift finger to the base of the gear lever **(see illustration)**. It is likely that the plastic coupling will be damaged. Remove the cable and its end fitting.

Refitting

5 Refit in the reverse order to removal. No adjustment procedure is laid down for the cable: experiment with the grub screws which clamp the top of the cable until a satisfactory result is obtained.

5 Gearchange linkage - removal, refitting and adjustment

Removal

1 Slacken the pinch-bolt on the gearchange rod coupling.
2 Remove the screws which hold the gearchange rod protective tube to the underbody. Pull back the rubber cover and disengage the eye in the intermediate lever from the base of the gearchange lever **(see illustration)**.
3 Withdraw the linkage from the vehicle. Remove the rubber cover and bellows from the protective tube.

4.4 Drive out the roll pins

5.2 Protective boot at base of gear lever

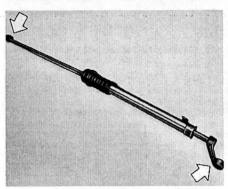

5.8 Intermediate lever to clamp alignment - arrowed

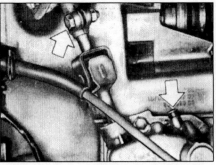

5.13 Transmission adjuster hole and clamp pinch-bolt - arrowed

5.14 Setting gearchange rod (shown with casing removed for clarity)

4 To dismantle the linkage, drive out the roll pin which secures the intermediate lever to the rod, then tap the rod out of the lever. The rod can then be removed from the protective tube.
5 The universal joint may be dismantled by grinding or filing off the rivet heads. Special pins and spring clips should be available for reassembly from your GM dealer, but check that this is so before destroying the rivets.
6 The bushes can be removed from the protective tube by driving them out with a rod.

Refitting

7 When reassembling, fill the grooves in the tube bushes with silicone grease before fitting.
8 Use a new roll pin to secure the intermediate lever to the rod making sure it is aligned as shown **(see illustration)**.
9 Fit the rubber cover and the bellows, applying silicone grease to their inner surfaces. Do not twist the bellows after installation.
10 Offer the linkage to the car, engaging the intermediate lever with the gearchange lever, and secure it with the screws. Refit the rubber cover around the base of the lever.
11 Adjust the linkage, as follows.

Adjustment

12 Remove the centre console, if fitted, as described in Chapter 11. Put the gear lever in the neutral position.
13 Working in the engine bay, prise out the adjuster hole plug and slacken the pinch-bolt

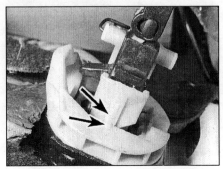

5.15 Alignment marks for neutral on lever and housing - arrowed

on the gearchange rod coupling **(see illustration)**.
14 Turn the selector rod protruding from the selector cover in an anti-clockwise direction (looking towards the front of the car) until a twist drill of diameter 4.5 mm can be inserted into the adjuster hole and into the correspondence hole in the selector lever **(see illustration)**.
15 Pull the rubber boot up from the base of the gear lever and move the lever, still in neutral, to the 1st/2nd gear plane. In this position the reference marks on the stop sleeve and lever housing will be aligned **(see illustration)**.
16 Have an assistant hold the gear lever in this position. Tighten the gearchange coupling pinch-bolt.
17 Remove the drill from the adjuster hole. Check that all gears can be engaged satisfactorily, then fit a new adjuster hole plug.
18 Refit the gear lever boot and (if applicable) the centre console.

6 Oil seals - renewal

Driveshaft oil seal

1 Position a suitable container beneath the transmission to catch any oil which may leak from the transmission during the following operation.
2 Working as described in Chapter 8, free the inner end of the driveshaft from the

7.4 Reverse lamp switch

transmission and position it clear of the seal, noting that there is no need to unscrew the driveshaft retaining nut; the driveshaft can be left secured to the hub. Support the driveshaft to avoid placing any strain on the driveshaft joints or gaiters.
3 Carefully prise the oil seal out of the transmission using a large flat-bladed screwdriver.
4 Remove all traces of dirt from the area around the oil seal aperture then apply a smear of grease to the outer lip of the new oil seal. Fit the new seal into its aperture and drive it squarely into position using a suitable tubular drift (such as a socket) which bears only on the hard outer edge of the seal, until it abuts its locating shoulder.
5 Refit the driveshaft (see Chapter 8).
6 Check and, if necessary top-up, the transmission oil level as described in Chapter 1.

Input shaft oil seal

7 Refer to Chapter 6, Section 6.

7 Reversing lamp switch - testing, removal and refitting

Testing

1 The reversing lamp circuit is controlled by a plunger-type switch that is screwed into the top of the transmission casing. If a fault develops in the circuit first ensure that the circuit fuse has not blown.
2 To test the switch, disconnect the wiring connector and use a multimeter (set to the resistance function) or a battery and bulb test circuit to check that there is continuity between the switch terminals only when reverse gear is selected. If this is not the case and there are no obvious breaks or other damage to the wires, the switch is faulty and must be renewed.

Removal

3 To improve access to the switch, remove the battery as described in Chapter 5.
4 Disconnect the wiring connector(s) from the switch then unscrew it from the transmission casing and remove it along with its sealing washer **(see illustration)**.

Refitting

5 Fit a new sealing washer to the switch then screw it back into position in the top of the transmission housing and tighten it to the specified torque setting. Reconnect the wiring connector(s) then refit the battery and test the operation of the circuit.

8 Speedometer drive - removal and refitting

Removal

1 Disconnect the speedometer cable from the transmission by unscrewing its knurled retaining ring.
2 Undo the retaining bolt and recover the speedometer drive retaining plate from the transmission housing.
3 Withdraw the speedometer drive assembly from the transmission.
4 Slide the drive gear out from its housing and remove the O-ring and seal from the housing.

Refitting

5 Press a new seal into the housing and fit a new O-ring to the housing groove. Apply a smear of oil to the seal and O-ring and slide the drive gear into position.
6 Refit the assembly to the transmission, making sure the drive gear engages correctly.
7 Refit the retaining plate, making sure it is correctly engaged with the drive gear, and securely tighten its retaining bolt.
8 Reconnect the speedometer cable.

9 Transmission - removal and refitting

Removal

1 Disconnect the battery earth lead.
2 Disconnect the clutch cable from the release lever (Chapter 6).
3 Disconnect the leads from the reversing lamp switch.
4 Disconnect the speedometer cable, or sender unit, at the transmission **(see illustration)**.

9.4 Disconnecting the speedometer cable

5 Slacken the gearchange rod coupling pinch-bolt and separate the coupling.
6 Remove the three bolts which secure the top of the transmission casing to the engine.
7 Slacken the front wheel bolts, raise and securely support the front of the vehicle (see "*Jacking and Vehicle Support*") and remove the front wheels.
8 It is now necessary to support the engine from above, either with a bar and hook braced across the engine bay, or with a crane or similar engine lifting tackle. Attach the tackle and adjust it to take the weight of the engine.
9 Unbolt the earth strap from the transmission end cover.
10 Disconnect the central arm balljoints on both sides.
11 Separate the driveshafts from the transmission, as described in Chapter 8. Be prepared for oil spillage. Plug the driveshaft apertures to reduce spillage and to keep out dirt.
12 Withdraw the clutch input shaft, as described in Chapter 6.
13 Remove the engine/transmission left-hand mounting completely.
14 Unbolt the engine/transmission rear mounting from the underframe. Also unbolt the exhaust pipe bracket.
15 Unbolt the clutch access plate, then remove the remaining engine-to-transmission bolts.
16 Withdraw the transmission from its dowels on the engine and lower it to the ground. Ideally a cradle and hydraulic jack should be used.
17 Take care not to damage projecting components when setting the transmission down. It should be stored in the same position it assumes in use.

Refitting

18 Commence refitting by offering the transmission to the engine, engaging the dowels and fitting the retaining bolts. Tighten the bolts to the specified torque.
19 Clean out the rear mounting bolt holes with a tap, or an old bolt with a slot nut in its threads. Fasten the rear mounting using new bolts coated with thread locking compound. Tighten the bolts to the specified torque.
20 Refit the left-hand mounting bracket and tighten its fastenings to the specified torque.
21 Refit the driveshafts, as described in Chapter 8.
22 Reconnect the control arm balljoints, tightening their securing nuts to the specified torque see Chapter 10.

23 Refit the clutch input shaft, as described in Chapter 6. Fit and tighten the end cover plug.
24 Secure the earth strap to the end cover.
25 Disconnect the engine support tackle, refit the roadwheels and lower the car to the ground. Tighten the wheel bolts.
26 Reconnect the speedometer cable, the reversing lamp switch and the clutch cable. Adjust the clutch cable, as described in Chapter 6.
27 Reconnect the gearchange rod coupling. Adjust the linkage, as described in Section 5, and tighten the pinch-bolt.
28 Refill the transmission with oil, as described in Section 2.

10 Transmission overhaul - general information
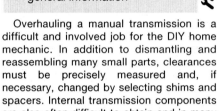

Overhauling a manual transmission is a difficult and involved job for the DIY home mechanic. In addition to dismantling and reassembling many small parts, clearances must be precisely measured and, if necessary, changed by selecting shims and spacers. Internal transmission components are also often difficult to obtain and in many instances, extremely expensive. Because of this, if the transmission develops a fault or becomes noisy, the best course of action is to have the unit overhauled by a specialist repairer or to obtain an exchange reconditioned unit.

Nevertheless, it is not impossible for the more experienced mechanic to overhaul the transmission if the special tools are available and the job is done in a deliberate step-by-step manner so that nothing is overlooked.

The tools necessary for an overhaul include internal and external circlip pliers, bearing pullers, a slide hammer, a set of pin punches, a dial test indicator and possibly a hydraulic press. In addition, a large, sturdy workbench and a vice will be required.

During dismantling of the transmission, make careful notes of how each component is fitted to make reassembly easier and accurate.

Before dismantling the transmission, it will help if you have some idea what area is malfunctioning. Certain problems can be closely related to specific areas in the transmission which can make component examination and replacement easier. Refer to the Fault diagnosis Section for more information.

Chapter 7B:
Automatic transmission

Contents

Degrees of difficulty

| Easy, suitable for novice with little experience | | Fairly easy, suitable for beginner with some experience | | Fairly difficult, suitable for competent DIY mechanic |  | Difficult, suitable for experienced DIY mechanic | | Very difficult, suitable for expert DIY or professional | |

Specifications

Type	General Motors Hydromatic Torque converter (fluidcoupling) with chain drive to gear trains. Three forward and one reverse gear
Designation	125 THM

Torque wrench settings	Nm	lbf ft
Fluid pan bolts	16	12
Fluid cooling hose connections to transmission	38	28
Fluid pipe bracket	24	18
Kickdown cable bracket	10	7
Torque converter housing-to-engine bolts	75	55
Selector lever to shaft	27	20
Torque converter-to-driveplate bolts:		
1.3 litre models	65	48
All other models	60	44
Fluid cooling hose to cooler	22	16
Mounting bracket bolts to transmission	22	16
Mounting bolts to bodyframe	40	30

1 General information

The automatic transmission is of General Motors design and manufacture and is optionally available on most models. The unit provides three forward speeds and reverse with a "kickdown" facility. As with manual transmission, the differential and final drive are built into the transmission casing.

The main components are a torque converter (fluid coupling), which transmits power to the gear trains through a chain drive, and a hydraulic circuit which regulates the selection of gears, clutches and brakes according to speed and engine load. Due to the close tolerances to which the unit operates, cleanliness is absolutely essential whenever fluid is being added or any component removed. Entry of grit or dirt into the transmission will cause a malfunction of the valves and possible damage to the internal components.

The automatic transmission is a complex piece of equipment and the home mechanic should limit himself to undertaking the operations described in the following Sections. More extensive operations should be left to your dealer or automatic transmission specialist.

2 Kickdown cable - removal, refitting and adjustment

Removal

1 Remove the air cleaner (see Chapter 4).
2 Disconnect the kickdown cable for the carburettor by pulling the clip from the support bracket and prising the ball end fitting from the ball-stud on the lever **(see illustration)**.
3 At the transmission end, remove the locking bolt from the cable sleeve, pull the sleeve upwards and disconnect the inner cable.
4 Release the cable adjusting mechanism from the support bracket by depressing the lugs.

Refitting

5 Fit the new cable by reversing the removal operations, then adjust it as follows.

Adjustment

6 Check that there is a small amount of slack in the accelerator cable with the pedal released. Adjust if necessary at the accelerator pedal stop screw.
7 Have an assistant depress the accelerator pedal slowly until it just contacts the kickdown switch. In this position the throttle plate in the carburettor must be wide open. Adjust if necessary at the carburettor end of the cable.
8 Have the assistant press the accelerator pedal beyond the kickdown detent to the floor. The ratchet of the self-adjusting mechanism should be heard to operate, confirming that adjustment has taken place.
9 No further adjustment of the cable is necessary.
10 Release the accelerator pedal and refit the air cleaner.

3 Speed selector control cable - removal, refitting and adjustment

Removal

1 Disconnect the battery earth lead.
2 Detach the selector lever surround by unscrewing and drawing back the centre console, removing the reflective strip and slot covering from the surround, and disengaging the surround from the console and the selector lever. Pull off the lamp base as the surround is withdrawn.
3 Disconnect the cable inner and outer components from the selector lever **(see illustration)**.
4 At the transmission, disconnect the cable inner by removing its retaining ring. Release the cable outer from its support **(see illustration)**.
5 Draw the cable into the engine bay and remove it. Installation of the new cable may be

simplified if a piece of string is drawn out by the end of the old cable, and used in fitting the new one.

Refitting and adjustment

6 When fitting the new cable, set the selector lever and the lever on the transmission in position P. Fit the cable so that it is neither taut nor slack.
7 Check that all positions can be engaged, and that the selector lever on the transmission is positively positioned in its correct detent and not under any tension in any position. Adjust if necessary at the console end.
8 Refit the remaining components in the reverse order to removal.

4 Starter inhibitor/reversing lamp switch - removal and refitting

Removal

1 Disconnect the battery earth lead.
2 Detach the selector lever surround, as described in Section 3.
3 Remove the two screws which secure the switch.
4 Detach the green/white cable from the selector illumination lamp base.
5 Strip back the wiring harness outer covering by about 10 cm, then cut the wiring harness. Deal with the wiring harness or the new switch in a similar fashion. Remove the old switch.

Refitting

6 Fit the new switch. Connect the wires using proprietary cable connectors or a terminal block, making sure that only wires of the same colour are joined together. All joints must be insulated.
7 Temporarily reconnect the battery. Switch on the ignition and check that the reversing lamps come on only in position 'R', and that the engine can be started only in position P and N. No provision is made for adjustment, but minor misalignment may be corrected by packing up one end of the switch with washers.

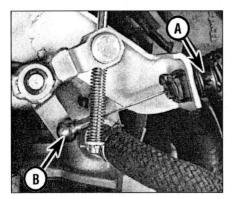

2.2 Kickdown cable connection at carburettor

A Cable adjuster   B Ball cap end fitting

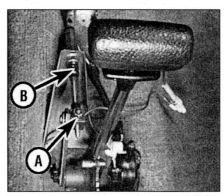

3.3 Selector cable attachment at hand control lever

A Clamp   B Sleeve

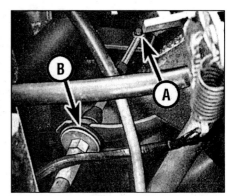

3.4 Selector cable retaining clip (A) and support (B)

8 Disconnect the battery, refit the selector lever surround and reconnect the battery.

5 Automatic transmission - removal and refitting

Removal

1 Disconnect the battery earth lead.
2 Remove the air cleaner, as described in Chapter 4.
3 Disconnect the earth strap from the transmission end cover.
4 Disconnect the kickdown cable at the carburettor end, then unbolt it from the transmission see Section 2.
5 Release the selector cable inner from the selector lever on the transmission, then unbolt the cable bracket. There is no need to remove the cable from the bracket.
6 Disconnect the speedometer cable from the transmission.
7 Remove the top three bolts which secure the transmission to the engine. Note that the centre bolt also secures a coolant pipe bracket.
8 Slacken the front wheel bolts, raise and securely support the front of the car (see "*Jacking and Vehicle Support*") and remove the front wheels.
9 Support the engine from above, either with a bar and adjustable hook braced across the engine bay, or with a crane or similar engine lifting tackle. Adjust the tackle to take the weight of the engine.
10 Disconnect the control arm balljoints on both sides.
11 Separate the driveshafts from the transmission, as described in Chapter 8. Be prepared for some fluid spillage. Plug the driveshaft apertures and tie the driveshafts up out of the way.

12 On models so equipped, disconnect and plug the oil cooler lines at the transmission. Be prepared for fluid spillage.
13 Remove the cover from the bottom of the torque converter housing .
14 Remove the screws which secure the torque converter to the flexplate, turning the engine as necessary to bring the screws into view.
15 Remove the remaining transmission-to-engine bolts.
16 Unbolt the engine/transmission rear mounting from the body. Also unbolt the exhaust bracket.
17 Support the transmission with a trolley jack, preferably using a cradle to spread the load and to stop it falling.
18 Remove the engine/transmission left-hand mounting completely.
19 Remove the two bolts which hold the transmission to the engine mounting bracket.
20 Carefully move the transmission away from the engine, lower it and withdraw it from below the vehicle. If the dipstick/oil filler tube gets in the way, it can be removed before the transmission is withdrawn, but be prepared to catch the considerable amount of fluid which will be released .
21 If the transmission is to be renewed, remember to salvage the mounting brackets and the oil cooler unions.

Refitting

22 Refit the transmission in the reverse order to removal, observing the following points.
  a) *Before offering the transmission to the engine, check that the torque converter is correctly meshed with the oil pump. To do this, measure dimension A. This should be between 9.00 and 10.00 mm. If it is not, rotate the converter, at the same time applying hand pressure, until it meshes with the pump* **(see illustration)**.

b) *Apply a smear of molybdenum disulphide paste, or other 'dry' lubricant, to the torque converter pilot spigot and to the corresponding recess in the tail of the crankshaft.*
c) *When bolting the torque converter to the flexplate, align the coloured spot on the converter as closely as possible with the white spot on the flexplate. Note that there will be a small clearance (0.4 to 1.5 mm) between the converter and the flexplate until the bolts are tightened. Tighten the bolts progressively to the specified torque.*
d) *Transmissions with codes EF and EK are not intended to have an oil cooler connected; do not attempt to uncap the cooler connection points.*
e) *Adjust the speed selector and kickdown cables, as described in Sections 2 and 3.*
f) *Fill the transmission with fluid, as described in Chapter 1.*

6 Automatic transmission overhaul - general information

In the event of a fault occurring on the transmission, it is first necessary to determine whether it is of an electrical, mechanical or hydraulic nature and to do this special test equipment is required. It is therefore essential to have the work carried out by a Vauxhall dealer if a transmission fault is suspected.

Do not remove the transmission from the car for possible repair before professional fault diagnosis has been carried out, since most tests require the transmission to be in the vehicle.

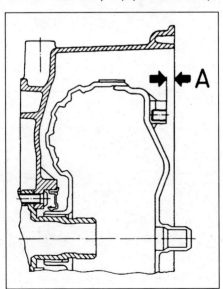

5.22 Torque converter installation diagram
A = 9. to 10. mm

Notes

Chapter 8
Driveshafts

Contents

Degrees of difficulty

Easy, suitable for novice with little experience	**Fairly easy,** suitable for beginner with some experience	**Fairly difficult,** suitable for competent DIY mechanic	**Difficult,** suitable for experienced DIY mechanic	**Very difficult,** suitable for expert DIY or professional

Specifications

Torque wrench settings	Nm	lbf ft
Driveshaft nut:		
Stage 1	100	74
Fully slacken the nut then tighten to:		
Stage 2	20	15
Stage 3*	Tighten through a further 90°	
Damper weight - right-hand driveshaft	10	7
Control arm balljoint pin nut	70	52
Roadwheel bolts	90	66

Turn nut back if necessary to align split pin hole. Do not tighten to align

1 General information

Drive is transmitted from the differential to the front wheels by means of two solid steel driveshafts of unequal length. The right-hand driveshaft is longer than the left-hand due to the position of the transmission. The longer right-hand shaft carries a damper weight to decrease vibration.

Both driveshafts are splined at their outer ends to accept the wheel hubs and are threaded so that each hub can be fastened by a large nut. The inner end of each driveshaft is splined to accept the differential sun gear.

Constant velocity (CV) joints are fitted to each end of the driveshafts to ensure that the smooth and efficient transmission of drive at all the angles possible as the roadwheels move up and down with the suspension, and as they turn from side to side under steering. Both inner and outer constant velocity joints are of the ball-and-cage type.

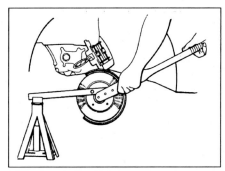

2.2 Undoing a driveshaft nut

2.4a Home made tool for releasing driveshafts

2.4b Releasing a driveshaft from the differential

2 Driveshaft - removal and refitting

Removal

1 Slacken the front wheel bolts on the side concerned, raise and support the front of the vehicle (see "*Jacking and Vehicle Support*") and remove the roadwheel.

2 Extract the split pin from the driveshaft retaining nut, then unscrew the nut using a socket and bar. Prevent the driveshaft from turning by having an assistant apply the footbrake hard, or by bolting a suitably drilled steel bar to the hub **(see illustration)**. Remove the nut and retrieve the washer.

3 Separate the control arm balljoint, as described in Chapter 10.

4 The driveshaft must now be released from the transmission. The makers specify a variety of tools for the different transmissions: they are wide metal forks with a good chamfer on the leading edge. A similarly chamfered bar, a tyre lever or even a large blunt screwdriver may serve instead. Drive the tool into the gap between the joint and the casing to release the circlip from the differential side gear **(see illustrations)**. A good blow will be needed to jar the circlip out of its groove. In exceptionally difficult cases it will be necessary to remove the differential cover plate and apply a flat chisel to the inboard end of the shaft.

5 On automatic transmission models only, the right-hand driveshaft should be released by means of a non-ferrous (soft metal) drift applied to the joint casing.

6 Once the circlip has been released, pull the joint out of the transmission by hand. Some oil or ATF will be spilt, so have a container handy. If possible, plug the hole to keep dirt out.

7 It should now be possible to push the outboard end of the shaft out of the splines in the hub **(see illustration)**. If this cannot be done by hand, it is best to use a screw or hydraulic pusher bolted to the hub. Blows from a soft-faced mallet will also work, but there is a risk of damage to the CV joint and/or hub bearing.

8 Note that, with the driveshaft removed from the hub, the two halves of the hub bearing are no longer positively located. **The vehicle must not be moved on its wheels in this state, or the bearing will be damaged.** If it is essential to move the vehicle without the driveshaft fitted, clamp the bearing with a dummy shaft or some stout studding, nuts and washers.

9 Do not allow a serviceable driveshaft to rest on its gaiter for long periods, or they may become permanently distorted.

Refitting

10 Before refitting the driveshaft, make sure that the contact faces of the outer CV joint and the hub bearing are perfectly clean. Check the condition of the circlip on the differential end of the shaft and renew it if its condition is suspect **(see illustrations)**.

11 Lubricate the shaft splines at the hub end with gear oil and insert the shaft into the hub. Fit a new washer and a new nut. Only tighten the nut finger tight at this stage.

12 Insert the inner end of the shaft in the transmission. Push it in by hand as far as it will go. Drive the joint home using a screwdriver or drift applied to the bead of the weld around the joint (not to the metal cover) until the circlip snaps into place **(see illustrations)**. Check that the circlip is home by pulling on the outer part of the CV joint. It is not possible to check for secure engagement by pulling on the shaft.

13 Reconnect the control arm balljoint, tighten its nut to the specified torque and secure with a new split pin.

14 Tighten the driveshaft nut to the Stage 1 specified torque. Back it off and retighten to the Stage 2 torque. Tighten the nut further through the angle specified for Stage 3.

15 Secure the nut with a new split pin. If the split pin holes are not aligned, back off the nut until they are - **do not** tighten it further to align.

16 If the damper weight on the right-hand shaft has been disturbed, make sure it is secured at the correct distance from the outboard gaiter **(see illustration)**.

2.7 Removing the driveshaft from the hub

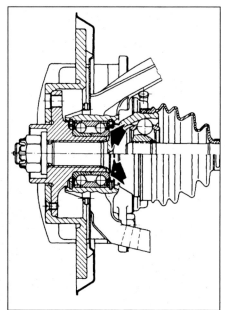

2.10a Sectional view of hub and driveshaft. Contact faces (arrowed) must be clean

2.10b Driveshaft circlip (arrowed) at differential end

2.12a Inserting a driveshaft into the transmission

17 Refit the roadwheels, lower the car and tighten the wheel bolts. Check the transmission oil level and top-up as necessary (Chapter 6).

3 Driveshaft gaiters - renewal

1 Remove the driveshaft (Section 2).
2 Remove the metal clips securing the gaiter to the driveshaft and constant velocity joint **(see illustration)**. Fold the gaiter back and slide it along the driveshaft to expose the internal components of the joint.
3 Secure the driveshaft in a vice, spread the retaining circlip with circlip pliers and tap the joint off the shaft using a soft-faced mallet **(see illustrations)**.
4 With the constant velocity joint removed, the gaiter can now be slid off the end of the driveshaft. If both are to be removed, the other one can be withdrawn from the same end of the driveshaft without having to remove the other joint.
5 Thoroughly clean away all traces of the old grease from the constant velocity joint using paraffin or a suitable solvent. Obtain new gaiter, new retaining clips and a suitable quantity of the special lubricating grease from a GM dealer.
6 Slide the gaiter onto the shaft until the smaller diameter engages with the groove on the shaft.
7 Wrap the small metal clip around the gaiter and, pulling the clip as tight as possible, engage the lug on the end of the clip with one

3.2 Driveshaft inboard joint showing gaiter clips (arrowed)

2.12b Securing a driveshaft joint to the transmission

of the slots. Use a screwdriver if necessary to push the clip as tight as possible before engaging the lug and slot. Now finally tighten the clip by compressing the raised square portion of the clip with pincers or pliers.
8 Fold the gaiter back and engage the constant velocity joint with the driveshaft splines. Using a soft-faced mallet, tap the joint onto the shaft until the circlip engages with its groove.
9 Fill all the spaces in the joint with the special lubricating grease, moving the joint around at the same time. Apply a liberal quantity of grease and make sure it enters all the spaces and cavities between the joint members.
10 Fold the gaiter back over the joint, making sure the larger diameter fits over the retaining clip groove in the joint outer diameter.
11 Expel all air from the gaiter and then fit the large retaining clip using the same procedure as for the small one.
12 The driveshaft can now be refitted to the car, as described in Section 2.

4 Driveshaft joint - renewal

All the information for joint renewal will be found in Section 3. A worn joint cannot be repaired, but must be renewed complete. **Note:** *If driveshaft joint wear is apparent on a vehicle that has covered in excess of 60 000 miles (100 000 km), the manufacturer recommends that the complete driveshaft assembly is renewed.*

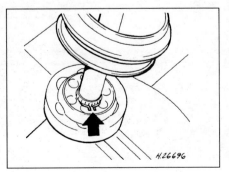

3.3a Driveshaft joint retaining circlip (arrowed)

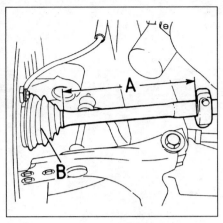

2.16 Driveshaft damper weight distance (A) from end of gaiter (B)
A = 260 mm

5 Driveshaft overhaul - general information

If any of the checks described in Chapter 1 reveal wear in any driveshaft joint, first remove the roadwheel trim or centre cap (as appropriate).
If the split pin is in position, the driveshaft nut should be correctly tightened. If in doubt remove the split pin then slacken the nut and tighten it through all the stages listed in the Specifications at the start of this Chapter. Once tightened, secure the nut in position with a new split pin then refit the centre cap or trim. Repeat this check on the remaining driveshaft nut.
Road test the vehicle and listen for a metallic clicking from the front as the vehicle is driven slowly in a circle on full lock. If a clicking noise is heard this indicates wear in the outer constant velocity joint. This means that the joint must be renewed; reconditioning is not possible.
If vibration, consistent with road speed, is felt through the car when accelerating, there is a possibility of wear in the inner constant velocity joints.
To check the joints for wear, remove the driveshafts, then dismantle them as described in Section 3; if any wear or free play is found, the affected joint must be renewed.

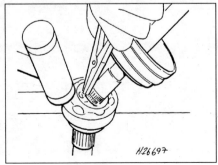

3.3b Tapping joint from the driveshaft

Notes

Chapter 9
Braking system

Contents

Degrees of difficulty

Easy, suitable for novice with little experience		**Fairly easy,** suitable for beginner with some experience		**Fairly difficult,** suitable for competent DIY mechanic		**Difficult,** suitable for experienced DIY mechanic		**Very difficult,** suitable for expert DIY or professional	

Specifications

Front brakes

Type	Disc, with single piston sliding caliper
Disc diameter:	
2.0 litre models	256 mm
All other models	236 mm
Disc thickness:	
New:	
1.2 and 1.3 litre Saloon and Hatchback models	10.0 mm
1.3 litre Van and Estate models	12.7 mm
1.6 litre models	12.7 mm
1.8 litre models	20.0 mm
2.0 litre models	24.0 mm
Minimum thickness (after refinishing*):	
1.2 and 1.3 litre Saloon and Hatchback models	8.0 mm
1.3 litre Van and Estate models	10.7 mm
1.6 litre models	10.7 mm
1.8 litre models	18.0 mm
2.0 litre models	22.0 mm
Brake pad thickness (including backing plate):	
New	15.5 to 15.9 mm
Minimum	7.0 mm

When this dimension is reached, only one more set of brake pads are permissible, then renew the discs

Rear brakes

Type:	
2.0 litre GTE models	Disc, with twin piston caliper
All other models	Single leading shoe drum
Drum diameter:	
New:	
Pre 1989 models:	
Hatchback and 1.3 litre Estates with manual transmission	200 mm
All other Estate models and all Vans	230 mm
1989 onwards models (all models)	200 mm

Rear brakes (continued)

Drum diameter (continued):

Maximum diameter:

Pre 1989 models:

Hatchback and 1.3 litre Estates with manual transmission .... 201 mm

All other Estate models and all Vans . . . . 231 mm

1989 onwards models (all models) . . . . 201 mm

Maximum drum out-of-round . . . . 0.1 mm

Minimum friction material-to-rivet head depth . . . . 0.5 mm

Disc diameter . . . . 260 mm

Disc thickness:

New . . . . 10.0 mm

Minimum thickness (after refinishing*) . . . . 8.0 mm

Brake pad thickness (including backing plate):

New . . . . 15.0 mm

Minimum . . . . 7.0 mm

*When this dimension is reached, only one more set of brake pads are permissible, then renew the discs

Torque wrench settings

	Nm	lbf ft
Bleed screws	9	7
Brake pipe/hose union	25	18
Front brake caliper:		
GMF caliper:		
Mounting bracket bolts	95	70
Caliper to mounting bracket bolts	95	70
ATE caliper:		
Mounting bracket bolts	95	70
Slide bolts	30	22
Rear brake caliper mounting bolts	60	44
Wheel cylinder mounting bolt	9	7
Master cylinder mounting nuts	18	13
Wheel cylinder hydraulic union	11	8
Pressure regulating valve:		
Rear axle mounted valve - Estate and Van	20	15
Master cylinder mounted valve:		
GMF cylinder	40	30
ATE cylinder	12	9
Master cylinder stop screw (ATE)	6	4
Servo to bracket	18	13
Servo bracket to bulkhead	18	13
Rear brake backplate bolts (use thread-locking compound)	30	22
Handbrake lever bolts	20	15
ABS components:		
Hydraulic unit to bracket bolts	8	6
Front wheel speed sensor bolt	8	6
Rear wheel speed sensor bolt	15	11

1 General description

The footbrake operates on all four wheels. On 2.0 litre GTE models disc brakes are fitted at both the front and rear, and on all other models, disc brakes are fitted at the front and self-adjusting drums at the rear. On all models, actuation is hydraulic with servo assistance.

The hydraulic system is split into two circuits, each circuit acting on one front and one diagonally opposite rear brake. In the event of rupture of the hydraulic system in one circuit, the remaining circuit will still function so that some braking capability remains. In such a case the pedal travel will increase and greater effort will be needed.

The hydraulic supply to the rear brakes is regulated so that the front brakes always lock first under heavy braking. On Hatchback models the regulation is by pressure-sensitive valves screwed into the master cylinder; on Estate and Van models the valve is load-sensitive and is located near the rear axle, by whose movement it is modulated.

The brake servo is of the direct-acting type, fitted between the pedal and the master cylinder. It is powered by vacuum developed in the inlet manifold. Should the servo fail, the brakes will still operate, but increased pedal pressure will be required.

The handbrake provides an independent mechanical means of rear brake application. On 2.0 litre GTE models the handbrake operates a set of brake shoes, the shoes act on the brake drum which is incorporated inside the rear disc. On all other models, the handbrake provides a mechanical means of operating the brake shoes.

Depending on operating territory and equipment level, warning lights may be fitted to indicate low brake fluid level, handbrake application and brake pad wear. Sometimes one warning light has a dual function: refer to the owner's handbook for details.

Note: *When servicing any part of the system, work carefully and methodically; also observe scrupulous cleanliness when overhauling any part of the hydraulic system. Always renew components (in axle sets, where applicable) if in doubt about their condition, and use only genuine Vauxhall/Opel replacement parts, or at least those of known good quality. Note the warnings given in 'Safety first' and at relevant points in this Chapter concerning the dangers of asbestos dust and hydraulic fluid.*

2 Hydraulic system - bleeding

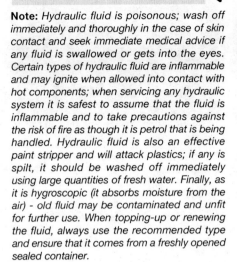

Note: *Hydraulic fluid is poisonous; wash off immediately and thoroughly in the case of skin contact and seek immediate medical advice if any fluid is swallowed or gets into the eyes. Certain types of hydraulic fluid are inflammable and may ignite when allowed into contact with hot components; when servicing any hydraulic system it is safest to assume that the fluid is inflammable and to take precautions against the risk of fire as though it is petrol that is being handled. Hydraulic fluid is also an effective paint stripper and will attack plastics; if any is spilt, it should be washed off immediately using large quantities of fresh water. Finally, as it is hygroscopic (it absorbs moisture from the air) - old fluid may be contaminated and unfit for further use. When topping-up or renewing the fluid, always use the recommended type and ensure that it comes from a freshly opened sealed container.*

General

1 The correct operation of any hydraulic system is only possible after removing all air from the components and circuit; this is achieved by bleeding the system.
2 During the bleeding procedure, add only clean, unused hydraulic fluid of the recommended type; never re-use fluid that has already been bled from the system. Ensure that sufficient fluid is available before starting work.
3 If there is any possibility of incorrect fluid being already in the system, the brake components and circuit must be flushed completely with uncontaminated, correct fluid and new seals should be fitted to the various components.
4 If hydraulic fluid has been lost from the system, or air has entered, because of a leak ensure that the fault is cured before proceeding further.
5 Park the vehicle on level ground, switch off the engine and select first or reverse gear, then chock the wheels and release the handbrake.
6 Check that all pipes and hoses are secure, unions tight and bleed screws closed. Clean any dirt from around the bleed screws.
7 Unscrew the master cylinder reservoir cap and top the master cylinder reservoir up to the `MAX` level line; refit the cap loosely and remember to maintain the fluid level at least above the `MIN` level line throughout the procedure or there is a risk of further air entering the system.
8 There are a number of one-man, do-it-yourself brake bleeding kits currently available from motor accessory shops. It is recommended that one of these kits is used whenever possible as they greatly simplify the bleeding operation and also reduce the risk of expelled air and fluid being drawn back into the system. If such a kit is not available the

basic (two-man) method must be used which is described in detail below.
9 If a kit is to be used, prepare the vehicle as described previously and follow the kit manufacturer's instructions as the procedure may vary slightly according to the type being used; generally they are as outlined below in the relevant sub-section.
10 Whichever method is used, the same sequence must be followed (paragraphs 11 and 12) to ensure that the removal of all air from the system.

Bleeding sequence

11 If the system has been only partially disconnected and suitable precautions were taken to minimise fluid loss, it should be necessary only to bleed that part of the system (ie. the primary or secondary circuit).
12 If the complete system is to be bled, then it should be done in the following sequence.

Non ABS models

a) Left-hand rear brake.
b) Right-hand front brake.
c) Right-hand rear brake.
d) Left-hand front brake.

Models equipped with ABS

a) Left-hand front brake.
b) Right-hand front brake.
c) Left-hand rear brake.
d) Right-hand rear brake.

Bleeding - basic (two-man) method

13 Collect a clean glass jar, a suitable length of plastic or rubber tubing which is a tight fit over the bleed screw and a ring spanner to fit the screw. The help of an assistant will also be required.
14 Remove the dust cap from the first screw in the sequence. Fit the spanner and tube to the screw, place the other end of the tube in the jar and pour in sufficient fluid to cover the end of the tube.
15 Ensure that the master cylinder reservoir fluid level is maintained at least above the `MIN` level line throughout the procedure.
16 Have the assistant fully depress the brake pedal several times to build up pressure, then maintain it on the final stroke.
17 While pedal pressure is maintained, unscrew the bleed screw (approximately one turn) and allow the compressed fluid and air to flow into the jar. The assistant should maintain pedal pressure, following it down to the floor if necessary and should not release it until instructed to do so. When the flow stops, tighten the bleed screw again, release the pedal slowly and recheck the reservoir fluid level.
18 Repeat the steps given in paragraphs 16 and 17 until the fluid emerging from the bleed screw is free from air bubbles. If the master cylinder has been drained and refilled and air is being bled from the first screw in the sequence, allow approximately five seconds between cycles for the master cylinder passages to refill.

19 When no more air bubbles appear, tighten the bleed screw securely, remove the tube and spanner and refit the dust cap. Do not overtighten the bleed screw.
20 Repeat the procedure on the remaining screws in the sequence until all air is removed from the system and the brake pedal feels firm again.

Bleeding - using a one-way valve kit

21 As their name implies, these kits consist of a length of tubing with a one-way valve fitted to prevent expelled air and fluid being drawn back into the system; some kits include a translucent container which can be positioned so that the air bubbles can be more easily seen flowing from the end of the tube.
22 The kit is connected to the bleed screw, which is then opened. The user returns to the driver's seat and depresses the brake pedal with a smooth, steady stroke and slowly releases it; this is repeated until the expelled fluid is clear of air bubbles.
23 Note that these kits simplify work so much that it is easy to forget the master cylinder reservoir fluid level; ensure that this is maintained at least above the `MIN` level line at all times.

Bleeding - using a pressure bleeding kit

24 These kits are usually operated by the reservoir of pressurised air contained in the spare tyre, although note that it will probably be necessary to reduce the pressure to a lower limit than normal; refer to the instructions supplied with the kit.
25 By connecting a pressurised, fluid-filled container to the master cylinder reservoir, bleeding can be carried out simply by opening each screw in turn (in the specified sequence) and allowing the fluid to flow out until no more air bubbles can be seen in the expelled fluid.
26 This method has the advantage that the large reservoir of fluid provides an additional safeguard against air being drawn into the system during bleeding.
27 Pressure bleeding is particularly effective when bleeding `difficult' systems or when bleeding the complete system at the time of routine fluid renewal.

All methods

28 On completion, when firm pedal feel is restored, wash off any spilt fluid, tighten the bleed screws securely and refit the dust caps.
29 Check the hydraulic fluid level and top-up if necessary (Chapter 1).
30 Discard any hydraulic fluid that has been bled from the system; it will not be fit for re-use.
31 Check the feel of the brake pedal. If it feels at all spongy, air must still be present in the system and further bleeding is required. Failure to bleed satisfactorily after a reasonable repetition of the bleeding procedure may be due to worn master cylinder seals.

3 Hydraulic pipes and hoses - renewal

Note: *Before starting work, refer to the note at the beginning of Section 2 concerning the dangers of hydraulic fluid.*

1 If any pipe or hose is to be renewed, minimise fluid loss by removing the master cylinder reservoir cap and then tightening it down onto a piece of polythene to obtain an airtight seal. Alternatively flexible hoses can be sealed, if required, using a proprietary brake hose clamp, while metal brake pipe unions can be plugged (if care is taken not to allow dirt into the system) or capped immediately they are disconnected. Place a wad of rag under any union that is to be disconnected to catch any spilt fluid.

2 If a flexible hose is to be disconnected, unscrew the brake pipe union nut before removing the spring clip which secures the hose to its mounting bracket.

3 To unscrew the union nuts it is preferable to obtain a brake pipe spanner of the correct size; these are available from most large motor accessory shops. Failing this a close-fitting open-ended spanner will be required, though if the nuts are tight or corroded their flats may be rounded-off if the spanner slips. In such a case a self-locking wrench is often the only way to unscrew a stubborn union, but it follows that the pipe and the damaged nuts must be renewed on reassembly. Always clean a union and surrounding area before disconnecting it. If disconnecting a component with more than one union make a careful note of the connections before disturbing any of them.

4 If a brake pipe is to be renewed it can be obtained, cut to length and with the union nuts and end flares in place, from Vauxhall/Opel dealers. All that is then necessary is to bend it to shape, following the line of the original, before fitting it to the car. Alternatively, most motor accessory shops can make up brake pipes from kits, but this requires very careful measurement of the original to ensure that the replacement is of the correct length. The safest answer is usually to take the original to the shop as a pattern.

4.4a Removing an anti-rattle spring

5 On refitting, do not overtighten the union nuts. It is not necessary to exercise brute force to obtain a sound joint.

6 Ensure that the pipes and hoses are correctly routed with no kinks and that they are secured in the clips or brackets provided. After fitting, remove the polythene from the reservoir and bleed the hydraulic system as described in Section 2. Wash off any spilt fluid and check carefully for fluid leaks.

4 Front brake pads - renewal

 Warning: Renew both sets of front brake pads at the same time - never renew the pads on only one wheel as uneven braking may result. Note that the dust created by wear of the pads may contain asbestos, which is a health hazard. Never blow it out with compressed air and don't inhale any of it. An approved filtering mask should be worn when working on the brakes. DO NOT use petroleum-based solvents to clean brake parts. Use brake cleaner or methylated spirit only.

1 Raise the front of the vehicle (see "*Jacking and Vehicle Support*"). If the roadwheels have been balanced on the vehicle (new vehicles are balanced this way in production) then mark the relative position of the roadwheel to the hub so that it can be aligned correctly when refitting.

4.4b Wear warning sensor clipped to pad

2 Inspect the thickness of the friction material on each pad. If any one is at or below the specified minimum, renew the pads as an axle set (four pads) in the following way.

GMF and early ATE type caliper

3 Drive out the pad retaining pins by applying a punch to their inboard ends.

4 Remove the springs and, where necessary, remove the pad wear warning sensor from the pad **(see illustrations)**.

5 Using a pair of pliers, withdraw the outboard pad **(see illustration)**.

6 Remove the inboard pad. If it is very tight, move the pad sideways slightly to depress the caliper piston **(see illustration)**.

7 In order to accommodate the new thicker pads, the caliper piston must be depressed fully into its cylinder using a flat bar of metal such as a tyre lever. The action of depressing the piston will cause the fluid in the reservoir to rise, so anticipate this by syphoning some off using an old (clean) hydrometer or similar.

8 Brush out the jaws of the caliper, *taking care not to inhale the dust.*

9 Insert the pads, making sure that the lining side is against the disc. When fitting disc pads supplied by the vehicle manufacturer, it may be found that two pads out of the four have white marks on their backing plates. Where this is the case, the pads with the marks should be fitted to the piston sides of the calipers.

10 Locate the springs correctly and drive in the retaining pins **(see illustrations)**.

11 Repeat the operations on the opposite brake.

4.5 Removing the outboard pad

4.6 Removing the inboard pad

4.10a Inserting disc pad pin

4.10b Pad retaining pins and anti rattle springs correctly fitted

4.16 On later ATE type calipers, unclip the pad wear sensor . . .

4.17 . . . then lever out the spring clip

12 Refit the roadwheels and lower the vehicle.

13 Apply the footbrake hard several times to position the pads against the discs.

14 Top-up the fluid reservoir to the correct level.

15 New brake pads need to be carefully bedded in and, where possible, heavy braking should be avoided during the first 120 miles (200 km).

Later ATE type caliper

16 Extract the pad wear warning sensor and move it aside **(see illustration)**.

17 Lever the ends of the spring clip from their locations and remove the clip **(see illustration)**.

18 Remove the dust caps from the slide bolts **(see illustration)**.

19 Using a 7 mm Allen key, unscrew the slide bolts and remove them.

20 Lift the caliper body and inboard pad off the disc. The outboard pad will stay on the bracket **(see illustration)**. Support the caliper body, or tie it up with a piece of wire, so that the flexible hose is not strained.

21 Unclip the inboard pad from the caliper piston and lift the outboard pad off the bracket **(see illustrations)**. Clean the caliper and bracket.

22 If new pads are to be fitted, press the piston back into its bore. As the piston is pushed back, the fluid level in the master cylinder will rise. Syphon some fluid out if necessary with an old (clean) poultry baster or battery hydrometer.

23 Make sure that the steps of the caliper piston are positioned as shown **(see illustration)**.

24 Fit the inboard pad to the piston and the outboard pad to the bracket. Fit the caliper to the bracket and secure it with the slide bolts

tightening them to the specified torque. Fit the dust caps.

25 Refit the pad wear warning sensor.

26 Carry out the operations described in paragraphs 11 to 15.

5 Rear brake pads - renewal

⚠️ *Warning: Disc brake pads must be renewed on both rear wheels at the same time. Never renew the pads on only one wheel as uneven braking may result. Also, the dust created by wear of the pads may contain asbestos, which is a health hazard. Never blow it out with compressed air and don't inhale any of it. An approved filtering mask should be worn when working on the brakes. DO NOT use petroleum-based solvents to clean brake parts. Use brake cleaner or methylated spirit only.*

1 Raise the front of the vehicle (see "*Jacking and Vehicle Support*"). If the roadwheels have been balanced on the vehicle (new vehicles are balanced this way in production) then mark the relative position of the roadwheel to the hub so that it can be aligned correctly when refitting.

2 Inspect the thickness of the friction material on each pad. If any one is at or below the specified minimum, renew the pads as an axle set (four pads) in the following way.

3 Using a pin punch, drive out the two pad retaining pins from the outside towards the

4.18 Removing a dust cap from a slide bolt

4.20 Lift the caliper off the disc . . .

4.21a . . . then unclip the inboard pad from the caliper piston . . .

4.21b . . . and remove the outboard pad from the caliper bracket

4.23 Prior to fitting the pads, ensure that the caliper steps are positioned as shown

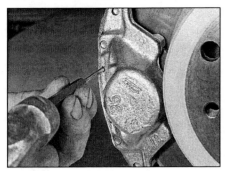

5.3 Driving out a rear disc pad retaining pin

5.9a Fitting a rear pad

5.9b Hooking the spring under one retaining pin

middle of the vehicle (see illustration). Recover the spring.

4 Remove the pads from the caliper. If they are tight, use a slide hammer or grip them with self-locking pliers.

5 Clean the caliper with a soft wire brush, paying attention to the warning at the beginning of this operation.

6 In order to accommodate the new thicker pads, the caliper piston must be depressed fully into its cylinder using a flat bar of metal such as a tyre lever. The action of depressing the piston will cause the fluid in the reservoir to rise, so anticipate this by syphoning some off using an old (clean) hydrometer or similar.

7 Inspect the brake disc for deep grooving, scoring or cracks. Renew the disc, or have it refinished if this is possible, if such damage is found. Excessive run-out may be caused by wheel bearing play, so bearing adjustment should be checked before assuming that the disc is at fault.

8 Apply a little disc brake anti-squeal or anti-seize compound to the backs of the new pads, and to the sides of the backplate. Be careful not to get any on the friction surface.

9 Insert the pads into the caliper with the friction material towards the disc. Fit one retaining pin (from the inside towards the outside) and tap it home. Hook one end of the spring under the pin (see illustrations).

10 Fit the other pin and tap it home, holding the other end of the spring down with a screwdriver so that the pin passes over it.

11 Repeat the operations on the opposite brake.

12 Refit the roadwheels and lower the vehicle.

13 Apply the footbrake hard several times to position the pads against the discs.

14 Top-up the fluid reservoir to the correct level.

15 New brake pads need to be carefully bedded in and, where possible, heavy braking should be avoided during the first 120 miles (200 km).

6 Rear brake shoes - renewal

⚠ *Warning: Drum brake shoes must be renewed on both rear wheels at the same time - never renew the shoes on only one wheel as uneven braking may result. Also, the dust created by wear of the shoes may contain asbestos, which is a health hazard Never blow it out with compressed air and don't inhale any of it. An approved filtering mask should be worn when working on the brakes. DO NOT use petroleum based solvents to clean brake parts. Use brake cleaner or methylated spirit only.*

1 Remove the brake drum (Section 9).

2 Working carefully and taking the necessary precautions, remove all traces of brake dust from the brake drum, backplate and shoes.

3 Measure the depth from the friction material to each of the rivets. If this is equal or less than the specified minimum, all four shoes must be renewed as a set. Also, the shoes should be renewed if any are fouled with oil or grease; there is no satisfactory way of degreasing friction material once contaminated.

4 If any of the brake shoes are worn unevenly or fouled with oil or grease, trace and rectify the cause before reassembly. If the shoes are to be renewed proceed as described below. If all is well refit the drums (Section 9).

5 Remove the steady pins, springs and washers by depressing the washers and turning them anti-clockwise. Renew them if they are damaged (see illustrations).

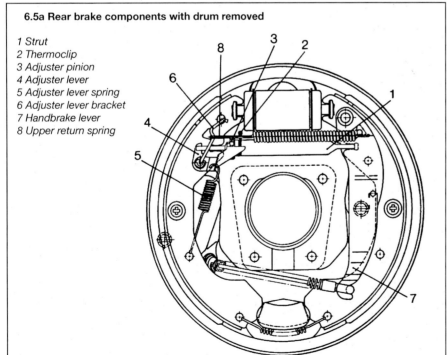

6.5a Rear brake components with drum removed

1 Strut
2 Thermoclip
3 Adjuster pinion
4 Adjuster lever
5 Adjuster lever spring
6 Adjuster lever bracket
7 Handbrake lever
8 Upper return spring

6.5b Brake shoe steady pin and washer (arrowed)

6.6 Handbrake cable attachment to operating lever (arrowed)

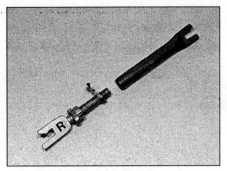

6.13 Self-adjusting strut components right-hand side

6.16 Handbrake lever secured by pin

6 Disconnect the handbrake cable from the operating lever **(see illustration)**. If there is insufficient slack at the cable, disconnect it at the equaliser yoke

7 The return springs may be unhooked now and the shoes removed separately, or the assembly of shoes, strut and springs may be removed together. The second course is particularly easy if the hub is removed (see Chapter 10), as has been done for some of the photographs. Be careful not to damage the wheel cylinder rubber boots.

8 If the shoes are to be removed for some time, secure the wheel cylinder pistons with a stout rubber band or a spring clip. In any event, do not press the brake pedal while the drum is removed.

9 Clean the brake backplate, again *being careful not to inhale the dust or to disperse it into the air*

10 Apply a smear of copper-based anti-seize compound to the shoe rubbing areas on the backplate.

11 Investigate and rectify any source of contamination of the linings (wheel cylinder or hub bearing oil seal leaking).

12 Unusually, linings are still available separately for these brake shoes. Renewal of the shoes complete with linings is to be preferred, however, unless the reader has the necessary skills and equipment to fit new linings to the old shoes.

13 Dismantle the shoes, strut and springs. Note how the springs are fitted, and which way round the strut goes. Be careful not to interchange left-hand and right-hand adjuster components; the threaded rod is marked L or R,

and the other 'handed' components are colour-coded: black for the left-hand side, and silver for the right **(see illustration)**.

14 Dismantle and clean the adjusting strut. Apply a smear of silicone-based lubricant to the adjuster threads. If new brake linings are being fitted, the thermoclip (in the middle of the strut) must be renewed too.

15 Examine the shoe return springs. If they are distorted or if they have seen much service, renewal is advisable. Weak springs may cause the brakes to bind.

16 If a new handbrake lever was not supplied with the new shoes, transfer the old lever. It may be secured with a pin and circlip **(see illustration)**, or by a rivet which will have to be drilled out.

17 Assemble the new shoes, springs and adjuster components. Expand the adjuster strut to ease fitting **(see illustrations)**.

18 Offer the shoes to the brake backplate. Be careful not to damage the wheel cylinder boots or to displace the pistons. Remember to remove the rubber band or spring clip from the wheel cylinder, if one was used.

19 When the shoes are in position, insert the steady pins and secure them with the springs and washers. Reconnect the handbrake cable, and refit and adjust the hub if it was removed.

20 If fitting the shoes and springs together is found too difficult, it is possible to fit the shoes and secure them with the steady pins, then to introduce the adjuster strut and fit the springs and adjuster.

21 Back off the adjuster pinion to reduce the length of the strut until the brake drum will

pass over the new linings. Make sure that the handbrake lever is correctly positioned (pin on the edge of the shoe web, not on top of it).

22 Refit and secure the brake drum as described in Section 9.

23 Repeat the operations on the other rear brake, then adjust the brakes by operating the footbrake at least 15 times. A clicking noise will be heard at the drums as the automatic adjusters operate; when the clicking stops, adjustment is complete.

24 Check the handbrake adjustment and correct it if necessary (see Chapter 1).

25 When new linings have been fitted, avoid harsh braking (if possible) for the first hundred miles or so to allow the linings to bed in.

7 Front brake disc - inspection, removal and refitting

Note: *Before starting work, refer to the note at the beginning of Section 4 concerning the dangers of asbestos dust.*

Inspection

Note: *If either disc requires renewal, both should be renewed at the same time to ensure even and consistent braking.*

1 Firmly apply the handbrake, jack up the front of the car and support it on axle stands (see "*Jacking and Vehicle Support*"). Remove the appropriate front roadwheel, marking its correct fitted position on the hub.

2 Slowly rotate the brake disc so that the full area of both sides can be checked; remove the brake pads if better access is required to the inner surface. Light scoring is normal in

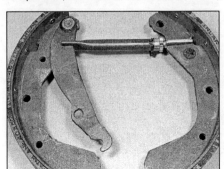

6.17a Self-adjusting strut correctly fitted

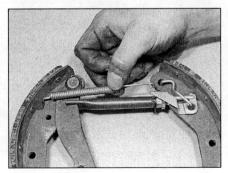

6.17b Fitting the upper return spring to the adjuster lever bracket

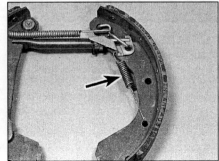

6.17c Adjuster lever spring (arrowed) fitted

8.3 Levering off the grease cap

the area swept by the brake pads, but if heavy scoring is found the disc must be renewed.

3 It is normal to find a lip of rust and brake dust around the disc's perimeter; this can be scraped off if required. If, however, a lip has formed due to excessive wear of the brake pad swept area then the disc's thickness must be measured using a micrometer. Take measurements at several places around the disc at the inside and outside of the pad swept area; if the disc has worn at any point to the specified minimum thickness or less, the disc must be renewed.

4 If the disc is thought to be warped it can be checked for run-out either using a dial gauge mounted on any convenient fixed point, while the disc is slowly rotated, or by using feeler blades to measure (at several points all around the disc) the clearance between the disc and a fixed point such as the caliper mounting bracket. To ensure that the disc is squarely seated on the hub, fit two wheel bolts complete with spacers approximately 10 mm thick and tighten them securely. If the measurements obtained are at the specified maximum or beyond, the disc is excessively warped and must be renewed; however it is worth checking first that the hub bearing is in good condition (Chapters 1 and/or 10).

5 Check the disc for cracks, especially around the wheel bolt holes, and any other wear or damage and renew if necessary.

Removal

6 Remove the brake pads (Section 4).

7 Extract the small retaining screw and then tilt the disc and withdraw it from the hub.

Refitting

8 Refitting is the reverse of the removal procedure, noting the following points.

   a) Ensure that the mating surfaces of the disc and hub are clean and flat.

   b) If a new disc has been fitted, use a suitable solvent to wipe any preservative coating from the disc before refitting the caliper.

   c) On vehicles which are equipped with light alloy roadwheels, a facing sleeve is mounted on the collar of the brake disc.

   d) Refit the brake pads as described in Section 4.

   e) Refit the roadwheel, aligning the marks

made on removal, then lower the vehicle to the ground and tighten the roadwheel bolts to the specified torque. On completion, repeatedly depress the brake pedal until normal (non-assisted) pedal pressure returns.

8 Rear brake disc - inspection, removal and refitting

Note: Before starting work, refer to the note at the beginning of Section 5 concerning the dangers of asbestos dust.

Inspection

1 Refer to Section 7.

Removal

2 Slacken and remove the two bolts securing the brake caliper in position. Slide off the caliper and position it clear of the brake disc, taking care not to strain the brake pipe.

3 Release the handbrake then remove the hub grease cap by levering or tapping it off (see illustration).

4 Remove the split pin from the hub nut. Remove the nut.

5 Pull the disc/hub unit off the stub axle, catching the washer and the bearing outer race (see illustration). If the handbrake shoes seem to be preventing removal, disconnect the handbrake cable from the lever on the brake backplate.

Refitting

6 Refitting is the reverse of the removal procedure, noting the following points:

   a) If a new disc has been fitted, use a suitable solvent to wipe any preservative coating from the disc before refitting the caliper.

   b) On refitting, adjust the hub bearings as described in Chapter 10.

   c) Use a new split pin, and if necessary a new grease cap.

   d) Adjust the handbrake (see Chapter 1).

9 Rear brake drum - removal, inspection and refitting

Note: Before starting work, refer to the note at the beginning of Section 6 concerning the dangers of asbestos dust.

Removal

1 Chock the front wheels then jack up the rear of the vehicle and support it on axle stands (see "Jacking and Vehicle Support").

2 Remove the appropriate rear wheel, marking its correct fitted position on the drum.

3 Remove the brake drum securing screw then release the handbrake and pull off the drum. If it is tight, collapse the brake shoes by removing the plug in the brake backplate and pushing the handbrake operating lever outwards with a screwdriver (see illustrations).

8.5 Removing the rear disc

Inspection

Note: If either drum requires renewal, both should be renewed at the same time to ensure even and consistent braking.

4 Working carefully, remove all traces of brake dust from the drum, but avoid inhaling the dust as it is injurious to health.

5 Scrub clean the outside of the drum and check it for obvious signs of wear or damage such as cracks around the roadwheel bolt holes; renew the drum if necessary.

6 Examine carefully the inside of the drum. Light scoring of the friction surface is normal, but if heavy scoring is found the drum must be renewed. It is usual to find a lip on the drum's inboard edge which consists of a mixture of rust and brake dust; this should be scraped away to leave a smooth surface which can be polished with fine (120 to 150 grade) emery paper. If, however, the lip is due to the friction

9.3a Removing a brake drum securing screw

9.3b Pushing back the handbrake lever

surface being recessed by excessive wear, then the drum must be renewed.

7 If the drum is thought to be excessively worn, or oval, its internal diameter must be measured at several points using an internal micrometer. Take measurements in pairs, the second at right angles to the first, and compare the two to check for signs of ovality. Provided that it does not enlarge the drum to beyond the specified maximum diameter, it may be possible to have the drum refinished by skimming or grinding; if this is not possible, the drums on both sides must be renewed. Note that if the drum is to be skimmed, both drums must be refinished to maintain a consistent internal diameter on both sides.

Refitting

8 If a new brake drum is to be installed, use a suitable solvent to remove any preservative coating that may have been applied to its interior.

9 Ensure that the drum and hub flange mating surfaces are clean and dry and remove all traces of corrosion.

10 Make sure that the handbrake lever stop peg is correctly repositioned against the edge of the brake shoe web then locate the drum on the hub. Note that it may be necessary to shorten the adjuster strut length by rotating the strut wheel to allow the drum to pass over the brake shoes.

11 Refit the drum retaining screw and tighten it securely.

12 Adjust the lining to drum clearance by repeatedly applying the footbrake at least fifteen times. Whilst applying the brake have

10.6a On the GMF caliper, remove the caliper bolt caps . . .

10.6b . . . then unscrew the caliper bolts . . .

an assistant listen to the rear drums to check that the adjuster strut is functioning correctly; if this is so a clicking sound will be emitted by the strut as the pedal is depressed.

13 With the lining to drum clearance set check and, if necessary, adjust the handbrake as described in Chapter 1.

14 Refit the roadwheel, aligning the marks made on removal, then lower the vehicle to the ground and tighten the wheel bolts to the specified torque setting.

10 Front brake caliper - removal, overhaul and refitting

Note: *Before starting work, refer to the note at the beginning of Section 2 concerning the dangers of hydraulic fluid and to the warning at the beginning of Section 4 concerning the dangers of asbestos dust.*

Removal

1 Apply the handbrake, then jack up the front of the vehicle and support it on axle stands (see "*Jacking and Vehicle Support*"). Remove the appropriate roadwheel, marking its correct fitted position on the wheel hub.

2 Minimise fluid loss either by removing the master cylinder reservoir cap and then tightening it down onto a piece of polythene to obtain an airtight seal, or by using a brake hose clamp, a G-clamp or a similar tool to clamp the flexible hose.

3 Clean the area around the caliper brake hose union. Slacken and remove the union bolt and recover the sealing washer from either side of the hose union; discard the washers new ones must be used on refitting. Plug the hose end and caliper hole to minimise fluid loss and prevent the ingress of dirt into the hydraulic system.

4 Remove the brake pads as described in paragraphs Section 4.

5 On models with early ATE type calipers, slacken and remove the two caliper mounting bolts and remove the caliper assembly from the vehicle.

6 On models with GMF type calipers, prise off the mounting bolt caps to gain access to the bolts. Slacken and remove the bolts and remove the caliper from the vehicle (**see illustrations**).

10.6c . . . and remove the caliper

Overhaul

Early ATE type caliper

7 With the caliper on the bench, wipe away all traces of dust and dirt, but *avoid inhaling the dust as it is injurious to health.*

8 Separate the caliper body from its bracket by sliding them apart. Recover the guide springs.

9 Using a screwdriver, prise off the retaining ring from the dust excluder then remove the excluder from the caliper.

10 Withdraw the partially ejected piston from the caliper body and remove the dust excluder. The piston can be withdrawn by hand, or if necessary pushed out by applying compressed air to the brake hose union hole. Only low pressure should be required such as is generated by a foot pump.

11 Once the piston has been removed, pick out the seal from its groove in the cylinder, using a plastic or wooden instrument.

12 Thoroughly clean all components using only methylated spirit, isopropyl alcohol or clean hydraulic fluid as a cleaning medium. Never use mineral-based solvents such as petrol or paraffin which will attack the hydraulic system's rubber components. Dry the components immediately using compressed air or a clean, lint-free cloth. Use compressed air to blow clear the fluid passages.

13 Check all components and renew any that are worn or damaged. Check particularly the cylinder bore and piston; these should be renewed (note that this means the renewal of the complete body assembly) if they are scratched, worn or corroded in any way.

14 If the assembly is fit for further use, obtain the necessary components from your Vauxhalll dealer. Renew the caliper seals as a matter of course; these should never be re-used.

15 On reassembly, ensure that all components are absolutely clean and dry.

16 Soak the piston and the new seal in clean hydraulic fluid.

17 Smear clean fluid on the cylinder bore surface.

18 Fit the new seal using only the fingers to manipulate it into the cylinder bore groove.

19 Fit the new dust seal to the piston and refit it to the cylinder bore using a twisting motion, and ensure that the piston enters squarely into the bore. Push the piston into the caliper bore making sure that the piston step is positioned as shown (**see illustration**).

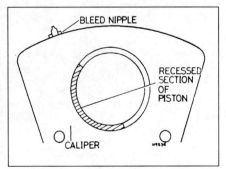

10.19 Caliper piston recess setting diagram - early type ATE caliper

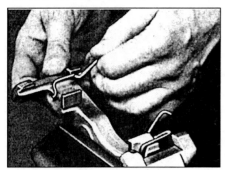

10.22 Fitting caliper bracket guide springs - early type ATE caliper

20 When the piston has been partially depressed, engage the dust excluder with the rim of the cylinder and fit the retaining clip.
21 Press the piston fully into its cylinder bore.
22 Secure the caliper bracket in a vice and install the guide springs **(see illustration)**.
23 Slide the caliper body into the bracket splines until the body and bracket are flush.

GMF type caliper

24 With the caliper on the bench, wipe away all traces of dust and dirt, but *avoid inhaling the dust as it is injurious to health*.
25 Prise the sliding sleeve inner dust caps from the caliper housing.
26 Push the caliper sliding sleeves inwards so that the dust caps can be disengaged from the sleeve grooves and removed.
27 Prise off the piston dust excluder.
28 Remove the piston dust excluder from the caliper.
29 Carry out the operations described earlier in paragraphs 10 to 12.
30 Press the sliding sleeves out from the caliper body, noting which way around they are fitted, and recover their sealing rings. Inspect the sleeves and caliper body for signs of wear or damage. Both should be undamaged and a reasonably tight, sliding fit in each other.
31 Check all components and renew any that are worn or damaged. Check particularly the cylinder bore and piston; these should be renewed (note that this means the renewal of the complete body assembly) if they are scratched, worn or corroded in any way.
32 If the assembly is fit for further use, obtain the necessary components from your Vauxhalll dealer. Renew the caliper seals as a matter of course; these should never be re-used.
33 On reassembly, ensure that all components are absolutely clean and dry.
34 Soak the piston and the new seal in clean hydraulic fluid. Smear clean fluid on the cylinder bore surface.
35 Fit the new seal using only the fingers to manipulate it into the cylinder bore groove.
36 Fit the new dust seal to the piston and refit it to the cylinder bore using a twisting motion, and ensure that the piston enters squarely into the bore.
37 When the piston has been partially depressed, engage the dust excluder with the rim of the cylinder then depress the piston fully into its cylinder bore.

38 Fit the new sealing rings to the sliding sleeve recesses and apply the grease supplied in the repair kit to the sleeves. Install the sleeves making sure they are fitted the correct way around.
39 Fit the inner dust caps, making sure they are correctly engaged with the sliding sleeves. Slide the sleeves into position and press the dust caps into position on the caliper body using a suitable tubular drift.

Later ATE type caliper

40 With the caliper on the bench, wipe away all traces of dust and dirt, but *avoid inhaling the dust as it is injurious to health*.
41 Press the sliding bolt sleeves out of their bore in the caliper body.
42 Carry out the operations described in paragraphs 10 to 19, positioning the piston as shown in **illustration 4.23**.
43 Ensure that the dust excluder is correctly located in the caliper body then coat the new slide bolt sleeves with washing-up liquid and press them into their bores by hand.

Refitting

44 On GMF and early ATE type calipers, prior to refitting, remove all traces of locking compound from the caliper mounting bolt threads and the hub carrier holes. Apply a drop of fresh locking compound to the bolt threads. Refit the caliper and insert the mounting bolts, tightening them to the specified torque setting.
45 On all calipers, refit the brake pads as described in Section 4 but do not depress the brake pedal yet.
46 Position a new sealing washer on each side of the hose union and connect the brake hose to the caliper. Ensure that the hose is correctly positioned against the caliper body lug then install the union bolt and tighten it to the specified torque setting.
47 Remove the brake hose clamp or polythene, where fitted, and bleed the hydraulic system as described in Section 2. Note that providing the precautions described were taken to minimise brake fluid loss, it should only be necessary to bleed the relevant front brake.
48 Refit the roadwheel, aligning the marks made on removal, then lower the vehicle to the ground and tighten the roadwheel bolts to the specified torque.

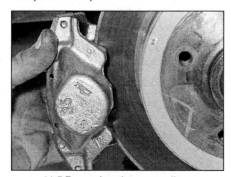

11.5 Removing the rear caliper

11 Rear brake caliper - removal, overhaul and refitting

Note: *Before starting work, refer to the note at the beginning of Section 2 concerning the dangers of hydraulic fluid and to the warning at the beginning of Section 5 concerning the dangers of asbestos dust.*

Removal

1 Apply the handbrake, then jack up the rear of the vehicle and support it on axle stands (see "*Jacking and Vehicle Support*"). Remove the appropriate roadwheel, marking its correct fitted position on the wheel hub.
2 Minimise fluid loss either by removing the master cylinder reservoir cap and then tightening it down onto a piece of polythene to obtain an airtight seal, or by using a brake hose clamp, a G-clamp or a similar tool to clamp the flexible hose at the nearest convenient point to the rear brake.
3 Clean the area around the caliper brake pipe union. Unscrew the union nut and disconnect the pipe from the caliper. Plug the pipe end and caliper hole to minimise fluid loss and prevent the ingress of dirt into the hydraulic system.
4 Remove the brake pads as described in paragraphs Section 5.
5 Slacken and remove the two caliper mounting bolts and remove the caliper assembly from the vehicle **(see illustration)**.

Overhaul

Note: *No attempt must be made to separate the caliper halves. If overhaul cannot be accomplished with the caliper assembled, it must be renewed.*

6 With the caliper on the bench, wipe away all traces of dust and dirt, but *avoid inhaling the dust as it is injurious to health*.
7 Prise off the piston dust excluders.
8 Clamp one of the pistons in its bore using a G-clamp and a thin piece of wood then extract the opposite piston and associated components as described in paragraphs 9 to 20 of Section 10, position the piston step as shown **(see illustration)**.

11.8 Correct position of rear caliper piston step, showing the inboard piston on the right-hand caliper. Opposite piston is the mirror image

9 Push the piston into its bore and repeat the operation on the opposite piston.

Refitting

10 Prior to refitting, remove all traces of locking compound from the caliper mounting bolt threads and the hub carrier holes. Apply a drop of fresh locking compound to the bolt threads. Refit the caliper and insert the mounting bolts, tightening them to the specified torque setting **(see illustration)**.

11 Reconnect the brake pipe to the caliper and tighten its union nut to the specified torque setting.

12 Refit the brake pads as described in Section 5.

13 Remove the brake hose clamp or polythene, where fitted, and bleed the hydraulic system as described in Section 2. Note that providing the precautions described were taken to minimise brake fluid loss, it should only be necessary to bleed the relevant rear brake.

14 Refit the roadwheel, aligning the marks made on removal, then lower the vehicle to the ground and tighten the roadwheel bolts to the specified torque.

12 Rear wheel cylinder - removal, overhaul and refitting

Note: *Before starting work, refer to the note at the beginning of Section 2 concerning the dangers of hydraulic fluid and to the warning at the beginning of Section 6 concerning the dangers of asbestos dust.*

Removal

1 Remove the brake drum (Section 9).

2 Using pliers, carefully unhook the upper brake shoe return spring and remove it from both brake shoes. Pull the upper ends of the shoes away from the wheel cylinder to disengage them from the pistons.

11.10 Tighten the rear caliper mounting bolts to the specified torque setting

3 Minimise fluid loss by either removing the master cylinder reservoir cap and then tightening it down onto a piece of polythene to obtain an airtight seal, or by using a brake hose clamp, a G-clamp or a similar tool to clamp the flexible hose at the nearest convenient point to the wheel cylinder.

4 Wipe away all traces of dirt around the brake pipe union at the rear of the wheel cylinder and unscrew the union nut. Carefully ease the pipe out of the wheel cylinder and plug or tape over its end to prevent dirt entry. Wipe off any spilt fluid immediately.

5 Unscrew the two wheel cylinder retaining bolts from the rear of the backplate and remove the cylinder taking great care not to allow surplus hydraulic fluid to contaminate the brake shoe linings.

Overhaul

6 Brush the dirt and dust from the wheel cylinder, taking care not to inhale it, and pull off the rubber dust excluders from the cylinder body **(see illustration)**.

7 The pistons will normally be ejected by pressure of the coil spring but if they are not, tap the end of the cylinder on a piece of hardwood or apply low air pressure from a tyre foot pump at the pipeline connection.

8 Inspect the surfaces of the piston and the cylinder bore for rust, scoring or metal-to-metal rubbed areas. If these are evident, renew the wheel cylinder complete.

9 If these components are in good order, discard the seals and dust excluders and obtain a repair kit which will contain all the renewable items.

10 Fit the piston seals (using the fingers only to manipulate them into position) so that the spring is between them. Dip the pistons in clean hydraulic fluid and insert them into the cylinder.

11 Fit the dust excluders.

Refitting

12 Ensure that the backplate and wheel cylinder mating surfaces are clean then spread the brake shoes and manoeuvre the wheel cylinder into position.

13 Engage the brake pipe and screw in the union nut two or three turns to ensure that the thread has started.

14 Insert the two wheel cylinder retaining bolts and tighten them to the specified torque setting. Now tighten the brake pipe union nut to the specified torque.

15 Remove the clamp from the flexible brake hose or the polythene from the master cylinder reservoir (as applicable).

16 Ensure that the brake shoes are correctly located in the cylinder pistons then carefully refit the brake shoe upper return spring, using a screwdriver to stretch the spring into position.

17 Refit the brake drum as described in Section 9.

18 Bleed the brake hydraulic system as described in Section 2. Providing suitable precautions were taken to minimise loss of fluid, it should only be necessary to bleed the relevant rear brake.

13 Master cylinder - removal and refitting

Note: *Before starting work, refer to the warning at the beginning of Section 2 concerning the dangers of hydraulic fluid.*

Removal

1 Remove the master cylinder reservoir cap and syphon the hydraulic fluid from the reservoir. **Note:** *Do not syphon the fluid by mouth, as it is poisonous; use a syringe or an old poultry baster.* Alternatively, open any convenient bleed screw in the system and gently pump the brake pedal to expel the fluid through a plastic tube connected to the screw (see Section 2).

2 Release the cable retainer from around the master cylinder body (where applicable).

3 Wipe clean the area around the brake pipe unions on the side of the master cylinder and place absorbent rags beneath the pipe unions to catch any surplus fluid. Make a note of the correct fitted positions of the unions then

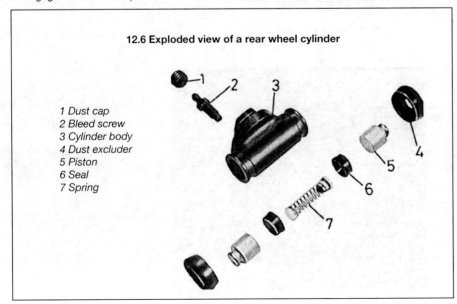
12.6 Exploded view of a rear wheel cylinder

1 Dust cap
2 Bleed screw
3 Cylinder body
4 Dust excluder
5 Piston
6 Seal
7 Spring

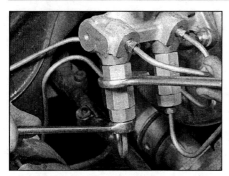

13.3 Slackening the brake pipe union from the pressure regulating valve

13.5 Removing the master cylinder

unscrew the union nuts and carefully withdraw the pipes **(see illustration)**. Plug or tape over the pipe ends and master cylinder orifices to minimise the loss of brake fluid and to prevent the entry of dirt into the system. Wash off any spilt fluid immediately with cold water.

4 Where necessary, unscrew the pressure regulating valve(s) from the master cylinder.

5 Unbolt the master cylinder from the brake vacuum servo unit (booster) **(see illustration)**.

Overhaul

Note: *On models equipped with ABS, the master cylinder is a sealed unit and cannot be overhauled. If the cylinder is faulty it must be renewed.*

ATE type cylinder

6 With the master cylinder removed, clean away all external dirt.

7 Prise the fluid reservoir from the cylinder body **(see illustration)**.

8 Depress the primary (rear) piston slightly and remove its retaining circlip.

9 Withdraw the primary piston. Make sure that the stop washers do not catch in the circlip groove.

10 Depress the secondary (front) piston with a suitable rod and remove the stop screw from the cylinder body.

11 Shake or tap out the secondary piston.

12 Clean all the parts in brake fluid or methylated spirit. Examine the pistons and the cylinder bore for scoring, rust, or evidence of metal-to-metal contact; if found, renew the cylinder complete. Strip the seals from the primary piston if it is to be re-used noting which way round they are fitted.

13 The makers do not supply a seal kit alone, but provide a repair kit consisting of a complete secondary piston and the other necessary seals springs, washers etc in a special assembly tube. Should a proprietary seal kit be available, fit new seals using the fingers only, and make sure that the new seals are fitted the same way round as the old ones. The remainder of this Section describes the fitting of the maker's repair kit.

14 Lubricate the cylinder bore with brake fluid or brake rubber grease.

15 Clamp the cylinder in a soft-jawed vice with the bore more or less horizontal. Screw in the stop screw a little way, but not so far that it protrudes into the bore.

16 Remove the large plug from the assembly tube. Remove all the components from the short part of the tube and push the short part into the long part until they are flush.

17 Insert the assembly tube into the cylinder bore as far as the collar on the short sleeve. Use a blunt rod to push the secondary piston into the bore until it contacts the end of the cylinder. Nip up the stop screw, withdraw the rod and sleeve and tighten the stop screw fully.

18 Reposition the master cylinder in the vice with the bore opening facing upwards.

19 Smear the primary piston skirt and seal grooves with the special grease provided in the repair kit. Fit the stop washer to the piston.

20 Adjust the assembly tube so that the end of the long part is flush with the inner shoulder of the short part.

21 Fit the front seal to the primary piston with the open end of the seal facing the front of the master cylinder. Place the assembly tube over the cylinder to compress the seal, insert the piston and tube part way into the bore and withdraw the tube.

22 Place the intermediate ring on the primary piston, then fit the other seal using the assembly tube in a similar manner.

23 Place the end washer on the primary piston, then depress the piston slightly and fit the circlip. Make sure that the circlip is properly seated and that the piston is free to move.

24 Fit new sealing rings and press the fluid reservoir into position.

25 Prime the cylinder by pouring clean brake fluid into the reservoir and working the pistons with a rod until fluid is ejected from all orifices.

GMF type cylinder

26 With the master cylinder removed, clean off all external dirt **(see illustration)**.

27 Remove the fluid reservoir by carefully pulling it away from the master cylinder, at the same time releasing the circlips with a screwdriver.

28 Clamp the cylinder in a soft-jawed vice, rear end uppermost, and prise out the pushrod seal.

29 Use a blunt rod to depress the primary (rear) piston by 10 mm or so until it can be retained in the depressed position by inserting a smooth rod (eg a knitting needle) onto the primary inlet hole.

30 Carefully extract the circlip from the end of the cylinder by prising it out with a screwdriver.

31 Knock, shake or blow the pistons out of the cylinder.

32 Clean all parts with brake fluid or methylated spirit. Examine the pistons and the cylinder bore for scoring, rust or evidence of metal-to-metal contact; if found, renew the cylinder complete.

33 The makers do not supply a kit of seals alone, but provide a repair kit consisting of both pistons in a special assembly tube. Should a proprietary seal kit be obtained, note the direction of fitting of the seals before removing them from the pistons.

34 Lubricate the cylinder bore with brake

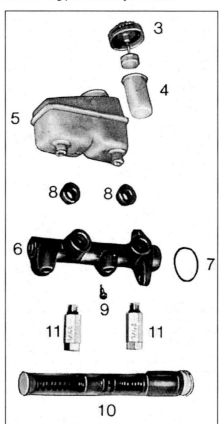

13.7 Exploded view of ATE master cylinder

3 Reservoir cap/low level switch
4 Float guide sleeve
5 Reservoir
6 Cylinder body
7 O-ring
8 Seals
9 Stop screw
10 Repair kit in assembly tube
11 Pressure regulating valve

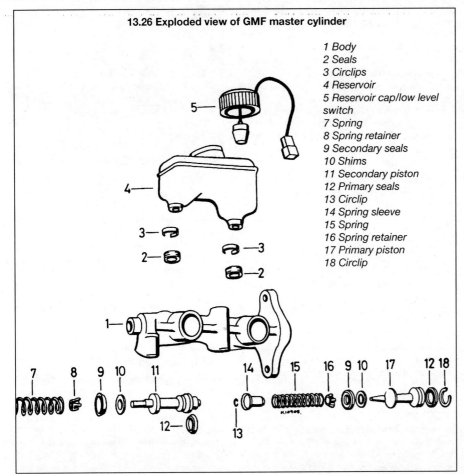

13.26 Exploded view of GMF master cylinder

1 Body
2 Seals
3 Circlips
4 Reservoir
5 Reservoir cap/low level switch
7 Spring
8 Spring retainer
9 Secondary seals
10 Shims
11 Secondary piston
12 Primary seals
13 Circlip
14 Spring sleeve
15 Spring
16 Spring retainer
17 Primary piston
18 Circlip

fluid or brake rubber grease. Clamp the cylinder with the bore horizontal.

35 Remove the plug from the assembly tube and insert the short part of the tube into the cylinder bore as far as the shoulder on the tube. Use a blunt rod to push the piston out of the tube and into the bore; retain the pistons in the bore with the smooth rod or needle used when dismantling. Withdraw the rod and the tube.

36 Fit a new circlip to the end of the cylinder. Depress the primary piston and withdraw the retaining rod or needle. Make sure that the circlip is properly seated and that the pistons are free to move.

37 Fit new sealing rings to the master cylinder and new circlips to the reservoir. Press the reservoir into position until the circlips click into place.

38 Prime the cylinder by pouring clean brake fluid into the reservoir and working the pistons with a rod until fluid is ejected from all orifices.

Refitting

39 Refitting is a reversal of removal, use new reservoir rubber seals and tighten all nuts and bolts to the specified torque settings (where given). On completion bleed the complete hydraulic system as described in Section 2.

14 Pressure regulating valves - testing, removal and refitting

Testing

1 Accurate testing of either type of pressure regulating valve (master cylinder mounted or underbody mounted) is not possible without special equipment. Malfunction may be suspected if the rear brakes lock prematurely in heavy braking, or if they seem not to be functioning at all.

2 A quick check of the underbody mounted valve fitted to Estate and Van models may be made by observing the valve whilst an assistant makes sharp applications of the brake pedal. (The weight of the vehicle must be on its wheels.) The lever on the valve must be seen to move as the pedal is depressed and released; if not, the valve is certainly defective.

Removal

Hatchback and Saloon models

Note: *Renew both valves as a matched pair to ensure that the braking is not adversely effected.*

3 Empty the master cylinder reservoir, as described in paragraph 1 of Section 13.

4 Wipe clean the area around the valves and place absorbent rags beneath the pipe unions to catch any surplus fluid. Make a note of the correct fitted positions of the unions then unscrew the union nuts and carefully withdraw the pipes. Plug or tape over the pipe ends and master cylinder orifices to minimise the loss of brake fluid and to prevent the entry of dirt into the system. Wash off any spilt fluid immediately with cold water.

5 Unscrew the valves from the master cylinder.

Estate and Van

6 Minimise fluid loss by first removing the master cylinder reservoir cap, and tightening it down onto a piece of polythene to obtain an airtight seal.

7 Raise and securely support the rear of the vehicle (see *"Jacking and Vehicle Support"*).

8 Slacken the valve spring bracket, push the bracket rearwards and unhook the spring from it **(see illustration)**.

9 Clean around the hydraulic unions. Identify the unions with tape or dabs of paint, then unscrew them from the valve. Be prepared for fluid spillage.

10 Unbolt and remove the valve.

Refitting

Hatchback and Saloon models

11 Make sure that both new valves are of the same type and are stamped with the same numbers (indicating their calibration). The valves must always be renewed in pairs, even if only one seems to be defective.

12 Fit the valves to the master cylinder and tighten them to the specified torque.

13 Reconnect the brake pipes, tightening the union nuts to the specified torque.

14 Bleed the complete hydraulic system, as described in Section 2.

Estate and Van

15 Transfer the stone guard to the new valve.

16 Bolt the new valve to the underbody and tighten the mounting bolts to the specified torque.

17 Connect the brake pipes, tightening the union nuts to the specified torque.

18 Bleed the complete hydraulic system, as described in Section 2.

14.8 Load-dependent pressure regulating valve, spring and bracket - Estate and Van models

15.2 Brake servo vacuum connection at inlet manifold (fuel injection model)

19 Attach the spring to the valve and to the spring bracket. Adjust the position of the spring bracket so that the spring is neither taut nor slack, then secure the bracket.

20 Lower the vehicle. Perform a road test to confirm that rear brake operation is satisfactory. Note that increasing the spring tension increases the pressure to the rear brakes, and *vice versa.*

15 Brake servo vacuum hose and non-return valve - renewal

1 The plastic hose fitted as original equipment cannot be re-used; to renew the valve, the hose must therefore be renewed as well. A serviceable valve can, however, be transferred to the new hose.

16.8 Removing a servo bracket screw

2 Unscrew the hose union nut at the inlet manifold (see illustration).
3 Pull or prise the elbow connector out of the servo (see illustration).
4 Cut the hose off the non-return valve, the elbow and the manifold connectors.
5 Cut the new hose to length - it is sold by the yard - and secure it to the valve and fittings using hose clips. Make sure that the arrows on the valve point towards the manifold.
6 Refit the connectors to the manifold and to the servo.

16 Vacuum servo unit - testing, removal and refitting

Testing

1 To establish whether or not the servo is operating, proceed as follows.
2 With the engine not running, apply the brake pedal several times to exhaust any residual vacuum.
3 Hold the brake pedal depressed and start the engine. The pedal should be felt to move down when the engine starts. If not, check the vacuum hose and non-return valve.
4 If the vacuum system is satisfactory, the servo itself is faulty and must be renewed.

Removal

Right-hand drive

5 Remove the vacuum connector from the servo.
6 Remove the nuts which secure the master cylinder to the servo and draw the cylinder away from the servo. There is no need to disconnect the hydraulic pipes, but be careful not to strain them.
7 Inside the car, remove the stop-lamp switch and disconnect the brake pedal clevis - see Section 17.
8 The servo must now be removed from its bracket. The recommended method is to undo the two 6 mm Allen screws which hold the bracket halves together. Access to these screws is obtained by removing the wiper arms, wind deflector and water deflector; the screws are then accessible through two holes which may have rubber plugs in them. The

15.3 Brake servo vacuum connection at servo

screws are extremely tight, and without doubt a well-fitting key and square drive adapter will be needed (see illustration).
9 If the Allen screws cannot be undone, it is possible to reach behind the servo and undo the four nuts which hold it to the bracket (see illustration). Small hands, some dexterity and a good deal of patience will be needed. The nuts are of the self-locking type and resist removal all the way.
10 With the screws or nuts removed, the servo can be removed from the car.

Left-hand drive

11 The procedure is similar to that just described, but access to the servo bracket fastenings is much easier. If power steering is fitted, a flexible head socket drive will be needed to reach the lower nut without disturbing the steering gear (see illustrations). On all models it will be necessary to remove the windscreen washer reservoir.

Refitting

12 If a new servo is to be fitted, transfer the clevis and locknut to it. On right-hand drive models, measure the fitted position of the clevis on the old servo pushrod and fit it in the same position on the new one. On left-hand drive models, when transferring the clevis and threaded sleeve to the new servo, set the clevis-to-servo distance as shown (see illustration).
13 The remainder of refitting is a reverse of removal, noting the following points:

16.9 Three of the four servo-to-bracket nuts (arrowed) servo and bracket removed for clarity

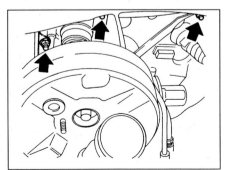

16.11a Three servo mounting nuts (arrowed) - Left-hand drive models

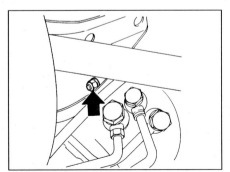

16.11b Servo mounting nut (arrowed) obscured by steering gear - Left-hand drive models

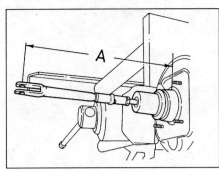

16.12 Servo clevis adjustment - Left-hand drive models
A = 278.5 mm (10.97 in)

a) Use sealing compound on the bracket halves if they were separated **(see illustration)**.

b) Make sure the vacuum connection point is in the correct position **(see illustration)**.

c) Use thread locking compound or new self-locking nuts, as appropriate.

17 Brake pedal - removal and refitting

Removal

1 Remove the stop-lamp switch by turning it 90° left or right and withdrawing it from its bracket **(see illustration)**.
2 Unhook the pedal return spring.
3 Detach the clevis from the brake pedal by

17.1 Stop-lamp switch 'keyhole' mounting (arrowed)

17.6 Stop-lamp switch plunger in extended position (top) and after fitting (bottom)

16.13a Servo mounting bracket lower half remains on bulkhead

removing the clevis pin retainer (split pin or spring clip) and pushing the pin out.
4 Remove the split pin from the end of the brake pedal shaft. Undo the shaft nut, remove the washer and push the shaft out towards the steering column. The pedal can now be removed.

Refitting

5 Refit in the reverse order to removal, using new split pins or other safety securing devices. Lubricate the pivot points with grease.
6 Before fitting the stop-lamp switch, pull its plunger out as far as it will go. The switch will adjust itself once it is fitted **(see illustration)**.

18 Handbrake cable - removal and refitting

Removal

1 Unscrew the yoke adjustment nut completely and remove the yoke.
2 On models with rear drum brakes, remove the brake drums, as described in Section 9.
3 Free the cable from the brackets on the underbody, fuel tank and rear axle.
4 Unhook the ends of the inner cable from the handbrake operating lever. On models with rear drum brakes the levers are on the leading brake shoes and on models with rear disc brakes the lever is situated at the rear of the backplate.
5 Prise out the retaining ring and free the

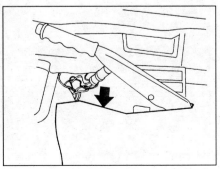

19.4 Cut the carpet along the line shown (arrowed)

16.13b Fit the servo with the vacuum connector (arrowed) positioned as shown

plastic sleeve from each brake backplate.
6 Withdraw the cable from the backplates and remove it.

Refitting

7 Refit in the reverse order to removal, noting that the dark cable guide is fitted uppermost at the yoke, adjusting the handbrake as described in Chapter 1.

19 Handbrake lever - removal and refitting

Removal

1 Unscrew the yoke adjustment nut completely and remove the yoke. Also remove the rubber boot from the pull-rod.
2 Remove the driver's seat by unbolting its rails from the floor.
3 Free the centre console by removing its single securing screw, which is concealed by a plastic plug. Remove the electric window and/or electric mirror switches, when fitted, then slide the console rearwards to free it and lift it off the handbrake lever.
4 Cut the carpet, as shown **(see illustration)**.
5 Remove the two securing bolts and withdraw the handbrake lever **(see illustration)**.
6 The handbrake warning switch can be unbolted from the lever. The ratchet pawl and segment can be renewed if facilities exist for removing and refitting their fastening bushes and rivets.

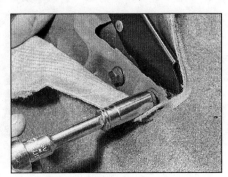

19.5 Unbolting the handbrake lever

Refitting

7 Commence refitting by bolting the handbrake lever in place. Tighten the bolts to the specified torque.

8 Secure the carpet with glue and/or sticky tape. (The cut area will be covered by the console.)

9 Refit and secure the console, and its switches when applicable.

10 Refit and secure the front seat.

11 Refit the rubber boot and yoke. Adjust the handbrake, as described in Section 22.

20 Handbrake shoes (rear disc brake models) - renewal

⚠️ *Warning: Note that the dust created by wear of the shoes may contain asbestos, which is a health hazard. Never blow it out with compressed air and don't inhale any of it. An approved filtering mask should be worn when working on the brakes. DO NOT use petroleum-based solvents to clean brake parts. Use brake cleaner or methylated spirit only.*

1 Remove the rear brake disc (Section 8).

2 Disconnect the handbrake cable and the return spring from the backplate **(see illustration)**.

3 Remove the steady washers and springs by depressing the washers and turning them through 90°. Remove the rear steady pin. The front pin is captive on the backplate **(see illustrations)**.

4 Remove the shoes complete with springs, adjuster and expander mechanism **(see illustration)**. Unhook the springs and separate the components.

5 Clean the components and renew worn or damaged items. Apply a little high melting-point grease or anti-seize compound to the adjuster threads, then screw the adjuster in so that it is as short as possible.

6 Apply a smear of anti-seize compound to the shoe rubbing areas on the brake backplate **(see illustration)**.

7 Assemble the shoes, adjuster and expander. Hook the springs into the holes in the shoes **(see illustration)**.

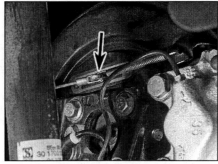

20.2 Handbrake cable and spring attachment (arrowed) on brake backplate - rear disc brake models

8 Offer the shoes to the backplate, fitting the leading shoe over the captive steady pin. Fit the other steady pin and the steady springs and washers.

9 Reconnect the handbrake cable and the return spring.

10 Refit the brake disc as described in Section 8.

11 Adjust the handbrake as described in Chapter 1.

21 Anti-lock braking system (ABS) - general information

The anti-lock braking system (ABS) is available as an option on most models from 1989. The system monitors the rotational speed of each wheel and prevents lock-up during braking by reducing the hydraulic pressure to any wheel cylinder or caliper where lock-up is occurring. This is particularly valuable when braking on loose or slippery surfaces, or during emergency braking when steering corrections may also be taking place. However the system will not protect against skids caused by excessively fast cornering or heavy acceleration on poor surfaces.

The main components of the system are shown in **illustration 21.2**. Magnetic pulses are induced in the wheel speed sensors by a toothed disc which is part of the brake disc or drum. The pulses are monitored by the electronic control unit (ECU). The ECU alters the hydraulic pressure when necessary by means of solenoid valves located in the hydraulic unit. An electric pump in the hydraulic

20.3a Removing a steady washer . . .

20.3b . . . and the rear steady pin

the master cylinder alone.

In use, the onset of the anti-lock function is indicated to the driver by a pulsating of the brake pedal. Any malfunction in the system is indicated by a warning light on the instrument panel. When the system is working correctly, the warning light will illuminate for a few seconds when the ignition is switched on, but will then go out and remain out. If it comes on during driving, there is a fault. Normal braking is not affected by malfunction of the ABS.

The ECU is mounted under the facia on the left-hand side. It is protected against voltage surges by a surge arrester relay and fuse mounted together under the bonnet. The ECU has its own fault diagnosis program, but this is only accessible to Vauxhall dealers or other specialists with the necessary test equipment.

No routine maintenance of the ABS components is required. The hydraulic pipes and unions must be inspected for condition and security in the same way as any other

20.4 Removing the handbrake shoe assembly

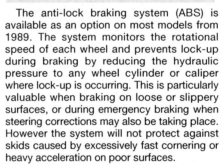

20.6 Anti-seize compound applied to rubbing points (arrowed)

20.7 Handbrake shoe assembly ready for refitting

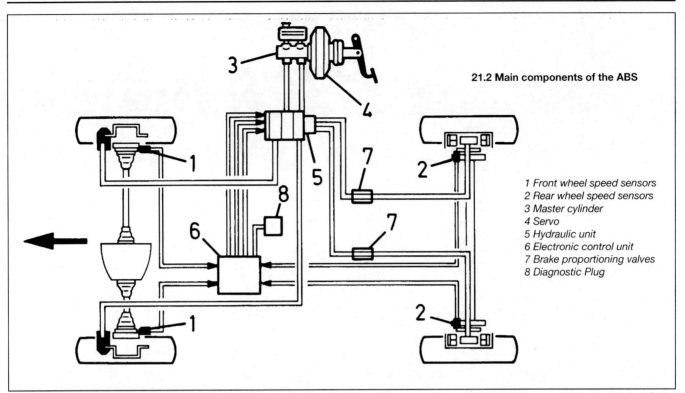

21.2 Main components of the ABS

1 Front wheel speed sensors
2 Rear wheel speed sensors
3 Master cylinder
4 Servo
5 Hydraulic unit
6 Electronic control unit
7 Brake proportioning valves
8 Diagnostic Plug

part of the brake hydraulic system

Note that the ECU is electrically fragile and should be treated with the same precautions as the fuel injection system control unit.

22.2a ABS rear wheel speed sensor on brake backplate securing screw arrowed

22.2b ABS front wheel speed sensor

22 Anti-lock braking system (ABS) components - removal and refitting

Wheel speed sensor

Note: The rear wheel speed sensor on 1992 model year vehicles has its pulse pick-up point unit integral in the hub housing. In the event of the pick-up unit malfunctioning, it will need to be renewed complete with the rear wheel hub unit as described in Chapter 10.

1 Disconnect the battery earth (negative) lead.

2 Remove the single securing screw and withdraw the sensor (see illustrations).

3 Follow the wiring back from the sensor to the connector. Unclip the connector and separate the two halves (see illustrations).

4 Refitting is the reverse of the removal procedure, but apply a smear of grease or

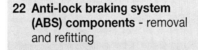

22.2c Removing a front wheel speed sensor

anti-seize compound to the body of the sensor. Check for correct operation of the ABS on completion.

Electronic control unit (ECU)

5 Disconnect the battery earth (negative) lead.

6 Remove the under-dash trim on the passenger (left-hand) side. This is secured by four clips.

7 Remove the ECU from its bracket. Release the spring clip, disconnect the multi-plug and remove the ECU.

8 Refitting is the reverse of the removal procedure. Check for correct operation of the ABS on completion.

ABS surge arrester relay

9 Disconnect the battery earth (negative) lead.

10 Unscrew or unclip the relay bracket. It is on the left-hand suspension turret; the relay is

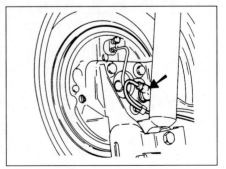

22.2d ABS rear wheel speed sensor (arrowed) on models with rear drum brakes

22.3a Rear sensor connectors next to petrol tank (earlier models)

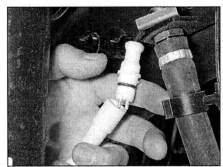

22.3b Separating a front sensor connector

22.10 ABS surge arrester relay (arrowed)

22.15 Two screws (arrowed) which secure the hydraulic unit cover

22.16a Removing the relays from the hydraulic unit

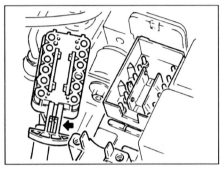

22.16b Squeeze the multi-plug catch (arrowed) to realise it

the one nearest the ABS hydraulic unit **(see illustration)**. Disconnect the multi-plug from the relay and remove it.

11 Note that the relay carries its own fuse. This fuse should be checked before condemning the relay.

12 Refitting is the reverse of the removal procedure.

ABS hydraulic unit removal and refitting

13 Disconnect the battery earth (negative) lead.

14 To minimise hydraulic fluid loss, top-up the reservoir to the maximum level and seal the cap by tightening it down over a piece of

cling film, or by blocking the vent hole temporarily with a piece of tape.

15 Remove the hydraulic unit cover, which is secured by two screws **(see illustration)**.

16 Remove the two relays from the unit. Release the multi-plug catch by squeezing its two halves together and disconnect the multi-plug **(see illustrations)**.

17 Clean around the hydraulic unions on the unit. Make identifying marks if necessary so that each pipe can be refitted to its original location, then disconnect the hydraulic pipes from the unit. Cap or plug open pipes and unions.

18 Undo the three mounting bolts. (Where

slotted mounting holes are used there is no need to remove the bolts completely.) Disconnect the earth strap from the hydraulic unit pump and remove the unit.

19 A defective hydraulic unit must be exchanged or renewed. Retain the relays from the old unit and fit them to the new one. The relay nearest the hydraulic connectors controls the solenoid valves and the other one controls the pump motor.

20 Refitting is the reverse of the removal procedure, noting the following points:
a) Tighten the mounting bolts to the specified torque
b) Bleed the hydraulic system on completion

Chapter 10
Suspension and steering

Contents

Degrees of difficulty

Easy, suitable for novice with little experience	**Fairly easy,** suitable for beginner with some experience	**Fairly difficult,** suitable for competent DIY mechanic	**Difficult,** suitable for experienced DIY mechanic	**Very difficult,** suitable for expert DIY or professional

Specifications

Front suspension
Type . . . . Independent, MacPherson strut, with anti-roll bar on most models

Rear suspension
Type:
   Astramax models . . . . Tubular axle with leaf springs and telescopic shock absorbers
   All other models . . . . Semi-independent, trailing link with coil springs and telescopic shock
                                                                                   absorbers. Level control system optional; anti-roll bar on some models

Steering
Type . . . . Rack and pinion. Power assistance on some models

Wheel alignment and steering angles
Front wheels:
   Toe setting . . . . 1.0 mm ± 1.0 mm toe-out
   Camber (non-adjustable):
      Standard* . . . . -1° 15' + 0° 15'
      Maximum difference between sides . . . . 1°
   Castor (non-adjustable):
      Standard* . . . . 0° to 2°45'
      Maximum difference between sides . . . . 1°
Rear wheels:
   Toe setting (non-adjustable):
      Standard* . . . . 0° 10' toe-out to 0° 40' toe-in
      Maximum difference between sides . . . . 0° 15'
   Camber (non-adjustable):
      Standard*:
         Rear drum brake models . . . . 0° to -1°
         Rear disc brake models . . . . -1°10' to -2°10'
      Maximum difference between sides . . . . 0° 30'

*With 70 kg in each front seat, fuel tank half full and (where necessary) the level control system inflated to 1 bar

Roadwheels

Type	Pressed-steel or aluminium alloy (depending on model)
Size	4.5J x 13, 5J x 13, 5.5J x 13 or 5.5J x 14

Tyres

Size:

4.5J x 13	145 R 13
5J x 13	155 R 13
5.5J x 13	155 R 13 or 175/70 R 13
5.5J x 14	175/65 R 14, 185/60 R 14 or 185/65 R 14

Pressures - refer to Chapter 1 Specifications

Torque wrench settings

	Nm	lbf ft
Front suspension		
Control arm pivot bolt	140	103
Control arm clamp bolts	70	52
Control arm balljoint pin nut	70	52
Control arm balljoint securing nuts	65	48
Suspension strut top mounting nuts	30	22
Suspension strut piston rod nut	55	41
Suspension strut ring nut	200	148
Steering tie-rod balljoint nut	60	44
Anti-roll bar brackets	40	30
Rear suspension		
Axle arm mountings to underbody	105	77
Rear anti-roll bar to rear axle	80	59
Rear auxiliary anti-roll bar - 2.0 litre 16-valve models	30	22
Shock absorber lower mountings:		
Hatchback, Saloon and Astramax	70	52
Estate and Van	10	7
Shock absorber top mountings:		
Hatchback and Saloon	See text	
Estate, Van and Astramax	70	52
Rear hub bearing nut:		
Stage 1	25	18
Stage 2	See text	
Leaf spring suspension components (Astramax):		
U-bolt nuts	45	33
Bump stop cup nut	20	15
Bump stop	50	37
Brake pressure regulating valve spring bracket	20	15
Steering		
Adjuster screw locknut	60	44
Flexible coupling clamp bolts	22	16
Steering wheel nut	25	18
Steering gear mountings	15	11
Pinion nut	40	30
Steering damper mounting (pinion end)	12	9
Steering damper mounting (moving end)	See text	
Tie-rod to rack	110	81
Tie-rod balljoint nut	60	44
Tie-rod and balljoint clamp bolts	20	15
Steering column support to bulkhead	22	16
Steering column bracket self - locking nut	15	11
Power steering fittings:		
Hydraulic unions on rack	37	27
Hydraulic unions on pump	28	21
Union nut - flexible hose to high pressure pipe	42	31
Pump support to block	40	30
Pump brackets to support	15	11
Tensioner strap to pump	40	30
Tensioner strap to support	15	11
Tensioner locknuts	40	30
Roadwheels		
Wheel bolts	90	66

1 General information

The front suspension is fully independent. It consists of MacPherson struts; the coil springs surrounding the shock absorbers. An anti-roll bar is fitted to most models **(see illustration)**.

Rear suspension is by axle tube and twin trailing arms. Coil springs and telescopic shock absorbers are used, mounted independently of each other. Again, an anti-roll bar is fitted to most models **(see illustration)**. On 2.0 litre 16-valve models and auxiliary anti-roll bar is also fitted.

A driver-operated level control system is available as an option on some models. The system enables the vehicle ride height and attitude to be maintained regardless of loading.

The steering gear is of rack and pinion type.

A collapsible steering column is fitted; on some models the top part of the column is adjustable to provide different steering wheel positions.

A steering damper is fitted to certain models without power assistance to reduce the feedback of shocks to the steering wheel.

Power assistance is available as an option on the larger-engined models. Assistance is by hydraulic pressure, generated in a pump driven from the crankshaft pulley.

1.1 Exploded view of the front suspension components

1 Suspension assembly (LH)
2 Cap
3 Piston rod nut
4 Strut mounting nut
5 Strut top mounting
6 Thrustwasher
7 Spring seat
8 Guide ring
9 Damper ring
10 Spring
11 Bellows
12 Ring nut
13 Shock absorber cartridge
14 Steering eye
15 Steering knuckle
16 Brake disc shield
17 Circlips
18 Hub bearing
19 Hub
20 Brake disc
21 Driveshaft nut
22 Brake caliper
23 Control arm balljoint
24 Balljoint nut
25 Control arm clamp
26 Control arm rear bush
27 Control arm
28 Mounting point
29 Control arm pivot bush
30 Control arm pivot bolt
31 Anti-roll bar link bolt
32 Anti-roll bar link
33 Anti-roll bar
34 Anti-roll bar mounting
35 Anti-roll bar clamp
36 Driveshaft

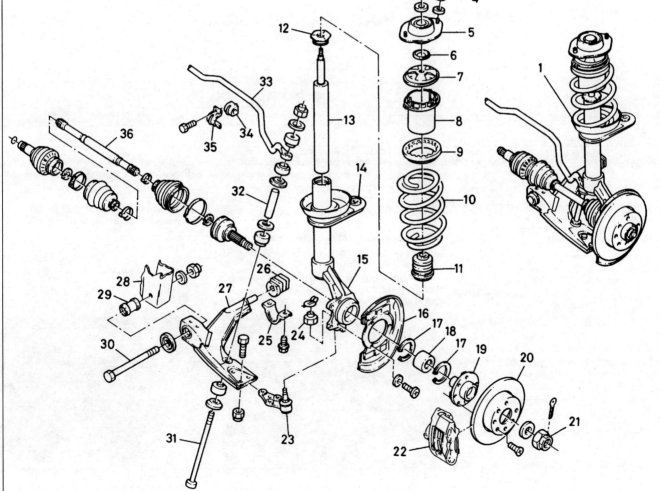

1.2 Exploded view of rear suspension components

1 Shock absorber (Estate)	5 Hub nut	9 Inner bearing	13 Axle arm bush
2 Spring*	6 Thrustwasher	10 Oil seal	14 Anti-roll bar
3 Shock absorber (Hatchback)	7 Outer bearing	11 Stub axle	15 Rubber damper
4 Spring*	8 Hub	12 Axle arm	

Typical - alternative type may be fitted

2 Front suspension strut - removal and refitting

Removal

1 Slacken the front wheel bolts, raise and support the vehicle (see "*Jacking and Vehicle Support*") and remove the front wheel.
2 Remove the split pin and undo the driveshaft retaining nut (see Chapter 8 for details). Remove the nut and washer.
3 Unbolt the brake caliper and tie it up out of the way so that the hydraulic hose is not strained (See Chapter 9 for details).
4 Disconnect the tie-rod and control arm balljoints using a balljoint separator.
5 Push the driveshaft out of the hub and tie it up out of the way (see Chapter 8). Remember that the vehicle must not be moved on its wheels without the hub bearing being clamped.
6 Undo the two securing nuts from the suspension turret and remove the strut downwards.

Refitting

7 Commence refitting by offering the strut to the turret. Secure it with new self-locking nuts, tightened to the specified torque.
8 Lubricate the driveshaft splines and pass

the driveshaft into the hub. Fit a new washer and castellated nut, but only tighten the nut finger tight at this stage.
9 Reconnect the control arm balljoint. Tighten the pin nut to the specified torque and secure it with a new split pin.
10 Reconnect the tie-rod balljoint. Fit a new self-locking nut and tighten it to the specified torque.
11 Clean out the brake caliper mounting bolt holes, then refit the caliper and secure with new bolts coated with thread locking compound. Tighten the bolts to the specified torque (see Chapter 9 Specifications).
12 Tighten the driveshaft nut (see Chapter 8).

3.3a Removing the hub from the carrier

13 Refit the roadwheel, lower the vehicle and tighten the wheel bolts.

3 Front hub bearings - renewal

1 Remove the suspension strut (Section 2).
2 Remove the securing screw and take off the brake disc.
3 Support the steering knuckle and press or drive out the hub. Alternatively, draw off the hub by screwing two wheel bolts onto progressively thicker packing pieces **(see illustrations)**.

3.3b Hub removed from the carrier

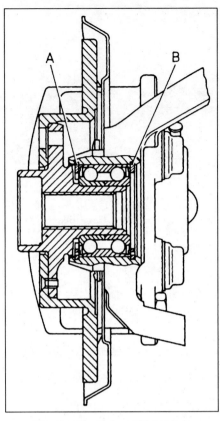

3.5a Sectional view of front hub

A Outboard circlip   B Inboard circlip

4 Remove the brake disc shield.
5 Remove the two circlips **(see illustrations)** and press or drive the bearing outer races out of the steering knuckle.
6 If the bearing inner race stayed on the hub, press or pull it off.
7 Fit the outboard circlip to its groove in the steering knuckle so that the ends of the circlip will point downwards when the strut is installed.
8 Press the new bearing into position, acting only on the outer race, until it contacts the outboard circlip.
9 Fit the inboard circlip, again with the ends pointing downwards.

4.6b Removing the strut ring nut

3.5b Removing a hub bearing circlip

10 Refit the brake disc shield.
11 Support the bearing inner race with a tube and press the hub into position.
12 Refit and secure the brake disc.
13 Refit the suspension strut as described in Section 2.

4 Front suspension strut - overhaul

> **Warning: Before attempting to dismantle the front/rear suspension strut a suitable tool to hold the coil spring in compression must be obtained Adjustable coil spring compressors are readily available and are recommended for this operation. Any attempt to dismantle the strut without such a tool is likely to result in damage or personal injury.**

1 Remove the suspension strut (Section 2).
2 Clamp the strut in a vice. Fit the spring compressor and tighten it to unload the pressure on the upper seat.
3 Hold the flats on the piston rod to stop it rotating and unscrew the piston rod nut. A 19 mm ring spanner with a deep offset will be needed.
4 Remove the top mounting and ball-bearing.
5 Carefully release the spring compressor. Remove the spring seat, guide ring, damper ring and bellows, followed by the spring itself. On later models also remove the rubber damping ring.

4.7 Removing the shock absorber cartridge

4.6a One method of unscrewing the strut ring nut

6 To remove the shock absorber cartridge, unscrew the ring nut from the top of the strut tube. This nut is very tight: one way of undoing it is to invert the strut so that the nut is clamped in the vice, then levering the strut round using a long bar and a bolt passed through the steering eye **(see illustrations)**.
7 With the ring nut removed, the cartridge can be withdrawn and the new one fitted **(see illustration)**. Secure it with a new ring nut, tightened to the specified torque. Do not clean the wax off the new nut.
8 Refit the rubber damping ring (where fitted) then compress the spring and refit it. (Strictly speaking it can be left in place when renewing the cartridge, but unless special tools are available for dealing with the ring nut, it will be too much in the way.)
9 Lubricate the top mounting ball-bearing with grease to GM spec 19 41 574. (The bearing cannot be renewed independently of the mounting) **(see illustration)**.
10 Fit the top mounting to the strut piston rod, making sure that the lower thrustwasher is fitted with the raised edge upwards **(see illustration)**. Hold the piston rod still and fit a new self-locking nut; tighten the nut to the specified torque.

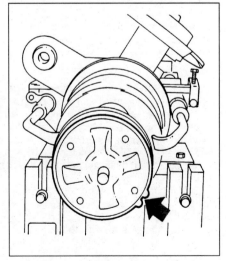

4.9 Lug on spring seat (arrowed) points forwards on LH strut, rearwards on RH strut

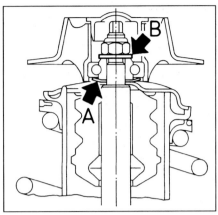

4.10 Sectional view of strut top mounting

A Lower thrustwasher   B Upper thrustwasher

11 Release the spring compressor. Make sure that the ends of the springs are correctly seated.
12 Release the strut from the vice and refit it to the vehicle, as described in Section 2.
13 If new springs or shock absorbers are being fitted, it is good practice to fit new components to both sides. A great variety of springs is available: consult your GM dealer to be sure of obtaining the correct ones.

5 Front suspension control arm - removal and refitting

Removal

1 Slacken the front wheel bolts, raise and support the vehicle (see "*Jacking and Vehicle Support*") and remove the front wheel.
2 When fitted, unbolt the anti-roll bar from the control arm.
3 Remove the split pin and slacken the control arm balljoint nut **(see illustration)**. Separate the balljoint with a proprietary separator and remove the nut.
4 Unscrew the clamp bolts and the pivot bolts from the inboard end of the arm **(see illustration)**. Withdraw the arm.

Refitting

5 Before refitting, clean out the clamp bolt holes with a tap or a bolt with a slot cut in it.
6 Commence refitting by bolting the arm loosely into position. Fit the pivot bolt with its head facing towards the front of the vehicle and use a new self-locking nut.
7 Use new clamp bolts and coat their threads with locking compound.
8 Jack up under the control arm so that it is more or less horizontal, then tighten the pivot bolt to the specified torque.
9 Tighten the clamp bolts to the specified torque. Lower the jack under the control arm.
10 Tighten the balljoint pin nut to the specified torque and secure with a new split pin.

5.3 Control arm balljoint nut (arrowed)

11 Reconnect the anti-roll bar (if applicable). Refer to Section 8 for tightening procedure.
12 Refit the roadwheel, lower the vehicle and tighten the wheel bolts.

6 Control arm bushes - renewal

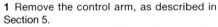

1 Remove the control arm, as described in Section 5.
2 Press out the front bush using suitable pieces of tube and a vice or a long bolt and washers. The bush should be removed from front to rear.
3 Fit the new front bush in the same direction (front to rear), using liquid detergent as a lubricant. The inner sleeve collar faces rearwards. When correctly fitted, the bush should overhang equally on both sides.
4 Support the front of the rear bush. Note which way round it is fitted, then press the arm out of it.
5 Lubricate the rear spigot with liquid detergent, then press on the new rear bush, making sure it is the right way round (flattened surface towards balljoint pin).
6 Refit the control arm, as described in Section 5.

7 Control arm balljoint - renewal

1 Remove the control arm (Section 5).
2 Drill out the rivets which secure the old balljoint. Use a pillar drill with a 12 mm bit,

8.2 Front anti-roll bar end link

5.4 Control arm clamp bolts (arrowed)

and drill accurately into a centre punch mark on each rivet head. Have this work done professionally if need be: sloppy drilling will render the arm scrap.
3 Fit the new balljoint and secure it with the bolts and self-locking nuts provided. The nuts should be fitted on the underside of the arm. Tighten the nuts to the specified torque.
4 Refit the control arm, as described in Section 5.

8 Front anti-roll bar - removal and refitting

Removal

1 Raise and support the front of the vehicle (see "*Jacking and Vehicle Support*").
2 Unbolt both ends of the anti-roll bar from the control arms **(see illustration)**.
3 Unbolt the two brackets from the bulkhead.
4 Remove the anti-roll bar through one of the wheel arches, turning the steering wheel as necessary to obtain sufficient clearance.

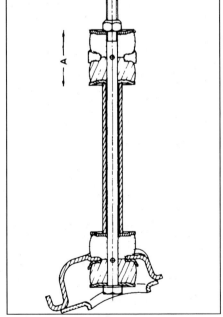

8.7 Anti-roll bar cushion link setting
A = 38mm

5 Renew the rubber mountings as necessary. Use a silicone-based lubricant on the bulkhead bracket bushes.

Refitting

6 When refitting, fasten the two brackets first; tightening their bolts to the specified torque.
7 Tighten the end mountings to achieve a dimension A, as shown using new self-locking nuts **(see illustration)**.
8 Lower the vehicle when the anti-roll bar is secured.

9 Rear hub bearings - adjustment

Early (pre 1992) models

1 Chock the front wheels. engage a gear (or P) and release the handbrake.
2 Remove the wheel trim. If the roadwheels have no central hole, slacken the wheel bolts.
3 Raise and support the rear of the vehicle (see "*Jacking and Vehicle Support*") so that the wheel is free to turn. If it has no central hole, remove it.
4 Prise off the hub grease cap using a stout screwdriver.
5 Remove the split pin from the hub nut. Tighten the nut to 25 Nm, at the same time turning the wheel or brake drum in order to settle the bearings.
6 Slacken the hub nut until the thrustwasher behind the nut can just be moved by poking it with a screwdriver. Do not lever or twist against the hub nut or brake drum when testing the washer for freedom of movement
7 Insert a new split pin to secure the hub nut. If the split pin holes are not aligned, tighten the nut to align the nearest holes, temporarily insert the split pin and check to see if the washer can still be moved. If it cannot, remove the split pin and back off the nut to the next set of holes.
8 When adjustment is correct, spread the legs of the split pin around the nut. Refit the grease cap, and the roadwheel is removed, and lower the vehicle. Tighten the wheel bolts if they were disturbed and refit the wheel trim.
9 If adjustment fails to cure noise or roughness, the bearings should be renewed, as described in the next Section.

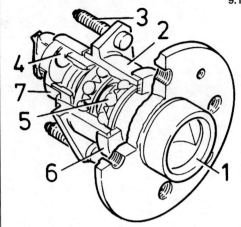

9.10 Rear wheel hub assembly - later (1992 onwards) models

1 Hub
2 Bearing housing
3 Stud
4 End cap (with integral wheel speed sensor - models with ABS)
5 Bearings
6 Sealing ring
7 Pulse gear (ABS vehicles only)

Later (1992 onwards) models

10 On later models, adjustment of the rear hub bearings is not possible. The taper roller bearings fitted to earlier models are replaced with double-row roller type bearings which are sealed and are intended to last the vehicle's entire service life **(see illustration)**. **Note:** *Never overtighten the hub nut beyond the specified torque setting in an attempt to "adjust" the bearing.* If there is excess play in the hub bearing, the bearings must be renewed.

10 Rear hub - removal and refitting

Removal

Early (pre 1992) models

1 Remove the brake drum/disc, as described in Chapter 9.
2 Prise off the hub grease cap, remove the split pin and undo the hub nut **(see illustration)**.
3 Pull the hub off the stub axle. Catch the thrustwasher and the outer bearing race, which will be displaced.

Later (1992) models

4 Remove the brake drum/disc as described in Chapter 9.

5 Disconnect the ABS wheel speed sensor wiring connector (where necessary) then undo the four retaining nuts and remove the hub assembly from the vehicle.

Refitting

Early (pre 1992) models

6 Fit the hub to the stub axle, being careful not to damage the oil seal. Fit the outer bearing race, the thrustwasher and the castellated nut **(see illustrations)**.
7 Tighten the nut finger tight, then refit the brake drum/disc, as described in Chapter 9.
8 Adjust the bearings, as described in Section 9.

Later (1992 onwards) models

9 Ensure that the hub and carrier mating surfaces are clean and dry then fit the hub assembly. Refit the retaining nuts and tighten them securely
10 Reconnect the ABS sensor wiring connector (where necessary) and refit the drum/disc as described in Chapter 9.

11 Rear hub bearings - renewal

Early (pre 1992) models

1 Remove the hub assembly as described in Section 10.

10.2 Rear hub nut split pin

10.6a Fit the outer bearing race . . .

10.6b . . . the washer and the castellated nut

2 Prise the oil seal out of the inboard side of the hub.

3 Extract the inner bearing race, then press or drive the bearing outer tracks from the hub.

4 Clean out the old grease from the hub cavity. Make sure the bearing seats are undamaged, then press or drive the new tracks squarely into the hub.

5 Generously grease the bearing races, the new oil seal and the bearing tracks. Half fill the space between the tracks with grease.

6 Fit the inner race and then the oil seal; lips inwards. Tap the seal into place with a tube or a piece of wood.

7 Refit the hub as described in Section 10.

Later (1992 onwards) models

8 On later models if the bearings are worn the complete hub assembly must be renewed; it is not possible to renew the bearings separately.

12 Rear shock absorbers - removal and refitting

Note: *Refer to Section 17 for information on the Astramax*

1 Shock absorbers should be renewed in pairs, but they should only be removed from one side at a time. Proceed as described under the relevant sub-heading

Hatchback and Saloon

2 Inside the vehicle, remove the cap from the shock absorber top mounting. Grip the flats on the piston rod with pliers or a small

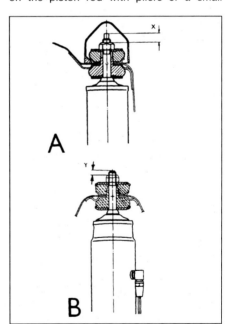

12.9 Rear shock absorber top mounting setting

A Without level control
B With level control or two locknuts

$X = 9$ mm $Y = 6$ mm

12.2 Rear shock absorber upper mounting - Hatchback

spanner and unscrew the top mounting nut. Remove the nut, washer and rubber buffer **(see illustration)**.

3 Raise and support the rear of the vehicle (see "*Jacking and Vehicle Support*").

4 On vehicles with the level control system disconnect the pressure line from the shock absorber by undoing the union nut.

5 Unbolt the shock absorber lower mounting **(see illustration)**. Free the shock absorber from the bracket and remove it from the vehicle.

6 Commence refitting by introducing the shock absorber to the lower mounting bracket. Use a plastic or wooden mallet if need be.

7 Wedge the shock absorber so that the lower mounting hole is aligned. Fit the lower mounting bolt, tapping it gently through the shock absorber eye, and tighten it to the specified torque.

8 Partly lower the vehicle, guiding the top of the shock absorber into position. Make sure that the washer and rubber buffer for the underside of the top mounting are in position.

9 Lower the vehicle to the ground. Fit the top mounting rubber buffer and washer. Tighten the mounting nut or nuts to achieve an exposed piston rod length as shown **(see illustration)**. Refit the cap.

10 Repeat the operations on the other side of the vehicle. Where necessary, on completion, reconnect the pressure line unions and inflate the system to 0.8 bar.

Estate and Van

11 Raise and support the rear of the vehicle (see "*Jacking and Vehicle Support*").

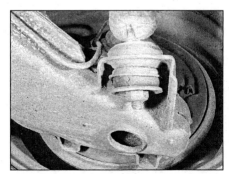

12.13 Rear shock absorber lower mounting - Estate

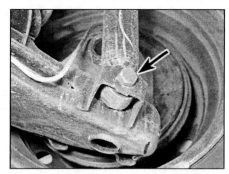

12.5 Rear shock absorber lower mounting bolt (arrowed) - Hatchback

12 On vehicles with the level control system, disconnect the pressure line from the shock absorber by undoing the union nut.

13 Unload the shock absorber mounting by jacking up under the axle arm. Remove the lower mounting nut, washer and rubber buffer **(see illustration)**. Lower the jack.

14 Remove the top mounting bolt **(see illustration)** and extract the shock absorber from its mountings.

15 Commence refitting by securing the top end of the shock absorber, but only tighten the bolt loosely at first.

16 Secure the bottom mounting, making sure that the rubber buffers and washers are in position, and tighten the cap nut to the specified torque.

17 Tighten the top mounting to the specified torque.

18 Repeat the operations on the other side of the vehicle, then lower it to the ground. Where necessary, on completion, reconnect the pressure line unions and inflate the system to 0.8 bar.

13 Rear anti-roll bar - removal and refitting

Main roll bar

Removal

1 Slacken the rear wheel bolts on one side only. Raise and support the rear of the vehicle (see "*Jacking and Vehicle Support*") and remove the roadwheel.

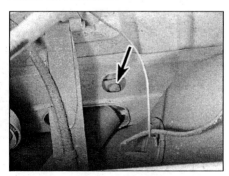

12.14 Rear shock absorber top mounting bolt (arrowed) - Estate

13.2 Rear anti-roll bar mounting nut and bolt (arrowed)

2 Remove the mounting nut and bolt from both ends of the anti-roll bar (see illustration).
3 Remove the rubber damper from the centre of the axle.
4 Remove the anti-roll bar from the side on which the wheel was removed. If it is reluctant to move, drive it from the other side.

Refitting

5 Refit in the reverse order to removal. Use liquid detergent as a lubricant when fitting the rubber damper. Tighten the anti-roll bar mountings to the specified torque.

Auxiliary anti-roll bar - 2.0 litre 16-valve models

Removal

6 Raise and support the rear of the car (see "Jacking and Vehicle Support").
7 Remove the two nuts and bolts from each end of the anti-roll bar (see illustration).

Refitting

8 Refitting is the reverse of the removal procedure. Tighten the fastenings to the specified torque.

14 Rear springs - removal and refitting

Note: Refer to Section 17 for information on the Astramax
1 Rear springs should be renewed in pairs.
2 On vehicles with a level control system, depressurise it at the filling valve.

13.7 Auxiliary anti-roll bar mounting - 2. litre 16-valve models

3 Raise and support the rear of the vehicle (see "Jacking and Vehicle Support").

Hatchback and Saloon

4 Unload the shock absorber mounting on one side by jacking up under the axle arm. A tool made up to the dimensions shown is useful for this (see illustration).
5 Unbolt the shock absorber lower mounting. Free the lower end of the shock absorber from its bracket.
6 Lower the jack and remove the spring and rubber dampers. Lever the axle arm downwards slightly if necessary to remove the spring.
7 If the spring is to be renewed, it is sound policy to renew the rubber dampers also.
8 Insert the new spring and dampers, raise the axle arm and make fast the shock absorber lower mounting. Where conical type springs are fitted, ensure that the upper ends are correctly located in the spring seat (see illustration).
9 Repeat the operations on the other side of the vehicle. On completion, inflate the level control system (where fitted) to 0.8 bar.

Estate and Van

10 Jack up under one axle arm and unbolt the shock absorber lower mounting. Lower the jack and repeat the operation on the other side, leaving the jack in place.
11 Remove the springs and lower dampers, lowering the jack as necessary.
12 If renewing the sprung upper dampers, glue them in position with impact adhesive to aid fitting.

13 Fit the new spring and dampers. Where conical type springs are fitted, ensure that the upper ends are correctly located in the spring seat (see illustration 14.8).
14 Raise the jack and reconnect the shock absorber lower mounting on that side, then transfer the jack to the other side and secure the other shock absorber.
15 Tighten the shock absorber lower mountings to the specified torque. On completion, inflate the level control system (where fitted) to 0.8 bar.

15 Rear axle assembly - removal and refitting

Note: Refer to Section 17 for information on the Astramax

Removal

1 Slacken the rear wheel bolts, raise and support the rear of the vehicle (see "Jacking and Vehicle Support") and remove the rear wheels.
2 On vehicles with a level control system, depressurise it at the filling valve.
3 Disconnect the handbrake cable at the equaliser yoke and free it from the underbody guides.
4 Unhook the rear part of the exhaust system from its rubber mountings.
5 Disconnect the brake flexible hose at the rear axle brackets. Plug or cap the hoses to reduce fluid spillage.
6 On Estate and Van models, unbolt the brake pressure regulating valve spring bracket.
7 Remove the rear springs, as described in Section 14.
8 Support the centre of the rear axle with a jack and a block of wood or a cradle. Unhook the axle arm mountings from the underbody (see illustration) and lower the jack. An assistant should steady the assembly whilst it is being unbolted and lowered.
9 Pass the handbrake cable over the exhaust system and remove the axle assembly.
10 Strip the axle of brake components, hubs, anti-roll bar etc, if needed for transfer to a new axle. Refer to the appropriate Chapters and Sections for details.

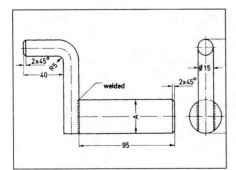

14.4 Rear axle arm jacking adapter. All dimensions in mm; diameter A to suit jack

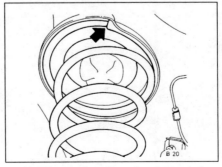

14.8 Correct location of upper end of spring (arrowed) - conical type shown

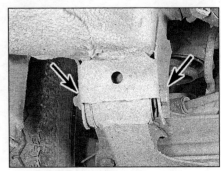

15.8 Axle arm mounting nut and bolt (arrowed)

Refitting

11 With the aid of an assistant, offer the new axle to the vehicle, remembering to pass the handbrake cable over the exhaust system. Insert the axle arm mounting bolts, but do not tighten them yet.
12 Fit the springs and secure the shock absorbers, as described in Section 14.
13 Reconnect the brake flexible hoses, then bleed the hydraulic system (Chapter 9).
14 On Estate and Van models, secure the brake pressure regulating valve spring bracket, as described in Chapter 9.
15 Secure the exhaust system to its mountings.
16 Secure the handbrake cable to its guides and to the yoke.
17 Adjust the rear wheel bearings, as described in Section 9.
18 Adjust the brakes by making at least 10 applications of the brake pedal, then adjust the handbrake, as described in Chapter 1.
19 Fit the roadwheels, lower the vehicle and tighten the wheel bolts.
20 Load the vehicle by having two assistants sit in the front seats, then tighten the axle arm mounting bolts to the specified torque.
21 When a level control system is fitted, inflate it to 0.8 bar.

16 Rear axle mounting bushes - renewal

1 The mounting bushes must always be renewed in pairs. Without doubt the opportunity should be taken to renew them if the axle is removed for some other reason. They can be renewed with the axle in situ as follows.

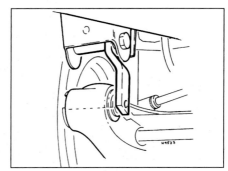
16.8 Cranked link used to support axle arm

2 Depressurise the level control system, when fitted.
3 Remove the rear springs, as described in Section 14, then reattach the shock absorber lower mountings.
4 On Estate and Van models, unbolt the brake pressure regulating valve spring bracket.
5 Unclip the brake flexible hose from the brackets on the underbody. If care is taken there is no need to disconnect the hoses.
6 Support the axle centrally with a hydraulic jack and a block of wood or a cradle.
7 Remove the axle arm mounting bolts and carefully lower the axle until the bushes are accessible. Bend the brake pipes slightly if necessary to avoid straining the flexible hoses.
8 Cut or chisel the flange from the outboard face of one bush. In order to restrain the axle from moving during this operation, the makers specify the use of a cranked link, one end of which bolts to the axle arm mounting, the other end carrying a pin which locates in the inner side of the bush **(see illustration)**. Be

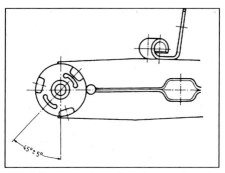
16.10 Correct orientation of rear axle arm bush

careful not to knock the axle off the jack: provide additional supports if possible.
9 Draw the old bush out from the inboard side to the outboard, using suitable tubes, bolts and washers. (The maker's special tool set for this job, consisting of the tubes etc plus the cranked link, is numbered KM-452-A). Removal of the bush will be easier if the axle arm around it is heated to 50° to 70°C using hot air, steam or a soldering iron. **Do not** use a naked flame: the fuel tank is not far away.
10 Coat the new bush with liquid detergent and draw it into place, observing the correct orientation, until the flange rests against the edge of the axle arm **(see illustration)**.
11 Repeat the operations on the other side of the vehicle.
12 Raise and secure the axle, but do not tighten the axle arm bolts yet.
13 Secure the brake flexible hose to their brackets.
14 Refit the springs (Section 14).
15 On Estate and Van models, refit the pressure regulating valve spring bracket, as described in Chapter 9, Section 15.
16 Lower the vehicle onto its wheels, have two assistants sit in the front seats and tighten the axle arm mounting bolts to the specified torque.
17 When fitted, pressurise the level control system to 0.8 bar.

17 Leaf spring rear suspension components (Astramax) - removal and refitting

Rear shock absorber

1 Raise and support the rear of the vehicle (see "Jacking and Vehicle Support") **(see illustration)**.

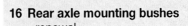
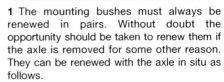
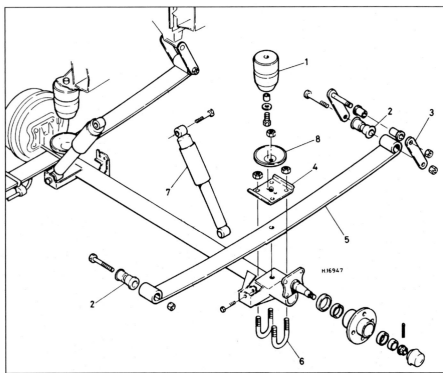

17.1 Exploded view of Astramax rear suspension

1 Bump stop	5 Leaf spring
2 Bushes	6 U-bolt
3 Shackle	7 Shock absorber
4 Tensioning pin	8 Bump stop cup

2 Unload the shock absorber mounting by jacking up under the axle arm.
3 Slacken and remove the upper and lower mounting bolts and remove the shock absorber from the vehicle.
4 Refitting is the reverse of removal, tightening the shock absorber bolts to the specified torque.
5 Repeat the operations on the other side of the vehicle, then lower it to the ground.

Rear leaf spring

6 Raise the rear of the vehicle and support it securely. Support the rear axle with another jack.
7 Remove the handbrake cable bracket from the spring.
8 Disconnect the brake pressure regulating valve spring from the leaf spring.
9 Unbolt the front leaf spring-to-body attachment and remove the bolt.
10 Unbolt the rear spring-to-shackle attachment and remove the bolt.
11 Remove the bump stop nut and washer, and the cup itself.
12 Unscrew the U-bolt nuts. Remove the tensioning plate and the U-bolts.
13 Remove the leaf spring from the vehicle.
14 If the spring is being renewed, transfer the brake pressure regulating valve spring bracket to the new spring.
15 To renew the spring bushes, press or drive out the old bushes and press in the new ones using a long bolt, some tubing and washers. Coat the new bushes with liquid detergent as an assembly lubricant.
16 Refitting is the reverse of the removal procedure, noting the following points:
 a) The shorter section of the spring faces the front of the vehicle.
 b) The hole in the tensioning plate for the bump stop cup locating lug must be towards the centre of the vehicle.
 c) The exposed lengths of thread on the U-bolts must not differ by more than 3 mm.
 d) Adjust the position of the brake pressure regulating valve spring bracket so that the spring is neither tight nor slack.

Bump stop

17 Raise and support the rear of the vehicle (see "Jacking and Vehicle Support").
18 Unscrew the bump stop bolt and remove the bump stop.
19 Refitting is the reverse of the removal procedure.

Rear axle

20 Slacken the rear wheel bolts, raise and support the rear of the vehicle and remove the rear wheels.
21 Remove the brake drums/discs and disconnect the handbrake cable (Chapter 9).
22 Disconnect the brake flexible hoses at the bracket on the axle. Plug or cap the open unions.
23 Support the centre of the rear axle with a

jack and a block of wood or a cradle.
24 Remove the shock absorber lower mounting bolts on both sides.
25 Remove the bump stop cups from both sides. They are each secured by a single nut and washer.
26 Unscrew the U-bolt nuts on one side of the axle. Remove the tensioning plate and the U-bolts.
27 Repeat the procedure on the other side.
Note: The axle may tip to one side or the other if it is not centrally supported.
28 Lower the jack and remove the axle from the vehicle.
29 Strip off the hubs, brake components etc if needed for transfer to another axle.
30 Refitting is the reverse of the removal procedure, noting the following points:
 a) The hole in the tensioning plate for the bump stop cup locating lug must be towards the centre of the vehicle.
 b) The exposed lengths of thread on the U-bolts must not differ by more than 3 mm.
 c) Tighten all fastenings to the specified torque.
 d) Bleed the brake hydraulic system and adjust the handbrake on completion.

18 Level control system - description and maintenance

1 On vehicles equipped with this system ride height can be controlled by pressurising the rear shock absorbers with air. The shock absorbers are connected to each other, and to the filling valve, by a high pressure pipeline. The filling valve is similar to a tyre inflation valve; it is located on the right-hand side of the load area.
2 For normal (unladen) running, the system should be pressurised to 0.8 bar. Before loading the vehicle, measure the ride height between the rear bumper and the ground. After loading, restore the ride height by increasing the system pressure using tyre inflation equipment. Do not exceed 5 bar.
3 Do not drive the vehicle unladen with a high pressure in the system, nor inflate the system to the maximum pressure before loading.

19.2 Removing the steering wheel central cap

4 Maintenance consists of checking the pressure lines and unions for security and good condition.

19 Steering wheel - removal and refitting

Removal

1 Disconnect the battery earth lead.
2 Prise off the central cap from the steering wheel. Disconnect the horn contact wires and remove the cap **(see illustration)**.
3 Set the steering in the straight-ahead position.
4 Relieve the locktabs and undo the central retaining nut **(see illustration)**.
5 Depending on the work to be done, it may ease refitting to mark the relationship of the wheel centre to the shaft splines.
6 Pull the wheel off the shaft splines. If pulling by hand, be careful not to injure yourself if the wheel suddenly comes free. Use a puller if it is tight. **Do not** use a hammer: damage to the column may result.
7 If wished, the horn contact ring can now be unclipped. Note that the direction indicator return segment on the ring points to the left.

Refitting

8 Before refitting, make sure that the washer and spring are in place on the shaft. Fit the steering wheel onto the splines, making sure it is correctly aligned.
9 Fit a new lockwasher and refit the nut. Tighten the nut to the specified torque and bend up the lockwasher tabs.
10 Reconnect the horn contact wires and press the central cap into place.
11 Reconnect the battery earth lead.

20 Steering column - removal and refitting

Removal

1 Disconnect the battery earth lead.
2 Although not strictly necessary, access will be improved if the steering wheel is removed. See Section 19.

19.4 Steering wheel retaining nut and locktabs (arrowed)

20.3a Removing an upper shroud securing screw

20.3b Removing a lower shroud securing screw adjustable wheel

3 Remove the upper and lower switch shrouds. These are secured by eight screws with the fixed steering wheel, or five screws with the adjustable wheel (see illustrations).
4 Remove the steering lock cylinder, as described in Section 23.
5 Disconnect the ignition switch multi-plug.
6 Remove the multi-function switches by depressing their retaining clips. With the adjustable wheel it may be necessary to undo the switch housing screws and draw the housing away from the dashboard to provide sufficient clearance.
7 Make sure that the steering is in the straight-ahead position, then remove the flexible coupling clamp bolt from the base of the column. Unbolt the column support from the bulkhead and recover the washer.
8 Remove the column upper mounting bracket nut and bolt. The bolt is of the shear-head type: drill it and extract it with a proprietary stud extractor, or it may be possible to unscrew the bolt by driving its head round with a chisel or punch. The nut is a self-locking type and should be renewed.
9 Withdraw the column slightly to free it from the flexible coupling, then remove it from the vehicle. Avoid knocking or dropping it as this could damage the collapsible section.
10 If a new column assembly is to be fitted, a large plastic washer will be found at the base of the column tube. This is to centre the shaft in the tube and should be removed when fitting is complete.

Refitting

11 Commence refitting by making sure that the roadwheels are still in the straight-ahead position, and that the flexible coupling is positioned so that the column clamp bolt will be horizontal and on top.
12 Offer the column assembly to its mountings, inserting the base of the shaft into the coupling. Insert the mounting nuts and bolts, but only tighten them finger tight at this stage. Do not try to force the column into position or damage may result.
13 Tighten the column bulkhead support bolt to the specified torque. Make sure the washer is in place.
14 Tighten the upper mounting bracket fastenings: the shear-head bolt should be

tightened until its head breaks off. The new self-locking nut should be tightened to the specified torque.
15 Pull the shaft upwards as far as it will go and tighten the flexible coupling clamp bolt to the specified torque.
16 Prise out the plastic washer from the base of the column tube. It can stay on the shaft.
17 Reconnect the ignition switch and refit the multi-function switches.
18 Refit the remaining components in the reverse order to removal.

21 Steering column - overhaul

The steering column incorporates a telescopic safety feature. In the event of a front end crash, the shaft housing collapses and prevents the steering wheel injuring the driver. Before refitting the steering column examine the column and mountings for signs of damage and deformation and check the steering shaft for signs of free play in the column bushes. If there are signs of damage or play, the column must be renewed. Overhaul of the column is possible but this is a fiddly task and should be entrusted to a Vauxhall/Opel dealer. Consult your Vauxhall/Opel dealer for further information.

22 Steering column flexible coupling - removal and refitting

Removal

1 Position the steering in the straight-ahead position
2 Slacken the steering rack mountings on the bulkhead.
3 Remove both clamp bolts from the coupling.
4 Push the coupling upwards, remove it from the pinion shaft, tilt it and withdraw it from the column shaft.

Refitting

5 Before refitting, make sure that the roadwheels are still in the straight-ahead position and that the steering wheel spokes are centred and pointing downwards.

6 Fit the coupling in such a position that the column clamp bolt will be horizontal and on top.
7 Push downwards on the coupling and tighten the pinion side clamp bolt to the specified torque.
8 Tighten the steering gear mountings to the specified torque.
9 Pull the steering shaft upwards as far as it will go and tighten the clamp bolt to the specified torque.
10 Make sure that the roadwheels and the steering wheel are still in the straight-ahead position.

23 Steering lock cylinder and ignition switch wiring block - removal and refitting

1 To renew either the ignition switch or the steering lock cylinder, first remove the lower half of the steering column shroud by undoing and removing the securing screws. Disconnect the battery negative terminal and proceed as described under the relevant sub-heading.

Ignition switch wiring block

2 Disconnect the wiring block from the ignition switch.
3 Slacken the two small retaining screws and withdraw the wiring block from the end of the lock housing.
4 Refitting is the reverse of removal, ensuring that the switch centre is correctly engaged with the lock cylinder rod flats.

Steering lock cylinder

5 Disconnect the battery earth lead and, after removing the lower half of the steering column shroud, insert the ignition key and turn it to the "II" position.
6 Using a piece of wire or a drill shank (3 mm dia), depress the lock spring retaining the cylinder and carefully withdraw the cylinder from its housing (see illustration). It is important that the ignition switch is not removed or disturbed while the lock cylinder is not fitted.
7 Before fitting a new lock cylinder insert the ignition key and turn it to the "II" position. Insert the assembly into the steering lock

23.6 Releasing the steering lock detent spring with an Allen key (arrowed)

24.2 Tie-rod balljoint separator in use It is better practice to leave the balljoint nut loosely fitted

housing and press it down until the retaining spring engages before removing the key.

8 Reconnect the battery earth lead and test the operation of the ignition switch before fitting the lower half shroud.

24 Tie-rod balljoints - removal and refitting

Removal

1 Remove the roadwheel on the side concerned.

2 Slacken the balljoint nut, release the ball-pin using a balljoint separator and remove the nut. Extract the balljoint from the steering arm **(see illustration)**.

3 Slacken the clamp bolt which secures the balljoint to the threaded adjustment pin. Mark the position of the balljoint on the adjustment pin with paint or tape, then unscrew the balljoint from the pin.

4 Note that the balljoints are handed. The right-hand balljoint is marked R; the left-hand balljoint has no marking.

Refitting

5 Screw in the new balljoint onto the adjustment pin to approximately the same position as was occupied by the old one. Secure it with the clamp bolt.

6 Connect the balljoint to the steering arm. Secure it with a new self-locking nut, tightened to the specified torque.

7 Refit the roadwheel, lower the vehicle and tighten the wheel bolts.

8 Check the front wheel alignment and adjust if necessary. No harm will result from driving the vehicle a short distance to have the alignment checked.

25 Steering rack bellows - removal and refitting

Removal

1 Remove the steering gear, as described in Section 27.

2 Remove the mounting bracket and rubber insulator from the end of the rack furthest from the pinion.

3 On power-assisted racks, disconnect the hydraulic pipe union adjacent to the end of the bellows.

4 Remove the clamping wires and slide both bellows and the connecting tube off the rack. Separate the bellows from the tube.

Refitting

5 Fit the new bellows and the tube to the rack. Secure the bellows with new wire clips, positioned so that when the rack is in the car the ends of the clips will point upwards. Make sure that the bellows are not twisted.

6 On power-assisted only, reconnect the hydraulic pipe union using new sealing rings. Tighten the union to the specified torque.

7 Refit the rubber insulator and mounting bracket. The concave end of the mounting bracket flange must point downwards when the rack is fitted.

8 If the pinion sealing cap has been disturbed, make sure it is refitted with its notch engaged with the rib on the pinion housing.

9 Refit the steering gear (Section 27).

26 Steering damper - removal and refitting

Removal

1 When fitted, the steering damper is removed as follows.

2 Remove the securing nut at the moving end of the damper **(see illustration)**. Recover the washer.

3 Unbolt the damper from the bracket at the pinion end and remove it.

Refitting

4 When refitting, secure the pinion end of the damper first and tighten its mounting bolt to the specified torque.

5 Tighten the securing nut at the moving end of the damper to obtain a dimension A as shown **(see illustration)**.

27 Steering gear - removal and refitting

Manual steering

Removal

1 Disconnect the battery earth lead.

2 On carburettor models only, remove the air cleaner, as described in Chapter 3.

3 On models with a headlamp washer system, release the fluid reservoir and move it to one side.

4 Remove both tie-rod bolts from the centre of the rack **(see illustration)**. Recover the bolt locks, the spacer plate and the washers.

5 If a steering damper is fitted, unbolt it at the pinion end and remove it, complete with the moving end tube and bracket.

6 Set the steering in the straight-ahead position.

7 Slacken both clamp bolts on the flexible coupling. Push the coupling upwards as far as it will go.

8 Remove the front right-hand wheel.

9 Unbolt the steering gear mounting brackets from the bulkhead. Make sure that the pinion is free of the coupling, then withdraw the steering gear through the wheel arch.

Refitting

10 Commence refitting by fastening the steering gear to the bulkhead. Tighten the mounting bracket bolts to the specified torque. Use new self-locking nuts on the mounting studs.

26.2 Steering damper securing nut (arrowed)

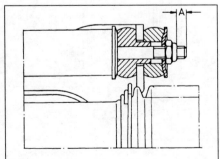

26.5 Steering damper securing nut setting
A = 6 mm

27.4 Tie-rod connection to steering rack

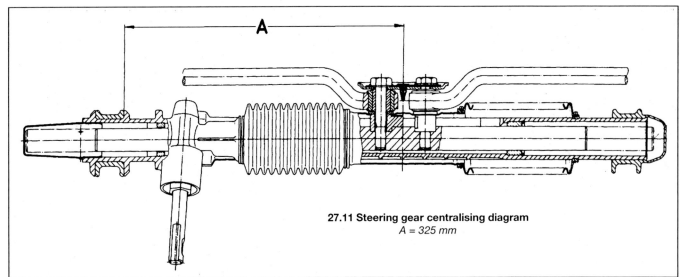

27.11 Steering gear centralising diagram
A = 325 mm

11 Before connecting the flexible coupling make sure the steering gear is in the straight-ahead position (see illustration).
12 Reconnect the flexible coupling as described in Section 6.
13 Reconnect the tie-rods to the rack, remembering to fit the washers under the rod ends. (Note that the tie-rods are handed: they are fitted correctly when their clamp bolts are fitted from below). Fit the spacer plate or damper bracket and tighten the bolts to the specified torque, using new lockplates.
14 Refit the remaining components in the reverse order to removal.

Power steering

Removal

15 Refer to paragraphs 1 to 9, but additionally the flow and return pipes must be disconnected from the pinion housing. Allow the fluid to drain from the open unions, then plug the holes to keep dirt out. Introduction of dirt may seriously damage the hydraulic system.

Refitting

16 Refer to paragraphs 10 to 14. Top-up and bleed the system on completion, as described in Section 29.

28 Steering gear - overhaul

1 Examine the steering gear assembly for signs of wear or damage and check that the rack moves freely throughout the full length of its travel with no signs of roughness or excessive free play between the steering gear pinion and rack. It is possible to overhaul the steering gear assembly housing components but this task should be entrusted to a Vauxhall dealer. The only components which can be renewed easily by the home mechanic are the steering gear bellows and the tie-rod ends which are covered elsewhere in this Chapter.

2 On models equipped with power-assisted steering inspect all the steering gear fluid unions for signs of leakage and check that all union nuts are securely tightened.
3 Inspect the rubber mountings and pinion gear cover renew them if the rubbers shown signs of wear or deterioration.

29 Power-assisted steering - bleeding

1 After any of the hydraulic unions has been disturbed, or if the fluid level has been allowed to fall so low that air has been introduced into the system, bleeding should be carried out as follows.
2 Top-up the reservoir with fresh clean fluid of the specified type. Fluid drained from the system must not be re-used.
3 If the pump is dry, start the engine momentarily and then switch it off. Top-up the reservoir to the lower mark on the dipstick, run the engine briefly again and repeat the process

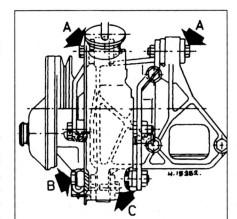

30.3 Steering pump mountings

A Pump pivot bolts
B Tensioner strap pivot bolt
C Tensioner strap mounting bolt

until the fluid level stabilises. It is important that the pump is not allowed to run dry.
4 With the engine running at idle speed, turn the steering wheel approximately 45° to left and right of centre, then from lock to lock. Do not hold the wheel on either lock, as this improves some strain on the hydraulic system.
5 Switch off the engine and correct the fluid level.

30 Power steering pump - removal and refitting

Removal

1 Remove the pump drivebelt, as described in Chapter 1.
2 Disconnect the fluid feed and return hoses from the pump. Be prepared for fluid spillage. Plug the openings; being careful not to introduce dirt.
3 Unbolt and remove the pump (see illustration).
4 A defective pump must be renewed: no spares are available.

Refitting

5 Refit in the reverse order to removal. Tension the drivebelt, as described in Chapter 1, before tightening the pump mountings.
6 Bleed the system, as described in Section 29. Pay particular attention to the procedure required to prime the pump if a new pump has been fitted.

31 Power steering fluid reservoir - removal and refitting

Removal

1 Slacken the reservoir clamp bolt.
2 Disconnect both hoses from the reservoir. Be prepared for fluid spillage. Remove the reservoir.

Refitting

3 Refit in the reverse order to removal. Bleed the system on completion, as described in Section 29.

32 Wheel alignment and steering angles - general information

Accurate front wheel alignment is essential for precise steering and handling, and for even tyre wear. Before carrying out any checking or adjusting operations, make sure that the tyres are correctly inflated, that all steering and suspension joints and linkages are in sound condition and that the wheels are not buckled or distorted, particularly around the rims. It will also be necessary to have the car positioned on flat level ground with enough space to push the car backwards and forwards through about half its length.

Front wheel alignment consists of four factors:

Camber is the angle at which the roadwheels are set from the vertical when viewed from the front or rear of the vehicle. Positive camber is the angle (in degrees) that the wheels are tilted outwards at the top from the vertical.

Castor is the angle between the steering axis and a vertical line when viewed from each side of the vehicle. Positive castor is indicated when the steering axis is inclined towards the rear of the vehicle at its upper end.

Steering axis inclination is the angle, when viewed from the front or rear of the vehicle, between the vertical and an imaginary line drawn between the upper and lower front suspension strut mountings.

Toe setting is the amount by which the distance between the front inside edges of the roadwheel differs from that between the rear inside edges, when measured at hub height. If the distance between the front edges is less than that at the rear, the wheels are said to toe-in. If it is greater than at the rear, the wheels toe-out.

Camber, castor and steering axis inclination are set during manufacture and are not adjustable. Unless the vehicle has suffered accident damage, or there is gross wear in the suspension mountings or joints, it can be assumed that these settings are correct. If for any reason it is believed that they are not correct, the task of checking them should be left to a GM dealer who will have the necessary special equipment needed to measure the small angles involved.

It is, however, within the scope of the home mechanic to check and adjust the front wheel toe setting. To do this a tracking gauge must first be obtained. Two types of gauges are available and can be obtained from motor accessory shops. The first type measures the distance between the front and rear inside edges of the roadwheels, as previously described, with the car stationary. The second type, known as a scuff plate, measures the actual position of the contact surface of the tyre, in relation to the road surface, with the vehicle in motion. This is done by pushing or driving the front tyre over a plate which then moves slightly according to the scuff of the tyre and shows this movement on a scale. Both types have their advantages and disadvantages, but either can give satisfactory results if used correctly and carefully.

Many tyre specialists will also check toe settings free or for a nominal charge.

Make sure that the steering is in the straight-ahead position when making measurements.

If adjustment is found to be necessary, clean the ends of the tie-rods in the area of the adjustment pin and clamp bolts.

Slacken the clamp bolts (one on each tie-rod balljoint and one on each tie-rod) and turn the adjustment pin on each tie-rod by the same amount in the same direction **(see illustration)**. Only turn each pin by a quarter turn at a time before rechecking.

When adjustment is correct, tighten the clamp bolts to the specified torque. Check that the tie-rod lengths are equal to within 5 mm and that the steering wheel spokes are in the correct straight-ahead position.

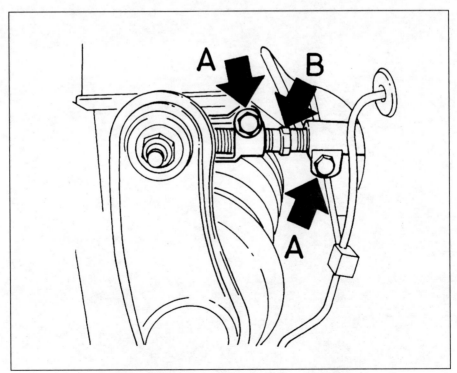

32.8 Toe adjustment points (only one side shown)

A Clamp bolts   *B Adjustment pin*

Notes

Chapter 11
Bodywork and fittings

Contents

Degrees of difficulty

Easy, suitable for novice with little experience	Fairly easy, suitable for beginner with some experience	Fairly difficult, suitable for competent DIY mechanic	Difficult, suitable for experienced DIY mechanic	Very difficult, suitable for expert DIY or professional

Specifications

Torque wrench settings	Nm	lbf ft
Bonnet hinges	20	15
Tailgate hinges	20	15
Tailgate lock striker	20	15
Front and rear trim panel nuts	12	9
Tailgate strut attachments	20	15
Seat belt mountings	35	25
Rear crossmember-to- lock bolts	55	43
Rear body panel-to-lock bolts	20	15
Front seat mountings	20	15
Front seat back-to-frame bolts	30	22

1 General information

The main body structure is a welded construction of individually shaped panels which make up a 'monocoque' bodyshell, without a separate chassis. Various areas are strengthened to provide for suspension, steering and engine attachments and load distribution. The whole shell is very strong and rigid for its weight.

The front wings are bolted in position and can be renewed without special equipment.

Interior fittings are of an extremely high standard, even on basic models.

2 Maintenance - bodywork and underframe

1 The general condition of a vehicle's bodywork is the one thing that significantly affects its value. Maintenance is easy but needs to be regular. Neglect, particularly after minor damage, can lead quickly to further deterioration and costly repair bills. It is important also to keep watch on those parts of the vehicle not immediately visible, for instance the underside, inside all the wheel arches and the lower part of the engine compartment.

2 The basic maintenance routine for the bodywork is washing preferably with a lot of water, from a hose. This will remove all the loose solids which may have stuck to the vehicle. It is important to flush these off in such a way as to prevent grit from scratching the finish. The wheel arches and underframe need washing in the same way to remove any accumulated mud which will retain moisture and tend to encourage rust. Strange as it may seem, the best time to clean the underframe and wheel arches is in wet weather when the mud is thoroughly wet and soft. In very wet weather the underframe is usually cleaned of large accumulations automatically and this is a good time for inspection.

3 Periodically, except on vehicles with a wax-based underbody protective coating, it is a good idea to have the whole of the underframe of the vehicle steam cleaned, engine compartment included, so that a thorough inspection can be carried out to see what minor repairs and renovations are necessary. Steam cleaning is available at many garages and is necessary for removal of the accumulation of oily grime which sometimes is allowed to become thick in certain areas. If steam cleaning facilities are not available, there are one or two excellent grease solvents available which can be brush applied. The dirt can then be simply hosed off. Note that these methods should not be used on vehicles with wax-based underbody protective coating or the coating will be removed. Such vehicles should be inspected annually, preferably just prior to winter, when the underbody should be washed down and any damage to the wax coating repaired. Ideally, a completely fresh coat should be applied. It would also be worth considering the use of such wax-based protection for injection into door panels, sills, box sections, etc, as an additional safeguard against rust damage where such protection is not provided by the vehicle manufacturer.

4 After washing paintwork, wipe off with a chamois leather to give an unspotted clear finish. A coat of clear protective wax polish, will give added protection against chemical pollutants in the air. If the paintwork sheen has dulled or oxidised, use a cleaner/polisher combination to restore the brilliance of this shine. This requires a little effort, but such dulling is usually caused because regular washing has been neglected. Care needs to be taken with metallic paintwork, as special non abrasive cleaner/polisher is required to avoid damage to the finish. Always check that the door and sill drain holes and pipes are completely clear so that water can be drained out **(see illustrations)**. Bright work should be treated in the same way as paint work. Windscreens and windows can be kept clear of the smeary film which often appears, by the use of a proprietary glass cleaner. Never use any form of wax or other body or chromium polish on glass.

Convertible

5 A manual or electrically operated hood is fitted to Convertible models. Maintenance of the hood and its operating mechanism is minimal, but the following points should be noted to ensure that the hood has a long life and is satisfactory in operation.

6 Before lowering the hood, make sure it is clean and dry and that the heated rear window is switched off. (Operating the heated rear window whilst the hood is lowered can cause permanent damage.)

7 Clean the hood regularly, using a soft brush, warm water and a mild detergent. Do not use strong detergents or solvents. Stubborn stains can be removed with special products designed for cleaning plastics.

8 The use of automatic car washes is not recommended for convertible models, as there is a risk of introducing water between the layers of the hood fabric.

3 Maintenance - upholstery and carpets

Mats and carpets should be brushed or vacuum cleaned regularly to keep them free of grit. If they are badly stained remove them from the vehicle for scrubbing or sponging and make quite sure they are dry before refitting. Seats and interior trim panels can be kept clean by wiping with a damp cloth and a proprietry car interior wax polish. If they do become stained (which can be more apparent on light coloured upholstery) use a little liquid detergent and a soft nail brush to scour the grime out of the grain of the material. Do not forget to keep the headlining clean in the same way as the upholstery. When using liquid cleaners inside the vehicle do not over-wet the surfaces being cleaned. Excessive damp could get into the seams and padded interior causing stains, offensive odours or even rot. If the inside of the vehicle gets wet accidentally it is worthwhile taking some trouble to dry it out properly, particularly where carpets are involved. Do not leave oil or electric heaters inside the vehicle for this purpose.

4 Minor body damage - repair

Note: *For more detailed information about bodywork repair, the Haynes Publishing Group publish a book by Lindsay Porter called The Car Bodywork Repair Manual. This incorporates information on such aspects as rust treatment, painting and glass-fibre repairs, as well as details on more ambitious repairs involving welding and panel beating.*

Repairs of minor scratches in bodywork

1 If the scratch is very superficial, and does not penetrate to the metal of the bodywork, repair is very simple. Lightly rub the area of the scratch with a paintwork renovator, or a very fine cutting paste, to remove loose paint from the scratch

and to clear the surrounding bodywork of wax polish. Rinse the area with clean water.

2 Apply touch-up paint to the scratch using a fine paint brush; continue to apply fine layers of paint until the surface of the paint in the scratch is level with the surrounding paintwork. Allow the new paint at least two weeks to harden, then blend it into the surrounding paintwork by rubbing the scratch area with a paintwork renovator or a very fine cutting paste

3 Where the scratch has penetrated right through to the metal of the bodywork, causing the metal to rust, a different repair technique is required. Remove any loose rust from the bottom of the scratch with a penknife, then apply rust inhibiting paint to prevent the formation of rust in the future. Using a rubber or nylon applicator fill the scratch with bodystopper paste. If required, this paste can be mixed with cellulose thinners, to provide a very thin paste which is ideal for filling narrow scratches. Before the stopper-paste in the scratch hardens, wrap a piece of smooth cotton rag around the top of a finger. Dip the finger in cellulose thinners and quickly sweep it across the surface of the stopper-paste in the scratch; this will ensure that the surface of the stopper-paste is slightly hollowed. The scratch can now be painted over as described earlier in this Section.

Repairs of dents in bodywork

4 When deep denting of the vehicle's bodywork has taken place, the first task is to pull the dent out, until the affected bodywork almost attains its original shape. There is little point in trying to restore the original shape completely, as the metal in the damaged area will have stretched on impact and cannot be reshaped fully to its original contour. It is better to bring the level of the dent up to a point which is about 3 mm below the level of the surrounding bodywork. In cases where the dent is very shallow anyway, it is not worth trying to pull it out at all. If the underside of the dent is accessible, it can be hammered out gently from behind, using a mallet with a wooden or plastic head. Whilst doing this, hold a suitable block of wood firmly against the outside of the panel to absorb the impact from the hammer blows and thus prevent a large area of the bodywork from being `belled-out'.

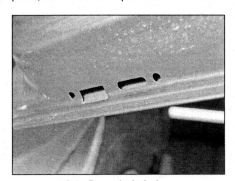
2.4a Door drain holes

2.4b Clearing a sill drain hole

5 Should the dent be in a section of the bodywork which has a double skin or some other factor making it inaccessible from behind, a different technique is called for. Drill several small holes through the metal inside the area - particularly in the deeper section. Then screw long self-tapping screws into the holes just sufficiently for them to gain a good purchase in the metal. Now the dent can be pulled out by pulling on the protruding heads of the screws with a pair of pliers.

6 The next stage of the repair is the removal of the paint from the damaged area, and from an inch or so of the surrounding 'sound' bodywork. This is accomplished most easily by using a wire brush or abrasive pad on a power drill, although it can be done just as effectively by hand using sheets of abrasive paper. To complete the preparation for filling, score the surface of the bare metal with a screwdriver or the tang of a file, or alternatively, drill small holes in the affected area. This will provide a really good 'key' for the filler paste.

7 To complete the repair see the Section on filling and respraying.

Repairs of rust holes or gashes in bodywork

8 Remove all paint from the affected area and from an inch or so of the surrounding 'sound' bodywork, using an abrasive pad or a wire brush on a power drill. If these are not available a few sheets of abrasive paper will do the job most effectively. With the paint removed you will be able to judge the severity of the corrosion and therefore decide whether to renew the whole panel (if this is possible) or to repair the affected area. New body panels are not as expensive as most people think and it is often quicker and more satisfactory to fit a new panel than to attempt to repair large areas of corrosion.

9 Remove all fittings from the affected area except those which will act as a guide to the original shape of the damaged bodywork (eg. headlights etc). Then, using tin snips or a hacksaw blade, remove all loose metal and any other metal badly affected by corrosion. Hammer the edges of the hole inwards in order to create a slight depression for the filler paste.

10 Wire brush the affected area to remove the powdery rust from the surface of the remaining metal. Paint the affected area with rust inhibiting paint if the back of the rusted area is accessible treat this also.

11 Before filling can take place it will be necessary to block the hole in some way. This can be achieved by the use of aluminium or plastic mesh, or aluminium tape.

12 Aluminium or plastic mesh or glass fibre matting is probably the best material to use for a large hole. Cut a piece to the approximate size and shape of the hole to be filled, then position it in the hole so that its edges are below the level of the surrounding bodywork. It can be retained in position by several blobs of filler paste around its periphery.

13 Aluminium tape should be used for small or very narrow holes. Pull a piece off the roll and trim it to the approximate size and shape required, then pull off the backing paper (if used) and stick the tape over the hole; it can be overlapped if the thickness of one piece is insufficient. Burnish down the edges of the tape with the handle of a screwdriver or similar, to ensure that the tape is securely attached to the metal underneath.

Bodywork repairs - filling and respraying

14 Before using this Section, see the Sections on dent, deep scratch, rust holes and gash repairs.

15 Many types of bodyfiller are available, but generally speaking those proprietary kits which contain a tin of filler paste and a tube of resin hardener are best for this type of repair which can be used directly from the tube. A wide, flexible plastic or nylon applicator will be found invaluable for imparting a smooth and well contoured finish to the surface of the filler.

16 Mix up a little filler on a clean piece of card or board - measure the hardener carefully (follow the maker's instructions on the pack) otherwise the filler will set too rapidly or too slowly. Alternatively, a no-mix brand can be used straight from the tube without mixing, but daylight is required to cure it. Using the applicator apply the filler paste to the prepared area; draw the applicator across the surface of the filler to achieve the correct contour and to level the surface. As soon as a contour that approximates to the correct one is achieved, stop working the paste - if you carry on too long the paste will become sticky and begin to 'pick-up' on the applicator. Continue to add thin layers of filler paste at twenty minute intervals until the level of the filler is just proud of the surrounding bodywork.

17 Once the filler has hardened, excess can be removed using a metal plane or file. From then on, progressively finer grades of abrasive paper should be used, starting with a 40 grade production paper and finishing with a 400 grade wet-and-dry paper. Always wrap the abrasive paper around a flat rubber, cork, or wooden block - otherwise the surface of the filler will not be completely flat. During the smoothing of the filler surface the wet-and-dry paper should be periodically rinsed in water. This will ensure that a very smooth finish is imparted to the filler at the final stage.

18 At this stage the 'dent' should be surrounded by a ring of bare metal, which in turn should be encircled by the finely 'feathered' edge of the good paintwork. Rinse the repair area with clean water, until all of the dust produced by the rubbing-down operation has gone.

19 Spray the whole area with a light coat of primer, - this will show up any imperfections in the surface of the filler. Repair these imperfections with fresh filler paste or

bodystopper, and once more smooth the surface with abrasive paper. If bodystopper is used, it can be mixed with cellulose thinners to form a really thin paste which is ideal for filling small holes. Repeat this spray and repair procedure until you are satisfied that the surface of the filler, and the feathered edge of the paintwork are perfect. Clean the repair area with clean water and allow to dry fully.

20 The repair area is now ready for final spraying. Paint spraying must be carried out in a warm, dry, windless and dust free atmosphere. This condition can be created artificially if you have access to a large indoor working area, but if you are forced to work in the open, you will have to pick your day very carefully. If you are working indoors, dousing the floor in the work area with water will help to settle the dust which would otherwise be in the atmosphere. If the repair area is confined to one body panel, mask off the surrounding panels; this will help to minimise the effects of a slight mis-match in paint colours. Bodywork fittings (eg. trim strips, door handles etc) will also need to be masked off. Use genuine masking tape and several thicknesses of newspaper for the masking operations.

21 Before commencing to spray, agitate the aerosol can thoroughly, then spray a test area (an old tin, or similar) until the technique is mastered. Cover the repair area with a thick coat of primer; the thickness should be built up using several thin layers of paint rather than one thick one. Using 400 grade wet-and-dry paper, rub down the surface of the primer until it is really smooth. While doing this, the work area should be thoroughly doused with water, and the wet-and-dry paper periodically rinsed in water. Allow to dry before spraying on more paint.

22 Spray on the top coat, again building up the thickness by using several thin layers of paint. Start spraying in the centre of the repair area and then, using a circular motion, work outwards until the whole repair area and about 2 inches of the surrounding original paintwork is covered. Remove all masking material 10 to 15 minutes after spraying on the final coat of paint.

23 Allow the new paint at least two weeks to harden, then, using a paintwork renovator or a very fine cutting paste to the edges of the paint. Finally, apply wax polish.

Plastic components

24 With the use of more and more plastic body components by the vehicle manufacturers (eg. bumpers, spoilers, and in some cases major body panels), rectification of more serious damage to such items has become a matter of either entrusting repair work to a specialist in this field, or renewing complete components. Repair of such damage by the DIY owner is not really feasible owing to the cost of the equipment and materials required for effecting such repairs. The basic technique involves making a groove along the line of the crack in the plastic using a rotary burr in a power drill. The damaged part is then welded back together by using a hot air gun to heat up and fuse a plastic filler rod into the groove. Any excess plastic is then removed and the area rubbed down to a smooth finish. It is important that a filler rod of the correct plastic is used, as body components can be made of a variety of different types (eg. polycarbonate, ABS, polypropylene).

25 Damage of a less serious nature (abrasions, minor cracks etc) can be repaired by the DIY owner using a two-part epoxy filler repair material, or a no-mix filler which can be used directly from the tube. Once mixed in equal proportions (or applied directly from the tube in the case of a no-mix filler), this is used in similar fashion to the bodywork filler used on metal panels. The filler is usually cured in twenty to thirty minutes, ready for sanding and painting.

26 If the owner is renewing a complete component himself, or if he has repaired it with epoxy filler, he will be left with the problem of finding a suitable paint for finishing which is compatible with the type of plastic used. At one time the use of a universal paint was not possible owing to the complex range of plastics encountered in body component applications. Standard paints, generally speaking, will not bond to plastic or rubber satisfactorily, but a professional spraymatch paints to match any plastic or rubber finish can be obtained from dealers. However, it is now possible to obtain a plastic body parts finishing kit which consists of a pre-primer treatment, a primer and coloured top coat. Full instructions are normally supplied with a kit, but basically the method of use is to first apply the pre-primer to the component concerned and allow it to dry for up to 30 minutes. Then the primer is applied and left to dry for about an hour before finally applying the special coloured top coat. The result is a correctly coloured component where the paint will flex with the plastic or rubber, a property that standard paint does not normally posses.

5 Major body damage - repair

Where serious damage has occurred, or large areas need renewal due to neglect, it means that complete new panels will need welding in, and this is best left to professionals. If the damage is due to impact, it will also be necessary to check completely the alignment of the bodyshell, and this can only be carried out accurately by a Vauxhall/Opel dealer using special jigs. If the body is left misaligned, it is primarily dangerous as the car will not handle properly, and secondly, uneven stresses will be imposed on the steering, suspension and possibly transmission, causing abnormal wear, or complete failure, particularly to such items as the tyres.

6.3 Removing a bonnet hinge bolt

6 Bonnet - removal and refitting

Removal

1 Open and prop the bonnet.
2 When an under-bonnet light is fitted, disconnect its electrical lead.
3 Mark around the hinge bolts with a soft lead pencil as a guide for refitting. Have an assistant support the bonnet, then remove the hinge bolts from each side **(see illustration)**.
4 Lift away the bonnet. If it is to be re-used, rest it carefully on rags or cardboard. If a new bonnet is to be fitted, transfer serviceable items (rubber buffers, lock striker etc) to it.

Refitting

5 Refit in the reverse order to removal, using the hinge bolt alignment marks for guidance when applicable.
6 If the lock striker was disturbed, adjust it to the dimension shown before tightening its locknut **(see illustration)**.
7 Adjust the hinge bolts and front buffers until a good fit is obtained with the bonnet closed.

7 Bonnet release cable - removal and refitting

Removal

1 Open up the bonnet and unbolt the cable clip from the rear of the bonnet lock platform.
2 Prise the cable and fitting out of the release

8.2 Undoing a front trim panel screw

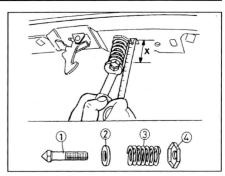

6.6 Bonnet lock striker adjustment

1 Striker 4 Locknut
2 Washer X = 40 to 45 mm
3 Coil spring

slide, using a screwdriver against the spring tension.
3 Inside the car, free the cable from the release lever and bracket.
4 Release the grommet from the bulkhead and withdraw the cable from under the bonnet.

Refitting

5 Fit the new cable in the reverse order to removal. Adjust the position of the cable under the front panel clip so that, with the release lever at rest, the inner cable is just slack. Check that the release slide moves when an assistant operates the release lever, then close the bonnet and check for correct operation.

8 Front trim panel - removal and refitting

Removal

1 The front trim panel incorporates the radiator grille and the front bumper.
2 Remove the three screws which secure the panel to the bonnet lock platform **(see illustration)**.
3 From under the vehicle remove the two nuts which secure the lower part of the panel **(see illustration)**.
4 Pull the panel forwards so that it slides off the side mountings. If front foglights are fitted,

8.3 Front trim panel securing nut (arrowed)

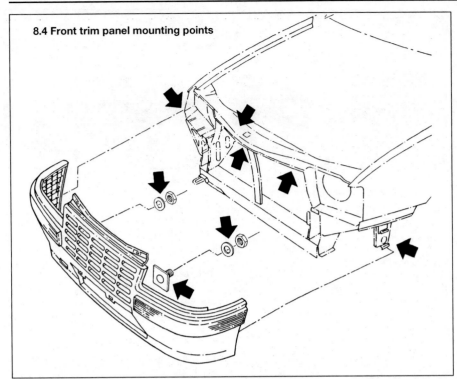

8.4 Front trim panel mounting points

disconnect them as the panel is withdrawn (**see illustration**). Also disconnect the headlamp washer pipes (when fitted).

Refitting

5 Refit in the reverse order to removal. The side mountings are riveted in position and can be renewed if wished after drilling out the rivets.

9.2 Rear trim panel securing nut

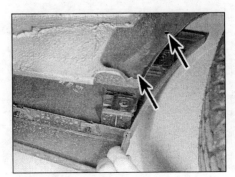

9.3 Freeing one end of the rear trim panel - screw holes arrowed

9 Rear trim panel - removal and refitting

Removal

1 Remove the number plate lamps (see Chapter 12).
2 Inside the car, free the soft trim from the rear panel to expose the two securing nuts (**see illustration**). Remove the nuts.
3 Remove the two screws from inside each wheel arch to free the ends of the rear trim panel (**see illustration**). Withdraw the panel, disconnecting the rear foglight wires as it is withdrawn.

Refitting

4 Refit in the reverse order to removal.

10 Front wing - removal and refitting

Removal

1 Remove the front trim panel, as described in Section 8.
2 Remove the direction indicator lamp unit (see Chapter 12).
3 Remove the wheel arch protective panelling by pushing the centres out of the plastic rivets and unclipping it from the edge of the wing. Remove the headlamp washer reservoir, when fitted.
4 Remove the twelve bolts which secure the wing to the car. Free the wing from the sealing compound on its flanges and remove it.

Refitting

5 Clean all sealant away from the body flange; commence refitting by applying a thick bead of new sealant.
6 Offer the wing to the vehicle and bolt it loosely into position. When it is correctly aligned with the surrounding bodywork, fully tighten the bolts.
7 Coat the inside of the wing with protective wax or similar compound; when necessary, paint the outside of the wing to match the rest of the car.
8 Refit the headlamp washer reservoir, when applicable.
9 Refit the wheel and protective panelling, using new plastic rivets or other proprietary fasteners.
10 Refit the direction indicator lamp and the front trim panel.

11 Wind deflector - removal and refitting

Removal

1 The wind deflector fills the gap between the rear of the bonnet and the base of the windscreen.
2 Remove both windscreen wiper arms (see Chapter 12).
3 Remove the wind deflector securing screws (**see illustrations**).
4 Free the wind deflector from its clips and remove it. Disconnect the windscreen washer hoses as it is withdrawn.

11.3a Wind deflector screw at the wing

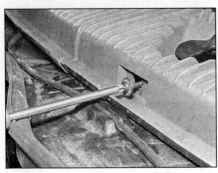

11.3b Wind deflector screw near the wiper

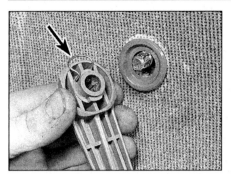

12.2 Window winder handle spring clip (arrowed)

5 The two halves of the wind deflector can be separated if wished by pulling them apart. Each half may also be removed individually, leaving the other in place.

Refitting

6 Refit in the reverse order to removal.

12 Door inner trim panel - removal and refitting

Removal

1 Procedure is described for a front door; rear doors are similar, except where noted.
2 Except on models with electric windows, the window winder handle must first be removed. In the absence of special tool KM-31 7-A, release the handle securing clip by introducing a strip of rag between the handle and the door trim panel and working it back and forth to pick up the ends of the clip. Remove the handle, clip and trim plate (see illustration).
3 Prise the surround from the remote control handle (see illustration).
4 Unscrew the interior lock button (see illustration).
5 When a door pocket is fitted, prise out the screw cover and remove the securing screw (see illustrations). Remove the two screws at the bottom of the pocket, if fitted, then remove the pocket. On rear doors, unclip the ashtray housing.
6 Remove the armrest. Precise details of fixing will vary with trim level, but usually there

12.3 Removing the surround from the remote control handle

are two Torx screws at the fore end (see illustrations). Some armrests also have an ordinary self-tapping screw at the rear end.
7 With some trim levels there is a self-tapping screw securing the trim to the door shut face. Remove this if present (see illustration).
8 Uncap the retaining clips with a broad-bladed screwdriver or a palette knife and remove the panel. The degree of force needed to release the clips is not far off that which will break them: obtain new clips for refitting if necessary.
9 Free the plastic sheets from the door or trim panel as appropriate.

Refitting

10 Refit in the reverse order to removal. make sure that the plastic sheet is intact and securely glued round the bottom and sides on the door: if it is broken or detached, rainwater may leak into the vehicle or damage the door trim.

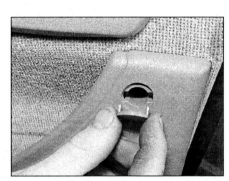

12.5a Door pocket screw cover

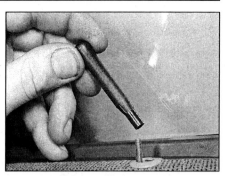

12.4 Unscrewing the lock button

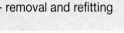

13 Door - removal and refitting

Removal

1 The door hinges are welded onto the door and onto the hinge pillar. The only remedy for worn hinges, unless oversize pins can be procured, is to renew the door and/or pillar.
2 To remove a door, open it fully and support its lower edge with well-padded blocks. Disconnect any door component wiring harness (mirrors, windows, central locking etc).
3 Disconnect the check strap and have an assistant support the door whilst the hinge pins are extracted. The pins should be extracted upwards, using a slide hammer, after removing their caps.

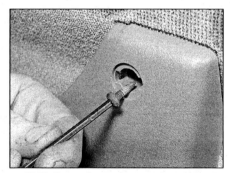

12.5b Removing a door pocket screw

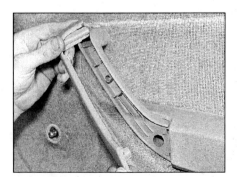

12.6a Removing the armrest screw cover

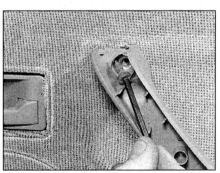

12.6b Removing an armrest screw

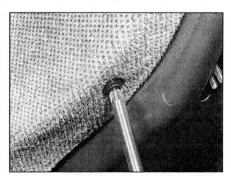

12.7 Trim securing screw on the door shut face - rear door shown

13.4 Adjusting a door lock striker

Refitting

4 Refit the door in the reverse order to removal, using new hinge pins. Gross adjustment of the door position is possible by bending the hinges or hinge eyes. Fine adjustment to obtain satisfactory shutting is made by turning the socket-headed lock striker **(see illustration)**.

14 Door lock - removal and refitting

Removal

1 Remove the door trim panel (Section 12).
2 Remove the three screws which secure the lock to the door shut face **(see illustration)**.

14.2 Door lock securing screws (arrowed)

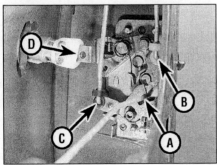

14.4 Door lock attachments inside the door

A Remote control handle rod
B Lock button rod
C Exterior handle rod
D Lock cylinder arm

3 Disconnect the control rods and remove the lock. (In the case of the front door, do not disconnect the interior lock button rod, but withdraw the lock and rod complete.)

Refitting

4 Refit in the reverse order to removal. When refitting the front door lock, make sure that the tongue on the lock engages with the slot in the cylinder arm **(see illustration)**.
5 Check for correct operation before refitting the door trim panel.

15 Door exterior handle - removal and refitting

Removal

1 Remove the door trim panel, as described in Section 12.
2 Wind up the window fully.
3 Unclip the handle-to-lock rod from the lock.
4 Unbolt the handle from inside the door and remove it. Some manipulation will be needed to get the goose-neck and the operating rod through the hole.

Refitting

5 Refit in the reverse order to removal. Check for correct operation before refitting the trim panel.

16 Door remote control handle - removal and refitting

Removal

1 Remove the door trim panel, as described in Section 12.
2 Slide the handle rearwards to free it **(see illustration)**. Unhook the link rod and remove it from the door.

Refitting

3 Refit in the reverse order to removal. Check for correct operation before refitting the trim panel.

17 Front door lock cylinder - removal and refitting

Removal

1 Remove the door trim panel, as described in Section 12.
2 Release the lock cylinder retaining clip by prising it forwards. Withdraw the cylinder and associated components from the outside of the door.
3 The cylinder may be separated from the other items by inserting the key in the slot, then using a screwdriver to prise off the end piece and arm. Withdraw the cylinder from the housing and recover the circlip **(see illustration)**.

Refitting

4 Reassemble in the reverse order, noting the position of the spring legs and their relationship to the arm.
5 Refit in the reverse order to removal. Check for correct operation before refitting the trim panel.

18 Window lifting mechanism - removal and refitting

Removal

1 Remove the door trim panel, as described in Section 12.
2 Various types of mechanism may be fitted: scissors or cable, manual or electric. In all cases the principles of removal are similar. The electric motors cannot be repaired, though sometimes they can be renewed separately from the lifting mechanism. **Note:** *On Convertible models with electric windows, prior to removal position the window lifting mechanism and secure it in position with some stout wire as shown* **(see illustration)**. *This will prevent the mechanism being suddenly released as it is disconnected.*
3 Lower the window to the halfway position and wedge it securely.
4 Disconnect the wiring harness from the electrically-operated mechanism.
5 Drill the heads off the rivets and remove the mechanism from the door. The cable

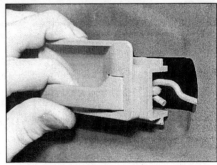

16.2 Removing a remote control handle

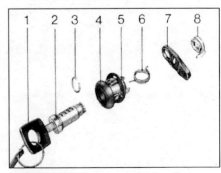

17.3 Exploded view of lock cylinder

1 Key
2 Cylinder
3 Circlip
4 Housing
5 Seal
6 Spring
7 Arm
8 End piece

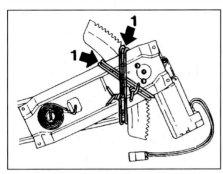

18.2 Convertible electric window lifter arm secured (1) prior to removal of the regulator unit

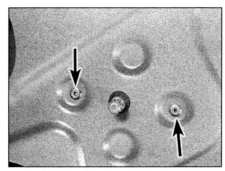

18.5a Two window lifting mechanism securing rivets (arrowed)

18.5b Window lifting channel bolts (arrowed)

18.6 Scissors lifting mechanism slider

mechanism lifter must also be unbolted from the window channel **(see illustrations)**.

Refitting

6 Refit in the reverse order to removal, using new blind rivets. Lubricate the sliders and channel of the scissors type mechanism with silicone grease **(see illustration)**. Tension the cable on the electric mechanism by turning the adjusters through 90°.
7 Check for correct operation before refitting the door trim. On Convertible models the operation of the window can be adjusted by slackening the mounting bolts and repositioning the window guide. Find the place where the window operates the smoothest the securely tighten the bolts.

19 Door window - removal and refitting

Removal

1 Remove the door trim panel as described in Section 12.
2 Remove the window weatherstrip from the top of the opening in the door.
3 In the case of the rear door, unbolt and remove the rear guide rail, then remove the fixed part of the window complete with seal.
4 If a scissors type lifter is fitted to the front door remove the rear guide rail. If a cable type lifter is fitted, unbolt the lifter from the glass channel.

5 Carefully lift the window out through its opening in the door. It will have to be tilted at a considerable angle.

Refitting

6 Refit in the reverse order to removal. Adjust the angle of the rear door window guide rail by means of the adjustment screw and locknuts until smooth operation is achieved **(see illustration)**. Note that there are two locknuts, one on each side of the panel.

20 Tailgate - removal and refitting

Removal

1 Open the tailgate and have an assistant support it.
2 Disconnect the rear screen washer tube and any wiring that enters the tailgate - this will vary according to model and equipment. Remove the tailgate trim panel if necessary to carry out the disconnections.
3 Disconnect the struts from the tailgate - see Section 22.
4 Extract the hinge pin circlips and press or drive out the hinge pins **(see illustration)**. Lift away the tailgate.

Refitting

5 Refit in the reverse order to removal. Note that the circlip ends of the hinge pins face outwards. Lubricate the pins before fitting.

19.6 Adjusting the rear window guide rail There is another locknut behind the panel

21 Tailgate hinge - removal and refitting

Removal

1 Open the tailgate and have an assistant support it.
2 Disconnect the strut on the side being worked on see Section 22.
3 Extract the circlip and press or drive out the hinge pin.
4 Unclip the roof trim panels and loosen the headlining to gain access to the hinge screws.
5 Undo the two screws with an offset screwdriver and remove the hinge, seal and screw plate.

Refitting

6 Refit in the reverse order to removal. Tighten the hinge screws to the specified torque. Lubricate the hinge pin before fitting; fit the pin with its circlip end facing outwards.

22 Tailgate strut - removal and refitting

Removal

1 Open the tailgate and have an assistant support it.
2 Release the strut from its mounting balljoints by prising the spring clips a little way out and pulling the strut off the balljoints **(see illustration)**. If the strut is to be re-used, do

20.4 Tailgate hinge showing circlip (arrowed)

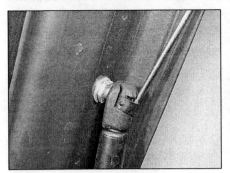

22.2 Releasing a tailgate strut spring clip

not remove the spring clips completely, nor prise them out further than 6 mm (0.24 in).
3 Dispose of used struts carefully, since they contain gas under pressure.

Refitting

4 Refit in the reverse order to removal.

23 Tailgate lock - removal and refitting

Removal

1 Remove the tailgate trim panel by releasing its retaining clips.
2 Remove the retaining screws from the lock **(see illustration)**. There are three retaining screws on the Hatchback, four on the Estate and Van.

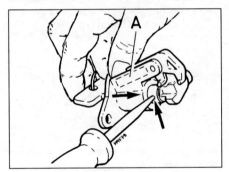

24.3 Tailgate lock cylinder removal - roll pin and circlip arrowed
A Key number

25.4 Boot lid hinge bolts

23.2 Tailgate lock retaining screws (arrowed) - Hatchback

3 Unhook the operating rod from the lock cylinder arm **(see illustration)**. It may be necessary to unbolt the lock cylinder in order to disengage the rod. Remove the lock and rod together.
4 If a new lock is being fitted, transfer the spring and rod to it.

Refitting

5 Refit in the reverse order to removal. Check for correct operation before refitting the trim panel.

24 Tailgate lock cylinder - removal and refitting

Removal

1 Remove the tailgate trim panel by releasing its retaining clips.
2 Remove the two retaining nuts, disengage the lock operating rod and remove the lock cylinder, complete with housing.
3 Remove the lock cylinder from the housing by driving out the roll pin, moving aside the catch and extracting the circlip **(see illustration)**. Remove the cylinder with the key inserted.
4 Fit the new cylinder and secure with the circlip and roll pin.

Refitting

5 Refitting is a reversal of the removal procedure. Check for correct operation before refitting the trim panel.

25.5a Torsion rod central housing bracket

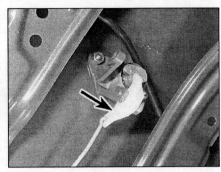

23.3 Lock operating rod connection to arm (arrowed)

25 Boot lid and torsion rods - removal and refitting

Removal

1 Open the boot.
2 Draw alignment marks between the boot lid and the hinge brackets on both sides of the vehicle.
3 On models with central locking, disconnect the lock motor connector. The connector is located in the left-hand corner of the boot.
4 With the aid of an assistant, support the boot lid and undo the hinge bolts **(see illustration)**. Remove the boot lid.
5 The torsion rods are held in place by their own spring tension. They can be removed by carefully unhooking them first from the central housing bracket, then from the hinge brackets **(see illustrations)**.

Refitting

6 Refitting is the reverse of the removal procedure. Observe the alignment marks if refitting the original lid. If fitting a new lid, just nip up the hinge bolts at first until satisfied with the fit, then carry out final tightening. **Note:** *On early models it may be found that despite correct alignment the boot lid contacts the rear screen at the centre of its front edge. This can be remedied by fitting rubber bump stops to limit the height of travel of the lid (see illustration 25.5b).*

25.5b Hinge bracket assembly

1 Torsion rod   2 Bump stop

26.2 Boot lid lock securing screws

26 Boot lid lock components - removal and refitting

Boot lid lock assembly - removal and refitting

1 Mark a line around the outer edge of the lock assembly on the boot lid.
2 Remove the securing screws **(see illustration)** and lift away the lock.
3 Refitting is the reverse of the removal procedure. Use the line marked before removal as a guide to positioning the lock.
4 Check the operation of the lock by opening and closing the boot lid several times. If necessary adjust the position of the lock or catch.

Boot lock catch - removal, refitting and adjustment

5 Remove the protective trim panel from the boot lip.
6 Remove the retaining bolt. Disengage the catch spigots and remove it **(see illustration)**.
7 Refitting is the reverse of the removal procedure.
8 The height of the catch may be adjusted by slackening the retaining bolt and moving the catch up or down to provide satisfactory closing and a snug fit with the edge seal.

Boot lid handle - removal and refitting

9 Open the boot and remove the two nuts, accessible from inside, which secure the handle **(see illustration)**.

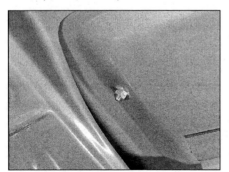

26.9 Boot lid handle retaining nut

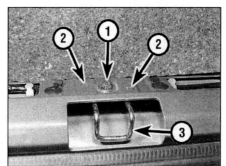

26.6 Boot lock catch retaining bolt (1), spigots (2) and catch (3)

10 Refitting is the reverse of the removal procedure.

27 Windscreen and other fixed glass - removal and refitting

1 With the exception of the small fixed windows in the rear passenger door, whose removal is covered in Section 19, the fixed glass is glued in position with adhesive.
2 Special tools, equipment and expertise are required for successful removal and refitting of glass fixed by this method. The work must therefore be left to a GM dealer, a windscreen specialist or other competent professional.
3 The same remarks apply if sealing of the windscreen or other glass surround is necessary.

28 Rear quarterlight (opening type) - removal and refitting

Removal

1 Unclip the interior trim panels from around the quarterlight.
2 Remove the three screws which secure the catch to the body.
3 Unscrew the two special nuts which hold the hinges to the front of the quarterlight. Remove the quarterlight and recover the hinge securing components.
4 Transfer the catch to the new quarterlight, if applicable, by drilling out the connecting pin and unscrewing the glass fitting. Use a new connecting pin on reassembly.

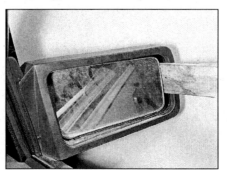

30.2a Remove the glass by levering with a wooden wedge

Refitting

5 Refit in the reverse order to removal.

29 Rear quarterlight (opening type) - weatherstrip renewal

1 Remove the quarterlight, as described in the previous Section.
2 Cut the old weatherstrip and rubber mount from the body flange. Clean up the flange, but do not remove the old adhesive completely.
3 Clean the mating face of the new weatherstrip with petrol or other suitable solvent, taking appropriate precautions.
4 Apply a 6 mm bead of polyurethane-based glass adhesive on top of the remains of the old adhesive.
5 Fit the new weatherstrip, refit the quarterlight and keep it closed for at least four hours (or as advised by the makers of the adhesive) to allow the adhesive to set.

30 Exterior rear view mirror components - removal and refitting

Mirror glass

1 On all types, the mirror glass may be renewed separately.
2 Prise out the old glass (if intact) with a wooden wedge, and when applicable disconnect the electrical cables. Engage the new glass with the linkage, connect the wires if applicable and snap the glass home **(see illustrations)**. Be careful when pressing the glass home: the sudden movement as the ball enters its socket may cause the glass to break.

Mirror motor - electric mirror

3 To renew an electric mirror motor, prise out the glass as just described, undo the motor securing screws and disconnect its multi-plug. Fit the new motor in the reverse order to removal.

Complete mirror - manual mirror

4 To remove a manually adjusted mirror, pull off the adjuster handle and unclip the corner

30.2b Engage the linkage and press the ball into the socket (arrowed)

30.4 Mirror retaining screws (arrowed)

31.1 Seat rail trim removal

31.2a Seat rail front retaining bolt (one of two)

trim. Undo the three retaining screws and remove the mirror **(see illustration)**.

5 Refitting is the reverse of removal.

Complete mirror - electric mirror

6 Removal of the electrically adjusted mirror is similar, but instead of pulling off the handle, the wiring harness must be disconnected. The harness connector is inside the door cavity.

7 Refitting is a reversal of the removal procedure.

31 Front seat - removal and refitting

Removal

1 Remove the trim which covers the seat outboard rail. This trim is secured by a single self-tapping screw at the front **(see illustration)**.

2 Remove the four bolts which secure the seat rails to the floor **(see illustrations)**. Remove the seat, complete with rails; disconnecting the seat heating wires (when fitted).

3 The seat can be separated from the rails if wished, for example if attention to the adjustment mechanisms is necessary.

Refitting

4 Refit in the reverse order to removal, but observe the following tightening sequence for the rail bolts:

a) *Nip up the rear bolts.*
b) *Tighten the front bolts to the specified torque.*
c) *Tighten the outboard rear bolt to the specified torque.*
d) *Tighten the inboard rear bolt to the specified torque and refit the seat rail trim.*

32 Head restraints - removal and refitting

Removal

1 Both front and rear head restraints are removed in the same way.

2 Pull the head restraint up as far as it will go.

3 Release the catch spring by pushing it rearwards and remove the head restraint. The catch springs are located on the left-hand side on front seats and on the right-hand side on rear seats.

4 The guide sleeves can be removed if necessary by releasing the retaining lugs with a screwdriver and pulling them upwards **(see illustration)**.

Refitting

5 Refit in the reverse order to removal.

31.2b Seat rail rear retaining bolt (one of two)

33 Rear seat - removal and refitting

Removal

1 Uncover the hinges at the front of the seat. Free them by extracting the circlips and removing the hinge pins **(see illustration)**. The bench section(s) of the seat can now be removed if wished.

2 Unclip the carpet from the backrest **(see illustration)**.

3 Free the backrest from its catches, unscrew the side hinges and remove the backrest. If a split seat is fitted, also separate the centre bearing. On Saloon models the rear seat backrest catch is retained by a nut, accessible from inside the boot **(see illustrations)**.

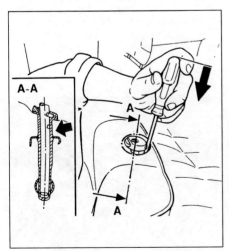

32.4 Removing a head restraint guide sleeve - push down with screwdriver to release retaining lugs (arrowed)

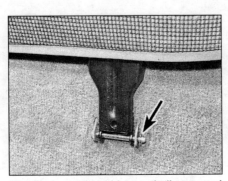

33.1 Rear seat front hinge - circlip arrowed

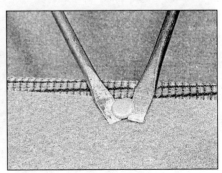

33.2 Removing a carpet securing plug

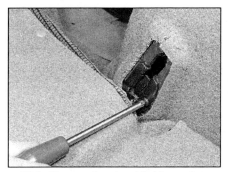

33.3a Unscrewing the side hinge plate

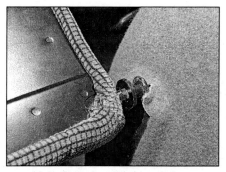

33.3b Seat pivot lifts out of hinge

33.3c Unscrewing the centre hinge cover

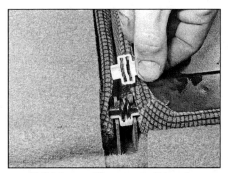

33.3d Centre hinge top half bearing

33.3e Rear seat backrest catch retaining nut - Saloon

33.5a Seat backrest catch striker - Hatchback

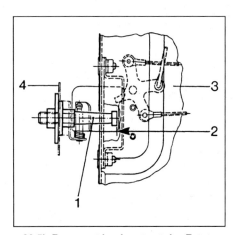

33.5b Rear seat backrest catch - Estate
1 Striker
2 Distance to other striker = 1162 ± 2.5 mm
3 Backrest
4 Rear quarter panel

Refitting

4 Refit in the reverse order to removal. When securing the split type backrest start at the centre and work outwards.

5 If adjustment of the catch striker is necessary, slacken the nut at the back of the striker pin, engage the seat backrest and then tighten the nut. This applies to Hatchback models. No procedure is laid down for Estate models; details of the catch construction are as shown (see illustrations).

34 Luggage area trim panel removal - general information

The 'soft' trim panels and carpets are mostly retained by plastic plugs. These can be levered out, but sometimes break. Where more frequent removal is envisaged, eg for access to the spare wheel and tools, the plugs are of a different design and incorporate pulling straps.

The side covers may be removed by unbolting them and (when applicable) disconnecting the loudspeaker wires (see illustration). They carry the rear parcel shelf catches on some models; the catches can be removed simply by pulling them towards the centre of the vehicle.

Other 'hard' trim Panels are either clipped or screwed into position.

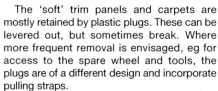

34.2 Removing a luggage area side panel

35 Centre console - removal and refitting

Removal

1 The centre console is in two parts: the rear half, surrounding the handbrake lever, and the front half, which sits below the heater controls.

2 Commence removal with the rear half. Prise out the screw cover and remove the securing screw (see illustrations).

3 Slide the console rearwards to free it. Removal of the front half may proceed without further disturbing the rear; to remove the rear half completely, disconnect or remove any switches from it and lift it over the handbrake lever.

4 Unclip the cover from around the base of

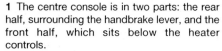

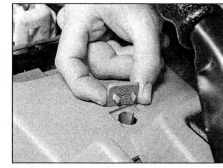

35.2a Centre console rear half screw cover

35.2b Removing the centre console rear half screw

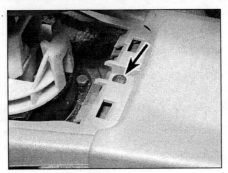

35.4a Centre console screw (arrowed) to rear of gear lever

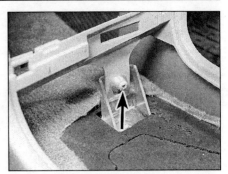

35.4b Centre console screw (arrowed) in front of gear lever

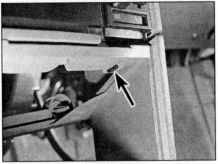

35.6 Centre console screw (arrowed) below heater control panel

the gear lever. There is no need to remove the gear lever boot itself. Undo the two screws to front and rear of the gear lever **(see illustrations)**. On automatic transmission versions, remove the selector lever cover.

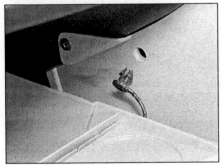

36.1 Glovebox check strap disconnected

5 Release the two retaining clips and remove the oddments box from below the heater control panel.
6 Remove the two screws which secure the console to the heater control panel **(see illustration)**. Withdraw the console.

Refitting

7 Refit in the reverse order to removal.

36 Glovebox - removal and refitting

Removal

1 Open the glovebox and prise out the two check strap plugs **(see illustration)**.
2 Support the glovebox and remove the two hinge bolts **(see illustration)**. The glovebox can now be removed.

Refitting

3 Refit in the reverse order to removal. Note that the hinge bolt holes are slotted to allow for fine adjustment when fitting.

37 Seat belts - general

 Warning: If the vehicle has been involved in an accident in which structural damage was sustained all the seat belt components must be renewed.

1 Inertia reel front seat belts are fitted to all models. According to trim level, these may have adjustable upper mountings. Rear seat belts are available as an optional extra at time of purchase, or as a kit for aftermarket fitting.
2 Keep the belts untwisted so that they retract into their reels when not in use. Occasionally check the function of the inertia reel units by braking sharply from 5 mph (traffic permitting): the belts should lock. A defective unit must be renewed.
3 Only use soap and water to clean the belts. Strong detergents, bleaches or dyes may weaken the webbing. After cleaning, keep the belts extended until they are dry.
4 Belts which have been subject to impact loads must be renewed.
5 When renewing a belt, note carefully the fitted sequence of mounting washers and spacers. Use new mounting components when these are supplied, and tighten the mountings to the specified torque **(see illustration)**.
6 Access to the adjustable top mounting is not immediately obvious. It is necessary to remove the floor level trim strip, then free the door seal from the pillar. The pillar trim can then be pulled inwards to free its top and centre mountings, then slid downwards to release the bottom lip. Notice how the belt feeds through the pillar trim **(see illustrations)**.
7 Access to the rear inertia reel is gained by removing most of the rear quarter trim panels;

36.2 Glovebox hinge bolt

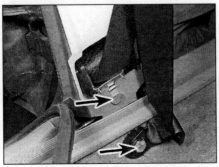

37.5 Front seat belt inertia reel and lower mounting bolts (arrowed)

37.6a Front seat belt adjustable top mounting

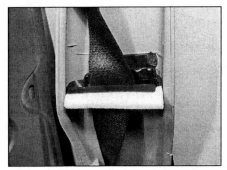

37.6b Belt feeds through guide in pillar trim

37.7a Rear seat belt inertia reel

37.7b Rear seat belt upper mounting

on 5-door models the door seal will have to be disturbed to remove the panels. Access to the floor mountings is gained by folding the seat forwards **(see illustrations)**.

38 Sunroof - operation and maintenance

1 A slide-and-tilt glass panel sunroof is available as an optional extra on most models. It is operated by a crank handle. After depressing the release button, turning the handle anti-clockwise open the roof. Turning the handle clockwise when the roof is closed causes its rear end to tilt up for ventilation.

2 A louvered panel, known as a sunshade, can be drawn out under the glass. This should only be done when the glass is closed or in the 'tilt' position.

3 Maintenance is confined to checking periodically that the drain hoses are not blocked at their lower ends.

4 No lubrication or other maintenance is specified.

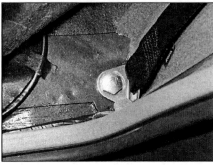

37.7c Rear seat belt floorpan mounting

Chapter 12
Body electrical system

Contents

Degrees of difficulty

Easy, suitable for novice with little experience	Fairly easy, suitable for beginner with some experience	Fairly difficult, suitable for competent DIY mechanic	Difficult, suitable for experienced DIY mechanic	Very difficult, suitable for expert DIY or professional

Specifications

General
System type . . . . 12 volt, negative earth

Fuses - early models

Fuse	Rating (amps)	Circuit(s) protected
1	10	LH side and tail lamps
2	10	RH side and tail lamps, instrument and engine compartment illumination
3	10	LH main beam
4	10	RH main beam
5	10	LH dipped beam
6	10	RH dipped beam
7	10	Not used
8	10	Direction indicators, stop lamps and foglamp relay
9	30	Wipers and washers
10	10	Rear foglamp
11	30	Horn and radiator fan
12	20	Heater blower
13	20	Reversing lamps, cigarette lighter, carburettor pre-heating, electric mirrors and glovebox lamp
14	20	Interior lights, hazard warning flasher, clock and radio
15	20	Trailer feed (terminal 30)
16	20	Fuel injection control unit
17	20	Front foglamps
18	20	Heated rear window

Note: *Not all items fitted to all models*

Fuses - later models

Fuse	Rating (amps)	Circuit(s) protected
1	10	LH side and tail lamps, instrument and engine compartment illumination, "lights-on" warning buzzer
2	10	RH side and tail lamps, number plate lamps
3	10	LH main beam
4	10	RH main beam
5	10	LH dipped beam
6	10	RH dipped beam
7	10	Not used
8	15	Direction indicators, stop lamps and foglamp relay, ABS relay
9	30	Wipers and washers
10	10	Rear foglamp
11	30	Horn and radiator fan
12	20	Heater blower
13	20	Reversing lamps, cigarette lighter, carburettor pre-heating, electric mirrors and glovebox lamp
14	20	Trailer feed (terminal 30)
15	15	Interior lights, hazard warning flasher, clock and radio
16	20	Fuel injection control unit
17	20	Front foglamps
18	20	Heated rear window
19	20	Central locking
20	30	Electric windows

Note: *Not all items fitted to all models. Fuses 19 and 20 are located on the underside of the fusebox. On Convertible models (where applicable), the fuse for the power hood system is located on the left-hand suspension strut in the engine compartment.*

Bulbs

Lamp	Wattage
Headlamp	60/55
Front parking lamp	4
Front foglamp	55
Direction indicator lamp	21
Stop/tail lamp	21/5
Rear number plate lamp	10
Reversing lamp	21
Engine compartment lamp	10
Luggage compartment lamp	10
Glovebox:	
Early models	5
Later models	10
Instrument warning lamps	1.2
Cigar lighter illumination	1.2
Switch illumination	1.2
Rear foglamps	21
Ashtray lamp	1.2
Clock illumination	1.2
Selector lever index (automatic transmission)	1.2
Direction indicator side repeater lamp	5
Vehicle interior lamp	10

1 General information

Warning: Before carrying out any work on the electrical system, read through the precautions given in Safety First! at the beginning of this manual and Chapter 5

The electrical system is of the 12 volt negative earth type. Power for the lights and all electrical accessories is supplied by a lead/acid type battery which is charged by the alternator.

This Chapter covers repair and service procedures for the various electrical components not associated with engine.

Information on the battery, alternator and starter motor can be found in Chapter 5A.

It should be noted that prior to working on any component in the electrical system, the battery negative terminal should first be disconnected to prevent the possibility of electrical short circuits and/or fires.

2 Electrical fault finding - general information

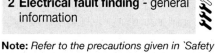

Note: *Refer to the precautions given in 'Safety first!' and in Section 1 of this Chapter before starting work. The following tests relate to testing of the main electrical circuits, and should not be used to test delicate electronic circuits (such as anti-lock braking systems),* particularly where an electronic control module is used.

General

1 A typical electrical circuit consists of an electrical component, any switches, relays, motors, fuses, fusible links or circuit breakers related to that component, and the wiring and connectors which link the component to both the battery and the chassis. To help to pinpoint a problem in an electrical circuit, wiring diagrams are included at the end of this Manual.

2 Before attempting to diagnose an electrical fault, first study the appropriate wiring diagram to obtain a complete understanding of the components included in the particular circuit concerned. The possible sources of a

fault can be narrowed down by noting if other components related to the circuit are operating properly. If several components or circuits fail at one time, the problem is likely to be related to a shared fuse or earth connection.

3 Electrical problems usually stem from simple causes, such as loose or corroded connections, a faulty earth connection, a blown fuse, a melted fusible link, or a faulty relay (refer to Section 3 for details of testing relays). Visually inspect the condition of all fuses, wires and connections in a problem circuit before testing the components. Use the wiring diagrams to determine which terminal connections will need to be checked in order to pinpoint the trouble spot.

4 The basic tools required for electrical fault-finding include a circuit tester or voltmeter (a 12-volt bulb with a set of test leads can also be used for certain tests); a self-powered test light (sometimes known as a continuity tester); an ohmmeter (to measure resistance); a battery and set of test leads; and a jumper wire, preferably with a circuit breaker or fuse incorporated, which can be used to bypass suspect wires or electrical components. Before attempting to locate a problem with test instruments, use the wiring diagram to determine where to make the connections.

5 To find the source of an intermittent wiring fault (usually due to a poor or dirty connection, or damaged wiring insulation), a 'wiggle' test can be performed on the wiring. This involves wiggling the wiring by hand to see if the fault occurs as the wiring is moved. It should be possible to narrow down the source of the fault to a particular section of wiring. This method of testing can be used in conjunction with any of the tests described in the following sub-Sections.

6 Apart from problems due to poor connections, two basic types of fault can occur in an electrical circuit - open circuit, or short circuit.

7 Open circuit faults are caused by a break somewhere in the circuit, which prevents current from flowing. An open circuit fault will prevent a component from working, but will not cause the relevant circuit fuse to blow.

8 Short circuit faults are caused by a 'short' somewhere in the circuit, which allows the current flowing in the circuit to 'escape' along an alternative route, usually to earth. Short circuit faults are normally caused by a breakdown in wiring insulation, which allows a feed wire to touch either another wire, or an earthed component such as the bodyshell. A short circuit fault will normally cause the relevant circuit fuse to blow.

Finding an open circuit

9 To check for an open circuit, connect one lead of a circuit tester or voltmeter to either the negative battery terminal or a known good earth.

10 Connect the other lead to a connector in the circuit being tested, preferably nearest to the battery or fuse.

11 Switch on the circuit, bearing in mind that some circuits are live only when the ignition switch is moved to a particular position.

12 If voltage is present (indicated either by the tester bulb lighting or a voltmeter reading, as applicable), this means that the section of the circuit between the relevant connector and the battery is problem-free.

13 Continue to check the remainder of the circuit in the same fashion.

14 When a point is reached at which no voltage is present, the problem must lie between that point and the previous test point with voltage. Most problems can be traced to a broken, corroded or loose connection.

Finding a short circuit

15 To check for a short circuit, first disconnect the load(s) from the circuit (loads are the components which draw current from a circuit, such as bulbs, motors, heating elements, etc).

16 Remove the relevant fuse from the circuit, and connect a circuit tester or voltmeter to the fuse connections.

17 Switch on the circuit, bearing in mind that some circuits are live only when the ignition switch is moved to a particular position.

18 If voltage is present (indicated either by the tester bulb lighting or a voltmeter reading, as applicable), this means that there is a short circuit.

19 If no voltage is present, but the fuse still blows with the load(s) connected, this indicates an internal fault in the load(s).

Finding an earth fault

20 The battery negative terminal is connected to 'earth' - the metal of the engine/transmission and the car body - and most systems are wired so that they only receive a positive feed, the current returning via the metal of the car body. This means that the component mounting and the body form part of that circuit. Loose or corroded mountings can therefore cause a range of electrical faults, ranging from total failure of a circuit, to a puzzling partial fault. In particular, lights may shine dimly (especially when another circuit sharing the same earth point is in operation), motors (eg. wiper motors or the radiator cooling fan motor) may run slowly, and the operation of one circuit may have an apparently unrelated effect on another. Note that on many vehicles, earth straps are used between certain components, such as the engine/transmission and the body, usually where there is no metal-to-metal contact between components due to flexible rubber mountings, etc.

21 To check whether a component is properly earthed, disconnect the battery and connect one lead of an ohmmeter to a known good earth point. Connect the other lead to the wire or earth connection being tested. The resistance reading should be zero; if not, check the connection as follows:

22 If an earth connection is thought to be faulty, dismantle the connection and clean back to bare metal both the bodyshell and the wire terminal or the component earth connection mating surface. Be careful to remove all traces of dirt and corrosion, then use a knife to trim away any paint, so that a clean metal-to-metal joint is made. On reassembly, tighten the joint fasteners securely; if a wire terminal is being refitted, use serrated washers between the terminal and the bodyshell to ensure a clean and secure connection. When the connection is remade, prevent the onset of corrosion in the future by applying a coat of petroleum jelly or silicone-based grease or by spraying on (at regular intervals) a proprietary ignition sealer.

3 Fuses and relays - general information

1 All the car's electrical circuits are protected by fuses; most of the fuses are found in a fuse/relay box located under a cover to the right of and below the steering column **(see illustration)**.

2 Typical fuse applications are given in the Specifications; model specific information will be found printed on the fuse/relay box lid.

3 The fuses are of the 'blade' type. Their ratings are printed on their backs and additionally they are colour-coded. A blown fuse may be recognised by its melted or missing wire link.

4 When renewing a fuse, switch off the circuit(s) concerned first. If the new fuse blows immediately when switching on, find and rectify the cause. The most usual cause of a blown fuse if a short-circuit to earth somewhere along the wire feeding the component concerned. The wire may be disconnected, trapped or frayed. Pay special attention to wire runs through grommets, under carpets etc.

5 Where a blown fuse serves more than one component, the defective circuit can be traced by switching on each component in turn until the replacement fuse blows.

6 **Never** attempt to bypass a fuse with silver foil or wire, nor fit a fuse of a higher rating than specified. Serious damage, or even fire, may result.

3.1 Removing the cover from the fuse/relay box

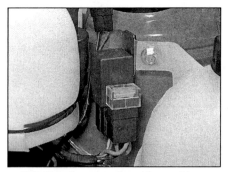

3.7a Headlamp washer relay and fuse

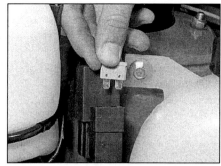

3.7b Removing the headlamp washer fuse

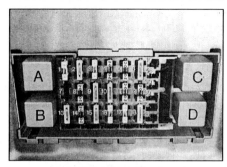

3.8a Relay identification

A   Flasher unit
B   Heated rear window relay
C   Windscreen wiper relay/delay unit
D   Front foglamp relay

7 Models with a full range of optional equipment may carry one or two fuses on the other side of the fuse/relay box. When a headlamp washer system is fitted, its fuse and relay are mounted under the bonnet on the left-hand suspension turret **(see illustrations)**.
8 All models have some relays on the accessible side of the fuse/relay box; according to equipment level, some other relays may be found on the reverse side. Unclip the box to gain access. The relays are as shown **(see illustrations)**..
9 A relay is essentially an electrically-operated switch. If a circuit served by a relay becomes inoperative, remember that the relay could be at fault. Test by substitution of a known good relay.

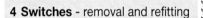
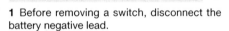

4 Switches - removal and refitting

1 Before removing a switch, disconnect the battery negative lead.

Lighting master switch

2 Release the spring clips at the side of the switch by pressing them with a bent screwdriver or similar tool. Draw the switch out of the facia, disconnect its wiring plug and remove it **(see illustration)**. If the switch cannot be released, remove the instrument panel surround, as described in Section 8.
3 To refit, connect the wiring plug to the switch and press the switch home until the clips snap into place.

Hazard warning switch

4 This is removed and refitted in the same way as the lighting master switch.

Foglamp switch

5 Carefully prise the switch from its location, disconnect its wires and withdraw it **(see illustration)**.
6 Refit in the reverse order to removal.

Instrument illumination control

7 Remove the instrument panel surround, as described in Section 8.
8 Slacken the securing screw and remove the illumination control **(see illustration)**.
9 Refit in the reverse order to removal.

Heater blower/heated rear window switch

10 This switch is released in a similar way to the lighting master switch. If the switch cannot be released, withdraw the heater control panel, as described in Chapter 3.
11 Refit in the reverse order to removal.

Steering column switches

12 Although not strictly necessary, access will be improved if the steering wheel is removed, as described in Chapter 10. Otherwise, remove the wheel centre trim.
13 Remove the upper and lower switch shrouds. These are held in place by eight screws with the fixed type steering wheel, or five screws with the adjustable wheel.
14 In theory it is now possible to unclip and

3.8b Fuse and relay identification (reverse side of fusebox)

E   Trip computer relay
F   Rear wiper relay (not GTE)
G   Day running lamp relay (not UK)
H   Headlamp cut-out (not UK)
I   "Lights-on" warning buzzer
19   Central locking fuse
20   Electric window winder fuse

withdraw either of the multi-function switches. In practice it was found necessary, when the adjustable wheel was fitted, to undo the two switch housing screws and draw the switch assembly up the column slightly. The switch in question can then be unplugged, unclipped and removed **(see illustrations)**.
15 Refit in the reverse order to removal.

4.2 Removing the lighting master switch - one of the spring clips is arrowed

4.5 Removing a foglamp switch

4.8 Removing the instrument illumination control

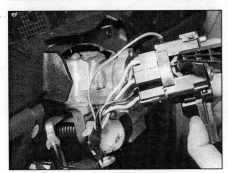

4.14a Drawing the steering column switches up the column

Ignition/starter switch

16 Refer to Chapter 5.

Stop-lamp switch

17 Remove the stop-lamp switch by turning it 90° left or right and withdrawing it from its bracket.

18 Before fitting the stop-lamp switch, pull its plunger out as far as it will go. The switch will adjust itself once it is fitted.

Handbrake warning switch

19 Proceed as described in Chapter 9, Section 19, but without disconnecting the handbrake lever from the yoke.

Electric mirror switch

20 Free the rear half of the centre console, as described in Chapter 11.

21 Disconnect and unclip the switch.

22 Refit in the reverse order to removal.

Electric window winder switch

23 Proceed as described above for the electric mirror switch.

Interior light switches

24 The main interior light is operated by door plunger switches. Similar switches control the luggage area and glovebox light, when fitted.

25 Removal is similar in every case. After displacing any trim which may be in the way, the switch is unscrewed or unclipped and withdrawn from its location **(see illustrations)**. The electrical lead(s) can then be unplugged and the switch removed. Tape the wires if necessary to avoid losing them inside the switch hole.

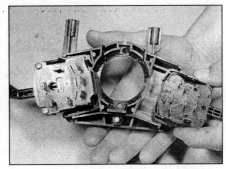

4.14b Unclipping a steering column switch - assembly removed for clarity

26 Refit in the reverse order to removal. Check for correct operation before refitting any trim.

5 Horn(s) - removal and refitting

Removal

1 The horn itself is located in front of the radiator, unless an oil cooler is fitted, when it is located behind the battery. Disconnect and unbolt the horn to remove it; remove the front trim panel if necessary for access.

2 On models with twin horns, the second horn is mounted behind the front grille on the left-hand side. To gain access to it, either the front grille or the radiator must be removed.

3 If the horn does not work, check with a 12 volt test lamp that voltage is present at the horn terminals when the horn push is operated. If the horn itself is defective it must be renewed.

Refitting

4 Refit in the reverse order to removal.

6 Clock - removal and refitting

Removal

1 Disconnect the battery earth lead.

2 Carefully pull the clock from its location. Disconnect the supply and illumination leads from the clock and remove it **(see illustration)**.

Refitting

3 Refit in the reverse order to removal.

7 Cigarette lighter - removal and refitting

Removal

1 Disconnect the battery earth lead.

2 Extract the heater element from the lighter socket.

3 Carefully prise the lighter socket out of the illuminating ring. Unplug the socket and remove it.

Refitting

4 Refit in the reverse order to removal. When inserting the socket into the illuminating ring, make sure that the ring lugs pass over a smooth part of the socket; twist the socket clockwise when home to engage the lugs.

8 Instrument panel - removal and refitting

Removal

1 Disconnect the battery earth lead.

2 Remove the horn push from the steering wheel.

3 Remove the steering column switch upper shroud, which is secured by four screws. Unlock the steering and turn the wheel as necessary to gain access to two of the screws.

4 Remove the four screws which secure the instrument panel surround and bottom trim strip. There are two screws at the top and one in each bottom corner; they may be covered by cosmetic caps **(see illustration)**.

5 Withdraw the instrument panel surround, disconnecting the wires from the various switches **(see illustration)**.

6 Except on the LCD instrument panel, disconnect the speedometer cable by depressing its retaining clip and pulling it away from the speedometer.

7 Remove the single securing screw and withdraw the instrument panel **(see illustrations)**. Disconnect the electrical leads if the panel is to be removed completely,

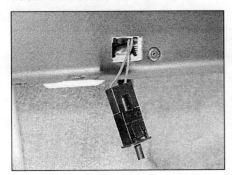

4.25a Glovebox light switch unclipped from its location

4.25b Luggage area light switch (arrowed) next to contact plate on tailgate sill

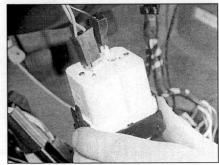

6.2 Removing the clock

8.4 Removing an instrument panel surround screw

8.5 Withdrawing the instrument panel surround

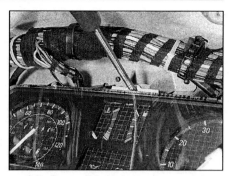

8.7a Removing the instrument panel securing screw

making notes if there is any possibility of confusion later. When an econometer is fitted, disconnect the vacuum hose.

Refitting

8 Refit in the reverse order of removal. On models with an LCD display, prior to refitting, ensure that the speedometer frequency code switch is set to the correct position **(see illustration)**. On models with 175/70 R 13 or 185/60 R 14 tyres set the switch to position 1, and on all other models set the switch to position 2.

9 Instrument panel - dismantling and reassembly

1 No attempt must be made to dismantle the LCD type instrument panel: its bulbs can be renewed, but that is all. Consult a GM dealer if an instrument fault is suspected: special test equipment is required for accurate diagnosis.
2 Individual instruments can be removed from the conventional instrument panel after removing the cover, which is secured by two screws at the top and three lugs at the bottom. The instruments are secured by screws or nuts **(see illustration)**.
3 Illumination and warning lamp bulbs can be removed by turning the combined bulb and holder anti-clockwise and withdrawing it from the rear of the panel. There is no need to remove the instrument panel completely to do

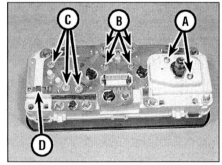

9.2 Instrument panel rear view (typical)

A Speedometer retaining screws
B Fuel/temperature gauge retaining nuts
C Tachometer retaining nuts
D Instrument voltage stabiliser

8.7b Withdrawing the instrument panel

this - just withdraw it far enough to gain access to the printed circuit.
4 The printed circuit can be renewed if all the instruments etc are transferred from the old one.

10 Speedometer cable - removal and refitting

Removal

1 A mechanical cable is not used with the LCD instrument panel; the electrical sender bolts onto the gearbox in the same position as the conventional cable.
2 To renew a mechanical cable, first disconnect it from the speedometer head. If it is not possible to reach up behind the instrument panel, partly withdraw it, as described in Section 8 **(see illustration)**.

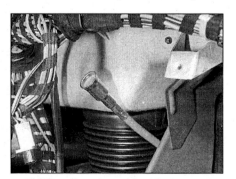

10.2 Speedometer cable at instrument panel end

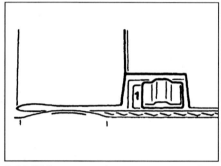

8.8 LCD instrument frequency code switch shown in position 1

3 Working under the bonnet, free the cable grommet from the bulkhead and draw the cable into the engine bay. Recover the grommet.
4 Undo the knurled nut which secures the cable to the transmission (or trip computer speed sender, when fitted). Remove the cable.

Refitting

5 Refit in the reverse order to removal. The cable must not be kinked or made to bend sharply. If lubricant is applied to the inner cable, do not put any on the top 15 cm or so, in case it gets into the speedometer head.

11 Bulbs - renewal

General

1 Whenever a bulb is renewed, note the following points.
   a) *Disconnect the battery negative lead before starting work.*
   b) *Remember that if the light has just been in use the bulb may be extremely hot.*
   c) *Always check the bulb contacts and holder, ensuring that there is clean metal-to-metal contact between the bulb and its live(s) and earth. Clean off any corrosion or dirt before fitting a new bulb.*
   d) *Wherever bayonet-type bulbs are fitted (see Specifications) ensure that the live contact(s) bear firmly against the bulb contact.*

11.2a Disconnecting the headlamp wiring plug

11.2b Rubber cover removed to expose the spring clip

11.3 Removing a headlamp bulb

e) *Always ensure that the new bulb is of the correct rating and that it is completely clean before fitting it; this applies particularly to headlight/foglight bulbs.*

Headlamp

2 Open the bonnet and disconnect the wiring plug from the rear of the headlamp unit. Remove the rubber cover to expose the spring clip which secures the bulb **(see illustrations)**.
3 Release the spring clip and withdraw the bulb **(see illustration)**. Be careful if it has just been in use, it may be very hot.
4 Do not touch the bulb glass with the fingers: traces of grease can blacken the glass and shorten bulb life. Use a clean cloth moistened with methylated spirit to clean a bulb which has been accidentally touched.
5 Fit the new bulb in the reverse order to removal. Make sure that the lugs on the bulb engage in the recesses in the bulb holder.

Sidelamp (front parking lamp)

6 Open the bonnet and disconnect the wiring plug from the sidelamp bulb holder.
7 Remove the bulb holder by depressing it and twisting it anti-clockwise **(see illustration)**.
8 Extract the old bulb from the holder and insert the new one. Refit and reconnect the bulb holder.

Front direction indicator

9 Open the bonnet. Remove the bulb holder by squeezing its legs together and twisting it anti-clockwise **(see illustration)**.
10 Fit the new bulb and refit the bulb holder.

Front foglamp

11 Working under the front bumper, remove the rear cover from the lamp unit by twisting it anti-clockwise.

12 Unclip and remove the bulb, separating its electrical connector at the first junction, not at the bulb itself.
13 Do not touch the bulb glass: see paragraph 4.
14 Connect the new bulb. secure it and refit the lamp cover.

Rear lamp cluster

15 Remove the trim panel or access cover from the area of the rear lamp cluster.
16 Disconnect the wiring plug, depress the bulb holder retaining lug And withdraw the bulb holder **(see illustrations)**.
17 The rear lamp unit itself can be removed after undoing the three retaining screws (two on Estates) **(see illustrations)**.
18 Refit in the reverse order to removal. If the lamp unit has been removed, make sure its retaining plates are correctly fitted before tightening the retaining screws.

11.7 Removing a sidelamp bulb and holder

11.9 Removing a direction indicator bulb and holder

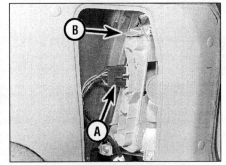

11.16a Rear lamp cluster wiring plug (A) and retaining lug (B)

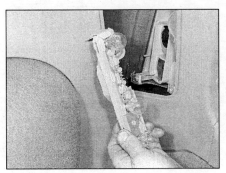

11.16b Rear lamp cluster bulbs and holder

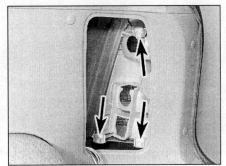

11.17a Rear lamp unit retaining screws (arrowed) Hatchback

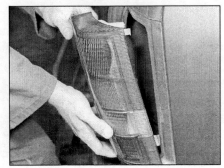

11.17b Removing a rear lamp lens

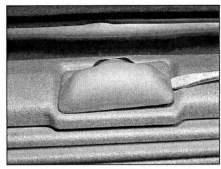

11.19 Removing a rear foglamp lens

11.22 Prising out the number plate lamp

11.23 Number plate lamp bulb holder and lens separated

11.25a Under-bonnet lamp unclipped note earth screw (arrowed)

11.25b Luggage area lamp unclipped

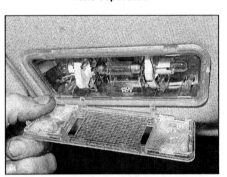

11.25c Removing the cover from the main interior lamp

Rear foglamp

19 Remove the lens from the foglamp by undoing its two retaining screws (see illustration).
20 Extract the bayonet fitting bulb and fit the new one.
21 Refit and secure the lens.

Number plate lamp

22 Prise the lamp unit out of the rear bumper and disconnect its wiring plug (see illustration).
23 Unclip the two halves of the lamp unit to gain access to the bulb (see illustration).
24 Refit in the reverse order to removal.

Interior lamps

25 Bulb renewal is similar for all types of interior lamp, and for the under-bonnet lamp (when fitted). Either unclip the lamp cover, or

carefully prise the lamp unit from its location (see illustrations).
26 Extract the old bulb. fit the new one and refit the lamp or cover.

Instrument illumination and warning lamps

27 Instrument panel illumination and warning lamp bulbs can be removed by turning the combined bulbholder assembly anti-clockwise and withdrawing it from the rear of the panel (see illustration). There is no need to withdraw the panel completely to do this - just withdraw it far enough to gain access to the printed circuit.

Switch illumination bulbs

28 Switches such as the lighting master switch and the heated rear window/heater blower control are illuminated by bulbs which can be renewed after removal of the switch (see illustration).

29 The pilot illumination in switches such as that controlling the foglamps is integral with the switch and cannot be renewed separately.

Check control display lamps

30 Carefully prise the check control unit from its location. The bulb holders are accessible from below.
31 Refit in the reverse order to removal.

12 Headlamp/direction indicator lens assembly - removal and refitting

Removal

1 Remove the direction indicator, headlamp and sidelamp bulbs (Section 11).
2 Undo the securing screw and withdraw the direction indicator lens (see illustrations).

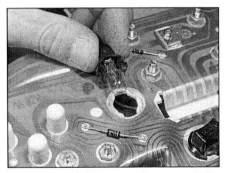

11.27 Removing an instrument panel bulb

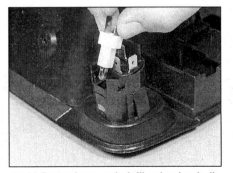

11.28 Removing a switch illumination bulb

12.2a Undoing a direction indicator lens screw

12.2b Removing a direction indicator lens

12.3a Headlamp lens outboard securing screw (arrowed)

12.3b Headlamp lens inboard securing screw (A). Do not disturb alignment adjusting screw (B)

12.3c Removing a headlamp lens

3 Remove the two screws which secure the headlamp unit, free it from its clips and withdraw it (see illustrations). Do not disturb the alignment adjusting screws.

Refitting

4 Refit in the reverse order to removal. Make sure that the front panel sealing lip aligns with the headlamp; use sealing tape if necessary. If a new unit has been fitted, or if the headlamp alignment has been otherwise disturbed, have the alignment checked and adjusted (see Section 13).

13 Headlamp beam adjustment - general information

1 Accurate adjustment of the headlight beam is only possible using optical beam setting equipment and this work should therefore be carried out by a Vauxhall/Opel dealer or suitably equipped workshop.
2 For reference the headlights can be adjusted using the adjuster assemblies fitted to the top and bottom of each light unit. In an emergency, adjustments can be made on a 'trial and error' basis. The vertical adjustment screws are accessible from under the bonnet (see illustration). The lateral adjustment screws are positioned as shown in illustration 12.3b. Note: *Adjustment of the front foglights is correct when the inclination of the beam is 20 cm over a distance of 10 m. Adjustment is made by turning the adjuster screw, on the rear of each lamp as required.*

14 Headlamp dim-dip system (UK models only) - general information

Fitted to UK models produced after October 1986, to prevent the possibility of vehicles being driven on parking lights only and to comply with new lighting legislation, all UK models produced from the above date are fitted with a dim-dip system in the headlamp circuit. The function of the system is to ensure that the car cannot be driven on parking lights only.
The system is activated by a dim-dip control unit which, when activated, reduces the voltage supply to the headlamps. This system is designed as a safeguard only and normal lighting legislation requirements still apply and must be observed.

15 Trip computer - general information and component renewal

General information

1 A trip computer is fitted to some top line models, The computer collects fuel consumption and distance data and integrates them with respect to time. In this way it can provide estimates of fuel consumption (both instantaneous and average), speed and range on fuel remaining. Normal time clock and stopwatch functions

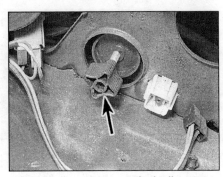

13.2 Headlamp beam vertical adjustment screw (arrowed)

are available, and an external temperature sensor is also provided.
2 For detailed operating instructions, refer to the owner's handbook supplied with the vehicle.
3 Testing of the computer and its satellite components is beyond the scope of the average DIY mechanic, but there is no reason why defective components should not be renewed, as described in the next Section.

Component renewal

Temperature sensor

4 Separate the temperature sensor lead at the multi-plug near the left-hand headlamp.
5 Pull the temperature sensor from the front bumper, unclip its lead and remove it.
6 Refit in the reverse order to removal.

Distance sender

7 The distance sender is located on the speedometer cable take-off point on the transmission; except with LCD instruments the speedometer cable screws into the sender.
8 Separate the sender multi-plug, then unclip the sender unit from the transmission
9 Unscrew the speedometer cable (when fitted) from the sender and remove the sender.
10 Refit in the reverse order to removal.

Fuel flow meter

11 The fuel flow meter is located on the wheel housing.
12 Disconnect the battery earth lead.
13 Disconnect the fuel flow meter multi-plug.
14 Identify the fuel hoses, then disconnect and plug them. Be prepared for fuel spillage.
15 Unbolt and remove the fuel flow meter.
16 Refit in the reverse order to removal.

Computer unit

17 Disconnect the battery earth lead.
18 Remove the radio (Section 25).
19 Carefully press the computer out of its location. Unplug its electrical connector and remove it.
20 Refit in the reverse order to removal. A new computer will have to be calibrated on the vehicle; this should be done by a GM dealer.

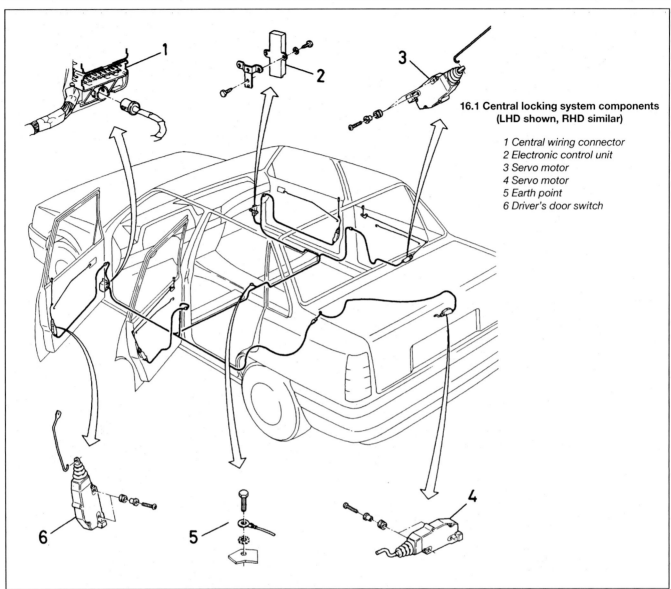

16.1 Central locking system components (LHD shown, RHD similar)

1 Central wiring connector
2 Electronic control unit
3 Servo motor
4 Servo motor
5 Earth point
6 Driver's door switch

Computer display lighting

21 Remove the computer, as just described.
22 Grip the bulb holder carefully with pliers and twist it to remove it. The capless bulb can then be extracted and renewed.
23 Refit in the reverse order to removal.

16 Central locking system - general information and component renewal

General information

1 On models so equipped, electric servo motors cause all the passenger door locks and the tailgate lock to follow the position of the driver's door lock. The major components of the system are as shown **(see illustration)**.
2 An electronic control unit, located in the passenger footwell, generates the electrical pulses needed to operate the lock motors.

Component renewal

Driver's door switch

3 Remove the door inner trim panel, as described in Chapter 11. Peel away the waterproof sheet in the area of the switch.

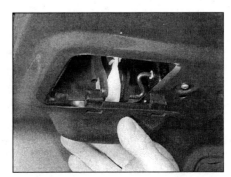

16.7 On Saloon models, unclip the cover from the boot lid lock . . .

4 Remove the two securing screws, disconnect the switch plug and unhook the switch from the lock actuating rod. Remove the switch.
5 Refit in the reverse order to removal: make sure that the electrical plug is connected the right way round. Renew the rubber mountings if necessary.

Passenger door and tailgate servo motors

6 Proceed as just described for the driver's door switch. Removal of the tailgate trim panel is achieved by carefully releasing its retaining clips.

Boot lid servo motor (Saloon models)

7 Open the boot lid and remove the plastic cover **(see illustration)**.
8 Remove the two nuts which secure the latch mechanism and the two screws which secure the servo motor **(see illustration)**. Separate the servo motor from the latch,

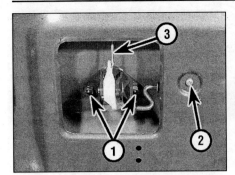

16.8 . . . to gain access to the boot latch nuts (1), servo unit mounting screw (2) and the manual release control rod (3)

disconnect its wiring plug and remove it.
9 Refitting is the reverse of removal.

Control unit

10 Remove the trim panel from the passenger side footwell.
11 On fuel injection models, release and move aside the fuel injection control unit and its bracket.
12 Remove the single screw which secures the control unit bracket to the A-Pillar.
13 Extract the control unit and bracket. Disconnect the electrical plug and unscrew the unit from the bracket to remove it completely.
14 Refit in the reverse order to removal.

17 Heated seats - general information

1 In some territories, electric heating elements for the front seats can be specified as an option. The heating elements are controlled by facia-mounted switches, they also incorporate a thermostatic control.
2 Do not use the heating elements when the engine is not running, or the battery will quickly be discharged.
3 In the event of malfunction, first check the wiring and connectors.
4 Element renewal should be referred to a GM dealer or upholstery specialist.

19.3 Wiper arm retaining nut

18.3 Removing the tailgate contact pins

1 +ve permanent feed (wiper parking) - black/violet
2 Heater rear window - black
3 Wiper (switch) - blue

18 Tailgate contact pins and plate - removal and refitting

Removal

1 A three-pole contact unit transfers electrical power for the tailgate units (heated window, wiper motor) when the tailgate is shut. The unit consists of a contact plate in the load area sill and spring-loaded pins in the tailgate.
2 To remove the plate or the pins, first disconnect the battery earth lead.
3 Remove the tailgate trim or rear sill trim, as appropriate. Unclip the contact plate or pins from its location and disconnect the wire **(see illustration)**.

Refitting

4 Refit in the reverse order to removal. The component mountings are inhibited to prevent incorrect fitting.

19 Wiper blades and arms - removal and refitting

Removal

1 To remove a wiper blade, lift the wiper arm away from the glass. Swivel the blade on the arm, depress the catch on the U-shaped

20.4 Wiper spindle clamp nut (arrowed)

19.1 Removing a wiper blade from its arm

retainer and slide the blade off the arm **(see illustration)**.
2 Before removing a wiper arm, make sure that the motor is in its parked position. Mark the position of the blade on the screen with sticky tape or wax crayon as a guide to refitting.
3 Lift up the cover and unscrew the arm retaining nut **(see illustration)**.
4 Pull the arm off the splined shaft. If it has not been moved for a long time it will be tight: apply some penetrating fluid.

Refitting

5 Refit in the reverse order to removal.

20 Windscreen wiper motor and linkage - removal and refitting

Removal

1 Remove the windscreen wiper arms, as described in the previous Section.
2 Disconnect the battery earth lead.
3 Remove the four screws and take off both halves of the wind deflector panel See Chapter 11, Section 11.
4 Remove the clamp nuts from both wiper spindles **(see illustration)**.
5 Free the bulkhead rubber seal, remove the single securing screw and take off the water deflector.
6 Release the retainer and disconnect the electrical multi-plug from the motor **(see illustration)**.

20.6 Releasing the wiper motor electrical plug

20.7 Wiper motor securing screw (arrowed)

20.8a Wiper motor spindle nut (arrowed)

20.8b Undoing the wiper motor securing

20.9 Choice of wiper motor mounting holes - RHD arrowed

7 Undo the single securing screw and remove the motor and linkage (see illustration).
8 The motor may be separated from the linkage by undoing the spindle nut. To remove

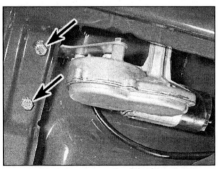

21.6 Rear wiper motor securing screws (arrowed) - tailgate-mounted motor

the motor from its bracket, also remove the three securing screws (see illustrations).

Refitting

9 Refit in the reverse order to removal. Note that two sets of motor mounting holes are provided, to provide for different sweep and parking requirements for RHD and LHD cars (see illustration).

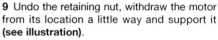

21 Rear window wiper motor - removal and refitting

Removal

Tailgate-mounted motor

1 Disconnect the battery earth lead.
2 Remove the wiper arm, as described in Section 19.
3 Remove the clamp nut from the wiper spindle.
4 Remove the tailgate inner trim panel.
5 Remove the contact pin nut (Section 18) and disconnect the wiper motor wire from it. (On Estate models, simply disconnect the motor from the tailgate harness.)
6 Remove the two securing screws and carefully withdraw the motor and its wiring (see illustration).

Window-mounted motor

7 Disconnect the battery earth lead.
8 Remove the rear wiper arm and withdraw the rubber cover from the spindle (see illustration).

9 Undo the retaining nut, withdraw the motor from its location a little way and support it (see illustration).
10 Remove the tailgate inner trim panel by prising free the plastic retainers.
11 Remove the tailgate contact pins as described in Section 18.
12 Detach the motor wiring from the retainer inside the tailgate. Remove the motor with its wiring and bracket.
13 To inspect the motor and control circuitry, remove the two screws which secure the bracket to the cover and the four screws which secure the cover to the motor. Remove the cover (see illustrations).

Refitting

14 Refit in the reverse order to removal, but check for correct operation before refitting the trim panel.

21.9 Removing the window-mounted motor

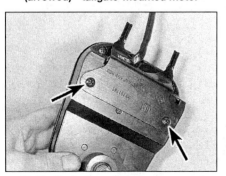

21.13a Undo the retaining screws and remove the mounting bracket . . .

21.13b . . . then undo the retaining screws . . .

21.13c . . . and remove the motor cover to gain access to the motor wiring

22 Windscreen/rear window washer system - general information

1 All models are fitted with an electrically-operated windscreen washer. The reservoir is mounted on the left-hand side of the engine bay; the pump is a push fit into a grommet in the base of the reservoir.

2 When a rear window washer is fitted, this uses a second pump which shares the same reservoir. A small bore tube carries the water through the car to the tailgate.

3 To renew a pump, first drain the reservoir (if necessary). Disconnect the electrical plug from the pump and rock the pump out of its grommet. Cut the tube off as close as possible to the pump outlet stub.

4 Use a new grommet when fitting a new pump. A short length of rubber hose should be used to connect the tube to the pump, as the tube is too stiff to pass over the outlet stub easily.

5 Washer jet aim can be adjusted by inserting a pin and carefully moving the jet.

23 Headlamp washer system - general information

1 When fitted, the headlamp washer system has its own reservoir and high pressure pump. The reservoir is located in the engine bay, except on models with fuel injection and/or a trip computer, when it is located under the left-hand wheel arch.

2 A relay controls the headlamp washer pump so that it operates when the windscreen washer is in use and the headlamps are on.

3 The washer jets are located in the bumper overriders. They can only be renewed as an assembly; the front trim panel must be removed first (Chapter 11).

4 Pump renewal is similar to that of the windscreen and rear window washer pumps (Section 22). To remove the wheel arch protective panelling, press the centres out of the plastic rivets; use new rivets or clips on reassembly. The reservoir can be removed from under the wing after unscrewing its filler neck and removing the securing screw.

24 Check control system - general information

1 Fitted to some higher specifications models, the check control system monitors important fluid levels, brake pad wear and bulb failure. A bank of six or seven warning lights to the left of the instrument panel conveys the information to the driver.

2 All the warning lights should come on for a few seconds when the ignition is first switched on; they should then all go out, except for the stop-lamp warning light, which will go out once the brake pedal is operated. If

25.2a Inserting the special clips for radio removal

any warning light stays on, or comes on during operation, the components or system indicated should be checked.

3 The main bulb failure indicator light monitors dipped headlights and tail lights; the stop-lamp indicator light monitors the stop-lamps and stop-lamp switch.

4 The bulb failure monitor unit is located under the facia panel on the passenger side. It is secured by two screws which are accessible after removing the trim and opening the glovebox.

5 The oil level warning light receives information from a sender on the engine. Obviously a correct reading will only be obtained if the car is parked on level ground. On early models the sender is incorporated in a dipstick and on later models it is bolted onto the side of the sump.

6 The brake fluid level warning light is controlled by a float switch in the master cylinder reservoir.

7 Brake pad wear is detected by wear sensors incorporated into the pads. This warning light will illuminate during braking if attention is required.

8 Screen washer fluid level is monitored by a float switch in the reservoir. On later models the coolant level in the expansion tank is also monitored by a similar float switch.

9 Renewal of the check control warning light bulbs is covered in Section 4.

10 Note that fitting bulbs of incorrect wattage may cause the bulb failure unit to give false alarms. For the same reason, the advice of a GM dealer should be sought if it is proposed to wire in a trailer socket.

25.4 Removing the radio surround

25.2b Removing the radio from its aperture

25 Radio/cassette unit - removal and refitting

Removal

1 All models are fitted with at least a radio, and most leave the factory with a combined radio/cassette player. This Section outlines removal and refitting procedures for the standard fitment equipment.

Early models

2 Radio/cassette units are to the latest DIN standard; they are released by inserting two special clips into the holes on each side of the unit. The clips are pressed in until they snap into place, then used to pull the radio out of its aperture. The various plugs can then be removed from the rear of the radio (see illustrations).

3 The special clips used to release the radio should have been supplied with the car; if not, they can be obtained from a car entertainment specialist.

4 With the radio removed, its surround can be removed if necessary by unclipping it (see illustration).

5 To refit the radio, reconnect its plugs and push it home until the retaining springs click into place.

Later (1989 onwards) models

6 For the 1989 model year, various anti-theft measures were introduced on the factory-fitted radio/cassette players. These are as follows:
   a) Blanking screws in removal holes.
   b) Serial number embossed in housing.
   c) Electronic coding of most units.

7 The blanking screws must be removed with an Allen key before the unit can be removed (see illustration). Removal is then carried out by inserting two special clips as described in paragraph 2.

8 The wiring connections on later units are made automatically by special connectors which engage as the unit is pushed home. Adapters are available to enable later units to be fitted to earlier models, and vice versa.

9 Units with electronic coding will not function after an interruption of the power supply until a 3-figure security code,

25.7 On later models it will be necessary to remove the blanking screws to be able to insert the removal tools

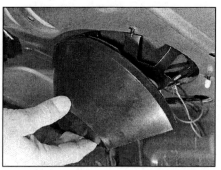

26.2a On Saloon models, unclip the plastic covers to gain access to the underside of the rear speakers . . .

26.2b . . . the speakers are retained by four screws

determined by the original owner of the unit, is keyed in. Only 8 attempts at coding are allowed, after this the unit will be mute and will have to be returned to the manufacturer for decoding. More details of this procedure are contained in the operating instructions supplied with the unit.

26 Loudspeakers - removal and refitting

Removal

1 Loudspeakers are positioned one at each end of the facia panel, and (on some models) one at each end of the parcel shelf or in the tailgate. Removal and refitting are self-explanatory once the appropriate trim has been removed (see Chapter 11).

2 On Saloon models the rear loudspeakers are mounted in the rear parcel shelf. Access to them is gained from the boot area. Unclip the plastic cover from the base of the speaker and disconnect the electrical leads then return to the inside of the car, undo the retaining screws and lift out the speaker **(see illustrations)**.

Refitting

3 Refitting is the reverse of removal.

27 Radio aerial - removal and refitting

Removal

1 The radio aerial is mounted on the right-hand front wing. To remove it, first remove the wheel arch protective panelling by pressing out the centres of the plastic rivets. The aerial can then be released from its bracket and the top mounting nut be undone.

2 If the aerial cable (and motor cables, when applicable) cannot be disconnected at the aerial end, they will have to be disconnected at the radio and fed back through the inner wing. Removal of some facia trim may be necessary to gain adequate access.

Refitting

3 When refitting the aerial, make sure that a good earth connection is made at the mounting bracket.

Key to Diagram 1 - all models to 1986 (Not all items are fitted to all models)

No	Description	Track
E1	RH sidelamp	235
E2	RH tail lamp	237, 440
E3	Number plate lamp	238, 451
E4	LH sidelamp	231
E5	LH tail lamp	232, 438
E6	Engine bay lamp	240
E7	RH main beam	246
E8	LH main beam	245
E9	RH dipped beam	249, 444
E10	LH dipped beam	248, 442
E11	Instrument illumination	242
E12	Auto transmission selector lamp	346
E13	Luggage area lamp	285
E14	Interior lamp	291
E15	Glovebox lamp	339
E16	Cigarette lighter lamp	338
E17	RH reversing lamp	336
E18	LH reversing lamp	335
E19	Heated rear window	202
E20	LH front foglamp	257
E21	RH front foglamp	258
E24	Rear foglamp	253
E25	LH seat heater	368
E30	RH seat heater	372
E32	Clock illumination	297
E33	Ashtray lamp	347
E34	Heater control lamp	242
E38	Computer illumination	355
E39	Rear foglamp	254
E40	Number plate lamp (Estate)	239, 452
E41	Interior lamp with delay unit	287, 289
E42	Radio illumination	431, 433
F1 to F2	Fuses	Various
F22	Fuse (mixture preheating)	164
F25	Instrument voltage stabiliser	213
G1	Battery	101
G2	Alternator	113
H1	Radio	429, 431
H2	Horn	211
H3	Direction indicator repeater	279
H4	Oil pressure warning lamp	221
H5	Brake fluid level warning lamp	219
H6	Hazard warning repeater	276
H7	No charge warning lamp	113
H8	Main beam pilot lamp	247
H9	RH stop-lamp	269, 448
H10	LH stop-lamp	268, 446
H11	RH front direction indicator	281
H12	RH rear direction indicator	282
H13	LH front direction indicator	277
H14	LH rear direction indicator	278
H16	Glow plug light (Diesel)	195
H17	Trailer direction indicator repeater	273
H19	Buzzer (headlamps on)	293
H20	Choke warning lamp	340
H21	Handbrake warning lamp	218
H23	Radio receiver (with automatic aerial)	432, 433
H25	Mirror heating pilot light	383, 392
K1	Heated rear window relay	201, 202
K2	Flasher unit	274
K5	Front foglamp relay	258, 259
K8	Wiper delay relay	305 to 308
K9	Headlamp washer relay	312 to 314
K10	Trailer flasher unit	273, 274

No	Description	Track
K15	Fuel injection control module	173 to 183
K20	Ignition module (electronic ignition)	118, 119
K25	Preheater relay (Diesel)	195 to 198
K28	Day running light relay (not UK)	421, 422
K30	Rear window wiper relay	319 to 321
K31	Fuel pump relay (fuel injection)	169 to 171
K35	Mirror heating timer	397, 399
K36	Computer relay	360 to 362
K37	Central locking relay	402 to 408
K39	Dashpot relay (not UK)	160, 162
K45	Preheater relay (not UK)	164 to 166
K46	Ignition timing control (not UK)	145 to 150
K52	Ignition module (not UK)	142, 143
K53	Ignition timing control (not UK)	134 to 139
L1	Ignition coil (contact breaker system)	109
L2	Ignition coil (electronic system)	117, 126, 143
L3	Ignition coil (not UK)	136
M1	Starter motor	105 to 107
M2	Windscreen wiper motor	303 to 306
M5	Heater blower motor	205 to 207
M4	Radiator cooling fan	210
M3	Windscreen washer pump	302
M8	Rear window wiper motor (not GTE)	317 to 319
M9	Rear window washer pump	322, 330
M12	Starter motor (Diesel)	193, 194
M14	LH front window motor	411
M15	RH front window motor	417
M16	LH rear window motor	413
M17	RH rear window motor	415
M18	Front passenger door lock actuator	404, 407
M19	LH rear door lock actuator	404, 407
M20	RH rear door lock actuator	404, 407
M21	Fuel pump (fuel injection)	169
M24	Headlamp washer pump	314
M26	Radio aerial motor	433, 434
M30	LH electric mirror	368 to 381, 387 to 390
M31	RH electric mirror	394 to 397
M36	Rear window wiper motor (GTE only)	327 to 330
M37	Tailgate lock actuator	404, 407
P1	Fuel gauge	214
P2	Temperature gauge	206
P3	Clock	296
P4	Fuel gauge sender	214, 471
P5	Temperature gauge sender	216, 481
P7	Tachometer	225
P10	Oil pressure sensor	488
P11	Airflow meter (fuel injection)	188 to 190
P12	Temperature sensor (fuel injection)	188 to 190
P13	Temperature sensor (ambient air)	360
P14	Distance recorder	133, 134, 156, 157, 351, 352, 492, 493
P15	Fuel flow meter	353, 354
P23	Vacuum sensor (not UK)	135 to 137
P24	Temperature sensor (not UK)	138, 139
P25	Bulb failure sensor	438 to 448
P26	Engine oil level sensor	457, 458
P27	LH brake pad wear sensor	460
P28	RH brake pad wear sensor	461
R1	Ballast resistor (points ignition)	109
R2	Carburettor heater	341
R3	Cigarette lighter	337
R5	Glow plugs (Diesel)	188 to 190
R7	Mixture preheating	164
R11	Instrument illumination rheostat	475

Key to Diagram 1 - all models to 1986 (Not all items are fitted to all models) (continued)

No	Description	Track
R12	Automatic choke heater	343
S1	Ignition/starter switch	106, 107
S2.1	Main lighting switch	239, 240, 439, 440
S2.2	Interior light switch	289
S3	Heater blower/	
	heated rear window switch	203 to 207
S5.2	Dipswitch	247,248,444
S5.3	Direction indicator switch	280,281
S5.5	Horn switch	211
S6	Distributor (contact breaker type)	109, 111
S7	Reversing lamp switch	335
S8	Stop-lamp switch	268,446
S9.2	Windscreen wiper switch	302 to 306
S9.3	Rear window wiper switch (not GTE)	320,321
S9.4	Rear window wiper switch (GTE)	329,330
S10	Starter inhibitor switch (automatic)	107
S11	Brake fluid level switch	219
S13	Handbrake switch	218,484
S14	Oil pressure switch	221,486
S15	Luggage area light switch	285
S16	RH door switch	290
S17	LH door switch	291
S18	Glovebox lamp switch	339
S21	Front foglamp switch	260,262
S22	Rear foglamp switch	253,255
S29	Radiator fan thermoswitch	210
S30	LH seat heating switch	368,370
S37	Window switches	410 to 418
S41	Central locking switch	402,403
S44	Throttle valve switch (fuel injection)	188 to 190
S47	Door switch (with headlamp buzzer)	292,293
S50	Choke warning switch	340
S52	Hazard warning switch	274 to 278
S55	RH seat heating switch	372 to 374
S60	Clutch pedal switch (not UK)	159
S66	Vacuum switch (not UK)	148
S68.1	Mirror adjustment switch	377 to 380, 385 to 389
S68.2	Mirror heating switch	383,392
S68.3	Mirror changeover switch	386 to 390
S73	Mixture preheating switch	165
S74	Engine temperature switch (not UK)	151
S75	Oil temperature switch (not UK)	151
S77	Distance switch (not UK)	153 to 156
S81	Brake fluid level switch	459
S82	Washer fluid level switch	462
U1	Day running light transformer (not UK)	422 to 426
U3	Computer board	352 to 361
U3.1	Clock priority switch	359
U3.2	Function select switch	359
U3.3	Reset/adjust switch	359
U5	Check control display	454 to 462

No	Description	Track
U5.1	Bulb failure warning lamp	454
U5.2	Stop-lamp failure warning lamp	456
U5.3	Oil level warning lamp	457
U5.4	Brake fluid level warning lamp	458
U5.5	Brake pad wear warning lamp	460
U5.6	Washer fluid level warning lamp	461
U6	LCD instrument panel	469 to 492
U6.1	No charge warning symbol	469
U6.2	Voltmeter	470 to 472
U6.3	Fuel gauge	471
U6.4	Oil pressure warning symbol	486
U6.5	Oil pressure gauge	488
U6.6	Temperature gauge	481
U6.7	Running lights pilot lamp	478
U6.8	Speedometer	491, 492
U6.9	Main beam pilot lamp	482
U6.10	Direction indicator repeater (LH)	486
U6.11	Direction indicator repeater (RH)	488
U6.13	Handbrake warning lamp	484
U6.14	Tachometer	484
U6.15	Trailer direction indicator repeater	480
U6.21	Relay (display lighting)	474 to 476
U6.22	Display lighting	475, 476
U6.23	Speedometer illumination	491
U6.24	Miles/km changeover switch	493
U6.25	Calibration switch	478
V4	Blocking diode (rear foglamps)	253
V5	Blocking diode (rear foglamps)	257
V6	Blocking diode (park lights, not UK)	240
X1	Trailer socket	Various
X2	Auxiliary connectors	Various
X5	Engine wiring harness connector	Various
X6	Rear wiring harness connector	Various
X7	Front wiring harness connector	Various
X8	LCD instrument connector (26-way)	469 to 492
X9	LCD instrument connector (16-way)	476 to 490
X10	Ignition timing connector (not UK)	138 to 140
Y5	Solenoid valve (Diesel)	199
Y6	Auxiliary air valve (fuel injectors)	188 to 190
Y7	Fuel injectors	188 to 190
Y10	Distributor (with Hall sensor)	122
Y11	Hall sensor	108, 109, 145 to 147
Y14	Inductive sensor (not UK)	135 to 137
Y15	Inductive sensor with ignition module	125, 126
Y17	Idle cut-off solenoid	342
Y18	Dashpot solenoid (not U K)	159
Y22	Distributor (not UK)	147
Y23	Distributor (with inductive sensor)	129
Y24	Distributor (not UK)	139

Colour codes

BL	Blue
BR	Brown
GE	Yellow
GN	Green
GR	Grey
HBL	Light blue
LI	Lilac
RT	Red
SW	Black
VI	Violet
WS	White

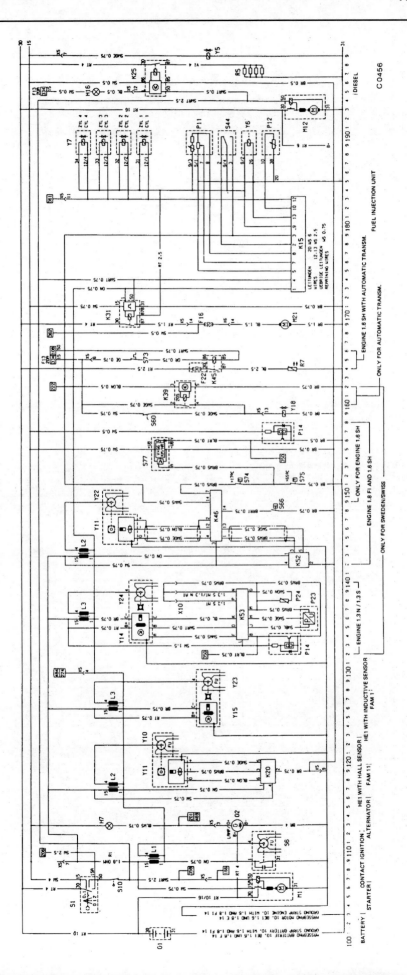

Diagram 1 - all models to 1986

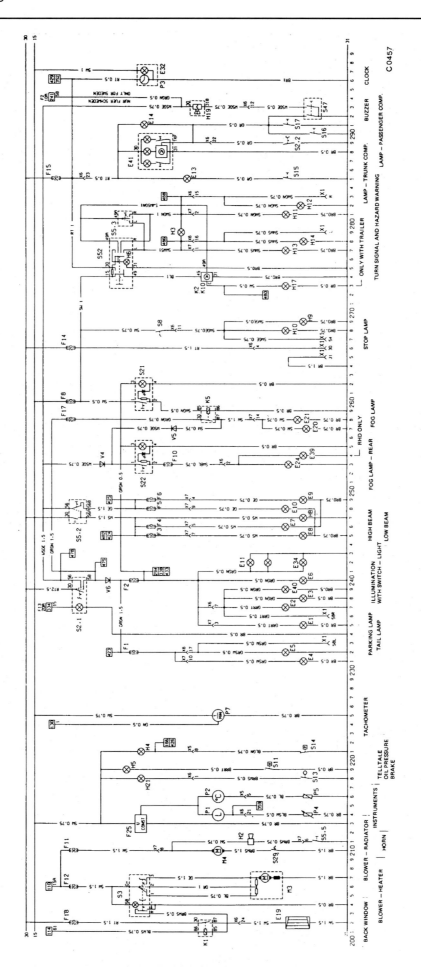

Diagram 1 - all models to 1986 (continued)

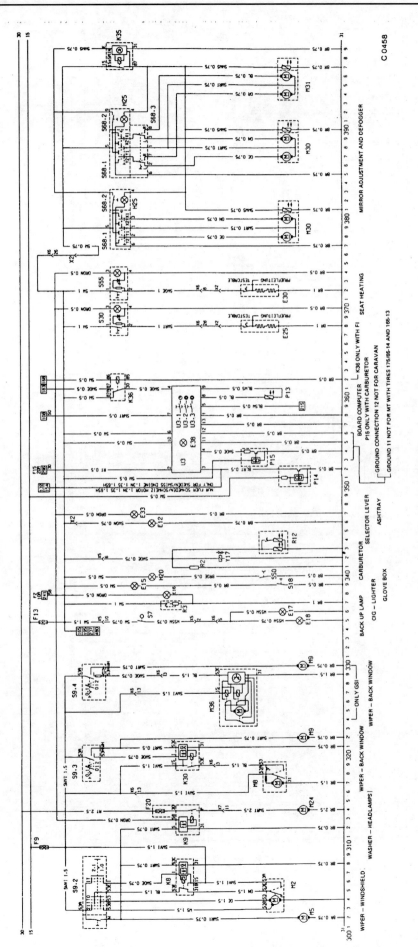

Diagram 1 - all models to 1986 (continued)

C 0458

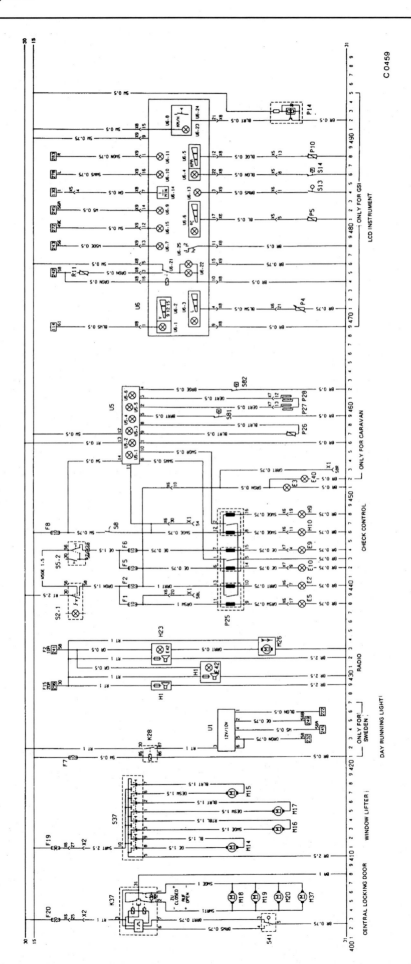

Diagram 1 - all models to 1986 (continued)

C 0459

Key to diagram 2 - all 1987 models
Not all items are fitted to all models; not all engines or systems are found in UK models

No	Description	Track	No	Description	Track
E1	Parking lamp left	328	H30	Engine systems warning lamp	151, 209
E2	Tail lamp left	329, 528	H33	Direction indicator repeater- left	376
E3	Number plate lamp	551	H34	Direction indicator repeater right	380
E4	Parking lamp right	332	K1	Relay heated rear window	301, 302
E5	Tail lamp right	334, 540	K2	Flasher unit	374
E6	Lamp engine compartment	337	K5	Foglamp relay	358, 359
E7	High beam left	341	K8	Relay windscreen wiper delay	405, 408
E8	High beam right	342	K9	Relay headlamp washer	412, 414
E9	Low beam left	344, 542	K10	Trailer flasher unit	373, 374
E10	Low beam right	345, 544	K15	Control unit (injection) (L3 Jetronic)	284, 291
E11	Lamps instrument	339	K30	Relay - rear wiper delay	419, 421
E12	Selector lever lamp (automatic transmission)	446	K35	Relay - heated mirror	497, 499
E13	Luggage area lamp	385	K36	Relay - trip computer	460, 462
E14	Interior lamp	391	K37	Relay - central locking	502, 508
E15	Glovebox lamp	439	K45	Relay - manifold heater	186, 187, 263, 264
E16	Cigarette lighter lamp	438	K53	Control unit EZ61 ignition	272 to281
E17	Reversing lamp left	435	K57	Control unit TBI (not UK)	145, 164
E18	Reversing lamp right	436	K58	Relay - fuel pump, TBI	165, 166
E19	Heated rear window	302	K61	Control unit Motronic	204, 228
E20	Front foglamp - left	357	K62	Control unit dim-dip system	347, 351
E21	Front foglamp - right	358	K63	Relay twin horns	173, 174
E24	Rear foglamp left	353	K68	Relay fuel injection	229, 232, 295 to 299
E25	Seat heating mat front left	468	K73	Ignition module EZ 61	269, 270
E26	Light switch lamp	334	K74	Control unit ignition system (MZV)	177, 185
E30	Seat heating mat front right	472	K75	Relay idle control (not UK)	131, 132
E32	Clock lamp	397	L1	Ignition coil (points system)	109, 110
E33	Ashtray lamp	447	L3	Ignition coil (electronic system)	Various
E34	Heater control lamp	339	L4	Ignition coil (EZ 61)	270, 271
E38	Trip computer lamp	455	M1	Starter motor	105, 107
E39	Rear foglamp - right	354	M2	Windscreen wiper motor	403, 406
E40	Number plate lamp	336, 552	M3	Heater blower motor	305, 307
E41	Interior lamp (with delay)	386, 389	M4	Radiator fan motor	171
E42	Radio lamp	531, 533	M5	Windscreen washer pump	402
F1 to 18	Fuses in fusebox	Various	M8	Rear wiper motor (except GSi)	417, 419
F19	Fuse window lift motors	511	M9	Rear screen washer pump	422, 430
F20	Fuse central locking	503	M14	Window lift motor front left	511, 512
F21	Fuse headlamp washer	414	M15	Window lift motor - front right	517, 518
F22	Fuse manifold heater	186, 264	M16	Window lift motor, rear left	513, 514
F25	Voltage stabiliser	313	M17	Window lift motor, rear right	515, 516
F27	Fuse twin horns	174	M19	Door lock actuator, rear left	504, 507
F31	Fuse electronic carburettor	238	M20	Door lock actuator, rear right	504, 507
G1	Battery	101	M21	Fuel pump	166, 230, 295
G2	Alternator	113	M24	Headlamp washer pump	414
H1	Radio	529, 531	M26	Electric aerial motor	533, 534
H2	Horn	172, 173	M30	Electric mirror left	478, 481, 487, 490
H3	Direction indicator repeater	378	M31	Electric mirror right	494, 497
H4	Oil pressure warning lamp	321	M32	Door lock actuator passenger door	504, 507
H5	Brake fluid warning lamp	319	M33	Idle speed actuator (Motronic)	216, 217
H6	Hazard warning repeater	376	M36	Rear wiper motor (GSi only)	427, 429
H7	Charging system warning lamp	323	M37	Tailgate lock actuator	504, 507
H8	High beam warning lamp	343	P1	Fuel gauge	314
H9	Stop-lamp left	368, 546	P2	Temperature gauge	316
H10	Stop-lamp right	369, 548	P3	Clock	396
H11	Direction indicator lamp front left	377	P4	Fuel gauge sender	314, 571
H12	Direction indicator lamp - rear left	378	P5	Coolant temperature sensor (gauge)	316, 581
H13	Direction indicator lamp front(right	381	P7	Tachometer	325
H14	Direction indicator lamp - rear right	382	P10	Oil pressure sensor	588
H18	Second horn	174	P11	Airflow meter	216,221
H19	'Headlamps on' warning buzzer	393, 394	P12	Coolant temperature sensor (L3 Jetronic)	211, 289
H20	Choke warning lamp	133	P13	Air temperature sensor (trip)	460, 461
H21	Handbrake warning lamp	318	P14	Distance sensor (Motronic/ trip computer)	144, 202, 451
H23	Radio with electric aerial	532, 533			
H25	Mirror heating warning lamp	483, 492	P15	Fuel flow meter (trip computer)	453, 454

Key to diagram 2 - all 1987 models (continued)

No	Description	Track	No	Description	Track
P23	Manifold vacuum sensor	125, 127, 158, 160, 177, 179	U3.1	Clock switch	459
P24	Oil temperature sensor	128, 129, 182, 183, 276, 277	U3.2	Function select switch	459
P25	Bulb failure sensor	537, 550	U3.3	Reset/clock adjustment switch	459
P26	Oil level sensor	557, 558	U5	Check control display unit	554, 563
P27	Brake pad wear sensor front left	560	U5.1	Bulb failure warning (running lights)	554
P28	Brake pad wear sensor front right	561	U5.2	Bulb failure warning (stop-lamps)	556
P29	Manifold temperature sensor	245, 246	U5.3	Oil level warning	557
P30	Coolant temperature sensor (not UK)	156, 157, 248, 249	U5.4	Brake fluid level warning	558
P31	Throttle potentiometer (not UK)	248, 250	U5.5	Brake pad wear warning	560
P32	Oxygen (Lambda) sensor	226, 227	U5.6	Washer fluid level warning	561
P34	Throttle position sensor (not UK)	161, 163	U5.7	Coolant level warning	563
P35	Inductive sensor (crankshaft)	222, 224, 257, 259, 273, 275	U6	LCD instrument panel	569 to 593
R1	Ballast resistor cable	109	U6.1	Charging system warning lamp	569
R2	Carburettor heater	196, 262	U6.2	Voltmeter	570, 572
R3	Cigarette lighter	437	U6.3	Fuel gauge	571
R5	Glow plugs (Diesel)	193, 194	U6.4	Oil pressure warning lamp	586
R7	Manifold heater	186, 264	U6.5	Oil pressure gauge	588
R11	Instrument illumination rheostat	575	U6.6	Temperature gauge	581
R15	Octane coding plug	162, 180, 181, 212, 278, 279	U6.7	'Lights on' indicator	578
S1	Ignition/starter switch	106, 107	U6.8	Speedometer	592, 593
S2.1	Main lighting switch	334, 337, 539, 540	U6.9	High beam indicator	582
S2.2	Interior lamp switch	389	U6.10	Direction indicator repeater left	586
S3	Heater blower/heated rear window switch	303, 307	U6.11	Direction indicator repeater right	588
S5.2	Dipswitch	343, 344, 544	U6.13	Handbrake 'on' warning lamp	584
S5.3	Direction indicator switch	380, 381	U6.14	Tachometer	584
S6	Distributor (contact breaker type)	111	U6.15	Trailer direction indicator repeater	580
S7	Reversing lamp switch (manual)	435	U6.21	Panel lighting relay	574, 576
S8	Stop-lamp switch	368, 546	U6.22	Panel lamp bulbs	575, 576
S9.2	Windscreen wiper switch	402, 406	U6.23	Speedometer illumination	592
S9.3	Rear wiper switch (except GSi)	420, 421	U6.24	Miles/km changeover switch	593
S9.4	Rear wiper switch (GSi)	429, 430	U6.25	Changeover switch	578
S10.1	Starter Inhibitor switch (automatic)	107	U6.27	Engine malfunction warning lamp	590
S10.2	Reversing lamp switch (automatic)	434	V1	Diode (brake fluid warning bulb test)	320
S10.3	Park/neutral switch (not UK)	156	X1	Trailer socket	Various
S11	Brake fluid warning level switch	319	X2	Auxiliary connector	Various
S13	Handbrake 'on' warning switch	318, 584	X5	Engine wiring harness connector	Various
S14	Oil pressure warning switch	321, 586	X6	Body wiring harness connector	Various
S15	Luggage area lamp switch	385	X7	Front wiring harness connector	Various
S16	Door switch left	390	X8	LCD instrument 26-pin connector	569 to 592
S17	Door switch right	391	X9	LCD instrument 16-pin connector	576 to 590
S18	Glovebox lamp switch	439	X10	Ignition timing basic coding plug	129, 130, 184, 184
S21	Front foglamp switch	360, 362	X11	Harness connector (not UK)	147 to 169
S22	Rear foglamp switch	353, 355	X13	Test connector	Various
S29	Radiator fan thermoswitch	171	X15A	Fuel injection harness connector (Motronic)	204 to 230
S30	Seat heating switch front left	468, 470	X15B	Fuel injection harness connector (L3 Jetronic)	283, 291, 293
S37	Window lift switch	510, 518	X16	Ignition harness connector	238, 245, 255, 257, 262
S41	Central locking driver's door switch	502, 503	Y5	Fuel shut-off valve (Diesel)	195
S44	Throttle valve switch	206, 207, 285, 286	Y6	Auxiliary air valve (L3 Jetronic)	292, 293
S47	Contact switch headlamps on warning	392, 393	Y7	Fuel injectors	219 to 226, 279 to 286
S50	Choke warning switch	133	Y14	Inductive sensor (MZV ignition system)	176 to 179
S52	Hazard warning	374, 378	Y15	Inductive sensor (1.3 models, electronic ignition)	116, 117
S55	Seat heating switch front right	472, 474	Y17	Idle cut-off solenoid	197
S60	Clutch pedal switch (not UK)	131	Y23	Ignition distributor (1.3 models, electronic ignition)	119, 120
S64	Horn switch	172	Y24	Ignition distributor (MZW ignition)	182
S68.1	Mirror adjustment switch	477, 480, 485, 489	Y26	Throttle valve positioner (not UK)	238 to 244
S68.2	Mirror heating switch	483, 492	Y27	Pre-throttle valve (not UK)	252, 253
S68.3	Mirror left/right switch	486, 490	Y32	Injection valve (not UK)	146
S73	Manifold heater switch (not UK)	187	Y33	Ignition distributor (fuel injection)	207, 260, 273
S81	Blake fluid check control switch	559	Y44	Idle control solenoid (not UK)	131
S82	Washer fluid check control switch	562			
S91	Oil pressure switch (not UK)	168, 169			
S93	Coolant check control switch	563			
U3	Trip computer assembly	452 to 461			

Refer to page 12•16 for colour codes

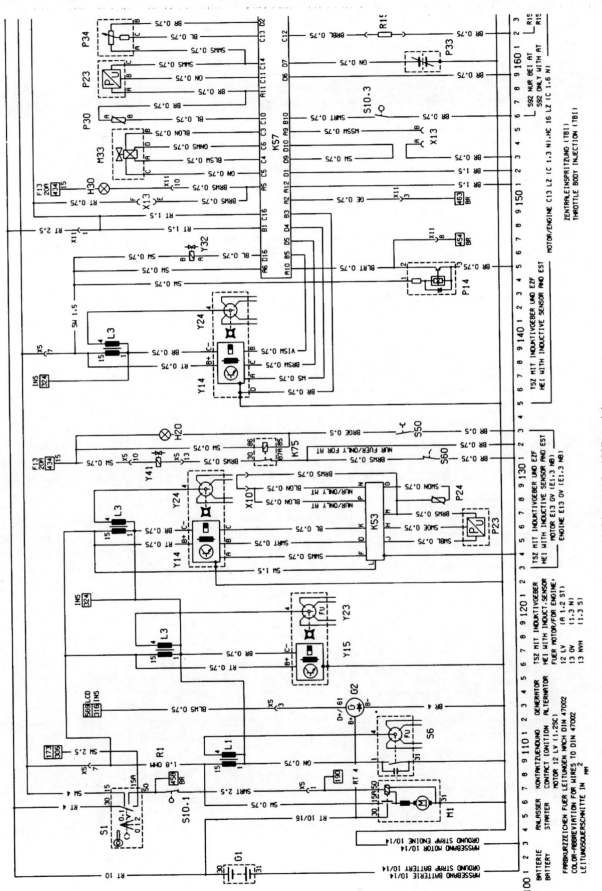

Diagram 2 - 1987 models

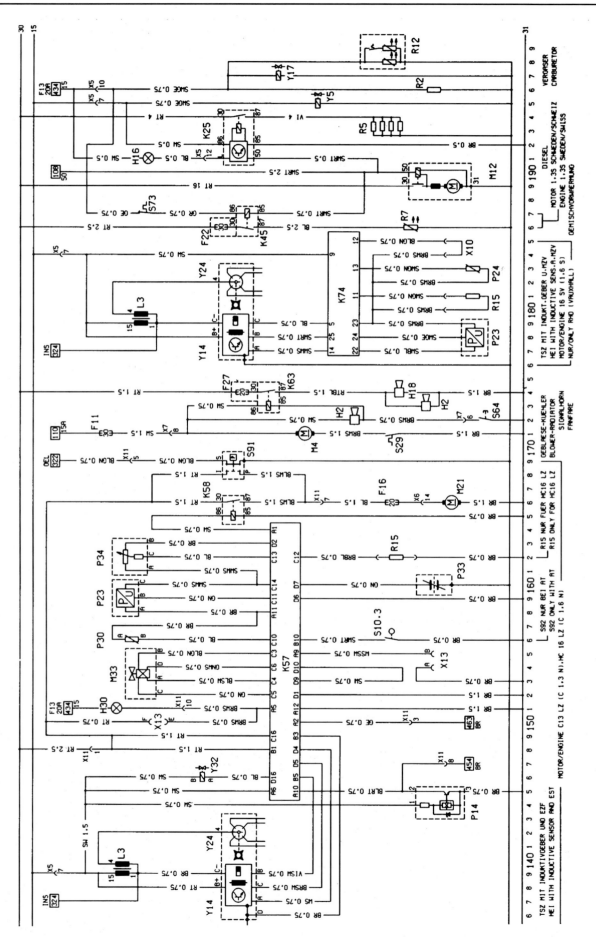

Diagram 2 - 1987 models (continued)

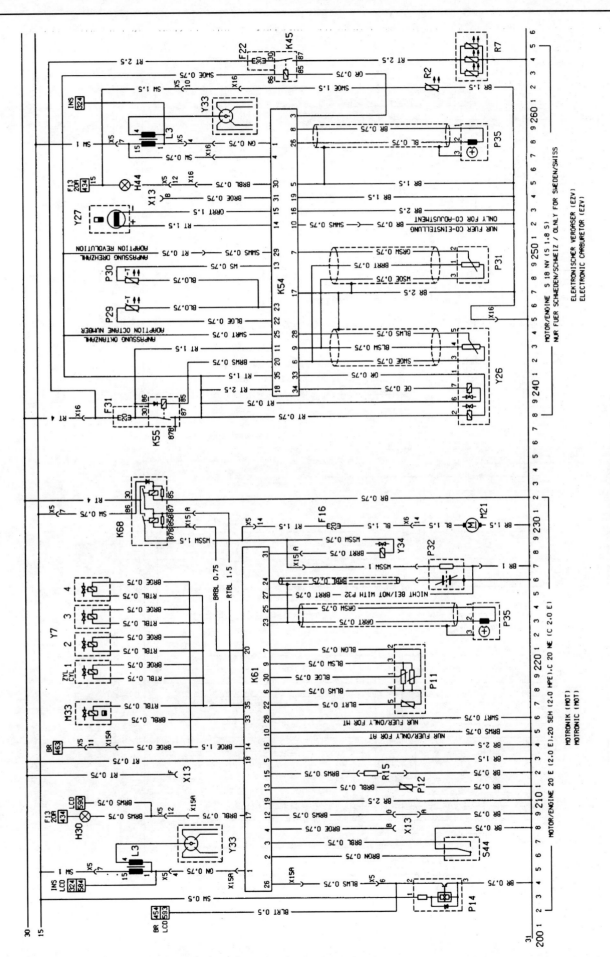

Diagram 2 - 1987 models (continued)

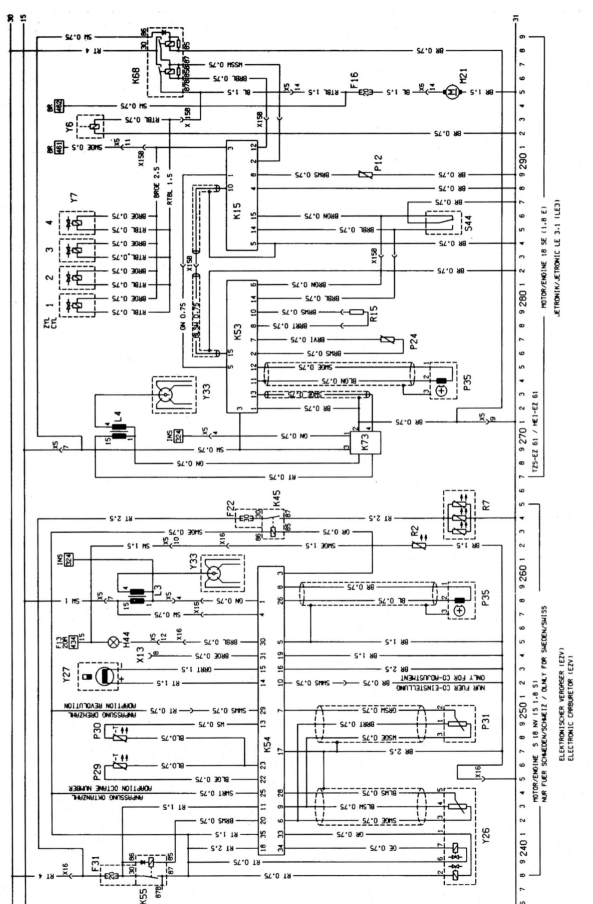

Diagram 2 - 1987 models (continued)

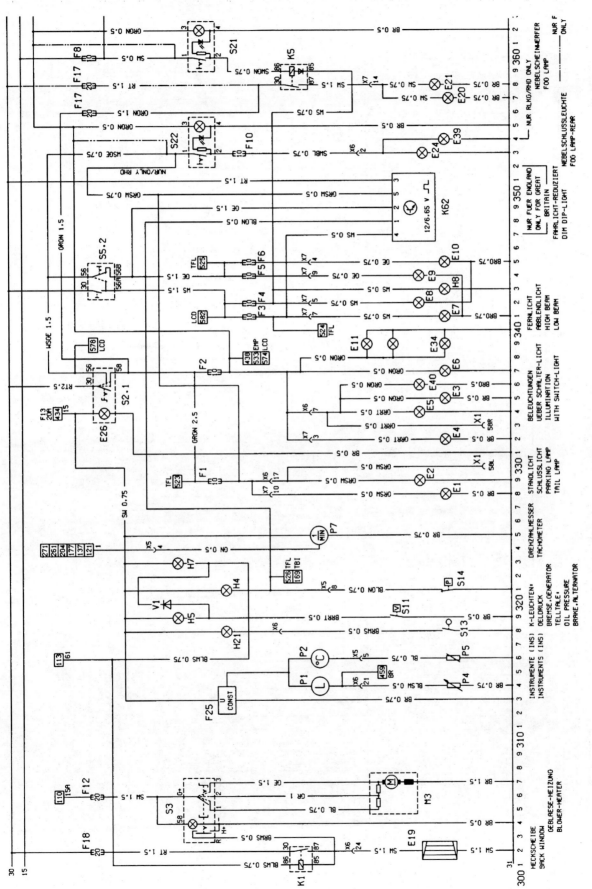

Diagram 2 - 1987 models (continued)

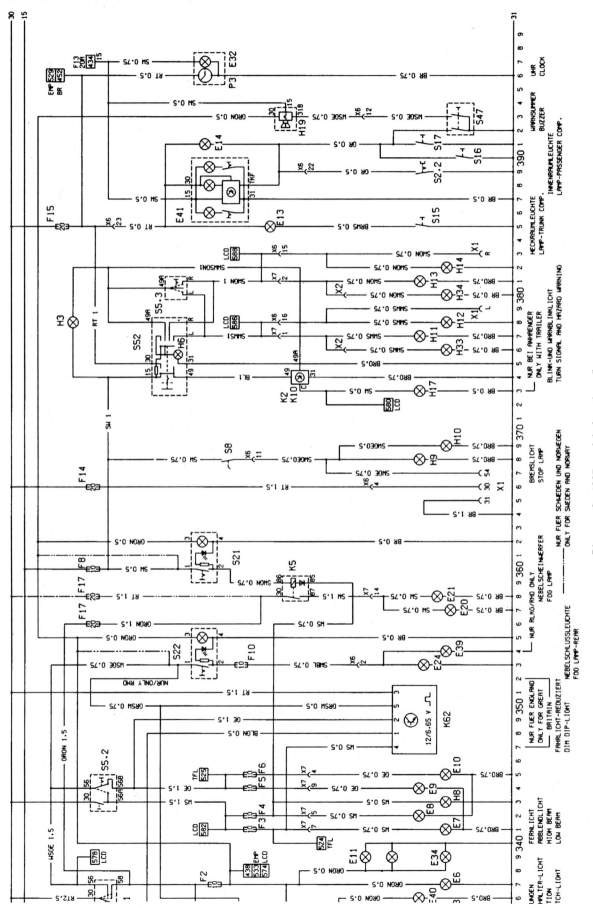

Diagram 2 - 1987 models (continued)

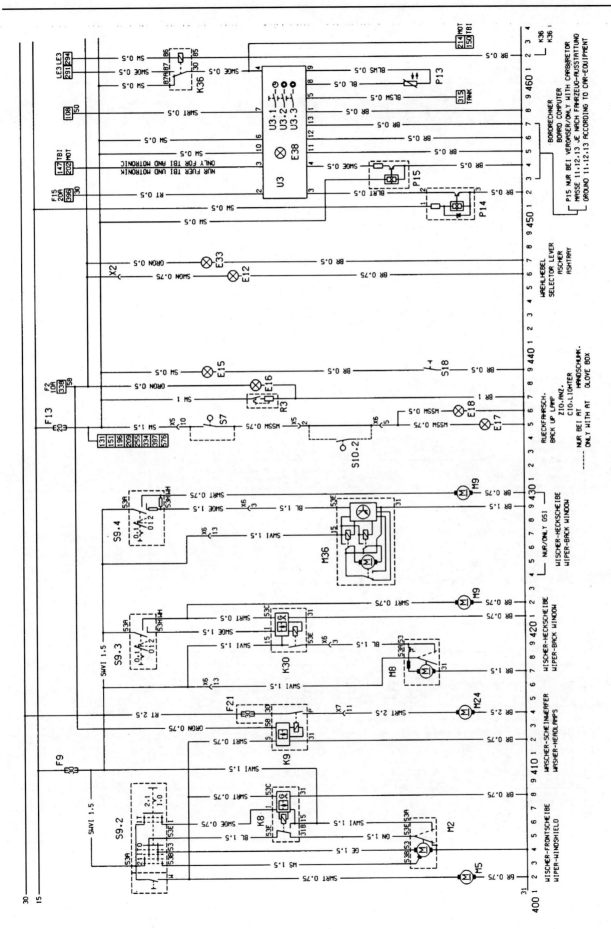

Diagram 2 - 1987 models (continued)

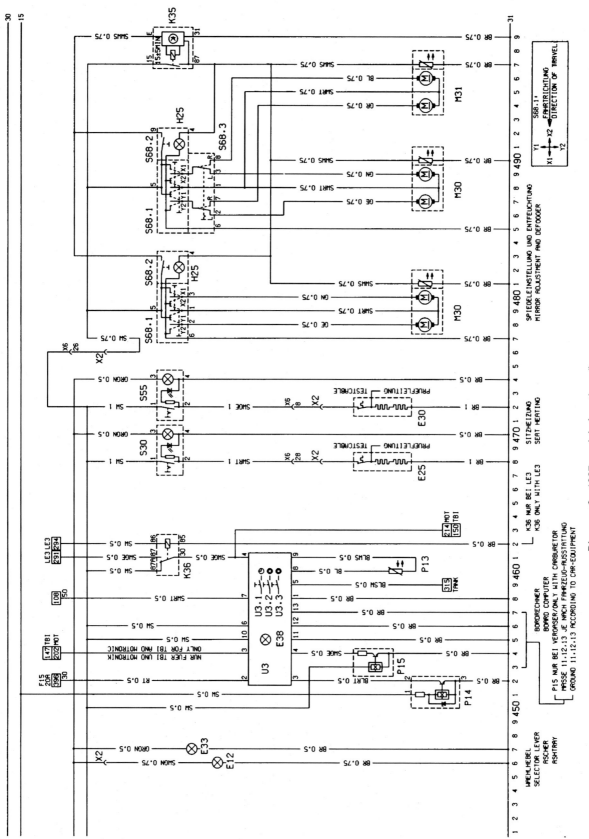

Diagram 2 - 1987 models (continued)

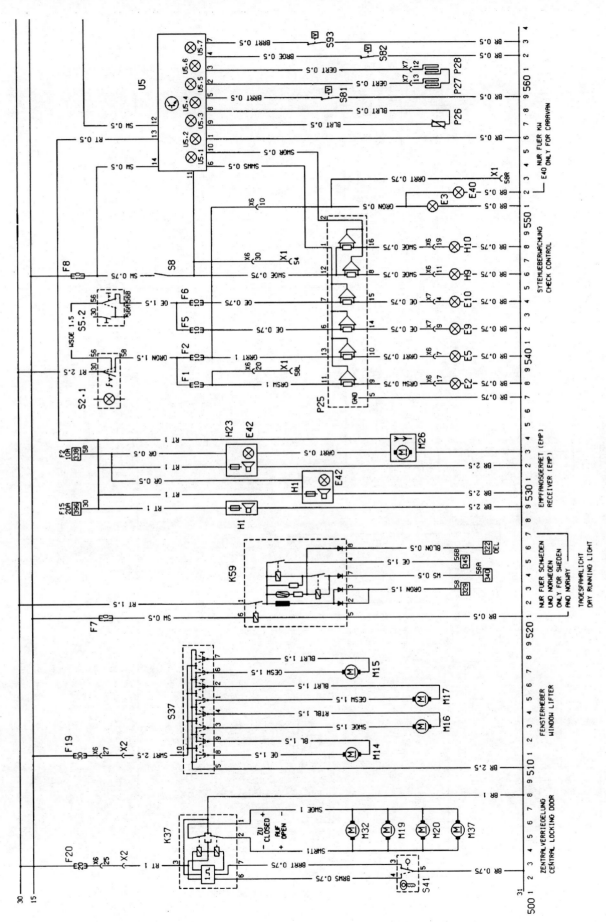

Diagram 2 - 1987 models (continued)

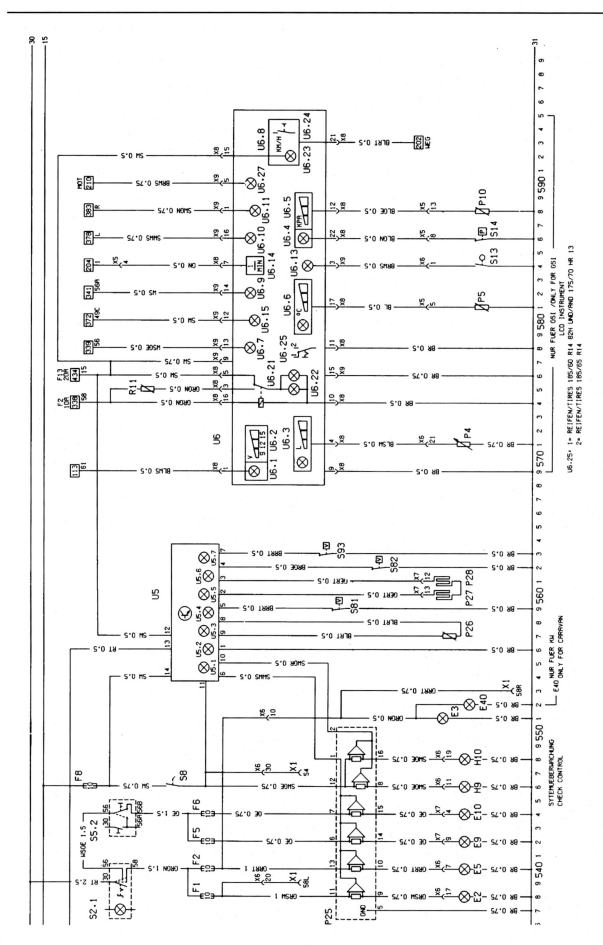

Diagram 2 - 1987 models (continued)

Key to diagram 3 - all models from 1990 on
Not all items are fitted to all models; not all engines or systems are found in UK models

No	Description	Track
E1	Parking lamp left	328
E2	Tail lamp left	329, 550
E3	Number plate lamp	335
E4	Parking lamp right	332
E5	Tail lamp right	334, 552
E6	Engine compartment lamp	337
E7	High beam left	341
E8	High beam right	342
E9	Low beam left	344, 554
E10	Low beam right	345, 556
E11	Lamps instrument	339
E12	Selector lever lamp (automatic)	446
E13	Luggage area lamp	385
E14	Interior lamp	391
E15	Glovebox lamp	443
E16	Cigarette lighter lamp	442
E17	Reversing lamp left	439
E18	Reversing lamp right	440
E19	Heated rear window (except Estate)	302
E20	Front foglamp left	357
E21	Front foglamp right	358
E24	Rear foglamp left	353
E25	Seat heating mat front left	468
E26	Light switch lamp	334
E30	Seat heating mat front right	472
E32	Clock lamp	397
E33	Ashtray lamp	447
E34	Heater control lamp	339
E38	Trip computer lamp	455
E39	Rear foglamp right	354
E40	Number plate lamp (Estate)	336
E41	Interior lamp (with delay)	386, 389
E42	Radio lamp	531, 533
E60	Heated rear window (Estate)	304
F1 - 20	Fuses in fuse box	Various
F21	Fuse headlamp washer	413
F25	Voltage stabiliser	313
F27	Fuse twin horns	174
G1	Battery	101
G2	Alternator	113
H1	Radio	529, 531
H2	Horn (single)	172
H3	Direction indicator repeater	378
H4	Oil pressure warning lamp	321
H5	Brake fluid warning lamp	319
H6	Hazard warning repeater	376
H7	Charging system warning lamp	323
H8	High beam warning lamp	343
H9	Stop-lamp left	368, 558
H10	Stop-lamp right	369, 560
H11	Direction indicator lamp front left	377
H12	Direction indicator lamp rear left	378
H13	Direction indicator lamp front right	381
H14	Direction indicator lamp rear right	382
H17	Direction indicator repeater (trailer)	373
H18	Horn (twin)	174
H19	'Headlamps on' warning buzzer	393, 394
H20	Choke warning lamp	133
H21	Handbrake warning lamp	318
H23	Radio with electric aerial	532, 533
H25	Mirror heating warning lamp	483, 492
H26	ABS warning lamp	722
H30	Engine malfunction warning lamp	Various
H33	Direction indicator repeater left	376
H34	Direction indicator repeater right	380
H48	Horn (twin)	173
K1	Heated rear window relay	301, 302
K2	Flasher unit	373, 374
K5	Foglamp relay	358, 359
K8	Relay windscreen wiper delay	405, 408

No	Description	Track
K9	Relay headlamp washer	411, 413
K15	L3 Jetronic control unit	284 to 291, 749 to 761
K20	Ignition module	Various
K30	Relay rear wiper delay	417 to 419
K32	Relay rear wiper delay (Estate)	431 to 433
K35	Relay heated mirror	497, 499
K37	Relay central locking	502, 508
K47	ABS surge protection relay	702, 703
K50	ABS control unit	702 to 721
K53	Ignition advance control unit	123 to 129, 272 to 281
K57	TBI control unit (C/E 16 NZ)	145 to 164
K58	Fuel pump relay (TBI)	165, 166, 262
K61	Control unit - Motronic	606 to 636
K62	Control unit dim-dip system	347, 351
K63	Horn relay	173, 174
K68	Fuel injection relay	Various
K75	Idle control relay (not UK)	131, 132
K84	Ignition control unit (EZ Plus)	187 to 198, 733 to 746
K86	Control unit check control	539 to 560
K91	Motronic control unit	202 to 226
K100	TBI control unit (C 14 NZ)	240 to 259
L1	Ignition coil	Various
M1	Starter motor	105 to 107
M2	Windscreen wiper motor	403, 406
M3	Heater blower motor	307 to 309
M4	Radiator fan	171, 699
M5	Windscreen washer pump	400
M8	Rear wiper motor (except GSi)	415 to 417
M14	Window lift motor front left	511, 512
M15	Window lift motor front right	517, 518
M16	Window lift motor rear left	513, 514
M17	Window lift motor rear right	515, 516
M19	Door lock actuator rear left	504, 507
M20	Door lock actuator - rear right	504, 507
M21	Fuel pump	166, 229, 262, 295, 639, 764
M24	Headlamp washer pump	413
M25	Rear screen washer pump	429 to 431
M26	Electric aerial motor	533, 534
M30	Electric mirror left	478, 481, 487, 490
M31	Electric mirror - right	494, 497
M32	Door lock actuator passenger door	504, 507
M33	Idle adjuster	Various
M36	Rear wiper motor (GSi only)	421, 426
M37	Tailgate lock actuator	504, 507
M39	Headlamp levelling motor	774 to 776
M40	Headlamp levelling motor	778 to 780
M55	Front & rear screen washer pump	420, 427, 434
M56	Rear wiper motor (Estate)	433 to 435
P1	Fuel gauge	314
P2	Temperature gauge	316
P3	Clock	396
P4	Fuel gauge sender	314, 571
P5	Coolant temperature sensor (gauge)	316, 583
P7	Tachometer	325
P10	Oil pressure sensor	589
P11	Airflow meter	217 to 221
P12	Coolant temperature sensor	214, 289, 613, 759
P13	Air temperature sensor	460, 461
P14	Distance sensor	451, 680, 681
P17	ABS wheel speed sensor - front left	707
P18	ABS wheel speed sensor - front right	709
P19	ABS wheel speed sensor - rear left	711
P20	ABS wheel speed sensor - rear right	713
P23	Manifold vacuum sensor	Various
P24	Oil temperature sensor	128, 129, 192, 276, 277, 737
P27	Brake pad wear sensor - front left	544
P28	Brake pad wear sensor front right	544
P30	Coolant temperature sensor	155, 156, 251
P32	Oxygen (Lambda) sensor (Motronic)	226, 227, 630, 631
P33	Oxygen (Lambda) sensor (TBI)	161, 254

Key to diagram 3 - all models from 1990 on (continued)

No	Description	Track	No	Description	Track
P34	Throttle position sensor	160 to 162, 212/3, 256 to 258	U5.1	Brake pad wear warning	539
P35	Inductive sensor (crankshaft)	221 to 223, 273 to 275, 619	U5.2	Brake fluid level warning	540
P44	Air mass meter	633 to 637	U5.3	Oil level warning	541
P46	Knock control sensor	623, 624	U5.4	Coolant level warning	542
P47	Hall sensor (Motronic M 2.5)	625 to 627	U5.5	Washer fluid level warning	543
R1	Ballast resistor cable	109	U5.6	Bulb failure warning (running lights)	544
R2	Carburettor heater	177	U5.7	Bulb failure warning (stop-lamps)	545
R3	Cigarette lighter	441	U6	LCD instrument panel	569 to 594
R11	Instrument illumination rheostat	575	U6.1	Charging system warning lamp	569
R12	Automatic choke	179	U6.2	Voltmeter	570, 572
R15	CO adjustment potentiometer	163,164	U6.3	Fuel gauge	571
S1	Ignition/starter switch	106, 107, 648, 649, 670, 671	U6.4	Oil pressure warning lamp	587
S2.1	Main lighting switch	334, 337	U6.5	Oil pressure gauge	589
S2.2	Interior lamp switch	389	U6.6	Temperature gauge	583
S3	Heater blower/heated rear window switch	305 to 309	U6.7	'Lights on' indicator	581
S5.2	Dipswitch	343, 344	U6.8	Speedometer	579
S5.3	Direction indicator switch	380, 381	U6.9	High beam indicator	583
S6	Distributor (contact breaker type)	111	U6.10	Direction indicator repeater left	585
S7	Reversing lamp switch (manual)	439	U6.11	Direction indicator repeater right	587
S8	Stop-lamp switch	368,562	U6.13	Handbrake 'on' warning lamp	594
S9.2	Windscreen wiper switch	403 to 406	U6.14	Tachometer	579
S9.5	Rear wipe/wash switch (except GSi)	418 to 420,432 to 434	U6.15	Trailer direction indicator repeater	589
S9.6	Rear wipe/wash switch (GSi)	426 to 428	U6.18	ABS warning lamp	591
S9.7	Windscreen washer switch	400,401	U6.21	Panel lighting relay	574, 576
S10.1	Starter inhibitor switch (automatic)	107	U6.22	Panel lamp bulbs	575, 576
S10.2	Reversing lamp switch (automatic)	438	U6.23	Speedometer illumination	578
S10.3	Park/neutral switch (auto with TBI)	159, 256	U6.24	Miles/km changeover switch	580
S11	Brake fluid warning level switch	319	U6.25	Changeover switch	592
S13	Handbrake 'on' warning switch	318, 594	U6.27	Engine malfunction warning lamp	593
S14	Oil pressure warning switch	321, 587	U11.1	Fuel deceleration cut-off valve	197
S15	Luggage area lamp switch	385	U11.2	Throttle valve switch	198
S16	Door switch left	390	V1	Diode (brake fluid warning bulb test)	320
S17	Door switch right	391	X1	Trailer socket	Various
S18	Glovebox lamp switch	443	X2	Auxiliary connector	Various
S21	Front foglamp switch	360, 362	X3	Connector, alternator	674 to 676
S22	Rear foglamp switch	353, 355	X4	Connector, glow plug timer	672 to 695
S29	Coolant temperature switch	171	X5	Connector, engine and instruments	Various
S30	Seat heating switch front left	468, 470	X6	Connector, body and instruments	Various
S37	Window lift switch	510, 518	X7	Connector, Jetronic and engine	283, 293
S41	Central locking driver's door switch	502, 503	X8	LCD instrument 26-pin connector	569 to 589
S44	Throttle valve switch	285, 286, 618, 619, 756, 757	X9	LCD instrument 16-pin connector	581 to 594
S47	Switch 'headlamps on' warning	392, 393	X10	Ignition timing basic coding plug	129, 130
S50	Choke warning lamp switch	133	X11	Connector. TBI	147. 150. 156. 166. 247 to 261
S52	Hazard warning switch	374, 378	X12	Connector, L3 Jetronic/E 16 SE	749 to 766
S55	Seat heating switch front right	472, 474	X13	Connector, diagnostic link	Various
S60	Clutch pedal switch (not UK)	131	X14	Connector, Motronic and instruments	202, 203, 212, 214
S61	Pressure switch (power steering)	299	X15	Octane rating plug	Various
S64	Horn switch	172	X16	Connector, TBI	236, 237, 245, 256
S68.1	Mirror adjustment switch	477, 480, 485, 489	X17	Connector, instruments	314 to 330,343,374,382
S68.2	Mirror heating switch	483, 492	X18	Connector, Motronic M 1.5	206 to 229
S68.3	Mirror left/right switch	486, 490	X19	Connector, Motronic M 2.5	602 to 639
S81	Brake fluid check control switch	539	X20	Connector, check control unit	549 to 560
S82	Washer fluid check control switch	540	X21	Connector, check control unit	539 to 549
S93	Coolant check control switch	541	X22	Connector, check control display	539 to 546
S95	Oil level check control switch	542	X23	Coding plug, Motronic M 2.5	611, 612
S98	Headlamp levelling switch	773 to 775	Y5	Fuel cut-off valve (Diesel)	657, 692
U3	Trip computer assembly	452 to 461	Y6	Auxiliary air valve	292, 762
U3.1	Clock switch	459	Y7	Fuel injectors	Various
U3.2	Function select switch	459	Y10	Distributor (with Hall sensor)	Various
U3.3	Reset/clock adjustment switch	459	Y17	Idle cut-off solenoid	178
U4	ABS hydraulic unit	705 to 718	Y23	Distributor (electronic ignition,1.3/1.4 models)	116 to 120
U4.1	ABS pump relay	706 to 709	Y24	Distributor (not UK)	124 to 129, 136 to 142
U4.2	ABS solenoid valve relay	714 to 718	Y25	Idle up valve (power steering)	299
U4.3	ABS hydraulic pump	705	Y30	Idle up valve (Diesel)	660
U4.5	ABS solenoid valve - front left	710	Y32	Injection valve (TBI)	146, 246
U4.6	ABS solenoid valve front right	711	Y33	Distributor (Motronic/Jetronic)	202, 273, 600 to 602
U4.7	ABS solenoid valve - rear	712	Y34	Fuel tank vent valve	220, 631
U5	Check control display unit	539 to 546	Y41	Idle control valve (not UK)	131

Refer to page 12•16 for colour codes

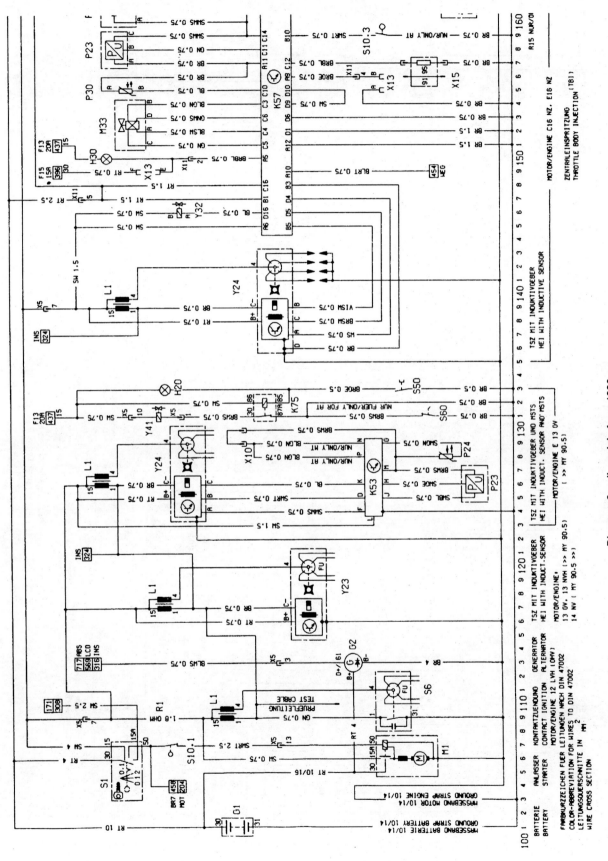

Diagram 3 - all models from 1990 on

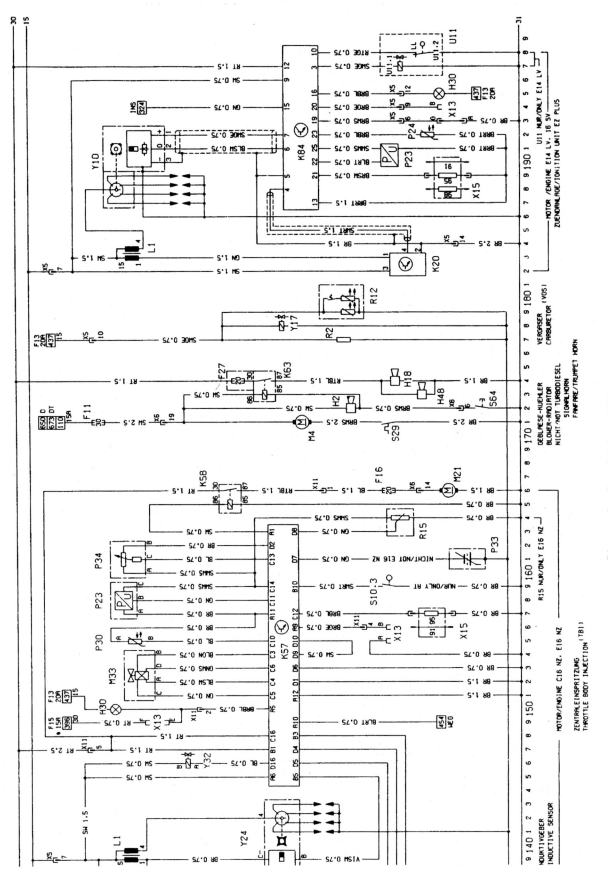

Diagram 3 - all models from 1990 on
(continued)

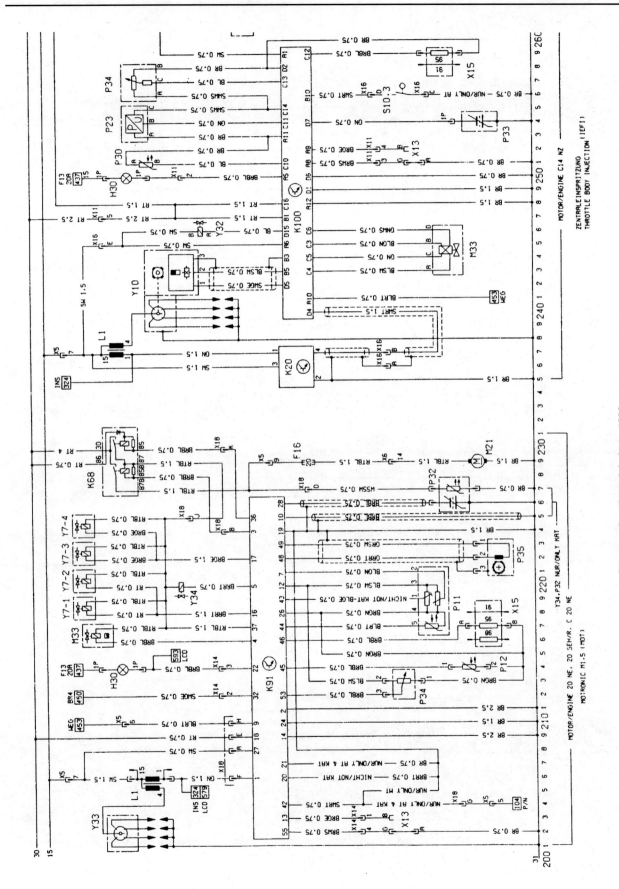

Diagram 3 - all models from 1990 on
(continued)

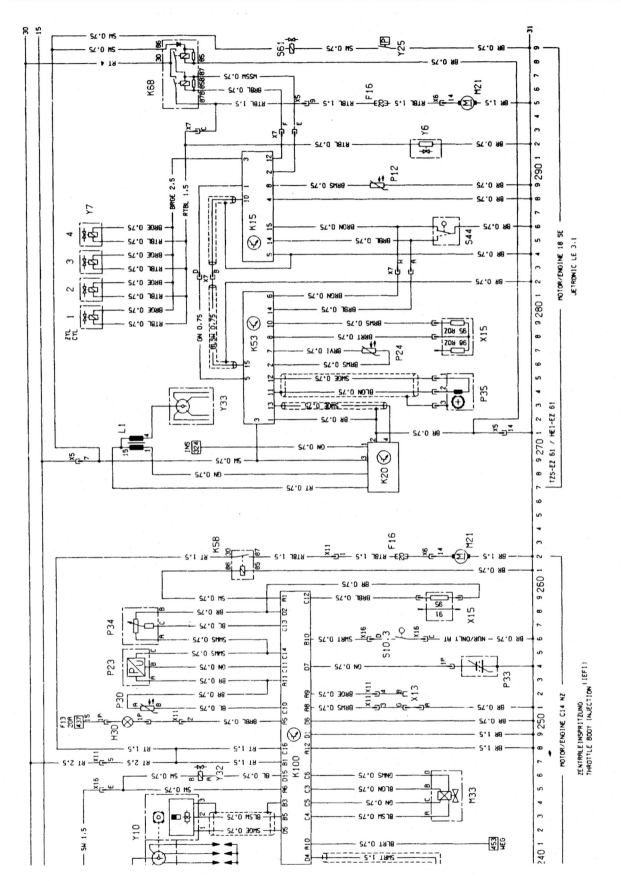

Diagram 3 - all models from 1990 on (continued)

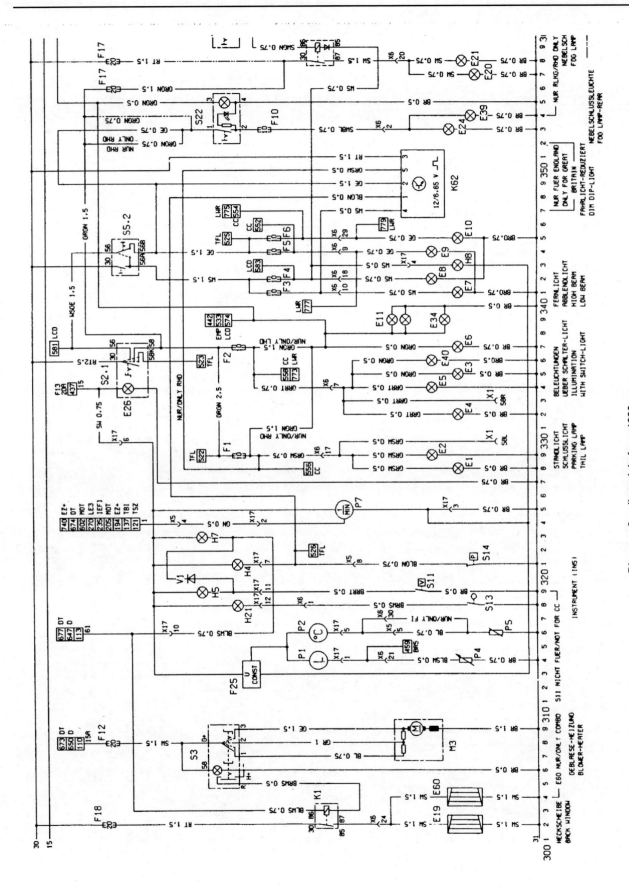

Diagram 3 - all models from 1990 on
(continued)

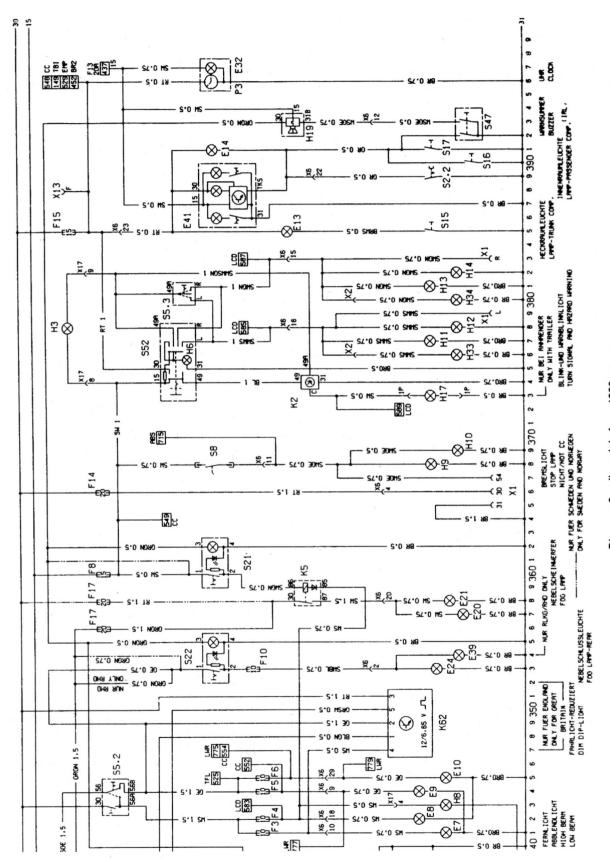

Diagram 3 - all models from 1990 on (continued)

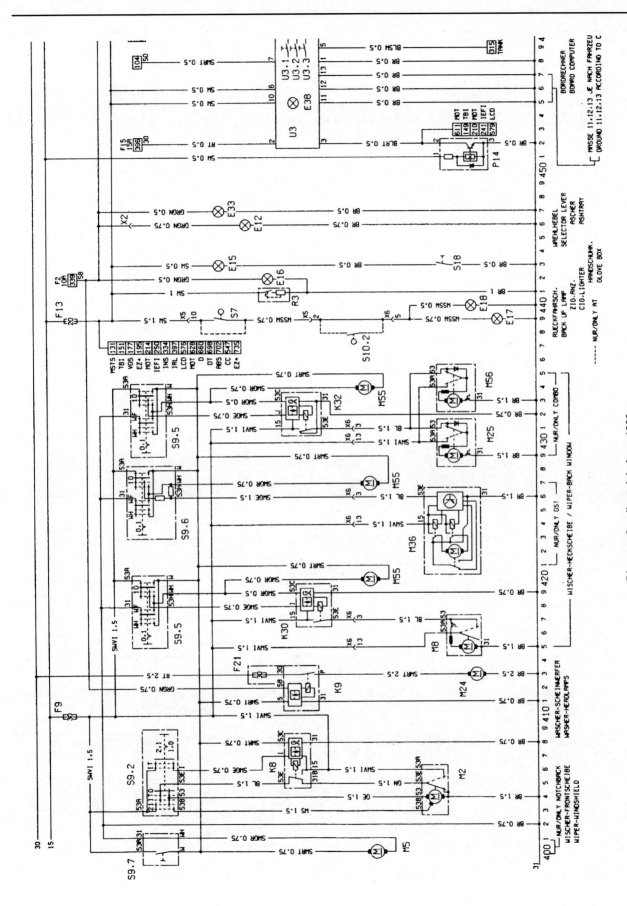

Diagram 3 - all models from 1990 on
(continued)

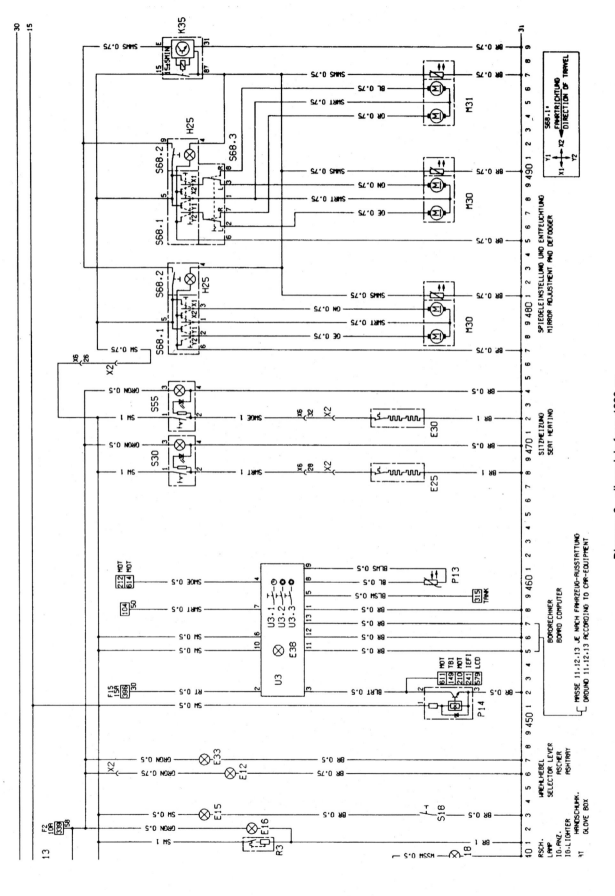

Diagram 3 - all models from 1990 on
(continued)

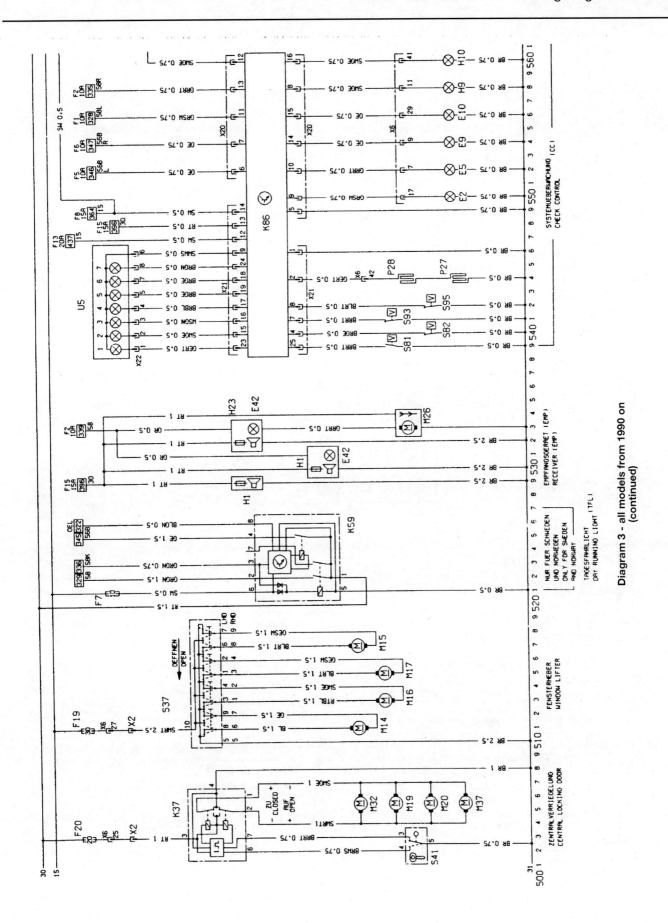

Diagram 3 - all models from 1990 on
(continued)

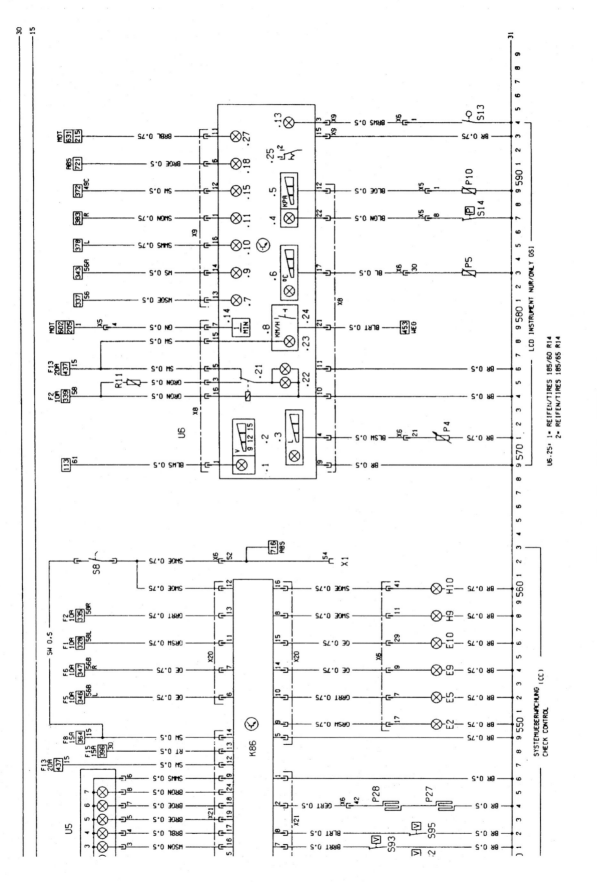

Diagram 3 - all models from 1990 on
(continued)

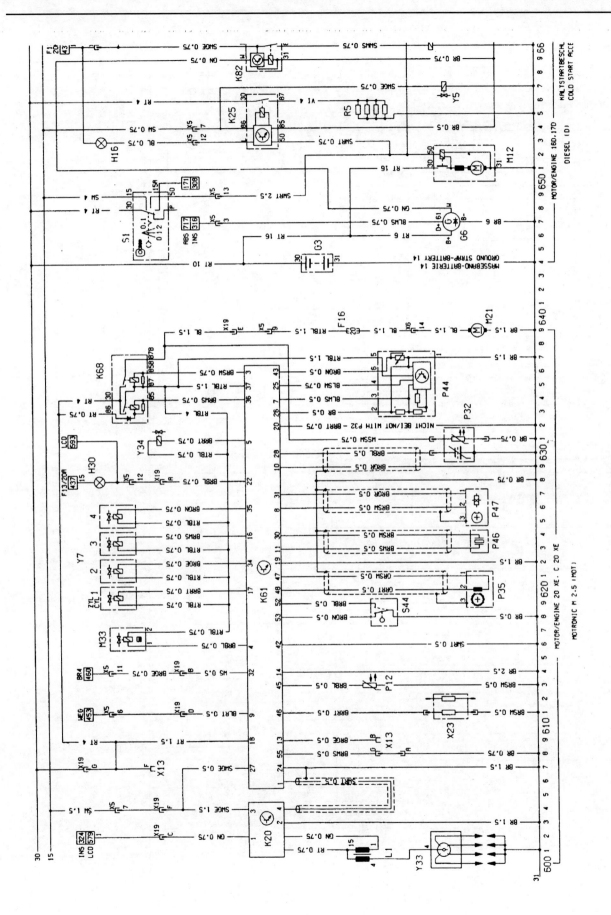

Diagram 3 - all models from 1990 on (continued)

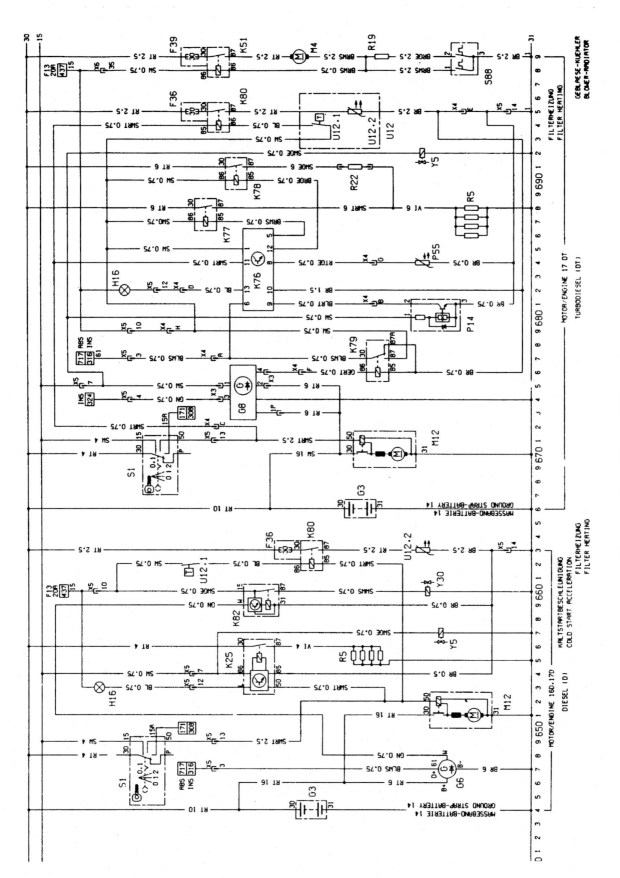

Diagram 3 - all models from 1990 on
(continued)

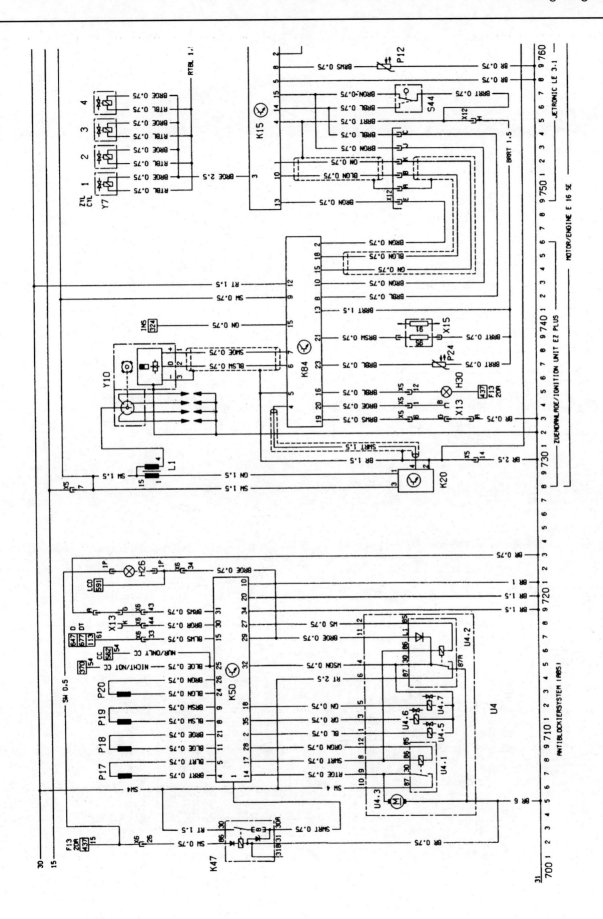

Diagram 3 - all models from 1990 on
(continued)

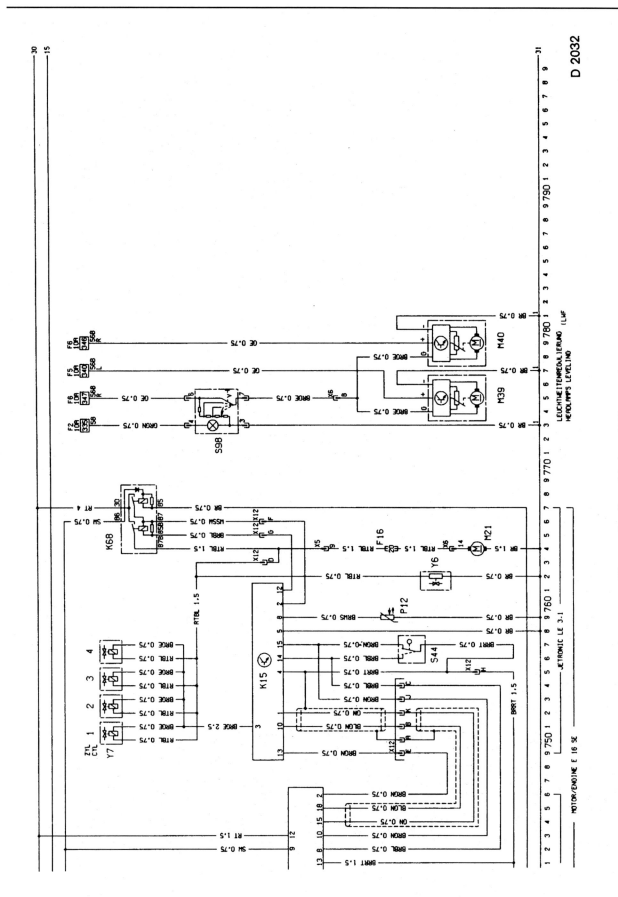

Diagram 3 - all models from 1990 on
(continued)

D 2032

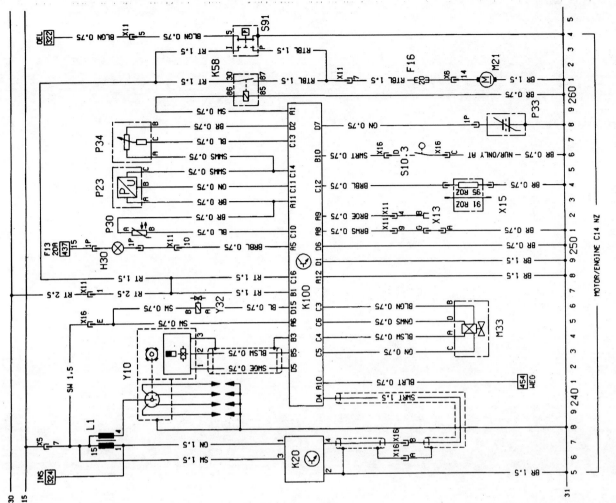

Wiring diagram for the MULTEC Central Fuel injection system fitted to later C 14 NZ engines

Key to wiring diagram for the MULTEC Central Fuel injection system fitted to later C 14 NZ engines

No	Description	Track
F18	Fuse(in fuse box)	261
H30	Engine telltale (in instrument	250
K20	Ignition coil ignition module	235 to 237
K58	Fuel pump relay	260, 261
K100	IEFI control unit	240, 259
L1	Ignition coil	236, 237
M21	Fuel pump	261
M33	Idle air control stepper motor	243 to 246
P23	Absolute pressure sensor	253 to 255
P30	Coolant temperature sensor	251
P33	Oxygen sensor	258
P34	Throttle valve potentiometer	256 to 258
S91	Oil pressure switch	236 to 264
S10.3	Park/Neutral switch	256
Y10	Ignition distributor Hall sensor	238 to 244
Y32	Injection valve	246
X5	Instrument panel and engine 14p	237
X6	Instrument panel and body 30p	261
X11	Instrument panel and TBI 14p	247 to 264
X13	ALDL Plug 10p	249 to 251
X15	Octane number plug 3p	253 to 254
X16	Engine and TBI 5p (basis 3p)	237 to 238

Notes

Dimensions and weights

Note: All figures are approximate, and may vary according to model. Refer to manufacturer's data for exact figures.

Dimensions

Overall height:
  Hatchback:
    GTE models . . . . 1395 mm
    All other models . . . . 1400 mm
  Saloon . . . . 1400 mm
  Estate . . . . 1430 mm
  Van . . . . 1440 mm
  Astramax . . . . 1680 mm
Overall width:
  Hatchback . . . . 1663 mm
  Saloon models . . . . 1658 mm
  Estate, Van and Astramax . . . . 1670 mm
Overall length:
  Hatchback . . . . 3998 mm
  Saloon . . . . 4218 mm
  Estate and Van . . . . 4228 mm
  Astramax . . . . 4220 mm
Wheelbase . . . . 2520 mm

Weights

Kerb weight*:
  Hatchback:
    1.2 litre models . . . . 830 to 865 kg
    1.3 litre models . . . . 845 to 915 kg
    1.4 litre models . . . . 865 to 900 kg
    1.6 litre models . . . . 885 to 975 kg
    1.8 litre models . . . . 900 to 960 kg
    2.0 litre models . . . . 960 to 990 kg
  Saloon models:
    1.3 and 1.4 litre models . . . . 850 to 950 kg
    1.6 litre models . . . . 922 to 957 kg
    1.8 litre models . . . . 972 to 1002 kg
  Estate models:
    1.3 litre models . . . . 900 to 1000 kg
    1.6 litre models . . . . 965 to 1045 kg
  Van models:
    1.3 litre models . . . . 880 to 920 kg
    1.6 litre models . . . . 945 to 970 kg
  Convertible models:
    1.6 litre models . . . . 970 to 1000 kg
    2.0 litre models . . . . 1045 kg
Maximum roof rack load . . . . 100 kg
Maximum towing weight*:
  Braked trailer . . . . 600 to 1200 kg
  Unbraked trailer . . . . 400 to 500 kg
Maximum trailer nose weight . . . . 50 kg

*The kerb weights and maximum permissible towing weights given are for general reference. The weights can differ according to model and year, therefore, if specific weight requirements are wanted for a particular model, consult your vehicle handbook or a Vauxhall dealer

Length (distance)

Inches (in)	x 25.4	= Millimetres (mm)	x 0.0394	= Inches (in)
Feet (ft)	x 0.305	= Metres (m)	x 3.281	= Feet (ft)
Miles	x 1.609	= Kilometres (km)	x 0.621	= Miles

Volume (capacity)

Cubic inches (cu in; in³)	x 16.387	= Cubic centimetres (cc; cm³)	x 0.061	= Cubic inches (cu in; in³)
Imperial pints (Imp pt)	x 0.568	= Litres (l)	x 1.76	= Imperial pints (Imp pt)
Imperial quarts (Imp qt)	x 1.137	= Litres (l)	x 0.88	= Imperial quarts (Imp qt)
Imperial quarts (Imp qt)	x 1.201	= US quarts (US qt)	x 0.833	= Imperial quarts (Imp qt)
US quarts (US qt)	x 0.946	= Litres (l)	x 1.057	= US quarts (US qt)
Imperial gallons (Imp gal)	x 4.546	= Litres (l)	x 0.22	= Imperial gallons (Imp gal)
Imperial gallons (Imp gal)	x 1.201	= US gallons (US gal)	x 0.833	= Imperial gallons (Imp gal)
US gallons (US gal)	x 3.785	= Litres (l)	x 0.264	= US gallons (US gal)

Mass (weight)

Ounces (oz)	x 28.35	= Grams (g)	x 0.035	= Ounces (oz)
Pounds (lb)	x 0.454	= Kilograms (kg)	x 2.205	= Pounds (lb)

Force

Ounces-force (ozf; oz)	x 0.278	= Newtons (N)	x 3.6	= Ounces-force (ozf; oz)
Pounds-force (lbf; lb)	x 4.448	= Newtons (N)	x 0.225	= Pounds-force (lbf; lb)
Newtons (N)	x 0.1	= Kilograms-force (kgf; kg)	x 9.81	= Newtons (N)

Pressure

Pounds-force per square inch (psi; lbf/in²; lb/in²)	x 0.070	= Kilograms-force per square centimetre (kgf/cm²; kg/cm²)	x 14.223	= Pounds-force per square inch (psi; lbf/in²; lb/in²)
Pounds-force per square inch (psi; lbf/in²; lb/in²)	x 0.068	= Atmospheres (atm)	x 14.696	= Pounds-force per square inch (psi; lbf/in²; lb/in²)
Pounds-force per square inch (psi; lbf/in²; lb/in²)	x 0.069	= Bars	x 14.5	= Pounds-force per square inch (psi; lbf/in²; lb/in²)
Pounds-force per square inch (psi; lbf/in²; lb/in²)	x 6.895	= Kilopascals (kPa)	x 0.145	= Pounds-force per square inch (psi; lbf/in²; lb/in²)
Kilopascals (kPa)	x 0.01	= Kilograms-force per square centimetre (kgf/cm²; kg/cm²)	x 98.1	= Kilopascals (kPa)
Millibar (mbar)	x 100	= Pascals (Pa)	x 0.01	= Millibar (mbar)
Millibar (mbar)	x 0.0145	= Pounds-force per square inch (psi; lbf/in²; lb/in²)	x 68.947	= Millibar (mbar)
Millibar (mbar)	x 0.75	= Millimetres of mercury (mmHg)	x 1.333	= Millibar (mbar)
Millibar (mbar)	x 0.401	= Inches of water (inH₂O)	x 2.491	= Millibar (mbar)
Millimetres of mercury (mmHg)	x 0.535	= Inches of water (inH₂O)	x 1.868	= Millimetres of mercury (mmHg)
Inches of water (inH₂O)	x 0.036	= Pounds-force per square inch (psi; lbf/in²; lb/in²)	x 27.68	= Inches of water (inH₂O)

Torque (moment of force)

Pounds-force inches (lbf in; lb in)	x 1.152	= Kilograms-force centimetre (kgf cm; kg cm)	x 0.868	= Pounds-force inches (lbf in; lb in)
Pounds-force inches (lbf in; lb in)	x 0.113	= Newton metres (Nm)	x 8.85	= Pounds-force inches (lbf in; lb in)
Pounds-force inches (lbf in; lb in)	x 0.083	= Pounds-force feet (lbf ft; lb ft)	x 12	= Pounds-force inches (lbf in; lb in)
Pounds-force feet (lbf ft; lb ft)	x 0.138	= Kilograms-force metres (kgf m; kg m)	x 7.233	= Pounds-force feet (lbf ft; lb ft)
Pounds-force feet (lbf ft; lb ft)	x 1.356	= Newton metres (Nm)	x 0.738	= Pounds-force feet (lbf ft; lb ft)
Newton metres (Nm)	x 0.102	= Kilograms-force metres (kgf m; kg m)	x 9.804	= Newton metres (Nm)

Power

Horsepower (hp)	x 745.7	= Watts (W)	x 0.0013	= Horsepower (hp)

Velocity (speed)

Miles per hour (miles/hr; mph)	x 1.609	= Kilometres per hour (km/hr; kph)	x 0.621	= Miles per hour (miles/hr; mph)

Fuel consumption*

Miles per gallon (mpg)	x 0.354	= Kilometres per litre (km/l)	x 2.825	= Miles per gallon (mpg)

Temperature

Degrees Fahrenheit = (°C x 1.8) + 32   Degrees Celsius (Degrees Centigrade; °C) = (°F - 32) x 0.56

It is common practice to convert from miles per gallon (mpg) to litres/100 kilometres (l/100km), where mpg x l/100 km = 282

Spare parts are available from many sources; for example, Vauxhall garages, other garages and accessory shops, and motor factors. Our advice regarding spare part sources is as follows.

Officially-appointed Vauxhall garages - This is the best source for parts which are peculiar to your car, and are not generally available (eg complete cylinder heads, internal gearbox components, badges, interior trim etc). It is also the only place at which you should buy parts if the vehicle is still under warranty. To be sure of obtaining the correct parts, it will be necessary to give the storeman your car's vehicle identification number, and if possible, take the old parts along for positive identification. Many parts are available under a factory exchange scheme - any parts returned should always be clean. It obviously makes good sense to go straight to the specialists on your car for this type of part, as they are best equipped to supply you.

Other garages and accessory shops - These are often very good places to buy materials and components needed for the maintenance of your car (eg oil filters, spark plugs, bulbs, drivebelts, oils and greases, touch-up paint, filler paste, etc). They also sell general accessories, usually have convenient opening hours, charge lower prices, and can often be found not far from home.

Motor factors - Good factors will stock all the more important components which wear out comparatively quickly (eg exhaust systems, brake pads, seals and hydraulic parts, clutch components, bearing shells, pistons, valves etc). Motor factors will often provide new or reconditioned components on a part-exchange basis - this can save a considerable amount of money.

Vehicle identification numbers

Modifications are a continuing and unpublicised process in vehicle manufacture, quite apart from major model changes. Spare parts manuals and lists are compiled upon a numerical basis, the individual vehicle identification numbers being essential to correct identification of the component concerned.

When ordering spare parts, always give as much information as possible. Quote the car model, year of manufacture, body and engine numbers as appropriate.

The *Vehicle Identification Number (VIN)* plate is riveted to the top of the body front crossmember, and can be viewed once the bonnet is open. The plate carries the VIN and vehicle weight information, and paint and trim colour codes **(see illustration)**.

The *engine number* is stamped onto a machined flat on the front face of the cylinder block **(see illustration)**.

The *chassis number* is stamped into the body floor panel, between the driver's seat and the door sill **(see illustration)**.

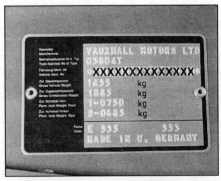

Vehicle identification plate

Engine number and VIN plate locations (arrowed)

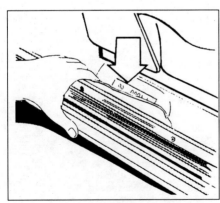

Chassis number location (arrowed)

Whenever servicing, repair or overhaul work is carried out on the car or its components, it is necessary to observe the following procedures and instructions. This will assist in carrying out the operation efficiently and to a professional standard of workmanship.

Joint mating faces and gaskets

When separating components at their mating faces, never insert screwdrivers or similar implements into the joint between the faces in order to prise them apart. This can cause severe damage which results in oil leaks, coolant leaks, etc upon reassembly. Separation is usually achieved by tapping along the joint with a soft-faced hammer in order to break the seal. However, note that this method may not be suitable where dowels are used for component location.

Where a gasket is used between the mating faces of two components, ensure that it is renewed on reassembly, and fit it dry unless otherwise stated in the repair procedure. Make sure that the mating faces are clean and dry, with all traces of old gasket removed. When cleaning a joint face, use a tool which is not likely to score or damage the face, and remove any burrs or nicks with an oilstone or fine file.

Make sure that tapped holes are cleaned with a pipe cleaner, and keep them free of jointing compound, if this is being used, unless specifically instructed otherwise.

Ensure that all orifices, channels or pipes are clear, and blow through them, preferably using compressed air.

Oil seals

Oil seals can be removed by levering them out with a wide flat-bladed screwdriver or similar implement. Alternatively, a number of self-tapping screws may be screwed into the seal, and these used as a purchase for pliers or some similar device in order to pull the seal free.

Whenever an oil seal is removed from its working location, either individually or as part of an assembly, it should be renewed.

The very fine sealing lip of the seal is easily damaged, and will not seal if the surface it contacts is not completely clean and free from scratches, nicks or grooves. If the original sealing surface of the component cannot be restored, and the manufacturer has not made provision for slight relocation of the seal relative to the sealing surface, the component should be renewed.

Protect the lips of the seal from any surface which may damage them in the course of fitting. Use tape or a conical sleeve where possible. Lubricate the seal lips with oil before fitting and, on dual-lipped seals, fill the space between the lips with grease.

Unless otherwise stated, oil seals must be fitted with their sealing lips toward the lubricant to be sealed.

Use a tubular drift or block of wood of the appropriate size to install the seal and, if the seal housing is shouldered, drive the seal down to the shoulder. If the seal housing is unshouldered, the seal should be fitted with its face flush with the housing top face (unless otherwise instructed).

Screw threads and fastenings

Seized nuts, bolts and screws are quite a common occurrence where corrosion has set in, and the use of penetrating oil or releasing fluid will often overcome this problem if the offending item is soaked for a while before attempting to release it. The use of an impact driver may also provide a means of releasing such stubborn fastening devices, when used in conjunction with the appropriate screwdriver bit or socket. If none of these methods works, it may be necessary to resort to the careful application of heat, or the use of a hacksaw or nut splitter device.

Studs are usually removed by locking two nuts together on the threaded part, and then using a spanner on the lower nut to unscrew the stud. Studs or bolts which have broken off below the surface of the component in which they are mounted can sometimes be removed using a proprietary stud extractor. Always ensure that a blind tapped hole is completely free from oil, grease, water or other fluid before installing the bolt or stud. Failure to do this could cause the housing to crack due to the hydraulic action of the bolt or stud as it is screwed in.

When tightening a castellated nut to accept a split pin, tighten the nut to the specified torque, where applicable, and then tighten further to the next split pin hole. Never slacken the nut to align the split pin hole, unless stated in the repair procedure.

When checking or retightening a nut or bolt to a specified torque setting, slacken the nut or bolt by a quarter of a turn, and then retighten to the specified setting. However, this should not be attempted where angular tightening has been used.

For some screw fastenings, notably cylinder head bolts or nuts, torque wrench settings are no longer specified for the latter stages of tightening, "angle-tightening" being called up instead. Typically, a fairly low torque wrench setting will be applied to the bolts/nuts in the correct sequence, followed by one or more stages of tightening through specified angles.

Locknuts, locktabs and washers

Any fastening which will rotate against a component or housing in the course of tightening should always have a washer between it and the relevant component or housing.

Spring or split washers should always be renewed when they are used to lock a critical component such as a big-end bearing retaining bolt or nut. Locktabs which are folded over to retain a nut or bolt should always be renewed.

Self-locking nuts can be re-used in non-critical areas, providing resistance can be felt when the locking portion passes over the bolt or stud thread. However, it should be noted that self-locking stiffnuts tend to lose their effectiveness after long periods of use, and in

such cases should be renewed as a matter of course.

Split pins must always be replaced with new ones of the correct size for the hole.

When thread-locking compound is found on the threads of a fastener which is to be re-used, it should be cleaned off with a wire brush and solvent, and fresh compound applied on reassembly.

Special tools

Some repair procedures in this manual entail the use of special tools such as a press, two or three-legged pullers, spring compressors, etc. Wherever possible, suitable readily-available alternatives to the manufacturer's special tools are described, and are shown in use. In some instances, where no alternative is possible, it has been necessary to resort to the use of a manufacturer's tool, and this has been done for reasons of safety as well as the efficient completion of the repair operation. Unless you are highly-skilled and have a thorough understanding of the procedures described, never attempt to bypass the use of any special tool when the procedure described specifies its use. Not only is there a very great risk of personal injury, but expensive damage could be caused to the components involved.

Environmental considerations

When disposing of used engine oil, brake fluid, antifreeze, etc, give due consideration to any detrimental environmental effects. Do not, for instance, pour any of the above liquids down drains into the general sewage system, or onto the ground to soak away. Many local council refuse tips provide a facility for waste oil disposal, as do some garages. If none of these facilities are available, consult your local Environmental Health Department for further advice.

With the universal tightening-up of legislation regarding the emission of environmentally-harmful substances from motor vehicles, most current vehicles have tamperproof devices fitted to the main adjustment points of the fuel system. These devices are primarily designed to prevent unqualified persons from adjusting the fuel/air mixture, with the chance of a consequent increase in toxic emissions. If such devices are encountered during servicing or overhaul, they should, wherever possible, be renewed or refitted in accordance with the vehicle manufacturer's requirements or current legislation.

Note: It is antisocial and illegal to dump oil down the drain. To find the location of your local oil recycling bank, call this number free.

OIL CARE
OIL BANK LINE
0800 66 33 66

Introduction

A selection of good tools is a fundamental requirement for anyone contemplating the maintenance and repair of a motor vehicle. For the owner who does not possess any, their purchase will prove a considerable expense, offsetting some of the savings made by doing-it-yourself. However, provided that the tools purchased meet the relevant national safety standards and are of good quality, they will last for many years and prove an extremely worthwhile investment.

To help the average owner to decide which tools are needed to carry out the various tasks detailed in this manual, we have compiled three lists of tools under the following headings: *Maintenance and minor repair, Repair and overhaul*, and *Special*. Newcomers to practical mechanics should start off with the *Maintenance and minor repair* tool kit, and confine themselves to the simpler jobs around the vehicle. Then, as confidence and experience grow, more difficult tasks can be undertaken, with extra tools being purchased as, and when, they are needed. In this way, a *Maintenance and minor repair* tool kit can be built up into a *Repair and overhaul* tool kit over a considerable period of time, without any major cash outlays. The experienced do-it-yourselfer will have a tool kit good enough for most repair and overhaul procedures, and will add tools from the *Special* category when it is felt that the expense is justified by the amount of use to which these tools will be put.

Maintenance and minor repair tool kit

The tools given in this list should be considered as a minimum requirement if routine maintenance, servicing and minor repair operations are to be undertaken. We recommend the purchase of combination spanners (ring one end, open-ended the other); although more expensive than open-ended ones, they do give the advantages of both types of spanner.

- [ ] *Combination spanners:*
  Metric - 8 to 19 mm inclusive
- [ ] *Adjustable spanner - 35 mm jaw (approx.)*
- [ ] *Spark plug spanner (with rubber insert) - petrol models*
- [ ] *Spark plug gap adjustment tool - petrol models*
- [ ] *Set of feeler gauges*
- [ ] *Brake bleed nipple spanner*
- [ ] *Screwdrivers:*
  Flat blade - 100 mm long x 6 mm dia
  Cross blade - 100 mm long x 6 mm dia
  Torx - various sizes (not all vehicles)
- [ ] *Combination pliers*
- [ ] *Hacksaw (junior)*
- [ ] *Tyre pump*
- [ ] *Tyre pressure gauge*
- [ ] *Oil can*
- [ ] *Oil filter removal tool*
- [ ] *Fine emery cloth*
- [ ] *Wire brush (small)*
- [ ] *Funnel (medium size)*
- [ ] *Sump drain plug key (not all vehicles)*

Repair and overhaul tool kit

These tools are virtually essential for anyone undertaking any major repairs to a motor vehicle, and are additional to those given in the *Maintenance and minor repair* list. Included in this list is a comprehensive set of sockets. Although these are expensive, they will be found invaluable as they are so versatile - particularly if various drives are included in the set. We recommend the half-inch square-drive type, as this can be used with most proprietary torque wrenches.

The tools in this list will sometimes need to be supplemented by tools from the *Special* list:

- [ ] *Sockets (or box spanners) to cover range in previous list (including Torx sockets)*
- [ ] *Reversible ratchet drive (for use with sockets)*
- [ ] *Extension piece, 250 mm (for use with sockets)*
- [ ] *Universal joint (for use with sockets)*
- [ ] *Flexible handle or sliding T "breaker bar" (for use with sockets)*
- [ ] *Torque wrench (for use with sockets)*
- [ ] *Self-locking grips*
- [ ] *Ball pein hammer*
- [ ] *Soft-faced mallet (plastic or rubber)*
- [ ] *Screwdrivers:*
  Flat blade - long & sturdy, short (chubby), and narrow (electrician's) types
  Cross blade – long & sturdy, and short (chubby) types
- [ ] *Pliers:*
  Long-nosed
  Side cutters (electrician's)
  Circlip (internal and external)
- [ ] *Cold chisel - 25 mm*
- [ ] *Scriber*
- [ ] *Scraper*
- [ ] *Centre-punch*
- [ ] *Pin punch*
- [ ] *Hacksaw*
- [ ] *Brake hose clamp*
- [ ] *Brake/clutch bleeding kit*
- [ ] *Selection of twist drills*
- [ ] *Steel rule/straight-edge*
- [ ] *Allen keys (inc. splined/Torx type)*
- [ ] *Selection of files*
- [ ] *Wire brush*
- [ ] *Axle stands*
- [ ] *Jack (strong trolley or hydraulic type)*
- [ ] *Light with extension lead*
- [ ] *Universal electrical multi-meter*

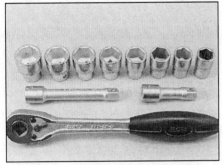
Sockets and reversible ratchet drive

Brake bleeding kit

Torx key, socket and bit

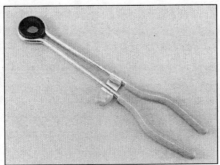
Hose clamp

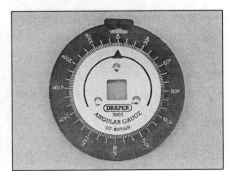
Angular-tightening gauge

Special tools

The tools in this list are those which are not used regularly, are expensive to buy, or which need to be used in accordance with their manufacturers' instructions. Unless relatively difficult mechanical jobs are undertaken frequently, it will not be economic to buy many of these tools. Where this is the case, you could consider clubbing together with friends (or joining a motorists' club) to make a joint purchase, or borrowing the tools against a deposit from a local garage or tool hire specialist. It is worth noting that many of the larger DIY superstores now carry a large range of special tools for hire at modest rates.

The following list contains only those tools and instruments freely available to the public, and not those special tools produced by the vehicle manufacturer specifically for its dealer network. You will find occasional references to these manufacturers' special tools in the text of this manual. Generally, an alternative method of doing the job without the vehicle manufacturers' special tool is given. However, sometimes there is no alternative to using them. Where this is the case and the relevant tool cannot be bought or borrowed, you will have to entrust the work to a dealer.

☐ *Angular-tightening gauge*
☐ *Valve spring compressor*
☐ *Valve grinding tool*
☐ *Piston ring compressor*
☐ *Piston ring removal/installation tool*
☐ *Cylinder bore hone*
☐ *Balljoint separator*
☐ *Coil spring compressors (where applicable)*
☐ *Two/three-legged hub and bearing puller*
☐ *Impact screwdriver*
☐ *Micrometer and/or vernier calipers*
☐ *Dial gauge*
☐ *Stroboscopic timing light*
☐ *Dwell angle meter/tachometer*
☐ *Fault code reader*
☐ *Cylinder compression gauge*
☐ *Hand-operated vacuum pump and gauge*
☐ *Clutch plate alignment set*
☐ *Brake shoe steady spring cup removal tool*
☐ *Bush and bearing removal/installation set*
☐ *Stud extractors*
☐ *Tap and die set*
☐ *Lifting tackle*
☐ *Trolley jack*

Buying tools

Reputable motor accessory shops and superstores often offer excellent quality tools at discount prices, so it pays to shop around.

Remember, you don't have to buy the most expensive items on the shelf, but it is always advisable to steer clear of the very cheap tools. Beware of 'bargains' offered on market stalls or at car boot sales. There are plenty of good tools around at reasonable prices, but always aim to purchase items which meet the relevant national safety standards. If in doubt, ask the proprietor or manager of the shop for advice before making a purchase.

Care and maintenance of tools

Having purchased a reasonable tool kit, it is necessary to keep the tools in a clean and serviceable condition. After use, always wipe off any dirt, grease and metal particles using a clean, dry cloth, before putting the tools away. Never leave them lying around after they have been used. A simple tool rack on the garage or workshop wall for items such as screwdrivers and pliers is a good idea. Store all normal spanners and sockets in a metal box. Any measuring instruments, gauges, meters, etc, must be carefully stored where they cannot be damaged or become rusty.

Take a little care when tools are used. Hammer heads inevitably become marked, and screwdrivers lose the keen edge on their blades from time to time. A little timely attention with emery cloth or a file will soon restore items like this to a good finish.

Working facilities

Not to be forgotten when discussing tools is the workshop itself. If anything more than routine maintenance is to be carried out, a suitable working area becomes essential.

It is appreciated that many an owner-mechanic is forced by circumstances to remove an engine or similar item without the benefit of a garage or workshop. Having done this, any repairs should always be done under the cover of a roof.

Wherever possible, any dismantling should be done on a clean, flat workbench or table at a suitable working height.

Any workbench needs a vice; one with a jaw opening of 100 mm is suitable for most jobs. As mentioned previously, some clean dry storage space is also required for tools, as well as for any lubricants, cleaning fluids, touch-up paints etc, which become necessary.

Another item which may be required, and which has a much more general usage, is an electric drill with a chuck capacity of at least 8 mm. This, together with a good range of twist drills, is virtually essential for fitting accessories.

Last, but not least, always keep a supply of old newspapers and clean, lint-free rags available, and try to keep any working area as clean as possible.

Micrometers

Dial test indicator ("dial gauge")

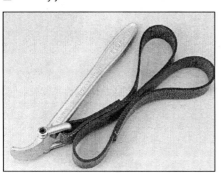

Strap wrench

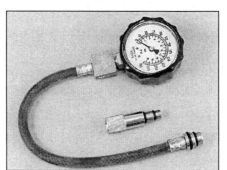

Compression tester

Fault code reader

This is a guide to getting your vehicle through the MOT test. Obviously it will not be possible to examine the vehicle to the same standard as the professional MOT tester. However, working through the following checks will enable you to identify any problem areas before submitting the vehicle for the test.

Where a testable component is in borderline condition, the tester has discretion in deciding whether to pass or fail it. The basis of such discretion is whether the tester would be happy for a close relative or friend to use the vehicle with the component in that condition. If the vehicle presented is clean and evidently well cared for, the tester may be more inclined to pass a borderline component than if the vehicle is scruffy and apparently neglected.

It has only been possible to summarise the test requirements here, based on the regulations in force at the time of printing. Test standards are becoming increasingly stringent, although there are some exemptions for older vehicles. For full details obtain a copy of the Haynes publication Pass the MOT! (available from stockists of Haynes manuals).

An assistant will be needed to help carry out some of these checks.

The checks have been sub-divided into four categories, as follows:

1 Checks carried out **FROM THE DRIVER'S SEAT**

2 Checks carried out **WITH THE VEHICLE ON THE GROUND**

3 Checks carried out **WITH THE VEHICLE RAISED AND THE WHEELS FREE TO TURN**

4 Checks carried out on **YOUR VEHICLE'S EXHAUST EMISSION SYSTEM**

---

1 Checks carried out **FROM THE DRIVER'S SEAT**

Handbrake

☐ Test the operation of the handbrake. Excessive travel (too many clicks) indicates incorrect brake or cable adjustment.

☐ Check that the handbrake cannot be released by tapping the lever sideways. Check the security of the lever mountings.

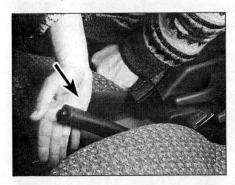

Footbrake

☐ Depress the brake pedal and check that it does not creep down to the floor, indicating a master cylinder fault. Release the pedal, wait a few seconds, then depress it again. If the pedal travels nearly to the floor before firm resistance is felt, brake adjustment or repair is necessary. If the pedal feels spongy, there is air in the hydraulic system which must be removed by bleeding.

☐ Check that the brake pedal is secure and in good condition. Check also for signs of fluid leaks on the pedal, floor or carpets, which would indicate failed seals in the brake master cylinder.

☐ Check the servo unit (when applicable) by operating the brake pedal several times, then keeping the pedal depressed and starting the engine. As the engine starts, the pedal will move down slightly. If not, the vacuum hose or the servo itself may be faulty.

Steering wheel and column

☐ Examine the steering wheel for fractures or looseness of the hub, spokes or rim.

☐ Move the steering wheel from side to side and then up and down. Check that the steering wheel is not loose on the column, indicating wear or a loose retaining nut. Continue moving the steering wheel as before, but also turn it slightly from left to right.

☐ Check that the steering wheel is not loose on the column, and that there is no abnormal

movement of the steering wheel, indicating wear in the column support bearings or couplings.

Windscreen and mirrors

☐ The windscreen must be free of cracks or other significant damage within the driver's field of view. (Small stone chips are acceptable.) Rear view mirrors must be secure, intact, and capable of being adjusted.

290mm

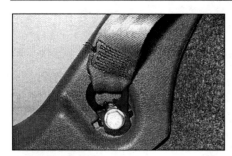

Seat belts and seats

Note: *The following checks are applicable to all seat belts, front and rear.*

☐ Examine the webbing of all the belts (including rear belts if fitted) for cuts, serious fraying or deterioration. Fasten and unfasten each belt to check the buckles. If applicable, check the retracting mechanism. Check the security of all seat belt mountings accessible from inside the vehicle.

☐ The front seats themselves must be securely attached and the backrests must lock in the upright position.

Doors

☐ Both front doors must be able to be opened and closed from outside and inside, and must latch securely when closed.

2 Checks carried out WITH THE VEHICLE ON THE GROUND

Vehicle identification

☐ Number plates must be in good condition, secure and legible, with letters and numbers correctly spaced – spacing at (A) should be twice that at (B).

☐ The VIN plate (A) and homologation plate (B) must be legible.

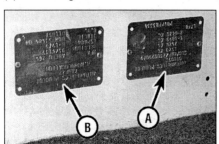

Electrical equipment

☐ Switch on the ignition and check the operation of the horn.

☐ Check the windscreen washers and wipers, examining the wiper blades; renew damaged or perished blades. Also check the operation of the stop-lights.

☐ Check the operation of the sidelights and number plate lights. The lenses and reflectors must be secure, clean and undamaged.

☐ Check the operation and alignment of the headlights. The headlight reflectors must not be tarnished and the lenses must be undamaged.

☐ Switch on the ignition and check the operation of the direction indicators (including the instrument panel tell-tale) and the hazard warning lights. Operation of the sidelights and stop-lights must not affect the indicators - if it does, the cause is usually a bad earth at the rear light cluster.

☐ Check the operation of the rear foglight(s), including the warning light on the instrument panel or in the switch.

Footbrake

☐ Examine the master cylinder, brake pipes and servo unit for leaks, loose mountings, corrosion or other damage.

☐ The fluid reservoir must be secure and the fluid level must be between the upper (A) and lower (B) markings.

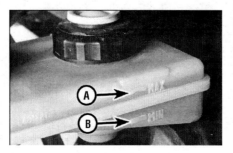

☐ Inspect both front brake flexible hoses for cracks or deterioration of the rubber. Turn the steering from lock to lock, and ensure that the hoses do not contact the wheel, tyre, or any part of the steering or suspension mechanism. With the brake pedal firmly depressed, check the hoses for bulges or leaks under pressure.

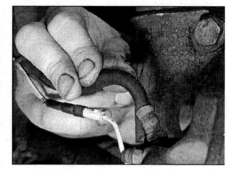

Steering and suspension

☐ Have your assistant turn the steering wheel from side to side slightly, up to the point where the steering gear just begins to transmit this movement to the roadwheels. Check for excessive free play between the steering wheel and the steering gear, indicating wear or insecurity of the steering column joints, the column-to-steering gear coupling, or the steering gear itself.

☐ Have your assistant turn the steering wheel more vigorously in each direction, so that the roadwheels just begin to turn. As this is done, examine all the steering joints, linkages, fittings and attachments. Renew any component that shows signs of wear or damage. On vehicles with power steering, check the security and condition of the steering pump, drivebelt and hoses.

☐ Check that the vehicle is standing level, and at approximately the correct ride height.

Shock absorbers

☐ Depress each corner of the vehicle in turn, then release it. The vehicle should rise and then settle in its normal position. If the vehicle continues to rise and fall, the shock absorber is defective. A shock absorber which has seized will also cause the vehicle to fail.

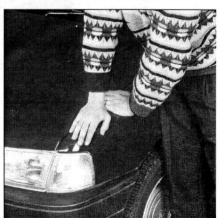

Exhaust system

☐ Start the engine. With your assistant holding a rag over the tailpipe, check the entire system for leaks. Repair or renew leaking sections.

3 Checks carried out WITH THE VEHICLE RAISED AND THE WHEELS FREE TO TURN

Jack up the front and rear of the vehicle, and securely support it on axle stands. Position the stands clear of the suspension assemblies. Ensure that the wheels are clear of the ground and that the steering can be turned from lock to lock.

Steering mechanism

☐ Have your assistant turn the steering from lock to lock. Check that the steering turns smoothly, and that no part of the steering mechanism, including a wheel or tyre, fouls any brake hose or pipe or any part of the body structure.

☐ Examine the steering rack rubber gaiters for damage or insecurity of the retaining clips. If power steering is fitted, check for signs of damage or leakage of the fluid hoses, pipes or connections. Also check for excessive stiffness or binding of the steering, a missing split pin or locking device, or severe corrosion of the body structure within 30 cm of any steering component attachment point.

Front and rear suspension and wheel bearings

☐ Starting at the front right-hand side, grasp the roadwheel at the 3 o'clock and 9 o'clock positions and shake it vigorously. Check for free play or insecurity at the wheel bearings, suspension balljoints, or suspension mountings, pivots and attachments.

☐ Now grasp the wheel at the 12 o'clock and 6 o'clock positions and repeat the previous inspection. Spin the wheel, and check for roughness or tightness of the front wheel bearing.

☐ If excess free play is suspected at a component pivot point, this can be confirmed by using a large screwdriver or similar tool and levering between the mounting and the component attachment. This will confirm whether the wear is in the pivot bush, its retaining bolt, or in the mounting itself (the bolt holes can often become elongated).

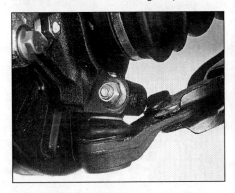

☐ Carry out all the above checks at the other front wheel, and then at both rear wheels.

Springs and shock absorbers

☐ Examine the suspension struts (when applicable) for serious fluid leakage, corrosion, or damage to the casing. Also check the security of the mounting points.

☐ If coil springs are fitted, check that the spring ends locate in their seats, and that the spring is not corroded, cracked or broken.

☐ If leaf springs are fitted, check that all leaves are intact, that the axle is securely attached to each spring, and that there is no deterioration of the spring eye mountings, bushes, and shackles.

☐ The same general checks apply to vehicles fitted with other suspension types, such as torsion bars, hydraulic displacer units, etc. Ensure that all mountings and attachments are secure, that there are no signs of excessive wear, corrosion or damage, and (on hydraulic types) that there are no fluid leaks or damaged pipes.

☐ Inspect the shock absorbers for signs of serious fluid leakage. Check for wear of the mounting bushes or attachments, or damage to the body of the unit.

Driveshafts (fwd vehicles only)

☐ Rotate each front wheel in turn and inspect the constant velocity joint gaiters for splits or damage. Also check that each driveshaft is straight and undamaged.

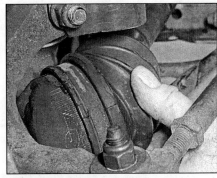

Braking system

☐ If possible without dismantling, check brake pad wear and disc condition. Ensure that the friction lining material has not worn excessively, (A) and that the discs are not fractured, pitted, scored or badly worn (B).

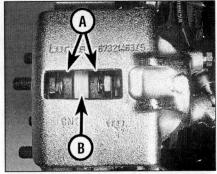

☐ Examine all the rigid brake pipes underneath the vehicle, and the flexible hose(s) at the rear. Look for corrosion, chafing or insecurity of the pipes, and for signs of bulging under pressure, chafing, splits or deterioration of the flexible hoses.

☐ Look for signs of fluid leaks at the brake calipers or on the brake backplates. Repair or renew leaking components.

☐ Slowly spin each wheel, while your assistant depresses and releases the footbrake. Ensure that each brake is operating and does not bind when the pedal is released.

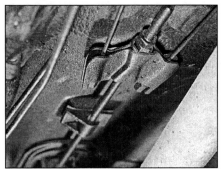

☐ Examine the handbrake mechanism, checking for frayed or broken cables, excessive corrosion, or wear or insecurity of the linkage. Check that the mechanism works on each relevant wheel, and releases fully, without binding.

☐ It is not possible to test brake efficiency without special equipment, but a road test can be carried out later to check that the vehicle pulls up in a straight line.

Fuel and exhaust systems

☐ Inspect the fuel tank (including the filler cap), fuel pipes, hoses and unions. All components must be secure and free from leaks.

☐ Examine the exhaust system over its entire length, checking for any damaged, broken or missing mountings, security of the retaining clamps and rust or corrosion.

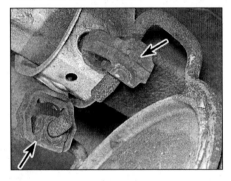

Wheels and tyres

☐ Examine the sidewalls and tread area of each tyre in turn. Check for cuts, tears, lumps, bulges, separation of the tread, and exposure of the ply or cord due to wear or damage. Check that the tyre bead is correctly seated on the wheel rim, that the valve is sound and

properly seated, and that the wheel is not distorted or damaged.

☐ Check that the tyres are of the correct size for the vehicle, that they are of the same size and type on each axle, and that the pressures are correct.

☐ Check the tyre tread depth. The legal minimum at the time of writing is 1.6 mm over at least three-quarters of the tread width. Abnormal tread wear may indicate incorrect front wheel alignment.

Body corrosion

☐ Check the condition of the entire vehicle structure for signs of corrosion in load-bearing areas. (These include chassis box sections, side sills, cross-members, pillars, and all suspension, steering, braking system and seat belt mountings and anchorages.) Any corrosion which has seriously reduced the thickness of a load-bearing area is likely to cause the vehicle to fail. In this case professional repairs are likely to be needed.

☐ Damage or corrosion which causes sharp or otherwise dangerous edges to be exposed will also cause the vehicle to fail.

4 Checks carried out on YOUR VEHICLE'S EXHAUST EMISSION SYSTEM

Petrol models

☐ Have the engine at normal operating temperature, and make sure that it is in good tune (ignition system in good order, air filter element clean, etc).

☐ Before any measurements are carried out, raise the engine speed to around 2500 rpm, and hold it at this speed for 20 seconds. Allow the engine speed to return to idle, and watch

for smoke emissions from the exhaust tailpipe. If the idle speed is obviously much too high, or if dense blue or clearly-visible black smoke comes from the tailpipe for more than 5 seconds, the vehicle will fail. As a rule of thumb, blue smoke signifies oil being burnt (engine wear) while black smoke signifies unburnt fuel (dirty air cleaner element, or other carburettor or fuel system fault).

☐ An exhaust gas analyser capable of measuring carbon monoxide (CO) and hydrocarbons (HC) is now needed. If such an instrument cannot be hired or borrowed, a local garage may agree to perform the check for a small fee.

CO emissions (mixture)

☐ At the time or writing, the maximum CO level at idle is 3.5% for vehicles first used after August 1986 and 4.5% for older vehicles. From January 1996 a much tighter limit (around 0.5%) applies to catalyst-equipped vehicles first used from August 1992. If the CO level cannot be reduced far enough to pass the test (and the fuel and ignition systems are otherwise in good condition) then the carburettor is badly worn, or there is some problem in the fuel injection system or catalytic converter (as applicable).

HC emissions

☐ With the CO emissions within limits, HC emissions must be no more than 1200 ppm (parts per million). If the vehicle fails this test at idle, it can be re-tested at around 2000 rpm; if the HC level is then 1200 ppm or less, this counts as a pass.

☐ Excessive HC emissions can be caused by oil being burnt, but they are more likely to be due to unburnt fuel.

Diesel models

☐ The only emission test applicable to Diesel engines is the measuring of exhaust smoke density. The test involves accelerating the engine several times to its maximum unloaded speed.

Note: *It is of the utmost importance that the engine timing belt is in good condition before the test is carried out.*

☐ Excessive smoke can be caused by a dirty air cleaner element. Otherwise, professional advice may be needed to find the cause.

Engine

- [ ] Engine fails to rotate when attempting to start
- [ ] Engine rotates, but will not start
- [ ] Engine difficult to start when cold
- [ ] Engine difficult to start when hot
- [ ] Starter motor noisy or excessively-rough in engagement
- [ ] Engine starts, but stops immediately
- [ ] Engine idles erratically
- [ ] Engine misfires at idle speed
- [ ] Engine misfires throughout the driving speed range
- [ ] Engine hesitates on acceleration
- [ ] Engine stalls
- [ ] Engine lacks power
- [ ] Engine backfires
- [ ] Oil pressure warning light illuminated with engine running
- [ ] Engine runs-on after switching off
- [ ] Engine noises

Cooling system

- [ ] Overheating
- [ ] Overcooling
- [ ] External coolant leakage
- [ ] Internal coolant leakage
- [ ] Corrosion

Fuel and exhaust systems

- [ ] Excessive fuel consumption
- [ ] Fuel leakage and/or fuel odour
- [ ] Excessive noise or fumes from exhaust system

Clutch

- [ ] Pedal travels to floor - no pressure or very little resistance
- [ ] Clutch fails to disengage (unable to select gears)
- [ ] Clutch slips (engine speed increases, with no increase in vehicle speed)
- [ ] Judder as clutch is engaged
- [ ] Noise when depressing or releasing clutch pedal

Manual gearbox

- [ ] Noisy in neutral with engine running
- [ ] Noisy in one particular gear
- [ ] Difficulty engaging gears
- [ ] Jumps out of gear
- [ ] Vibration
- [ ] Lubricant leaks

Automatic transmission

- [ ] Fluid leakage
- [ ] Transmission fluid brown, or has burned smell
- [ ] General gear selection problems
- [ ] Transmission will not downshift (kickdown) with accelerator fully depressed
- [ ] Engine will not start in any gear, or starts in gears other than Park or Neutral
- [ ] Transmission slips, shifts roughly, is noisy, or has no drive in forward or reverse gears

Driveshafts

- [ ] Clicking or knocking noise on turns (at slow speed on full-lock)
- [ ] Vibration when accelerating or decelerating

Braking system

- [ ] Vehicle pulls to one side under braking
- [ ] Noise (grinding or high-pitched squeal) when brakes applied
- [ ] Excessive brake pedal travel
- [ ] Brake pedal feels spongy when depressed
- [ ] Excessive brake pedal effort required to stop vehicle
- [ ] Judder felt through brake pedal or steering wheel when braking
- [ ] Brakes binding
- [ ] Rear wheels locking under normal braking

Suspension and steering systems

- [ ] Vehicle pulls to one side
- [ ] Wheel wobble and vibration
- [ ] Excessive pitching and/or rolling around corners, or during braking
- [ ] Wandering or general instability
- [ ] Excessively-stiff steering
- [ ] Excessive play in steering
- [ ] Lack of power assistance
- [ ] Tyre wear excessive

Electrical system

- [ ] Battery will not hold a charge for more than a few days
- [ ] Ignition/no-charge warning light remains illuminated with engine running
- [ ] Ignition/no-charge warning light fails to come on
- [ ] Lights inoperative
- [ ] Instrument readings inaccurate or erratic
- [ ] Horn inoperative, or unsatisfactory in operation
- [ ] Windscreen/tailgate wipers inoperative, or unsatisfactory in operation
- [ ] Windscreen/tailgate washers inoperative, or unsatisfactory in operation
- [ ] Electric windows inoperative, or unsatisfactory in operation
- [ ] Central locking system inoperative, or unsatisfactory in operation

Introduction

The vehicle owner who does his or her own maintenance according to the recommended service schedules should not have to use this section of the manual very often. Modern component reliability is such that, provided those items subject to wear or deterioration are inspected or renewed at the specified intervals, sudden failure is comparatively rare. Faults do not usually just happen as a result of sudden failure, but develop over a period of time. Major mechanical failures in particular are usually preceded by characteristic symptoms over hundreds or even thousands of miles. Those components which do occasionally fail without warning are often small and easily carried in the vehicle.

With any fault-finding, the first step is to decide where to begin investigations. Sometimes this is obvious, but on other occasions, a little detective work will be necessary. The owner who makes half a dozen haphazard adjustments or replacements may be successful in curing a fault (or its symptoms), but will be none the wiser if the fault recurs, and ultimately may have spent more time and money than was necessary. A calm and logical approach will be found to be more satisfactory in the long run. Always take into account any warning signs or abnormalities that may have been noticed in the period preceding the fault - power loss, high or low gauge readings, unusual smells, etc - and remember that failure of components such as fuses or spark plugs may only be pointers to some underlying fault.

The pages which follow provide an easy-reference guide to the more common problems which may occur during the operation of the vehicle. These problems and their possible causes are grouped under headings denoting various components or systems, such as Engine, Cooling system, etc. The Chapter and/or Section which deals with the problem is also shown in brackets. Whatever the fault, certain basic principles apply. These are as follows:

Verify the fault. This is simply a matter of being sure that you know what the symptoms are before starting work. This is particularly important if you are investigating a fault for someone else, who may not have described it very accurately.

Don't overlook the obvious. For example, if the vehicle won't start, is there petrol in the tank? (Don't take anyone else's word on this particular point, and don't trust the fuel gauge either!) If an electrical fault is indicated, look for loose or broken wires before digging out the test gear.

Cure the disease, not the symptom. Substituting a flat battery with a fully-charged one will get you off the hard shoulder, but if the underlying cause is not attended to, the new battery will go the same way. Similarly, changing oil-fouled spark plugs for a new set will get you moving again, but remember that the reason for the fouling (if it wasn't simply an incorrect grade of plug) will have to be established and corrected.

Don't take anything for granted. Particularly, don't forget that a "new" component may itself be defective (especially if it's been rattling around in the boot for months), and don't leave components out of a fault diagnosis sequence just because they are new or recently-fitted. When you do finally diagnose a difficult fault, you'll probably realise that all the evidence was there from the start.

Engine

Engine fails to rotate when attempting to start

☐ Battery terminal connections loose or corroded (Chapter 1).
☐ Battery discharged or faulty (Chapter 5A).
☐ Broken, loose or disconnected wiring in the starting circuit (Chapter 5A).
☐ Defective starter solenoid or switch (Chapter 5A).
☐ Defective starter motor (Chapter 5A).
☐ Starter pinion or flywheel ring gear teeth loose or broken (Chapters 2 and 5A).
☐ Engine earth strap broken or disconnected (Chapter 5A).
☐ Automatic transmission not in Park/Neutral position or starter inhibitor switch faulty (Chapter 7B).

Engine rotates, but will not start

☐ Fuel tank empty.
☐ Battery discharged (engine rotates slowly) (Chapter 5A).
☐ Battery terminal connections loose or corroded (Chapter 1).
☐ Ignition components damp or damaged (Chapters 1 and 5B or 5C).
☐ Broken, loose or disconnected wiring in the ignition circuit (Chapters 1 and 5B or 5C).
☐ Worn, faulty or incorrectly-gapped spark plugs (Chapter 1).
☐ Carburettor/fuel injection system fault (Chapter 4A or 4B).
☐ Major mechanical failure (eg camshaft drive) (Chapter 2).

Engine difficult to start when cold

☐ Battery discharged (Chapter 5A).
☐ Battery terminal connections loose or corroded (Chapter 1).
☐ Worn, faulty or incorrectly-gapped spark plugs (Chapter 1).
☐ Choke mechanism faulty - carburettor models (Chapter 4A).
☐ Faulty fuel cut-off solenoid - carburettor models (Chapter 4A).
☐ Fuel injection system fault - fuel-injected models (Chapter 4B).
☐ Other ignition system fault (Chapters 1 and 5B or 5C).
☐ Low cylinder compressions (Chapter 2).

Engine difficult to start when hot

☐ Air filter element dirty or clogged (Chapter 1).
☐ Choke mechanism faulty - carburettor models (Chapter 4A).
☐ Faulty fuel cut-off solenoid - carburettor models (Chapter 4A).
☐ Fuel injection system fault - fuel-injected models (Chapter 4B).
☐ Other ignition system fault (Chapters 1 and 5B or 5C).
☐ Low cylinder compressions (Chapter 2).

Starter motor noisy or excessively-rough in engagement

☐ Starter pinion or flywheel ring gear teeth loose or broken (Chapters 2 or 5A).
☐ Starter motor mounting bolts loose or missing (Chapter 5A).
☐ Starter motor internal components worn or damaged (Chapter 5A).

Engine starts, but stops immediately

☐ Loose or faulty electrical connections in the ignition circuit (Chapters 1 and 5B or 5C).
☐ Vacuum leak at the carburettor/throttle body or inlet manifold (Chapter 4A or 4B).
☐ Blocked carburettor jet(s) or internal passages - carburettor models (Chapter 4A).
☐ Blocked injector/fuel injection system fault - fuel-injected models (Chapter 4B).

Engine idles erratically

☐ Air filter element clogged (Chapter 1).
☐ Vacuum leak at the carburettor/throttle body or inlet manifold (Chapter 4A or 4B).
☐ Worn, faulty or incorrectly-gapped spark plugs (Chapter 1).
☐ Uneven or low cylinder compressions (Chapter 2).
☐ Camshaft lobes worn (Chapter 2A).
☐ Camshaft toothed belt incorrectly fitted (Chapter 2A).
☐ Blocked carburettor jet(s) or internal passages - carburettor models (Chapter 4A).
☐ Blocked injector/fuel injection system fault - fuel-injected models (Chapter 4B).

Engine misfires at idle speed

☐ Worn, faulty or incorrectly-gapped spark plugs (Chapter 1).
☐ Faulty spark plug HT leads (Chapter 1).
☐ Vacuum leak at the carburettor/throttle body, inlet manifold or associated hoses (Chapter 4A or 4B).
☐ Blocked carburettor jet(s) or internal passages - carburettor models (Chapter 4A).
☐ Blocked injector/fuel injection system fault - fuel-injected models (Chapter 4B).
☐ Distributor cap cracked or tracking internally (Chapter 1).
☐ Uneven or low cylinder compressions (Chapter 2).
☐ Disconnected, leaking, or perished crankcase ventilation hoses (Chapter 2).

Engine misfires throughout the driving speed range

☐ Fuel filter choked (Chapter 1).
☐ Fuel pump faulty, or delivery pressure low (Chapter 4A or 4B).
☐ Fuel tank vent blocked, or fuel pipes restricted (Chapter 4A or 4B).
☐ Vacuum leak at the carburettor/throttle body, inlet manifold or associated hoses (Chapter 4A or 4B).
☐ Worn, faulty or incorrectly-gapped spark plugs (Chapter 1).
☐ Faulty spark plug HT leads (Chapter 1).
☐ Distributor cap cracked or tracking internally (Chapter 1).
☐ Faulty ignition coil (Chapter 5B or 5C).
☐ Uneven or low cylinder compressions (Chapter 2).

☐ Blocked carburettor jet(s) or internal passages - carburettor models (Chapter 4A).

☐ Blocked injector/fuel injection system fault - fuel-injected models (Chapter 4B).

Engine hesitates on acceleration

☐ Worn, faulty or incorrectly-gapped spark plugs (Chapter 1).
☐ Vacuum leak at the carburettor/throttle body, inlet manifold or associated hoses (Chapter 4A or 4B).
☐ Blocked carburettor jet(s) or internal passages - carburettor models (Chapter 4A).
☐ Blocked injector/fuel injection system fault - fuel-injected models (Chapter 4B).

Engine stalls

☐ Vacuum leak at the carburettor/throttle body, inlet manifold or associated hoses (Chapter 4A or 4B).
☐ Fuel filter choked (Chapter 1).
☐ Fuel pump faulty, or delivery pressure low (Chapter 4A or 4B).
☐ Fuel tank vent blocked, or fuel pipes restricted (Chapter 4A or 4B).
☐ Blocked carburettor jet(s) or internal passages - carburettor models (Chapter 4A).
☐ Blocked injector/fuel injection system fault - fuel-injected models (Chapter 4B).

Engine lacks power

☐ Camshaft toothed belt incorrectly fitted (Chapter 2).
☐ Fuel filter choked (Chapter 1).
☐ Fuel pump faulty, or delivery pressure low (Chapter 4A or 4B).
☐ Uneven or low cylinder compressions (Chapter 2).
☐ Worn, faulty or incorrectly-gapped spark plugs (Chapter 1).
☐ Vacuum leak at the carburettor/throttle body, inlet manifold or associated hoses (Chapter 4A or 4B).
☐ Blocked carburettor jet(s) or internal passages - carburettor models (Chapter 4A).
☐ Blocked injector/fuel injection system fault - fuel-injected models (Chapter 4B or 4C).
☐ Brakes binding (Chapters 1 and 9).
☐ Clutch slipping - manual transmission models (Chapter 6).

Engine backfires

☐ Camshaft toothed timing belt incorrectly fitted (Chapter 2).
☐ Vacuum leak at the carburettor/throttle body, inlet manifold or associated hoses (Chapter 4A or 4B).
☐ Blocked carburettor jet(s) or internal passages - carburettor models (Chapter 4A).
☐ Blocked injector/fuel injection system fault - fuel-injected models (Chapter 4B).

Oil pressure warning light illuminated with engine running

☐ Low oil level, or incorrect oil grade (Chapter 1).
☐ Faulty oil pressure sensor (Chapter 5A).
☐ Worn engine bearings and/or oil pump (Chapter 2).
☐ High engine operating temperature (Chapter 3).
☐ Oil pressure relief valve defective (Chapter 2).
☐ Oil pick-up strainer clogged (Chapter 2).

Engine runs-on after switching off

☐ Excessive carbon build-up in engine (Chapter 2).
☐ High engine operating temperature (Chapter 3).
☐ Faulty fuel cut-off solenoid - carburettor models (Chapter 4A).
☐ Fuel injection system fault - fuel injection models (Chapter 4B).

Engine noises

Pre-ignition (pinking) or knocking during acceleration or under load

☐ Ignition timing incorrect/ignition system fault (Chapters 1 and 5B or 5C).
☐ Incorrect grade of spark plug (Chapter 1).
☐ Incorrect grade of fuel (Chapter 1).
☐ Vacuum leak at the carburettor/throttle body, inlet manifold or associated hoses (Chapter 4A or 4B).
☐ Excessive carbon build-up in engine (Chapter 2).
☐ Blocked carburettor jet(s) or internal passages - carburettor models (Chapter 4A).
☐ Blocked injector/fuel injection system fault - fuel-injected models (Chapter 4B).

Whistling or wheezing noises

☐ Leaking inlet manifold or carburettor/throttle body gasket (Chapter 4A or 4B).
☐ Leaking exhaust manifold gasket or pipe-to-manifold joint (Chapter 4A or 4B).
☐ Leaking vacuum hose (Chapters 4A, 4B and 9).
☐ Blowing cylinder head gasket (Chapter 2).

Tapping or rattling noises

☐ Worn valve gear or camshaft (Chapter 2).
☐ Ancillary component fault (water pump, alternator, etc) (Chapters 3, 5, etc).

Knocking or thumping noises

☐ Worn big-end bearings (regular heavy knocking, perhaps less\ under load) (Chapter 2).
☐ Worn main bearings (rumbling and knocking, perhaps worsening under load) (Chapter 2).
☐ Piston slap (most noticeable when cold) (Chapter 2).
☐ Ancillary component fault (water pump, alternator, etc) (Chapters 3, 5, etc).

Cooling system

Overheating

☐ Insufficient coolant in system (Chapter 1).
☐ Thermostat faulty (Chapter 3).
☐ Radiator core blocked, or grille restricted (Chapter 3).
☐ Electric cooling fan or thermoswitch faulty (Chapter 3).
☐ Pressure cap faulty (Chapter 3).
☐ Ignition timing incorrect (Chapters 1 and 5B or 5C).
☐ Inaccurate temperature gauge sender unit (Chapter 3).
☐ Airlock in cooling system (Chapter 1).

Overcooling

☐ Thermostat faulty (Chapter 3).
☐ Inaccurate temperature gauge sender unit (Chapter 3).

External coolant leakage

☐ Deteriorated or damaged hoses or hose clips (Chapter 1).
☐ Radiator core or heater matrix leaking (Chapter 3).
☐ Pressure cap faulty (Chapter 3).
☐ Water pump seal leaking (Chapter 3).
☐ Boiling due to overheating (Chapter 3).
☐ Core plug leaking (Chapter 2).

Internal coolant leakage

☐ Leaking cylinder head gasket (Chapter 2).
☐ Cracked cylinder head or cylinder bore (Chapter 2).

Corrosion

☐ Infrequent draining and flushing (Chapter 1).
☐ Incorrect coolant mixture or inappropriate coolant type (Chapter 1).

Fuel and exhaust systems

Excessive fuel consumption

☐ Air filter element dirty or clogged (Chapter 1).
☐ Choke mechanism faulty - carburettor models (Chapter 4A).
☐ Fuel injection system fault - fuel-injected models (Chapter 4B).
☐ Ignition timing incorrect/ignition system fault (Chapters 1 and 5B or 5C).
☐ Tyres under-inflated (Chapter 1).

Fuel leakage and/or fuel odour

☐ Damaged or corroded fuel tank, pipes or connections (Chapter 4A or 4B).
☐ Carburettor float chamber flooding (float height incorrect) (Chapter 4A).

Excessive noise or fumes from exhaust system

☐ Leaking exhaust system or manifold joints (Chapters 1 and 4A or 4B).
☐ Leaking, corroded or damaged silencers or pipe (Chapters 1 and 4A or 4B).
☐ Broken mountings causing body or suspension contact (Chapter 1).

Clutch

Pedal travels to floor - no pressure or very little resistance

☐ Broken clutch cable (Chapter 6).
☐ Incorrect clutch cable adjustment (Chapter 6).
☐ Broken clutch release bearing or fork (Chapter 6).
☐ Broken diaphragm spring in clutch pressure plate (Chapter 6).

Clutch fails to disengage (unable to select gears)

☐ Incorrect clutch cable adjustment (Chapter 6).
☐ Clutch disc sticking on gearbox input shaft splines (Chapter 6).
☐ Clutch disc sticking to flywheel or pressure plate (Chapter 6).
☐ Faulty pressure plate assembly (Chapter 6).
☐ Clutch release mechanism worn or incorrectly assembled (Chapter 6).

Clutch slips (engine speed increases, with no increase in vehicle speed)

☐ Incorrect clutch cable adjustment (Chapter 6).
☐ Clutch disc linings excessively worn (Chapter 6).

☐ Clutch disc linings contaminated with oil or grease (Chapter 6).
☐ Faulty pressure plate or weak diaphragm spring (Chapter 6).

Judder as clutch is engaged

☐ Clutch disc linings contaminated with oil or grease (Chapter 6).
☐ Clutch disc linings excessively worn (Chapter 6).
☐ Clutch cable sticking or frayed (Chapter 6).
☐ Faulty or distorted pressure plate or diaphragm spring (Chapter 6).
☐ Worn or loose engine or gearbox mountings (Chapter 2).
☐ Clutch disc hub or gearbox input shaft splines worn (Chapter 6).

Noise when depressing or releasing clutch pedal

☐ Worn clutch release bearing (Chapter 6).
☐ Worn or dry clutch pedal bushes (Chapter 6).
☐ Faulty pressure plate assembly (Chapter 6).
☐ Pressure plate diaphragm spring broken (Chapter 6).
☐ Broken clutch disc cushioning springs (Chapter 6).

Manual gearbox

Noisy in neutral with engine running

☐ Input shaft bearings worn (noise apparent with clutch pedal released, but not when depressed) (Chapter 7A).*
☐ Clutch release bearing worn (noise apparent with clutch pedal depressed, possibly less when released) (Chapter 6).

Noisy in one particular gear

☐ Worn, damaged or chipped gear teeth (Chapter 7A).*

Difficulty engaging gears

☐ Clutch fault (Chapter 6).
☐ Worn or damaged gear linkage (Chapter 7A).
☐ Incorrectly-adjusted gear linkage (Chapter 7A).
☐ Worn synchroniser units (Chapter 7A).*

Jumps out of gear

☐ Worn or damaged gear linkage (Chapter 7A).

☐ Incorrectly-adjusted gear linkage (Chapter 7A).
☐ Worn synchroniser units (Chapter 7A).*
☐ Worn selector forks (Chapter 7A).*

Vibration

☐ Lack of oil (Chapter 1).
☐ Worn bearings (Chapter 7A).*

Lubricant leaks

☐ Leaking differential output oil seal (Chapter 7A).
☐ Leaking housing joint (Chapter 7A).*
☐ Leaking input shaft oil seal (Chapter 7A).*

Although the corrective action necessary to remedy the symptoms described is beyond the scope of the home mechanic, the above information should be helpful in isolating the cause of the condition, so that the owner can communicate clearly with a professional mechanic.

Automatic transmission

Note: *Due to the complexity of the automatic transmission, it is difficult for the home mechanic to properly diagnose and service this unit. For problems other than the following, the vehicle should be taken to a dealer service department or automatic transmission specialist.*

Fluid leakage

☐ Automatic transmission fluid is usually deep red in colour. Fluid leaks should not be confused with engine oil, which can easily be blown onto the transmission by air flow.

☐ To determine the source of a leak, first remove all built-up dirt and grime from the transmission housing and surrounding areas, using a degreasing agent, or by steam-cleaning. Drive the vehicle at low speed, so air flow will not blow the leak far from its source. Raise and support the vehicle, and determine where the leak is coming from. The following are common areas of leakage.
a) Oil pan.
b) Dipstick tube.

Transmission fluid brown, or has burned smell

☐ Transmission fluid level low, or fluid in need of renewal (Chapter 1).

General gear selection problems

☐ Chapter 7B deals with checking and adjusting the selector cable on automatic transmissions. The following are common problems which may be caused by a poorly-adjusted cable.

a) Engine starting in gears other than Park or Neutral.
b) Indicator on gear selector lever pointing to a gear other than the one actually being used.
c) Vehicle moves when in Park or Neutral.
d) Poor gearshift quality or erratic gearchanges.

Transmission will not downshift (kickdown) with accelerator pedal fully depressed

☐ Low transmission fluid level (Chapter 1).
☐ Incorrect selector cable adjustment (Chapter 7B).
☐ Incorrect kickdown cable adjustment (Chapter 7B).

Engine will not start in any gear, or starts in gears other than Park or Neutral

☐ Incorrect starter inhibitor switch adjustment (Chapter 7B).
☐ Incorrect selector cable adjustment (Chapter 7B).

Transmission slips, shifts roughly, is noisy, or has no drive in forward or reverse gears

☐ There are many probable causes for the above problems, but the home mechanic should be concerned with only one possibility - fluid level. Before taking the vehicle to a dealer or transmission specialist, check the fluid level and condition of the fluid as described in Chapter 1. Correct the fluid level as necessary, or change the fluid and filter if needed. If the problem persists, professional help will be necessary.

Driveshafts

Clicking or knocking noise on turns (at slow speed on full-lock)

☐ Lack of constant velocity joint lubricant, possibly due to damaged gaiter (Chapter 8).
☐ Worn outer constant velocity joint (Chapter 8).

Vibration when accelerating or decelerating

☐ Worn inner constant velocity joint (Chapter 8).

☐ Bent or distorted driveshaft (Chapter 8).

Braking system

Note: *Before assuming that a brake problem exists, make sure that the tyres are in good condition and correctly inflated, that the front wheel alignment is correct, and that the vehicle is not loaded with weight in an unequal manner. Apart from checking the condition of all pipe and hose connections.*

Vehicle pulls to one side under braking

☐ Worn, defective, damaged or contaminated front brake pads or rear brake shoes/pads on one side (Chapters 1 and 9).
☐ Seized or partially-seized front brake caliper or rear wheel caliper/cylinder piston (Chapters 1 and 9).
☐ A mixture of brake pad/shoe lining materials fitted between sides (Chapters 1 and 9).
☐ Front brake caliper mounting bolts loose (Chapter 9).
☐ Rear brake backplate mounting bolts loose (Chapter 9).
☐ Worn or damaged steering or suspension components (Chapters 1 and 10).

Noise (grinding or high-pitched squeal) when brakes applied

☐ Brake pad or shoe friction lining material worn down to metal backing (Chapters 1 and 9).
☐ Excessive corrosion of brake disc or drum. (May be apparent after the vehicle has been standing for some time (Chapters 1 and 9).
☐ Foreign object (stone chipping, etc) trapped between brake disc and shield (Chapters 1 and 9).

Excessive brake pedal travel

☐ Rear brakes incorrectly adjusted - early models (Chapter 9)
☐ Inoperative rear brake self-adjust mechanism - later drum brake models (Chapters 1 and 9).
☐ Faulty master cylinder (Chapter 9).
☐ Air in hydraulic system (Chapters 1 and 9).
☐ Faulty vacuum servo unit (Chapter 9).

Brake pedal feels spongy when depressed

☐ Air in hydraulic system (Chapters 1 and 9).
☐ Deteriorated flexible rubber brake hoses (Chapters 1 and 9).
☐ Master cylinder mounting nuts loose (Chapter 9).
☐ Faulty master cylinder (Chapter 9).

Excessive brake pedal effort required to stop vehicle

☐ Faulty vacuum servo unit (Chapter 9).
☐ Disconnected, damaged or insecure brake servo vacuum hose (Chapter 9).
☐ Primary or secondary hydraulic circuit failure (Chapter 9).
☐ Seized brake caliper or wheel cylinder piston(s) (Chapter 9).
☐ Brake pads or brake shoes incorrectly fitted (Chapters 1 and 9).
☐ Incorrect grade of brake pads or brake shoes fitted (Chapters 1 and 9).
☐ Brake pads or brake shoe linings contaminated (Chapters 1 and 9).

Judder felt through brake pedal or steering wheel when braking

- [ ] Excessive run-out or distortion of front discs or rear discs/drums (Chapters 1 and 9).
- [ ] Brake pad or brake shoe linings worn (Chapters 1 and 9).
- [ ] Brake caliper or rear brake backplate mounting bolts loose (Chapter 9).
- [ ] Wear in suspension or steering components or mountings (Chapters 1 and 10).

Suspension and steering

Note: *Before diagnosing suspension or steering faults, be sure that the trouble is not due to incorrect tyre pressures, mixtures of tyre types, or binding brakes.*

Vehicle pulls to one side

- [ ] Defective tyre (Chapter 1).
- [ ] Excessive wear in suspension or steering components (Chapters 1 and 10).
- [ ] Incorrect front wheel alignment (Chapter 10).
- [ ] Accident damage to steering or suspension components (Chapter 1).

Wheel wobble and vibration

- [ ] Front roadwheels out of balance (vibration felt mainly through the steering wheel) (Chapters 1 and 10).
- [ ] Rear roadwheels out of balance (vibration felt throughout the vehicle) (Chapters 1 and 10).
- [ ] Roadwheels damaged or distorted (Chapters 1 and 10).
- [ ] Faulty or damaged tyre (Chapter 1).
- [ ] Worn steering or suspension joints, bushes or components (Chapters 1 and 10).
- [ ] Wheel bolts loose (Chapters 1 and 10).

Excessive pitching and/or rolling around corners, or during braking

- [ ] Defective shock absorbers (Chapters 1 and 10).
- [ ] Broken or weak spring and/or suspension component (Chapters 1 and 10).
- [ ] Worn or damaged anti-roll bar or mountings (Chapter 10).

Wandering or general instability

- [ ] Incorrect front wheel alignment (Chapter 10).
- [ ] Worn steering or suspension joints, bushes or components (Chapters 1 and 10).
- [ ] Roadwheels out of balance (Chapters 1 and 10).
- [ ] Faulty or damaged tyre (Chapter 1).
- [ ] Wheel bolts loose (Chapters 1 and 10).
- [ ] Defective shock absorbers (Chapters 1 and 10).

Excessively-stiff steering

- [ ] Lack of steering gear lubricant (Chapter 10).
- [ ] Seized track rod end balljoint or suspension balljoint (Chapters 1 and 10).

Brakes binding

- [ ] Seized brake caliper or wheel cylinder piston(s) (Chapter 9).
- [ ] Incorrectly-adjusted handbrake mechanism (Chapter 9).
- [ ] Faulty master cylinder (Chapter 9).

Rear wheels locking under normal braking

- [ ] Rear brake shoe linings contaminated (Chapters 1 and 9).
- [ ] Faulty brake pressure regulator valve(s) (Chapter 9).

- [ ] Broken or incorrectly-adjusted auxiliary drivebelt (Chapter 1).
- [ ] Incorrect front wheel alignment (Chapter 10).
- [ ] Steering rack or column bent or damaged (Chapter 10).

Excessive play in steering

- [ ] Worn steering track rod end balljoints (Chapters 1 and 10).
- [ ] Worn rack-and-pinion steering gear (Chapter 10).
- [ ] Worn steering or suspension joints, bushes or components (Chapters 1 and 10).

Lack of power assistance

- [ ] Broken or incorrectly-adjusted auxiliary drivebelt (Chapter 1).
- [ ] Incorrect power steering fluid level (Chapter 1).
- [ ] Restriction in power steering fluid hoses (Chapter 1).
- [ ] Faulty power steering pump (Chapter 10).
- [ ] Faulty rack-and-pinion steering gear (Chapter 10).

Tyre wear excessive

Tyres worn on inside or outside edges

- [ ] Tyres under-inflated (wear on both edges) (Chapter 1).
- [ ] Incorrect camber or castor angles (wear on one edge only) (Chapter 10).
- [ ] Worn steering or suspension joints, bushes or components (Chapters 1 and 10).
- [ ] Excessively-hard cornering.
- [ ] Accident damage.

Tyre treads exhibit feathered edges

- [ ] Incorrect toe setting (Chapter 10).

Tyres worn in centre of tread

- [ ] Tyres over-inflated (Chapter 1).

Tyres worn on inside and outside edges

- [ ] Tyres under-inflated (Chapter 1).

Tyres worn unevenly

- [ ] Tyres/wheels out of balance (Chapter 1).
- [ ] Excessive wheel or tyre run-out (Chapter 1).
- [ ] Worn shock absorbers (Chapters 1 and 10).
- [ ] Faulty tyre (Chapter 1).

Electrical system

Note: *For problems associated with the starting system, refer to the faults listed under "Engine" earlier in this Section.*

Battery will not hold a charge for more than a few days

- [ ] Battery defective internally (Chapter 5A).
- [ ] Battery terminal connections loose or corroded (Chapter 1).
- [ ] Auxiliary drivebelt worn or incorrectly adjusted (Chapter 1).
- [ ] Alternator not charging at correct output (Chapter 5A).

- [ ] Alternator or voltage regulator faulty (Chapter 5A).
- [ ] Short-circuit causing continual battery drain (Chapters 5A and 12).

Ignition/no-charge warning light remains illuminated with engine running

- [ ] Auxiliary drivebelt broken, worn, or incorrectly adjusted (Chapter 1).
- [ ] Alternator brushes worn, sticking, or dirty (Chapter 5A).
- [ ] Alternator brush springs weak or broken (Chapter 5A).

☐ Internal fault in alternator or voltage regulator (Chapter 5A).
☐ Broken, disconnected, or loose wiring in charging circuit (Chapter 5A).

Ignition/no-charge warning light fails to come on

☐ Warning light bulb blown (Chapter 12).
☐ Broken, disconnected, or loose wiring in warning light circuit (Chapter 12).
☐ Alternator faulty (Chapter 5A).

Lights inoperative

☐ Bulb blown (Chapter 12).
☐ Corrosion of bulb or bulbholder contacts (Chapter 12).
☐ Blown fuse (Chapter 12).
☐ Faulty relay (Chapter 12).
☐ Broken, loose, or disconnected wiring (Chapter 12).
☐ Faulty switch (Chapter 12).

Instrument readings inaccurate or erratic

Instrument readings increase with engine speed

☐ Faulty voltage regulator (Chapter 12).

Fuel or temperature gauges give no reading

☐ Faulty gauge sender unit (Chapters 3 or 4).
☐ Wiring open-circuit (Chapter 12).
☐ Faulty gauge (Chapter 12).

Fuel or temperature gauges give continuous maximum reading

☐ Faulty gauge sender unit (Chapters 3 or 4).
☐ Wiring short-circuit (Chapter 12).
☐ Faulty gauge (Chapter 12).

Horn inoperative, or unsatisfactory in operation

Horn operates all the time

☐ Horn push either earthed or stuck down (Chapter 12).
☐ Horn cable-to-horn push earthed (Chapter 12).

Horn fails to operate

☐ Blown fuse (Chapter 12).
☐ Cable or cable connections loose, broken or disconnected (Chapter 12).
☐ Faulty horn (Chapter 12).

Horn emits intermittent or unsatisfactory sound

☐ Cable connections loose (Chapter 12).
☐ Horn mountings loose (Chapter 12).
☐ Faulty horn (Chapter 12).

Windscreen/tailgate wipers inoperative, or unsatisfactory in operation

Wipers fail to operate, or operate very slowly

☐ Wiper blades stuck to screen, or linkage seized or binding (Chapters 1 and 12).
☐ Blown fuse (Chapter 12).
☐ Cable or cable connections loose, broken or disconnected (Chapter 12).
☐ Faulty relay (Chapter 12).
☐ Faulty wiper motor (Chapter 12).

Wiper blades sweep over too large or too small an area of the glass

☐ Wiper arms incorrectly positioned on spindles (Chapter 1).
☐ Excessive wear of wiper linkage (Chapter 12).
☐ Wiper motor or linkage mountings loose or insecure (Chapter 12).

Wiper blades fail to clean the glass effectively

☐ Wiper blade rubbers worn or perished (Chapter 1).
☐ Wiper arm tension springs broken, or arm pivots seized (Chapter 12).
☐ Insufficient windscreen washer additive to adequately remove road film (Chapter 1).

Windscreen/tailgate washers inoperative, or unsatisfactory in operation

One or more washer jets inoperative

☐ Blocked washer jet (Chapter 1).
☐ Disconnected, kinked or restricted fluid hose (Chapter 12).
☐ Insufficient fluid in washer reservoir (Chapter 1).

Washer pump fails to operate

☐ Broken or disconnected wiring or connections (Chapter 12).
☐ Blown fuse (Chapter 12).
☐ Faulty washer switch (Chapter 12).
☐ Faulty washer pump (Chapter 12).

Washer pump runs for some time before fluid is emitted from jets

☐ Faulty one-way valve in fluid supply hose (Chapter 12).

Electric windows inoperative, or unsatisfactory in operation

Window glass will only move in one direction

☐ Faulty switch (Chapter 12)

Window glass slow to move

☐ Incorrectly-adjusted door glass guide channels (Chapter 11).
☐ Regulator seized or damaged, or in need of lubrication (Chapter 11).
☐ Door internal components or trim fouling regulator (Chapter 11).
☐ Faulty motor (Chapter 11).

Window glass fails to move

☐ Incorrectly-adjusted door glass guide channels (Chapter 11).
☐ Blown fuse (Chapter 12).
☐ Faulty relay (Chapter 12).
☐ Broken or disconnected wiring or connections (Chapter 12).
☐ Faulty motor (Chapter 11).

Central locking system inoperative, or unsatisfactory in operation

Complete system failure

☐ Blown fuse (Chapter 12).
☐ Faulty relay (Chapter 12).
☐ Broken or disconnected wiring or connections (Chapter 12).
☐ Faulty control unit (Chapter 11).

Latch locks but will not unlock, or unlocks but will not lock

☐ Faulty master switch (Chapter 12).
☐ Broken or disconnected latch operating rods or levers (Chapter 11).
☐ Faulty relay (Chapter 12).
☐ Faulty control unit (Chapter 11).

One solenoid/motor fails to operate

☐ Broken or disconnected wiring or connections (Chapter 12).
☐ Faulty solenoid/motor (Chapter 11).
☐ Broken, binding or disconnected latch operating rods or levers (Chapter 11).
☐ Fault in door latch (Chapter 11).

A

ABS (Anti-lock brake system) A system, usually electronically controlled, that senses incipient wheel lockup during braking and relieves hydraulic pressure at wheels that are about to skid.

Air bag An inflatable bag hidden in the steering wheel (driver's side) or the dash or glovebox (passenger side). In a head-on collision, the bags inflate, preventing the driver and front passenger from being thrown forward into the steering wheel or windscreen.

Air cleaner A metal or plastic housing, containing a filter element, which removes dust and dirt from the air being drawn into the engine.

Air filter element The actual filter in an air cleaner system, usually manufactured from pleated paper and requiring renewal at regular intervals.

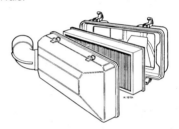

Air filter

Allen key A hexagonal wrench which fits into a recessed hexagonal hole.

Alligator clip A long-nosed spring-loaded metal clip with meshing teeth. Used to make temporary electrical connections.

Alternator A component in the electrical system which converts mechanical energy from a drivebelt into electrical energy to charge the battery and to operate the starting system, ignition system and electrical accessories.

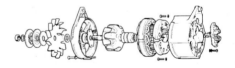

Alternator (exploded view)

Ampere (amp) A unit of measurement for the flow of electric current. One amp is the amount of current produced by one volt acting through a resistance of one ohm.

Anaerobic sealer A substance used to prevent bolts and screws from loosening. Anaerobic means that it does not require oxygen for activation. The Loctite brand is widely used.

Antifreeze A substance (usually ethylene glycol) mixed with water, and added to a vehicle's cooling system, to prevent freezing of the coolant in winter. Antifreeze also contains chemicals to inhibit corrosion and the formation of rust and other deposits that would tend to clog the radiator and coolant passages and reduce cooling efficiency.

Anti-seize compound A coating that reduces the risk of seizing on fasteners that are subjected to high temperatures, such as exhaust manifold bolts and nuts.

Anti-seize compound

Asbestos A natural fibrous mineral with great heat resistance, commonly used in the composition of brake friction materials. Asbestos is a health hazard and the dust created by brake systems should never be inhaled or ingested.

Axle A shaft on which a wheel revolves, or which revolves with a wheel. Also, a solid beam that connects the two wheels at one end of the vehicle. An axle which also transmits power to the wheels is known as a live axle.

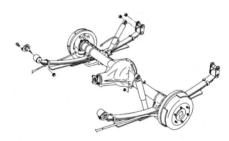

Axle assembly

Axleshaft A single rotating shaft, on either side of the differential, which delivers power from the final drive assembly to the drive wheels. Also called a driveshaft or a halfshaft.

B

Ball bearing An anti-friction bearing consisting of a hardened inner and outer race with hardened steel balls between two races.

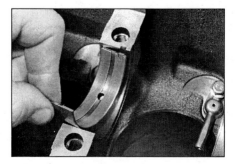

Bearing

Bearing The curved surface on a shaft or in a bore, or the part assembled into either, that permits relative motion between them with minimum wear and friction.

Big-end bearing The bearing in the end of the connecting rod that's attached to the crankshaft.

Bleed nipple A valve on a brake wheel cylinder, caliper or other hydraulic component that is opened to purge the hydraulic system of air. Also called a bleed screw.

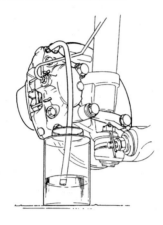

Brake bleeding

Brake bleeding Procedure for removing air from lines of a hydraulic brake system.

Brake disc The component of a disc brake that rotates with the wheels.

Brake drum The component of a drum brake that rotates with the wheels.

Brake linings The friction material which contacts the brake disc or drum to retard the vehicle's speed. The linings are bonded or riveted to the brake pads or shoes.

Brake pads The replaceable friction pads that pinch the brake disc when the brakes are applied. Brake pads consist of a friction material bonded or riveted to a rigid backing plate.

Brake shoe The crescent-shaped carrier to which the brake linings are mounted and which forces the lining against the rotating drum during braking.

Braking systems For more information on braking systems, consult the *Haynes Automotive Brake Manual*.

Breaker bar A long socket wrench handle providing greater leverage.

Bulkhead The insulated partition between the engine and the passenger compartment.

C

Caliper The non-rotating part of a disc-brake assembly that straddles the disc and carries the brake pads. The caliper also contains the hydraulic components that cause the pads to pinch the disc when the brakes are applied. A caliper is also a measuring tool that can be set to measure inside or outside dimensions of an object.

Camshaft A rotating shaft on which a series of cam lobes operate the valve mechanisms. The camshaft may be driven by gears, by sprockets and chain or by sprockets and a belt.

Canister A container in an evaporative emission control system; contains activated charcoal granules to trap vapours from the fuel system.

Canister

Carburettor A device which mixes fuel with air in the proper proportions to provide a desired power output from a spark ignition internal combustion engine.

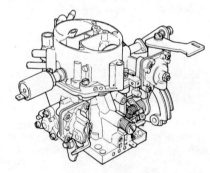

Carburettor

Castellated Resembling the parapets along the top of a castle wall. For example, a castellated balljoint stud nut.

Castellated nut

Castor In wheel alignment, the backward or forward tilt of the steering axis. Castor is positive when the steering axis is inclined rearward at the top.

Catalytic converter A silencer-like device in the exhaust system which converts certain pollutants in the exhaust gases into less harmful substances.

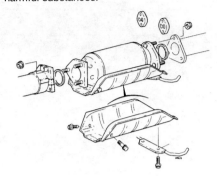

Catalytic converter

Circlip A ring-shaped clip used to prevent endwise movement of cylindrical parts and shafts. An internal circlip is installed in a groove in a housing; an external circlip fits into a groove on the outside of a cylindrical piece such as a shaft.

Clearance The amount of space between two parts. For example, between a piston and a cylinder, between a bearing and a journal, etc.

Coil spring A spiral of elastic steel found in various sizes throughout a vehicle, for example as a springing medium in the suspension and in the valve train.

Compression Reduction in volume, and increase in pressure and temperature, of a gas, caused by squeezing it into a smaller space.

Compression ratio The relationship between cylinder volume when the piston is at top dead centre and cylinder volume when the piston is at bottom dead centre.

Constant velocity (CV) joint A type of universal joint that cancels out vibrations caused by driving power being transmitted through an angle.

Core plug A disc or cup-shaped metal device inserted in a hole in a casting through which core was removed when the casting was formed. Also known as a freeze plug or expansion plug.

Crankcase The lower part of the engine block in which the crankshaft rotates.

Crankshaft The main rotating member, or shaft, running the length of the crankcase, with offset "throws" to which the connecting rods are attached.

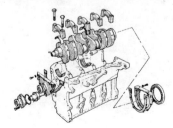

Crankshaft assembly

Crocodile clip See Alligator clip

D

Diagnostic code Code numbers obtained by accessing the diagnostic mode of an engine management computer. This code can be used to determine the area in the system where a malfunction may be located.

Disc brake A brake design incorporating a rotating disc onto which brake pads are squeezed. The resulting friction converts the energy of a moving vehicle into heat.

Double-overhead cam (DOHC) An engine that uses two overhead camshafts, usually one for the intake valves and one for the exhaust valves.

Drivebelt(s) The belt(s) used to drive accessories such as the alternator, water pump, power steering pump, air conditioning compressor, etc. off the crankshaft pulley.

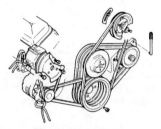

Accessory drivebelts

Driveshaft Any shaft used to transmit motion. Commonly used when referring to the axleshafts on a front wheel drive vehicle.

Driveshaft

Drum brake A type of brake using a drum-shaped metal cylinder attached to the inner surface of the wheel. When the brake pedal is pressed, curved brake shoes with friction linings press against the inside of the drum to slow or stop the vehicle.

Drum brake assembly

E

EGR valve A valve used to introduce exhaust gases into the intake air stream.

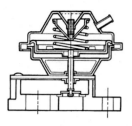

EGR valve

Electronic control unit (ECU) A computer which controls (for instance) ignition and fuel injection systems, or an anti-lock braking system. For more information refer to the *Haynes Automotive Electrical and Electronic Systems Manual*.

Electronic Fuel Injection (EFI) A computer controlled fuel system that distributes fuel through an injector located in each intake port of the engine.

Emergency brake A braking system, independent of the main hydraulic system, that can be used to slow or stop the vehicle if the primary brakes fail, or to hold the vehicle stationary even though the brake pedal isn't depressed. It usually consists of a hand lever that actuates either front or rear brakes mechanically through a series of cables and linkages. Also known as a handbrake or parking brake.

Endfloat The amount of lengthwise movement between two parts. As applied to a crankshaft, the distance that the crankshaft can move forward and back in the cylinder block.

Engine management system (EMS) A computer controlled system which manages the fuel injection and the ignition systems in an integrated fashion.

Exhaust manifold A part with several passages through which exhaust gases leave the engine combustion chambers and enter the exhaust pipe.

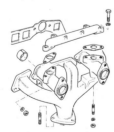

Exhaust manifold

F

Fan clutch A viscous (fluid) drive coupling device which permits variable engine fan speeds in relation to engine speeds.

Feeler blade A thin strip or blade of hardened steel, ground to an exact thickness, used to check or measure clearances between parts.

Feeler blade

Firing order The order in which the engine cylinders fire, or deliver their power strokes, beginning with the number one cylinder.

Flywheel A heavy spinning wheel in which energy is absorbed and stored by means of momentum. On cars, the flywheel is attached to the crankshaft to smooth out firing impulses.

Free play The amount of travel before any action takes place. The "looseness" in a linkage, or an assembly of parts, between the initial application of force and actual movement. For example, the distance the brake pedal moves before the pistons in the master cylinder are actuated.

Fuse An electrical device which protects a circuit against accidental overload. The typical fuse contains a soft piece of metal which is calibrated to melt at a predetermined current flow (expressed as amps) and break the circuit.

Fusible link A circuit protection device consisting of a conductor surrounded by heat-resistant insulation. The conductor is smaller than the wire it protects, so it acts as the weakest link in the circuit. Unlike a blown fuse, a failed fusible link must frequently be cut from the wire for replacement.

G

Gap The distance the spark must travel in jumping from the centre electrode to the side

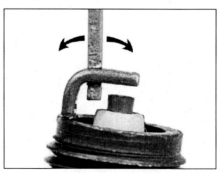

Adjusting spark plug gap

electrode in a spark plug. Also refers to the spacing between the points in a contact breaker assembly in a conventional points-type ignition, or to the distance between the reluctor or rotor and the pickup coil in an electronic ignition.

Gasket Any thin, soft material - usually cork, cardboard, asbestos or soft metal - installed between two metal surfaces to ensure a good seal. For instance, the cylinder head gasket seals the joint between the block and the cylinder head.

Gasket

Gauge An instrument panel display used to monitor engine conditions. A gauge with a movable pointer on a dial or a fixed scale is an analogue gauge. A gauge with a numerical readout is called a digital gauge.

H

Halfshaft A rotating shaft that transmits power from the final drive unit to a drive wheel, usually when referring to a live rear axle.

Harmonic balancer A device designed to reduce torsion or twisting vibration in the crankshaft. May be incorporated in the crankshaft pulley. Also known as a vibration damper.

Hone An abrasive tool for correcting small irregularities or differences in diameter in an engine cylinder, brake cylinder, etc.

Hydraulic tappet A tappet that utilises hydraulic pressure from the engine's lubrication system to maintain zero clearance (constant contact with both camshaft and valve stem). Automatically adjusts to variation in valve stem length. Hydraulic tappets also reduce valve noise.

I

Ignition timing The moment at which the spark plug fires, usually expressed in the number of crankshaft degrees before the piston reaches the top of its stroke.

Inlet manifold A tube or housing with passages through which flows the air-fuel mixture (carburettor vehicles and vehicles with throttle body injection) or air only (port fuel-injected vehicles) to the port openings in the cylinder head.

J

Jump start Starting the engine of a vehicle with a discharged or weak battery by attaching jump leads from the weak battery to a charged or helper battery.

L

Load Sensing Proportioning Valve (LSPV) A brake hydraulic system control valve that works like a proportioning valve, but also takes into consideration the amount of weight carried by the rear axle.

Locknut A nut used to lock an adjustment nut, or other threaded component, in place. For example, a locknut is employed to keep the adjusting nut on the rocker arm in position.

Lockwasher A form of washer designed to prevent an attaching nut from working loose.

M

MacPherson strut A type of front suspension system devised by Earle MacPherson at Ford of England. In its original form, a simple lateral link with the anti-roll bar creates the lower control arm. A long strut - an integral coil spring and shock absorber - is mounted between the body and the steering knuckle. Many modern so-called MacPherson strut systems use a conventional lower A-arm and don't rely on the anti-roll bar for location.

Multimeter An electrical test instrument with the capability to measure voltage, current and resistance.

N

NOx Oxides of Nitrogen. A common toxic pollutant emitted by petrol and diesel engines at higher temperatures.

O

Ohm The unit of electrical resistance. One volt applied to a resistance of one ohm will produce a current of one amp.

Ohmmeter An instrument for measuring electrical resistance.

O-ring A type of sealing ring made of a special rubber-like material; in use, the O-ring is compressed into a groove to provide the sealing action.

O-ring

Overhead cam (ohc) engine An engine with the camshaft(s) located on top of the cylinder head(s).

Overhead valve (ohv) engine An engine with the valves located in the cylinder head, but with the camshaft located in the engine block.

Oxygen sensor A device installed in the engine exhaust manifold, which senses the oxygen content in the exhaust and converts this information into an electric current. Also called a Lambda sensor.

P

Phillips screw A type of screw head having a cross instead of a slot for a corresponding type of screwdriver.

Plastigage A thin strip of plastic thread, available in different sizes, used for measuring clearances. For example, a strip of Plastigage is laid across a bearing journal. The parts are assembled and dismantled; the width of the crushed strip indicates the clearance between journal and bearing.

Plastigage

Propeller shaft The long hollow tube with universal joints at both ends that carries power from the transmission to the differential on front-engined rear wheel drive vehicles.

Proportioning valve A hydraulic control valve which limits the amount of pressure to the rear brakes during panic stops to prevent wheel lock-up.

R

Rack-and-pinion steering A steering system with a pinion gear on the end of the steering shaft that mates with a rack (think of a geared wheel opened up and laid flat). When the steering wheel is turned, the pinion turns, moving the rack to the left or right. This movement is transmitted through the track rods to the steering arms at the wheels.

Radiator A liquid-to-air heat transfer device designed to reduce the temperature of the coolant in an internal combustion engine cooling system.

Refrigerant Any substance used as a heat transfer agent in an air-conditioning system. R-12 has been the principle refrigerant for many years; recently, however, manufacturers have begun using R-134a, a non-CFC substance that is considered less harmful to

the ozone in the upper atmosphere.

Rocker arm A lever arm that rocks on a shaft or pivots on a stud. In an overhead valve engine, the rocker arm converts the upward movement of the pushrod into a downward movement to open a valve.

Rotor In a distributor, the rotating device inside the cap that connects the centre electrode and the outer terminals as it turns, distributing the high voltage from the coil secondary winding to the proper spark plug. Also, that part of an alternator which rotates inside the stator. Also, the rotating assembly of a turbocharger, including the compressor wheel, shaft and turbine wheel.

Runout The amount of wobble (in-and-out movement) of a gear or wheel as it's rotated. The amount a shaft rotates "out-of-true." The out-of-round condition of a rotating part.

S

Sealant A liquid or paste used to prevent leakage at a joint. Sometimes used in conjunction with a gasket.

Sealed beam lamp An older headlight design which integrates the reflector, lens and filaments into a hermetically-sealed one-piece unit. When a filament burns out or the lens cracks, the entire unit is simply replaced.

Serpentine drivebelt A single, long, wide accessory drivebelt that's used on some newer vehicles to drive all the accessories, instead of a series of smaller, shorter belts. Serpentine drivebelts are usually tensioned by an automatic tensioner.

Serpentine drivebelt

Shim Thin spacer, commonly used to adjust the clearance or relative positions between two parts. For example, shims inserted into or under bucket tappets control valve clearances. Clearance is adjusted by changing the thickness of the shim.

Slide hammer A special puller that screws into or hooks onto a component such as a shaft or bearing; a heavy sliding handle on the shaft bottoms against the end of the shaft to knock the component free.

Sprocket A tooth or projection on the periphery of a wheel, shaped to engage with a chain or drivebelt. Commonly used to refer to the sprocket wheel itself.

Starter inhibitor switch On vehicles with an

automatic transmission, a switch that prevents starting if the vehicle is not in Neutral or Park.

Strut See MacPherson strut.

T

Tappet A cylindrical component which transmits motion from the cam to the valve stem, either directly or via a pushrod and rocker arm. Also called a cam follower.

Thermostat A heat-controlled valve that regulates the flow of coolant between the cylinder block and the radiator, so maintaining optimum engine operating temperature. A thermostat is also used in some air cleaners in which the temperature is regulated.

Thrust bearing The bearing in the clutch assembly that is moved in to the release levers by clutch pedal action to disengage the clutch. Also referred to as a release bearing.

Timing belt A toothed belt which drives the camshaft. Serious engine damage may result if it breaks in service.

Timing chain A chain which drives the camshaft.

Toe-in The amount the front wheels are closer together at the front than at the rear. On rear wheel drive vehicles, a slight amount of toe-in is usually specified to keep the front wheels running parallel on the road by offsetting other forces that tend to spread the wheels apart.

Toe-out The amount the front wheels are closer together at the rear than at the front. On front wheel drive vehicles, a slight amount of toe-out is usually specified.

Tools For full information on choosing and using tools, refer to the *Haynes Automotive Tools Manual.*

Tracer A stripe of a second colour applied to a wire insulator to distinguish that wire from another one with the same colour insulator.

Tune-up A process of accurate and careful adjustments and parts replacement to obtain the best possible engine performance.

Turbocharger A centrifugal device, driven by exhaust gases, that pressurises the intake air. Normally used to increase the power output from a given engine displacement, but can also be used primarily to reduce exhaust emissions (as on VW's "Umwelt" Diesel engine).

U

Universal joint or U-joint A double-pivoted connection for transmitting power from a driving to a driven shaft through an angle. A U-joint consists of two Y-shaped yokes and a cross-shaped member called the spider.

V

Valve A device through which the flow of liquid, gas, vacuum, or loose material in bulk may be started, stopped, or regulated by a movable part that opens, shuts, or partially obstructs one or more ports or passageways. A valve is also the movable part of such a device.

Valve clearance The clearance between the valve tip (the end of the valve stem) and the rocker arm or tappet. The valve clearance is measured when the valve is closed.

Vernier caliper A precision measuring instrument that measures inside and outside dimensions. Not quite as accurate as a micrometer, but more convenient.

Viscosity The thickness of a liquid or its resistance to flow.

Volt A unit for expressing electrical "pressure" in a circuit. One volt that will produce a current of one ampere through a resistance of one ohm.

W

Welding Various processes used to join metal items by heating the areas to be joined to a molten state and fusing them together. For more information refer to the *Haynes Automotive Welding Manual.*

Wiring diagram A drawing portraying the components and wires in a vehicle's electrical system, using standardised symbols. For more information refer to the *Haynes Automotive Electrical and Electronic Systems Manual.*

Note: *References throughout this index are in the form - "Chapter number" • "page number"*

Notes

Notes

Haynes Manuals – The Complete **UK Car** List

Title	Book No.
ALFA ROMEO Alfasud/Sprint (74 - 88) up to F *	0292
Alfa Romeo Alfetta (73 - 87) up to E *	0531
AUDI 80, 90 & Coupe Petrol (79 - Nov 88) up to F	0605
Audi 80, 90 & Coupe Petrol (Oct 86 - 90) D to H	1491
Audi 100 & 200 Petrol (Oct 82 - 90) up to H	0907
Audi 100 & A6 Petrol & Diesel (May 91 - May 97) H to P	3504
Audi A3 Petrol & Diesel (96 - May 03) P to 03	4253
Audi A4 Petrol & Diesel (95 - 00) M to X	3575
Audi A4 Petrol & Diesel (01 - 04) X to 54	4609
AUSTIN A35 & A40 (56 - 67) up to F *	0118
Austin/MG/Rover Maestro 1.3 & 1.6 Petrol (83 - 95) up to M	0922
Austin/MG Metro (80 - May 90) up to G	0718
Austin/Rover Montego 1.3 & 1.6 Petrol (84 - 94) A to L	1066
Austin/Rover Montego 2.0 Petrol (84 - 95) A to M	1067
Mini (59 - 69) up to H *	0527
Mini (69 - 01) up to X	0646
Austin/Rover 2.0 litre Diesel Engine (86 - 93) C to L	1857
Austin Healey 100/6 & 3000 (56 - 68) up to G *	0049
BEDFORD CF Petrol (69 - 87) up to E	0163
Bedford/Vauxhall Rascal & Suzuki Supercarry (86 - Oct 94) C to M	3015
BMW 316, 320 & 320i (4-cyl) (75 - Feb 83) up to Y *	0276
BMW 320, 320i, 323i & 325i (6-cyl) (Oct 77 - Sept 87) up to E	0815
BMW 3- & 5-Series Petrol (81 - 91) up to J	1948
BMW 3-Series Petrol (Apr 91 - 99) H to V	3210
BMW 3-Series Petrol (Sept 98 - 03) S to 53	4067
BMW 520i & 525e (Oct 81 - June 88) up to E	1560
BMW 525, 528 & 528i (73 - Sept 81) up to X *	0632
BMW 5-Series 6-cyl Petrol (April 96 - Aug 03) N to 03	4151
BMW 1500, 1502, 1600, 1602, 2000 & 2002 (59 - 77) up to S *	0240
CHRYSLER PT Cruiser Petrol (00 - 03) W to 53	4058
CITROËN 2CV, Ami & Dyane (67 - 90) up to H	0196
Citroën AX Petrol & Diesel (87 - 97) D to P	3014
Citroën Berlingo & Peugeot Partner Petrol & Diesel (96 - 05) P to 55	4281
Citroën BX Petrol (83 - 94) A to L	0908
Citroën C15 Van Petrol & Diesel (89 - Oct 98) F to S	3509
Citroën C3 Petrol & Diesel (02 - 05) 51 to 05	4197
Citroën C5 Petrol & Diesel (01-08) Y to 08	4745
Citroën CX Petrol (75 - 88) up to F	0528
Citroën Saxo Petrol & Diesel (96 - 04) N to 54	3506
Citroën Visa Petrol (79 - 88) up to F	0620
Citroën Xantia Petrol & Diesel (93 - 01) K to Y	3082
Citroën XM Petrol & Diesel (89 - 00) G to X	3451
Citroën Xsara Petrol & Diesel (97 - Sept 00) R to W	3751
Citroën Xsara Picasso Petrol & Diesel (00 - 02) W to 52	3944
Citroen Xsara Picasso (03-08)	4784
Citroën ZX Diesel (91 - 98) J to S	1922
Citroën ZX Petrol (91 - 98) H to S	1881
Citroën 1.7 & 1.9 litre Diesel Engine (84 - 96) A to N	1379
FIAT 126 (73 - 87) up to E *	0305
Fiat 500 (57 - 73) up to M *	0090
Fiat Bravo & Brava Petrol (95 - 00) N to W	3572
Fiat Cinquecento (93 - 98) K to R	3501
Fiat Panda (81 - 95) up to M	0793
Fiat Punto Petrol & Diesel (94 - Oct 99) L to V	3251
Fiat Punto Petrol (Oct 99 - July 03) V to 03	4066
Fiat Punto Petrol (03-07) 03 to 07	4746
Fiat Regata Petrol (84 - 88) A to F	1167
Fiat Tipo Petrol (88 - 91) E to J	1625
Fiat Uno Petrol (83 - 95) up to M	0923
Fiat X1/9 (74 - 89) up to G *	0273
FORD Anglia (59 - 68) up to G *	0001
Ford Capri II (& III) 1.6 & 2.0 (74 - 87) up to E *	0283
Ford Capri II (& III) 2.8 & 3.0 V6 (74 - 87) up to E	1309
Ford Cortina Mk I & Corsair 1500 ('62 - '66) up to D*	0214
Ford Cortina Mk III 1300 & 1600 (70 - 76) up to P *	0070
Ford Escort Mk I 1100 & 1300 (68 - 74) up to N *	0171
Ford Escort Mk I Mexico, RS 1600 & RS 2000 (70 - 74) up to N *	0139
Ford Escort Mk II Mexico, RS 1800 & RS 2000 (75 - 80) up to W *	0735
Ford Escort (75 - Aug 80) up to V *	0280
Ford Escort Petrol (Sept 80 - Sept 90) up to H	0686
Ford Escort & Orion Petrol (Sept 90 - 00) H to X	1737
Ford Escort & Orion Diesel (Sept 90 - 00) H to X	4081
Ford Fiesta (76 - Aug 83) up to Y	0334
Ford Fiesta Petrol (Aug 83 - Feb 89) A to F	1030
Ford Fiesta Petrol (Feb 89 - Oct 95) F to N	1595
Ford Fiesta Petrol & Diesel (Oct 95 - Mar 02) N to 02	3397
Ford Fiesta Petrol & Diesel (Apr 02 - 07) 02 to 57	4170
Ford Focus Petrol & Diesel (98 - 01) S to Y	3759
Ford Focus Petrol & Diesel (Oct 01 - 05) 51 to 05	4167
Ford Galaxy Petrol & Diesel (95 - Aug 00) M to W	3984
Ford Granada Petrol (Sept 77 - Feb 85) up to B *	0481
Ford Granada & Scorpio Petrol (Mar 85 - 94) B to M	1245
Ford Ka (96 - 02) P to 52	3570
Ford Mondeo Petrol (93 - Sept 00) K to X	1923
Ford Mondeo Petrol & Diesel (Oct 00 - Jul 03) X to 03	3990
Ford Mondeo Petrol & Diesel (July 03 - 07) 03 to 56	4619
Ford Mondeo Diesel (93 - 96) L to N	3465
Ford Orion Petrol (83 - Sept 90) up to H	1009
Ford Sierra 4-cyl Petrol (82 - 93) up to K	0903
Ford Sierra V6 Petrol (82 - 91) up to J	0904
Ford Transit Petrol (Mk 2) (78 - Jan 86) up to C	0719
Ford Transit Petrol (Mk 3) (Feb 86 - 89) C to G	1468
Ford Transit Diesel (Feb 86 - 99) C to T	3019
Ford Transit Diesel (00-06)	4775
Ford 1.6 & 1.8 litre Diesel Engine (84 - 96) A to N	1172
Ford 2.1, 2.3 & 2.5 litre Diesel Engine (77 - 90) up to H	1606
FREIGHT ROVER Sherpa Petrol (74 - 87) up to E	0463
HILLMAN Avenger (70 - 82) up to Y	0037
Hillman Imp (63 - 76) up to R *	0022
HONDA Civic (Feb 84 - Oct 87) A to E	1226
Honda Civic (Nov 91 - 96) J to N	3199
Honda Civic Petrol (Mar 95 - 00) M to X	4050
Honda Civic Petrol & Diesel (01 - 05) X to 55	4611
Honda CR-V Petrol & Diesel (01-06)	4747
Honda Jazz (01 - Feb 08) 51 - 57	4735
HYUNDAI Pony (85 - 94) C to M	3398
JAGUAR E Type (61 - 72) up to L *	0140
Jaguar MkI & II, 240 & 340 (55 - 69) up to H *	0098
Jaguar XJ6, XJ & Sovereign; Daimler Sovereign (68 - Oct 86) up to D	0242
Jaguar XJ6 & Sovereign (Oct 86 - Sept 94) D to M	3261
Jaguar XJ12, XJS & Sovereign; Daimler Double Six (72 - 88) up to F	0478
JEEP Cherokee Petrol (93 - 96) K to N	1943
LADA 1200, 1300, 1500 & 1600 (74 - 91) up to J	0413
Lada Samara (87 - 91) D to J	1610
LAND ROVER 90, 110 & Defender Diesel (83 - 07) up to 56	3017
Land Rover Discovery Petrol & Diesel (89 - 98) G to S	3016
Land Rover Discovery Diesel (Nov 98 - Jul 04) S to 04	4606
Land Rover Freelander Petrol & Diesel (97 - Sept 03) R to 53	3929
Land Rover Freelander Petrol & Diesel (Oct 03 - Oct 06) 53 to 56	4623
Land Rover Series IIA & III Diesel (58 - 85) up to C	0529
Land Rover Series II, IIA & III 4-cyl Petrol (58 - 85) up to C	0314
MAZDA 323 (Mar 81 - Oct 89) up to G	1608
Mazda 323 (Oct 89 - 98) G to R	3455
Mazda 626 (May 83 - Sept 87) up to E	0929
Mazda B1600, B1800 & B2000 Pick-up Petrol (72 - 88) up to F	0267
Mazda RX-7 (79 - 85) up to C *	0460
MERCEDES-BENZ 190, 190E & 190D Petrol & Diesel (83 - 93) A to L	3450
Mercedes-Benz 200D, 240D, 240TD, 300D & 300TD 123 Series Diesel (Oct 76 - 85)	1114
Mercedes-Benz 250 & 280 (68 - 72) up to L *	0346
Mercedes-Benz 250 & 280 123 Series Petrol (Oct 76 - 84) up to B *	0677
Mercedes-Benz 124 Series Petrol & Diesel (85 - Aug 93) C to K	3253
Mercedes-Benz A-Class Petrol & Diesel (98-04) S to 54	4748
Mercedes-Benz C-Class Petrol & Diesel (93 - Aug 00) L to W	3511
Mercedes-Benz C-Class (00-06)	4780
MG A (55 - 62) *	0475
MGB (62 - 80) up to W	0111
MG Midget & Austin-Healey Sprite (58 - 80) up to W *	0265
MINI Petrol (July 01 - 05) Y to 05	4273
MITSUBISHI Shogun & L200 Pick-Ups Petrol (83 - 94) up to M	1944
MORRIS Ital 1.3 (80 - 84) up to B	0705
Morris Minor 1000 (56 - 71) up to K	0024
NISSAN Almera Petrol (95 - Feb 00) N to V	4053
Nissan Almera & Tino Petrol (Feb 00 - 07) V to 56	4612
Nissan Bluebird (May 84 - Mar 86) A to C	1223
Nissan Bluebird Petrol (Mar 86 - 90) C to H	1473
Nissan Cherry (Sept 82 - 86) up to D	1031
Nissan Micra (83 - Jan 93) up to K	0931
Nissan Micra (93 - 02) K to 52	3254
Nissan Micra Petrol (03-07) 52 to 57	4734
Nissan Primera Petrol (90 - Aug 99) H to T	1851
Nissan Stanza (82 - 86) up to D	0824
Nissan Sunny Petrol (May 82 - Oct 86) up to D	0895
Nissan Sunny Petrol (Oct 86 - Mar 91) D to H	1378
Nissan Sunny Petrol (Apr 91 - 95) H to N	3219
OPEL Ascona & Manta (B Series) (Sept 75 - 88) up to F *	0316
Opel Ascona Petrol (81 - 88)	3215
Opel Astra Petrol (Oct 91 - Feb 98)	3156
Opel Corsa Petrol (83 - Mar 93)	3160
Opel Corsa Petrol (Mar 93 - 97)	3159
Opel Kadett Petrol (Nov 79 - Oct 84) up to B	0634
Opel Kadett Petrol (Oct 84 - Oct 91)	3196
Opel Omega & Senator Petrol (Nov 86 - 94)	3157
Opel Rekord Petrol (Feb 78 - Oct 86) up to D	0543
Opel Vectra Petrol (Oct 88 - Oct 95)	3158
PEUGEOT 106 Petrol & Diesel (91 - 04) J to 53	1882
Peugeot 205 Petrol (83 - 97) A to P	0932
Peugeot 206 Petrol & Diesel (98 - 01) S to X	3757
Peugeot 206 Petrol & Diesel (02 - 06) 51 to 06	4613
Peugeot 306 Petrol & Diesel (93 - 02) K to 02	3073
Peugeot 307 Petrol & Diesel (01 - 04) Y to 54	4147
Peugeot 309 Petrol (86 - 93) C to K	1266
Peugeot 405 Petrol (88 - 97) E to P	1559
Peugeot 405 Diesel (88 - 97) E to P	3198
Peugeot 406 Petrol & Diesel (96 - Mar 99) N to T	3394
Peugeot 406 Petrol & Diesel (Mar 99 - 02) T to 52	3982

* Classic reprint

Title	Book No.
Peugeot 505 Petrol (79 - 89) up to G	0762
Peugeot 1.7/1.8 & 1.9 litre Diesel Engine (82 - 96) up to N	0950
Peugeot 2.0, 2.1, 2.3 & 2.5 litre Diesel Engines (74 - 90) up to H	1607
PORSCHE 911 (65 - 85) up to C	0264
Porsche 924 & 924 Turbo (76 - 85) up to C	0397
PROTON (89 - 97) F to P	3255
RANGE ROVER V8 Petrol (70 - Oct 92) up to K	0606
RELIANT Robin & Kitten (73 - 83) up to A *	0436
RENAULT 4 (61 - 86) up to D *	0072
Renault 5 Petrol (Feb 85 - 96) B to N	1219
Renault 9 & 11 Petrol (82 - 89) up to F	0822
Renault 18 Petrol (79 - 86) up to D	0598
Renault 19 Petrol (89 - 96) F to N	1646
Renault 19 Diesel (89 - 96) F to N	1946
Renault 21 Petrol (86 - 94) C to M	1397
Renault 25 Petrol & Diesel (84 - 92) B to K	1228
Renault Clio Petrol (91 - May 98) H to R	1853
Renault Clio Diesel (91 - June 96) H to N	3031
Renault Clio Petrol & Diesel (May 98 - May 01) R to Y	3906
Renault Clio Petrol & Diesel (June '01 - '05) Y to 55	4168
Renault Espace Petrol & Diesel (85 - 96) C to N	3197
Renault Laguna Petrol & Diesel (94 - 00) L to W	3252
Renault Laguna Petrol & Diesel (Feb 01 - Feb 05) X to 54	4283
Renault Mégane & Scénic Petrol & Diesel (96 - 99) N to T	3395
Renault Mégane & Scénic Petrol & Diesel (Apr 99 - 02) T to 52	3916
Renault Megane Petrol & Diesel (Oct 02 - 05) 52 to 55	4284
Renault Scenic Petrol & Diesel (Sept 03 - 06) 53 to 06	4297
ROVER 213 & 216 (84 - 89) A to G	1116
Rover 214 & 414 Petrol (89 - 96) G to N	1689
Rover 216 & 416 Petrol (89 - 96) G to N	1830
Rover 211, 214, 216, 218 & 220 Petrol & Diesel (Dec 95 - 99) N to V	3399
Rover 25 & MG ZR Petrol & Diesel (Oct 99 - 04) V to 54	4145
Rover 414, 416 & 420 Petrol & Diesel (May 95 - 98) M to R	3453
Rover 45 / MG ZS Petrol & Diesel (99 - 05) V to 55	4384
Rover 618, 620 & 623 Petrol (93 - 97) K to P	3257
Rover 75 / MG ZT Petrol & Diesel (99 - 06) S to 06	4292
Rover 820, 825 & 827 Petrol (86 - 95) D to N	1380
Rover 3500 (76 - 87) up to E *	0365
Rover Metro, 111 & 114 Petrol (May 90 - 98) G to S	1711
SAAB 95 & 96 (66 - 76) up to R *	0198
Saab 90, 99 & 900 (79 - Oct 93) up to L	0765
Saab 900 (Oct 93 - 98) L to R	3512
Saab 9000 (4-cyl) (85 - 98) C to S	1686
Saab 9-3 Petrol & Diesel (98 - Aug 02) R to 02	4614
Saab 9-3 Petrol & Diesel (02-07) 52 to 57	4749
Saab 9-5 4-cyl Petrol (97 - 04) R to 54	4156
SEAT Ibiza & Cordoba Petrol & Diesel (Oct 93 - Oct 99) L to V	3571
Seat Ibiza & Malaga Petrol (85 - 92) B to K	1609
SKODA Estelle (77 - 89) up to G	0604
Skoda Fabia Petrol & Diesel (00 - 06) W to 06	4376
Skoda Favorit (89 - 96) F to N	1801
Skoda Felicia Petrol & Diesel (95 - 01) M to X	3505
Skoda Octavia Petrol & Diesel (98 - Apr 04) R to 04	4285
SUBARU 1600 & 1800 (Nov 79 - 90) up to H *	0995

Title	Book No.
SUNBEAM Alpine, Rapier & H120 (67 - 74) up to N *	0051
SUZUKI SJ Series, Samurai & Vitara (4-cyl) Petrol (82 - 97) up to P	1942
Suzuki Supercarry & Bedford/Vauxhall Rascal (86 - Oct 94) C to M	3015
TALBOT Alpine, Solara, Minx & Rapier (75 - 86) up to D	0337
Talbot Horizon Petrol (78 - 86) up to D	0473
Talbot Samba (82 - 86) up to D	0823
TOYOTA Avensis Petrol (98 - Jan 03) R to 52	4264
Toyota Carina E Petrol (May 92 - 97) J to P	3256
Toyota Corolla (80 - 85) up to C	0683
Toyota Corolla (Sept 83 - Sept 87) A to E	1024
Toyota Corolla (Sept 87 - Aug 92) E to K	1683
Toyota Corolla Petrol (Aug 92 - 97) K to P	3259
Toyota Corolla Petrol (July 97 - Feb 02) P to 51	4286
Toyota Hi-Ace & Hi-Lux Petrol (69 - Oct 83) up to A	0304
Toyota RAV4 Petrol & Diesel (94-06) L to 55	4750
Toyota Yaris Petrol (99 - 05) T to 05	4265
TRIUMPH GT6 & Vitesse (62 - 74) up to N *	0112
Triumph Herald (59 - 71) up to K *	0010
Triumph Spitfire (62 - 81) up to X	0113
Triumph Stag (70 - 78) up to T *	0441
Triumph TR2, TR3, TR3A, TR4 & TR4A (52 - 67) up to F *	0028
Triumph TR5 & 6 (67 - 75) up to P *	0031
Triumph TR7 (75 - 82) up to Y *	0322
VAUXHALL Astra Petrol (80 - Oct 84) up to B	0635
Vauxhall Astra & Belmont Petrol (Oct 84 - Oct 91) B to J	1136
Vauxhall Astra Petrol (Oct 91 - Feb 98) J to R	1832
Vauxhall/Opel Astra & Zafira Petrol (Feb 98 - Apr 04) R to 04	3758
Vauxhall/Opel Astra & Zafira Diesel (Feb 98 - Apr 04) R to 04	3797
Vauxhall/Opel Astra Petrol (04 - 08)	4732
Vauxhall/Opel Astra Diesel (04 - 08)	4733
Vauxhall/Opel Calibra (90 - 98) G to S	3502
Vauxhall Carlton Petrol (Oct 78 - Oct 86) up to D	0480
Vauxhall Carlton & Senator Petrol (Nov 86 - 94) D to L	1469
Vauxhall Cavalier Petrol (81 - Oct 88) up to F	0812
Vauxhall Cavalier Petrol (Oct 88 - 95) F to N	1570
Vauxhall Chevette (75 - 84) up to B	0285
Vauxhall/Opel Corsa Diesel (Mar 93 - Oct 00) K to X	4087
Vauxhall Corsa Petrol (Mar 93 - 97) K to R	1985
Vauxhall/Opel Corsa Petrol (Apr 97 - Oct 00) P to X	3921
Vauxhall/Opel Corsa Petrol & Diesel (Oct 00 - Sept 03) X to 53	4079
Vauxhall/Opel Corsa Petrol & Diesel (Oct 03 - Aug 06) 53 to 06	4617
Vauxhall/Opel Frontera Petrol & Diesel (91 - Sept 98) J to S	3454
Vauxhall Nova Petrol (83 - 93) up to K	0909
Vauxhall/Opel Omega Petrol (94 - 99) L to T	3510
Vauxhall/Opel Vectra Petrol & Diesel (95 - Feb 99) N to S	3396
Vauxhall/Opel Vectra Petrol & Diesel (Mar 99 - May 02) T to 02	3930
Vauxhall/Opel Vectra Petrol & Diesel (June 02 - Sept 05) 02 to 55	4618
Vauxhall/Opel 1.5, 1.6 & 1.7 litre Diesel Engine (82 - 96) up to N	1222
VW 411 & 412 (68 - 75) up to P *	0091
VW Beetle 1200 (54 - 77) up to S	0036
VW Beetle 1300 & 1500 (65 - 75) up to P	0039

Title	Book No.
VW 1302 & 1302S (70 - 72) up to L *	0110
VW Beetle 1303, 1303S & GT (72 - 75) up to P	0159
VW Beetle Petrol & Diesel (Apr 99 - 07) T to 57	3798
VW Golf & Jetta Mk 1 Petrol 1.1 & 1.3 (74 - 84) up to A	0716
VW Golf, Jetta & Scirocco Mk 1 Petrol 1.5, 1.6 & 1.8 (74 - 84) up to A	0726
VW Golf & Jetta Mk 1 Diesel (78 - 84) up to A	0451
VW Golf & Jetta Mk 2 Petrol (Mar 84 - Feb 92) A to J	1081
VW Golf & Vento Petrol & Diesel (Feb 92 - Mar 98) J to R	3097
VW Golf & Bora Petrol & Diesel (April 98 - 00) R to X	3727
VW Golf & Bora 4-cyl Petrol & Diesel (01 - 03) X to 53	4169
VW Golf & Jetta Petrol & Diesel (04 - 07) 53 to 07	4610
VW LT Petrol Vans & Light Trucks (76 - 87) up to E	0637
VW Passat & Santana Petrol (Sept 81 - May 88) up to E	0814
VW Passat 4-cyl Petrol & Diesel (May 88 - 96) E to P	3498
VW Passat 4-cyl Petrol & Diesel (Dec 96 - Nov 00) P to X	3917
VW Passat Petrol & Diesel (Dec 00 - May 05) X to 05	4279
VW Polo & Derby (76 - Jan 82) up to X	0335
VW Polo (82 - Oct 90) up to H	0813
VW Polo Petrol (Nov 90 - Aug 94) H to L	3245
VW Polo Hatchback Petrol & Diesel (94 - 99) M to S	3500
VW Polo Hatchback Petrol & Diesel (00 - Jan 02) V to 51	4150
VW Polo Petrol & Diesel (02 - May 05) 51 to 05	4608
VW Scirocco (82 - 90) up to H *	1224
VW Transporter 1600 (68 - 79) up to V	0082
VW Transporter 1700, 1800 & 2000 (72 - 79) up to V *	0226
VW Transporter (air-cooled) Petrol (79 - 82) up to Y *	0638
VW Transporter (water-cooled) Petrol (82 - 90) up to H	3452
VW Type 3 (63 - 73) up to M *	0084
VOLVO 120 & 130 Series (& P1800) (61 - 73) up to M *	0203
Volvo 142, 144 & 145 (66 - 74) up to N *	0129
Volvo 240 Series Petrol (74 - 93) up to K	0270
Volvo 262, 264 & 260/265 (75 - 85) up to C *	0400
Volvo 340, 343, 345 & 360 (76 - 91) up to J	0715
Volvo 440, 460 & 480 Petrol (87 - 97) D to P	1691
Volvo 740 & 760 Petrol (82 - 91) up to J	1258
Volvo 850 Petrol (92 - 96) J to P	3260
Volvo 940 petrol (90 - 98) H to R	3249
Volvo S40 & V40 Petrol (96 - Mar 04) N to 04	3569
Volvo S40 & V50 Petrol & Diesel (Mar 04 - Jun 07) 04 to 07	4731
Volvo S60 Petrol & Diesel (01-08)	4793
Volvo S70, V70 & C70 Petrol (96 - 99) P to V	3573
Volvo V70 / S80 Petrol & Diesel (98 - 05) S to 55	4263

DIY MANUAL SERIES

Title	Book No.
The Haynes Air Conditioning Manual	4192
The Haynes Car Electrical Systems Manual	4251
The Haynes Manual on Bodywork	4198
The Haynes Manual on Brakes	4178
The Haynes Manual on Carburettors	4177
The Haynes Manual on Diesel Engines	4174
The Haynes Manual on Engine Management	4199
The Haynes Manual on Fault Codes	4175
The Haynes Manual on Practical Electrical Systems	4267
The Haynes Manual on Small Engines	4250
The Haynes Manual on Welding	4176

* Classic reprint

CL24.08/09

Preserving Our Motoring Heritage

< *The Model J Duesenberg Derham Tourster. Only eight of these magnificent cars were ever built – this is the only example to be found outside the United States of America*

Almost every car you've ever loved, loathed or desired is gathered under one roof at the Haynes Motor Museum. Over 300 immaculately presented cars and motorbikes represent every aspect of our motoring heritage, from elegant reminders of bygone days, such as the superb Model J Duesenberg to curiosities like the bug-eyed BMW Isetta. There are also many old friends and flames. Perhaps you remember the 1959 Ford Popular that you did your courting in? The magnificent 'Red Collection' is a spectacle of classic sports cars including AC, Alfa Romeo, Austin Healey, Ferrari, Lamborghini, Maserati, MG, Riley, Porsche and Triumph.

A Perfect Day Out

Each and every vehicle at the Haynes Motor Museum has played its part in the history and culture of Motoring. Today, they make a wonderful spectacle and a great day out for all the family. Bring the kids, bring Mum and Dad, but above all bring your camera to capture those golden memories for ever. You will also find an impressive array of motoring memorabilia, a comfortable 70 seat video cinema and one of the most extensive transport book shops in Britain. The Pit Stop Cafe serves everything from a cup of tea to wholesome, home-made meals or, if you prefer, you can enjoy the large picnic area nestled in the beautiful rural surroundings of Somerset.

> *John Haynes O.B.E., Founder and Chairman of the museum at the wheel of a Haynes Light 12.*

< *Graham Hill's Lola Cosworth Formula 1 car next to a 1934 Riley Sports.*

The Museum is situated on the A359 Yeovil to Frome road at Sparkford, just off the A303 in Somerset. It is about 40 miles south of Bristol, and 25 minutes drive from the M5 intersection at Taunton.
Open 9.30am - 5.30pm (10.00am - 4.00pm Winter) 7 days a week, *except Christmas Day, Boxing Day and New Years Day*
Special rates available for schools, coach parties and outings Charitable Trust No. 292048